SERVICES MARKETING

**Integrating Customer Focus
Across the Firm**

Fourth Edition

Valarie A. Zeithaml
University of North Carolina

Mary Jo Bitner
Arizona State University

Dwayne D. Gremler
Bowling Green State University

Mc
Graw
Hill

Boston   Burr Ridge, IL   Dubuque, IA   Madison, WI   New York   San Francisco   St. Louis
Bangkok   Bogotá   Caracas   Kuala Lumpur   Lisbon   London   Madrid   Mexico City
Milan   Montreal   New Delhi   Santiago   Seoul   Singapore   Sydney   Taipei   Toronto

The McGraw·Hill Companies

SERVICES MARKETING: INTEGRATING CUSTOMER FOCUS ACROSS THE FIRM
International Edition 2006

Exclusive rights by McGraw-Hill Education (Asia), for manufacture and export. This book cannot be re-exported from the country to which it is sold by McGraw-Hill. The International Edition is not available in North America.

10 09 08 07 06 05 04 03 02 01
20 09 08 07 06 05
CTF   BJE

Library of Congress Control Number: 2004065642

When ordering this title, use ISBN 007-124496-4

Printed in Singapore

www.mhhe.com

To Hugo, my lifelong friend.

—V.A.Z.

To my family—husband, Rich, and daughters Andrea and Christa—for their unfailing love and support.

—M.J.B.

To my mother, Pat, for her years of support, and in memory of my father, David.

—D.D.G.

ABOUT THE AUTHORS

Mary Jo Bitner (left), Valarie Zeithaml and Dwayne Gremler

Valarie A. Zeithaml
University of North Carolina—Chapel Hill

VALARIE ZEITHAML is the Roy and Alice H. Richards Bicentennial Professor and MBA Associate Dean at the Kenan-Flagler Business School of the University of North Carolina at Chapel Hill. Since receiving her MBA and PhD in marketing from the Robert H. Smith School of Business at the University of Maryland in 1980, Professor Zeithaml has devoted her career to researching and teaching the topics of service quality and services management. She is the co-author of *Delivering Quality Service: Balancing Customer Perceptions and Expectations* (Free Press, 1990), now in its 13th printing; and *Driving Customer Equity: How Customer Lifetime Value Is Reshaping Corporate Strategy* (with Roland Rust and Katherine Lemon, Free Press, 2000). In 2002, *Driving Customer Equity* won the first Berry–American Marketing Association Book Prize for the best marketing book of the past three years.

In 2004, Professor Zeithaml received both the Innovative Contributor to Marketing Award given by the Marketing Management Association and the Outstanding Marketing Educator Award given by the Academy of Marketing Science. In 2001, she received the American Marketing Association's Career Contributions to the Services Discipline Award.

Professor Zeithaml has won five teaching awards, including the Gerald Barrett Faculty Award from the University of North Carolina and The Fuqua School Outstanding MBA Teaching Award from Duke University. She is also the recipient of numerous research awards, including the Robert Ferber Consumer Research Award from the *Journal of Consumer Research,* the Harold H. Maynard Award from the *Journal of Marketing,* the MSI Paul Root Award from the *Journal of Marketing,* the Jagdish Sheth Award from the *Journal of the Academy of Marketing Science,* and the William F. O'Dell Award from the *Journal of Marketing Research.* She has consulted with more than 50 service and product companies.

Professor Zeithaml served on the Board of Directors of the American Marketing Association from 2000 to 2003 and is currently an Academic Trustee of the Marketing Science Institute.

Mary Jo Bitner
Arizona State University

MARY JO BITNER is the PETsMART Chair in Services Leadership in the Marketing Department at the W. P. Carey School of Business, Arizona State University. She also serves as Academic Director for the Center for Services Leadership at ASU. Dr. Bitner was a founding faculty member of the Center for Services Leadership and has been a leader in its emergence as a premier university-based center for the study of services marketing and management. In the mid-1990s she led the development of the W. P. Carey MBA Services Marketing and Management specialization. Alumni of this program now work in companies across the United States, leading the implementation of services and customer-focused strategies. Dr. Bitner has published more than 50 articles and has received a number of awards for her research in leading journals, including the *Journal of Marketing, Journal of the Academy of Marketing Science, Journal of Business Research, Journal of Retailing, International Journal of Service Industry Management,* and *Academy of Management Executive.* She has consulted with and presented seminars and workshops for numerous businesses, including Yellow Roadway Corporation, Ford Motor Company, Caremark, IBM Global Services, and RR Donnelley. In 2003, Dr. Bitner was honored with the Career Contributions to the Services Discipline award by the American Marketing Association's Services Special Interest Group.

Dwayne D. Gremler
Bowling Green State University

DWAYNE D. GREMLER is Associate Professor of Marketing at Bowling Green State University. He received his MBA and PhD degrees from the W. P. Carey School of Business at Arizona State University. Throughout his academic career, Dr. Gremler has been a passionate advocate for the research and instruction of services marketing issues. He has served as Chair of the American Marketing Association's Services Marketing Special Interest Group and has helped organize services marketing conferences in Australia, The Netherlands, France, and the United States. Dr. Gremler has been invited to conduct seminars and present research on services marketing issues in several countries. Dr. Gremler's research addresses customer loyalty in service businesses, customer-employee interactions in service delivery, service guarantees, and word-of-mouth communication. He has published articles in the *Journal of Service Research, International Journal of Service Industry Management, Journal of the Academy of Marketing Science,* and *Journal of Marketing Education.* He has also been the recipient of several research awards at BGSU, including the College of Business Administration Outstanding Scholar Award and the Robert A. Patton Scholarly Achievement Award. While a professor at the University of Idaho, Dr. Gremler received the First Interstate Bank Student Excellence in Award for teaching, an award determined by students in the College of Business and Economics.

PREFACE

This text is for students and businesspeople who recognize the vital role that services play in the economy and its future. The advanced economies of the world are now dominated by services, and virtually all companies view service as critical to retaining their customers today and in the future. Even manufacturing companies that, in the past, have depended on their physical products for their livelihood now recognize that service provides one of their few sustainable competitive advantages.

We wrote this book in recognition of the ever-growing importance of services and the unique challenges faced by managers of services.

WHY A SERVICES MARKETING TEXT?

Since the beginning of our academic careers in marketing, we have devoted our research and teaching efforts to topics in services marketing. We strongly believe that services marketing is different from goods marketing in significant ways and that it requires strategies and tactics that traditional marketing texts do not fully reflect. This text is unique in both content and structure, and we hope that you will learn from it as we have in writing it.

Content Overview

The foundation of the text is the recognition that services present special challenges that must be identified and addressed. Issues commonly encountered in service organizations—the inability to inventory, difficulty in synchronizing demand and supply, and challenges in controlling the performance quality of human interactions—need to be articulated and tackled by managers. Many of the strategies include information and approaches that are new to marketing. We wrote the text to help students and managers understand and address these special challenges of services marketing.

The development of strong customer relationships through quality service (and services) are at the heart of the book's content. The topics covered are equally applicable to organizations whose core product is service (such as banks, transportation companies, hotels, hospitals, educational institutions, professional services, telecommunication) and to organizations that depend on service excellence for competitive advantage (high-technology manufacturers, automotive and industrial products, and so on).

Rarely do we repeat material from marketing principles or marketing strategy texts. Instead, we adjust, when necessary, standard content on topics such as distribution, pricing, and promotion to account for service characteristics of intangibility, heterogeneity, inseparability, and perishability.

The book's content focuses on knowledge needed to implement service strategies for competitive advantage across industries. Included are frameworks for customer-focused management, and strategies for increasing customer satisfaction and retention through service. In addition to standard marketing topics (such as pricing), this text introduces students to entirely new topics that include management and measurement of service quality, service recovery, the linking of customer measurement to performance measurement, service blueprinting, customer coproduction, and cross-functional treatment of issues through integration of marketing with disciplines such as operations and human resources. Each of these topics represents pivotal content for tomorrow's businesses as they structure around process rather than task, engage in one-to-one marketing, mass customize their offerings, and attempt to build strong relationships with their customers.

Distinguishing Content Features

The distinguishing features of our text and the new features in this edition include the following:

1. Greater emphasis on the topic of service quality than existing marketing and service marketing texts.

2. Increased focus on customer expectations and perceptions and what they imply for marketers.

3. A new feature called "Strategy Insight" in each chapter—a feature that focuses on emerging or existing strategic initiatives involving services.

4. Increased coverage of business-to-business applications.

5. Increased technology and Internet coverage, including updated "Technology Spotlight" boxes in each chapter.

6. A chapter on service recovery that includes a conceptual framework for understanding the topic.

7. A chapter on the financial and economic impact of service quality.

8. A chapter on customer-defined service standards.

9. Cross-functional treatment of issues through integration of marketing with other disciplines such as operations and human resources management.

10. Consumer-based pricing and value pricing strategies.

11. A chapter on integrated services marketing communications.

12. Description of a set of tools that must be added to basic marketing techniques when dealing with services rather than goods.

13. Introduction of three service Ps to the traditional marketing mix and increased focus on customer relationships and relationship marketing strategies.

14. An entire chapter that recognizes human resource challenges and human resource strategies for delivering customer-focused services.

15. Coverage of new service development processes and a detailed and complete introduction to service blueprinting—a tool for describing, designing, and positioning services.

16. Coverage of the customer's role in service delivery and strategies for making customers productive partners in service creation.

17. A chapter on the role of physical evidence, particularly the physical environment or "servicescape."

18. Global features in each chapter and expanded examples of global services marketing.

19. Exercises in each chapter.

20. Updated or new examples throughout the text.

Conceptual and Research Foundations

We synthesized research and conceptual material from many talented academics and practitioners to create this text. We relied on pioneering work of researchers and businesspeople from diverse disciplines such as marketing, human resources, operations, and management. Because the field of services marketing is international in its roots, we also drew from work originating around the globe. We have continued this strong conceptual grounding in the fourth edition by integrating new research into every chapter. The framework of the book is managerially focused, with every chapter presenting company examples and strategies for addressing issues in the chapter.

Conceptual Frameworks in Chapters

We developed integrating frameworks in most chapters. For example, we created new frameworks for understanding service recovery strategies, service pricing, integrated marketing communications, customer relationships, customer roles, and internal marketing.

Unique Structure

The text features a structure completely different from the standard 4P (marketing mix) structure of introductory marketing texts. The text is organized around the gaps model of service quality, which is described fully in Chapter 2. Beginning with Chapter 3, the text is organized into parts around the gaps model. For example, Chapters 3, 4, and 5 each deal with an aspect of the customer gap—customer behavior, expectations, and perceptions, respectively—to form the focus for services marketing strategies. The managerial content in the rest of the chapters is framed by the gaps model using part openers that build the model gap by gap. Each part of the book includes multiple chapters with strategies for understanding and closing these critical gaps.

Fully Integrated Text

In the 1980s and early 1990s, the field of services marketing was so new that insufficient material had been written on the topic to create a traditional text. For that reason, the books used as texts contained cases and readings that had to be interpreted by educators for their students. These early services marketing books were therefore different from standard texts—where the major function is to synthesize and conceptualize the material—and placed a burden on the professor to blend the components. This book contains integrated text materials, thereby removing from professors and students the tremendous burden of synthesis and compilation.

WHAT COURSES AND STUDENTS CAN USE THE TEXT?

In our years of experience teaching services marketing, we have found that a broad cross section of students is drawn to learning about services marketing. Students with career interests in services industries as well as goods industries with high service components (such as industrial products, high-tech products, and durable products) want and need to understand these topics. Students who wish to become consultants and entrepreneurs want to learn the strategic view of marketing, which involves not just physical goods but also the myriad services that envelop these goods. Virtually all students—even those who will work for packaged goods firms—will face employers needing to understand the basics of services marketing and management.

Although services marketing courses are usually designated as marketing electives, a large number of enrollees in our classes have been finance students seeking to broaden their knowledge and career opportunities in financial services. Business students with human resource, information technology, accounting, and operations majors also enroll, as do nonbusiness students from such diverse disciplines as health administration, recreation and parks, public and nonprofit administration, law, and library science.

Students need only a basic marketing course as a prerequisite for a services marketing course and this text. The primary target audience for the text is services marketing classes at the undergraduate (junior or senior elective courses), graduate (both masters and doctoral courses), and executive student levels. Other target audiences are (1) service management classes at both the undergraduate and graduate levels and (2) marketing management classes at the graduate level in which a professor wishes to provide more comprehensive teaching of services than is possible with a standard marketing management text. A subset of chapters would also provide a more concise text for use in a quarter-length or mini-semester course. A further reduced set of chapters may be used to supplement undergraduate and graduate basic marketing courses to enhance the treatment of services.

WHAT CAN WE PROVIDE EDUCATORS TO TEACH SERVICES MARKETING?

As a team, we have accumulated more than 55 years of experience teaching the subject of services marketing. We set out to create a text that represents the approaches we have found most effective. We incorporated all that we have learned in our many years of teaching services marketing—teaching materials, student exercises, case analyses, research, and PowerPoint slides on a CD-ROM. We also offer a comprehensive instructor's manual and test bank.

HOW MANY PARTS AND CHAPTERS ARE INCLUDED, AND WHAT DO THEY COVER?

The text material includes 18 chapters divided into six parts. Part 1 includes an introduction in Chapter 1 and an overview of the gaps model in Chapter 2. Part 2 discusses the focus on the customer. Part 3 focuses on listening to customer requirements, including chapters covering marketing research for services, building customer relationships, and service recovery. Part 4 involves aligning service strategy through design and standards and includes chapters on service development and design, customer-defined service standards, and physical evidence and the servicescape. Part 5 concerns the delivery and performance of service and has chapters on employees' and customers' roles in service delivery, conveying service through intermediaries and electronic channels, and managing demand and capacity. Part 6 focuses on managing services promises and includes chapters on integrated services marketing communications and pricing of services. Finally, Part 7 examines the financial and economic effect of service quality.

THE SUPPLEMENTARY MATERIALS

Instructor's Manual

The *Instructor's Manual* includes sample syllabi, suggestions for in-class exercises and projects, teaching notes for each of the cases included in the text, and answers to end-of-chapter discussion questions and exercises. The *Instructor's Manual* uses the "active learning" educational paradigm, which involves students in constructing their own learning experiences and exposes them to the collegial patterns present in work situations. Active learning offers an educational underpinning for the pivotal workforce skills required in business, among them oral and written communication skills, listening skills, and critical thinking and problem solving.

PowerPoint CD-ROM

We offer a CD-ROM that contains figures and tables from the text that are useful for instructors in class. The full-color PowerPoint slides contained on the CD-ROM were created to present a coordinated look for course presentation.

ACKNOWLEDGMENTS

We owe a great deal to the pioneering service researchers and scholars who developed the field of services marketing. They include John Bateson, Leonard Berry, Bernard Booms, Dave Bowen, Steve Brown, Larry Crosby, John Czepiel, Ray Fisk, William George, Christian Gronroos, Steve Grove, Evert Gummesson, Chuck Lamb, Christopher Lovelock, Parsu Parasuraman, Ben Schneider, Lynn Shostack, and Carol Surprenant. We also owe gratitude to the second generation of service researchers who broadened and enriched the services marketing field. When we attempted to compile a list of those researchers, we realized that it was too extensive to include here. The length of that list is testament to the influence of the early pioneers and to the importance that services marketing has achieved both in academia and practice.

We remain indebted to Parsu Parasuraman and Len Berry, who have been research partners of Dr. Zeithaml's since 1982. The gaps model around which the text is structured was developed in collaboration with them, as was the model of customer expectations used in Chapter 4. Much of the research and measurement content in this text was shaped by what the team found in a 15-year program of research on service quality.

Dr. Zeithaml also expresses special thanks to Maria Elena Vazquez who provided examples of international services marketing and has been a friend and valued colleague. She also wishes to thank her colleagues, MBA students, and EMBA students at the University of North Carolina. The students' interest in the topic of services marketing, their creativity in approaching the papers and assignments, and their continuing contact are appreciated. She also thanks the Marketing Science Institute, of which she is an academic trustee, for the ongoing inspiration from their many conferences and working papers. She is especially indebted to Marni Clippinger, David Reibstein, Susan Keane, Leigh McAllister, J. B. Steenkamp, and Sunil Gupta for their support and talent.

Dr. Bitner expresses special thanks to Steve Brown, Michael Mokwa, and the Center for Services Leadership, and the Department of Marketing of Arizona State. Their support and encouragement has been invaluable throughout the multiple editions of this book. She also acknowledges Bernard Booms and Michael Hutt for their valued advice, mentorship, and support.

She also acknowledges and thanks Amy Ostrom for her support and invaluable assistance in sharing examples, new research, and creative teaching innovations. Dr. Bitner also acknwledges and is grateful to the fine group of Arizona State services doctoral graduates she has worked with who have shaped her thinking and supported the text: Lois Mohr, Bill Faranda, Amy Rodie, Kevin Gwinner, Matt Meuter, Steve Tax, Dwayne Gremler, Lance Bettencourt, Susan Cadwallader, and Felicia Morgan.

Dr. Bitner acknowledges the many ideas and examples provided by the member companies of the Center for Services Leadership; American Automobile Association; American Express; Annenberg Center for Health Sciences; AT&T; Avaya, Inc.; Avnet; Inc.; Blue Cross And Blue Shield; Cardinal Health; Caremark; Charles Schwab and Co.; The Co-operators; Evanston Northwestern Healthcare; Exult, Inc.; Ford Motor Company; Harley-Davidson Motor Company; Harrah's Entertainment; Hewlett-Packard Company; Hill-Rom Company, Inc.; IBM Global Services; The INSIGHT Group; Intermec; J.P. Morgan Chase and Co.; LensCrafters, Inc.; Marriott International, Inc.; Marsh; Mayo Clinic; McKesson Corporation; McKinsey & Company, Inc.; Neoforma, Inc.; neoIT; PETsMART; RR Donnelley; SAP; Siemens; Southwest Airlines Company; State Farm Insurance Companies; Synovate Symmetrics; TriWest Healthcare Alliance; United Stationers; Valley Crest Landscape Maintenance; Yellow Roadway Corporation; and Zanes Cycles.

Dr. Gremler expresses thanks to several people, including his mentor, Steve Brown, for advice and encouragement. He thanks other Arizona State University faculty who have also served as role models and encouragers, including John Schlacter, Michael Mokwa, Kenn Rowe, David Altheide, Dave Gourley, and Ken Evans. Dr. Gremler also thanks those colleagues with whom he has worked on service marketing research projects, including Steve Brown, Mary Jo Bitner, Kevin Gwinner, Thorsten Hennig-Thurau, Mike McCollough, Ken Evans, Doug Hoffman, Sue Keaveney, Lauren Wright, Jeff Bailey, Cathy Goodwin, and David Martin Ruiz. He acknowledges the fellowship with and support of fellow doctoral student colleagues from Arizona State University, including Kevin Gwinner, Lance Bettencourt, Amy Rodie, Matt Meuter, Steve Tax, Bill Faranda, Mark Houston, Debbie Laverie, Gary Wolfe, Tim Christiansen, Lois Mohr, and John Eaton. Dr. Gremler also expresses thanks to colleagues at various universities who have invited him to speak in their countries and have provided insight into services marketing issues internationally, including Jos Lemmink, Ko de Ruyter, Mark Colgate, Janelle McPhail, Chiara Orsingher, Alberto Marcati, Stefan Michel, Thorsten Hennig-Thurau, Silke Michalski, and Brigitte Auriacombe. Finally, a special thanks to Candy Gremler for her unending willingness to serve as copy editor, encourager, wife, and friend.

We would like to acknowledge the suggestions and improvements made by the reviewers, including Diane Halstead, University of Tennessee, Chattanooga; Lynn Harris, Shippensburg University; Scott Kelley, University of Kentucky; Peter McClure, University of Massachusetts, Boston; Daryl McKee, Louisiana State University, Baton Rouge; Paula Saunders, Wright State University; Alex Sharland, Hofstra University.

The panel of academics who helped us by completing a survey included Avery Abernathy, Auburn University; Bruce Allen, Central Michigan University; Dean Alimon, University of West Florida; David Andrus, Kansas State University; Stacey Menzel Baker, Ph.D., Bowling Green State University; Sharon Beatty, University of Alabama; Sandy Becker, Rutgers University; Gary Benson, Chadron State College; Michael Brady, Boston College; Dr. Eileen Bridges, Kent State University; Rich Brown, Freed-Hardeman University; Gary J. Brunswick, Northern Michigan University; Kent Byus, Ph.D., Northeastern State University; James W. Camerius, Northern

Michigan University; Hope V. Clark, Pitt Community College; Clare Comm, University of Massachusetts, Lowell; Douglas Cords, California State University, Fresno; Duane Davis, University of Central Florida; Roger Davis, Baylor University; J. Robert B. Field, Lake Superior State University; Dr. S.J. Garner, Eastern Kentucky University; Carol Gaumer, Frostburg State University; Dr. Audrey Guskey, Duquesne University; Paul Herbig, Tri State University; Donna Hill, Bradley University; Rajesh Iyer, Valdosta State University; Richard Jacobs, Adams State College; Joby John, Bentley College; Scott Johnson, San Jose State University; Andrew Joniak, Buffalo State College; Dr. Ali Kara, Penn State York; Susan Keaveney, University of Colorado, Denver; Dr. Rita McMillan, Dillard University; Kevin McNeilly, Miami University; Daniel McQuiston, Butler University; Matthew Meuter, California State University, Chico; James Mullin Jr., Villanova University; A. Ben Oumlil, University of Dayton; Richard Pomazal, Wheeling Jesuit University; Richard R. Purdue, University of Colorado; Henry Rodkin, DePaul University; Drue Schuler, St. Cloud State University; Jim Stephens, Emporia State University; Thaddeus Stupi, Southern West Virginia CTC; Scott Swanson, University of Wisconsin, Whitewater; Patricia K. Voli, Ph.D., University of North Carolina, Wilmington; Timothy Wilson, Clarion University; Kathy Winsfed, Pace University; Neil Younkin, Saint Xavier University

Finally, we would like to acknowledge the professional efforts of the McGraw-Hill/Irwin staff. Our sincere thanks to Andy Winston, Barrett Koger, Dan Silverburg, Amy Luck, Marlena Pechan, Debra Sylvester, Artemio Ortiz, Jeremy Cheshareck, and Betty Hadala.

Valarie A. Zeithaml

Mary Jo Bitner

Dwayne D. Gremler

BRIEF CONTENTS

CONTENTS

Chapter 4
Customer Expectations of Service   80

Chapter 5
Customer Perceptions of Service   105

Cases 572

Index 695

LIST OF BOXES

FOUNDATIONS FOR SERVICES MARKETING

This first part of the text provides you with the foundations needed to begin your study of services marketing. The first chapter identifies up-to-date trends, issues, and opportunities in services as a backdrop for the strategies addressed in remaining chapters. The second chapter introduces the gaps model of service quality, the framework that provides the structure for the text. The remaining parts of the book will include information and strategies to address specific gaps, giving you the tools and knowledge to become a services marketing leader.

Chapter 1

INTRODUCTION TO SERVICES

This chapter's objectives are to

1. Explain what services are and identify important trends in services.

2. Explain the need for special services marketing concepts and practices and why the need has developed and is accelerating.

3. Explore the profound impact of technology on service.

4. Outline the basic differences between goods and services and the resulting challenges and opportunities for service businesses.

5. Introduce the expanded marketing mix for services and the philosophy of customer focus, as powerful frameworks and themes that are fundamental to the rest of the text.

"Services are going to move in this decade to being the front edge of the industry."

Louis V. Gerstner, 2001

This quote from IBM's former CEO, Louis V. Gerstner, illustrates the changes sweeping across industry today. Many businesses that were once viewed as manufacturing giants are shifting their focus to services. IBM has led the pack in its industry. Mr. Gerstner predicts that in the IT industry over the next decade services will lead the market instead of hardware and software to the extent that "hardware and software will be sold inside a services wrapper." Actions of current IBM CEO, Sam Palmisano, have reinforced this view. In his tenure, Mr. Palmisano has led IBM in the expansion of its outsourcing businesses and accentuated its focus on client solutions. He also led IBM in its purchase of PriceWaterhouseCoopers in 2002 to gain broader strategic services consulting expertise.

In a company brochure IBM states that it is the largest *service* business in the world. Through its Global Services division, IBM offers product support services, professional consulting services, and network computing services around the globe. Many businesses have outsourced entire service functions to IBM, counting on the company to provide the services better than anyone else.

Currently the services side of IBM brings in $43 billion, over half the company's total revenue. The services strategy has been very successful for IBM to date and promises to be the engine of growth into the future (see the "New Wave of Services" graphic). Going forward, IBM's strategy is to focus on total solutions and to be a truly valued, trusted, and indispensable partner for its key clients. This strategy means providing clients with total service solutions in such wide-ranging areas as human resources, marketing, product design, and customer relationship management.

No one in IBM would suggest that these positive results have been easily achieved. Switching from a manufacturing to a service and customer focus is indeed a challenge. It requires changes in management mind-set, changes in culture, changes in the ways people work and are rewarded, and new ways of implementing customer solutions. At IBM this change has evolved over decades. It is suggested that Lou Gerstner's legacy at IBM may well be the definitive switch that the company has made from hardware to services and the strategic focus on customers.

Many companies (such as Hewlett-Packard, Sun Microsystems, and Cisco) have viewed IBM's success and are attempting to make the same transition to services. It is not as easy as it looks. In moving into services, companies discover what service businesses such as hospitality, consulting, health care, financial services, and telecommunications have known for years: services marketing and management are different—not totally unique, but different. Selling and delivering a computer is not the same as selling and delivering a service that solves a customer's problem.[1]

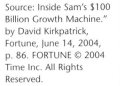

Source: Inside Sam's $100 Billion Growth Machine." by David Kirkpatrick, Fortune, June 14, 2004, p. 86. FORTUNE © 2004 Time Inc. All Rights Reserved.

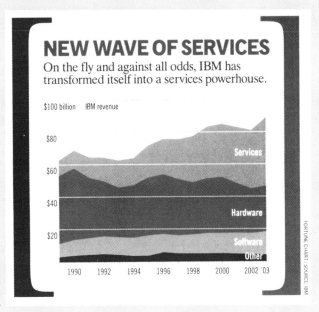

NEW WAVE OF SERVICES
On the fly and against all odds, IBM has transformed itself into a services powerhouse.

$100 billion   IBM revenue

Services

Hardware

Software

Other

1990   1992   1994   1996   1998   2000   2002 '03

FORTUNE CHART / SOURCE: IBM

As the opening vignette suggests, services are not limited to service industries, services can be very profitable, and services are challenging to manage and market. Services represent a huge and growing percentage of the world economy; yet particularly in the United States, customer perceptions of service are not good.[2] In fact, the University of Michigan's American Customer Satisfaction Index has shown consistently lower scores for services when compared to other products.[3] Given the economic growth in services, their profit and competitive advantage potential, and the overall decline in customer satisfaction with services, it seems that the potential and opportunities for companies who can excel in services marketing, management, and delivery have never been greater.

This text will give you a lens with which to approach the marketing and management of services. What you learn can be applied in a company like IBM with a traditional manufacturing history or in pure service businesses. You will learn tools, strategies, and approaches for developing and delivering profitable services that can provide competitive advantage to firms. At the base of services marketing and management you will find a strong customer focus that extends across all functions of the firm—thus the subtitle of this book, "integrating customer focus across the firm."

WHAT ARE SERVICES?

Put in the most simple terms, *services are deeds, processes, and performances.* Our opening vignette illustrates what is meant by this definition. The services offered by IBM are not tangible things that can be touched, seen, and felt, but rather are intangible deeds and performances. To be concrete, IBM offers repair and maintenance service for its equipment, consulting services for IT and e-commerce applications, training services, Web design and hosting, and other services. These services may include a final, tangible report, a website, or in the case of training, tangible instructional materials. But for the most part, the entire service is represented to the client through problem analysis activities, meetings with the client, follow-up calls, and reporting—a series of deeds, processes, and performances. Similarly, the core offerings of hospitals, hotels, banks, and utilities comprise primarily deeds and actions performed for customers.

Although we will rely on the simple, broad definition of *services,* you should be aware that over time *services* and the *service sector of the economy* have been defined in subtly different ways. The variety of definitions can often explain the confusion or disagreements people have when discussing services and when describing industries that comprise the service sector of the economy. Compatible with our simple, broad definition is one that defines services to include "all economic activities whose output is not a physical product or construction, is generally consumed at the time it is produced, and provides added value in forms (such as convenience, amusement, timeliness, comfort, or health) that are essentially intangible concerns of its first purchaser."[4] The breadth of industries making up the service sector of the U.S. economy is illustrated in Figure 1.1.

Services Industries, Services as Products, Customer Service, and Derived Service

As we begin our discussion of services marketing and management, it is important to draw distinctions between *service industries and companies, services as products, customer service,* and *derived service.* Sometimes when people think of service, they think

FIGURE 1.1 **Contributions of Service Industries to U.S. Gross Domestic Product, 2003**

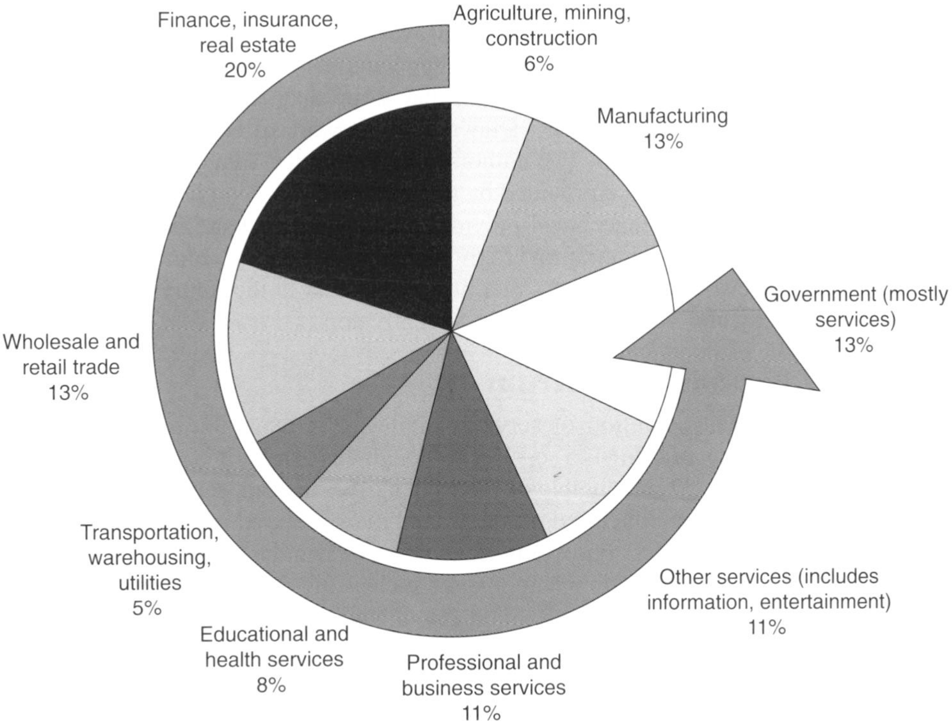
Finance, insurance, real estate 20%
Agriculture, mining, construction 6%
Manufacturing 13%
Government (mostly services) 13%
Wholesale and retail trade 13%
Transportation, warehousing, utilities 5%
Educational and health services 8%
Professional and business services 11%
Other services (includes information, entertainment) 11%

Source: Inside Sam's $100 Billion Growth Machine, by David Kirkpatrick, *Fortune,* June 14, 2004, p 86. © 2004 Time Inc. All rights reserved.

only of customer service, but service can be divided into four distinct categories. The tools and strategies you will learn in this text can be applied to any of these categories.

Service industries and companies include those industries and companies typically classified within the service sector whose core product is a service. All of the following companies can be considered pure service companies: Marriott International (lodging), American Airlines (transportation), Charles Schwab (financial services), Mayo Clinic (health care). The total services sector comprises a wide range of service industries, as suggested by Figure 1.1. Companies in these industries sell services as their core offering.

Services as products represent a wide range of intangible product offerings that customers value and pay for in the marketplace. Service products are sold by service companies and by nonservice companies such as manufacturers and technology companies. For example, IBM and Hewlett-Packard offer information technology consulting services to the marketplace, competing with firms such as EDS and Accenture, which are traditional pure services firms. Other industry examples include department stores, like Macy's that sell services such as gift wrapping and shipping, and pet stores like PETsMART that sell pet grooming and training services.

Customer service is also a critical aspect of what we mean by "service." Customer service is the service provided in support of a company's core products. Companies typically do not charge for customer service. Customer service can occur on-site (as when a retail employee helps a customer find a desired item or answers a question), or it can occur over the phone or via the Internet. Many companies operate customer service call centers, often staffed around the clock. Quality customer service is essential to building customer relationships. It should not, however, be confused with the services provided for sale by the company.

Derived service is yet another way to look at what service means. In a recent article in the *Journal of Marketing*, Steve Vargo and Bob Lusch argue for a new dominant logic for marketing that suggests that all products and physical goods are valued for the services they provide.[5] Drawing on the work of respected economists, marketers, and philosophers, the two authors suggest that the value derived from physical goods is really the service provided by the good, not the good itself. For example, they suggest that a pharmaceutical provides medical services, a razor provides barbering services, and computers provide information and data manipulation services. Although this view is somewhat abstract, it suggests that in the future we may think even more broadly about services than we currently do.

Tangibility Spectrum

The broad definition of services implies that intangibility is a key determinant of whether an offering is a service. Although this is true, it is also true that very few products are purely intangible or totally tangible. Instead, services tend to be *more intangible* than manufactured products, and manufactured products tend to be *more tangible* than services. For example, the fast-food industry, while classified as a service, also has many tangible components such as the food, the packaging, and so on. Automobiles, while classified within the manufacturing sector, also supply many intangibles, such as transportation. The tangibility spectrum shown in Figure 1.2 captures this idea. Throughout this text, when we refer to services we will be assuming the broad definition of services and acknowledging that there are very few "pure services" or "pure goods." The issues and approaches we discuss are directed toward those offerings that lie on the right side, the intangible side, of the spectrum shown in Figure 1.2.

Trends in the Service Sector

Although you often hear and read that many modern economies are dominated by services, the United States and other countries did not become service economies overnight. As early as 1929, 55 percent of the working population was employed in the

FIGURE 1.2 **Tangibility Spectrum**

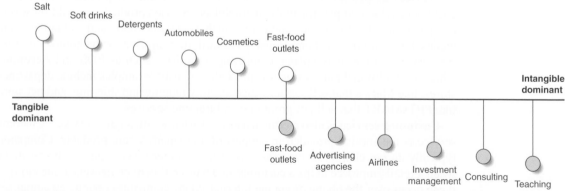

Source: G. Lynn Shostack, "Breaking Free from Product Marketing," *Journal of Marketing* 41 (April 1977), pp. 73–80. Reprinted with permission of the American Marketing Association.

FIGURE 1.3
Percentage of U.S. Labor Force by Industry

Source: U.S. Department of Labor, Bureau of Labor Statistics, *Industry at a Glance,* Dec 31, 2003; *Survey of Current Business,* February 2001, Table B.8, July 1988, Table 6.6B, and July 1992, Table 6.4C; E. Ginzberg and G. J. Vojta, "The Service Sector of the U.S. Economy," *Scientific American* 244, no. 3 (1981), pp. 31–39.

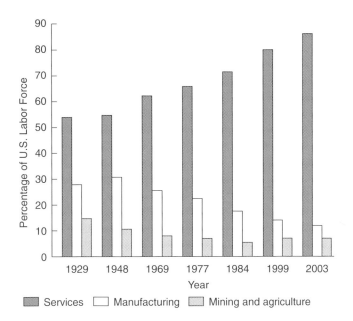

FIGURE 1.4
Percentage of U.S. Gross Domestic Product by Industry

Source: *Survey of Current Business,* June 2004, p. 26, Table D; *Survey of Current Business,* February 2001, Table B.3, and August 1996, Table 11; E. Ginzberg and G. J. Vojta, "The Service Sector of the U.S. Economy," *Scientific American* 244, no. 3 (1981), pp. 31–39.

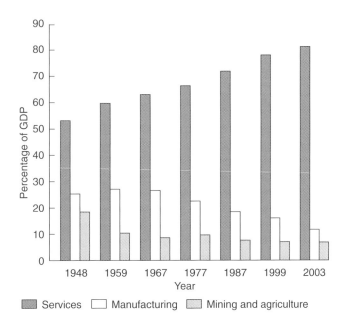

service sector in the United States, and approximately 54 percent of the gross national product was generated by services in 1948. The data in Figures 1.3 and 1.4 show that the trend toward services has continued, until in 2003 services represented 81 percent of the gross domestic product (GDP) and 81 percent of employment. Note also that these data do not include services provided by manufacturing companies. The number of employees and value of the services they produce would be classified as manufacturing sector data.

WHY SERVICES MARKETING?

Why is it important to learn about services marketing, service quality, and service management? What are the differences in services versus manufactured-goods marketing that have led to the demand for books and courses on services? Many forces have led to the growth of services marketing, and many industries, companies, and individuals have defined the scope of the concepts, frameworks, and strategies that define the field. The field of services marketing and management has evolved as a result of these combined forces.

Service-Based Economies

First, services marketing concepts and strategies have developed in response to the tremendous growth of service industries, resulting in their increased importance to the U.S. and world economies. As was noted, in 2003 the service sector represented just over 80 percent of total employment and gross domestic product of the United States. Almost all the absolute growth in numbers of jobs and the fastest growth rates in job formation are in service industries.

Another indicator of the economic importance of services is that trade in services is growing worldwide. In fact, while the U.S. balance of trade in goods remains in the red, in 2000 there was an $81 billion trade *surplus* in services.[6] World-class providers of services such as American Express, McDonald's, and Marriott Hotels, together with many small service companies, are exporting information, knowledge, creativity, and technology that the world badly needs.

There is a growing market for services and increasing dominance of services in economies worldwide, not just in the United States (see the accompanying table). The tremendous growth and economic contributions of the service sector have drawn increasing attention to the issues and challenges of service sector industries worldwide.

Country	Percent of GDP Attributed to Services
United States	80
United Kingdom	74
Netherlands	73
Australia	72
Canada	72
France	71
Singapore	70
Sweden	69
Germany	68
Japan	68
New Zealand	67
Brazil	54
India	48
China	34

Source: *The World Factbook 2004,* published by the Central Intelligence Agency, www.odci.gov/cia/publications/factbook.

Service as a Business Imperative in Manufacturing and IT

Early in the development of the field of services marketing and management, most of the impetus came from service industries such as banking, transportation, and health care. As these traditional service industries evolve and become more competitive, the need for effective services management and marketing strategies continues. Now, however, manufacturing and technology industries such as automobiles, computers, and software are also recognizing the need to provide quality service and revenue-producing services in order to compete worldwide.

From General Electric and IBM to Cardinal Health, Hewlett-Packard, and Siemens, companies are recognizing the opportunity to grow and profit through services.[7] Why? Because the quick pace of developing technologies and increasing competition make it difficult to gain strategic competitive advantage through physical products alone. Plus, customers are more demanding. Not only do they expect excellent, high-quality goods and technology, they also expect high levels of customer service and total service solutions along with them.

At GE the services strategy began in the mid-1990s under then-CEO Jack Welch when he launched what has been termed the "third revolution." A major thrust of the third revolution was to push GE's growth strategies even deeper into services such as aftermarket services, financial services, broadcasting, management consulting, and other services as far afield as health care and utilities. In 2000, GE generated approximately 75 percent of its revenues from services.[8] The move into services has continued with GE's new CEO, Jeffrey Immelt. Under Immelt's new initiatives, GE offers a broad range of expertise and services to its customers in an effort to make them more productive and competitive. For GE, the theory behind this broad push is "the more successful our customers are, the more successful we will be."[9] In 2004, services and customer-focused strategies represent two of GE's four key areas to drive growth (along with technology and globalization).

As manufacturers such as GE and IT companies such as IBM (see the opening vignette and Figure 1.5) transition to become services organizations, the need for special concepts and approaches for managing and marketing services is increasingly apparent.[10]

Deregulated Industries and Professional Service Needs

Specific demand for services marketing concepts has come from the deregulated industries and professional services as both these groups have gone through rapid changes in the ways they do business. In the past several decades many very large service industries, including airlines, banking, telecommunications, and trucking, have been deregulated by the U.S. government. Similar deregulatory moves have taken place in many other countries as well. As a result, marketing decisions that used to be tightly controlled by the government are now partially, and in some cases totally, within the control of individual firms.[11] For example, until 1978 all airline fares, routes, and commissions paid to travel agents were determined and monitored by the government. Since that time airlines have been free to set their own pricing structures and determine which routes they will fly. Needless to say, deregulation created turmoil in the airline industry, accelerating the need for more sophisticated, customer-based, and competition-sensitive marketing.

Providers of professional services (such as physicians, lawyers, accountants, engineers, and architects) have also demanded new concepts and approaches for their businesses as these industries have become increasingly competitive and as professional standards have been modified to allow advertising. Whereas traditionally the professions avoided even using the word *marketing,* they are now seeking better ways to understand and segment their customers, to ensure the delivery of quality services, and to strengthen their positions amid a growing number of competitors.

FIGURE 1.5
Services are driving IBM's growth in the 21st century.

Source: Reprinted with permission of IBM Global Services. (IBM)

IBM Global Services	
Overview:	IBM Global Services is people. Strategists. Problem solvers. Implementers. Over 100,000 people worldwide who have worked in all kinds of industries. People who understand how technology can solve real business problems, or take advantage of new opportunities. People who help you make sense of technology, who work with you — making sure the solution you want is the solution you get.
Phone:	1 800 IBM 7777, ask for Services
Web:	www.ibm.com/services/info

IBM Global Services
People who think. People who do. People who get it.

@business people

IBM.

Services Marketing Is Different

As the forces described above coincided and evolved, businesspeople realized that marketing and managing services presented issues and challenges not faced in manufacturing and packaged goods companies. These differences and challenges were captured in a series of interviews by management consultant Gary Knisely in 1979 (see Exhibit 1.1).[12] For example, when a firm's core offering is a deed performed by an employee (such as engineering consulting), how can the firm ensure consistent product quality to the marketplace? As service businesses began to turn to marketing and decided to hire marketing people, they naturally recruited from the best marketers in the world—Procter & Gamble, General Foods, Kodak. People who moved from marketing in packaged goods industries to marketing in health care, banking, and other service industries found that their skills and experiences were not directly transferable. They faced issues and dilemmas in marketing services that their experiences in packaged goods and manufacturing had not prepared them for. These people realized the need for new concepts and approaches for marketing and managing service businesses.

Service marketers responded to these forces and began to work across disciplines and with academics and business practitioners from around the world to develop and document marketing practices for services. As the field evolved, it expanded to address the concerns and needs of *any* business in which service is an integral part of the offering. Frameworks, concepts, and strategies developed to address the fact that "services marketing is different." As the field continues to evolve in the 21st century, new trends will shape the field and accelerate the need for services marketing concepts and tools.

Service Equals Profits

Through the 1980s and early 1990s many firms jumped on the service bandwagon, investing in service initiatives and promoting service quality as ways to differentiate themselves and create competitive advantage. Many of these investments were based on faith and intuition by managers who believed in serving customers well and who believed in their hearts that quality service made good business sense. Indeed, a dedication to quality service has been the foundation for success for many firms, across industries. In his book *Discovering the Soul of Service,* Leonard Berry describes in detail 14 such companies.[13] The companies featured in his book had been in business an average of 31 years in 1999 when the book was written. These companies had been profitable in all but 5 of their combined 407 years of existence. Dr. Berry discovered through his research that these successful businesses share devotion to nine common service themes, among them values-driven leadership, commitment to investments in employee success, and trust-based relationships with customers and other partners at the foundation of the organization.

Since the mid-1990s firms have demanded hard evidence of the bottom-line effectiveness of service strategies. And researchers are building a convincing case that service strategies, implemented appropriately, can be very profitable. Work sponsored by the Marketing Science Institute suggests that corporate strategies focused on customer satisfaction, revenue generation, and service quality may actually be more profitable than strategies focused on cost cutting or strategies that attempt to do both simultaneously.[14] Research out of the Harvard Business School builds a case for the "service–profit chain," linking internal service and employee satisfaction to customer value and ultimately to profits.[15] And considerable research shows linkages from customer satisfaction (often driven by service outcomes) to profits.[16] From the University of Michigan American Customer Satisfaction Index (ACSI) even comes data suggesting that customer satisfaction is directly linked to shareholder value. Firms in the top 50 percent of the ACSI rankings show significantly higher shareholder value than do firms in the bottom 50 percent.[17]

An important key to these successes is that the right strategies are chosen and that these strategies are implemented appropriately and well. Much of what you learn from this text will guide you in making such correct choices and in providing superior implementation. Throughout the text we will point out the profit implications and trade-offs to be made with service strategies. See this chapter's Strategy Insight for four ways that firms successfully and profitably compete through service. In Chapter 18 we will come back to this issue by providing integrated coverage of the financial and profit impact of service.

But "Service Stinks"

Despite the importance of service and the bottom-line profit potential for service, consumers perceive that overall the quality of service is declining.[18] We see *BusinessWeek* magazine blatantly condemning service in its cover story "Why Service Stinks."[19] And although there are exceptions in every industry, American Customer Satisfaction Index (ACSI) scores for service industries are generally lower than the average for all industries. Particularly low are ACSI scores in the transportation, communications, and utilities sectors. For example, whereas the national ACSI average across all industries has risen to 74.4, cable and satellite television and the wireless telecommunication industries overall receive ratings in the low to mid 60s, and most airlines score in the mid 60s.[20]

Firms can compete profitably through services in a variety of different ways. Through our work with companies across industries and through benchmarking other companies, we see four strategic themes emerge as the primary ways that firms can compete through service. Although firms tend to emphasize one or two of these strategic choices at a given time, it may be possible to do more.

EXEMPLARY OUT-OF-THE-BOX CUSTOMER SERVICE

There are some organizations whose competitive advantage is their reputation for out-of-the-box customer service. Southwest Airlines, Mayo Clinic, Gallery Furniture (a hugely successful furniture store in Texas), and Zanes Cycles (a small bicycle shop in Connecticut) are just a few examples. These organizations focus on going out of their way for customers and providing customer service in unique ways. Special services that these companies provide include

- at Southwest Airlines, a distinctive sense of humor among employees as well as in-flight games and jokes

- at Mayo Clinic, a grand piano in the lobby and doctors who sit physically close to patients, look them in the eye, and truly believe that "the best interest of the patient is the only interest to be considered"

- at Gallery Furniture, free food and day care for children

- at Zanes Cycles, a "flat tire club"

INNOVATIVE, CUTTING-EDGE SERVICES

Other organizations compete through providing innovative and cutting-edge services—being the first and/or best in their industry or being on the forefront of new inventions, technology, or science. Examples here include Amazon.com, the first company to introduce really effective and innovative online retailing. Mayo Clinic falls into this category as well. It is on the leading edge of medicine in the United States and typically only sees patients who have hard-to-diagnose or complex problems. The clinic's research-based, team-oriented, consultative model of medicine keeps it on the forefront.

Being innovative doesn't necessarily mean that the organization invents something totally new; perhaps its services approach is simply new to that industry. Yellow Roadway Corporation, an old-line trucking company, reinvented itself as a transportation company by successfully introducing guarantees, express services, and time-definite delivery into this somewhat stodgy industry.

VALUE-ADDED, REVENUE-PRODUCING SERVICES

A major trend in manufacturing, information technology, and other nonservice industries in recent years is the introduction of value-added, revenue-producing services. Firms in these industries have recognized that they cannot compete on the sales and margins produced by their manufactured products alone. Many firms, such as IBM, Hewlett-Packard, Siemens, and General Electric, have integrated services into their mix of offerings. In some

continued

cases, as with IBM (see the opening vignette in this chapter), services have actually taken over as the growth engine for the company.

This focus on revenue-producing services also extends to retailers. For example, PETs-MART, the largest pet retailer in the United States, has introduced a host of new services in recent years as a way to compete effectively in this relatively low-margin industry. The company targets "pet parents" in its advertising, and its special services include pet training, grooming, and overnight care.

A SERVICE CULTURE THAT DIFFERENTIATES

Finally, a firm can compete by nurturing a service culture that attracts the very best workers in the industry. In attracting the best workers, the company has an advantage over the competition in terms of providing the very best services and thus becoming both the "employer of choice" and the "provider of choice" in its industry. This approach is used, for example, by Southwest Airlines, Mayo Clinic, and Marriott Hotels. At Marriott, the underlying company philosophy is "take care of your employees and they will take care of your guests." This philosophy permeates all the Marriott brands, from Fairfield Inns to the Ritz Carlton, giving Marriott a worldwide competitive advantage in its industry.

Source: Center for Services Leadership, W. P. Carey School of Business, Arizona State University (www.wpcarey.asu.edu/csl). Reprinted by permission of Mary Jo Bitner, co-author, Center for Services Leadership.

This condemnation of service is troubling when, at some level, service has never been better. For example, think of just one industry—health care. The ability to prevent and treat diseases has never been greater, resulting in an ever-increasing life expectancy in the United States and in most industrialized countries. Or take the communications industries—communicating quickly, effectively, and cheaply with people all over the world has never been easier. Access to vast quantities of information, entertainment, and music is unbelievable compared to what people had just 10 years ago. So clearly, in some ways and in many industries, services are better than ever.

Despite these obvious improvements, there is hard evidence that consumers perceive a lower quality of service overall and are less satisfied. There are many theories as to why this decline in customer satisfaction with services has occurred, but it is difficult to point precisely to the reason. Plausible theories include these:

- With more companies offering tiered service based on the calculated profitability of different market segments, many customers are in fact getting less service than they have in the past.

- Increasing use by companies of self-service and technology-based service is perceived as less service because no human interaction or human personalization is provided.

- Technology-based services (automated voice systems, Internet-based services, technology kiosks) are hard to implement, with many failures and with poorly designed systems in place.

- Customer expectations are higher because of the excellent service they receive from some companies. Thus, they expect the same from all and are frequently disappointed.

- Organizations have cut costs to the extent that they are too lean and too understaffed to provide quality service.

- The competitive job market results in less-skilled people working in front-line service jobs; talented workers soon get promoted or leave for better opportunities.

- Many companies give lip service to customer focus and service quality, but they fail to provide the training, compensation, and support needed to actually deliver quality service.

- Delivering consistent, high-quality service is not easy, yet many companies promise it.

These theories as to the causes of declining customer satisfaction can be debated. But for managers, students, and teachers of services marketing and management, the message is clear: There is plenty of work to be done. Services can be profitable, customers demand services, and yet overall quality perceptions and customer satisfaction are declining. In this text we will provide many examples of best practices—companies that understand how to get it right and are succeeding with service. We will also delineate many tools, concepts, and strategies that can help to reverse the "service stinks" mind-set.

SERVICE AND TECHNOLOGY

The preceding sections examined the roots of services marketing and the reasons why the field exists. Another major trend—technology, specifically information technology—is currently shaping the field and profoundly influencing the practice of services marketing. In this section we explore trends in technology (positive *and* negative) to set the stage for topics that will be discussed throughout this text. In each chapter you will find a Technology Spotlight box that highlights the influence of technology on issues related to the particular chapter. We will also raise technology and service issues as appropriate throughout the general discussion in the text and have included several cases that explore the opportunities and challenges of services and technology. Together with globalization, the influence of technology is the most profound trend affecting services marketing today.

Potential for New Service Offerings

Looking to the recent past, it is apparent how technology has been the basic force behind service innovations now taken for granted. Automated voice mail, interactive voice response systems, fax machines, ATMs, and other common services were possible only because of new technologies. Just think how dramatically different your world would be without these basic technology services.

More recently, people have seen the explosion of the Internet, resulting in a host of new services. Internet-based companies like amazon.com and eBay offer services previously unheard of. And established companies find that the Internet provides a way to offer new services as well.[21] For example, Dow Jones, publisher of *The Wall Street*

Journal, offers an interactive edition that allows customers to organize the newspaper's content to suit their individual preferences and needs.

Many new technology services are on the horizon. For example, some researchers project that the "connected car" will allow people to access all kinds of existing and new services while on the road. Already many cars are equipped with map and routing software that direct drivers to specific locations. In the future, in-car systems may provide recommendations for shopping by informing drivers when they are within a certain number of miles of their preferred retailer. On a road trip, the system may provide weather forecasts and warnings, and when it is time to stop for the night, the car's system could book a room at a nearby hotel, recommend a restaurant, and make dinner reservations.[22]

New Ways to Deliver Service

In addition to providing opportunities for new service offerings, technology is providing vehicles for delivering existing services in more accessible, convenient, productive ways. Technology facilitates basic customer service functions (bill paying, questions, checking account records, tracking orders), transactions (both retail and business-to-business), and learning or information seeking. Our Technology Spotlight traces how, through history, evolving technologies have changed customer service forever. Companies have moved from face-to-face service to telephone-based service to widespread use of interactive voice response systems to Internet-based customer service and now to wireless service. Interestingly, many companies are coming full circle and now offer human contact as the ultimate form of customer service!

Technology also facilitates transactions by offering a direct vehicle for making purchases. In the financial services field, Charles Schwab transformed itself from a traditional broker to an online financial services company that currently conducts more than 70 percent of its customer transactions online. Technology giant Cisco Systems offers virtually all its customer service and ordering functions to its business customers via technology. Over 90 percent of its transactions with customers are completed online. On the consumer side, online shopping and transactions have already revolutionized the music and book businesses. Predictions suggest that online ordering will also rewrite the rules for purchasing jewelry, real estate, hotel rooms, and software. For example, more than 70 percent of home buyers shop online before completing a home purchase, compared to 41 percent three years ago.[23]

Finally, technology, specifically the Internet, provides an easy way for customers to learn and research. Access to information has never been easier. For example, over 20,000 websites currently offer health-related information. Many provide answers to specific disease, drug, and treatment questions. In a study of online health care information usage, the Pew organization found that among Americans with Internet access, 62 percent had looked for health or medical information on the Web.[24]

Enabling Both Customers and Employees

Technology enables both customers and employees to be more effective in getting and providing service.[25] Through self-service technologies, customers can serve themselves more effectively. Via online banking, customers can access their accounts, check balances, apply for loans, shift money among accounts, and take care of just about any banking need they might have—all without the assistance of the bank's employees. Wells Fargo, the first bank to offer online services in the United States, finds that its online customers are its most satisfied customers. These online banking

Technology Spotlight
The Changing Face of Customer Service

Excellent customer service—the daily, ongoing support of a company's offerings—is critical in creating brand identity and ultimate success. It includes answering questions, taking orders, dealing with billing issues, handling complaints, scheduling appointments, and similar activities. These essential functions can make or break an organization's relationships with its customers. The quality of customer care can significantly impact brand identity for service, manufacturing, and consumer products companies. Because of its importance in creating impressions and sustaining customer relationships, customer service has sometimes been called the "front door" of the organization or its "face."

So how has the "face" of customer service changed with the influx of technology? Long ago all customer service was provided face-to-face through direct personal interaction between employees and customers. To get service you had to visit stores or service providers in person. The telephone changed this, allowing customers to call companies and speak directly with employees, typically Monday–Friday, 8 A.M.–5 P.M. Customer service became less personal, but without a doubt more efficient, through use of the telephone. With the evolution of computer technology, customer service representatives (CSRs) became even more efficient. Through computer information systems and customer data files, CSRs are able to call up customer records at their workstations to answer questions on the spot.

Over time, because communication and computer technologies allowed it, large organizations began to centralize their customer service functions, consolidating into a few large call centers that could be located anywhere in the country or the world. For example, a large percentage of IBM's customer service calls in North America are handled out of its sales and service center in Toronto, Canada, and calls can be handled 24 hours per day. But still, in these types of call centers, customer service is for the most part an interpersonal event with customers talking directly, one-on-one with an employee.

The advent and rapid proliferation of the efficient, but much maligned, automated voice response systems have changed personal customer service in many organizations into menu-driven, automated exchanges. In almost every industry and any business context, consumers encounter these types of systems, and many are quite frustrating—for example, when a system has a long, confusing set of menu options or when no menu option seems to fit the purpose of the call. Similarly, consumers become angered when they cannot get out of the automated system easily, or when there is no option to speak to a live person.

continued

services are just one example of the types of self-service technologies that are proliferating across industries.

For employees, technology can provide tremendous support in making them more effective and efficient in delivering service. Customer relationship management and sales support software are broad categories of technology that can aid frontline employees in providing better service. By having immediate access to information about their product and service offerings as well as about particular customers, employees are better able to serve them. This type of information allows employees to customize services to fit the customer's needs. They can also be much more efficient and timely than in the old days when most customer and product information was in paper files or in the heads of sales and customer service representatives.

Extending the Global Reach of Services

Technology infusion results in the potential for reaching out to customers around the globe in ways not possible before. The Internet itself knows no boundaries, and therefore information, customer service, and transactions can move across countries and

Technology Spotlight
The Changing Face of Customer Service—continued

Some companies have overcome these obstacles, however, and have well-designed automated telephone systems that work well for customers. Charles Schwab provides a notable example. Schwab completes more than 75 percent of its 82 million annual calls through speech and touch-tone automated response systems. Its automated voice response system has been designed to give quick answers with a minimum of navigation beyond the first menu. This efficiency is accomplished through a form of natural-language speech recognition technology that allows customers to easily interact through the telephone in ways that are much like talking to a real person. Further, a human contact is always easy to get to if needed. Customer satisfaction at Schwab is rated among the highest in any industry. One of the keys may be that at Charles Schwab, the vice president of retail voice technology occupies a senior management position, showing the importance placed on this function. In general, satisfaction levels for automated speech recognition systems are higher than satisfaction with touch-tone systems and in some cases are higher than for live agents.

Beyond automated telecom systems, explosion of the Internet is also dramatically changing customer service for many companies. Service can now be provided on the Internet via e-mails, website robots, FAQs, and online chats. In these cases there is no direct human interaction, and customers actually perform their own ser-

vice. An example is Ford Motor Company's technology that allows dealership customers to set their own service appointments, send messages regarding their specific repair needs, and monitor the status of their vehicles, all online.

With the relentless proliferation of technology solutions, firms are finding that expectations for customer service have changed. Customers are demanding choices in how they get customer service, whether it be via phone, automated voice system, fax, e-mail, or Internet self-service. Although customers often enjoy technology-based service and even demand it in many cases, they dislike it when it doesn't work reliably (a common problem), when it doesn't seem to have any advantages over the interpersonal service alternatives, and when there are no systems in place to recover from failures. Interestingly, when things don't work as they are supposed to on an Internet site or through an automated response system, customers are quick to look for more traditional interpersonal (in person or via telephone) options, coming full circle to where they started!

Sources: J. A. Nickell, "To Voice Mail Hell and Back," *Business 2.0,* July 10, 2001, pp. 49–53; D. Ward, "The Web's Killer App: A Human Being," *Revolution,* March 2000, pp. 82–88; M. L. Meuter, A. L. Ostrom, R. I. Roundtree, and M. J. Bitner, "Self-Service Technologies: Understanding Customer Satisfaction with Technology-Based Service Encounters," *Journal of Marketing* 64 (July 2000), pp. 50–64.

across continents, reaching any customer who has access to the Web. Technology also allows employees of international companies to stay in touch easily—to share information, to ask questions, to serve on virtual teams together. All this technology facilitates the global reach as well as the effectiveness of service businesses. Our Global Feature focuses on the migration of service jobs and the ability to produce services almost anywhere.

The Internet *Is* a Service

An interesting way to look at the influence of technology is to realize that the Internet is just "one big service." All businesses and organizations that operate on the Internet are essentially providing services—whether they are giving information, performing basic customer service functions, or facilitating transactions. Thus all the tools, concepts, and strategies you learn in studying services marketing and management have direct application in an Internet or e-business world. Although technology and the Internet are profoundly changing how people do business and what offerings are possible, it is clear that customers still want basic service. They want what they have always wanted: dependable outcomes, easy access, responsive systems, flexibility, apologies,

With the ever-growing sophistication of information technology, the global reach of organizations is increasing at a spectacular rate. Activities that used to require close proximity and personal contact can now often be accomplished via the Internet, video, and telecommunication technologies. This advancement means that the jobs that produce and support these activities can be done almost anywhere in the world. The result has been referred to as a "migration of service jobs" out of countries such as the United States and the United Kingdom to countries such as India, Pakistan, the Philippines, and Eastern European countries.

This globalization of services is in many ways inevitable, but it comes with considerable controversy. One clear concern is that some of the highest-paying service jobs are being "lost" to lower-wage countries, and this concern is very real for the individuals whose jobs are lost. However, the numbers are not as large as perhaps imagined. Forrester Research in Cambridge, Massachusetts, estimates that by the year 2015, 3.3 million high-tech and service jobs will move overseas from the United States. On the other side of this concern are arguments that offshore jobs will spur innovation, job creation in other areas, and increases in productivity that will benefit the consumer and keep companies competitive in the global marketplace. In fact, the Bureau of Labor Statistics estimates that between 2000 and 2010, 22 million new U.S. jobs (mostly in business services, health care, social services, transportation, and communications) will be created. Although the specific outcomes of service job migration are not totally known, it is safe to say that the globalization of services will continue, resulting in further shrinking of the boundaries among people and countries.

Service job migration involves not just call centers and IT help lines, but also services that span industries and levels of skills. Software development, IT consulting, chip design, financial analysis, industrial engineering, analytics, and drug research are just a few examples of services performed in India for global firms. Even medical diagnoses and reading of medical records can be done remotely via video, Internet, and scanning technologies.

Why is service job migration happening now? The root of the acceleration is the rapid development and accessibility of sophisticated information technologies. Services are information intensive, and information can now be shared readily without direct personal contact. For example, at the John F. Welch Technology Center in Bangalore, 1,800 Indian engineers (a quarter of whom have PhDs) engage in research for General Electric's 13 divisions. Projects span such diverse areas as developing materials for use in DVDs, boosting productivity of GE plants, and tweaking the designs of turbine engine blades. The design work can be done in India (perhaps even teaming with engineers elsewhere), and the results can be sent instantaneously wherever they are needed. Other examples: 20,000 U.S. tax returns were prepared and filed by CPAs working in India; Indian financial analysts digested the latest disclosures of U.S. companies and filed reports the next day; and other workers in India sorted through mounds of consumer data provided by non-Indian company clients to determine behavior patterns and develop ideas for marketing. In each of these cases, *where* the work is done is not important or meaningful to the client as long as it is done well and on time.

A major reason that this movement of jobs is possible is that countries outside the developed world are now producing highly skilled, well-educated workforces, particularly in

continued

China and India. These workers typically work for far less compensation than their U.S. or U.K. counterparts, allowing global companies to reduce labor costs on the one hand and increase overall productivity on the other. The quality of the work can be very high as well, with many companies citing quality and performance among their reasons for moving service jobs overseas.

Source: Indranil Mukerjee/Getty Images

Sources: U. Karmarkar, "Will You Survive the Services Revolution?" *Harvard Business Review,* June 2004, pp. 100–107; M. Kripalani and P. Engardio, "The Rise of India," *BusinessWeek,* December 8, 2003; "Mapping Offshore Markets," white paper by neoIT, at www.neoIT.com; S. A. Teicher, "A Not So Simple Path," *Christian Science Monitor,* February 23, 2004; M. N. Baily and D. Farrell, "Exploding the Myths of Offshoring," *The McKinsey Quarterly,* online at www.mckinseyquarterly.com, July 2004.

and compensation when things go wrong. But now they expect these same outcomes from technology-based businesses and from e-commerce solutions.[26] With hindsight it is obvious that many dot-com start-ups suffered and even failed because of lack of basic customer knowledge and failure of implementation, logistics, and service follow-up.[27]

The Paradoxes and Dark Side of Technology and Service

Although there is clearly great potential for technology to support and enhance services, there are potential negative outcomes as well. Mick and Fournier, well-regarded consumer researchers, have pointed out the many paradoxes of technology products and services for consumers, as shown in Table 1.1.[28] This section highlights some of the general concerns.

Customer concerns about privacy and confidentiality raise major issues for firms as they seek to learn about and interact directly with customers through the Internet. These types of concerns are what have stymied and precluded many efforts to advance technology applications in the health care industry, for example. Nor are all customers equally interested in using technology as a means of interacting with companies. Research exploring "customer technology readiness" suggests that some customers are simply not interested or ready to use technology.[29] Employees can also be reluctant to accept and integrate technology into their work lives—especially when they perceive, rightly or wrongly, that the technology will substitute for human labor and perhaps eliminate their jobs.

TABLE 1.1   **Eight Central Paradoxes of Technological Products**

Paradox	Description
Control/chaos	Technology can facilitate regulation or order, and technology can lead to upheaval or disorder.
Freedom/enslavement	Technology can facilitate independence or fewer restrictions, and technology can lead to dependence or more restrictions.
New/obsolete	New technologies provide the user with the most recently developed benefits of scientific knowledge, and new technologies are already or soon to be outmoded as they reach the marketplace.
Competence/incompetence	Technology can facilitate feelings of intelligence or efficacy, and technology can lead to feelings of ignorance or ineptitude.
Efficiency/inefficiency	Technology can facilitate less effort or time spent in certain activities, and technology can lead to more effort or time in certain activities.
Fulfills/creates needs	Technology can facilitate the fulfillment of needs or desires, and technology can lead to the development or awareness of needs or desires previously unrealized.
Assimilation/isolation	Technology can facilitate human togetherness, and technology can lead to human separation.
Engaging/disengaging	Technology can facilitate involvement, flow, or activity, and technology can lead to disconnection, disruption, or passivity.

Source: D. G. Mick and S. Fournier, "Paradoxes of Technology: Consumer Cognizance, Emotions, and Coping Strategies," *Journal of Consumer Research* 25 (September 1998), pp. 123–47. Copyright © 1998 University of Chicago Press. Reprinted by permission.

With technology infusion comes a loss of human contact, which many people believe is detrimental purely from a quality of life and human relationships perspective. Parents may lament that their children spend hours in front of computer screens, interacting with games, seeking information, and relating to their friends only through instant messaging without any face-to-face human contact. And workers in organizations become more and more reliant on communicating through technology—even communicating via e-mail with the person in the next office!

Finally, the payback in technology investments is often uncertain. It may take a long time for an investment to result in productivity or customer satisfaction gains. Sometimes it never happens. For example, McKinsey & Company reports that a firm projected a $40 million savings from moving its billing and service calls to the Web. Instead it suffered a $16 billion loss as a result of lower usage by customers than projected, unanticipated follow-up calls and e-mails to the call center from those who had used the Web application initially, and loss of revenue from lack of cross-selling opportunities.[30]

CHARACTERISTICS OF SERVICES COMPARED TO GOODS

There is general agreement that differences between goods and services exist and that the distinctive characteristics discussed in this section result in challenges (as well as advantages) for managers of services.[31] It is also important to realize that each of these characteristics could be arranged on a continuum similar to the tangibility spectrum show in Figure 1.1. That is, services tend to be more heterogeneous, more intangible, more difficult to evaluate than goods, but the differences between goods and services are not black and white by any means.[32]

Table 1.2 summarizes the differences between goods and services and the implications of these characteristics. Many of the strategies, tools, and frameworks in this text

TABLE 1.2   **Goods versus Services**

Goods	Services	Resulting Implications
Tangible	Intangible	Services cannot be inventoried. Services cannot be easily patented. Services cannot be readily displayed or communicated. Pricing is difficult.
Standardized	Heterogeneous	Service delivery and customer satisfaction depend on employee and customer actions. Service quality depends on many uncontrollable factors. There is no sure knowledge that the service delivered matches what was planned and promoted.
Production separate from consumption	Simultaneous production and consumption	Customers participate in and affect the transaction. Customers affect each other. Employees affect the service outcome. Decentralization may be essential. Mass production is difficult.
Nonperishable	Perishable	It is difficult to synchronize supply and demand with services. Services cannot be returned or resold.

Source: A. Parasuraman, V.A. Zeithaml, and L. L. Berry, "A Conceptual Model of Service Quality and It's Implications for Future Research." *Journal of Marketing* 49 (Fall 1985) pp. 41–50. Reprinted by permission of the American Marketing Association.

were developed to address these characteristics, which, until the 1980s, had been largely ignored by marketers. Recently it has been suggested that these distinctive characteristics should not be viewed as unique to services but that they are also relevant to goods, that "all products are services," and that "economic exchange is fundamentally about service provision."[33] Although this view is rather abstract, it does suggest that all types of organizations may be able to gain valuable insights from services marketing frameworks, tools, and strategies.

Intangibility

The most basic distinguishing characteristic of services is intangibility. Because services are performances or actions rather than objects, they cannot be seen, felt, tasted, or touched in the same manner that you can sense tangible goods. For example, health care services are actions (such as surgery, diagnosis, examination, and treatment) performed by providers and directed toward patients and their families. These services cannot actually be seen or touched by the patient, although the patient may be able to see and touch certain tangible components of the service (like the equipment or hospital room). In fact, many services such as health care are difficult for the consumer to grasp even mentally. Even after a diagnosis or surgery has been completed the patient may not fully comprehend the service performed, although tangible evidence of the service (e.g., incision, bandaging, pain) may be quite apparent.

Resulting Marketing Implications   Intangibility presents several marketing challenges. Services cannot be inventoried, and therefore fluctuations in demand are often difficult to manage. For example, there is tremendous demand for resort accommodations in Phoenix in February, but little demand in July. Yet resort owners have the same number of rooms to sell year-round. Services cannot be easily patented, and new service concepts can therefore easily be copied by competitors. Services cannot be readily displayed or easily communicated to customers, so quality may be difficult for consumers to assess. Decisions about what to include in advertising and other promotional materials are challenging, as is pricing. The actual costs of a "unit of service" are hard to determine, and the price–quality relationship is complex.

Heterogeneity

Because services are performances, frequently produced by humans, no two services will be precisely alike. The employees delivering the service frequently are the service in the customer's eyes, and people may differ in their performance from day to day or even hour to hour. Heterogeneity also results because no two customers are precisely alike; each will have unique demands or experience the service in a unique way. Thus the heterogeneity connected with services is largely the result of human interaction (between and among employees and customers) and all of the vagaries that accompany it. For example, a tax accountant may provide a different service experience to two different customers on the same day depending on their individual needs and personalities and on whether the accountant is interviewing them when he or she is fresh in the morning or tired at the end of a long day of meetings.

Resulting Marketing Implications   Because services are heterogeneous across time, organizations, and people, ensuring consistent service quality is challenging. Quality actually depends on many factors that cannot be fully controlled by the service supplier, such as the ability of the consumer to articulate his or her needs, the ability and willingness of personnel to satisfy those needs, the presence (or absence) of other customers, and the level of demand for the service. Because of these complicating factors, the service manager cannot always know for sure that the service is being delivered in a manner consistent with what was originally planned and promoted. Sometimes services may be provided by a third party, further increasing the potential heterogeneity of the offering.

Simultaneous Production and Consumption

Whereas most goods are produced first, then sold and consumed, most services are sold first and then produced and consumed simultaneously. For example, an automobile can be manufactured in Detroit, shipped to San Francisco, sold two months later, and consumed over a period of years. But restaurant services cannot be provided until they have been sold, and the dining experience is essentially produced and consumed at the same time. Frequently this situation also means that the customer is present while the service is being produced and thus views and may even take part in the production process. Simultaneity also means that customers will frequently interact with each other during the service production process and thus may affect each others' experiences. For example, strangers seated next to each other in an airplane may well affect the nature of the service experience for each other. That passengers understand this fact is clearly apparent in the way business travelers will often go to great lengths to be sure they are not seated next to families with small children. Another outcome of simultaneous production and consumption is that service producers find themselves playing a role as part of the product itself and as an essential ingredient in the service experience for the consumer.

Resulting Marketing Implications   Because services often are produced and consumed at the same time, mass production is difficult. The quality of service and customer satisfaction will be highly dependent on what happens in "real time," including actions of employees and the interactions between employees and customers. Clearly the real-time nature of services also results in advantages in terms of opportunities to customize offerings for individual consumers. Simultaneous production and consumption also means that it is not usually possible to gain significant economies of scale through centralization. Often, operations need to be relatively decentralized so that the service can be delivered directly to the consumer in convenient locations, although the growth of technology-delivered services is changing this requirement for many services. Also because of simultaneous production and consumption, the customer is involved in and observes the production process and thus may affect (positively or negatively) the outcome of the service transaction.

Perishability

Perishability refers to the fact that services cannot be saved, stored, resold, or returned. A seat on an airplane or in a restaurant, an hour of a lawyer's time, or telephone line capacity not used cannot be reclaimed and used or resold at a later time. Perishability is in contrast to goods that can be stored in inventory or resold another day, or even returned if the consumer is unhappy. Wouldn't it be nice if a bad haircut could be returned or resold to another consumer? Perishability makes this action an unlikely possibility for most services.

Resulting Marketing Implications   A primary issue that marketers face in relation to service perishability is the inability to inventory. Demand forecasting and creative planning for capacity utilization are therefore important and challenging decision areas. The fact that services cannot typically be returned or resold also implies a need for strong recovery strategies when things do go wrong. For example, although a bad haircut cannot be returned, the hairdresser can and should have strategies for recovering the customer's goodwill if and when such a problem occurs.

Challenges and Questions for Service Marketers

Because of the basic characteristics of services, marketers of services face some very real and distinctive challenges. Answers to questions such as the ones listed here still elude managers of services:

How can service quality be defined and improved when the product is intangible and nonstandardized?

How can new services be designed and tested effectively when the service is essentially an intangible process?

How can the firm be certain it is communicating a consistent and relevant image when so many elements of the marketing mix communicate to customers and some of these elements are the service providers themselves?

How does the firm accommodate fluctuating demand when capacity is fixed and the service itself is perishable?

How can the firm best motivate and select service employees who, because the service is delivered in real time, become a critical part of the product itself?

How should prices be set when it is difficult to determine actual costs of production and price may be inextricably intertwined with perceptions of quality?

How should the firm be organized so that good strategic and tactical decisions are made when a decision in any of the functional areas of marketing, operations, and human resources may have significant impact on the other two areas?

How can the balance between standardization and personalization be determined to maximize both the efficiency of the organization and the satisfaction of its customers?

How can the organization protect new service concepts from competitors when service processes cannot be readily patented?

How does the firm communicate quality and value to consumers when the offering is intangible and cannot be readily tried or displayed?

How can the organization ensure the delivery of consistent quality service when both the organization's employees and the customers themselves can affect the service outcome?

SERVICES MARKETING MIX

The preceding questions are some of the many raised by managers and marketers of services that will be addressed throughout the text through a variety of tools and strategies. Sometimes these tools are adaptations of traditional marketing tools, as with the services marketing mix presented here. Other times they are radically new, as in the case of service blueprinting presented in Chapter 9.

Traditional Marketing Mix

One of the most basic concepts in marketing is the marketing mix, defined as the elements an organization controls that can be used to satisfy or communicate with customers. The traditional marketing mix is composed of the four Ps: *product, price, place* (distribution), and *promotion*.[34] These elements appear as core decision variables in any marketing text or marketing plan. The notion of a mix implies that all the variables are interrelated and depend on each other to some extent. Further, the marketing mix philosophy implies an optimal mix of the four factors for a given market segment at a given point in time.

Key strategy decision areas for each of the four Ps are captured in the first four columns in Table 1.3. Careful management of product, place, promotion, and price will clearly also be essential to the successful marketing of services. However, the strategies for the four Ps require some modifications when applied to services. For example, traditionally promotion is thought of as involving decisions related to sales, advertising, sales promotions, and publicity. In services these factors are also important, but because services are produced and consumed simultaneously, service delivery people (such as clerks, ticket takers, nurses, and phone personnel) are involved in real-time promotion of the service even if their jobs are typically defined in terms of the operational function they perform.

Expanded Mix for Services

Because services are usually produced and consumed simultaneously, customers are often present in the firm's factory, interact directly with the firm's personnel, and are actually part of the service production process. Also, because services are intangible, customers will often be looking for any tangible cue to help them understand the nature of the service experience. For example, in the hotel industry the design and decor of the hotel as well as the appearance and attitudes of its employees will influence customer perceptions and experiences.

TABLE 1.3
Expanded Marketing
Mix for Services

Product	Place	Promotion	Price
Physical good features	Channel type	Promotion blend	Flexibility
Quality level	Exposure	Salespeople	Price level
Accessories	Intermediaries	Selection	Terms
Packaging	Outlet locations	Training	Differentiation
Warranties	Transportation	Incentives	Discounts
Product lines	Storage	Advertising	Allowances
Branding	Managing channels	Media types	
		Types of ads	
		Sales promotion	
		Publicity	
		Internet/Web strategy	

People	Physical Evidence	Process
Employees	Facility design	Flow of activities
Recruiting	Equipment	Standardized
Training	Signage	Customized
Motivation	Employee dress	Number of steps
Rewards	Other tangibles	Simple
Teamwork	Reports	Complex
Customers	Business cards	Customer
Education	Statements	involvement
Training	Guarantees	

Acknowledgment of the importance of these additional variables has led services marketers to adopt the concept of an expanded marketing mix for services shown in the three remaining columns in Table 1.3.[35] In addition to the traditional four Ps, the services marketing mix includes *people, physical evidence,* and *process.*

People   All human actors who play a part in service delivery and thus influence the buyer's perceptions: namely, the firm's personnel, the customer, and other customers in the service environment.

All the human actors participating in the delivery of a service provide cues to the customer regarding the nature of the service itself. How these people are dressed, their personal appearance, and their attitudes and behaviors all influence the customer's perceptions of the service. The service provider or contact person can be very important. In fact, for some services, such as consulting, counseling, teaching, and other professional relationship-based services, the provider *is* the service. In other cases the contact person may play what appears to be a relatively small part in service delivery— for instance, a telephone installer, an airline baggage handler, or an equipment delivery dispatcher. Yet research suggests that even these providers may be the focal point of service encounters that can prove critical for the organization.

In many service situations, customers themselves can also influence service delivery, thus affecting service quality and their own satisfaction. For example, a client of a consulting company can influence the quality of service received by providing needed and timely information and by implementing recommendations provided by the consultant. Similarly, health care patients greatly affect the quality of service they receive when they either comply or don't comply with health regimens prescribed by the provider.

Customers not only influence their own service outcomes, but they can influence other customers as well. In a theater, at a ballgame, or in a classroom, customers can influence the quality of service received by others—either enhancing or detracting from other customers' experiences.

Physical evidence   The environment in which the service is delivered and where the firm and customer interact, and any tangible components that facilitate performance or communication of the service.

The physical evidence of service includes all the tangible representations of the service such as brochures, letterhead, business cards, report formats, signage, and equipment. In some cases it includes the physical facility where the service is offered—the "servicescape"—for example, the retail bank branch facility. In other cases, such as telecommunication services, the physical facility may be irrelevant. In this case other tangibles such as billing statements and appearance of the repair truck may be important indicators of quality. Especially when consumers have little on which to judge the actual quality of service they will rely on these cues, just as they rely on the cues provided by the people and the service process. Physical evidence cues provide excellent opportunities for the firm to send consistent and strong messages regarding the organization's purpose, the intended market segments, and the nature of the service.

Process   The actual procedures, mechanisms, and flow of activities by which the service is delivered—the service delivery and operating systems.

The actual delivery steps that the customer experiences, or the operational flow of the service, also give customers evidence on which to judge the service. Some services are very complex, requiring the customer to follow a complicated and extensive series of actions to complete the process. Highly bureaucratized services frequently follow this pattern, and the logic of the steps involved often escapes the customer. Another distinguishing characteristic of the process that can provide evidence to the customer is whether the service follows a production-line/standardized approach or whether the process is an empowered/customized one. None of these characteristics of the service is inherently better or worse than another. Rather, the point is that these process characteristics are another form of evidence used by the consumer to judge service. For example, two successful airline companies, Southwest and Singapore Airlines, follow extremely different process models. Southwest is a no-frills (no food, no assigned seats), low-priced airline that offers frequent, relatively short domestic flights. All the evidence it provides is consistent with its vision and market position, as illustrated in Exhibit 1.2. Singapore Airlines, on the other hand, focuses on the business traveler and is concerned with meeting individual traveler needs. Thus, its process is highly customized to the individual, and employees are empowered to provide nonstandard service when needed. Both airlines have been very successful.

The three new marketing mix elements (people, physical evidence, and process) are included in the marketing mix as separate elements because they are within the control of the firm *and* because any or all of them may influence the customer's initial decision to purchase a service as well as the customer's level of satisfaction and repurchase decisions. The traditional elements as well as the new marketing mix elements will be explored in depth in future chapters.

Exhibit 1.2 **SOUTHWEST AIRLINES: ALIGNING PEOPLE, PROCESSES, AND PHYSICAL EVIDENCE**

Southwest Airlines occupies a solid position in the minds of U.S. air travelers as a reliable, convenient, fun, low-fare, no-frills airline. Translated, this position means high value—a position reinforced by all elements of Southwest's services marketing mix. It has maintained this position consistently for over 30 years while making money every year; no other U.S. airline comes close to this record. As further evidence of the airline's financial stability, Southwest was the only airline to remain profitable in the months immediately following the September 11, 2001, tragedies in the United States that sent many airlines to near bankruptcy.

Success has come for a number of reasons. One is the airline's low cost structure. It flies only one type of plane (Boeing 737s), which lowers costs because of the fuel efficiency of the aircraft itself combined with the ability to standardize maintenance and operational procedures. The airline also keeps its costs down by not serving meals, having no preassigned seats, and keeping employee turnover very low. Southwest Airlines' Herb Kelleher (president of Southwest from its inception until 2001, and currently serving as chairman) is famous for his belief that employees come first, not customers. The Dallas-based carrier has managed to be the low-cost provider and a preferred employer while enjoying high levels of customer satisfaction and strong customer loyalty. Southwest Airlines has the best customer service record in the airline industry and has won the industry's "Triple Crown" for best baggage handling, best on-time performance, and best customer complaint statistics many years in a row.

Observing Southwest Airlines' success, it is clear that all of its marketing mix is aligned around its highly successful market position. The three new marketing mix elements all strongly reinforce the value image of the airline:

- **People** Southwest uses its people and its customers very effectively to communicate its position. Employees are unionized, yet they are trained to have fun, allowed to define what "fun" means, and given authority to do what it takes to make flights lighthearted and enjoyable. People are hired at Southwest for their attitudes; technical skills can be and are trained. And they are the most productive workforce in the U.S. airline industry. Customers also are included in the atmosphere of fun, and many get into the act by joking with the crew and each other and by flooding the airline with letters expressing their satisfaction.

- **Process** The service delivery process at Southwest also reinforces its position. There are no assigned seats on the aircraft, so passengers line up and are "herded" by number onto the plane, where they jockey for seats. The airline does not transfer baggage to connecting flights on other airlines. Food is not served in flight. In all, the process is very efficient, standardized, and low-cost, allowing for quick turnaround and low fares. Customers are very much part of the service process, taking on their roles willingly.

- **Physical evidence** All the tangibles associated with Southwest further reinforce the market position. Southwest's aircraft are orange and mustard brown, which accentuates their uniqueness and low-cost orientation. Employees dress casually, wearing shorts in the summer to reinforce the "fun" and further emphasize the airline's commitment to its employees' comfort. No in-flight meal service confirms the low-price image through the absence of tangibles—no food. Because many people joke about airline food, its absence for many is not viewed as a value detractor. Southwest's simple, easy-to-use website is yet another form of consistent, tangible evidence that supports the airline's strong positioning and reinforces its image.

The consistent positioning using the services marketing mix reinforces the unique image in the customer's mind, giving Southwest Airlines its high-value position, which has resulted in a huge and committed following of satisfied customers and consistently increasing profits.

Source: K. Freiberg and J. Freiberg, *Nuts! Southwest Airlines' Crazy Recipe for Business and Personal Success* (Austin, TX: Bard Press, Inc., 1996); and K. Labich, "Is Herb Kelleher America's Best CEO?" *Fortune,* May 2, 1994; H. Kelleher and K. Brooker, "The Chairman of the Board Looks Back," *Fortune,* May 28, 2001, pp. 62–76.

STAYING FOCUSED ON THE CUSTOMER

A critical theme running throughout the text is *customer focus.* In fact, the subtitle of the book is "integrating customer focus across the firm." From the firm's point of view, all strategies are developed with an eye on the customer, and all implementations are carried out with an understanding of their impact on the customer. From a practical perspective, decisions regarding new services and communication plans will integrate the customer's point of view; operations and human resource decisions will be considered in terms of their impact on customers. All the tools, strategies, and frameworks included in this text have customers at their foundation. The services marketing mix just described is clearly an important tool that addresses the uniqueness of services, keeping the customer at the center.

In this text, we also view customers as assets to be valued, developed, and retained. The strategies and tools we offer thus focus on customer relationship building and loyalty as opposed to a more transactional focus in which customers are viewed as one-time revenue producers. This text looks at customer relationship management not as a software program but as an entire architecture or business philosophy. Every chapter in the text can be considered a component needed to build a complete customer relationship management approach.

Summary

This chapter has set the stage for further learning about services marketing by presenting information on changes in the world economy and business practice that have driven the focus on service: the fact that services dominate the modern economies of the world; the focus on service as a competitive business imperative; specific needs of the deregulated and professional service industries; the role of new service concepts growing from technological advances; and the realization that the characteristics of services result in unique challenges and opportunities. The chapter presented a broad definition of services as deeds, processes, and performances, and it drew distinctions among pure services, value-added services, customer service, and derived service.

Building on this fundamental understanding of the service economy, the chapter went on to present the key characteristics of services that underlie the need for distinct strategies and concepts for managing service businesses. These basic characteristics are that services are intangible, heterogeneous, produced and consumed simultaneously, and perishable. Because of these characteristics, service managers face a number of challenges in marketing, including the complex problem of how to deliver quality services consistently.

The chapter ended by describing two themes that provide the foundation for future chapters: the expanded marketing mix for services; and customer focus as a unifying theme. The remainder of the text focuses on exploring the unique opportunities and challenges faced by organizations that sell and deliver services and on developing solutions that will help you become an effective services champion and manager.

Discussion Questions

1. What distinguishes service offerings from customer service? Provide specific examples.
2. How is technology changing the nature of service?
3. What are the basic characteristics of services vs. goods? What are the implications of these characteristics for IBM Global Service or for Southwest Airlines?
4. One of the underlying frameworks for the text is the services marketing mix. Discuss why each of the three new mix elements (process, people, and physical evidence) is included. How might each of these communicate with or help to satisfy an organization's customers?

5. Think of a service job you have had or currently have. How effective, in your opinion, was or is the organization in managing the elements of the services marketing mix?

6. Again, think of a service job you have had or currently have. How did or does the organization handle relevant challenges listed in Table 1.2?

7. How can quality service be used in a manufacturing context for competitive advantage? Think of your answer to this question in the context of automobiles or computers or some other manufactured product you have actually purchased.

Exercises

1. Roughly calculate your budget for an average month. What percentage of your budget goes for services versus goods? Do the services you purchase have value? In what sense? If you had to cut back on your expenses, what would you cut out?

2. Visit two local retail service providers that you believe are positioned very differently (such as Kmart and Nordstrom, or Burger King and a fine restaurant). From your own observations, compare their strategies on the elements of the services marketing mix.

3. Try a service you have never tried before on the Internet. Analyze the benefits of this service. Was enough information provided to make the service easy to use? How would you compare this service to other methods of obtaining the same benefits?

Notes

1. D. Kirkpatrick, "Inside Sam's $100 Billion Growth Machine," *Fortune,* June 14, 2004, pp. 80–98; D. Kirkpatrick, "IBM, from Big Blue Dinosaur to E-Business Animal," *Fortune,* April 26, 1999, pp. 116–26; W. M. Bulkeley, "These Days, Big Blue Is About Big Services Not Just Big Boxes," *The Wall Street Journal,* June 11, 2001, p. A1.

2. D. Brady, "Why Service Stinks," *BusinessWeek,* October 23, 2000, pp. 118–28.

3. www.theacsi.org.

4. J. B. Quinn, J. J. Baruch, and P. C. Paquette, "Technology in Services," *Scientific American* 257, no. 6 (December 1987), pp. 50–58.

5. S. L. Vargo and R. F. Lusch, "Evolving to a New Dominant Logic for Marketing," *Journal of Marketing* 68 (January 2004), pp. 1–17.

6. C. L. Bach, "U.S. International Transactions, Fourth Quarter and Year 2000," *Survey of Current Business,* April 2001, pp. 21–68.

7. M. Sawhney, S. Balasubramanian, and V. V. Krishnan, "Creating Growth with Services," *Sloan Management Review,* Winter 2004, pp. 34–43.

8. T. Smart, "Jack Welch's Encore," *BusinessWeek,* October 28, 1996, pp. 155–60; and GE company data, 2000.

9. D. Brady, "Will Jeff Immelt's New Push Pay Off for GE?" *BusinessWeek,* October 13, 2003, pp. 94–98.

10. J. A. Alexander and M. W. Hordes, *S-Business: Reinventing the Services Organization* (New York: SelectBooks, 2003); R. Oliva and R. Kallenberg, "Managing the Transition from Products to Services," *International Journal of Service Industry Management* 14, no. 2 (2003), pp. 160–72.

11. R. H. K. Vietor, *Contrived Competition* (Cambridge, MA: Harvard University Press, 1994).

12. This discussion is based on interviews conducted by Gary Knisely that appeared in *Advertising Age* on January 15, 1979; February 19, 1979; March 19, 1979; and May 14, 1979.

13. L. Berry, *Discovering the Soul of Service* (New York: The Free Press, 1999).

14. R. T. Rust, C. Moorman, and P. R. Dickson, "Getting Return on Quality: Revenue Expansion, Cost Reduction, or Both?" *Journal of Marketing* 66 (October 2002), pp. 7–24.

15. J. L. Heskett, T. O. Jones, G. W. Loveman, W. E. Sasser Jr., and L. A. Schlesinger, "Putting the Service–Profit Chain to Work," *Harvard Business Review,* March–April 1994, pp. 164–74.

16. E. W. Anderson and V. Mittal, "Strengthening the Satisfaction–Profit Chain," *Journal of Service Research* 3, no. 2 (November 2000), pp. 107–20.

17. "Predictive Capabilities," www.theacsi.org, accessed October 13, 2004.

18. C. Fishman, "But Wait, You Promised . . . ," *Fast Company,* April 2001, pp. 116–27.

19. D. Brady, "Why Service Stinks," *BusinessWeek,* October 23, 2000, pp. 116–28.

20. "Latest Increase in ACSI Bodes Well for the Economy," www.theacsi.org/releases. Posted June 4, 2004, accessed October 13, 2004.

21. L. P. Willcocks and R. Plant, "Getting from Bricks to Clicks," *Sloan Management Review,* Spring 2001, pp. 50–59.

22. "Revolution Digital Tomorrow Report: Technologies That Will Change Marketing," *Revolution,* February 2001, pp. 51–65.

23. T. J. Mullaney, "E-Biz Strikes Again!" *BusinessWeek,* May 10, 2004, pp. 80–90.

24. "Vital Decisions," Washington, DC: *The Pew Internet and American Life Project,* http://www.pewinternet.org., 2002.

25. M. J. Bitner, S. W. Brown, and M. L. Meuter, "Technology Infusion in Service Encounters," *Journal of the Academy of Marketing Science* 28, (Winter 2000), pp. 138–49.

26. M. J. Bitner, "Self-Service Technologies: What Do Customers Expect?" *Marketing Management,* Spring 2001, pp. 10–11.

27. R. Hallowell, "Service in E-Commerce: Findings from Exploratory Research," Harvard Business School, Module Note, N9-800-418, May 31, 2000.

28. D. G. Mick and S. Fournier, "Paradoxes of Technology: Consumer Cognizance, Emotions, and Coping Strategies," *Journal of Consumer Research* 25 (September 1998), pp. 123–47.

29. A. Parasuraman and C. L. Colby, *Techno-Ready Marketing: How and Why Your Customers Adopt Technology* (New York: The Free Press, 2001).

30. "Customer Care in a New World," McKinsey & Company, 2001.

31. Discussion of these issues is found in many services marketing publications. The discussion here is based on V. A. Zeithaml, A. Parasuraman, and L. L. Berry, "Problems and Strategies in Services Marketing," *Journal of Marketing* 49 (Spring 1985), pp. 33–46.

32. For research supporting the idea of goods–services continua, see D. Iacobucci, "An Empirical Examination of Some Basic Tenets in Services: Goods–Services Continua," in *Advances in Services Marketing and Management,* T. A. Swartz, D. E. Bowen, and S. W. Brown ed. (Greenwich, CT: JAI Press, 1992), vol. 1, pp. 23–52.

33. S. L. Vargo and R. F. Lusch, "The Four Service Marketing Myths," *Journal of Service Research* 6, (May 2004), pp. 324–35.

34. E. J. McCarthy and W. D. Perrault Jr., *Basic Marketing: A Global Managerial Approach* (Burr Ridge, IL: Richard D. Irwin, 1993).

35. B. H. Booms and M. J. Bitner, "Marketing Strategies and Organizational Structures for Service Firms," in *Marketing of Services,* ed. J. H. Donnelly and W. R. George (Chicago: American Marketing Association, 1981), pp. 47–51.

Chapter 2

CONCEPTUAL FRAMEWORK OF THE BOOK: THE GAPS MODEL OF SERVICE QUALITY

This chapter's objectives are to

1. Introduce a framework, called the gaps model of service quality, which is used to organize this textbook.

2. Demonstrate that the gaps model is a useful framework for understanding service quality in an organization.

3. Demonstrate that the most critical service quality gap to close is the customer gap, the difference between customer expectations and perceptions.

4. Show that four gaps that occur in companies, which we call provider gaps, are responsible for the customer gap.

5. Identify the factors responsible for each of the four provider gaps.

Service Quality at the Island Hotel, Cedar Key, Florida

For those of you accustomed to staying at hotel chains when you travel, consider your experience with the Island Hotel, a bed-and-breakfast located in Cedar Key, a small barrier reef on the gulf side of the Florida coast. You telephone the inn to reserve a guest room and speak directly to one of the owners, who sounds very happy to take your call. She tells you that the hotel, built in 1859, is on the National Register of Historic Buildings and that each of its 13 guest rooms is uniquely decorated. She discusses each of the available rooms until you find the one that sounds right for you. When you arrive at the Hotel, she and her husband and the inn's famous chef Jahn McCumbers meet you in the lobby and welcome you personally. The husband, not a bellhop, carries your bags to your room, which is charming and has an old-fashioned claw-footed bathtub right in the corner. After you open your bags and freshen up, you go to the restaurant downstairs, renowned as the superior seafood restaurant in Cedar Key and the surrounding area. You choose the house specialties, Crab Bisque and Heart of Palm Salad, and say hello to the chef when she stops by your table to ask if all is OK. You stop in the small bar that has a large mural of King Neptune and his court stretching across the wall and find that the bartender and all the customers welcome you as if you were a regular. When you return to your room, the owner is putting fresh towels on your bed and wishes you a good evening. You make one more stop before you sleep: You step out on the balcony to sit on a large rocking chair and look out over the bay and marina, feeling as if you have just spent a day with a warm, caring family in an impeccable home rather than in a hotel. This feeling is repeated every day of your stay, and when you leave, the owners and chef are in the lobby to personally thank you for coming and send you on your way.

Most of you will agree that the service experience at the Island Hotel is exceptional. The reservation is tailored to you; the employees (in this case, owners and chef and bartender) are concerned and genuinely caring about your comfort; the setting is ideal; the other guests and customers are friendly; the food is superb; and—perhaps most impressive—the whole experience from reservation to stay to checkout is coordinated to make you feel known and special.

Do you typically receive this experience from a stay at the Hilton or Radisson or even the more upscale Hyatt? If not, why not? This chapter will introduce you to some of the ways that organizations fall short in delivering quality service and to the underlying reasons why these gaps occur. You may have guessed that small organizations like the Island Hotel have fewer difficulties than do large organizations in controlling all the factors that influence service delivery. You probably do not yet realize how many different factors must be organized and managed to deliver what the Island Hotel delivers. This chapter will provide that perspective.

Effective services marketing is a complex undertaking that involves many different strategies, skills, and tasks. Executives of service organizations have long been confused about how to approach this complicated topic in an organized manner. This textbook is designed around one approach: viewing services in a structured, integrated way called the *gaps model of service quality*.[1] This model positions the key concepts, strategies, and decisions in services marketing and will be used to guide the structure of the rest of this book; sections of the book are tied to each of the gaps described in this chapter.

THE CUSTOMER GAP

The *customer gap* is the difference between customer expectations and perceptions (see Figure 2.1). Customer expectations are standards or reference points that customers bring into the service experience, whereas customer perceptions are

FIGURE 2.1
The Customer Gap

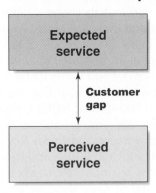

The Customer Gap

subjective assessments of actual service experiences. Customer expectations often consist of what a customer believes should or will happen. For example, when you visit an expensive restaurant, you expect a high level of service, one that is considerably superior to the level you would expect in a fast-food restaurant. Closing the gap between what customers expect and what they perceive is critical to delivering quality service; it forms the basis for the gaps model.

Because customer satisfaction and customer focus are so critical to competitiveness of firms, any company interested in delivering quality service must begin with a clear understanding of its customers. This understanding is relatively easy for an organization as small as the Island Hotel but very difficult for a large organization in which managers are not in direct contact with customers. For this reason, we will devote the first section of the textbook to describing the relevant customer concepts so that the focus of everything can relate back to these concepts. Considerable evidence exists that consumer evaluation processes differ for goods and services and that these differences affect the way service providers market their organizations. Unfortunately, much of what is known and written about consumer evaluation processes pertains specifically to goods. The assumption appears to be that services, if not identical to goods, are at least similar enough in the consumer's mind that they are chosen and evaluated in the same manner. We will detail what is known about customer behavior in services in Chapter 3.

The sources of customer expectations are marketer-controlled factors (such as pricing, advertising, sales promises) as well as factors that the marketer has limited ability to affect (innate personal needs, word-of-mouth communications, competitive offerings). In a perfect world, expectations and perceptions would be identical: Customers would perceive that they have received what they thought they would and should. In practice these concepts are often, even usually, separated by some distance. Broadly, it is the goal of services marketing to bridge this distance, and we will devote virtually the entire textbook to describing strategies and practices designed to close this customer gap. We will describe customer expectations in detail in Chapter 4 and customer perceptions in Chapter 5.

THE PROVIDER GAPS

To close the all-important customer gap, the gaps model suggests that four other gaps—the *provider gaps*—need to be closed. These gaps occur within the organization providing the service (hence the term *provider gaps*) and include

Gap 1: Not knowing what customers expect

Gap 2: Not selecting the right service designs and standards

Gap 3: Not delivering to service designs and standards

Gap 4: Not matching performance to promises

The rest of this chapter is devoted to a description of the full gaps model.

Provider Gap 1: Not Knowing What Customers Expect

Provider gap 1 is the difference between customer expectations of service and company understanding of those expectations. A primary cause in many firms for not meeting customers' expectations is that the firm lacks accurate understanding of exactly what those expectations are. Many reasons exist for managers not being aware of what customers expect: They may not interact directly with customers, they may be unwilling to ask about expectations, or they may be unprepared to address them. When people with the authority and responsibility for setting priorities do not fully understand customers' service expectations, they may trigger a chain of bad decisions and suboptimal resource allocations that results in perceptions of poor service quality. In this text, we broaden the responsibility for the first provider gap from managers alone to any employee in the organization with the authority to change or influence service policies and procedures. In today's changing organizations, the authority to make adjustments in service delivery is often delegated to empowered teams and frontline people. In business-to-business situations, in particular, account teams make their own decisions about how to address their clients' unique expectations.

Figure 2.2 shows the key factors responsible for provider gap 1. An inadequate marketing research orientation is one of the critical factors. When management or empowered employees do not acquire accurate information about customers' expectations, provider gap 1 is large. Formal and informal methods to capture information

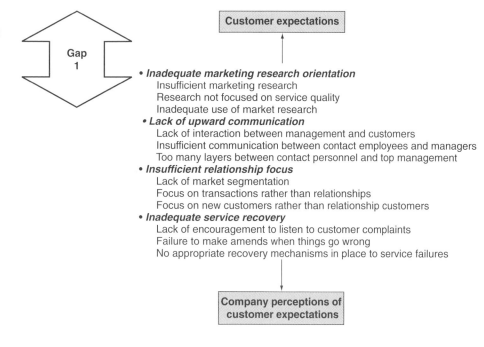

FIGURE 2.2
Key Factors Leading to Provider Gap 1

Customer expectations

Gap 1

• *Inadequate marketing research orientation*
  Insufficient marketing research
  Research not focused on service quality
  Inadequate use of market research
• *Lack of upward communication*
  Lack of interaction between management and customers
  Insufficient communication between contact employees and managers
  Too many layers between contact personnel and top management
• *Insufficient relationship focus*
  Lack of market segmentation
  Focus on transactions rather than relationships
  Focus on new customers rather than relationship customers
• *Inadequate service recovery*
  Lack of encouragement to listen to customer complaints
  Failure to make amends when things go wrong
  No appropriate recovery mechanisms in place to service failures

Company perceptions of customer expectations

Finding out what customers expect is the first step in closing all the gaps in the organization to provide service excellence. In Chapter 6 we will talk about many ways that companies determine customer perceptions, including customer surveys and complaints, but understanding what customers expect can often be more challenging. Putting customers in the "wish mode" is an innovative approach to closing gap 1 that proved successful for IKEA, the world's largest furniture retailer, when it opened its Chicago retail outlet.

In this approach, nine groups of a dozen customers each were asked to dream up their ideal IKEA shopping experience. They were told to pretend that all IKEA stores had been destroyed and that new ones had to be designed from scratch. How would the store look? What would the shopping experience be like? Jason Magidson, who helped IKEA create the process, reported that customers responded with statements like the following:

"I never feel disoriented because I always know exactly where I am in relation to every department."

"If I am buying one item, all of the other items that go with it are nearby."

"Shopping is a pleasant, relaxing experience."

Even though they were not technical experts, customers were asked to actually draw up a design for a store that would satisfy their needs.

What is significant about IKEA's approach is not just that the company asked customers what they expected but that they subsequently incorporated these expectations into the service design for the store. Designers created a multistory octagonal building with an atrium in the center that formed a home base for shoppers, addressing their concern about being able to find items easily. In keeping with another customer expectation, items were grouped together with related products. When shoppers were tired or hungry, they could go to the cafeteria-style restaurant on the upper floor that served Swedish food. IKEA's cus-

Source: Michael Newman/Photo Edit

tomers were so satisfied with the store (85 percent rated it as "excellent" or "very good") that they returned more and spent about an hour longer than they did in other IKEA stores. These actions close gap 2 because service design was based on customer expectations.

IKEA has done an excellent job of closing all four provider gaps. The company's supplier network is carefully chosen and managed to ensure quality and consistency. Despite the fact that the company has stores in more than 20 countries, it keeps standards, designs, and approaches very consistent everywhere, thereby reducing gap 2. Servicescapes—the indoor and outdoor physical environments—are unique and customer focused, further closing gap 2. IKEA is also well known for its strong employee culture and careful hiring and training, factors that help reduce gap 3. In Chapter 13, we will tell you about another way the company closes gap 3: its innovative service concept that involves customers in the delivery, assembly and creation of its products. To accomplish this service, the company educates its customers thoroughly with its scriptlike catalogs, thereby helping to close gap 4.

Sources: Jason Magidson and Gregg Brandyberry, "Putting Customers in the 'Wish Mode,'" *Harvard Business Review,* September 2001, pp. 26–27; Barbara Solomon, "A Swedish Company Corners the Business: Worldwide," *Management Review,* April 1991, pp. 10–13; Richard Normann and Rafael Ramfrez, "From Value Chain to Value Constellation: Designing Interactive Strategy," *Harvard Business Review,* July–August 1993, pp. 65–77.

about customer expectations must be developed through marketing research. Techniques involving a variety of traditional research approaches—among them customer interviews, survey research, complaint systems, and customer panels—must be used to stay close to the customer. More innovative techniques, such as structured brainstorming and service quality gap analysis, are often needed. This chapter's Global Feature discusses one of these innovative techniques that IKEA and other companies have used to identify customer expectations.

Another key factor that is related to provider gap 1 is lack of upward communication. Frontline employees often know a great deal about customers; if management is not in contact with frontline employees and does not understand what they know, the gap widens.

Also related to provider gap 1 is a lack of company strategies to retain customers and strengthen relationships with them, an approach called relationship marketing. When organizations have strong relationships with existing customers, provider gap 1 is less likely to occur. Relationship marketing is distinct from transactional marketing, the term used to describe the more conventional emphasis on acquiring new customers rather than on retaining them. Relationship marketing has always been a practice with large clients of business-to-business firms (such as IBM or Boeing), but firms that sell to end customers often view such situations as sales or transactions rather than as ongoing customers. When companies focus too much on attracting new customers, they may fail to understand the changing needs and expectations of their current customers. Technology affords companies the ability to acquire and integrate vast quantities of data on customers that can be used to build relationships. Frequent flyer travel programs conducted by airlines, car rental companies, and hotels are among the most familiar programs of this type.

The final key factor associated with provider gap 1 is lack of service recovery. Even the best companies, with the best of intentions and clear understanding of their customers' expectations, sometimes fail. It is critical for an organization to understand the importance of service recovery—why people complain, what they expect when they complain, and how to develop effective service recovery strategies for dealing with inevitable service failures. Such strategies might involve a well-defined complaint-handling procedure and an emphasis on empowering employees to react on the spot, in real time, to fix the failure; other times it involves a service guarantee or ways to compensate the customer for the unfulfilled promise.

To address the factors in provider gap 1, this text will cover topics that include how to understand customers through multiple research strategies (Chapter 6), how to build strong relationships and understand customer needs over time (Chapter 7), and how to implement recovery strategies when things go wrong (Chapter 8). Through these strategies, provider gap 1 can be minimized.

Provider Gap 2: Not Having the Right Service Quality Designs and Standards

Accurate perceptions of customers' expectations are necessary, but not sufficient, for delivering superior quality service. Another prerequisite is the presence of service designs and performance standards that reflect those accurate perceptions. A recurring theme in service companies is the difficulty experienced in translating customer expectations into service quality specifications that employees can understand and execute. These problems are reflected in provider gap 2, the difference between company understanding of customer expectations and development of customer-driven service designs and standards. Customer-driven standards are different from the conventional performance standards that companies establish for service in that they are based on pivotal customer requirements that are visible to and measured by customers. They are operations standards set to correspond to customer expectations and priorities rather than to company concerns such as productivity or efficiency.

As shown in Figure 2.3, provider gap 2 exists in service organizations for a variety of reasons. Those people responsible for setting standards, typically management, sometimes believe that customer expectations are unreasonable or unrealistic. They may also believe that the degree of variability inherent in service defies standardization and therefore that setting standards will not achieve the desired goal. Although some of these assumptions are valid in some situations, they are often only rationalizations of management's reluctance to tackle head-on the difficult challenges of creating service standards to deliver excellent service.

FIGURE 2.3
Key Factors Leading to Provider Gap 2

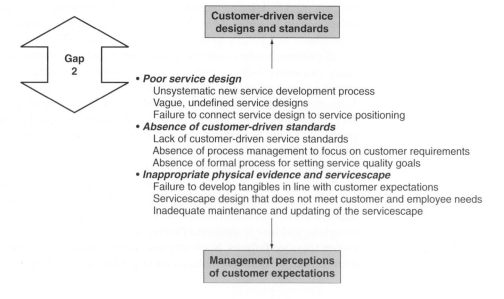

Because services are intangible, they are difficult to describe and communicate. This difficulty becomes especially evident when new services are being developed. It is critical that all people involved (managers, frontline employees, and behind-the-scenes support staff) be working with the same concepts of the new service, based on customer needs and expectations. For a service that already exists, any attempt to improve it will also suffer unless everyone has the same vision of the service and associated issues. One of the most important ways to avoid provider gap 2 is to clearly design services without oversimplification, incompleteness, subjectivity, and bias. To do so, tools are needed to ensure that new and existing services are developed and improved in as careful a manner as possible. Chapter 9 describes the tools that are most effective in service development and design, including service blueprinting, a unique tool for services.

The quality of service delivered by customer contact personnel is critically influenced by the standards against which they are evaluated and compensated. Standards signal to contact personnel what the management priorities are and which types of performance really count. When service standards are absent or when the standards in place do not reflect customers' expectations, quality of service as perceived by customers is likely to suffer. When standards do reflect what customers expect, the quality of service they receive is likely to be enhanced. The Technology Spotlight in this chapter shows how Amazon.com uses customer-defined standards as the basis for its excellent service performance. Chapter 10 develops further the topic of customer-defined service standards and shows that if they are developed appropriately they can have a powerful positive impact on closing both provider gap 2 and the customer gap.

In Chapter 11 we focus on the roles of physical evidence in service design and in meeting customer expectations. By *physical evidence,* we mean everything from business cards to reports, signage, Internet presence, equipment, and facilities used to deliver the service. The *servicescape,* the physical setting where the service is delivered, is a particular focus of Chapter 11. Think of a restaurant, a hotel, a theme park, a health club, a hospital, or a school. The servicescape—the physical facility—is critical in these industries in terms of communicating about the service and making the entire experience pleasurable. In these cases the servicescape plays a variety of roles, from serving as a visual metaphor for what the company stands for to actually facilitating the activities of both consumers and employees. In Chapter 11 we explore the importance of physical evidence, the variety of roles it plays, and strategies for effectively designing physical evidence and the servicescape to meet customer expectations.

Provider Gap 3: Not Delivering to Service Designs and Standards

Once service designs and standards are in place, it would seem that the firm is well on its way to delivering high-quality services. This assumption is true, but is still not enough to deliver excellent service. The firm must have systems, processes, and people in place to ensure that service delivery actually matches (or is even better than) the designs and standards in place.

Provider gap 3 is the discrepancy between development of customer-driven service standards and actual service performance by company employees. Even when guidelines exist for performing services well and treating customers correctly, high-quality service performance is not a certainty. Standards must be backed by appropriate resources (people, systems, and technology) and also must be enforced to be effective—that is, employees must be measured and compensated on the basis of performance along those standards. Thus, even when standards accurately reflect customers'

Technology Spotlight
Amazon.com Closes the Gaps

Can an online company be an excellent service provider, identifying customer expectations and meeting them by closing the four provider gaps? Amazon.com is a company that exemplifies the use of the strategies needed to provide consistent, accurate, and even personalized service.

Understanding customer expectations is a strategy that Amazon begins when a customer first starts shopping at its online store. From the very first time customers make choices, the company's computers begin profiles on them, offering selections based on a database of previous customers that read similar books or listened to similar music. In the beginning some offerings may not seem on target, but the longer customers shop at Amazon, the more accurately the company identifies their preferences and the more appropriate suggestions become. In time, the company even begins to send e-mails that are so specific ("We noticed that you purchased the last book by Jonathan Kellerman and we want you to know that he has just published a new book.") that it almost seems like the local librarian is calling to let you know your new book is in. One of the company's unique features is "Your Store," a tab on the home page that sends customers to a selection of items that past purchases indicate would be of interest to them.

Customer-defined standards exist for virtually all activities at Amazon, from delivery to communication to service recovery. When you buy a product from Amazon, you select the mode of delivery and the company tells you the expected number of days it will take to receive your merchandise. Standard shipping is three to five days, but two- and one-day shipping are also available. The company has standards for how quickly you are informed when a product is unavailable (immediately), how fast you find out whether an out-of-print book can be located (three weeks), how long you can return items

(30 days), and whether you pay return shipping costs (not if it is Amazon's error).

Service performance is where Amazon excels. Orders almost always arrive ahead of the promised date, are accurate, and are in excellent condition because of careful shipping practices. The company's copyrighted One-click Ordering allows regular customers to make purchases instantaneously without creating a shopping cart. Customers can track packages and review previous orders at any time. Amazon also makes sure that all its partners, who sell used and new books and other items direct to customers, perform to Amazon's standards. The company verifies performance of each purchase by asking the customer how well the merchant performed, then it posts scores where customers can see them easily.

Managing promises is handled by clear and careful communication on the website. Virtually every page is easy to understand and navigate. For example, the page dealing with returns eliminates customer misunderstanding by clearly spelling out what can be returned (almost everything) and what cannot (items that are gas powered or have flammable liquids, large televisions, opened CDs). The page describes how to repack items and when refunds are given. The page dealing with a customer's account shows all previous purchases and exactly where every ordered item is in the shipping process.

Amazon's strategies have been well received by its customers. According to the American Customer Satisfaction Index (discussed in Chapter 5), customer satisfaction with Amazon.com is higher than with any other electronic retailer in the United States. Our Technology Spotlight in Chapter 5 provides more specifics on Amazon's overall success to date as well as its future plans—all focused on the customer.

Source: www.Amazon.com

expectations, if the company fails to provide support for those standards—if it does not facilitate, encourage, and require their achievement—standards do no good. When the level of service delivery falls short of the standards, it falls short of what customers expect as well. Narrowing gap 3—by ensuring that all the resources needed to achieve the standards are in place—reduces the customer gap.

Research has identified many of the critical inhibitors to closing gap 3 (see Figure 2.4). These factors include employees who do not clearly understand the roles they are to play in the company, employees who experience conflict between customers and company management, poor employee selection, inadequate technology, inappropriate compensation and recognition, and lack of empowerment and teamwork. These factors all relate to the company's human resource function and involve internal practices such as recruitment, training, feedback, job design, motivation, and organizational structure. To deliver better service performance, these issues must be addressed across functions (such as with both marketing and human resources).

Another important variable in provider gap 3 is the customer. Even if contact employees and intermediaries are 100 percent consistent in their service delivery, the uncontrollable variables of the customer can introduce variability in service delivery. If customers do not perform their roles appropriately—if, for example, they fail to provide all the information necessary to the provider or neglect to read and follow instructions—service quality is jeopardized. Customers can also negatively influence the quality of service received by others if they are disruptive or take more than their share of a service provider's time. Understanding customer roles and how customers themselves can influence service delivery and outcomes are critical.

A third difficulty associated with provider gap 3 involves the challenge in delivering service through such intermediaries as retailers, franchisees, agents, and brokers. Because quality in service occurs in the human interaction between customers and service providers, control over the service encounter by the company is crucial, yet it rarely is fully possible. Most service (and many manufacturing) companies face an even more formidable task: attaining service excellence and consistency in the presence of intermediaries who represent them and interact with their customers yet are not under their direct control. Franchisers of services depend on their franchisees to execute service delivery as they have specified it. And it is in the execution by the franchisee that the customer evaluates the service quality of the company. With franchises and other types of intermediaries, someone other than the producer is responsible for

FIGURE 2.4
Key Factors Leading to Provider Gap 3

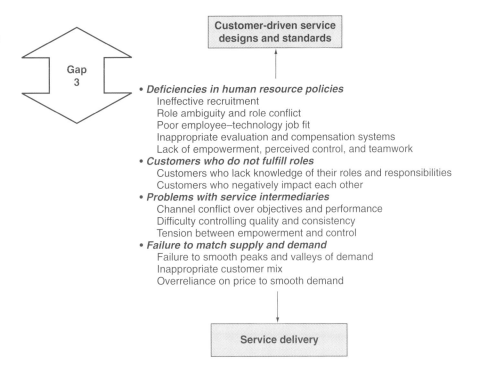

the fulfillment of quality service. For this reason, a firm must develop ways to either control or motivate these intermediaries to meet company goals.

Another issue in provider gap 3 is the need in service firms to synchronize demand and capacity. Because services are perishable and cannot be inventoried, service companies frequently face situations of overdemand or underdemand. Lacking inventories to handle overdemand, companies lose sales when capacity is inadequate to handle customer needs. On the other hand, capacity is frequently underutilized in slow periods. Most companies rely on operations strategies such as cross-training or varying the size of the employee pool to synchronize supply and demand. Marketing strategies for managing demand—such as price changes, advertising, promotion, and alternative service offerings—can supplement approaches for managing supply.

We will discuss strategies to deal with the roles of employees in Chapter 12, customers in Chapter 13, intermediaries in Chapter 14, and demand and capacity in Chapter 15.

Provider Gap 4: Not Matching Performance to Promises

Provider gap 4 illustrates the difference between service delivery and the service provider's external communications. Promises made by a service company through its media advertising, sales force, and other communications may potentially raise customer expectations, the standards against which customers assess service quality. The discrepancy between actual and promised service therefore has an adverse effect on the customer gap. Broken promises can occur for many reasons: overpromising in advertising or personal selling, inadequate coordination between operations and marketing, and differences in policies and procedures across service outlets. Figure 2.5 shows the key factors that lead to provider gap 4.

FIGURE 2.5
Key Factors Leading to Provider Gap 4

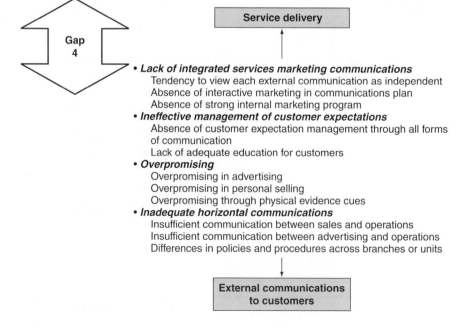

In addition to unduly elevating expectations through exaggerated claims, there are other, less obvious ways in which external communications influence customers' service quality assessments. Service companies frequently fail to capitalize on opportunities to educate customers to use services appropriately. They also neglect to manage customer expectations of what will be delivered in service transactions and relationships.

One of the major difficulties associated with provider gap 4 is that communications to consumers involve issues that cross organizational boundaries. Because service advertising promises what people do, and because what *people* do cannot be controlled like machines that produce physical goods can be controlled, this type of communication involves functions other than the marketing department. This type of marketing is what we call *interactive marketing*—the marketing between contact people and customers—and it must be coordinated with the conventional types of *external marketing* used in product and service firms. When employees who promote the service do not fully understand the reality of service delivery, they are likely to make exaggerated promises or fail to communicate to customers aspects of the service intended to serve them well. The result is poor service quality perceptions. Effectively coordinating actual service delivery with external communications, therefore, narrows provider gap 4 and favorably affects the customer gap as well.

Another issue in provider gap 4 is associated with the pricing of services. In packaged goods (and even in durable goods), customers possess enough price knowledge before purchase to be able to judge whether a price is fair or in line with competition. With services, customers often have no internal reference points for prices before purchase and consumption. Pricing strategies such as discounting, "everyday prices," and couponing obviously need to be different in service cases in which the customer has no initial sense of prices. Techniques for developing prices for services are more complicated than those for pricing tangible goods.

In summary, external communications—whether from marketing communications or pricing—can create a larger customer gap by raising expectations about service delivery. In addition to improving service delivery, companies must also manage all communications to customers so that inflated promises do not lead to higher expectations. Chapter 16 will discuss integrated services marketing communications, and Chapter 17 will cover pricing to accomplish these objectives.

PUTTING IT ALL TOGETHER: CLOSING THE GAPS

The full conceptual model shown in Figure 2.6 on page 46 conveys a clear message to managers wishing to improve their quality of service: The key to closing the customer gap is to close provider gaps 1 through 4 and keep them closed. To the extent that one or more of provider gaps 1 through 4 exist, customers perceive service quality shortfalls. The gaps model of service quality serves as a framework for service organizations attempting to improve quality service and services marketing. The Strategy Insight provides a service quality gaps audit based on the model.

The model begins where the process of improving service quality begins: with an understanding of the nature and extent of the customer gap. Given the service organization's need to focus on the customer and to use knowledge about the customer to drive business strategy, we believe that this foundation of emphasis is warranted.

The gaps model featured in this chapter and used as a framework for this textbook is a useful way to audit the service performance and capabilities of an organization. The model has been used by many companies as an assessment or service audit tool because it is comprehensive and offers a way for companies to examine all the factors that influence service quality. To use the tool, a company documents what it knows about each gap and the factors that affect the size of the gap. Although you will learn much more about each of these gaps throughout the book, we provide here a basic gaps audit. In Exercise 1 at the end of the chapter, we propose that you use this audit with a company to determine its service quality gaps. As practice, you could evaluate the Island Hotel, the inn featured in the opening vignette, to see how its approaches work to close each of the gaps.

Service Quality Gaps Model Audit

For each of the following factors in the gaps, indicate the effectiveness of the organization on that factor. Use a 1 to 10 scale where I is "poor" and 10 is "excellent."

Customer Gap	*1 = poor* *10 = excellent*
1. How well does the company understand customer expectations of service quality? 2. How well does the company understand customer perceptions of service?	

Provider Gap I	*1 = poor* *10 = excellent*

1. **Market Research Orientation**
   Is the amount and type of market research adequate to understand customer expectations of service?
   Does the company use this information in decisions about service provision?
2. **Upward Communication**
   Do managers and customers interact enough for management to know what customers expect?
   Do contact people tell management what customers expect?
3. **Relationship Focus**
   To what extent does the company understand the expectations of different customer segments?
   To what extent does the company focus on relationships with customers rather than transactions?
4. **Service Recovery**
   How effective are the service recovery efforts of the organization?
   How well does the organization plan for service failures?
   Score for Provider Gap 1	

Provider Gap 2	*1 = poor* *10 = excellent*

5. **Systematic Service Design**
   How effective is the company's service development process?
   How well are new services defined for customers and employees?	

6. **Presence of Customer-Defined Standards** How effective are the company's service standards? Are they defined to correspond to customer expectations? How effective is the process for setting and tracking service quality goals? 7. **Appropriate Physical Evidence and Servicescape** How appropriate, attractive, and effective are the company's physical facilities, equipment, and other tangibles? **Score for Provider Gap 2**	
Provider Gap 3 8. **Effective Human Resource Policies** How effectively does the company recruit, hire, train, compensate, and empower employees? Is service quality delivery consistent across employees, teams, units, and branches? 9. **Effective Role Fulfillment by Customers** Do customers understand their roles and responsibilities? Does the company manage customers to fulfill their roles, especially customers that are incompatible? 10. **Effective Alignment with Service Intermediaries** How well are service intermediaries aligned with the company? Is there conflict over objectives and performance, costs and rewards? Is service quality delivery consistent across the outlets? 11. **Alignment of Supply and Demand** How well is the company able to match supply with demand fluctuations? **Score for Provider Gap 3**	*1 = poor* *10 = excellent*
Provider Gap 4 12. **Integrated Services Marketing Communications** How well do all company communications—including the interactions between company employees and customers—express the same message and level of service quality? 13. **Effective Management of Customer Expectations** How well does the company communicate to customers about what will be provided to them? 14. **Accurate Promising in Advertising and Personal Selling** Does the company avoid overpromising and overselling? 15. **Adequate Horizontal Communications** How well do different parts of the organization communicate with each other so that service quality equals what is promised? **Score for Provider Gap 4**	*1 = poor* *10 = excellent*

The score for each gap should be compared to the maximum score possible. Are particular gaps weaker than others? Which areas in each gap need attention? As you go through the rest of the book, we will provide more detail about how to improve the factors in each of the gaps.

FIGURE 2.6
Gaps Model of
Service Quality

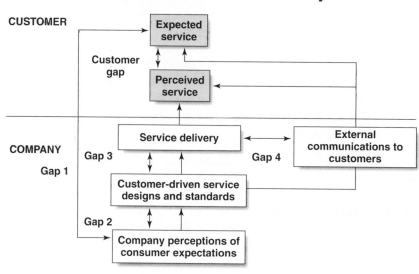

Gaps Model of Service Quality

Summary

This chapter presented the integrated gaps model of service quality (shown in Figure 2.6), a framework for understanding and improving service delivery. The entire text will be organized around this model of service quality, which focuses on five pivotal gaps in delivering and marketing service:

The customer gap: Difference between customer expectations and perceptions

Provider gap 1: Not knowing what customers expect

Provider gap 2: Not selecting the right service designs and standards

Provider gap 3: Not delivering to service designs and standards

Provider gap 4: Not matching performance to promises

The gaps model positions the key concepts, strategies, and decisions in services marketing in a manner that begins with the customer and builds the organization's tasks around what is needed to close the gap between customer expectations and perceptions. The final chapter in the book, Chapter 18, discusses the financial implications of service quality, reviewing the research and company data that indicates linkages between service quality and financial performance.

Discussion
Questions

1. Think about a service you receive. Is there a gap between your expectations and perceptions of that service? What do you expect that you do not receive?
2. Consider the "wish mode" discussion about IKEA. Think about a service that you receive regularly and put yourself in the wish mode. How would you change the service and the way it is provided?

3. If you were the manager of a service organization and wanted to apply the gaps model to improve service, which gap would you start with? Why? In what order would you proceed to close the gaps?

4. Can provider gap 4 be closed prior to closing any of the other three provider gaps? How?

5. Which of the four provider gaps do you believe is hardest to close? Why?

Exercises

1. Choose an organization to interview, and use the integrated gaps model of service quality as a framework. Ask the manager whether the organization suffers from any of the factors listed in the figures in this chapter. Which factor in each of Figures 2.2 through 2.5 does the manager consider the most troublesome? What does the company do to try to address the problems?

2. Use the Internet to locate the website of Walt Disney, Marriott, Ritz-Carlton or any other well-known, high-quality service organization. Which provider gaps has the company closed? How can you tell?

3. Interview a nonprofit or public sector organization in your area (it could be some part of your school if it is a state school). Find out if the integrated gaps model of service quality framework makes sense in the context of its organization.

Note

1. The gaps model of service quality that provides the structure for this text was developed by and is fully presented in Valarie A. Zeithaml, A. Parasuraman, and Leonard L. Berry, *Delivering Quality Service: Balancing Customer Perceptions and Expectations* (New York: The Free Press, 1990).

FOCUS ON THE CUSTOMER

THE CUSTOMER GAP

The figure shows a pair of boxes from the gaps model of service quality that correspond to two concepts—*customer expectations* and *customer perceptions*—that play a major role in services marketing. Customer expectations are the standards of performance or reference points for performance against which service experiences are compared, and are often formulated in terms of what a customer believes should or will happen. Customer perceptions are subjective assessments of actual service experiences.

The Customer Gap

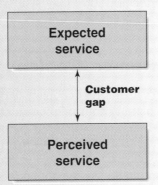

We devote the second part of the textbook to describing this gap and other relevant customer concepts because excellent services marketing requires a focus on the customer. We detail what is known about customer behavior relative to services in Chapter 3, customer expectations in Chapter 4, and customer perceptions in Chapter 5. Knowing what customers want and how they assess what they receive is the foundation for designing effective services.

Chapter 3

CONSUMER BEHAVIOR IN SERVICES

The chapter's objectives are to

1. Enhance understanding of how consumers choose and evaluate services, through focusing on factors that are particularly relevant for services.

2. Describe how consumers judge goods versus services in terms of search, experience, and credence criteria.

3. Develop the elements of consumer behavior that a services marketer must understand: choice behavior, consumer experiences, and postexperience evaluation.

4. Explore how differences among consumers (cultural differences, group decision making) affect consumer behavior and influence services marketing strategies.

Consumer Problem: Time Deficiency

Today's dual-career couples, single-parent families, and two-job families are realizing a burning consumer need: more time. Individuals in these and other nontraditional family configurations are overstressed with their work and home obligations and find that dealing with many of life's everyday tasks is overwhelming. In one study, 50 percent of dual-income primary shoppers with children and 35 percent of their single-income counterparts contend that shopping and service tasks contribute to life's stresses. For many customers, all types of shopping have become "drudgery or worse."[1] Faced with this dilemma, consumers have choices: They can continue to do all these tasks for themselves, or they can decide to employ the services of professionals or friends and relatives to help them out.[2]

The antidote to this time deficiency is found in many new services and service features that recover time for consumers. Innovative new services—pet sitting, plant watering, mail packaging, wedding advising, baby-proofing, executive organizing, personal shopping, even health form preparation—are emerging to deal with tasks that used to be performed by the household but now can be purchased by the time-buying consumer.[3] Conventional services such as retailing, banking, and restaurants[4] are also adding peripheral services to make shopping easier, increasing their hours to suit customer schedules, reducing transaction time, improving delivery, and providing merchandise or services at home or work. Increased use of the Internet is also saving time for customers. With the Web and home delivery, many shopping tasks can be carried out by customers without even leaving the house and at any time of the day or night.

And there is an increasingly popular parallel phenomenon in business today known as *outsourcing,* which means purchasing whole service functions (such as billing, payroll, secretarial support, maintenance, inventory, network operations, and marketing) from other firms rather than executing them in-house. The motivation for corporations is not so much saving time as it is saving money, better use of limited resources, and focusing on core competencies. Companies that use outsourcing effectively have discovered that in many cases purchasing services outright from another company can be far more economical than the payroll and capital costs of performing them inside. Another benefit, particularly for smaller businesses, is that outsourcing allows the company to focus on its core competencies without the distraction of less central tasks.

The primary objectives of services producers and marketers are identical to those of all marketers: to develop and provide offerings that satisfy consumer needs and expectations, thereby ensuring their own economic survival. To achieve these objectives, service providers need to understand how consumers choose, experience, and evaluate their service offerings. However, most of what is known about consumer evaluation processes pertains specifically to goods. The assumption appears to be that services, if not identical to goods, are at least similar enough in the consumer's mind that they are chosen, experienced, and evaluated in the same manner.

FIGURE 3.1
Service tasks contribute to consumers' time deficiency.

Source: Ryan McVay/Photodisc/Getty Images

This chapter challenges that assumption and shows that services' characteristics result in some differences in consumer evaluation processes compared to those used in assessing goods. Recognizing these differences and thoroughly understanding consumer evaluation processes are critical for the customer focus on which effective services marketing is based. Because the premise of this text is that the customer is the heart of effective services marketing, we begin with the customer and maintain this focus throughout the text.

Consumers have a more difficult time evaluating and choosing most services partly because services are intangible and nonstandardized and partly because consumption is so closely intertwined with production. These characteristics lead to differences in consumer evaluation processes for goods and services in all stages of the buying and consumption process.

SEARCH, EXPERIENCE, AND CREDENCE PROPERTIES

One framework for isolating differences in evaluation processes between goods and services is a classification of properties of offerings proposed by economists.[5] Economists first distinguished between two categories of properties of consumer products: **search qualities,** attributes that a consumer can determine before purchasing a product; and **experience qualities,** attributes that can be discerned only after purchase or during consumption. Search qualities include color, style, price, fit, feel, hardness, and smell; experience qualities include taste and wearability. Products such as automobiles, clothing, furniture, and jewelry are high in search qualities because their attributes can be almost completely determined and evaluated before purchase. Products such as vacations and restaurant meals are high in experience qualities because their attributes cannot be fully known or assessed until they have been purchased and are being consumed. A third category, **credence qualities,** includes characteristics that the consumer may find impossible to evaluate even after purchase and consumption.[6] Examples of offerings high in credence qualities are appendix operations and brake relinings on automobiles. Few consumers possess medical or mechanical skills sufficient to evaluate whether these services are necessary or are performed properly, even after they have been prescribed and produced by the seller.

Figure 3.2 arrays products high in search, experience, or credence qualities along a continuum of evaluation ranging from easy to evaluate to difficult to evaluate. Products high in search qualities are the easiest to evaluate (left end of the continuum).

FIGURE 3.2
Continuum of Evaluation for Different Types of Products

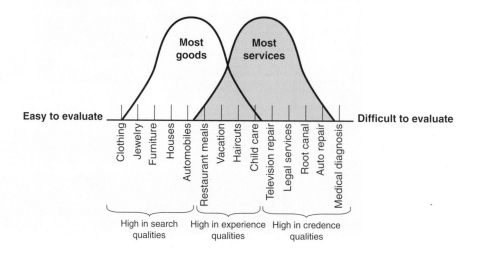

Products high in experience qualities are more difficult to evaluate because they must be purchased and consumed before assessment is possible (center of continuum). Products high in credence qualities are the most difficult to evaluate because the consumer may be unaware of or may lack sufficient knowledge to appraise whether the offerings satisfy given wants or needs even after consumption (right end of the continuum). The major premise of this chapter is that most goods fall to the left of the continuum, whereas most services fall to the right because of the distinguishing characteristics described in Chapter 1. These characteristics make services more difficult to evaluate than goods, particularly in advance of purchase. Difficulty in evaluation, in turn, forces consumers to rely on different cues and processes when assessing services.

The next sections of this chapter build from these basic differences to explore the stages of consumer decision making and evaluation for services. This discussion is organized around three broad stages of consumer behavior, as shown in Figure 3.3: consumer choice, consumer experience, and postexperience evaluation. Within each of these stages, you will see similarities and differences between goods and services.

CONSUMER CHOICE

The first important area of consumer behavior that marketers are concerned with is how customers choose and make decisions and the steps that lead to the purchase of a particular service. This process is similar to that used for goods in some ways and different in others. Customers follow a logical sequence, including need recognition, information search, evaluation of alternatives, and purchase. The following sections discuss this sequence, particularly focusing on the ways in which services decision making is different from goods decision making.

Need Recognition

The process of buying a service begins with the recognition that a need or want exists. Although there are many different ways to characterize needs, the most widely known is Maslow's hierarchy, which specifies five need categories arranged in a sequence from basic lower-level needs to higher-level needs. Services can fill all these needs, and they become increasingly important for higher-level social, ego, and self-actualization needs.

Physiological needs are *biological needs such as food, water, and sleep.* The recognition of these basic needs is fairly straightforward. Recall the last time you were on vacation, perhaps sightseeing in a new place. At some point around lunchtime, you recognized that you were thirsty and hungry and needed to stop and have lunch. Restaurants, coffee shops, bistros, and other service establishments that provided food and water likely became more noticeable. If you were sightseeing in Tokyo, you would

FIGURE 3.3 **Stages in Consumer Decision Making and Evaluation of Services**

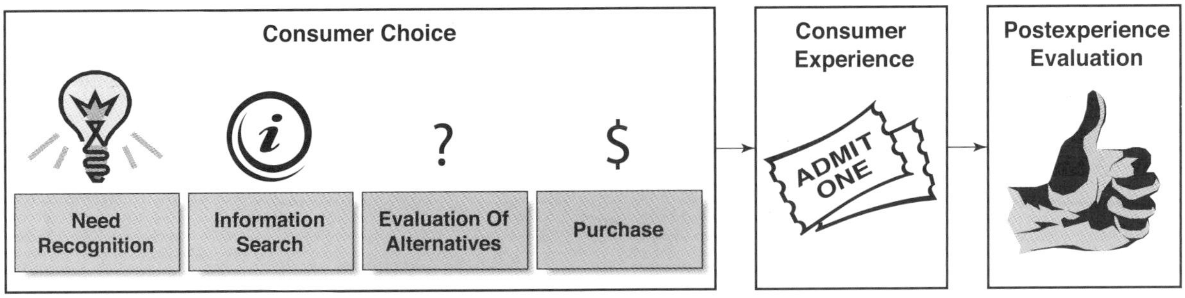

notice that virtually every other street contains a large vending machine with ice cold drinks to quench the thirst of citizens and visitors suffering from the intense heat.

Safety and security needs include *shelter, protection, and security.* Immediately following the terrorist attacks on New York and Washington, consumers began to recognize their vulnerability and sought ways to increase their safety and security. Instead of purchasing vacations and making business trips, consumers switched service purchases to bus tickets, movie rentals, insurance, and other services to satisfy their needs for safety and security.

Social needs are for *affection, friendship, and acceptance.* Social needs are critical to all cultures but are particularly important in the East. In countries like Japan and China, consumers place a great deal of value on social and belonging needs. They spend more time with their families and work colleagues than do Westerners and therefore consume more services that can be shared. The Japanese spend more annually per capita in restaurants, for example, than any other country—$1,670 per year compared to $936 in the United States, $767 in Britain, and a mere $466 in France.[7] Consumers in all cultures use many types of services to address social needs, including health and dance clubs, dating services, and vacations (like Club Med) in which socializing is encouraged.

Ego needs are for *prestige, success, accomplishment, and self-esteem.* Food, safety, and belonging are not enough for many consumers, especially those from Western cultures. Individuals also seek to look good to others and to feel good about themselves because of what they have accomplished. Needs to improve oneself and achieve success are responsible for the growth of education, training, and other services that increase the skills and prestige of consumers. Personal services such as spa services, plastic surgery, teeth whitening, and some forms of physical training and weight-loss also satisfy these needs (Figure 3.4).

Self-actualization involves *self-fulfillment and enriching experiences.* Consumers desire to live up to their full potential and enjoy themselves. Some consumers purchase experiences such as skydiving, jungle safaris, and bungee jumping for the pure thrill of the experience, a need quite different from the others in Maslow's hierarchy. Other peo-

FIGURE 3.4
Teeth whitening is a growing service that is driven by consumers' ego needs.

Source: Courtesy BriteSmile

ple self-actualize through classes in oil painting or poetry writing, thereby expressing feelings and meanings that are unrelated to the basic needs of day-to-day living.

The hierarchical nature of Maslow's need categorization has been disputed, and evidence exists that people with unfilled basic needs can be motivated to self-actualize. We are not concerned with the hierarchical nature in this section; we use it only as a way to discuss different drives that lead customers to the next stages of consumer behavior in services.

Information Search

Once they recognize a need, consumers obtain information about goods and services that might satisfy this need. Seeking information may be an extensive, formalized process if the service or good is important to the consumer or it represents a major investment (for example, a European vacation package or a professional landscape service). In other cases, the information search may be quick and relatively automatic (for example, a restaurant for a quick lunch, or a station for gasoline fill-up). Consumers use both personal sources (such as friends or experts) and nonpersonal sources (such as mass or selective media and websites) to gain information about goods and services. Seeking information is a way of reducing risk, helping consumers feel more confident about their choices.

Personal and Nonpersonal Sources

When purchasing goods, consumers make use of both personal and nonpersonal sources because both effectively convey information about search qualities. When purchasing services, on the other hand, consumers seek and rely to a greater extent on personal sources for several reasons.

First, mass and selective media can convey information about search qualities but can communicate far less about experience qualities. By asking friends or experts about services, however, the consumer can obtain information vicariously about experience qualities.

A second reason for greater use of personal sources of information for services is that many types of nonpersonal sources of information are not as readily available for services. Many service providers are local, independent merchants with neither the experience nor the funds to advertise. Furthermore, cooperative advertising (advertising funded jointly by the retailer and the manufacturer) is used infrequently with services because most local providers are both producer and retailer of the service. And, because professional associations banned advertising for so long, both professionals and consumers tend to resist its use even though it is now permitted.

Finally, because consumers can assess few attributes before purchase of a service, they may feel greater risk in selecting a little-known alternative. Personal influence becomes pivotal as product complexity increases and when objective standards by which to evaluate a product decrease (that is, when experience qualities are high).[8] Managers in service industries clearly recognize the strong influence of word-of-mouth communication (Figure 3.5).

Interestingly, consumers are now able through the Internet to seek more nonpersonal information about services in the form of visuals, photographs, and even virtual tours.[9] In addition to these tangible representations of the service experience, consumers can also seek the personal opinions of others via the Web through chat rooms, online ratings, and consumer complaint websites. Some consumer complaint websites even target a specific firm's current and prospective customers, offering unsolicited information.[10]

FIGURE 3.5
Consumers seek and rely on personal sources in purchasing experience goods and services.

Source: Mark Lewis/Getty Images

Perceived Risk

Although some degree of perceived risk probably accompanies all purchase transactions, more risk appears to be involved in the purchase of services than in the purchase of goods because services are typically more intangible, variable, and perishable. Risk can come in the form of financial risk, time risk, performance risk, social risk, or psychological risk, any of which may be greater for services.

The intangible nature of services and their high level of experience qualities imply that services generally must be selected on the basis of less prepurchase information than is the case for goods. There is clear evidence that greater intangibility (whether for goods or services) increases perceptions of risk.[11] And because services are non-standardized, the consumer will feel some uncertainty about the outcome and consequences each time a service is purchased. In addition, services purchases may involve more perceived risk than other purchases because, with some exceptions, services are not accompanied by warranties or guarantees. Dissatisfied customers can rarely "return" a service; they have already consumed it by the time they realize their dissatisfaction. Finally, many services are so technical or specialized that consumers possess neither the knowledge nor the experience to evaluate whether they are satisfied, even after they have consumed the service.

The increase in perceived risk in purchasing services suggests the use of strategies to reduce risk. Risk reduction can be accomplished through tactics that reduce risk directly (e.g., guarantees) or by addressing the factors that contribute to the perception of risk (e.g., making the service more tangible).[12] For example, UPS and FedEx provide tracking numbers for customers so they can follow their shipments online and know exactly where a package is. This system helps reduce the risk for consumers. Offering a free or reduced-cost trial period for a service would be another means to reduce risk. For example, child care centers often encourage a free trial day for prospective clients and their children to reduce the sense of risk in this important decision. To the extent possible, service providers should emphasize employee training and other procedures to standardize their offerings so that consumers learn to expect a given level of quality, again reducing perceived risk.

Evaluation of Service Alternatives

The evoked set of alternatives—that group of products that a consumer considers acceptable options in a given product category—is likely to be smaller with services than with goods. One reason involves differences in retailing between goods and services. To purchase goods, consumers generally shop in retail stores that display competing products in close proximity, clearly demonstrating the possible alternatives. To purchase services, on the other hand, the consumer visits an establishment (such as a bank, a dry cleaner, or a hair salon) that almost always offers only a single "brand" for sale. A second reason for the smaller evoked set is that consumers are unlikely to find more than one or two businesses providing the same services in a given geographic area, whereas they may find numerous retail stores carrying the identical manufacturer's product. A third reason for a smaller evoked set is the difficulty of obtaining adequate prepurchase information about services.

Faced with the task of collecting and evaluating experience qualities, consumers may simply select the first acceptable alternative rather than searching many alternatives. The Internet has the potential to widen the set of alternatives and already has done so in some industries. This trend is most notable in airlines and hotels where comparable information is available through providers such as Travelocity, Orbitz, and Expedia.

For nonprofessional services, consumers' decisions often entail the choice between performing the services for themselves or hiring someone to perform them.[13] Working people may choose between cleaning their own homes or hiring housekeepers, between altering their families' clothes or taking them to a tailor, even between staying home to take care of their children or engaging a day care center to provide child care. Consumers may consider themselves as sources of supply for many services, including lawn care, tax preparation, and preparing meals. Thus, the customer's evoked set frequently includes self-provision of the service. Self-service via technology is also a viable alternative for many services, as the Technology Spotlight demonstrates.

Service Purchase

Following consideration of alternatives (whether an extensive process or more automatic), consumers make the decision to purchase a particular service or to do it themselves. One of the most interesting differences between goods and services is that most goods are fully produced (at the factory) prior to being purchased by consumers. Thus, consumers, prior to making their final purchase decision, can see and frequently try the exact object that they will buy. For services, much is still unknown at the point of purchase. In many cases, the service is purchased and produced almost simultaneously—as with a restaurant meal or live entertainment. In other cases, consumers pay all or part of the purchase price up-front for a service they will not fully experience until it is produced for them much later. This situation arises with services such as vacation tours or home remodeling, or ongoing services such as health club memberships or university educations. In business-to-business situations, long-term contracts for services (such as payroll, network integration, or landscaping) may be signed prior to anything being produced at all.

Because of the inherent risk in the purchase decision for services, some providers offer "free" (or "deeply discounted") initial trials or extensive tours of their facilities (for example, prospective student and parent tours at universities) in order to reduce risk in the final purchase decision. In business-to-business situations, trust in the

Technology Spotlight
Self-Service Technologies: How Much Do Customers Like Providing Their Own Services?

One of the major recent changes in consumer behavior is the growing tendency for consumers to interact with technology to create services instead of interacting with a live service firm employee. *Self-service technologies (SSTs)* are technological interfaces that allow customers to produce services independent of direct service employee involvement. Examples of SSTs that you are probably very familiar with are automated teller machines, pay-at-the-pump terminals at gas stations, and automated hotel checkout and check-in. All forms of services over the Internet are also SSTs, many of which are very innovative. In some states, for example, users can file for divorce or evict a tenant using an automated kiosk rather than go through the traditional court system. Electronic self-ordering is being developed at fast-food chains, and self-scanning at grocery stores is available through companies such as Harris Teeter.

The chart in this box shows a comprehensive set of categories and examples of SSTs in use today. The columns of the matrix represent the types of technologies that companies are using to interface with customers in self-service encounters, and the rows show purposes of the technologies from the customer perspective. As you can see, customers use the technologies to provide customer service (deal with questions about accounts, bill paying, and delivery tracking), to conduct transactions (order, buy, and exchange resources with companies without direct interaction), and to provide self-help (learn, receive information, train themselves, and provide their own services).

A recent study asked customers across a wide range of industries and applications what they think of SSTs and found that customers have very strong feelings about them. They both love and hate SSTs depending on a few key conditions. Customers love them when:

- *SSTs bail them out of difficult situations.* A single parent with a sleeping child in the car needs to get gas and money for work the following morning. Using a pay-at-the-pump gas station and drive-up ATM allows the parent to accomplish these tasks without leaving the sleeping child.

- *SSTs are better than the interpersonal alternative.* SSTs have the potential to save customers time, money, and psychological costs. The Internet, in particular, allows customers to shop at any time and complete transactions more quickly than they could in person. Internet loans and mortgages also allow customers to avoid the anxiety of meeting a banker in person and feeling judged.

- *SSTs work.* When SSTs work as they are supposed to, customers are impressed. Many of you have had the experience of using one-click ordering at Amazon.com. When these transactions work smoothly, as they usually do after the proper setup, the transactions are satisfying.

On the other hand, customers hate SSTs when the following problems occur:

- *SSTs fail.* The researchers found that 60 percent of the negative stories they heard stemmed from failures of SSTs. Broken machines, failed PIN numbers, websites that were down, and items not shipped as promised all frustrate consumers.

- *SSTs are poorly designed.* Poorly designed technologies that are difficult to use or understand create hassles for customers, making them feel as though the SST is not worth using. Websites that are difficult to maneuver are particularly troublesome. If customers cannot

provider is paramount when customers sign long-term service contracts, and frequently the contracts themselves spell out in detail the service level agreements and penalties for nonperformance.

CONSUMER EXPERIENCE

Because the choice process for services is inherently risky with many unknowns, the experience itself often dominates the evaluation process. As noted, services are high

reach information they need within a few clicks (some researchers say that two clicks are all that customers will tolerate), then customers shun the website.

- *The customer messes up.* Customers dislike using technologies that they feel they cannot perform adequately. Even though they feel partial responsibility, they will avoid using them in the future. A common frustration today is having various user names and passwords for different websites. When confronted with a screen requiring this information—and not recalling it accurately—many customers will give up and go elsewhere.

- *There is no service recovery.* When the process or technology fails, SSTs rarely provide ways to recover on the spot. In these cases customers must then call or visit the company, precisely what they were trying to avoid by using the self-service technology.

It is increasingly evident that these technological innovations will be a critical component of customer–firm interactions. If these SSTs are to succeed, the researchers contend, they must become more reliable, be better than the interpersonal alternatives, and have recovery systems in place when they fail.

Sources: M. L. Meuter, A. L. Ostom, R. I. Roundtree, and M. J. Bitner, "Self-Service Technologies: Understanding Customer Satisfaction with Technology-Based Service Encounters," *Journal of Marketing* 64 (July 2000), pp. 50–64; M. J. Bitner, "Self-Service Technologies: What Do Customers Expect?" *Marketing Management,* Spring 2001, pp. 10–11.

Interface / Purpose	Categories and Examples of SSTs in Use			
	Telephone/Interactive Voice Response	**Online/Internet**	**Interactive Kiosks**	**Video/CD**
Customer Service	• Telephone banking • Flight information • Order status	• Package tracking • Account information	• ATMs • Hotel checkout	
Transactions	• Telephone banking • Prescription refills	• Retail purchasing • Financial transactions	• Pay at the pump • Hotel checkout • Car rental	
Self-Help	• Information telephone lines	• Internet information search • Distance learning	• Blood pressure machines • Tourist information	• Tax preparation software • Television/CD-based training

in experience and credence qualities relative to goods; thus, how consumers evaluate the actual experience of the service is very critical in their evaluation process and their decision to repurchase later. In fact, noted customer experience experts have stated that "the experience is the marketing."[14]

Much has been written recently about customer experiences and their important role in influencing consumer behavior. Goods and services companies alike are being admonished to create "memorable experiences for their customers."[15] Our Strategy Insight illustrates the prominent role that experiences have assumed in corporate strategy.

Customer experiences and experience management have become the foundations for important corporate strategies. According to Bernd Schmitt at Columbia University, customer experience management can be defined as the process of strategically managing customers' entire experience with a product—from how they learn about it, to how they consume it, to how they relate to the company that produces it. Firms across industries from health care to airlines and cosmetics to automobiles are developing strategies around providing meaningful customer experiences. Although experience management applies to goods and services, it is particularly relevant for services, given their process nature. Services are experiences. Whether they are managed strategically or not is a choice to be made.

Here are just a few companies that have recognized the value of strategically creating distinctive experiences for their customers. For these companies, "the experience is the marketing," as noted authors James Gilmore and Joseph Pine have said.

KRISPY KREME

What truly can be exciting or fun about buying a doughnut? Sure, they taste great, and people probably shouldn't eat too many, which makes them even more desirable. But why do people flock to Krispy Kreme stores, and why are they willing to wait in long lines to purchase a doughnut? It is not unheard of for people to wait 30 to 40 minutes in the drive-through line to buy doughnuts to take to work. Although it may seem mundane, purchasing a Krispy Kreme doughnut is a true experience. From the "Hot Doughnuts Now" signage to the "doughnut theater" and free samples, customers connect with Krispy Kreme. Through a large glass window, customers can watch the doughnuts being made. They can see the doughnuts cook for exactly 115 seconds in 365-degree vegetable shortening and then pass through a waterfall of sugar glazing before they trundle along the conveyer to be served. As they come off the line, Krispy Kreme employees hand out free samples to eagerly waiting customers who then proceed to buy more—many more. Despite the fact that carbohydrate-conscious customers are reducing their consumption of high-carb snacks, the experience of a Krispy Kreme outlet will always entice many others. The company spends almost nothing on national advertising and has no traditional media advertising budget—the experience is truly what sells Krispy Kreme doughnuts. (That, and the free doughnuts!)

KAISER PERMANENTE

Kaiser Permanente is the largest health maintenance organization in the United States. When IDEO, a strategic consulting firm out of Palo Alto, California, began working with Kaiser to develop a plan to increase Kaiser's long-term growth, the results were not predictable to most of the company's managers. Many assumed they would need to build new medical offices or invest in new hospital facilities. But what Kaiser managers learned through IDEO's innovative consumer research was that the customer experience itself needed a major overhaul. Patients were not happy. Kaiser needed to offer more comfortable waiting rooms and a lobby with clear instructions on where to go. The company needed to enlarge the size of its examining rooms to fit three or more people, with curtains for privacy. The registration and check-in process also needed to be improved. Kaiser learned that it is in the human experience business—not the building design business. What Kaiser and other health care clients of IDEO have learned is that whereas health care providers have traditionally focused on technology and medicines, their patients are concerned with service and information. In health care, patients want positive, informative, supportive, nonstressful experiences for themselves and their family members. Organizations that can design those types of experiences and deliver them consistently have a competitive advantage.

Source: Rhoda Sydney/The Image Works

PIKE PLACE FISH MARKET

With the distinctive salt sea smells, the constant chatter and auctioneer-like shouts of fish mongers, colorful sights, and the brisk fresh air, customers truly have an experience at the Pike Place Fish Market in Seattle. Many people are familiar with the Pike Place Fish Market because of the popularity of the *Fish!* books and training videos. What is not as well known is that the entire market itself is nearly 100 years old, drawing crowds year-round. Tourists and natives of the area all flock to the Pike Place Market because of the unique experience it affords. Abundant fresh flowers, fruit and vegetable displays, unique restaurants, and all kinds of arts, crafts, and tourist mementos line the narrow walkways of the market, which sits on a hill looking out over Puget Sound. The foghorns of 450-foot commuter ferries are audible, often through the fog and mist that blanket the Sound. On a clear day, kites fly overhead in the adjacent park. Deep within the market scene is the Pike Place Fish Market. Fish flying through the air, bantering employees, and fresh crab the size of small cats all provide elements of the experience that has made the place famous. Clearly patrons of the Pike Place Fish Market come for the experience—not just the outstanding fresh fish!

BUSINESS-TO-BUSINESS CUSTOMER EXPERIENCES

Although the previous examples have all been consumer companies, business-to-business firms are also recognizing the value of creating experiences. Executive briefing centers, for example, are corporate venues designed to enhance the otherwise mundane customer visit experience for business customers. Customer visits allow business-to-business customers to get to know their suppliers better through personal contact and information provided at the supplier's place of business. To create a memorable experience for its customers, Johnson Controls' flagship center in Milwaukee simulates for its customers inky, cold darkness on the one hand and arid heat on the other to demonstrate how its technologies can help customers avoid these conditions. And Nortel Networks provides guests with smart cards to activate and guide their experience with Nortel technology at its Executive Briefing Center in North Carolina. The design of the customer experience can be a distinctive corporate advantage and asset for organizations that use it strategically.

Sources: B. Nussbaum, "The Power of Design," *BusinessWeek* cover story, May 17, 2004, pp. 86–94; J. H. Gilmore and B. J. Pine II, "The Experience Is the Marketing," 2002, Strategic Horizons, LLP; B. H. Schmitt, *Customer Experience Management,* Hoboken, NJ: John Wiley & Sons, 2003; A. Serwer, "The Hole Story: How Krispy Kreme Became the Hottest Brand in America," *Fortune,* July 7, 2003, pp. 52–62.

In this section we describe elements of consumer behavior that are relevant to understanding service experiences and how customers evaluate them. We do not limit our discussion to fun, exciting, or memorable experiences only. Instead, we use the term *customer experience* to encompass service processes that span the mundane to the spectacular. Customers purchasing building maintenance and dry cleaning services still have experiences, albeit less exciting ones than customers of entertainment or travel services. All services *are* experiences—some are long in duration and some are short; some are complex and others are simple; some are mundane, whereas others are exciting and unique. Creating and managing effective processes and experiences are always essential management tasks for service organizations. Many subsequent chapters in this book will provide you with tools and approaches for managing specific elements of the customer experience—the heart of services marketing and management.

Services as Processes

Because services are actions or performances done for and with customers, they typically involve a sequence of steps, actions, and activities. Consider medical services. Some of the steps in medical care involve customers interacting with providers (e.g., patients interacting with their physician), other steps may be carried out by the customers themselves (e.g., "following the doctor's orders," taking medications), and other steps may involve third parties (e.g., going to a lab for blood work). The combination of these steps, and many others along the way, constitute a process, a service experience that is evaluated by the consumer. It is the combination of steps, the flow of the activities, or the "experience" that is evaluated by the customer. In many cases, the customer's experience comprises interactions with multiple, interconnected organizations, as in the case of medical services, automobile insurance, or home buying. Diverse sets of experiences across the network of firms (e.g., a doctor's office, medical laboratory, hospital, and physical therapy clinic) will likely influence consumers' overall impressions of their experience.[16] Whether or not the provider acknowledges it or seeks to control this experience in a particular way, it is inevitable that the customer will have an experience—good, bad, or indifferent.

FIGURE 3.6
At Disney World the delivery of service is conceived as drama.

Source: Freelance Consulting Services/Corbis

Service Provision as Drama

The metaphor of a theater is a useful framework for describing and analyzing service performances. Both the theater and service organizations aim to create and maintain a desirable impression before an audience and recognize that the way to accomplish this is by carefully managing the actors and the physical setting of their behavior.[17] The service marketer must play many drama-related roles—including director, choreographer, and writer—to be sure the performances of the actors are pleasing to the audience. The Walt Disney Company (Figure 3.6) explicitly considers its service provision a "performance," even using show business terms such as *cast member, onstage,* and *show* to describe the operations at Disneyland and Walt Disney World.[18]

The skill of the service **actors** in performing their routines, the way they appear, and their commitment to the "show" are all essential to service delivery. Although service actors are present in most service performances, their importance increases in three conditions. First, service actors are critical when the degree of direct personal contact is high. Consider the difference between a visit to Denny's and a trip to a Japanese restaurant like Benihana. In many cases customers go to Japanese steakhouses as much for the show as for the food, and they eagerly anticipate the performance of the real-time chef who twirls knives, jokes with the guests, and even flips shrimp into his hat or onto guests' plates. (It is interesting to note that in Japan the chef is not the focus of attention in this type of restaurant and prepares the food with quiet dignity.) The second condition in which service actors' skills are critical is when the services involve repeat contact. Nurses in hospitals, favorite waiters or tennis pros in resorts, or captains on cruises are essential characters in service theater, and their individual performances can make or break the success of the services. The third condition in which contact personnel are critical is when they have discretion in determining the nature of the service and how it is delivered. When you consider the quality of the education you are receiving in college, you are certain to focus much of your evaluation on your professors' delivery of classes. In education, as in other services such as medical and legal services, the professional is the key actor in the performance.[19]

Ray Fisk and Steve Grove, two experts in the area of service dramaturgy, point out that service actors' performances can be characterized as sincere or cynical.[20] A sincere performance occurs when an actor becomes one with the role that she is playing, whereas a cynical performance occurs when an actor views a performance only as a means to an end, such as getting paid for doing the job. When a service employee takes the time to listen and help, the performance is sincere and often noteworthy. Unfortunately, too many examples of cynical performances exist in which front-line "actors" seem to care little about the "audience" of customers. As Grove and Fisk point out, a single employee can ruin the service experience by ridiculing other cast members' efforts, failing to perform his role correctly, or projecting the wrong image. To create the right impression, three characteristics are necessary: loyalty, discipline, and circumspection.[21]

The **physical setting** of the service can be likened to the staging of a theatrical production, including scenery, props, and other physical cues to create desired impressions. Among a setting's features that may influence the character of a service are the colors or brightness of the service's surroundings; the volume and pitch of sounds in the setting; the smells, movement, freshness, and temperature of the air; the use of space; the style and comfort of the furnishings; and the setting's design and cleanliness.[22] As an example, the service provided by a cruise ship features its layout (broad and open), decor and comfort (large, cushioned deck chairs), furnishings (lots of polished wood and brass), and cleanliness ("shipshape"). The setting increases in importance when the environment distinguishes the service. Consider how critical the setting is for a downtown law firm, which must appear professional, capable, even imposing.[23] In essence, the delivery of service can be conceived as drama, where service personnel are the actors, service customers are the audience, physical evidence of the service is the setting, and the process of service assembly is the performance.[24]

The drama metaphor offers a useful way to improve service performances. Selection of personnel can be viewed as auditioning the actors. An actor's personal appearance, manner, facial expression, gestures, personality, and demographic profile can be determined in large part in the interview or audition. Training of personnel can become rehearsing. Clearly defining the role can be seen as scripting the performance. Creation of the service environment involves setting the stage. Finally, deciding which aspects of the service should be performed in the presence of the customer (onstage) and which should be performed in the back room (backstage) helps define the performances the customer experiences.

Service Roles and Scripts

Roles are combinations of social cues that guide and direct behavior in a given setting.[25] Just as there are roles in dramatic performances, there are roles in service delivery. For example, the role of a hostess in a restaurant is to acknowledge and greet customers, find out how many people are in their group, and then lead them to a table where they will eat. The success of any service performance depends in part on how well the role is performed by the service actor and how well the team of players—the "role set" of both service employees and customers—act out their roles.[26] Service employees need to perform their roles according to the expectations of the customer; if they do not, the customer may be frustrated and disappointed. If customers are informed and educated about their roles and if they cooperate with the provider in following the script, successful service provision is likely.

One factor that influences the effectiveness of role performance is the **script**—the logical sequence of events expected by the customer, involving her as either a participant or an observer.[27] Service scripts consist of sequences of actions associated with actors and objects that, through repeated involvement, define what the customer expects.[28] Receiving a dental checkup is a service experience for which a well-defined script exists. For a checkup the consumer expects the following sequence: Enter the reception area, greet a receptionist, sit in a waiting room, follow the dental hygienist to a separate room, recline in a chair while his teeth are cleaned by the hygienist, be examined by the dentist, then pay for the services. When the service conforms to this script, the customer has a feeling of confirmed expectations and satisfaction. Deviations from the service script lead to confusion and dissatisfaction. Suppose, on moving to a new town, you went to a dentist who had no receptionist and no waiting area, only a doorbell in a cubicle. Suppose, on answering the doorbell, an employee in shorts took you to a large room where all patients were in a dental chairs facing each other. These actions and objects are certainly not in the traditional service script for dentistry and might create considerable uncertainty and doubt in patients.

Some services are more scripted than others. Customers would expect very expensive, customized services such as spa vacations to be less scripted than mass-produced services such as fast food ("Have a nice day!") and airline travel.

The Compatibility of Service Customers

We have just discussed the roles of employees and customers receiving service. We now want to focus on the role of *other customers* receiving service at the same time. Consider how central the mere presence of other customers is in churches, restaurants, dances, bars, clubs, and spectator sports: If no one else shows up, customers will not get to socialize with others, one of the primary expectations in these types of services. However, if customers become so dense that crowding occurs, customers may also be dissatisfied.[29] The way other customers behave with many services—such as airlines, education, clubs, and social organizations—also exerts a major influence on a customer's experience.[30] In general, the presence, behavior, and similarity of other customers receiving services has a strong impact on the satisfaction and dissatisfaction of any given customer.[31]

Customers can be incompatible for many reasons—differences in beliefs, values, experiences, abilities to pay, appearance, age, and health, to name just a few. The service marketer must anticipate, acknowledge, and deal with heterogeneous consumers who have the potential to be incompatible. The service marketer can also bring homogeneous customers together and solidify relationships between them, which increases the cost to the customer of switching service providers.[32] Customer compatibility is a factor that influences customer satisfaction, particularly in high-contact services.

Customer Coproduction

In addition to being audience members, as suggested by the drama metaphor, service customers also play a coproduction role that can have profound influence on the service experience.[33] For example, counseling, personal training, or educational services have little value without the full participation of the client, who will most likely have extensive work to do between sessions. In this sense, the client coproduces the service. In business-to-business contexts such as consulting, architecture, accounting, and almost any outsourced service, customers also coproduce the service.[34] It has been suggested that customers therefore need to understand their roles and be "trained" in ways that are similar to the training of service employees, so that they will have the motivation, ability, and role clarity to perform.[35] The customer coproduction role is particularly relevant in self-service situations, as noted in this chapter's Technology Spotlight.

The idea of customers as "partners" in the cocreation of products is gaining ground across all industries, not just services.[36] Postmodern consumer behavior experts propose an even broader interpretation of this idea. They suggest that a fundamental characteristic of the postmodern era is consumers' assertiveness as active participants in creating their world—often evidenced in their demands to adjust, change, and use products in customized ways.[37]

Emotion and Mood

Emotion and mood are feeling states that influence people's (and therefore customers') perceptions and evaluations of their experiences. Moods are distinguished from emotions in that *moods* are transient feeling states that occur at specific times and in specific situations, whereas *emotions* are more intense, stable, and pervasive.[38]

Because services are experiences, moods and emotions are critical factors that shape the perceived effectiveness of service encounters. If a service customer is in a bad mood when she enters a service establishment, service provision will likely be in-

FIGURE 3.7
Positive moods of customers in a dance club heighten their service experiences.

Source: Mark Richards/Photo Edit

terpreted more negatively than if she were in a buoyant, positive mood. Similarly, if a service provider is irritable or sullen, his interaction with customers will likely be colored by that mood. Furthermore, when other customers in a service establishment are cranky or frustrated, whether from problems with the service or from existing emotions unrelated to the service, their mood affects the provision of service for all customers who sense the negative mood. In sum, any service characterized by human interaction is strongly dependent on the moods and emotions of the service provider, the service customer, and other customers receiving the service at the same time.

In what specific ways can mood affect the behavior of service customers? First, positive moods can make customers more obliging and willing to participate in behaviors that help service encounters succeed.[39] Customers in a good emotional state are probably more willing to follow an exercise regimen prescribed by a physical therapist, bus their own dishes at a fast-food restaurant, and overlook delays in service. Customers in a negative mood may be less likely to engage in behaviors essential to the effectiveness of the service: abstaining from chocolates when on a diet program with Weight Watchers, taking frequent aerobic classes from a health club, or completing homework assigned in a class.

A second way that moods and emotions influence service customers is to bias the way they judge service encounters and providers. Mood and emotions enhance and amplify experiences, making them either more positive or more negative than they might seem in the absence of the moods and emotions.[40] After losing a big account, a saleswoman catching an airline flight will be more incensed with delays and crowding than she might be on a day when business went well. Conversely, the positive mood of a services customer at a dance or restaurant will heighten the experience, leading to positive evaluations of the service establishment (Figure 3.7). The direction of the bias in evaluation is consistent with the polarity (positive or negative) of the mood or emotion.

Finally, moods and emotions affect the way information about service is absorbed and retrieved in memory. As memories about a service are encoded by a consumer, the feelings associated with the encounter become an inseparable part of the memory. If travelers fall in love during a vacation in the Bahamas, they may hold favorable assessments of the destination due more to their emotional state than to the destination itself. Conversely, if a customer first becomes aware of his poor level of fitness when on a guest pass in a health club, the negative feelings may be encoded and retrieved every time he thinks of the health club or, for that matter, any health club.

Because emotions and moods play such important roles in influencing customer experiences, "organizations must manage the emotional component of experiences with the same rigor they bring to the management of product and service functionality."[41] Organizations may observe customers' emotional responses and attempt to create places, processes, and interactions to enhance certain emotions. Some firms believe that consumers' emotional responses may be the best predictors of their ultimate loyalty. Thus, many companies are now beginning to measure emotional responses and connections as well—going beyond traditional measures of satisfaction and behavioral loyalty.

POSTEXPERIENCE EVALUATION

Following the service experience, customers form an evaluation that determines to a large degree whether they will return or continue to patronize the service organization (see Figure 3.3). Historically within the field of marketing, much more attention has been paid to prepurchase evaluations and consumer choice. Yet, postpurchase and postexperience evaluations are typically most important in predicting subsequent consumer behaviors and repurchase, particularly for services.

Postexperience evaluation is captured by companies in measures of satisfaction, service quality, loyalty, and sometimes emotional engagement. We devote an entire chapter (Chapter 5) to exploring the specifics of customer satisfaction and service quality. Another chapter (Chapter 7) will examine the topic of relationships and loyalty.

Word-of-Mouth Communication

Postexperience evaluations will significantly impact what consumers tell others about the service. Because service consumers are strongly influenced by the personal opinions of others, understanding and controlling word-of-mouth communication becomes even more important for service companies. The best way to get positive word of mouth is, of course, to create memorable and positive service experiences. When service is dissatisfactory, it is critical to have an effective service recovery strategy (see Chapter 8) to curb negative word of mouth.

Attribution of Dissatisfaction

When consumers are disappointed with purchases—because the products did not fulfill the intended needs, did not perform satisfactorily, or were not worth the price—they may attribute their dissatisfaction to a number of different sources, among them the producers, the retailers, or themselves. Because consumers participate to a greater extent in the definition and production of services, they may feel more responsible for their dissatisfaction when they purchase services than when they purchase goods. As an example, consider a consumer purchasing a haircut; receiving the cut she desires depends in part on her clear specifications of her needs to the stylist. If disappointed, she may blame either the stylist (for lack of skill) or herself (for choosing the wrong stylist or for not communicating her own needs clearly).

The quality of many services depends on the information the customer brings to the service encounter: A doctor's accurate diagnosis requires a conscientious case history and a clear articulation of symptoms; a dry cleaner's success in removing a spot depends on the consumer's knowledge of its cause; and a tax preparer's satisfactory performance relies on the receipts saved by the consumer. Failure to obtain satisfaction with any of these services may not be blamed completely on the retailer or producer, because consumers must adequately perform their part in the production process also.

With products, on the other hand, a consumer's main form of participation is the act of purchase. The consumer may attribute failure to receive satisfaction to her own decision-making error, but she holds the producer responsible for product performance. Goods usually carry warranties or guarantees with purchase, emphasizing that the producer believes that if something goes wrong, it is not the fault of the consumer. With services, consumers attribute some of their dissatisfaction to their own inability to specify or perform their part of the service. They also may complain less frequently about services than about goods because of their belief that they themselves are partly responsible for their dissatisfaction.

Positive or Negative Biases

There is a long history of research in psychology and consumer behavior that suggests that people remember negative events and occurrences more than positive ones and are more influenced by negative information than by positive information. Research and personal observation suggest that it is easier for consumers to remember the negative service experiences they have than to think of the many routine, or even positive, experiences.

There is also a long stream of research that says that customers will weigh negative information about a product attribute more heavily than positive information in forming their overall brand attitudes. Yet some very interesting and recent research suggests "positivity bias" for services.[42] The research showed that consumers tend to infer positive qualities for the firm and its employees if they have a good experience with one service employee. When individual service providers are regarded positively, customers' positive perceptions of other service providers in the company are also raised. On the other hand, customers who have a negative experience with one employee are less likely to draw a negative inference about all employees or the firm. That is, customers are more likely to attribute that negative experience to the individual provider, not the entire firm. Although this study is just one piece of research, the results and implications are very intriguing.

Brand Loyalty

The degree to which consumers are committed to particular brands of goods or services depends on a number of factors: the cost of changing brands (switching cost), the availability of substitutes, social ties to the company, the perceived risk associated with the purchase, and the satisfaction obtained in the past. Because it may be more costly to change brands of services, because awareness of substitutes is limited, and because higher risks may accompany services, consumers are more likely to remain customers of particular companies with services than with goods.

The difficulty of obtaining information about services means that consumers may be unaware of alternatives or substitutes for their brands, or they may be uncertain about the ability of alternatives to increase satisfaction over present brands. Monetary fees may accompany brand switching in many services: physicians often require complete physicals on the initial visit; dentists sometimes demand new X rays; and health clubs frequently charge "membership fees" at the outset to obtain long-term commitments from customers.

If consumers perceive greater risks with services, as is hypothesized here, they probably depend on brand names to a greater extent than when they purchase products. Brand loyalty, described as a means of economizing decision effort by substituting habit for repeated, deliberate decision, functions as a device for reducing the risks of consumer decisions.

A final reason that consumers may be more brand loyal with services is the recognition of the need for repeated patronage in order to obtain optimum satisfaction from the seller. Becoming a "regular customer" allows the seller to gain knowledge of the customer's tastes and preferences, ensures better treatment, and encourages more interest in the consumer's satisfaction. Thus a consumer may exhibit brand loyalty to cultivate a satisfying relationship with the seller.

Brand loyalty has two sides. The fact that a service provider's own customers are brand loyal is, of course, desirable. The fact that the customers of the provider's competition are difficult to capture, however, creates special challenges. The marketer may need to direct communications and strategy to the customers of competitors, emphasizing attributes and strengths that his firm possesses and the competitor lacks. Marketers can also facilitate switching from competitors' services by reducing switching costs.

UNDERSTANDING DIFFERENCES AMONG CONSUMERS

To this point in the chapter, we have discussed consumer decision-making and evaluation processes that are applicable across a wide range of consumers and types of services. In these last sections of the chapter, we examine two broad topics that shed light on some of the differences *among* consumers. First, we examine the role of national and ethnic cultures in shaping consumer behavior. Then we discuss some of the unique differences in consumer decision making for organizations and households.

Global Differences: The Role of Culture

Culture represents the common values, norms, and behaviors of a particular group and is often identified with nations or ethnicity. Culture is learned, shared, multidimensional, and transmitted from one generation to the next. Understanding cultural differences is important in services marketing because of its effects on the ways that customers evaluate and use services. Culture also influences how companies and their service employees interact with customers. Culture is important in international services marketing—taking services from one country and offering them in others—but it is also critical within countries. More and more, individual countries are becoming multicultural, and organizations need to understand how this factor affects evaluation, purchase, and use of services even within countries.

Research provides considerable evidence that there are differences in how consumers perceive services across cultures. For example, a study of service quality perceptions in Taiwan revealed that much greater emphasis is placed on the interpersonal dimensions of service than is generally true in studies of U.S. consumers.[43] Another study showed notable differences in how fast-food and grocery consumers in eight different countries (Australia, China, Germany, India, Morocco, the Netherlands, Sweden, and the United States) evaluate these services.[44] Research also recommends that firms carefully consider global differences in the ways they measure service quality in order to make valid comparisons across cultures.[45] Because of the importance of the

As we emphasize in this chapter, the way service experiences differ across cultures influences how consumers evaluate service. Until recently, service differences across cultures were observed anecdotally rather than systematically, and researchers had few guidelines or criteria on which to evaluate these differences. One notable exception is a study that examined differences in the service experience across two cultures, in the United States and Japan, and provided both vivid examples and solid evidence of cultural subtleties that affect service encounters. The examples came from interviews with Japanese students studying at an American university and are categorized by dimensions of service behavior. Following these examples, which come directly from the study, are a few of the interesting research findings.

- *Authenticity.* In Japan, "every clerk has the same type of smile…the smile is not natural," and "everything is done according to the manual." In the United States, clerks "act independently," and "there is more variation in treatment."

- *Caring.* Caring or concern is the most important dimension in Japan, where the "customer is God." In the United States, sales clerks are always answering "I don't know"; another comment was that "they don't seem to care."

- *Control.* Control seems very important to Americans. In Japan, on the other hand, customers are "kind of timid or nervous. They tend to give the controlling interest to the clerk." Control is not important in Japan.

- *Courtesy.* In Japan, "if we find something bad about the service like, for example, they didn't apologize for spilling water, we never go back there again." Courtesy is very important in Japan.

- *Formality.* In Japan, formal treatment is a requirement for all service. Treatment in the United States is much more informal.

- *Friendliness.* "In the U.S. I feel like I'm supposed to treat serving people as equals. In Japan, that is not so." In Japan, friendliness can be disrespectful, and formality is usually preferred. In the United States, friendliness is expected.

- *Personalization.* "In Japan, you are treated the same." The waiters "are almost faceless, too businesslike and whoever comes, they treat them like the same person." In the United States, service is much more personalized and names are used more frequently.

- *Promptness.* "In the U.S., the sales clerk and the customer expect to have a nice little chat…in Japan, many people would prefer a sales clerk who is quick but unfriendly."

After measuring and testing cultural dimensions across samples from the two countries, the study's author developed several compelling insights that are critical for understanding what service providers need to do to influence perceptions and evaluations of service encounters.

First, themes of friendliness, being personal, authenticity, and promptness dominate in the United States, whereas caring and concern are central in Japan. This difference can be explained by the cultural focus on individualism in the United States and the emphasis on empathy (being attentive, caring, and kind) in Japan. Civility, an important dimension in both countries, had different meanings: In the United States it meant paying attention and providing good service, whereas in Japan it meant being patient and fair. Authenticity is a relevant dimension in the United States but not in Japan, likely based on the Japanese focus on playing a role rather than expressing individual feelings.

It is evident from this study, and from others like it, that understanding culture is pivotal to being evaluated as an effective service provider. Providing the same service experience offered in the home country may not be successful when a service is extended to other cultural groups.

Source: Reprinted with permission of Elsevier Science Limited from K. F. Winsted, "The Service Experience in Two Cultures," *Journal of Retailing* 73, no. 3 (1997), pp. 337–60.

global dimensions of business and cultural differences among consumers, we include a Global Feature in every chapter of the text to illustrate how global differences affect services management as well as consumer behavior. Our Global Feature in this chapter illustrates differences in how consumers experience and evaluate services in the United States compared to Japan.

Despite the clear differences in cultures, human nature dictates that people tend to view other cultures through the often cluttered lens of their own.[46] One expert on culture, Edward T. Hall, observed that in the United States people tend to view foreigners as "underdeveloped Americans."[47] Another expert, Geert Hofstede, sums up the message of one of his books as follows:

Everybody looks at the world from behind the windows of a cultural home, and everybody prefers to act as if people from other countries have something special about them (a national character) but home is normal. Unfortunately, there is no normal position in cultural matters."[48]

Differences in how services are evaluated across cultures can be traced to basic factors that distinguish cultures from each other. In the next sections, we highlight some of the major differences that can influence how people choose, use, and evaluate services, including values and attitudes, manners and customers, material culture, aesthetics, and educational and social institutions. Language, another obvious cultural difference particularly important for services, is discussed in Chapter 16.

Values and Attitudes Differ across Cultures

Values and attitudes help determine what members of a culture think is right, important, and/or desirable. Because behaviors, including consumer behaviors, flow from values and attitudes, services marketers who want their services adopted across cultures must understand these differences.

Although American brands often have an "exotic" appeal to other cultures, U.S. firms should not count on this appeal as a long-term strategy. In the late 1990s Wal-Mart found that the cachet of U.S. brands was falling in Mexico. The Mexican news media alerted consumers to shoddy foreign goods, and some Wal-Mart customers turned to a spirit of nationalism. The retailer responded with an "Hecho en Mexico" program similar to the "Made in the U.S.A." program that was successful in the United States. In some situations it is more than a case of nationalism: brand attitudes are negatively influenced by specific prejudices toward "dominating" cultures. The Korean ban on Japanese movies and the French phobia about EuroDisney are good examples of the latter.

Manners and Customs

Manners and customs represent a culture's views of appropriate ways of behaving. It is important to monitor differences in manners and customs because they can have a direct effect on the service encounter. Central and Eastern Europeans are perplexed by Western expectations that unhappy workers put on a "happy face" when dealing with customers. As an example, McDonald's requires Polish employees to smile whenever they interact with customers. Such a requirement strikes many employees as artificial and insincere. The fast-food giant has learned to encourage managers in Poland to probe employee problems and to assign troubled workers to the kitchen rather to the food counter.[49]

Habits are similar to customs, and these tend to vary by culture. Japanese take very few vacations, and when they do they like to spend 7 to 10 days. Their vacations are unusually crammed with activities—Rome, Geneva, Paris, and London in 10 days is representative.[50] The travel industry has been responsive to the special preferences of these big-spending Japanese tourists. The Four Seasons Hotel chain provides special pillows, kimonos, slippers, and teas for Japanese guests. Virgin Atlantic Airways and other carriers have interactive screens available for each passenger, allowing viewing of Japanese (or American, French, and so on) movies, television, and even gambling if regulators approve.

Material Culture

Material culture consists of the tangible products of culture, or as comedian George Carlin puts it, "the stuff we own." What people own and how they use and display material possessions vary around the world. Cars, houses, clothes, and furniture are examples of material culture.

The majority of Mexicans do not own cars, limiting retailers' geographic reach. Further, most Mexicans own small refrigerators and have limited incomes that restrict the amount of groceries they can purchase at one time. Instead of the once-per-week shopping trip typical in the United States, Mexicans make frequent smaller trips. Promotional programs in Mexico are also constrained by the availability of media. Limited ownership of televisions and radios affects the ability of services marketers to reach target audiences.

Zoos as entertainment represent an interesting reflection of material culture's influence. Any American visiting the Tokyo Zoo is impressed by two things: the fine collection of animals and the small cages in which the animals are kept. To the Japanese who live in one of the most crowded countries in the world and own relatively small houses, the small cages seem appropriate, whereas to the American eye the small cages may look like mistreatment.

Terms of mortgages are another interesting area of cross-cultural differences in financial services. The typical mortgage in the United States is for 30 years, whereas in Canada mortgages are issued for five years, with repeated refinancing every five years. In Mexico, most people pay cash for houses because mortgages are virtually unavailable. And in Japan 100-year mortgages are quite common and often pass along with the house or flat to the next generation.

Aesthetics

Aesthetics refers to cultural ideas about beauty and good taste. These ideas are reflected in music, art, drama, and dance as well as the appreciation of color and form (Figure 3.8).

FIGURE 3.8
Ideas about aesthetics differ across cultures.

Source: Ryan
McVay/Photodisc/Getty Images

Perhaps Madonna and MTV sell well internationally, but even so the adage "There's no accounting for taste" still rings quite true with most consumers around the world. A summer stroll through one of Madrid's important tourist attractions, Parque de Retiro, provides a simple but memorable lesson in how aesthetics vary across cultures. Trash cans are everywhere, but somehow the refuse doesn't make it into them. Spaniards litter. From the American perspective, the litter detracts from the otherwise beautiful park. German tourists, used to the clean organization of their own fastidiously tidy forests, react with disgust. As another example of differences in aesthetic preferences, consider the earth tones in the decor of Japanese restaurants around the world versus the glossy reds evident in their Chinese competitors' establishments.

Educational and Social Institutions

Both educational and social institutions are affected by, and are transmission agents of, culture. The structure and functioning of each are heavily influenced by culture. Culture manifests itself most dramatically in the people-to-people contact of social institutions. Classroom interactions, for example, vary substantially around the world. Notice if the student from Japan sitting next to you in class verbally disagrees with your instructor. Japanese students are used to listening to lectures, taking notes, and asking questions only after class, if at all. In Japan the idea of grading class participation is nonsense. Alternatively, because Spaniards are used to huge undergraduate classes (hundreds rather than dozens), they tend to talk to their friends even when the instructor is talking.

Like education, health care delivery systems and doctor–patient interactions also reflect cultural differences. Americans ask questions and get second opinions about medical care in the United States, and innovative health care services are developed on the basis of extensive marketing research. Alternatively, the social hierarchy is heavily reflected in the Japanese health care system; instead of patients being most important, the doctors command deference. Thus the Japanese health care system, while delivering the best longevity statistics of any country, is relatively unresponsive to concerns of patients.

Group Decision Making

A group is defined as two or more individuals who have implicitly or explicitly defined relationships to one another such that their behavior is interdependent.[51] When groups make decisions about services—a household purchasing a family vacation or home remodeling services, or an organization purchasing information technology consulting or marketing research services—many of the same issues arise as for individuals. Groups purchasing services encounter greater perceived risk, more reliance on word-of-mouth communication, greater difficulty in comparing alternatives, and often a higher level of customer participation than do groups purchasing goods. For example, although many large organizations have very clear evaluation processes for buying goods, their processes and decision rules for purchasing services are often not as well defined. The intangibility and variability of business services make them more risky and often difficult to compare. Thus, organizations often rely on established partnerships, long-term relationships, or referrals from others when it comes to major service purchases. Similar issues arise for households who rely heavily on personal referrals in making significant services purchases such as home repair, remodeling, landscaping, medical care, and vacation trips. Even smaller household decisions—where to eat dinner or choice of a dry cleaner—may be influenced by referrals and may involve a great deal of risk, depending on the occasion. A special anniversary or birthday dinner or where to have Grandma's 40-year-old wedding dress dry-cleaned can be decisions that carry considerable personal risk.

Despite these similarities, some differences in group decision making should be considered for a fuller understanding of consumer behavior in services. Among the aspects that are different for group buying are collective decision making, mixed motives or goals, roles in the purchasing process, and group culture. We will highlight some of these differences for two major groups: households and organizations.

Households

When a family makes a service purchase decision, it has a collective style of decision making that often differs from what any of the individuals would use if making an independent choice. When a family chooses a vacation destination, for example, its style may involve one of the following: (1) one parent makes a unilateral decision that the family will go on vacation to Disneyland; (2) the family discusses possible vacation destinations at the dinner table, taking each person's ideas and suggestions into account, and selects three locations that a parent will investigate further; (3) the parents provide a budget and a list of the destinations that can be visited within that budget, then allow the children to choose among them. Once a destination has been chosen, the mix of motives or goals of the group comes into play. The mother may want to sightsee, the father to rest, and the children to visit local theme parks. In this and other group purchasing decisions, the needs and goals of the various members must be balanced so that the service (in this case the vacation) delivers optimal satisfaction for as many members as possible. Group roles are also a key consideration. In a household, one individual often identifies a need and initiates the purchase, someone else may influence which service provider is selected, someone else may pay, and someone else may become the ultimate user of the service. For example, the father may decide that the family needs to visit the dentist, a teenager may recommend a dentist that her friend uses, the mother may pay the bills, and all the family members may go to the dentist to receive treatment. Finally, national and ethnic culture affects household purchase and consumption behaviors. For example, ethnic groups vary, with some being very patriarchal, others egalitarian, and still others autocratic.

Organizations

Organizational consumers are a special category of group consumers. These days, companies spend millions on information technology services, call centers, travel management, and payroll services, and outsourced services for human resource management. Making the right decision on services purchases can be absolutely critical for an organization's success. How do companies make these important decisions? How, for example, did JetBlue Airways decide to purchase its contact center service solution from Avaya as described in recent advertisements?

For routine and even complex purchases, organizations often rely on a small number of buyers within the company, many of whom specialize in purchasing. These buyers are typically organized either formally or informally into buying centers, which include all people involved in the decision process.[52] Each of these roles may be taken by a different person, or one person may assume all roles in some cases.

- The *initiator* identifies the organization's service needs.

- The *gatekeeper* collects and controls information about the purchase.

- The *decider* determines what service to purchase.

- The *buyer* or purchasing agent physically acquires the service.

- The *user* consumes the service and may or may not have any influence over the purchase decision.

Among the characteristics that distinguish organizational from individual decision making are economic forces such as current business climate and technology trends; organizational strategies and culture; whether purchasing is a centralized or decentralized function; and the group forces that influence purchasing decisions.[53] Organizational purchases also tend to differ by magnitude and include new task purchases (large purchases that require careful consideration of needs and evaluation of alternative), straight rebuys (simple reorders of past service purchases), and modified rebuys (a mix of new and straight rebuy features).[54]

As companies outsource more services and particularly when these services are outsourced around the globe, purchase decisions become complex and difficult. Often companies must rely on outside expertise to help them with these multifaceted and financially risky decisions. NeoIT has built its successful business model around helping firms assess their readiness for outsourcing overseas and assisting them in the implementation of these strategies. NeoIT recognizes the inherent risk associated with shifting business operations offshore and has built a successful business by providing advice and planning to companies as well as helping them choose offshore providers who will be reliable and of high quality.[55]

Organizational purchasers also rely on references and the experience of other organizations in making their service purchase decisions. In its advertising mentioned earlier, Avaya uses JetBlue as a de facto endorser of its services by including the carrier in its ads. Referrals and testimonials can be very helpful to other organizations considering similar business service purchases. In fact, many business service providers have customer stories, cases, and testimonials on their websites to help reduce the risk of these complex decisions.

Summary

The intent of this chapter was to provide understanding for how consumers choose and evaluate services. Services possess high levels of experience and credence properties, which in turn make them challenging to evaluate, particularly prior to purchase. The chapter isolated and discussed three stages of consumer behavior for services, and it looked at how experience and credence properties result in challenges and opportunities in all three stages. The three stages are consumer choice (including need recognition, information search, evaluation of alternatives, and service purchase); consumer experience; and postexperience evaluation. Consumer behavior theories, current research, and insights for managers were highlighted in each of these sections.

Although the three stages are relevant for all types of consumer behavior in services, important differences exist in behavior across global cultures and for groups versus individuals. Global differences in consumer behavior were presented, particularly as they relate to service consumption. The chapter ended with a discussion of the differences in group versus individual consumer decision making related to households and organizations.

Discussion Questions

1. Based on the chapter, which aspects of consumer behavior are similar and which are different for services versus goods?
2. Where does a college education fit on the continuum of evaluation for different types of products? Where does computer software fit? Consulting? Retailing? Fast food? What are the implications for consumer behavior?
3. What are examples (other than those given in the chapter) of services that are high in credence properties? How do high credence properties affect consumer behavior for these services?
4. For what types of services might consumers depend on mass communication (nonpersonal sources of information, including the Internet) in the purchase decision?
5. Which of the aspects discussed in the chapter describe your behavior when it comes to purchasing services? Does your behavior differ for different types of services?
6. Why are consumer experiences so important in the evaluation process for services?
7. Using the service drama metaphor, describe the services provided by a health club, a fine restaurant, or a vacation cruise line.
8. What are some differences in service choice, purchase, and consumption processes for organizations and households compared to individuals? What are some similarities?

Exercises

1. Choose a particular end-consumer services industry and one type of service provided in that industry (such as the financial services industry for mortgage loans, the legal services industry for wills, or the travel industry for a vacation package). Talk to five customers who have purchased that service and determine to what extent the information in this chapter described their behavior in terms of consumer choice, consumer experience, and postexperience evaluation for that service.

2. Choose a particular business-to-business service industry and one type of service provided in that industry (such as the information services industry for computer maintenance services or the consulting industry for management consulting). Talk to five customers in that industry and determine to what extent the information in this chapter described their behavior in terms of consumer choice, consumer experience, and postexperience evaluation for that service.

3. Visit a service provider of your choice. Experience the service firsthand if possible and observe other customers for a period of time. Describe the consumer (service) experience in detail in terms of what happened throughout the process and how customers, including yourself, felt about it. How could the service experience be improved?

4. Interview three people who come from countries other than your own. Ask them about their consumer behavior patterns. Note the differences and similarities to your own consumer behavior. What are possible causes of the differences?

Notes

1. E. H. Fram, "Stressed-out Consumers Need Timesaving Innovations," *Marketing News,* March 2, 1992, p. 10.
2. M. J. Dorsch, S. J. Grove, and W. R. Darden, "Consumer Intentions to Use a Service Category," *Journal of Services Marketing* 14, no. 2 (2000), pp. 92–117.
3. L. L. Berry, "The Time-Buying Customer," *Journal of Retailing* 55, no. 4 (Winter 1979), pp. 58–69.
4. A Spector, "Menu Marketers Deliver Dinner, Incremental Sales," *Nation's Restaurant News,* May 19, 2003, p. 154.
5. P. Nelson, "Information and Consumer Behavior," *Journal of Political Economy* 78, no. 20 (1970), pp. 311–29.
6. M. R. Darby and E. Karni, "Free Competition and the Optimal Amount of Fraud," *Journal of Law and Economics* 16 (April 1973), pp. 67–86.
7. "USA Snapshots: A Look at Statistics That Shape Our Lives," *USA Today,* November 1, 1998, p. D-1.
8. T. S. Robertson, *Innovative Behavior and Communication* (New York: Holt, Rinehart & Winston, 1971).
9. P. Berthon, L. Pitt, C. S. Katsikeas, and J. P. Berthon, "Virtual Services Go International: International Services in the Marketspace," *Journal of International Marketing* 7, no. 3 (1999), pp. 84–105.
10. J. C. Ward and A. L. Ostrom, "Online Complaining via Customer-created Web Sites: A Protest Framing Perspective," working paper, W. P. Carey School of Business, Arizona State University, 2004.
11. M. Laroche, G. H. G. McDougall, J. Bergeron, and Z. Yang, "Exploring How Intangibility Affects Perceived Risk," *Journal of Service Research* 6, no. 4 (May 2004), pp. 373-89; K. B. Murray and J. L. Schlacter, "The Impact of Services versus Goods on Consumers' Assessment of Perceived Risk and Variability," *Journal of the Academy of Marketing Science* 18, (Winter 1990), pp. 51–65; M. Laroche, J. Bergeron, and C. Goutaland, "How Intangibility Affects Perceived Risk: The Moderating Role of Knowledge and Involvement," *Journal of Services Marketing* 17, no. 2 (2003), pp. 122–40.

12. M. Laroche et al., "Exploring How Intangibility Affects Perceived Risk."

13. R. F. Lusch, S. W. Brown, and G. J. Brunswick, "A General Framework for Explaining Internal vs. External Exchange," *Journal of the Academy of Marketing Science* 10, (Spring 1992), pp. 119–34; Dorsch, Grove and Darden, "Consumer Intentions to Use a Service Category."

14. J. H. Gilmore and B. J. Pine II, "The Experience Is the Marketing," report from Strategic Horizons LLP, 2002.

15. See, for example, B. J. Pine II and J. H. Gilmore, *The Experience Economy* (Boston: Harvard Business School Press, 1999); B. H. Schmitt, *Experiential Marketing* (New York: The Free Press, 1999); B. H. Schmitt, *Customer Experience Management* (Hoboken, NJ: John Wiley & Sons, 2003).

16. S. S. Tax and F. N. Morgan, "Toward a Theory of Service Delivery Networks," working paper, W. P. Carey School of Business, Arizona State University, 2004.

17. S. J. Grove and R. P. Fisk, "Service Theater: An Analytical Framework for Services Marketing," in *Services Marketing,* 4th ed., ed. Christopher Lovelock (Englewood Cliffs, NJ: Prentice Hall, 2001), pp. 83–92.

18. S. J. Grove, R. P. Fisk, and M. J. Bitner, "Dramatizing the Service Experience: A Managerial Approach," in *Advances in Services Marketing and Management,* vol. 1, ed. T. A. Swartz, D. E. Bowen, and S. W. Brown (Greenwich, CT: JAI Press, 1992), pp. 91–121.

19. Grove, Fisk, and Bitner, "Dramatizing the Service Experience."

20. Grove and Fisk, "Service Theater."

21. Ibid.

22. Grove, Fisk, and Bitner, "Dramatizing the Service Experience."

23. Ibid.

24. Ibid.

25. M. R. Solomon, C. Surprenant, J. A. Czepiel, and E. G. Gutman, "A Role Theory Perspective on Dyadic Interactions: The Service Encounter," *Journal of Marketing* 49 (Winter 1985), pp. 99–111.

26. Ibid.

27. R. F. Abelson, "Script Processing in Attitude Formation and Decision Making," in *Cognition and Social Behavior,* ed. J. S. Carroll and J. S. Payne (Hillsdale, NJ: Erlbaum, 1976).

28. R. A. Smith and M. J. Houston, "Script-Based Evaluations of Satisfaction with Services," in *Emerging Perspectives on Services Marketing,* ed. L. Berry, G. L. Shostack, and G. Upah (Chicago: American Marketing Association, 1982), pp. 59–62.

29. J. E. G. Bateson and M. K. M. Hui, "Crowding in the Service Environment," in *Creativity in Services Marketing: What's New, What Works, What's Developing,* ed. M. Venkatesan, D. M. Schmalensee, and C. Marshall (Chicago: American Marketing Association, 1986), pp. 85–88.

30. J. Baker, "The Role of the Environment in Marketing Services: The Consumer Perspective," in *The Services Challenge: Integrating for Competitive Advantage,* ed. J. A. Czepiel, C. A. Congram, and J. Shanahan (Chicago: American Marketing Association, 1987), pp. 79–84.

31. C. L. Martin and C. A. Pranter, "Compatibility Management: Customer-to-Customer Relationships in Service Environments," *Journal of Services Marketing* 3 (Summer 1989).

32. Ibid.

33. N. Bendapudi and R. P. Leone, "Psychological Implications of Customer Participation in Co-Production," *Journal of Marketing* 67 (January 2003), pp.14–28.

34. L. A. Bettencourt, A. L. Ostrom, S. W. Brown, and R. I. Roundtree, "Client Co-Production in Knowledge-Intensive Business Services," *California Management Review* 44, no. 4 (Summer 2002), pp. 100–128.

35. S. Dellande, M. C. Gilly, and J. L. Graham, "Gaining Compliance and Losing Weight: The Role of the Service Provider in Health Care Services," *Journal of Marketing* 68 (July 2004), pp. 78–91; M. L. Meuter, M. J. Bitner, A. L. Ostrom, and S. W. Brown, "Choosing among Alternative Service Delivery Modes: An Investigation of Customer Trials of Self-Service Technologies," *Journal of Marketing* (forthcoming 2005).

36. C. K. Prahalad and V. Ramaswamy, "The New Frontier of Experience Innovation," *Sloan Management Review* (Summer 2003), pp. 12–18.

37. A. F. Firat and A. Venkatesh, "Liberatory Postmodernism and the Reenchantment of Consumption," *Journal of Consumer Research* 22, no. 3 (December 1995), pp. 239–67.

38. M. P. Gardner, "Mood States and Consumer Behavior: A Critical Review," *Journal of Consumer Research* 12 (December 1985), pp. 281–300.

39. Ibid., p. 288.

40. S. S. Tomkins, "Affect as Amplification: Some Modifications in Theory," in *Emotion: Theory, Research, and Experience,* ed. R. Plutchik and H. Kellerman (New York: Academic Press, 1980), pp. 141–64.

41. L. L. Berry, L. P. Carbone, and S. H. Haeckel, "Managing the Total Customer Experience," *Sloan Management Review* (Spring 2002), pp. 85–89.

42. V. S. Folkes and V. M. Patrick, "The Positivity Effect in Perceptions of Services: Seen One, Seen Them All?" *Journal of Consumer Research* 30 (June 2003), pp. 125–37.

43. B. Imrie, J. W. Cadogan, and R. McNaughton, "The Service Quality Construct on a Global Stage," *Managing Service Quality* 12, no. 1 (2002), pg. 10–18.

44. B. D. Keillor, G. T. M. Hult, D. Kandemir, "A Study of the Service Encounter in Eight Countries," *Journal of International Marketing* 12, no. 1 (2004), pp. 9–35.

45. A. M. Smith and N. L. Reynolds, "Measuring Cross-Cultural Service Quality: A Framework for Assessment," *International Marketing Review* 19, no. 5 (2001), pp. 450–81.

46. R. B. Money, M. C. Gilly, and J. L. Graham, "Explorations of National Culture and Word-of-Mouth Referral Behavior in the Purchase of Industrial Services in the United States and Japan," *Journal of Marketing,* 62 (October 1998), pp. 76–87.

47. E. T. Hall, *Silent Language* (Garden City, NY: Anchor Press/Doubleday, 1959).

48. G. Hofstede, *Culture and Organizations: Software of the Mind* (New York: McGraw-Hill, 1991), p. 235.

49. D. E. Murphy, "New East Europe Retailers Told to Put on a Happy Face," *Los Angeles Times,* November 26, 1994, pp. A1, A18.

50. "Japanese Put Tourism on a Higher Plane," *International Herald Tribune,* February 3, 1992, p. 8.

51. E. Arnould, L. Price, and G. Zinkhan, *Consumers,* 2nd ed. (New York: McGraw-Hill, 2004).

52. For excellent coverage of buyer behavior in organizations, see M. D. Hutt and T. W. Speh, *Business Marketing Management,* 8th ed. (Mason, Ohio: South-Western, 2004), chapter 3.

53. Ibid., pp. 68–69.

54. Ibid., pp. 62–67.

55. www.neoIT.com: A Vashistha and A. Vashistha, *The Offshore Nation: The Rise of Services Globalization* (New York: McGraw-Hill, 2005, forthcoming).

Chapter 4

Customer Expectations of Service

This chapter's objectives are to

1. Recognize that customers hold different types of expectations for service performance.

2. Discuss the sources of customer expectations of service, including those that are controllable and uncontrollable by marketers.

3. Acknowledge that the types and sources of expectations are similar for end consumers and business customers, for pure service and product-related service, for experienced customers and inexperienced customers.

4. Delineate the most important current issues surrounding customer expectations.

Undoubtedly, the greatest gap between customer expectations and service delivery exists when the Japanese meet Russians. In Japan the customer is supreme. At the morning opening of large department stores in Tokyo, sales personnel line up to welcome patrons and bow as they enter! When one of us—who could speak no Japanese—visited Tokyo recently, as many as eight salespeople willingly tried to help me find a calligraphy pen. Although the pen was a very low-priced item, several attendants rushed from counter to counter to find someone to translate, several others spread out to find pens that might serve as the perfect gift, and still others searched for maps to other stores where the perfect pen could be found.

Because of the wonderful treatment Japanese customers are used to in their home country, they often have service expectations that exceed service delivery even when shopping in "civilized" countries such as Great Britain: "Hideo Majima, 57, a Japanese tourist, looked puzzled and annoyed. He was standing in a London department store while two shop assistants conversed instead of serving him. He left without buying anything."[1] His annoyance is understandable when you realize the standard of service treatment in Japan.

FIGURE 4.1
Tokyo sales personnel provide excellent customer service.

Source: © Charles Gupton/Stock Boston Inc./PictureQuest

Given how our friend Majima-san felt about shopping in Britain, try to imagine his perceptions of this actual dining experience in many Russian restaurants. Remember that in Russia's economy, products are still so scarce that suppliers rule. Sellers decide who gets what, and the concept of customer service is virtually meaningless. In a real-life experience, a customer visiting the Izmailova Hotel had to excuse the waiters if they were too busy to serve customers—they were playing chess. "'Can't you see we're one move away from checkmate?' yelled waiter Oleg Shamov, surrounded by six other waiters in a restaurant back room. The match kept customers waiting for 40 minutes."[2] Free enterprise is apparently having strong effects in the former Soviet Union. Professor Peter Shikkirev at the Graduate School of International Business in Moscow assures us that some Russian restaurants are now providing service comparable to fine American restaurants. However, we doubt that even that level of customer service would delight Japanese customers.

Customer expectations are beliefs about service delivery that serve as standards or reference points against which performance is judged. Because customers compare their perceptions of performance with these reference points when evaluating service quality, thorough knowledge about customer expectations is critical to services marketers. Knowing what the customer expects is the first and possibly most critical step in delivering quality service. Being wrong about what customers want can mean losing a customer's business when another company hits the target exactly. Being wrong can also mean expending money, time, and other resources on things that do not count to the customer. Being wrong can even mean not surviving in a fiercely competitive market.

Among the aspects of expectations that need to be explored and understood for successful services marketing are the following: What types of expectation standards do customers hold about services? What factors most influence the formation of these expectations? What role do these factors play in changing expectations? How can a service company meet or exceed customer expectations?

In this chapter we provide a framework for thinking about customer expectations.[3] The chapter is divided into three main sections: (1) the meaning and types of expected service, (2) factors that influence customer expectations of service, and (3) current issues involving customer service expectations.

MEANING AND TYPES OF SERVICE EXPECTATIONS

To say that expectations are reference points against which service delivery is compared is only a beginning. The level of expectation can vary widely depending on the reference point the customer holds. Although most everyone has an intuitive sense of what expectations are, service marketers need a far more thorough and clear definition of expectations in order to comprehend, measure, and manage them.

Let's imagine that you are planning to go to a restaurant. Figure 4.2 shows a continuum along which different possible types of service expectations can be arrayed from low to high. On the left of the continuum are different types or levels of expectations, ranging from high (top) to low (bottom). At each point we give a name to the type of expectation and illustrate what it might mean in terms of a restaurant you are considering. Note how important the expectation you held will be to your eventual assessment of the restaurant's performance. Suppose you went into the restaurant for which you held the minimum tolerable expectation, paid very little money, and were served immediately with good food. Next suppose that you went to the restaurant for which you had the highest (ideal) expectations, paid a lot of money, and were served good (but not fantastic) food. Which restaurant experience would you judge to be best? The answer is likely to depend a great deal on the reference point that you brought to the experience.

FIGURE 4.2
Possible Levels of Customer Expectations

Source: R. K. Expectations, Performance Evaluation and Consumers' Perceptions of Quality," Journal of Marketing, October 1993, pp. 18-34. Reprinted by permission of the American Marketing Association.

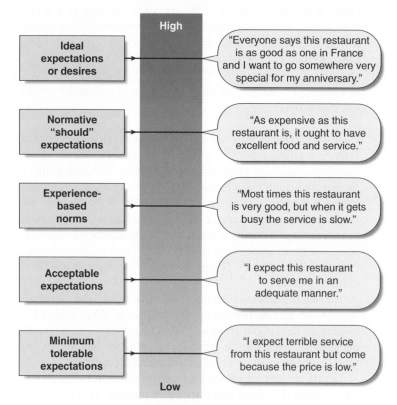

Because the idea of customer expectations is so critical to evaluation of service, we start this chapter by talking about the levels of expectations.

Expected Service: Levels of Expectations

As we showed in Figure 4.2, customers hold different types of expectations about service. For purposes of our discussion in the rest of this chapter, we focus on two types. The highest can be termed *desired service:* the level of service the customer hopes to receive—the "wished for" level of performance. Desired service is a blend of what the customer believes "can be" and "should be."[4] For example, consumers who sign up for a computer dating service expect to find compatible, attractive, interesting people to date and perhaps even someone to marry. The expectation reflects the hopes and wishes of these consumers; without these hopes and wishes and the belief that they may be fulfilled, consumers would probably not purchase the dating service. In a similar way, you will engage the services of your college's placement office when you are ready to graduate. What are your expectations of the service? In all likelihood you want the office to find you a job—the right job in the right place for the right salary—because that is what you hope and wish for.

However, you probably also see that the economy may constrain the availability of ideal job openings in companies. And not all companies you may be interested in having a relationship with your placement office. In this situation and in general, customers hope to achieve their service desires but recognize that this is not always possible. We call the threshold level of acceptable service *adequate service*—the level of service the customer will accept.[5] In the economic slowdown following the World Trade Center disaster, many college graduates who were trained for high-skilled jobs accepted entry-level positions at fast-food restaurants or internships for no pay. Their hopes and desires were still high, but they recognized that they could not attain those desires in the market that existed at the time. Their standard of adequate service was much lower than their desired service. Some graduates accepted any job for which they could earn a salary, and others agreed to nonpaying, short-term positions as interns to gain experience. Adequate service represents the "minimum tolerable expectation,"[6] the bottom level of performance acceptable to the customer.

Figure 4.3 shows these two expectation standards as the upper and lower boundaries for customer expectations. This figure portrays the idea that customers assess service performance on the basis of two standard boundaries: what they desire and what they deem acceptable.

Among the intriguing questions about service expectations is whether customers hold the same or different expectation levels for service firms in the same industry. For

FIGURE 4.3
Dual Customer Expectation Levels

To understand how consumers behave across cultures, we can identify five universal values across cultures. These universal values are well documented; they are based on a study using 72,215 employees working in 66 different national subsidiaries of IBM Corporation. The universal values, which collectively distinguish members of different cultures, include power distance, uncertainty avoidance, individualism–collectivism, masculinity–femininity, and Confucian dynamic or long-term orientation.[8] Here we explain how Hofstede, the author of this research, defined each of these subdimensions, and then we describe one of many ways they might affect consumer expectations in services.

- *Power distance* involves the way that the less powerful members of institutions and organizations within a country expect and accept that power is distributed unequally. Part of power distance involves human inequality in areas such as prestige, wealth, power, and law. People from cultures high in power distance are comfortable with power hierarchy, discrimination, and tolerance of inequalities.

- *Uncertainty avoidance* is the extent to which the members of a culture feel threatened by uncertain or unknown situations. People with high uncertainty avoidance like clear rules and explicit situations; people with low uncertainty avoidance can accept uncertainty without discomfort and tolerate inexplicit rules.

- *Individualism* exists in societies in which the ties between individuals are loose; all individuals are expected to look after themselves and their immediate family. *Collectivism*, the opposite, exists in societies in which people from birth onward are integrated into strong, cohesive groups that offer lifetime protection in exchange for loyalty. This subdimension can be summed up in three words: I versus we.

- *Masculinity* and *femininity* are the dominant sex role patterns in the vast majority of both traditional and modern societies. Masculine societies value assertiveness, performance,

example, are desired service expectations the same for all restaurants? Or just for all fast-food restaurants? Do the levels of adequate service expectations vary across restaurants? Consider the following quotation:

> Levels of expectation are why two organizations in the same business can offer far different levels of service and still keep customers happy. It is why McDonald's can extend excellent industrialized service with few employees per customer and why an expensive restaurant with many tuxedoed waiters may be unable to do as well from the customer's point of view.[7]

Customers typically hold similar desired expectations across categories of service, but these categories are not as broad as whole industries. Among subcategories of restaurants are expensive restaurants, ethnic restaurants, fast-food restaurants, and airport restaurants. A customer's desired service expectation for fast-food restaurants is quick, convenient, tasty food in a clean setting. The desired service expectation for an expensive restaurant, on the other hand, usually involves elegant surroundings, gracious employees, candlelight, and fine food. In essence, desired service expectations seem to be the same for service providers within industry categories or subcategories that are viewed as similar by customers.

ambition, and independence, whereas feminine societies value nurturance, quality of life, service, and interdependence.

- The *Confucian dynamic,* or *long-term versus short-term orientation dimension,* refers to the way people look at the future. Long-term orientation emphasizes perseverance, ordering relationships by status, thrift, and a sense of shame. On the other hand, short-term orientation focuses on personal steadiness and stability, saving face, respect for tradition, and reciprocation of greetings, favors, and gifts.

The impact of culture on consumer expectations can be illuminated using these five sub-dimensions of values and attitudes. In one study, for example, researchers found the following:[9]

- Consumers low on power distance have high overall expectations of service and particularly expect responsive and reliable service.

- Individualistic consumers have high overall service quality expectations and expect empathy and assurance from the service provider.

- Consumers high on uncertainty avoidance and short-term–oriented consumers have high overall service quality expectations.

As the authors of the study point out, marketing efforts will perform better when matched with cultural characteristics. This and other typologies that help us understand the differences in values across cultures will be of immense importance as service marketers develop and market service offerings.

Source: Based on background research and a study conducted by N. Donthu and B. Yoo, *Journal of Service Research* 1, no. 2 (November 1998), pp. 178–86.

The adequate service expectation level, on the other hand, may vary for different firms within a category or subcategory. Within fast-food restaurants, a customer may hold a higher expectation for McDonald's than for Burger King, having experienced consistent service at McDonald's over time and somewhat inconsistent service at Burger King. It is possible, therefore, that a customer can be more disappointed with service from McDonald's than from Burger King even though the actual level of service at McDonald's is higher than the level at Burger King. This chapter's Global Feature further discusses how culture influences expectations.

The Zone of Tolerance

As we discussed in earlier chapters of this textbook, services are heterogeneous in that performance may vary across providers, across employees from the same provider, and even with the same service employee. The extent to which customers recognize and are willing to accept this variation is called the *zone of tolerance* and is shown in Figure 4.4. If service drops below adequate service—the minimum level considered acceptable—customers will be frustrated and their satisfaction with the company will be undermined. If service performance is higher than the zone of tolerance at the top end—where performance exceeds desired service—customers will be very pleased and probably quite surprised as well. You might consider the zone of tolerance as the range or window in which customers do not particularly notice service performance. When it falls outside the range (either very low or very high), the service gets the customer's attention in either a positive or negative way. As an example, consider the service at a checkout line in a grocery store. Most customers hold a range of acceptable times for this service encounter—probably somewhere between 5 and 10 minutes. If service consumes that period of time, customers probably do not pay much attention to the wait. If a customer enters the line and finds sufficient checkout personnel to serve her in the first two or three minutes, she may notice the service and judge it as excellent. On the other hand, if a customer has to wait in line for 15 minutes, he may begin to grumble and look at his watch. The longer the wait is below the zone of tolerance, the more frustrated he becomes.

Customers' service expectations are characterized by a range of levels (like those shown in Figure 4.3), bounded by desired and adequate service, rather than a single level. This tolerance zone, representing the difference between desired service and the level of service considered adequate, can expand and contract within a customer. An airline customer's zone of tolerance will narrow when she is running late and is concerned about making her plane. A minute seems much longer, and her adequate service level increases. On the other hand, a customer who arrives at the airport early may have a larger tolerance zone, making the wait in line far less noticeable than when he is pressed for time. This example shows that the marketer must understand not just the size and boundary levels for the zone of tolerance but also when and how the tolerance zone fluctuates with a given customer.

Different Customers Possess Different Zones of Tolerance

Another aspect of variability in the range of reasonable services is that different customers possess different tolerance zones. Some customers have narrow zones of tolerance, requiring a tighter range of service from providers, whereas other customers allow a greater range of service. For example, very busy customers would likely always be pressed for time, desire short wait times in general, and also hold a constrained range for the length of acceptable wait times. When it comes to meeting plumbers or repair personnel at their homes for appliance problems, customers who work outside the home have a more restricted window of acceptable time duration for that appointment than do customers who work in their homes or do not work at all.

An individual customer's zone of tolerance increases or decreases depending on a number of factors, including company-controlled factors such as price. When prices increase, customers tend to be less tolerant of poor service. In this case, the zone of

FIGURE 4.4
The Zone of Tolerance

FIGURE 4.5
Zones of Tolerance for Different Service Dimensions

Source: L. L. Berry, A. Parasuraman, and V. A. Zeithaml, "Ten Lessons for Improving Service Quality," *Marketing Science Institute,* Report No. 93-104 (May 1993).

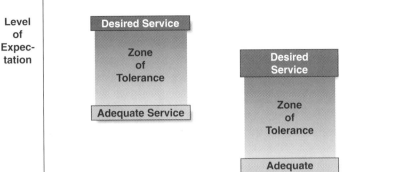

tolerance decreases because the adequate service level shifts upward. Later in this chapter we will describe many different factors, some company controlled and others customer controlled, that lead to the narrowing or widening of the tolerance zone.

Zones of Tolerance Vary for Service Dimensions

Customers' tolerance zones also vary for different service attributes or dimensions. The more important the factor, the narrower the zone of tolerance is likely to be. In general, customers are likely to be less tolerant about unreliable service (broken promises or service errors) than other service deficiencies, which means that they have higher expectations for this factor. In addition to higher expectations for the most important service dimensions and attributes, customers are likely to be less willing to relax these expectations than those for less important factors, making the zone of tolerance for the most important service dimension smaller and the desired and adequate service levels higher.[10] Figure 4.5 portrays the likely difference in tolerance zones for the most important and the least important factors.[11]

The fluctuation in the individual customer's zone of tolerance is more a function of changes in the adequate service level, which moves readily up and down because of situational circumstances, than in the desired service level, which tends to move upward incrementally because of accumulated experiences. Desired service is relatively idiosyncratic and stable compared with adequate service, which moves up and down and in response to competition and other factors. Fluctuation in the zone of tolerance can be likened to an accordion's movement, but with most of the gyration coming from one side (the adequate service level) rather than the other (the desired service level).

In summary, we can express the boundaries of customer expectations of service with two different levels of expectations: desired service and adequate service. The desired service level is less subject to change than the adequate service level. A zone of tolerance separates these two levels. This zone of tolerance varies across customers and expands or contracts with the same customer.

FACTORS THAT INFLUENCE CUSTOMER EXPECTATIONS OF SERVICE

Because expectations play such a critical role in customer evaluation of services, marketers need and want to understand the factors that shape them. Marketers would also

FIGURE 4.6
Factors That
Influence Desired
Service

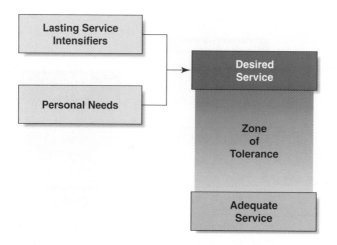

like to have control over these factors as well, but many of the forces that influence customer expectations are uncontrollable. In this section of the chapter we try to separate the many influences on customer expectations.

Sources of Desired Service Expectations

As shown in Figure 4.6, the two largest influences on desired service level are personal needs and philosophies about service. *Personal needs,* those states or conditions essential to the physical or psychological well-being of the customer, are pivotal factors that shape what customers desire in service. Personal needs can fall into many categories, including physical, social, psychological, and functional. A fan who regularly goes to baseball games right from work, and is therefore thirsty and hungry, hopes and desires that the food and drink vendors will pass by his section frequently, whereas a fan who regularly has dinner elsewhere has a low or zero level of desired service from the vendors. A customer with high social and dependency needs may have relatively high expectations for a hotel's ancillary services, hoping, for example, that the hotel has a bar with live music and dancing. The effect of personal needs on desired service is illustrated by the different expectations held by two business insurance customers:

> I expect [an insurance] broker to do a great deal of my work because I don't have the staff…I expect the broker to know a great deal about my business and communicate that knowledge to the underwriter.

> My expectations are different…I do have a staff to do our certificates, etc., and use the broker minimally.[12]

Some customers are more demanding than others, having greater sensitivity to, and higher expectations of, service. *Lasting service intensifiers* are individual, stable factors that lead the customer to a heightened sensitivity to service. One of the most important of these factors can be called *derived service expectations,* which occur when customer expectations are driven by another person or group of people. A niece from a big family who is planning a 90th birthday party for a favorite aunt is representing the entire family in selecting a restaurant for a successful celebration. Her needs are driven in part by the derived expectations from the other family members. A parent choosing a vacation for the family, a spouse selecting a home-cleaning service, an employee choosing an office for the firm—all these customers' individual expectations are intensified because they represent and must answer to other parties who will receive the service. In the context of business-to-business service, customer expectations are driven by the expectations of their own customers. The head of an information technology department in an insurance company, who is the business customer of a large computer vendor, has expectations based on those of the insurance customers she serves: when the computer equipment is down, her customers complain. Her need to keep the system up and running is not just her own expectation but is derived from the pressure of customers.

Business-to-business customers may also derive their expectations from their managers and supervisors. Employees of a marketing research department may speed up project cycles (increase their expectations for speed of delivery) when pressured by their management to deliver the study results. Purchasing agents may increase demands for faster delivery at lower costs when company management is emphasizing cost reduction in the company.

Another lasting service intensifier is *personal service philosophy*—the customer's underlying generic attitude about the meaning of service and the proper conduct of service providers. If you have ever been employed as a wait person in a restaurant, you are likely to have standards for restaurant service that were shaped by your training and experience in that role. You might, for example, believe that waiters should not keep customers waiting longer than 15 minutes to take their orders. Knowing the way a kitchen operates, you may be less tolerant of lukewarm food or errors in the order than customers who have not held the role of waitperson. In general, customers who are themselves in service businesses or have worked for them in the past seem to have especially strong service philosophies.

To the extent that customers have personal philosophies about service provision, their expectations of service providers will be intensified. Personal service philosophies and derived service expectations elevate the level of desired service.

Sources of Adequate Service Expectations

A different set of determinants affects adequate service, the level of service the customer finds acceptable. In general, these influences are short-term and tend to fluctuate more than the factors that influence desired service. In this section we explain the five factors shown in Figure 4.7 that influence adequate service: (1) temporary service intensifiers, (2) perceived service alternatives, (3) customer self-perceived service role, (4) situational factors, and (5) predicted service.

The first set of elements, *temporary service intensifiers,* consists of short-term, individual factors that make a customer more aware of the need for service. Personal emergency situations in which service is urgently needed (such as an accident and the need for automobile insurance or a breakdown in office equipment during a busy period) raise the level of adequate service expectation, particularly the level of responsiveness required and considered acceptable. A mail-order company that depends on toll-free phone lines for receiving all customer orders will tend to be more demanding of the telephone service during peak periods of the week, month, and year. Any system breakdown or lack of clarity on the lines will be tolerated less during these intense periods than at other times. The impact of temporary service intensifiers is evident in these comments by two participants in a research study conducted by one of us:

> An automobile insurance customer: The nature of my problem influences my expectations, for example, a broken window versus a DWI accident requiring brain surgery.

> A business equipment repair customer: I had calibration problems with the X-ray equipment. They should have come out and fixed it in a matter of hours because of the urgency.[13]

FIGURE 4.7
Factors That Influence Adequate Service

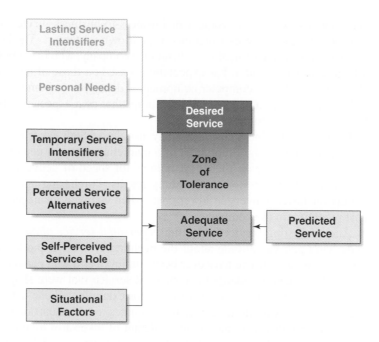

Problems with the initial service can also lead to heightened expectations. Performing a service right the first time is very important because customers value service reliability above all other dimensions. If the service fails in the recovery phase, fixing it right the second time (that is, being reliable in service recovery) is even more critical than it was the first time. Automobile repair service provides a case in point. If a problem with your automobile's brakes sends you to a car repair provider, you expect the company to fix the brakes. If you experience further problems with the brakes after the repair (a not-uncommon situation with car repair), your adequate service level will increase. In these and other situations where temporary service intensifiers are present, the level of adequate service will increase and the zone of tolerance will narrow.

Perceived service alternatives are other providers from whom the customer can obtain service. If customers have multiple service providers to choose from, or if they can provide the service for themselves (such as lawn care or personal grooming), their levels of adequate service are higher than those of customers who believe it is not possible to get better service elsewhere. An airline customer who lives in a small town with a tiny airport, for example, has a reduced set of options in airline travel. This customer will be more tolerant of the service performance of the carriers in the town because few alternatives exist. She will accept the scheduling and lower levels of service more than the customer in a big city who has myriad flights and airlines to choose from. The customer's perception that service alternatives exist raises the level of adequate service and narrows the zone of tolerance.

It is important that service marketers fully understand the complete set of options that customers view as perceived alternatives. In the small town–small airport example just discussed, the set of alternatives from the customer's point of view is likely to include more than just other airlines: limousine service to a nearby large city, rail service, or driving. In general, service marketers must discover the alternatives that the customer views as comparable rather than those in the company's competitive set. For example, airline companies must fully understand customer views of new service technologies (see our Technology Spotlight).

Technology Spotlight
Customer Expectations of New Technology Services at the Airport

One of the most difficult tasks that marketers face is understanding what customers expect from completely new services, and nowhere is this problem more evident than when these new services involve technology. Customers almost always resist new technology initially—perhaps because they do not understand it, perhaps because they fear change—even when the technology leads to improved service. Technology that makes obtaining service easier and faster is springing up all over, even in airports around the country. Customers are accepting some new service technologies and resisting others. Here we discuss two innovations that are meeting different fates.

One new service technology that is rapidly being accepted by customers is automatic airline check-in: Customers walk up to computer screens, slide credit cards, and use touch pads to retrieve their boarding passes and receipts. Unless the flight is international, customers can check luggage automatically as well, and an attendant takes their luggage from them before they go to their gates. The service takes less time than working with an attendant, and most airlines have added more computers than they previously had lines for attendants, saving customers considerable time. When these computer screens were first installed, customers were not sure what to expect and did not know how to use them. Airlines that supplied extra employees to stand and help customers use the computers found success in converting customers from the human handling to the technology. Today, most customers prefer the computers because of their speed and ease.

Another airport technology that is being accepted more slowly by customers is called Exit Express and is a technology substitute for toll booths as customers leave airport parking areas. It works like this: Before customers exit the airport, they use a machine (similar to a subway token machine) to pay their parking fees in advance. They insert their parking ticket, then their credit card or cash, and receive back their stamped parking ticket.

When they exit the parking lot, they use one of the many Exit Express lanes, insert their paid tickets, and leave. Airports typically still retain a small number of lanes that use live employees and operate in the traditional way. Surprisingly, many airports are finding that customers do not use Exit Express technology as much as expected. One of us, who loves the new technology and always uses it, typically finds herself alone in the Exit Express lanes while other customers line up in the live employee lane. Why are customers resisting this technology that clearly meets or exceeds their expectations of getting out of the airport quickly? One possible reason is that they do not understand how the system works, even though a loudspeaker in the parking lots trumpets the new system continuously. They also may not clearly see the benefits being provided, possibly because the airport did not communicate them well enough, leading customers to believe that the old system with toll booths was quick enough. Another reason is that most airports have not stationed employees near the technology to familiarize customers with it and to deal with service failures, as the airlines did with automatic check-in. Customers may also fear that if something goes wrong, they would be embarrassed and not know how to resolve the situation. A final compelling reason is that many customers distrust the technology the way they used to distrust automated teller machine (ATM) technology when it was first introduced.

If new services created by technology are to meet the expectations of customers, they must be trusted, understood, and introduced as valuable to customers. Otherwise, the promise of meeting or exceeding customer expectations will not be realized despite large investments.

Source: M. L. Meuter, M. J. Bitner, A. L. Ostrom, and S. W. Brown, "Choosing among Alternative Service Delivery Modes: An Investigation of Customer Trial of Self-Service Technologies," *Journal of Marketing*, (April) 2005. Reprinted by permission of the American Marketing Association.

A third factor affecting the level of adequate service is the *customer's self-perceived service role*. We define this as customer perceptions of the degree to which customers exert an influence on the level of service they receive. In other words, customers' expectations are partly shaped by how well they believe they are performing their own roles in service delivery.[14] One role of the customer is to specify the level of service expected. A customer who is very explicit with a waiter about how rare he wants his steak cooked in a restaurant will probably be more dissatisfied if the meat comes to the table overcooked than a customer who does not articulate the degree of doneness expected. The customer's active participation in the service also affects this factor. A customer who does not show up for many of her allergy shots will probably be more lenient on the allergist when she experiences symptoms than one who conscientiously shows up for every shot.

A final way the customer defines his or her role is in assuming the responsibility for complaining when service is poor. A dissatisfied customer who complains will be less tolerant than one who does not voice his or her concerns. An automobile insurance customer acknowledged his responsibility in service provision this way: "You can't blame it all on the insurance agent. You need to be responsible too and let the agent know what exactly you want." A truck-leasing customer recognized her role by stating, "There are a lot of variables that can influence how you get treated, including how you deal with them."[15]

Customers' zones of tolerance seem to expand when they sense they are not fulfilling their roles. When, on the other hand, customers believe they are doing their part in delivery, their expectations of adequate service are heightened and the zone of tolerance contracts. The comment of an automobile repair customer illustrates: "Service writers are not competent. I prepare my own itemized list of problems, take it to the service writer, and tell him or her, 'Fix these.'" This customer will expect more than one who did not prepare as well to receive the service.

Levels of adequate service are also influenced by *situational factors,* defined as service performance conditions that customers view as beyond the control of the service provider. For example, where personal emergencies such as serious automobile accidents would likely intensify customer service expectations of insurance companies (because they are temporary service intensifiers), catastrophes that affect a large number of people at one time (tornadoes or earthquakes) may lower service expectations because customers recognize that insurers are inundated with demands for their services. During the days following the World Trade Center disaster, telephone and Internet service was poor because so many people were trying to get in touch with friends and relatives. However, customers were forgiving because they understood the source of the problem. Customers who recognize that situational factors are not the fault of the service company may accept lower levels of adequate service given the context. In general, situational factors temporarily lower the level of adequate service, widening the zone of tolerance.

The final factor that influences adequate service is *predicted service* (Figure 4.8), the level of service that customers believe they are likely to get. This type of service expectation can be viewed as predictions made by customers about what is likely to happen during an impending transaction or exchange. Predicted service performance implies some objective calculation of the probability of performance or estimate of anticipated service performance level. If customers predict good service, their levels of adequate service are likely to be higher than if they predict poor service. For example, full-time residents in a college town usually predict faster restaurant service during the summer months when students are not on campus. This prediction will probably lead them to have higher standards for adequate service in restaurants during the summer than during school months. On the other hand, customers of telephone companies and utilities know that installation service from these firms will be difficult to obtain during

FIGURE 4.8
Factors That Influence Desired and Predicted Service

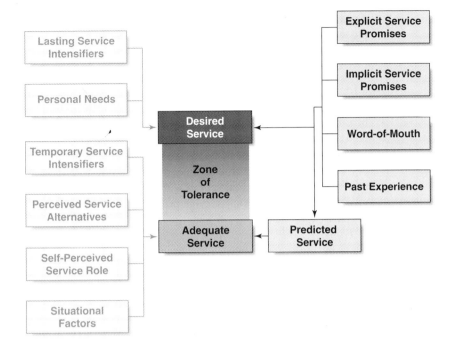

the first few weeks of school when myriad students are setting up their apartments for the year. In this case, levels of adequate service decrease and zones of tolerance widen.

Predicted service is typically an estimate or calculation of the service that a customer will receive in an individual transaction rather than in the overall relationship with a service provider. Whereas desired and adequate service expectations are global assessments comprising many individual service transactions, predicted service is almost always an estimate of what will happen in the next service encounter or transaction that the customer experiences. For this reason, predicted service is viewed in this model as an influencer of adequate service.

Because predictions are about individual service encounters, they are likely to be more concrete and specific than the types of expectation levels customers hold for adequate service or desired service. For example, your predicted service expectations about the length of time you will spend in the waiting room the next time you visit your doctor will likely be expressed in terms of the number of minutes or hours you have spent in the waiting room this time.

Service Encounter Expectations versus Overall Service Expectations

In Chapter 5 we discuss the difference between overall service quality and service encounter quality, viewing the service encounter as a discrete event occurring over a definable period of time (such as a particular hotel stay or a particular check-in experience at the hotel). Customers hold expectations of the quality of each service encounter, just as they hold expectations about the overall service quality of a firm. When the expectations are about individual service encounters, they are likely to be more specific and concrete (such as the number of minutes one must wait for a front desk clerk) than the expectations about overall service quality (like speedy service).

Sources of Both Desired and Predicted Service Expectations

When consumers are interested in purchasing services, they are likely to seek or take in information from several different sources. For example, they may call a store, ask a friend, or deliberately track newspaper advertisements to find the needed service at the lowest price. They may also receive service information by watching television or hearing an unsolicited comment from a colleague about a service that was performed well. In addition to these active and passive types of external search for information, consumers may conduct an internal search by reviewing the information held in memory about the service. This section discusses one internal and three external factors that influence both desired service and predicted service expectations: (1) explicit service promises, (2) implicit service promises, (3) word-of-mouth communications, and (4) past experience.

Explicit service promises are personal and nonpersonal statements about the service made by the organization to customers. The statements are personal when they are communicated by salespeople or service or repair personnel; they are nonpersonal when they come from advertising, brochures, and other written publications. Explicit service promises are one of the few influences on expectations that are completely in the control of the service provider.

Promising exactly what will ultimately be delivered would seem a logical and appropriate way to manage customer expectations and ensure that reality fits the promises. However, companies and the personnel who represent them often deliberately overpromise to obtain business or inadvertently overpromise by stating their best estimates about delivery of a service in the future. In addition to overpromising, company representatives simply do not always know the appropriate promises to make because services are often customized and therefore not easily defined and repeated; the representative may not know when or in what final form the service will be delivered.

All types of explicit service promises have a direct effect on desired service expectation. If the sales visit portrays a banking service that is available 24 hours a day, the customer's desires for that service (as well as the service of competitors) will be shaped by this promise. A hotel customer describes the impact of explicit promises on expectations: "They get you real pumped up with the beautiful ad. When you go in you expect the bells and whistles to go off. Usually they don't." A business equipment repair customer states, "When you buy a piece of equipment you expect to get a competitive advantage from it. Service is promised with the sale of the equipment." A particularly dangerous promise that many companies today make to their business customers is to provide a "total solution" to their business needs. This promise is very difficult to deliver.

Explicit service promises influence the levels of both desired service and predicted service. They shape what customers desire in general as well as what they predict will happen in the next service encounter from a particular service provider or in a certain service encounter.

Implicit service promises are service-related cues other than explicit promises that lead to inferences about what the service should and will be like. These quality cues are dominated by price and the tangibles associated with the service. In general, the higher the price and the more impressive the tangibles, the more a customer will expect from the service. Consider a customer who shops for insurance, finding two firms charging radically different prices. She may infer that the firm with the higher price should and will provide higher-quality service and better coverage. Similarly, a customer who stays at a posh hotel is likely to desire and predict a higher standard of service than from a hotel with less impressive facilities.

The importance of *word-of-mouth communication* in shaping expectations of service is well documented.[16] These personal and sometimes nonpersonal statements made by parties other than the organization convey to customers what the service will be like and influence both predicted and desired service. Word-of-mouth communication carries particular weight as an information source because it is perceived as unbiased. Word of mouth tends to be very important in services that are difficult to evaluate before purchase and before direct experience of them. Experts (including *Consumer Reports,* friends, and family) are also word-of-mouth sources that can affect the levels of desired and predicted service.

Past experience, the customer's previous exposure to service that is relevant to the focal service, is another force in shaping predictions and desires. The service relevant for prediction can be previous exposure to the focal firm's service. For example, you probably compare each stay in a particular hotel with all previous stays in that hotel. But past experience with the focal hotel is likely to be a very limited view of your past experience. You may also compare each stay with your experiences in other hotels and hotel chains. Customers also compare across industries: hospital patients, for example, compare hospital stays against the standard of hotel visits. Cable service customers tend to compare cable service with the standards set by telephone service, one reason cable service is often judged to be poor. In a general sense, past experience may incorporate previous experience with the focal brand, typical performance of a favorite brand, experience with the brand last purchased or the top-selling brand, and the average performance a customer believes represents a group of similar brands.[17]

How might a manager of a service organization use the information we have developed in this chapter to create, improve, or market services? First, managers need to know the pertinent expectation sources and their relative importance for a customer population, a customer segment, and perhaps even a particular customer. They need to know, for instance, the relative weight of word of mouth, explicit service promises, and implicit service promises in shaping desired service and predicted service. Some of these sources are more stable and permanent in their influence (such as lasting service intensifiers and personal needs) than the others, which fluctuate considerably over time (like perceived service alternatives and situational factors).

The different sources vary in terms of their credibility as well as their potential to be influenced by the marketer. Our Strategy Insight shows the breakdown of various factors and how services marketers can influence them. Chapter 16 will detail these and other strategies that services marketers can use to match delivery to promises and thereby manage expectations.

ISSUES INVOLVING CUSTOMER SERVICE EXPECTATIONS

The following issues represent current topics of particular interest to service marketers about customer expectations. In this section we discuss five of the most frequently asked questions about customer expectations:

1. What does a service marketer do if customer expectations are "unrealistic"?

2. Should a company try to delight the customer?

3. How does a company exceed customer service expectations?

FACTOR	POSSIBLE INFLUENCE STRATEGIES
Explicit service promises	Make realistic and accurate promises that reflect the service actually delivered rather than an idealized version of the service.
	Ask contact people for feedback on the accuracy of promises made in advertising and personal selling.
	Avoid engaging in price or advertising wars with competitors because they take the focus off customers and escalate promises beyond the level at which they can be met.
	Formalize service promises through a service guarantee that focuses company employees on the promise and that provides feedback on the number of times promises are not fulfilled.
Implicit service promises	Ensure that service tangibles accurately reflect the type and level of service provided.
	Ensure that price premiums can be justified by higher levels of performance by the company on important customer attributes.
Lasting service intensifiers	Use market research to determine sources of derived service expectations and their requirements. Focus advertising and marketing strategy on ways the service allows the focal customer to satisfy the requirements of the influencing customer.
	Use market research to profile personal service philosophies of customers and use this information in designing and delivering services.
Personal needs	Educate customers on ways the service addresses their needs.
Temporary service intensifiers	Increase service delivery during peak periods or in emergencies.
Perceived service alternatives	Be fully aware of competitive offerings, and where possible and appropriate, match them.
Self-perceived service role	Educate customers to understand their roles and perform them better.
Word-of-mouth communications	Simulate word of mouth in advertising by using testimonials and opinion leaders.
	Identify influencers and opinion leaders for the service and concentrate marketing efforts on them.
	Use incentives with existing customers to encourage them to say positive things about the service.
Past experience	Use marketing research to profile customers' previous experience with similar services.
Situational factors	Use service guarantees to assure customers about service recovery regardless of the situational factors that occur.
Predicted service	Tell customers when service provision is higher than what can normally be expected so that predictions of future service encounters will not be inflated.

4. Do customer service expectations continually escalate?

5. How does a service company stay ahead of competition in meeting customer expectations?

Exhibit 4.1   SERVICE CUSTOMERS WANT THE BASICS

Type of Servcie	Type of Customer	Principal Expectations
Automobile repair	Consumers	Be competent. ("Fix it right the first time.") Explain things. ("Explain why I need the suggested repairs—provide an itemized list.") Be respectful. ("Don't treat me like a dumb female.")
Automobile insurance	Consumers	Keep me informed. ("I shouldn't have to learn about insurance law changes from the newspaper.") Be on my side. ("I don't want them to treat me like a criminal just because I have a claim.") Play fair. ("Don't drop me when something goes wrong.") Protect me from catastrophe. ("Make sure my estate is covered in the event of a major accident.") Provide prompt service. ("I want fast settlement of claims.")
Hotel	Consumers	Provide a clean room. ("Don't have a deep-pile carpet that can't be completely cleaned…you can literally see germs down there.") Provide a secure room. ("Good bolts and peephole on door.") Treat me like a guest. ("It is almost like they're looking you over to decide whether they're going to let you have a room.") Keep your promise. ("They said the room would be ready, but it wasn't at the promised time.")
Property and casualty insurance	Business customers	Fulfill obligations. ("Pay up.") Learn my business and work with me. ("I expect them to know me and my company.") Protect me from catastrophe. ("They should cover my risk exposure so there is no single big loss.") Provide prompt service. ("Fast claim service.")
Equipment repair	Business customers	Share my sense of urgency. ("Speed of response. One time I had to buy a second piece of equipment because of the huge downtime with the first piece.") Be competent. ("Sometimes you are quoting stuff from their instruction manuals to their own people and they don't even know what it means.") Be prepared. ("Have all the parts ready.")
Truck and tractor rental/leasing	Business customers	Keep the equipment running. ("Need to have equipment working all of the time—that is the key.") Be flexible. ("The leasing company should have the flexibility to rent us equipment when we need it.") Provide full service. ("Get rid of all the paperwork and headaches.")

Source: Reprinted from "Understanding Customer Expectations of Service" by A. Parasuraman, LL Berry and VA Zeithaml, MIT Sloan Management Review, Spring 1991, pp. 33-46, by permission of publisher. Copyright © 1991 by Massachusetts Institute of Technology. All rights reserved.

What Does a Services Marketer Do If Customer Expectations Are "Unrealistic"?

One inhibitor to learning about customer expectations is management's and employees' fear of asking. This apprehension often stems from the belief that customer expectations will be extravagant and unrealistic and that by asking about them a company will set itself up for even loftier expectation levels (that is, "unrealistic" levels). Compelling evidence, shown in Exhibit 4.1, suggests that customers' main expectations of service are quite simple and basic: "Simply put, customers expect service companies to do what they are supposed to do. They expect fundamentals, not fanciness; performance, not empty promises."[18] Customers want service to be delivered as promised. They want planes to take off on time, hotel rooms to be clean, food to be hot, and service providers to show up when scheduled. Unfortunately, many service customers are disappointed and let down by companies' inability to meet these basic service expectations.

Asking customers about their expectations does not so much raise the levels of the expectations themselves but rather heightens the belief that the company will do something with the information that surfaces. Arguably the worst thing a company can do is show a strong interest in understanding what customers expect and then never act on the information. At a minimum, a company should acknowledge to customers that it has received and heard their input and that it will expend effort trying to address their issues. The company may not be able to—and indeed does not always have to—deliver to expressed expectations. An alternative and appropriate response would be to let customers know the reasons that desired service is not being provided at the present time and describe the efforts planned to address them. Another approach could be a campaign to educate customers about ways to use and improve the service they currently receive. Giving customers progress updates as service is improved to address their needs and desires is sensible because it allows the company to get credit for incremental efforts to improve service.

Some observers recommend deliberately underpromising the service to increase the likelihood of meeting or exceeding customer expectations.[19] While underpromising makes service expectations more realistic, thereby narrowing the gap between expectations and perceptions, it also may reduce the competitive appeal of the offer. Also, some research has indicated that underpromising may have the inadvertent effect of lowering customer *perceptions* of service, particularly in situations in which customers have little experience with a service.[20] In these situations customer expectations may be self-fulfilling; that is, if the customer goes into the service experience expecting good service, she will focus on the aspects of service provision that are positive, but if she expects low service she may focus on the negative. Thus a salesperson who pitches a customer with a realistic promise may lose the sale to another who inflates the offering. In Chapter 16 we describe various techniques for controlling a firm's promises, but for now consider two options. First, if the salesperson knows that no competitor can meet an inflated sales promise in an industry, he could point that fact out to the customer, thereby refuting the promise made by competitive salespeople.

The second option is for the provider to follow a sale with a "reality check" about service delivery. One of us bought a new house from a builder. Typical sales promises were made about the quality of the home, some less than accurate, in order to make the sale. Before closing on the house, the builder and I conducted a final check on the house. At the front door, the builder turned to me and pointed out that each new home has between 3,000 and 5,000 individual elements and that in his experience the typical new home had 100 to 150 defects. Armed with this reality check, I thought the 32 defects found in my house seemed minor. Consider my response in the absence of that reality check.

Should a Company Try to Delight the Customer?

Some management consultants urge service companies to "delight" customers to gain a competitive edge. The *delight* that they refer to is a profoundly positive emotional state that results from having one's expectations exceeded to a surprising degree.[21] One author describes the type of service that results in delight as "positively outrageous service"—that which is unexpected, random, extraordinary, and disproportionately positive.[22]

A way that managers can conceive of delight is to consider product and service features in terms of concentric rings.[23] The innermost bull's-eye refers to attributes that are central to the basic function of the product or service, called *musts.* Their provision isn't particularly noticeable, but their absence would be. Around the musts is a ring called *satisfiers:* features that have the potential to further satisfaction beyond the basic function of the product. At the next and final outer level are *delights,* or product features that are unexpected and surprisingly enjoyable. These features are things that consumers would not expect to find and are therefore highly surprised and sometimes excited when they receive them. For example, in your classes the musts consist of professors, rooms, syllabi, and class meetings. Satisfiers might include professors who are entertaining or friendly, interesting lectures, and good audiovisual aids. A delight might include a free textbook for students signing up for the course.

Delighting customers may seem like a good idea, but this level of service provision comes with extra effort and cost to the firm. Therefore, the benefits of providing delight must be weighed. Among the considerations are the staying power and competitive implications of delight.

Staying power involves the question of how long a company can expect an experience of delight to maintain the consumer's attention. If it is fleeting and the customer forgets it immediately, it may not be worth the cost. Alternatively, if the customer remembers the delight and adjusts her level of expectation upward accordingly, it will cost the company more just to satisfy, effectively raising the bar for the future. Recent research indicates that delighting customers does in fact raise expectations and make it more difficult for a company to satisfy customers in the future.[24]

The competitive implication of delight relates to its impact on expectations of other firms in the same industry. If a competitor in the same industry is unable to copy the delight strategy, it will be disadvantaged by the consumer's increased expectations. If you were offered that free textbook in one of your classes, you might then expect to receive one in each of your classes. Those classes not offering the free textbook might not have high enrollment levels compared to the delighting class. If a competitor can easily copy the delight strategy, however, neither firm benefits (although the consumer does!), and all firms may be hurt because their costs increase and profits erode. The implication is that if companies choose to delight, they should do so in areas that cannot be copied by other firms.

How Does a Company Exceed Customer Service Expectations?

Many companies today talk about exceeding customer expectations—delighting and surprising them by giving more than they expect. This philosophy raises the question, Should a service provider try simply to meet customer expectations or to exceed them?

First, it is essential to recognize that exceeding customer expectations of the basics is virtually impossible. Honoring promises—having the reserved room available, meeting deadlines, showing up for meetings, delivering the core service—is what the company is supposed to do. Companies are *supposed* to be accurate and dependable and provide the service they promised to provide.[25] As you examine the examples of basic expectations of customers in Exhibit 4.1, ask yourself if a provider doing any of these things would delight you. The conclusion you should reach is that it is very difficult to surprise or delight customers consistently by delivering reliable service.

How, then, does a company delight its customers and exceed their expectations? In virtually any service, developing a customer relationship is one approach for exceeding service expectations. The United States Automobile Association (USAA), a provider of insurance to military personnel and their dependents, illustrates how a large company that never interacts personally with its customers can surprise and delight them with its personalization of service and knowledge of the customer. Using a state-of-the-art imaging system, all USAA employees can access any customer's entire information file in seconds, giving them full knowledge of the customer's history and requirements and the status of the customer's recent interactions with the company. Expecting a lower level of personalization from an insurance company and from most any service interaction on the telephone, USAA's customers are surprised and impressed with the care and concern that employees demonstrate.

Using a similar type of information technology, Ritz-Carlton Hotels, a winner of the Malcolm Baldrige Quality Award, provides highly personalized attention to its customers. The company trains each of its employees to note guest likes and dislikes and to record these into a computerized guest history profile. The company now has information on the preferences of more than 240,000 repeat Ritz-Carlton guests, resulting in more personalized service. The aim is not simply to meet expectations of guests but to provide them with a "memorable visit." The company uses the guest history information to exceed customers' expectations of the way they will be treated. When a repeat customer calls the hotel's central reservations number to book accommodations, the reservation agent can call up the individual's preference information. The agent then sends this information electronically to the particular hotel at which the reservation is made. The hotel puts the data in a daily guest recognition and preference report that is circulated to employees. Employees then greet the repeat guest personally at check-in and ensure that the guest's needs/preferences are anticipated and met.[26]

How well does this approach work? According to surveys conducted for Ritz-Carlton by an independent research firm, 92 to 97 percent of the company's guests leave satisfied.[27]

Another way to exceed expectations is to deliberately underpromise the service to increase the likelihood of exceeding customer expectations. The strategy is to underpromise and overdeliver. If every service promise is less than what will eventually happen, customers can be delighted frequently. Although this reasoning sounds logical, a firm should weigh two potential problems before using this strategy.

First, customers with whom a company interacts regularly are likely to notice the underpromising and adjust their expectations accordingly, negating the desired benefit of delight. Customers will recognize the pattern of underpromising when time after time a firm promises one delivery time (we can not get that to you before 5 P.M. tomorrow) yet constantly exceeds it (by delivering at noon).

Second, underpromising in a sales situation potentially reduces the competitive appeal of an offering and must be tempered by what competition is offering. When competitive pressures are high, presenting a cohesive and honest portrayal of the service both explicitly (through advertising and personal selling) and implicitly (such as through the appearance of service facilities and the price of the service) may be wiser. Controlling the firm's promises, making them consistent with the deliverable service, may be a better approach.

A final way to exceed expectations without raising them in the future is to position unusual service as unique rather than the standard. On a flight between Raleigh-Durham and Charlotte, North Carolina, one of us experienced an example of this strategy. The flight is extremely short, less than half an hour, and typically too brief for beverage service. On the night in question, a crew member announced over the intercom that an unusually ambitious crew wanted to try to serve beverages anyway. He warned passengers that the crew may not get to all of them, and positioned the service as unique by imploring passengers not to expect beverage service on other flights. In this scenario, passengers seemed delighted but their expectations for regular service were not heightened by the action. (To this day, we have never received beverage service on that route, but are really not expecting it!)

Do Customer Service Expectations Continually Escalate?

As we illustrated in the beginning of this chapter, customer service expectations are dynamic. In the credit card industry, as in many competitive service industries, battling companies seek to best each other and thereby raise the level of service above that of competing companies. Service expectations—in this case adequate service expectations—rise as quickly as service delivery or promises rise. In a highly competitive and rapidly changing industry, expectations can thus rise quickly. For this reason companies need to monitor adequate service expectations continually—the more turbulent the industry, the more frequent the monitoring needed.

Desired service expectations, on the other hand, are far more stable. Because they are driven by more enduring factors, such as personal needs and lasting service intensifiers, they tend to be high to begin with and remain high.

How Does a Service Company Stay Ahead of Competition in Meeting Customer Expectations?

All else being equal, a company's goal is to meet customer expectations better than its competitors. Given the fact that adequate service expectations change rapidly in a turbulent environment, how can a company ensure that it stays ahead of competition?

The adequate service level reflects the minimum performance level expected by customers after they consider a variety of personal and external factors (Figure 4.7), including the availability of service options from other providers. Companies whose service performance falls short of this level are clearly at a competitive disadvantage, with the disadvantage escalating as the gap widens. These companies' customers may well be "reluctant" customers, ready to take their business elsewhere the moment they perceive an alternative.

If they are to use service quality for competitive advantage, companies must perform above the adequate service level. This level, however, may signal only a temporary advantage. Customers' adequate service levels, which are less stable than desired service levels, will rise rapidly when competitors promise and deliver a higher level of service. If a company's level of service is barely above the adequate service level to begin with, a competitor can quickly erode that advantage. Companies currently performing in the region of competitive advantage must stay alert to the need for service increases to meet or beat competition.

To develop a true customer franchise—immutable customer loyalty—companies must not only consistently exceed the adequate service level but also reach the desired service level. Exceptional service can intensify customers' loyalty to a point at which they are impervious to competitive options.

Summary

Using a conceptual framework of the nature and determinants of customer expectations of service, we showed in this chapter that customers hold different types of service expectations: (1) desired service, which reflects what customers want; (2) adequate service, or what customers are willing to accept; and (3) predicted service, or what customers believe they are likely to get.

Customer expectations are influenced by a variety of factors. The types and sources of expectations are the same for end consumers and business customers, for pure service and product-related service, and for experienced customers and inexperienced customers.

Discussion Questions

1. What is the difference between desired service and adequate service? Why would a services marketer need to understand both types of service expectations?

2. Consider a recent service purchase that you have made. Which of the factors influencing expectations were the most important in your decision? Why?

3. Why are desired service expectations more stable than adequate service expectations?

4. How do the technology changes discussed in the Technology Spotlight in this chapter influence customer expectations?

5. Describe several instances in which a service company's explicit service promises were inflated and led you to be disappointed with the service outcome.

6. Consider a small business preparing to buy a computer system. Which of the influences on customer expectations do you believe will be pivotal? Which factors will have the most influence? Which factors will have the least importance in this decision?

7. What strategies can you add to the Strategy Insight in this chapter for influencing the factors?

8. Do you believe that any of your service expectations are unrealistic? Which ones? Should a service marketer try to address unrealistic customer expectations?

9. In your opinion, what service companies have effectively built customer franchises (immutable customer loyalty)?

10. Intuitively, it would seem that managers would want their customers to have wide tolerance zones for service. But if customers do have these wide zones of tolerance for service, is it more difficult for firms with superior service to earn customer loyalty? Would superior service firms be better off to attempt to narrow customers' tolerance zones to reduce the competitive appeal of mediocre providers?

11. Should service marketers delight their customers?

Exercises

1. What factors do you think influenced your professor to adopt this text? In the case of text adoption, what do you think are the most important factors? After you have formulated your ideas, ask your professor in class to talk about the sources of his or her expectations.

2. Keep a service journal for a day and document your use of services. Ask yourself before each service encounter to indicate your predicted service of that encounter. After the encounter, note whether your expectations were met or exceeded. How does the answer to this question relate to your desire to do business with that service firm again?

3. List five incidents in which a service company has exceeded your expectations. How did you react to the service? Did these incidents change the way you viewed subsequent interactions with the companies? In what way?

Notes

1. "Japanese Put Tourism on a Higher Plane," *International Herald Tribune,* February 3, 1992, p. 8.
2. J. Kelley, "Service without a Smile, Russians Find a Friendly Face Works Better," *USA Today,* January 22, 1992, p. 1.
3. The model on which this chapter is based is taken from V. A. Zeithaml, L. L. Berry, and A. Parasuraman, "The Nature and Determinants of Customer Expectations of Service," *Journal of the Academy of Marketing Science* 21 (Winter 1993), no. 1 (1993), pp. 1–12.
4. See sources such as C. Gronroos, *Strategic Management and Marketing in the Service Sector* (Helsingfors, Sweden: Swedish School of Economics and Business Administration, 1982); U. Lehtinen and J. R. Lehtinen, "Service Quality: A Study of Quality Dimensions," unpublished working paper, Helsinki, Finland OY, Service Management Institute, 1982; and S. W. Brown and T. A. Swartz, "A Dyadic Evaluation of the Professional Services Encounter," *Journal of Marketing* 53 (April 1989), pp. 92–98.
5. R. B. Woodruff, E. R. Cadotte, and R. L. Jenkins, "Expectations and Norms in Models of Consumer Satisfaction," *Journal of Marketing Research* 24 (August 1987), pp. 305–14.
6. J. A. Miller, "Studying Satisfaction, Modifying Models, Eliciting Expectations, Posing Problems, and Making Meaningful Measurements," in *Conceptualization and Measurement of Consumer Satisfaction and Dissatisfaction,* ed. H. K. Hunt (Bloomington, IN: Indiana University School of Business, 1977), pp. 72–91.
7. W. H. Davidow and B. Uttal, "Service Companies: Focus or Falter," *Harvard Business Review,* July–August 1989, pp. 77–85.
8. G. Hofstede, *Cultures and Organizations: Software of the Mind* (Berkshire, UK: McGraw-Hill, 1991).
9. N. Donthu and B. Yoo, "Cultural Influences on Service Quality Expectations," *Journal of Service Research* 1, (November 1998), pp. 178–86.
10. A. Parasuraman, L. L. Berry, and V. A. Zeithaml, "Understanding Customer Expectations of Service," *Sloan Management Review* 32, (Spring 1991), p. 42.
11. L. L. Berry, A. Parasuraman, and V. A. Zeithaml, "Ten Lessons for Improving Service Quality," *Marketing Science Institute,* Report No. 93-104 (May 1993).
12. Zeithaml, Berry, and Parasuraman, "Customer Expectations of Service," p. 7.
13. Ibid., p. 8.

14. D. Bowen, "Leadership Aspects and Reward Systems of Customer Satisfaction," speech given at CTM Customer Satisfaction Conference, Los Angeles, March 17, 1989.

15. Zeithaml, Berry, and Parasuraman, "Customer Expectations of Service," p. 8.

16. D. L. Davis, J. G. Guiltinan, and W. H. Jones, "Service Characteristics, Consumer Research, and the Classification of Retail Services," *Journal of Retailing* 55 (Fall 1979), pp. 3–21; and W. R. George and L. L. Berry, "Guidelines for the Advertising of Services," *Business Horizons* 24 (May–June 1981), pp. 52–56.

17. E. R. Cadotte, R. B. Woodruff, and R. L. Jenkins, "Expectations and Norms in Models of Consumer Satisfaction," *Journal of Marketing Research* 14 (August 1987), pp. 353–64.

18. Parasuraman, Berry, and Zeithaml, "Understanding Customer Expectations," p. 40.

19. Davidow and Uttal, "Service Companies."

20. W. Boulding, A. Kalra, R. Staelin, and V. A. Zeithaml, "A Dynamic Process Model of Service Quality: From Expectations to Behavioral Intentions," *Journal of Marketing Research* 30 (February 1993), pp. 7–27.

21. R. T. Rust and R. L. Oliver, "Should We Delight the Customer," *Journal of the Academy of Marketing Science* 28 (Winter 2000), pp. 86–94.

22. T. S. Gross, *Positively Outrageous Service* (New York: Warner Books, 1994).

23. J. Clemmer, "The Three Rings of Perceived Value," *Canadian Manager* (Summer 1990), pp. 30–32.

24. Rust and Oliver, "Delight the Customer."

25. Parasuraman, Berry, and Zeithaml, "Understanding Customer Expectations," p. 41.

26. "How the Ritz-Carlton Hotel Company Delivers 'Memorable' Service to Customers," *Executive Report on Customer Satisfaction* 6, no. 5 (March 15, 1993), pp. 1–4.

27. Ibid.

5

CUSTOMER PERCEPTIONS OF SERVICE

This chapter's objectives are to

1. Provide a solid basis for understanding what influences customer perceptions of service and the relationships among customer satisfaction, service quality, and individual service encounters.

2. Demonstrate the importance of customer satisfaction—what it is, the factors that influence it, and the significant outcomes resulting from it.

3. Develop critical knowledge of service quality and its five key dimensions: reliability, responsiveness, empathy, assurance, and tangibles.

4. Show that service encounters or the "moments of truth" are the essential building blocks from which customers form their perceptions.

At Coors Field, Great Service Is More than Winning Games

For the 3.4 million baseball fans who attended one of the Colorado Rockies' 81 home games, hits, runs, and errors—along with a helping or two of peanuts, pop-corn, and Cracker Jacks—were probably the measure of a good day. But for the five groups that work together to provide customer service at every Rockies home game at Denver's Coors Field, a good day at the ballpark is measured as much by the number of lost Little Leaguers united with parents, valuables returned to their rightful owners, and special requests responded to, as it is by the box score of the game. The Rockies receive roughly 150 comment cards per game, which trans-lates into about 12,450 for the season. Some of these comments are simple re-quests for seat repair or missing cup holders, but about 40 each game receive a personal response from a member of the stadium services department—about 3,320 each season.

What does great service look like at Coors Field? It looks like Brian S., who spent an hour and a half after a Rockies game walking the surrounding neighborhood with a six-year-old child who had become separated from his older brother and couldn't remember his address. The boys had walked the 12 blocks from home to the game. And great service looks like Kelly G., who pushed a fan the 14 blocks from the park to his home when the battery on his electric wheelchair went dead. Not to be outdone, Rockies' service team member Stacy S. drove a family of four home to Ft. Collins, an hour and a half away, when they became separated from their car keys.

Taking care of customers sometimes extends beyond the members of the guest services team to the ballplayers themselves. During one game, a guest was hit by a foul ball off the bat of outfielder Dante Bichette. The next day Bichette visited the guest at her home—and ended up staying for dinner.

By the way, if you're ever at Coors Field and need a guest relations person, they're easy to find—they are, quite literally, the ones in the white hats.[1]

Great games, fun atmosphere, excellent service quality, lots of little extras, and the unexpected over-the-top kindness of service team members all add up to customer satisfaction for guests of the Colorado Rockies. The same is true for other landmark service companies such as Lands' End (see Exhibit 5.1), IBM Global Services, and Ritz-Carlton Hotels. In all of these companies, the quality of the core product and exemplary customer service result in high customer satisfaction ratings.

So what is it that brings about customer satisfaction? How do customers evaluate service quality? How do they form their perceptions of service? Answers to these questions are the subjects of this chapter.

CUSTOMER PERCEPTIONS

How customers perceive services, how they assess whether they have experienced quality service, and whether they are satisfied are the subjects of this chapter. We will be focusing on the *perceived service* box in the gaps model. As we move through this chapter, keep in mind that perceptions are always considered relative to expectations. Because expectations are dynamic, evaluations may also shift over time—from person to person and from culture to culture. What is considered quality service or the things that satisfy customers today may be different tomorrow. Also keep in mind that the entire discussion of quality and satisfaction is based on *customers' perceptions of the service*—not some predetermined objective criteria of what service is or should be.

Customers perceive services in terms of the quality of the service and how satisfied they are overall with their experiences. Companies today recognize that they can compete more effectively by distinguishing themselves with respect to service quality and improved customer satisfaction, as discussed in our Strategy Insight box.

Satisfaction versus Service Quality

Practitioners and writers in the popular press tend to use the terms *satisfaction* and *quality* interchangeably, but researchers have attempted to be more precise about the meanings and measurement of the two concepts, resulting in considerable debate.[2] Consensus is that the two concepts are fundamentally different in terms of their underlying causes and outcomes.[3] Although they have certain things in common, **satisfaction** is generally viewed as a broader concept, whereas **service quality** focuses specifically on dimensions of service. Based on this view, **perceived service quality** is a component of customer satisfaction. Figure 5.1 graphically illustrates the relationships between the two concepts.

Exhibit 5.1 LANDS' END DELIGHTED THIS CUSTOMER

Dear Lands' End,

Recognizing that all good things must come to an end, I was still a little sad opening my very last Rugby Bear under the soft lights of my family Christmas tree. The bears had been a cherished annual gift from my family since my freshman year of college, So Kid Kodiak marked the end of an era for me.

I immediately fell in love with Kid's cute scowl, pot-belly, and affinity for blueberry pies. But something was missing—one little thing that kept me from being totally happy at getting the final member of my team.

That one little thing? Big Daddy, from 1992. I don't know how, but somehow the bear for that year did not make it under the tree. I realized it too late and it appeared impossible to get him. Lands' End phone reps said it was too late and he couldn't be ordered anymore. So I dropped it and tried to be content that I had the other six bears. But still . . .

Imagine my surprise when I opened up one of my last presents from my boyfriend and found—BIG DADDY! I was absolutely stunned—how could he have gotten this if LE said it was not available anymore?

I don't have the complete details from him yet (and maybe it's best that way to keep some of the "magic" of Christmas), but apparently he spoke with someone in Customer Service who helped him track down the "owner" of the '26 Championship team with the use of an internal newsletter for the employees of Lands' End.

So, this is my little way of saying thanks to the mystery woman in Customer Service for helping beyond the call of duty, the mystery employee who contributed Big Daddy, and Lands' End for being the best company.

And if I may a huge public thank you for my boyfriend, Patrick. My Christmas present for him this year? A Lands' End travel golf bag, of course! (He loved it!)

Jennifer
Salisbury, NC

PS Are you sure I can't convince you to conjure up a few more teammates????

Source: by Ron Zemke. Copyright 1998 by AMA MGT. ASSN./AMACOM (B) in the format Texbook via Copyright Clearance Center.

FIGURE 5.1
Customer Perceptions of Quality and Customer Satisfaction

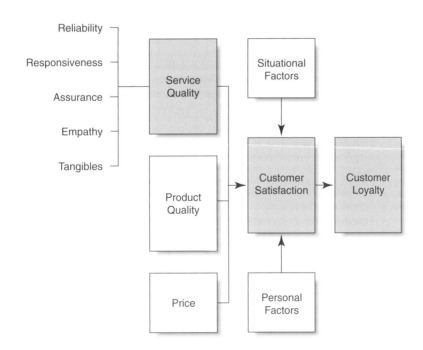

CEOs of many highly successful, growth-oriented companies are preoccupied with customer satisfaction, loyalty, and service. They see these corporate objectives as critical challenges but also as the keys to their companies' continued profitable growth. In fact, a survey of CEOs by The Conference Board in 2002 identified "customer loyalty and retention" as the leading management issue, ahead of many other critical issues including reducing costs, developing leaders, and increasing innovation. In many firms, these customer goals drive corporate strategies. Measures of improvement in satisfaction and loyalty often are a basis for managers' and employees' incentive compensation, stock performance, growth predictions, and product improvement strategies.

For example, at Enterprise Rent-A-Car, branch managers must meet or exceed corporate customer satisfaction and loyalty averages in order to be eligible for promotion. Clearly this requirement motivates them to develop cross-functional approaches and strategies that will improve satisfaction in their branches. Led by CEO Gary Loveman, Harrah's Entertainment links front-line employee rewards directly to customer satisfaction. Each and every employee—from slot attendants to valets, from receptionists to chefs—has been told: "If your service can persuade one customer to make one more visit a year with us, you've had a good shift. If you can persuade three, you've had a great shift." The company also implemented a bonus plan to reward hourly workers with extra cash for achieving improved customer satisfaction scores.

Because customer satisfaction, loyalty, and service quality are used to predict and reward performance, measuring them accurately and using the measures wisely are critical. A multitude of ways to measure customer satisfaction exist, and all are not equally good for prediction or diagnosis. Some are too complex, others are too simple, and yet others measure the wrong things. One extreme approach was suggested by loyalty expert Frederick

As shown in Figure 5.1, service quality is a focused evaluation that reflects the customer's perception of : reliability, assurance, responsiveness, empathy, and tangibles.[4] Satisfaction, on the other hand, is more inclusive: It is influenced by perceptions of service quality, product quality, and price as well as situational factors and personal factors. For example, *service quality* of a health club is judged on attributes such as whether equipment is available and in working order when needed, how responsive the staff are to customer needs, how skilled the trainers are, and whether the facility is well maintained. *Customer satisfaction* with the health club is a broader concept that will certainly be influenced by perceptions of service quality but that will also include perceptions of product quality (such as quality of products sold in the pro shop), price of membership,[5] personal factors such as the consumer's emotional state, and even uncontrollable situational factors such as weather conditions and experiences driving to and from the health club.[6]

Transaction versus Cumulative Perceptions

In considering perceptions, it is also important to recognize that customers will have perceptions of single, transaction-specific encounters as well as overall perceptions of a company based on all their experiences.[7] For example, a bank customer will have a

Reichheld based on 14 business case studies conducted by his firm. The research promotes *one* customer loyalty question as the best for most industries in terms of predicting repeat customer purchases or referrals. The question is "How likely is it that you would recommend [company X] to a friend or colleague?"

Although this one question may help firms determine where they stand with their customers, it is overly simplistic and doesn't provide the detail that companies need in order to improve. Additional, deeper, and more detailed assessment (as discussed in this chapter and chapter 6) can help firms evaluate potential issues and what improvements may be needed.

Source: Robin Nelson/PhotoEdit

Improving service and satisfaction most often involves a series of actions related to employees, service operations, and customers. A successful corporatewide customer satisfaction, loyalty, or service strategy will involve all functional areas that can influence it. It is clearly much more than a marketing, market-research or customer-research program. As it does for Enterprise and Harrah's, this type of corporate strategy can tie all functions together around the customer.

Sources: N. Kumar, *Marketing as Strategy: Understanding the CEO's Agenda for Driving Growth and Innovation* (Boston, MA: Harvard Business School Press, 2004); M. D. Johnson and A. Gustafsson, *Improving Customer Satisfaction, Loyalty, and Profit* (San Francisco: Jossey-Bass, 2000); F. F. Reichheld, "The One Number You Need to Grow," *Harvard Business Review* (December 2003), pp. 46–53; and C. D. Ittner and D. F. Larcker, "Coming Up Short on Nonfinancial Performance Measurement," *Harvard Business Review* (November 2003), pp. 88–95; G. Loveman, "Diamonds in the Data Mine," *Harvard Business Review* (May 2003), pp. 109–13.

perception of how he was treated in a particular encounter with a bank employee at a branch and will form a perception of that particular transaction based on elements of the service experienced during that specific transaction. That perception is at a very micro, transaction-specific level. That same bank customer will also have overall perceptions of the bank based on all his encounters over a period of time. These experiences might include multiple in-person encounters at the bank branch, online banking experiences, and experiences using the bank's ATMs across many different cities. At an even more general level, the customer may have perceptions of banking services or the whole banking industry as a result of all his experiences with banks and everything he knows about banking.

Research suggests that it is important to understand all these types of perceptions for different reasons and that the viewpoints are complementary rather than competing.[8] Understanding perceptions at the transaction-specific level is critical for diagnosing service issues and making immediate changes. These isolated encounters are also the building blocks for overall, cumulative experience evaluations, as you will learn later in this chapter. On the other hand, cumulative experience evaluations are likely to be better predictors of overall loyalty to a company. That is, customer loyalty most often results from the customer's assessment of all his experiences, not just one single encounter. (For an exception to this rule, look ahead to Exhibit 5.2).

CUSTOMER SATISFACTION

What Is Customer Satisfaction?

"Everyone knows what satisfaction is, until asked to give a definition. Then, it seems, nobody knows."[9] This quote from Richard L. Oliver, respected expert and long-time writer and researcher on the topic of customer satisfaction, expresses the challenge of defining this most basic of customer concepts. Building from previous definitions, Oliver offers his own formal definition (p. 13):

> Satisfaction is the consumer's fulfillment response. It is a judgment that a product or service feature, or the product or service itself, provides a pleasurable level of consumption-related fulfillment.

In less technical terms, we interpret this definition to mean that *satisfaction* is the customer's evaluation of a product or service in terms of whether that product or service has met the customer's needs and expectations. Failure to meet needs and expectations is assumed to result in *dissatisfaction* with the product or service.

In addition to a sense of *fulfillment* in the knowledge that one's needs have been met, satisfaction can also be related to other types of feelings, depending on the particular context or type of service.[10] For example, satisfaction can be viewed as *contentment*—more of a passive response that consumers may associate with services they do not think a lot about or services that they receive routinely over time. Satisfaction may also be associated with feelings of *pleasure* for services that make the consumer feel good or are associated with a sense of happiness. For those services that really surprise the consumer in a positive way, satisfaction may mean *delight*. In some situations, where the removal of a negative leads to satisfaction, the consumer may associate a sense of *relief* with satisfaction. Finally, satisfaction may be associated with feelings of *ambivalence* when there is a mix of positive and negative experiences associated with the product or service.

Although consumer satisfaction tends to be measured at a particular point in time as if it were static, satisfaction is a dynamic, moving target that may evolve over time, influenced by a variety of factors.[11] Particularly when product usage or the service experience takes place over time, satisfaction may be highly variable depending on which point in the usage or experience cycle one is focusing on. Similarly, in the case of very new services or a service not previously experienced, customer expectations may be barely forming at the point of initial purchase; these expectations will solidify as the process unfolds and the consumer begins to form his or her perceptions. Through the service cycle the consumer may have a variety of different experiences—some good, some not good—and each will ultimately impact satisfaction.

What Determines Customer Satisfaction?

As shown in Figure 5.1, customer satisfaction is influenced by specific product or service features, perceptions of product and service quality, and price. In addition, personal factors such as the customer's mood or emotional state and situational factors such as family member opinions will also influence satisfaction.

Product and Service Features

Customer satisfaction with a product or service is influenced significantly by the customer's evaluation of product or service features.[12] For a service such as a resort hotel, important features might include the pool area, access to golf facilities, restaurants, room comfort and privacy, helpfulness and courtesy of staff, room price, and so forth. In conducting satisfaction studies, most firms will determine through some means (often focus groups) what the important features and attributes are for their service and then measure perceptions of those features as well as overall service satisfaction. Research has shown that customers of services will make trade-offs among different service features (for example, price level versus quality versus friendliness of personnel versus level of customization), depending on the type of service being evaluated and the criticality of the service.[13]

Consumer Emotions

Customers' emotions can also affect their perceptions of satisfaction with products and services.[14] These emotions can be stable, preexisting emotions—for example, mood state or life satisfaction. Think of times when you are at a very happy stage in your life (such as when you are on vacation), and your good, happy mood and positive frame of mind have influenced how you feel about the services you experience. Alternatively, when you are in a bad mood, your negative feelings may carry over into how you respond to services, causing you to overreact or respond negatively to any little problem.

Specific emotions may also be induced by the consumption experience itself, influencing a consumer's satisfaction with the service. Research done in a river-rafting context showed that the river guides had a strong effect on their customers' emotional responses to the trip and that those feelings (both positive and negative) were linked to overall trip satisfaction.[15] Positive emotions such as happiness, pleasure, elation, and a sense of warm-heartedness enhanced customers' satisfaction with the rafting trip. In turn, negative emotions such as sadness, sorrow, regret, and anger led to diminished customer satisfaction. Overall, in the rafting context, positive emotions had a stronger effect than negative ones. (These positive emotions are apparent in the photo shown in Figure 5.2.) Similar effects of emotions on satisfaction were found in a Finnish study that looked at consumers' satisfaction with a government labor bureau service.[16] In that study, negative emotions including anger, depression, guilt, and humiliation had a strong effect on customers' dissatisfaction ratings.

FIGURE 5.2
River rafters experience many positive emotions, increasing their satisfaction with the service.

Source: River Odysseys West, www.rowinc.com

Attributions for Service Success or Failure

Attributions—the perceived causes of events—influence perceptions of satisfaction as well.[17] When they have been surprised by an outcome (the service is either much better or much worse than expected), consumers tend to look for the reasons, and their assessments of the reasons can influence their satisfaction. For example, if a customer of a weight-loss organization fails to lose weight as hoped for, she will likely search for the causes—was it something she did, was the diet plan ineffective, or did circumstances simply not allow her to follow the diet regimen—before determining her level of satisfaction or dissatisfaction with the weight-loss company.[18] For many services, customers take at least partial responsibility for how things turn out.

Even when customers do not take responsibility for the outcome, customer satisfaction may be influenced by other kinds of attributions. For example, research done in a travel agency context found that customers were less dissatisfied with a pricing error made by the agent if they felt that the reason was outside the agent's control or if they felt that it was a rare mistake, unlikely to occur again.[19]

Perceptions of Equity or Fairness

Customer satisfaction is also influenced by perceptions of equity and fairness.[20] Customers ask themselves: Have I been treated fairly compared with other customers? Did other customers get better treatment, better prices, or better quality service? Did I pay a fair price for the service? Was I treated well in exchange for what I paid and the effort I expended? Notions of fairness are central to customers' perceptions of satisfaction with products and services, particularly in service recovery situations. As you will learn in Chapter 8, satisfaction with a service provider following a service failure is largely determined by perceptions of fair treatment. The example of Sears Auto Centers division illustrates consumers' strong reactions to unfair treatment.[21] Over a decade ago the division was charged with defrauding customers in 44 states by performing unnecessary repairs. Sears employee rewards had been based on the quantity of repairs sold, resulting in substantial unnecessary charges to customers. The $27 million that Sears paid to settle complaints and the additional loss of business all resulted from extreme dissatisfaction of its customers over the unfair treatment.

Other Consumers, Family Members, and Coworkers

In addition to product and service features and one's own individual feelings and beliefs, consumer satisfaction is often influenced by other people.[22] For example, satisfaction with a family vacation trip is a dynamic phenomenon, influenced by the reactions and expressions of individual family members over the duration of the vacation. Later, what family members express in terms of satisfaction or dissatisfaction with the trip will be influenced by stories that are retold among the family and selective memories of the events. Similarly, the satisfaction of the rafters in Figure 5.2 is certainly influenced by individual perceptions, but it is also influenced greatly by the experiences, behavior, and views of the other rafters. In a business setting, satisfaction with a new service or technology—for example, a new customer relationship management software service—will be influenced not only by individuals' personal experiences with the software itself but also by what others say about it in the company, how others use it and feel about it, and how widely it is adopted in the organization.

National Customer Satisfaction Indexes

Because of the importance of customer satisfaction to firms and overall quality of life, many countries have a national index that measures and tracks customer satisfaction at a macro level.[23] Many public policymakers believe that these measures could and should be used as tools for evaluating the health of the nation's economy, along with traditional measures of productivity and price. Customer satisfaction indexes begin to get at the *quality* of economic output, whereas more traditional economic indicators tend to focus only on *quantity.* The first such measure was the Swedish Customer Satisfaction Barometer introduced in 1989.[24] Throughout the 1990s similar indexes were introduced in Germany (Deutsche Kundenbarometer, or DK, in 1992), the United States (American Customer Satisfaction Index, ACSI, in 1994), and Switzerland (Swiss Index of Customer Satisfaction, SWICS, in 1998).[25]

The American Customer Satisfaction Index

The American Customer Satisfaction Index (ACSI),[26] developed by researchers at the National Quality Research Center at the University of Michigan, is a measure of quality of goods and services as experienced by consumers. The measure tracks customer perceptions across 200 firms representing all major economic sectors, including government agencies. Within each industry group, major industry segments are included, and within each industry, the largest companies in that industry are selected to participate. For each company approximately 250 interviews are conducted with current customers. Each company, receives an ACSI score computed from its customers' perceptions of quality, value, satisfaction, expectations, complaints, and future loyalty.[27]

The 2003–04 ACSI results by industry are shown in Table 5.1.[28] The table shows that, overall, consumers tend to be most satisfied with nondurables (like soft drinks and personal care products), a bit less satisfied with durables (such as cars and household appliances), and the least satisfied with services (like airlines and wireless and cable services). In the year 2000 e-commerce retailers and services were assessed for the first time. With the exception of Internet retailers, which ranked at the top, other online services ranked near the middle. The observation that services tend to rank lower in the ACSI rankings than do durable and nondurable products is a trend observed across ten years of the ACSI's history. It is important to point out, however, that these rankings are industry averages. Virtually every industry has some strong performers in terms of customer satisfaction.

We can only conjecture about the reasons for lower satisfaction with services in general. Perhaps it is because downsizing and right-sizing in service businesses has resulted in stressed and overworked front-line service providers who are unable to provide the level of service demanded. Perhaps it is due to the inherent heterogeneity of services discussed in Chapter 1; in other words, because services are difficult to standardize, and each customer has his or her own unique expectations, the result may be greater variability and potentially lower overall satisfaction. Perhaps it is due to difficulty finding qualified front-line service providers for consumer-service businesses. Perhaps it is due to rising customer expectations rather than any real or absolute decline in actual service. Whatever the reason, there is much room for improvement in customer satisfaction ratings across service industries.

Outcomes of Customer Satisfaction

Why all this attention to customer satisfaction? As mentioned in the previous section, some public policymakers believe that customer satisfaction is an important indicator of national economic health. They believe that it is not enough to track economic efficiency and pricing statistics. Satisfaction, they believe, is just as important an indicator of quality of life. Further, many believe that customer satisfaction is correlated with other measures of economic health such as corporate earnings and stock value. Through the ACSI data, researchers at the University of Michigan have been able to

TABLE 5.1
American Customer Satisfaction Index— Ratings by Industry

Source: "American Customer Satisfaction Index—Ratings by Industry, ACSI website, *www.theacsi.org.* Reprinted by permission of American Customer Satisfaction Index, *www.theascsi.org.*"

Industry	Customer Satisfaction 2003–2004 Score	Change from Previous Year
Beverages, soft drinks	84	−1.2
Consumer electronics	84	3.7
Internet retailers	84	1.2
Personal care products	84	3.7
Beverages, beer	82	1.2
Pet foods	82	NC
Food processing	81	NC
Household appliances	81	−1.2
Parcel delivery, express mail	81	2.5
Automobiles, vans, light trucks	80	NC
Apparel, athletic shoes	79	NC
Insurance, casualty, property	78	1.3
Internet auctions	78	1.3
Insurance, life	77	−2.5
Department and discount stores	76	2.7
Hospitals	76	4.1
Internet brokerage services	76	4.1
Tobacco, cigarettes	76	NC
Commercial banks	75	1.4
Gasoline	75	−1.3
Restaurants, fast-food, pizza, carryout	74	4.2
Supermarkets	74	−1.3
U.S. Postal Service	74	2.8
Motion pictures	73	2.8
Energy utilities	72	−1.4
Hotels	72	−1.4
Personal computers	72	1.4
Telecommunications, fixed line	71	−1.4
Publishing, newspapers	68	6.3
Airlines, scheduled	66	-1.5
Broadcasting, national news	66	-2.9
Telecommunications, wireless	65	NA
Internal Revenue Service	62	NA
Telecommunications, cable	61	NC

NA = Not available. NC = No change.

document a clear correlational relationship between the ACSI average in a year and the S&P 500 earnings in the following year, suggesting strong relationships between customer satisfaction and important earnings outcomes. This relationship is depicted in Figure 5.3.[29]

Beyond these macroeconomic implications, however, individual firms have discovered that increasing levels of customer satisfaction can be linked to customer loyalty and profits.[30] As shown in Figure 5.4, there is an important relationship between customer satisfaction and customer loyalty. This relationship is particularly strong when customers are very satisfied. Thus firms that simply aim to satisfy customers may not be doing enough to engender loyalty—they must instead aim to more than satisfy or even delight their customers. Xerox Corporation was one of the first, if not the first, companies to pinpoint this relationship. In the 1980s Xerox discovered through its ex-

FIGURE 5.3
ACSI and Annual Percentage Growth in S&P 500 Earnings

Source: C. Fornell, "Customer Satisfaction and Corporate Earnings," commentary appearing on ACSI website, May 1, 2001. Reprinted by permission of American Customer Satisfaction Index, *www.theacsi.org.*

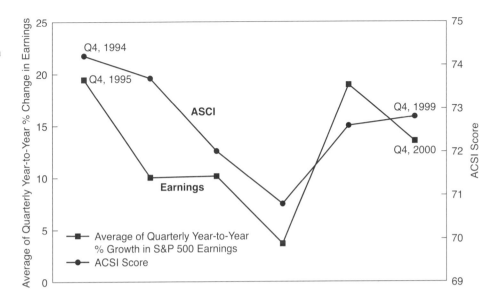

FIGURE 5.4
Relationship between Customer Satisfaction and Loyalty in Competitive Industries

Source: J. L. Heskett, W. E. Sasser Jr., and L. A. Schlesinger, *The Service Profit Chain: How Leading Companies Link Profit and Growth to Loyalty, Satisfaction, and Value* (New York: The Free Press, 1997), p. 83. Copyright © 1997 by J. L. Heskett, W. E. Sasser, Jr., and L. A. Schlesinger. Reprinted with the permission of The Free Press, a Division of Simon & Schuster, Inc.

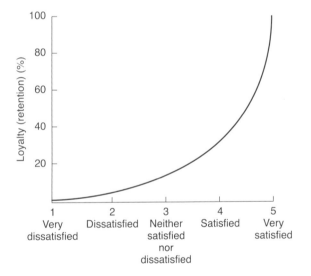

tensive customer research that customers giving Xerox a 5 (very satisfied) on a satisfaction scale were six times more likely to repurchase Xerox equipment than were those giving the company a 4 (somewhat satisfied).[31] As another example, Enterprise Rent-A-Car learned through its research that customers who gave the highest rating to their rental experience were three times more likely to rent again than were those who gave the company the second-highest rating.[32] Many other companies have drawn similar conclusions.

At the opposite end of the satisfaction spectrum, researchers have also found that there is a strong link between dissatisfaction and disloyalty—or defection. Customer loyalty can fall off precipitously when customers reach a particular level of dissatisfaction or when they are dissatisfied with critically important service attributes.[33] We discuss these relationships and the implications for relationship and loyalty marketing in Chapter 7, but suffice it to say here that clear linkages have been drawn between customer satisfaction, loyalty, and firm profitability. Thus, many companies are spending more time and money understanding the underpinnings of customer satisfaction and ways that they can improve.

SERVICE QUALITY

We now turn to *service quality,* a critical element of customer perceptions. In the case of pure services (e.g., health care, financial services, education), service quality will be the dominant element in customers' evaluations. In cases in which customer service or services are offered in combination with a physical product (e.g., IT services, auto services), service quality may also be very critical in determining customer satisfaction. Figure 5.1 highlighted these relationships. We will focus here on the left side of Figure 5.1, examining the underlying factors that form perceptions of service quality. First we discuss *what* customers evaluate; then we look specifically at the five dimensions of service that customers rely on in forming their judgments.

Outcome, Interaction, and Physical Environment Quality

What is it that consumers evaluate when judging service quality? Over the years, services researchers have suggested that consumers judge the quality of services based on their perceptions of the technical outcome provided, the process by which that outcome was delivered, and the quality of the physical surroundings where the service is delivered.[34] For example, in the case of a lawsuit, a legal services client will judge the quality of the technical outcome, or how the court case was resolved, and also the quality of the interaction. Interaction quality would include such factors as the lawyer's timeliness in returning phone calls, his empathy for the client, and his courtesy and listening skills. Similarly, a restaurant customer will judge the service on her perceptions of the meal (technical outcome quality) and on how the meal was served and how the employees interacted with her (interaction quality). The decor and surroundings (physical environment quality) of the restaurant will also impact the customer's perceptions of overall service quality.

This depiction of service quality as outcome quality, interaction quality, and physical environment quality is most recently captured by Michael Brady and Joseph Cronin in their empirical research published in the *Journal of Marketing.*[35] Other researchers have defined similar aspects of service in their examinations of service quality.[36]

Service Quality Dimensions

Research suggests that customers do not perceive quality in a unidimensional way but rather judge quality based on multiple factors relevant to the context. The dimensions of service quality have been identified through the pioneering research of Parsu Parasuraman, Valarie Zeithaml, and Leonard Berry. Their research identified five specific dimensions of service quality that apply across a variety of service contexts.[37] The five dimensions defined here are shown in Figure 5.1 as drivers of service quality. These five dimensions appear again in Chapter 6, along with the scale developed to measure them, SERVQUAL.

- *Reliability:* ability to perform the promised service dependably and accurately.

- *Responsiveness:* willingness to help customers and provide prompt service.

- *Assurance:* employees' knowledge and courtesy and their ability to inspire trust and confidence.

- *Empathy:* caring, individualized attention given to customers.

- *Tangibles:* appearance of physical facilities, equipment, personnel, and written materials.

These dimensions represent how consumers organize information about service quality in their minds. On the basis of exploratory and quantitative research, these five dimensions were found relevant for banking, insurance, appliance repair and maintenance, securities brokerage, long-distance telephone service, automobile repair service, and others. The dimensions are also applicable to retail and business services, and logic suggests they would be relevant for internal services as well. Sometimes customers will use all the dimensions to determine service quality perceptions, at other times not. For example, for an ATM, empathy is not likely to be a relevant dimension. And in a phone encounter to schedule a repair, tangibles will not be relevant. Research suggests that cultural differences will also affect the relative importance placed on the five dimensions, as discussed in our Global Feature. In the following pages we expand on each of the dimensions and provide illustrations of how customers judge them.

Reliability: Delivering on Promises

Of the five dimensions, reliability has been consistently shown to be the most important determinant of perceptions of service quality among U.S. customers.[38] **Reliability** is defined as the ability to perform the promised service dependably and accurately. In its broadest sense, reliability means that the company delivers on its promises—promises about delivery, service provision, problem resolution, and pricing. Customers want to do business with companies that keep their promises, particularly their promises about the service outcomes and core service attributes.

One company that effectively communicates and delivers on the reliability dimension is Federal Express (FedEx). The reliability message of FedEx—when it "absolutely, positively has to get there"—reflects the company's service positioning. But even when firms do not choose to position themselves explicitly on reliability, as FedEx has, this dimension is extremely important to consumers. All firms need to be aware of customer expectations of reliability. Firms that do not provide the core service that customers think they are buying fail their customers in the most direct way.

Responsiveness: Being Willing to Help

Responsiveness is the willingness to help customers and to provide prompt service. This dimension emphasizes attentiveness and promptness in dealing with customer requests, questions, complaints, and problems. Responsiveness is communicated to customers by the length of time they have to wait for assistance, answers to questions, or attention to problems. Responsiveness also captures the notion of flexibility and ability to customize the service to customer needs.

To excel on the dimension of responsiveness, a company must view the process of service delivery and the handling of requests from the customer's point of view rather than from the company's point of view. Standards for speed and promptness that reflect the company's view of internal process requirements may be very different from

The development of the service quality dimensions of reliability, responsiveness, assurance, empathy, and tangibles was based on research conducted across multiple contexts within the United States. As a general rule, reliability comes through as the most important dimension of service quality in the United States, with responsiveness also being relatively important when compared to the remaining three dimensions. But what happens when we look across cultures? Are the service quality dimensions still important? Which ones are most important? Answers to these questions can be extremely valuable for companies delivering services across cultures or in multicultural environments.

Researchers have used Hofstede's well-established cultural dimensions to assess whether service quality importance would vary across different cultural orientations. For example, *power distance* refers to the extent to which status differences are expected and accepted within a culture. Research has suggested that most Asian countries are characterized by high power distance, whereas many Western countries score lower on power distance measures. Broadly speaking, *individualism* reflects a self-orientation that is characteristic of Western culture whereas its opposite, *collectivism,* is more typical of the East. Similar comparisons across cultures have been made for the other dimensions: *masculinity, uncertainty avoidance,* and *long-term orientation.* The question is whether these types of cultural differences may affect the importance consumers place on the service quality dimensions.

The figure shown here from research published by Furrer, Liu, and Sudharshan suggests strong differences in the importance of service quality dimensions across clusters of customers defined by different cultural dimensions. The cultural profile of the clusters is described here:

Followers: Large power distance, high collectivism, high masculinity, neutral uncertainty avoidance, and short-term orientation.

Balance seekers: Small power distance, high collectivism, neutral masculinity, high uncertainty avoidance, and medium-term orientation.

Self-confidents: Small power distance, high individualism, medium femininity, low uncertainty avoidance, and long-term orientation.

Sensory seekers: Large power distance, medium individualism, high masculinity, low uncertainty avoidance, and short-term orientation.

Functional analyzers: Small power distance, medium individualism, high femininity, high uncertainty avoidance, and long-term orientation.

From this figure it is clear that the service quality dimensions are important across cultures, but their relative importance varies depending on cultural value orientation. For example, small power distance cultures with high to medium individualism and long-term

the customer's requirements for speed and promptness. To truly distinguish themselves on responsiveness, companies need well-staffed customer service departments as well as responsive front-line people in all contact positions. Responsiveness perceptions diminish when customers wait to get through to a company by telephone, are put on hold, are put through to a complex voice mail system, or have trouble accessing the firm's website.

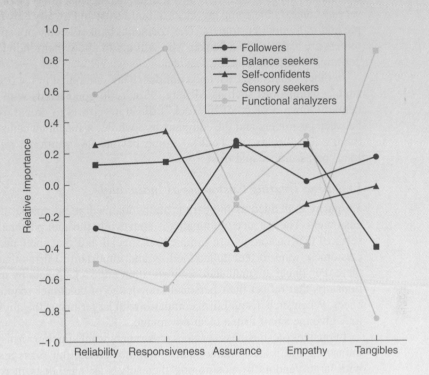

orientation (self-confidents and functional analyzers) rate reliability and responsiveness as most important. On the other hand, cultures with large power distance and high masculinity (followers and sensory seekers) rate these same dimensions as less important. The tangibles dimension shows the widest variation, with sensory seekers rating it most important and functional analyzers rating it least important.

The researchers in this study suggest a number of implications for companies serving multiple cultures. For example, if the target market has a follower cultural profile, service providers may want to emphasize training their employees to have professional knowledge and be trustworthy to gain the trust of these customers, combined with tangibles and empathy to convey service quality. On the other hand, to serve self-confidents, providers should emphasize equipping and empowering the employees so they are capable of providing reliable, responsive service.

Sources: G. Hofstede, *Cultures and Organizations: Software of the Mind* (New York, McGraw-Hill, 1991); O. Furrer, B. Shaw-Ching Liu, and D. Sudharshan, "The Relationships between Culture and Service Quality Perceptions," *Journal of Service Research* 2, no. 4 (May 2000), pp. 355–71.

Assurance: Inspiring Trust and Confidence

Assurance is defined as employees' knowledge and courtesy and the ability of the firm and its employees to inspire trust and confidence. This dimension is likely to be particularly important for services that customers perceive as high risk or for services of which they feel uncertain about their ability to evaluate outcomes—for example, banking, insurance, brokerage, medical, and legal services.

Trust and confidence may be embodied in the person who links the customer to the company, such as securities brokers, insurance agents, lawyers, or counselors. In such service contexts the company seeks to build trust and loyalty between key contact people and individual customers. The "personal banker" concept captures this idea: customers are assigned to a banker who will get to know them individually and who will coordinate all their banking services.

In other situations, trust and confidence are embodied in the organization itself. Insurance companies such as Allstate ("You're in good hands with Allstate") and Prudential ("Own a piece of the rock") illustrate efforts to create trusting relationships between customers and the company as a whole. A recent ad campaign by FedEx uses the tag line "Relax, it's FedEx," going beyond its traditional reliability message to focus on assurance and trust.

Empathy: Treating Customers as Individuals

Empathy is defined as the caring, individualized attention that the firm provides its customers. The essence of empathy is conveying, through personalized or customized service, that customers are unique and special and that their needs are understood. Customers want to feel understood by and important to firms that provide service to them. Personnel at small service firms often know customers by name and build relationships that reflect their personal knowledge of customer requirements and preferences. When such a small firm competes with larger firms, the ability to be empathetic may give the small firm a clear advantage.

In business-to-business services, customers want supplier firms to understand their industries and issues. Many small computer consulting firms successfully compete with large vendors by positioning themselves as specialists in particular industries. Even though larger firms have superior resources, the small firms are perceived as more knowledgeable about customers' issues and needs and are able to offer more customized services.

Tangibles: Representing the Service Physically

Tangibles are defined as the appearance of physical facilities, equipment, personnel, and communication materials. Tangibles provide physical representations or images of the service that customers, particularly new customers, will use to evaluate quality. Service industries that emphasize tangibles in their strategies include hospitality services in which the customer visits the establishment to receive the service, such as restaurants and hotels, retail stores, and entertainment companies.

Although tangibles are often used by service companies to enhance their image, provide continuity, and signal quality to customers, most companies combine tangibles with another dimension to create a service quality strategy for the firm. For example, Jiffy Lube emphasizes both responsiveness and tangibles—providing fast, efficient service and a comfortable, clean waiting area. In contrast, firms that do not pay attention to the tangibles dimension of the service strategy can confuse and even destroy an otherwise good strategy.

Table 5.2 provides examples of how customers judge each of the five dimensions of service quality across a variety of service contexts.

E-Service Quality

The growth of e-tailing and e-services has led many companies to wonder how consumers evaluate service quality on the Web and whether the criteria are different from

TABLE 5.2   Examples of How Customers Judge the Five Dimensions of Service Quality

	Reliability	Responsiveness	Assurance	Empathy	Tangibles
Car repair (consumer)	Problem fixed the first time and ready when promised	Accessible; no waiting; responds to requests	Knowledgeable mechanics	Acknowledges customer by name; remembers previous problems and preferences	Repair facility; waiting area; uniforms; equipment
Airline (consumer)	Flights to promised destinations depart and arrive on schedule	Prompt and speedy system for ticketing, in-flight baggage handling	Trusted name; good safety record; competent employees	Understands special individual needs; anticipates customer needs	Aircraft; ticketing counters; baggage area; uniforms
Medical care (consumer)	Appointments are kept on schedule; diagnoses prove accurate	Accessible; no waiting; willingness to listen	Knowledge; skills; credentials; reputation	Acknowledges patient as a person; remembers previous problems; listens well; has patience	Waiting room; exam room; equipment; written materials
Architecture (business)	Delivers plans when promised and within budget	Returns phone calls; adapts to changes	Credentials; reputation; name in the community; knowledge and skills	Understands client's industry; acknowledges and adapts to specific client needs; gets to know the client	Office area; reports; plans themselves; billing statements; dress of employees
Information processing (internal)	Provides needed information when requested	Prompt response to requests; not "bureaucratic"; deals with problems promptly	Knowledgeable staff; well trained; credentials	Knows internal customers as individuals; understands individual and departmental needs	Internal reports; office area; dress of employees
Internet brokerage (consumer and business)	Provides correct information and executes customer requests accurately	Quick website with easy access and no down time	Credible information sources on the site; brand recognition; credentials apparent on site	Responds with human interaction as needed	Appearance of the website and collateral

those used to judge the quality of non-Internet services.[39] Some commercial groups, such as BizRate.com and Gomez.com, capture customer perceptions of specific sites. A more systematic study, sponsored by the Marketing Science Institute, has been conducted to understand how consumers judge e-service quality.[40] In that study, e-SQ is defined as the extent to which a website facilitates efficient and effective shopping, purchasing, and delivery. Through exploratory focus groups and two phases of empirical data collection and analysis, this research identified seven dimensions that are critical for core service evaluation (four dimensions) and service recovery evaluation (three dimensions).

The four core dimensions that customers use to judge websites at which they experience no questions or problems are:

Efficiency: the ability of customers to get to the website, find their desired product and information associated with it, and check out with minimal effort.

Fulfillment: the accuracy of service promises, having products in stock, and delivering the products in the promised time.

Reliability: the technical functioning of the site, particularly the extent to which it is available and functioning properly.

Privacy: the assurance that shopping behavior data are not shared and that credit information is secure.

The study also revealed three dimensions that customers use to judge recovery service when they have problems or questions:

Responsiveness: the ability of e-tailers to provide appropriate information to customers when a problem occurs, to have mechanisms for handling returns, and to provide online guarantees.

Compensation: the degree to which customers are to receive money back and are reimbursed for shipping and handling costs.

Contact: the availability of live customer service agents online or through the phone.

In comparing the dimensions of traditional service quality and e-service quality, we can make several observations. First, the traditional dimensions can and should be considered for e-tailing and Internet-based services, as illustrated by the Internet brokerage example in Table 5.2. However, both similar and different dimensions emerge in the research on e-tailing. Reliability and responsiveness are shared dimensions, but new Internet-specific dimensions appear to be critical in that context. Efficiency and fulfillment are core dimensions in e-service quality, and both share some elements of the traditional reliability and responsiveness dimensions. The personal (that is, friendly, empathetic, and understanding) flavor of perceived service quality's empathy dimension is not required on the Internet except as it makes transactions more efficient or in nonroutine or problem situations. While not emerging as a dimension of e-service quality, tangibles are clearly relevant given that the entire service is delivered through technology. The tangible, visual elements of the site will be critical to efficiency as well as to overall perceptions of the firm and the brand.

SERVICE ENCOUNTERS: THE BUILDING BLOCKS FOR CUSTOMER PERCEPTIONS

We have just finished a discussion of customer perceptions, specifically customer satisfaction and service quality. Here we turn to what have been termed the building blocks for customer perceptions—service encounters, or "moments of truth." Service encounters are where promises are kept or broken and where the proverbial rubber meets the road—sometimes called "real-time marketing." It is from these service encounters that customers build their perceptions.

Service Encounters or Moments of Truth

From the customer's point of view, the most vivid impression of service occurs in the **service encounter** or **moment of truth,** when the customer interacts with the service firm. For example, among the service encounters that a hotel customer experiences are checking into the hotel, being taken to a room by a bellperson, eating a restaurant meal, requesting a wake-up call, and checking out. You could think of the linking of these moments of truth as a service encounter cascade (see Figure 5.5). It is in these encounters that customers receive a snapshot of the organization's service quality, and each encounter contributes to the customer's overall satisfaction and willingness to do business with the organization again. From the organization's point of view, each encounter thus presents an opportunity to prove its potential as a quality service provider and to increase customer loyalty, as suggested by the ad for Doubletree Hotels shown in Figure 5.6.

Some services have few service encounters, and others have many. The Disney Corporation estimates that each of its amusement park customers experiences about 74 service encounters and that a negative experience in any one of them can lead to a negative overall evaluation. Mistakes or problems that occur in the early levels of the service cascade may be particularly critical. Marriott Hotels learned this through their extensive customer research to determine what service elements contribute most to customer loyalty. They found that four of the top five factors came into play in the first 10 minutes of the guest's stay.[41]

The Importance of Encounters

Although early events in the encounter cascade are likely to be especially important, *any* encounter can potentially be critical in determining customer satisfaction and loy-

FIGURE 5.5
A Service Encounter Cascade for a Hotel Visit

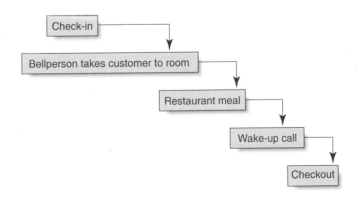

FIGURE 5.6
Every service encounter is an opportunity to build satisfaction and quality.

Source: Reprinted with permission, Hilton Hospitality, Inc./Doubletree ® Hotels, Suites, Resorts, Clubs. Photographer: Chris Schrameck.

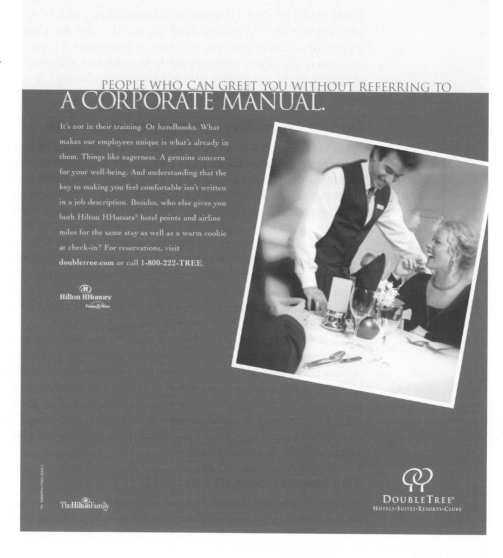

alty. If a customer is interacting with a firm for the first time, that initial encounter will create a first impression of the organization. In these first encounter situations, the customer frequently has no other basis for judging the organization, and the initial phone contact or face-to-face experience with a representative of the firm can take on excessive importance in the customer's perceptions of quality. A customer calling for repair service on a household appliance may well hang up and call a different company if he is treated rudely by a customer service representative, put on hold for a lengthy period, or told that two weeks is the soonest someone can be sent out to make the repair. Even if the technical quality of the firm's repair service is superior, the firm may not get the chance to demonstrate it if the initial telephone encounter drives the customer away.

Even when the customer has had multiple interactions with a firm, each individual encounter is important in creating a composite image of the firm in the customer's memory. Many positive experiences add up to a composite image of high quality, whereas many negative interactions will have the opposite effect. On the other hand, a combination of positive and negative interactions will leave the customer feeling unsure of the firm's quality, doubtful of its consistency in service delivery, and vulnerable to the appeals of competitors. For example, a large corporate customer of an institutional food provider that provides food service in all its company dining rooms and cafeterias could have a series of positive encounters with the account manager or salesperson who handles the account. These experiences could be followed by positive encounters with the operations staff who actually set up the food service facilities. However, even with these positive encounters, later negative experiences with the staff who serve the food or the accounting department that administers the billing procedures can result in a mixture of overall quality impressions. This variation in experiences could result in the corporate customer wondering about the quality of the organization and unsure of what to expect in the future. Each encounter with different people and departments representing the food service provider adds to or detracts from the potential for a continuing relationship.

Logic suggests that not all encounters are equally important in building relationships. For every organization, certain encounters are probably key to customer satisfaction. For Marriott Hotels, as noted, the early encounters are most important. In a hospital context, a study of patients revealed that encounters with nursing staff were more important in predicting satisfaction than were encounters with meal service or patient discharge personnel.[42] And research at GTE Laboratories documented that small business customers' relationships with GTE depended on specific installation, repair, and sales encounters.[43]

In addition to these key encounters, there are some momentous encounters that, like the proverbial "one bad apple," simply ruin the rest and drive the customer away no matter how many or what type of encounters have occurred in the past. These momentous encounters can occur in connection with very important events (such as the failure to deliver an essential piece of equipment before a critical deadline), or they may seem inconsequential, as in the story of the bank customer described in Exhibit 5.2. Similarly, momentous positive encounters can sometimes bind a customer to an organization for life.

Types of Service Encounters

A service encounter occurs every time a customer interacts with the service organization. There are three general types of service encounters: *remote encounters, phone encounters,* and *face-to-face encounters*.[44] A customer may experience any of these types of encounters, or a combination of all three, in his or her relations with a service firm.

First, encounters can occur without any direct human contact (**remote encounters**), such as when a customer interacts with a bank through the ATM system, with Ticketron through an automated ticketing machine, with a retailer through its Internet website, or with a mail-order service through automated touch-tone phone ordering. Remote encounters also occur when the firm sends its billing statements or communicates other types of information to customers by mail. Although there is no direct human contact in these remote encounters, each represents an opportunity for the firm to reinforce or establish quality perceptions in the customer. In remote encounters the tangible evidence of the service and the quality of the technical processes and systems become the primary bases for judging quality.

More and more services are being delivered through technology, particularly with the advent of Internet applications. Retail purchases, airline ticketing, repair and maintenance troubleshooting, and package and shipment tracking are just a few examples of services available via the Internet. All these types of service encounters can be considered remote encounters (see our Technology Spotlight).

In many organizations (such as insurance companies, utilities, and telecommunications), the most frequent type of encounter between an end customer and the firm occurs over the telephone (**phone encounters**). Almost all firms (whether goods manufacturers or service businesses) rely on phone encounters to some extent for customer service, general inquiry, or order-taking functions. The judgment of quality in phone encounters is different from remote encounters because there is greater potential variability in the interaction.[45] Tone of voice, employee knowledge, and effectiveness/efficiency in handling customer issues become important criteria for judging quality in these encounters.

A third type of encounter is the one that occurs between an employee and a customer in direct contact (**face-to-face encounters**). At Disney theme parks, face-to-face encounters occur between customers and ticket takers, maintenance personnel, actors in Disney character costumes, ride personnel, food and beverage servers, and others. For a company such as IBM, in a business-to-business setting direct encounters occur between the business customer and salespeople, delivery personnel, maintenance representatives, and professional consultants. Determining and understanding service quality issues in face-to-face contexts is the most complex of all. Both verbal and nonverbal behaviors are important determinants of quality, as are tangible cues such as employee dress and other symbols of service (equipment, informational brochures, physical setting). In face-to-face encounters the customer also plays a role in creating quality service for herself through her own behavior during the interaction.

Sources of Pleasure and Displeasure in Service Encounters

Because of the importance of service encounters in building perceptions, researchers have extensively analyzed service encounters in many contexts to determine the

Technology Spotlight
Customers Love Amazon.com

Although its stock price suffered in 2000–2001, along with just about every Internet-based company, and although the company had never reported a profit until early in 2002, customers have always loved Amazon.com. In 2003 the company completed its first full year of profitable quarters and the stock price was back up. The 2004 American Customer Satisfaction Index reflected a rating of 88 for Amazon—one of the highest ratings of any company in any industry, and certainly much higher than the 80 average rating for e-commerce endeavors and the 60–75 ratings for many other service businesses.

Jeff Bezos, CEO of Amazon, whose name has become a household word worldwide, believes that his customers come first. With a continued focus on customers, relationships, value, and the brand itself, Bezos and others believe that sales will continue to grow (over $5 billion in 2003) and profits will continue. According to Bezos, "Customers come first. If you focus on what customers want and build a relationship, they will allow you to make money."

Few would deny that Amazon is a master of technology and technology-based services for consumers. In fact, other companies, such as Toys R Us and Office Depot have sought a technology partnership with Amazon in order to benefit from the company's experience and success with customers. Amazon now provides Internet retail services for both these companies.

Amazon has taken a historically interpersonally dominated transaction and successfully transformed it to a Web-based service experience. Let's take a closer look at what the company is doing and why customers love it so much. Since its inception in July 1995, Amazon has grown to the point where it offers more book titles than any bricks-and-mortar bookstore could ever hope to stock. So selection and availability of titles are one key to its popularity with customers. But that is just the beginning.

In addition to a wide selection, Amazon has invested significant effort to simulate the feel of a neighborhood bookstore, where a patron can mingle with other customers, discuss books, and get recommendations from bookstore employees. Amazon allows customers to find related books on virtually any topic by simply typing key words and initiating a search of its massive database. Its one-to-one marketing system allows the company to track what individual consumers buy and let them know of additional titles that might interest them. This marketing is done while the customer is shopping as well as through periodic direct e-mail that identifies books specifically related to the customer's past purchase patterns and interests.

Currently, customers can buy much more than books from Amazon. In fact, Bezos hopes that they can buy just about anything they want through the Amazon website. His goal from the beginning was "to create the world's most customer-centric company, the place where you can find and buy anything you want online." Bezos continues to take risks that are combined with a long-term view of success, and to reflect all new ideas against a customer-focused filter. It is hard to predict where these basic strategies may lead in the future, but even doubters are beginning to believe that Amazon will continue to succeed and be around for a long time. As noted in our Technology Spotlight in Chapter 2, Amazon is a great example of a technology company that addresses all the gaps in the service quality gaps model.

Sources: S. Alsop, "I'm Betting on Amazon.com," *Fortune,* April 30, 2001, p. 48; ACSI results at www.theacsi.org; Robert D. Hof, "How Amazon Cleared That Hurdle," *BusinessWeek,* February 4, 2002, pp. 60–61; A. Deutschman, "Inside the Mind of Jeff Bezos," *Fast Company,* August 2004, pp. 52–58.

sources of customers' favorable and unfavorable impressions. The research uses the critical incident technique to get customers and employees to provide verbatim stories about satisfying and dissatisfying service encounters they have experienced.[46] With this technique, customers (either internal or external) are asked the following questions:

Think of a time when, as a customer, you had a particularly *satisfying* (or *dissatisfying*) interaction with_____.

When did the incident happen?

What specific circumstances led up to this situation?

Exactly what did the employee (or firm member) say or do?

What resulted that made you feel the interaction was *satisfying* (or *dissatisfying*)?

What could or should have been done differently?

Sometimes contact employees are asked to put themselves in the shoes of a customer and answer the same questions: "Put yourself in the shoes of *customers* of your firm. In other words, try to see your firm through your customers' eyes. Now think of a recent time when a customer of your firm had a particularly *satisfying/unsatisfying* interaction with you or a fellow employee." The stories are then analyzed to determine common themes of satisfaction/dissatisfaction underlying the events. On the basis of thousands of service encounter stories, four common themes—recovery (after failure), adaptability, spontaneity, and coping—have been identified as the sources of customer satisfaction/dissatisfaction in memorable service encounters.[47] Each of the themes is discussed here, and sample stories of both satisfying and dissatisfying incidents for each theme are given in Exhibit 5.3. The themes encompass service behaviors in encounters spanning a wide variety of industries.

Recovery—Employee Response to Service Delivery System Failures

The first theme includes all incidents in which there has been a failure of the service delivery system and an employee is required to respond in some way to consumer complaints and disappointments. The failure may be, for example, a hotel room that is not available, an airplane flight that is delayed six hours, an incorrect item sent from a mail-order company, or a critical error on an internal document. The content or form of the employee's response is what causes the customer to remember the event either favorably or unfavorably.

Adaptability—Employee Response to Customer Needs and Requests

A second theme underlying satisfaction/dissatisfaction in service encounters is how adaptable the service delivery system is when the customer has special needs or requests that place demands on the process. In these cases, customers judge service encounter quality in terms of the flexibility of the employees and the system. Incidents categorized within this theme all contain an implicit or explicit request for customization of the service to meet a need. Much of what customers see as special needs or requests may actually be rather routine from the employee's point of view; what is important is that the customer perceives that something special is being done for her based on her own individual needs. External customers and internal customers alike are pleased when the service provider puts forth the effort to accommodate and adjust the system to meet their requirements. On the flip side, they are angered and frustrated by an unwillingness to try to accommodate and by promises that are never followed through. Contact employees also see their abilities to adapt the system as being a prominent source of customer satisfaction, and often they are equally frustrated by constraints that keep them from being flexible.

Exhibit 5.3 SERVICE ENCOUNTER THEMES

THEME 1: RECOVERY

Satisfactory

They lost my room reservation but the manager gave me the V.P. suite for the same price.

Even though I did not make any complaint about the hour-and-a-half wait, the waitress kept apologizing and said the bill was on the house.

Dissatisfactory

We had made advance reservations at the hotel. When we arrived we found we had no room—no explanation, no apologies, and no assistance in finding another hotel.

One of my suitcases was all dented up and looked like it had been dropped from 30,000 feet. When I tried to make a claim for my damaged luggage, the employee insinuated that I was lying and trying to cheat them.

THEME 2: ADAPTABILITY

Satisfactory

I did not have an appointment to see a doctor; however, my allergy nurse spoke to a practitioner's assistant and worked me into the schedule. I received treatment after a 10-minute wait. I was very satisfied with the special treatment I received, the short wait, and the quality of the service.

It was snowing outside—my car broke down. I checked 10 hotels and there were no rooms. Finally, one understood my situation and offered to rent me a bed and set it up in a small banquet room.

Dissatisfactory

My young son, flying alone, was to be assisted by the flight attendant from start to finish. At the Albany airport she left him alone in the airport with no one to escort him to his connecting flight.

Despite our repeated requests, the hotel staff would not deal with the noisy people partying in the hall at 3 A.M.

THEME 3: SPONTANEITY

Satisfactory

We always travel with our teddy bears. When we got back to our room at the hotel we saw that the cleaning person had arranged our bears very comfortably in a chair. The bears were holding hands.

The anesthesiologist took extra time to explain exactly what I would be aware of and promised to take special care in making sure I did not wake up during surgery. It impressed me that the anesthesiologist came to settle my nerves and explain the medicine I was getting because of my cold.

Dissatisfactory

The lady at the front desk acted as if we were bothering her. She was watching TV and paying more attention to the TV than to the hotel guests.

I needed a few more minutes to decide on a dinner. The waitress said, "If you would read the menu and not the road map, you would know what you want to order."

THEME 4: COPING

Satisfactory

A person who became intoxicated on a flight started speaking loudly, annoying the other passengers. The flight attendant asked the passenger if he would be driving when the plane landed and offered him coffee. He accepted the coffee and became quieter and friendlier.

Dissatisfactory

An intoxicated man began pinching the female flight attendants. One attendant told him to stop, but he continued and then hit another passenger. The copilot was called and asked the man to sit down and leave the others alone, but the passenger refused. The copilot then "decked" the man, knocking him into his seat.

Spontaneity—Unprompted and Unsolicited Employee Actions

Even when there is no system failure and no special request or need, customers can still remember service encounters as being very satisfying or very dissatisfying. Employee spontaneity in delivering memorably good or poor service is the third theme. Satisfying incidents in this group represent very pleasant surprises for the customer (special attention, being treated like royalty, receiving something nice but not requested), whereas dissatisfying incidents in this group represent negative and unacceptable employee behaviors (rudeness, stealing, discrimination, ignoring the customer).

Coping—Employee Response to Problem Customers

The incidents categorized in this group came to light when employees were asked to describe service encounter incidents in which customers were either very satisfied or dissatisfied. In addition to describing incidents of the types outlined under the first three themes, employees described many incidents in which customers were the cause of their own dissatisfaction. Such customers were basically uncooperative—that is, unwilling to cooperate with the service provider, other customers, industry regulations, and/or laws. In these cases nothing the employee could do would result in the customer feeling pleased about the encounter. The term *coping* is used to describe these incidents because coping is the behavior generally required of employees to handle problem customer encounters. Rarely are such encounters satisfying from the customers' point of view.[48] Also of interest is that customers themselves did not relate any "problem customer" incidents. That is, customers either do not see, or choose not to remember or retell, stories of the times when they themselves were unreasonable to the point of causing their own dissatisfactory service encounter.

Table 5.3 summarizes the specific employee behaviors that cause satisfaction and dissatisfaction in service encounters according to the four themes just presented: recovery, adaptability, spontaneity, and coping. The left side of the table suggests what employees do that results in positive encounters, whereas the right side summarizes negative behaviors within each theme.

Technology-Based Service Encounters

All the research on service encounters described thus far and the resulting themes underlying service encounter evaluations are based on interpersonal services—that is, face-to-face encounters between customers and employees of service organizations. Recently researchers have begun to look at the sources of pleasure and displeasure in technology-based service encounters.[49] These types of encounters involve customers interacting with Internet-based services, automated phone services, kiosk services, and services delivered via CD or video technology. Often these systems are referred to as *self-service technologies* (SSTs) because the customer essentially provides his or her own service.

The research on SSTs reveals some different themes in terms of what drives customer satisfaction and dissatisfaction. The following themes were identified from analysis of hundreds of critical incident stories across a wide range of contexts, including Internet retailing, Internet-based services, ATMs, automated phone systems, and others:

For Satisfying SSTs

Solved an intensified need. Customers in this category were thrilled that the technology could bail them out of a difficult situation—for example, a cash

TABLE 5.3 **General Service Behaviors Based on Service Encounter Themes—Dos and Don'ts**

Theme	Do	Don't
Recovery	Acknowledge problem	Ignore customer
	Explain causes	Blame customer
	Apologize	Leave customer to fend for himself or herself
	Compensate/upgrade	Downgrade
	Lay out options	Act as if nothing is wrong
	Take responsibility	"Pass the buck"
Adaptability	Recognize the seriousness of the need	Ignore
	Acknowledge	Promise, but fail to follow through
	Anticipate	Show unwillingness to try
	Attempt to accommodate	Embarrass the customer
	Adjust the system	Laugh at the customer
	Explain rules/policies	Avoid responsibility
	Take responsibility	"Pass the buck"
Spontaneity	Take time	Exhibit impatience
	Be attentive	Ignore
	Anticipate needs	Yell/laugh/swear
	Listen	Steal from customers
	Provide information	Discriminate
	Show empathy	
Coping	Listen	Take customer's dissatisfaction personally
	Try to accommodate	Let customer's dissatisfaction affect others
	Explain	
	Let go of the customer	

machine that came to the rescue, allowing the customer to get cash to pay a cab driver and get to work on time when a car had broken down.

Better than the alternative. Many SST stories related to how the technology-based service was in some way better than the alternative—easy to use, saved time, available when and where the customer needed it, saved money.

Did its job. Because there are so many failures of technology, many customers are simply thrilled when the SST works as it should!

For Dissatisfying SSTs

Technology failure. Many dissatisfying SST stories relate to the technology simply not working as promised—it is not available when needed, PIN numbers do not work, or systems are off-line.

Process failure. Often the technology seems to work, but later the customer discovers that a back-office or follow-up process, which the customer assumed was connected, does not work. For example, a product order seems to be placed successfully, but it never arrives or the wrong product is delivered.

Poor design. Many stories relate to the customer's dissatisfaction with how the technology is designed, in terms of either the technical process (technology is confusing, menu options are unclear) or the actual service design (delivery takes too long, service is inflexible).

Customer-driven failure. In some cases the customers told stories of their own inabilities or failures to use the technology properly. These types of stories are (of course) much less common than stories blaming the technology or the company.

For all of the dissatisfying SST stories, there is clearly an element of service failure. Interestingly, the research revealed little attempt in these technology-based encounters to recover from the failure—unlike the interpersonal service encounters described earlier, where excellent service recovery can be a foundation for retaining and even producing very satisfied customers. As companies progress further with SSTs and become better at delivering service this way, we expect that growing numbers will be able to deliver superior service via technology. Many are doing it already, as our Technology Spotlight on Amazon.com illustrates. In the future we believe that many firms will be able to deliver highly reliable, responsive, customized services via technology and will offer easy and effective means for service recovery when failure does occur.[50]

The Evidence of Service

Because services are intangible, customers are searching for evidence of service in every interaction they have with an organization.[51] Figure 5.7 depicts the three major categories of evidence as experienced by the customer: people, process, and physical evidence. These categories together represent the service and provide the evidence that makes the offering tangible. Note the parallels between the elements of evidence of service and the new marketing mix elements presented in Chapter 1. The new mix elements essentially *are* the evidence of service in each moment of truth.

All these evidence elements, or a subset of them, are present in every service encounter a customer has with a service firm and are critically important in managing service encounter quality and creating customer satisfaction. For example, when an HMO patient has an appointment with a doctor in a health clinic, the first encounter of the visit is frequently with a receptionist in a clinic waiting area. The quality of that encounter will be judged by how the appointment registration *process* works (Is there a line? How long is the wait? Is the registration system computerized and accurate?), the actions and attitude of the *people* (Is the receptionist courteous, helpful, knowledgeable? Does he treat the patient as an individual? Does he handle inquiries fairly and efficiently?), and the *physical evidence* of the service (Is the waiting area clean and comfortable? Is the signage clear?). The three types of evidence may be differentially

FIGURE 5.7
The Evidence of Service (from the Customer's Point of View)

Source: From "Managing the Evidence of Service" by M. J. Bitner from *The Service Quality Handbook,* ed. E. E. Scheuing and W. F. Christopher; Reprinted by permission of the American Marketing Association.

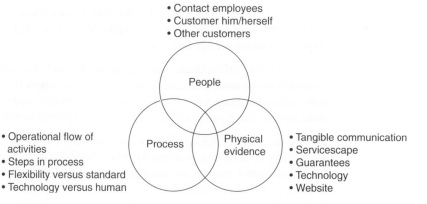

important depending on the type of service encounter (remote, phone, face-to-face). All three types will operate in face-to-face service encounters like the one just described.

Summary

This chapter described customer perceptions of service by first introducing you to two critical concepts: customer satisfaction and service quality. These critical customer perceptions were defined and discussed in terms of the factors that influence each of them. You learned that customer satisfaction is a broad perception influenced by features and attributes of the product as well as by customers' emotional responses, their attributions, and their perceptions of fairness. Service quality, the customer's perception of the service component of a product, is also a critical determinant of customer satisfaction. Sometimes, as in the case of a pure service, service quality may be the *most* critical determinant of satisfaction. You learned that perceptions of service quality are based on five dimensions: reliability, assurance, empathy, responsiveness, and tangibles.

Another major purpose of the chapter was to introduce the idea of service encounters, or "moments of truth," as the building blocks for both satisfaction and quality. You learned that every service encounter (whether remote, over the phone, or in person) is an opportunity to build perceptions of quality and satisfaction. The underlying themes of pleasure and displeasure in service encounters were also described. The importance of managing the evidence of service in each and every encounter was discussed.

Chapters 3, 4, and 5 have provided you with a grounding in customer issues relevant to services. The three chapters together are intended to give you a solid understanding of customer behavior issues and of service expectations and perceptions. Through the rest of the book, we illustrate strategies that firms can use to close the gap between customer expectations and perceptions.

Discussion Questions

1. What is customer satisfaction, and why is it so important? Discuss how customer satisfaction can be influenced by each of the following: product attributes and features, customer emotions, attributions for success or failure, perceptions of fairness, and family members or other customers.

2. What is the ACSI? Do you believe that such national indicators of customer satisfaction should be included as benchmarks of national economic well-being similar to GDP, price indicators, and productivity measures?

3. Why do service companies generally receive lower satisfaction ratings in the ACSI than nondurable and durable product companies?

4. Discuss the differences between perceptions of service quality and customer satisfaction.

5. List and define the five dimensions of service quality. Describe the services provided by a firm you do business with (your bank, your doctor, your favorite restaurant) on each of the dimensions. In your mind, has this organization distinguished itself from its competitors on any particular service quality dimension?

6. Describe a remote encounter, a phone encounter, and a face-to-face encounter that you have had recently. How did you evaluate the encounter, and what were the most important factors determining your satisfaction/dissatisfaction in each case?

7. Describe an "encounter cascade" for an airplane flight. In your opinion, what are the most important encounters in this cascade for determining your overall impression of the quality of the airline?

8. Why did the gentleman described in Exhibit 5.2 leave his bank after 30 years? What were the underlying causes of his dissatisfaction in that instance, and why would that cause him to leave the bank?

9. Assume that you are a manager of a health club. Discuss general strategies you might use to maximize customers' positive perceptions of your club. How would you know if you were successful?

Exercises

1. Keep a journal of your service encounters with different organizations (at least five) during the week. For each journal entry, ask yourself the following questions: What circumstances led up to this encounter? What did the employee say or do? How did you evaluate this encounter? What exactly made you evaluate the encounter that way? What should the organization have done differently (if anything)? Categorize your encounters according to the four themes of service encounter satisfaction/dissatisfaction (recovery, adaptability, spontaneity, coping).

2. Interview someone with a non-U.S. cultural background. Ask the person about service quality, whether the five dimensions of quality are relevant, and which are most important in determining quality of banking services (or some other type of service) in the person's country.

3. Think of an important service experience you have had in the last several weeks. Analyze the encounter according to the evidence of service provided (see Figure 5.7). Which of the three evidence components was (or were) most important for you in evaluating the experience, and why?

4. Interview an employee of a local service business. Ask the person to discuss each of the five dimensions of quality with you as it relates to the person's company. Which dimensions are most important? Are any dimensions *not* relevant in this context? Which dimensions does the company do best? Why? Which dimensions could benefit from improvement? Why?

5. Interview a manager, owner, or president of a business. Discuss with this person the strategies he or she uses to ensure customer satisfaction. How does service quality enter into the strategies, or does it? Find out how this person measures customer satisfaction and/or service quality.

6. Visit Amazon.com's website. Visit a traditional bookstore. How would you compare the two experiences? Compare and contrast the factors that most influenced your satisfaction and perceptions of service quality in the two different situations. When would you choose to use one versus the other?

Notes

1. K. Anderson and R. Zemke, *Tales of Knock Your Socks Off Service* (New York: AMACOM, 1998), pp. 56–57.

2. For more discussion of the debate on the distinctions between quality and satisfaction, see A. Parasuraman, V. A. Zeithaml, and L. L. Berry, "Reassessment of Expectations as a Comparison Standard in Measuring Service Quality: Implications for Future Research," *Journal of Marketing* 58 (January 1994), pp. 111–24; R. L. Oliver, "A Conceptual Model of Service Quality and Service Satisfaction: Compatible Goals, Different Concepts," in *Advances in Services Marketing and Management,* vol. 2, ed. T. A. Swartz, D. E. Bowen, and S. W. Brown (Greenwich, CT: JAI Press, 1994), pp. 65–85; M. J. Bitner and A. R. Hubbert, "Encounter Satisfaction vs. Overall Satisfaction vs. Quality: The Customer's Voice," in *Service Quality: New Directions in Theory and Practice,* ed. R. T. Rust and R. L. Oliver (Newbury Park, CA: Sage, 1993), pp. 71–93; and D. Iacobucci et al.,

"The Calculus of Service Quality and Customer Satisfaction: Theory and Empirical Differentiation and Integration," in *Advances in Services Marketing and Management,* vol. 3, ed. T. A. Swartz, D. E. Bowen, and S. W. Brown (Greenwich, CT: JAI Press, 1994), pp. 1–67; P. A. Dabholkar, C. D. Shepherd, and D. I. Thorpe, "A Comprehensive Framework for Service Quality: An Investigation of Critical Conceptual and Measurement Issues through a Longitudinal Study," *Journal of Retailing* 7, no. 2 (Summer 2000), pp. 139–73; J. J. Cronin, Jr., M. K. Brady, and G. T. M. Hult, "Assessing the Effects of Quality, Value, and Customer Satisfaction on Consumer Behavioral Intentions in Service Environments," *Journal of Retailing* 7 (Summer 2000), pp. 193–218.

3. See in particular, Parasuraman, Zeithaml, and Berry, "Reassessment of Expectations"; Oliver, "A Conceptual Model of Service Quality"; and M. K. Brady and J. J. Cronin Jr., "Some New Thoughts on Conceptualizing Perceived Service Quality: A Hierarchical Approach," *Journal of Marketing* 65 (July 2001), pp. 34–49.

4. A. Parasuraman, V. A. Zeithaml, and L. L. Berry, "SERVQUAL: A Multiple-Item Scale for Measuring Consumer Perceptions of Service Quality," *Journal of Retailing* 64 (Spring 1988), pp. 12–40.

5. Parasuraman, Zeithaml, and Berry, "Reassessment of Expectations."

6. Oliver, "A Conceptual Model of Service Quality."

7. See V. Mittal, P. Kumar, and M. Tsiros, "Attribute-Level Performance, Satisfaction, and Behavioral Intentions over Time," *Journal of Marketing* 63 (April 1999), pp. 88–101; L. L. Olsen and M. D. Johnson, "Service Equity, Satisfaction, and Loyalty: From Transaction-Specific to Cumulative Evaluations," *Journal of Service Research* 5 (February 2003), pp. 184-95.

8. Olsen and Johnson, "Service Equity, Satisfaction, and Loyalty."

9. R. L. Oliver, *Satisfaction: A Behavioral Perspective on the Consumer* (New York: McGraw-Hill, 1997).

10. For a more detailed discussion of the different types of satisfaction, see E. Arnould, L. Price, and G. Zinkhan, Consumers, 2nd ed., chap. 18, "Consumer Satisfaction" (New York: McGraw-Hill, 2004), pp. 754–96.

11. S. Fournier and D. G. Mick, "Rediscovering Satisfaction," *Journal of Marketing* 63 (October 1999), pp. 5–23.

12. Oliver, *Satisfaction,* chap. 2.

13. A. Ostrom and D. Iacobucci, "Consumer Trade-Offs and the Evaluation of Services," *Journal of Marketing* 59 (January 1995), pp. 17–28.

14. For more on emotions and satisfaction, see Oliver, *Satisfaction,* chap. 11; and L. L. Price, E. J. Arnould, and S. L. Deibler, "Consumers' Emotional Responses to Service Encounters," *International Journal of Service Industry Management* 6, no. 3 (1995), pp. 34–63.

15. L. L. Price, E. J. Arnould, and P. Tierney, "Going to Extremes: Managing Service Encounters and Assessing Provider Performance," *Journal of Marketing* 59 (April 1995), pp. 83–97.

16. V. Liljander and T. Strandvik, "Emotions in Service Satisfaction," *International Journal of Service Industry Management* 8, no. 2 (1997), pp. 148–69.

17. For more on attributions and satisfaction, see V. S. Folkes, "Recent Attribution Research in Consumer Behavior: A Review and New Directions," *Journal of Consumer Research* 14 (March 1988), pp. 548–65; and Oliver, *Satisfaction,* chap. 10.

18. A. R. Hubbert, "Customer Co-Creation of Service Outcomes: Effects of Locus of Causality Attributions," doctoral dissertation, Arizona State University, Tempe, Arizona, 1995.

19. M. J. Bitner, "Evaluating Service Encounters: The Effects of Physical Surrounding and Employee Responses," *Journal of Marketing* 54 (April 1990), pp. 69–82.

20. For more on fairness and satisfaction, see E. C. Clemmer and B. Schneider, "Fair Service," in *Advances in Services Marketing and Management,* vol. 5, ed. T. A. Swartz, D. E. Bowen, and S. W. Brown (Greenwich, CT: JAI Press, 1996), pp. 109–26; Oliver, *Satisfaction,* chap. 7; and Olsen and Johnson, "Service Equity, Satisfaction, and Loyalty."

21. As described in K. Seiders and L. L. Berry. "Service Fairness: What It Is and Why It Matters," *Academy of Management Executive* 12 (May 1998), pp. 8–20.

22. Fournier and Mick, "Rediscovering Satisfaction."

23. C. Fornell, M. D. Johnson, E. W. Anderson, J. Cha, and B. E. Bryant, "The American Customer Satisfaction Index: Nature, Purpose, and Findings," *Journal of Marketing* 60 (October 1996), pp. 7–18.

24. E. W. Anderson, C. Fornell, and D. R. Lehmann, "Customer Satisfaction, Market Share, and Profitability: Findings from Sweden," *Journal of Marketing* 58 (July 1994), pp. 53–66.

25. M. Bruhn and M. A. Grund, "Theory, Development and Implementation of National Customer Satisfaction Indices: The Swiss Index of Customer Satisfaction (SWICS)," *Total Quality Management* 11, no. 7 (2000), pp. S1017–S1028; A. Meyer and F. Dornach, "The German Customer Barometer," http://www. servicebarometer.de.or.

26. Fornell et al., "The American Customer Satisfaction Index."

27. For a listing of companies and their scores, go to the ACSI website at www.theacsi.org.

28. ACSI website, www.theacsi.org.

29. C. Fornell, "Customer Satisfaction and Corporate Earning," commentary appearing on ACSI website, date accessed May 21, 2001.

30. J. L. Heskett, W. E. Sasser Jr., and L. A. Schlesinger, *The Service Profit Chain* (New York: Free Press, 1997).

31. M. A. J. Menezes and J. Serbin, *Xerox Corporation: The Customer Satisfaction Program,* case no. 591-055 (Boston: Harvard Business School, 1991).

32. F. F. Reichheld, "The One Number You Need to Grow," *Harvard Business Review,* December 2003, pp. 47–54.

33. E. W. Anderson and V. Mittal, "Strengthening the Satisfaction–Profit Chain," *Journal of Service Research* 3 (November 2000), pp. 107–20.

34. Brady and Cronin, "Some New Thoughts on Conceptualizing Perceived Service Quality."

35. Ibid.

36. See: C. Gronroos, "A Service Quality Model and Its Marketing Implications," *European Journal of Marketing* 18, no. 4 (1984), pp. 36–44; R. T. Rust and R. L. Oliver, "Service Quality Insights and Managerial Implications from the Frontier," in *Service Quality: New Directions in Theory and Practice,* ed. R. T. Rust and R. L. Oliver (Thousand Oaks, CA: Sage, 1994), pp. 1–19; M. J. Bitner, "Managing the Evidence of Service," in *The Service Quality Handbook,* ed. E. E. Scheuing and W. F. Christopher (AMACOM, 1993), pp. 358–70.

37. Parasuraman, Zeithaml, and Berry, "SERVQUAL: A Multiple-Item Scale." Details on the SERVQUAL scale and the actual items used to assess the dimensions are provided in Chapter 6.

38. Ibid.

39. For a review of what is known about service quality delivery via the Web see, V. A. Zeithaml, A. Parasuraman, and A. Malhotra, "Service Quality Delivery

through Web Sites: A Critical Review of Extant Knowledge," *Journal of the Academy of Marketing Science* 30, no. 4 (2002), pp. 362–75.

40. V. Zeithaml, A. Parasuraman, and A. Malhotra, "A Conceptual Framework for Understanding e-Service Quality: Implications for Future Research and Managerial Practice," Marketing Science Institute Working Paper, Report No. 00-115, 2001.

41. "How Marriott Makes a Great First Impression," *The Service Edge* 6, no. 5 (May 1993), p. 5.

42. A. G. Woodside, L. L. Frey, and R. T. Daly, "Linking Service Quality, Customer Satisfaction, and Behavioral Intention," *Journal of Health Care Marketing* 9 (December 1989), pp. 5–17.

43. R. N. Bolton and J. H. Drew, "Mitigating the Effect of Service Encounters," *Marketing Letters* 3, no. 1 (1992), pp. 57–70.

44. G. L. Shostack, "Planning the Service Encounter," in *The Service Encounter,* ed. J. A. Czepiel, M. R. Solomon, and C. F. Surprenant (Lexington, MA: Lexington Books, 1985), pp. 243–54.

45. Ibid.

46. For detailed discussions of the Critical Incident Technique, see J. C. Flanagan, "The Critical Incident Technique," *Psychological Bulletin* 51 (July 1954), pp. 327–58; M. J. Bitner, J. D. Nyquist, and B. H. Booms, "The Critical Incident as a Technique for Analyzing the Service Encounter," in *Services Marketing in a Changing Environment,* ed. T. M. Bloch, G. D. Upah, and V. A. Zeithaml (Chicago: American Marketing Association, 1985), pp. 48–51; S. Wilson-Pessano, "Defining Professional Competence: The Critical Incident Technique 40 Years Later," presentation to the Annual Meeting of the American Educational Research Association, New Orleans, 1988; I. Roos, "Methods of Investigating Critical Incidents," *Journal of Service Research* 4 (February 2002), pp. 193–204; D. D. Gremler, "The Critical Incident Technique in Service Research," *Journal of Service Research* 7 (August 2004), pp. 65–89.

47. For a complete discussion of the research on which this section is based, see M. J. Bitner, B. H. Booms, and M. S. Tetreault, "The Service Encounter: Diagnosing Favorable and Unfavorable Incidents," *Journal of Marketing* 54 (January 1990), pp. 71–84; M. J. Bitner, B. H. Booms, and L. A. Mohr, "Critical Service Encounters: The Employee's View," *Journal of Marketing* 58, no. 4 (1994), pp. 95–106; D. Gremler and M. J. Bitner, "Classifying Service Encounter Satisfaction across Industries," in *Marketing Theory and Applications,* ed. C. T. Allen et al. (Chicago: American Marketing Association, 1992), pp. 111–18; and D. Gremler, M. J. Bitner, and K. R. Evans, "The Internal Service Encounter," *International Journal of Service Industry Management* 5, no. 2 (1994), pp. 34–56.

48. Bitner, Booms, and Mohr, "Critical Service Encounters."

49. This discussion is based on research and results presented in M. L. Meuter, A. L. Ostrom, R. I. Roundtree, and M. J. Bitner, "Self-Service Technologies: Understanding Customer Satisfaction with Technology-Based Service Encounters," *Journal of Marketing* 64 (July 2000), pp. 50–64.

50. M. J. Bitner, S. W. Brown, and M. L. Meuter, "Technology Infusion in Service Encounters," *Journal of the Academy of Marketing Science* 28 (1), pp. 138–49.

51. Bitner, "Managing the Evidence of Service."

UNDERSTANDING CUSTOMER REQUIREMENTS

Part 3

Provider Gap 1

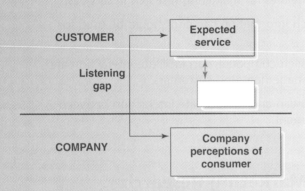

THE LISTENING GAP

Not knowing what customers expect is one of the root causes of not delivering to customer expectations. Provider gap 1 is the difference between customer expectations of service and company understanding of those expectations. Note that in the accompanying figure we created a link between the customer and the company, showing customer expectations above the line that dissects the model and provider perceptions of those expectations below the line. This alignment signifies that what customers expect is not always the same as what companies believe they expect.

Part 3 describes three ways to close provider gap 1. In Chapter 6, we detail ways that companies listen to customers through research. Both formal and informal methods of customer research are described, including surveys, critical incident studies, and complaint solicitation. Upward communication from front-line employees to managers, another key factor in listening to customers, is also discussed.

Chapter 7 covers company strategies to retain customers and strengthen relationships with them, an approach called relationship marketing. Relationship marketing is distinct from transactional marketing, the more conventional approach that tends to focus on acquiring new customers rather than retaining them. When organizations have strong relationships with existing customers, opportunities for in-depth listening increase over time, and provider gap l is less likely to occur. A variety of strategies, including the creation of switching barriers and the development of relationship bonds, are suggested as a means of relationship development and, ultimately, the cultivation of customer loyalty.

Chapter 8 describes service recovery, the other major strategy needed to close provider gap 1. Service recovery involves understanding why customers complain, what they expect when they complain, and how to deal with service failures. Firms engaged in service recovery must, along with other approaches, create a complaint-handling procedure, empower employees to react in real time to fix failures, and guarantee service. Excellent service recovery strategies seek to gain insight from service failures, allowing firms to better understand customers and their expectations.

Chapter 6

LISTENING TO CUSTOMERS THROUGH RESEARCH

This chapter's objectives are to

1. Present the types of and guidelines for marketing research in services.

2. Show how marketing research information can and should be used for services.

3. Describe the strategies by which companies can facilitate interaction and communication between management and customers.

4. Present ways that companies can and do facilitate interaction between contact people and management.

Wachovia Excels at Marketing Research in Services

Wachovia, a megabank originally located in North Carolina but now national, has the best customer satisfaction scores of all banks in the American Customer Satisfaction Index. Its satisfaction, quality, and loyalty scores have improved steadily since 1999, even during a merger with First Union Bank. A large part of Wachovia's success in delivering excellent service and customer satisfaction is attributable to its strong marketing research program.

Wachovia's service measurement program ensures that delivery in its financial centers and phone centers meets customer expectations. First, the company determined through focus group research the most important aspects of service delivery (such as "makes it easy to do business," "provides unmatched service and advice"), then it created a questionnaire. Every month, Wachovia surveys more than 25,000 customers who have been in the bank within the previous 24 hours. Although the bank has more than 12 million households and businesses who hold accounts at the bank, 25,000 surveys is a significant number no matter what the customer base.[1]

Working with Gallup, Wachovia asks these customers about the key service attributes, and every two weeks, the results are shared directly with the front-line employees who provided the service. Based on the survey results, coaching is offered to the employees in need of improvement. When the bank began its research, it aspired to achieve scores of 6 on the 7-point scale for the service attributes. Now Wachovia regularly achieves scores that exceed 6.65 on all the attributes that matter to customers.

On the same survey, the company also tracks overall customer satisfaction, likelihood to continue to use Wachovia, loyalty, and likelihood to recommend the bank to others. Because it knows that wait times are critical to customer satisfaction, it also measures and tracks the percent of teller wait times that are three minutes or less, aiming for a goal of 85 percent.

This service research is but one of Wachovia's many marketing research studies to listen to customers. The company recently conducted a major segmentation study to understand precise differences among its customer groups so that offerings and advertising messages can be more targeted. Based on other research, Wachovia has changed its online banking website to make it easier to use. Each month the company also collects information to track brand perceptions in all parts of the country, a research study that has been very important in setting bank strategy through the company's merger, logo, and color changes. Other studies gather information about wholesale customers and corporate customers. The company possesses an admirable portfolio of customer research that allows it to listen to and understand its customers clearly.

Despite a genuine interest in meeting customer expectations, many companies miss the mark by thinking inside out—they believe they know what customers *should* want and deliver that, rather than finding out what they *do* want. When this happens, companies provide services that do not match customer expectations: important features are left out, and the levels of performance on features that are provided are inadequate. Because services have few clearly defined and tangible cues, this difficulty may be considerably larger than it is in manufacturing firms. A far better approach involves thinking outside in—determining customer expectations and then delivering to them. Thinking outside in uses marketing research to understand customers and their requirements fully. Marketing research, the subject of this chapter, involves far more than conventional surveys. It consists of a portfolio of listening strategies that allow companies to deliver service to customer expectations.

USING MARKETING RESEARCH TO UNDERSTAND CUSTOMER EXPECTATIONS

Finding out what customers expect is essential to providing service quality, and marketing research is a key vehicle for understanding customer expectations and perceptions of services. In services, as with any offering, a firm that does no marketing research at all is unlikely to understand its customers. A firm that does marketing research, but not on the topic of customer expectations, may also fail to know what is needed to stay in tune with changing customer requirements. Marketing research must focus on service issues such as what features are most important to customers, what levels of these features customers expect, and what customers think the company can and should do when problems occur in service delivery. Even when a service firm is small and has limited resources to conduct research, avenues are open to explore what customers expect.

In this section we discuss the elements of services marketing research programs that help companies identify customer expectations and perceptions. In the sections that follow, we will discuss ways in which the tactics of general marketing research may need to be adjusted to maximize its effectiveness in services.

Research Objectives for Services

The first step in designing services marketing research is without doubt the most critical: defining the problem and research objectives. This is where the services marketer poses the questions to be answered or problems to be solved with research. Does the company want to know how customers view the service provided by the company, what customer requirements are, how customers will respond to a new service introduction, or what customers will want from the company five years from now? Each of these research questions requires a different research strategy. Thus it is essential to devote time and resources to define the problem thoroughly and accurately. In spite of the importance of this first stage, many marketing research studies are initiated without adequate attention to objectives.

Research objectives translate into action questions. While many different questions are likely to be part of a marketing research program, the following are the most common research objectives in services:

- To discover customer requirements or expectations for service.

- To monitor and track service performance.

- To assess overall company performance compared with that of competition.

- To assess gaps between customer expectations and perceptions.

- To identify dissatisfied customers, so that service recovery can be attempted.

- To gauge effectiveness of changes in service delivery.

- To appraise the service performance of individuals and teams for evaluation, recognition, and rewards.

- To determine customer expectations for a new service.

- To monitor changing customer expectations in an industry.

- To forecast future expectations of customers.

These research objectives are similar in many ways to the research conducted for physical products: both aim to assess customer requirements, dissatisfaction, and demand. Services research, however, incorporates additional elements that require specific attention.

First, services research must continually monitor and track service performance because performance is subject to human variability and heterogeneity. Conducting performance research at a single point in time, as might be done for a physical product such as an automobile, would be insufficient in services. A major focus of services research involves capturing human performance—at the level of individual employee, team, branch, organization as a whole, and competition. Another focus of services research involves documenting the process by which service is performed. Even when service employees are performing well, a service provider must continue to track performance because the potential for variation in service delivery always exists.

A second distinction in services research is the need to consider and monitor the gap between expectations and perceptions. This gap is dynamic because both perceptions and expectations fluctuate. Does the gap exist because performance is declining, because performance varies with demand and supply level, or because expectations are escalating?

Exhibit 6.1 lists a number of services research objectives. Once objectives such as these have been identified, they will point the way to decisions about the most appropriate type of research, methods of data collection, and ways to use the information. The additional columns in this table are described in sections of this chapter.

Criteria for an Effective Services Research Program

A **services research program** can be defined as the composite of separate research studies and types needed to address research objectives and execute an overall measurement strategy. Many types of research could be considered in a research program. Understanding the criteria for an effective services research program (see Figure 6.1) will help a company evaluate different types of research and choose the ones most appropriate for its research objectives. In this section we discuss these criteria.

Includes Qualitative and Quantitative Research

Marketing research is not limited to surveys and statistics. Some forms of research, called *qualitative research,* are exploratory and preliminary and are conducted to clarify problem definition, to prepare for more formal research, or to gain insight when more formal research is not necessary. Trader Joe's, the specialty food retailer that sells mostly private-label products, listens closely to customers using informal, qualitative research. This research is not done through focus groups or contact centers, and the company has neither a toll-free number nor a customer care e-mail address. The

FIGURE 6.1
Criteria for an Effective Services Research Program

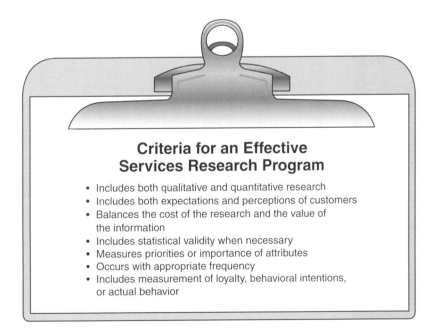

Criteria for an Effective Services Research Program

- Includes both qualitative and quantitative research
- Includes both expectations and perceptions of customers
- Balances the cost of the research and the value of the information
- Includes statistical validity when necessary
- Measures priorities or importance of attributes
- Occurs with appropriate frequency
- Includes measurement of loyalty, behavioral intentions, or actual behavior

Exhibit 6.1 ELEMENTS IN AN EFFECTIVE MARKETING RESEARCH PROGRAM FOR SERVICES

Type of Research	Primary Research Objectives	Qualitative/Quantitative	Costs of Information			Frequency
			Monetary	Time		
Complaint solicitation	To identify/attend to dissatisfied customers To identify common service failure points	Qualitative	Low	Low		Continuous
Critical incident studies	To identify "best practices" at transaction level To identify customer requirements as input for quantitative studies To identify common service failure points To identify systemic strengths and weaknesses in customer-contact services	Qualitative	Low	Moderate		Periodic
Requirements research	To identify customer requirements as input for quantitative research	Qualitative	Moderate	Moderate		Periodic
Relationship surveys and SERVQUAL surveys	To monitor and track service performance To assess overall company performance compared with that of competition To determine links between satisfaction and behavioral intentions To assess gaps between customer expectations and perceptions	Quantitative	Moderate	Moderate		Annual
Trailer calls	To obtain immediate feedback on performance of service transactions To measure effectiveness of changes in service delivery To assess service performance of individuals and teams To use as input for process improvements To identify common service failure points	Quantitative	Low	Low		Continuous

Research type	Research objective				
Service expectation meetings and reviews	To create dialogue with important customers To identify what individual large customers expect and then to ensure that it is delivered To close the loop with important customers	Qualitative	Moderate	Moderate	Annual
Process checkpoint evaluations	To determine customer perceptions of long-term professional services during service provision To identify service problems and solve them early in the service relationship	Quantitative	Moderate	Moderate	Periodic
Market-oriented ethnography	To research customers in natural settings To study customers from cultures other than America in an unbiased way	Qualitative	Moderate	Moderate	Periodic
Mystery shopping	To measure individual employee performance for evaluation, recognition, and rewards To identify systemic strengths and weaknesses in customer-contact services	Quantitative	Low	Low	Quarterly
Customer panels	To monitor changing customer expectations To provide a forum for customers to suggest and evaluate new service ideas	Qualitative	Moderate	Moderate	Continuous
Lost customer research	To identify reasons for customer defection To assess gaps between customer expectations and perceptions	Qualitative	Low	Low	Continuous
Future expectations research	To forecast future expectations of customers To develop and test new service ideas	Qualitative	High	High	Periodic
Database marketing research	To identify the individual requirements of customers using information technology and database information	Quantitative	High	High	Continuous

company finds out what customers want by talking to them—managers ("captains") spend most of the day on the floor, where there are always multiple product samplings taking place, and anyone on the sales staff ("crew members") can directly e-mail a buyer to tell them what people are liking or not.[2] Insights gained through one-on-one conversations like those at Trader Joe's, customer focus groups, critical incidents research (described in Chapter 5 and discussed more fully later in this chapter), and direct observation of service transactions show the marketer the right questions to ask of consumers. Because the results of qualitative research play a major role in designing quantitative research, it is often the first type of research done. Qualitative research can also be conducted after quantitative research to make the numbers in computer printouts meaningful by giving managers the perspective and sensitivity that are critical in interpreting data and initiating improvement efforts.[3]

Quantitative research in marketing is designed to describe the nature, attitudes, or behaviors of customers empirically and to test specific hypotheses that a services marketer wants to examine. Quantitative research clearly is essential to assessing and improving service delivery, and design for it provides managers data from which they can make inferences about customer groups. These studies are key for quantifying the customers' satisfaction, the importance of service attributes, the extent of service quality gaps, and perceptions of value. Such studies also provide managers with yardsticks for evaluating competitors. Finally, results from quantitative studies can highlight specific service deficiencies that can be more deeply probed through follow-up qualitative research.

Includes Both Perceptions and Expectations of Customers

As we discussed in Chapter 4, expectations serve as standards or reference points for customers. In evaluating service quality, customers compare what they perceive they get in a service encounter with their expectations of that encounter. For this reason, a measurement program that captures only perceptions of service is missing a critical part of the service quality equation. Companies need also to incorporate measures of customer expectations.

Measurement of expectations can be included in a research program in multiple ways. First, basic research that relates to customers' requirements—that identifies the service features or attributes that matter to customers—can be considered expectation research. In this form, the *content* of customer expectations is captured, initially in some form of qualitative research such as focus group interviews. Research on the *levels* of customer expectations also is needed. This type of research quantitatively assesses the levels of customer expectations and compares these with perception levels, usually by calculating the gap between expectations and perceptions.

Balances the Cost of the Research and the Value of the Information

An assessment of the cost of research compared with its benefits or value to the company is another key criterion. One cost is monetary, including direct costs to marketing research companies, payments to respondents, and internal company costs incurred by employees collecting the information. Time costs are also important, including the time commitment needed internally by employees to administer the research and the interval between data collection and availability for use by the firm. These and other costs must be weighed against the gains to the company in improved decision making, retained customers, and successful new product launches. As in many other marketing decisions, costs are easier to estimate than the value of the information. For this reason, we include only costs, not value, in Exhibit 6.1. In later chapters we describe approaches to estimating the value of customers to a company, approaches that are useful as input to the trade-off analysis needed to address this criterion.

Includes Statistical Validity When Necessary

We have already shown that research has multiple and diverse objectives. These objectives determine the appropriate type of research and methodology. To illustrate, some research is used by companies not so much to measure as to build relationships with customers—to allow contact employees to find out what customers desire, to diagnose the strengths and weaknesses of their and the firm's efforts to address the desires, to prepare a plan to meet requirements, and to confirm after a period of time (usually one year) that the company has executed the plan. The underlying objective of this type of research is to allow contact people to identify specific action items that will gain the maximum return in customer satisfaction for individual customers. This type of research does not need sophisticated quantitative analysis, anonymity of customers, careful control of sampling, or strong statistical validity.

On the other hand, research used to track overall service quality that will be used for bonuses and salary increases of salespeople must be carefully controlled for sampling bias and statistical validity. One of us (VZ) has worked with a company that paid salespeople on the basis of customers' satisfaction scores while allowing the salespeople to control the customers sampled. Obviously, the salespeople quickly learned that they could have surveys sent only to satisfied customers, artificially inflating the scores and—of course—undermining the confidence in the measurement system.

Not all forms of research have statistical validity, and not all forms need it. Most forms of qualitative research, for example, do not possess statistical validity.

Measures Priorities or Importance

Customers have many service requirements, but not all are equally important. One of the most common mistakes managers make in trying to improve service is spending resources on the wrong initiatives, only to become discouraged because the firm's service does not improve! Measuring the relative importance of service dimensions and attributes helps managers to channel resources effectively; therefore, research must document the priorities of the customer. Prioritization can be accomplished in multiple ways. *Direct importance measures* ask customers to prioritize items or dimensions of service. Several alternatives are available for measuring importance directly, among them asking respondents to rank-order service dimensions or attributes, or to rate them on a scale from "not at all important" to "extremely important." One effective approach involves asking respondents to allocate a total of 100 points across the various service dimensions. *Indirect importance measures* are estimated using the statistical procedures of correlation and regression analysis, which show the relative contribution of questionnaire items or requirements to overall service quality. Both indirect and direct importance measures provide evidence of customer priorities, and the technique that is chosen depends on the nature of the study and the number of dimensions or attributes that are being evaluated.

Occurs with Appropriate Frequency

Because customer expectations and perceptions are dynamic, companies need to institute a service quality research process, not just do isolated studies. A single study of service provides only a "snapshot" view of one moment in time. For full understanding of the marketplace's acceptance of a company's service, marketing research must be ongoing. Without a pattern of studies repeated with appropriate frequency,

Technology Spotlight
Conducting Marketing Research on the Web

One of the most intriguing applications of the Internet is online research, replacing comment cards and intrusive telephone calls with cyber-surveys that are challenging and fun for consumers. The application is growing rapidly: Less than $3 million was spent in the United States on Internet marketing research in 1996; by 2000 it was a global phenomenon, with estimated spending of $461 million; and it accounted for $800 million in 2004. The reasons are obvious—Internet research has been touted to have many benefits to marketers besides more willing respondents, including the following:

- *Speed.* Rather than three to four months required to collect data through mail questionnaires, or six to eight weeks needed to train interviewers and obtain data from telephone questionnaires, online surveys can be prepared and executed quickly. A sample of 300 to 400, large enough for many studies, can be completed in a weekend and available for viewing by clients on a secure website. One market research firm was able to complete 1,000 customer satisfaction surveys in only two hours.

- *Ability to target hard-to-reach populations.* One of the traditional difficulties in research, particularly segmentation research, is to identify and access respondents who fit a particular lifestyle or interest profile. The hard-to-reach business-to-business market accounts for about a quarter of all marketing research studies conducted by U.S. research firms. Doctors, lawyers, professionals, and working mothers are all valuable but difficult-to-access groups of customers. These people might read special interest magazines (such as professional or hobby publications) that are expensive to advertise in. They could be reached in surveys only by having the service company purchase

at great cost the mailing list of that magazine. However, online sites for special interests are quite simple to identify, access, and insert survey banners in.

- *Ability to target customers with money.* Online research allows service companies to reach customers who have higher incomes, higher education levels, and greater willingness to spend. Consumers with computers who use online services regularly tend to be in these demographic target groups, and they can be effectively surveyed with online research. Compared with the sample that would be obtained from traditional research using all telephone subscribers, the sample of online users is far better in terms of marketing potential.

- *Opportunity to use multimedia to present video and audio.* Telephone surveys are limited to voice alone, whereas mail surveys are constrained to two-dimensional visuals. In the past, to present the full range of audio and video needed to give respondents the true sense of a service being researched, surveys had to be conducted in person and were therefore very expensive ($30 to $150 per person depending on the topic and sample). Online research offers broader stimuli potential through all multimedia possibilities at a fraction of the cost.

- *No interviewers*—and therefore no interviewer errors or interviewer bias. Bias occurs when the interviewer is in a bad mood, tired, impatient, or not objective. These problems occur with human interviews but not cyber-interviews. Interviewer error is another age-old research problem, described well by a research professional:

managers cannot tell whether the firm is moving forward or falling back and which of their service improvement initiatives are working. Just what does "ongoing research" mean in terms of frequency? The answer is specific to the type of service and to the purpose and method of each type of service research a company might do. As we discuss the different types in the following section, you will see the frequency with which each type of research could be conducted.

Includes Measures of Loyalty, Behavioral Intentions, or Behavior

An important trend in services research involves measuring the positive and negative consequences of service quality along with overall satisfaction or service quality

"The first survey I ever designed was on the subject of home heating systems. When I went to observe the first day of field, I was surprised and horrified to realize that most of my interviewers could not pronounce many of the technical terms that I had used in the survey, and virtually none of them knew what those terms meant. It wasn't exactly the best way to collect data."

- *Control over data quality,* which can eliminate contradictory or nonsensical answers. With traditional surveys, researchers need a step called "data cleaning and editing" in which all data are checked for such problems; electronic checks can be built into online surveys that take care of this problem as it occurs.

- *Inexpensive research.* Data collection costs can be the most expensive part of a study, and the most expensive part of data collection can be paying subjects to participate. Online marketing research, astonishingly, is 10 to 80 percent less expensive than other approaches. The Internet also eliminates postage, phone, labor, and printing costs that are typical with other survey approaches. Respondents also seem to complete Web-based surveys in half the time it would take an interviewer to conduct the survey, perhaps contributing to the lack of need for incentives.

One additional but to date undersubstantiated benefit is higher response rate—reportedly as high as 70 percent—possibly stemming from the fact that the interactive nature of cyber-research can make answering surveys fun for respondents. While it is getting more difficult to get consumers to answer traditional surveys, the entertainment value of cyber-surveys makes it easy to recruit participants. One study shows that consumers are five times more likely to complete an electronic survey as they are to do the same survey with written materials and that researchers obtain the following three additional benefits: (1) consumers "play" an e-survey longer, answering more questions than in a traditional survey; (2) people tend to concentrate more fully on their answers; and (3) the entertainment value of an e-survey actually lowers the respondent's perceived time to complete the survey.

The advantages of online research likely far outnumber the disadvantages. However, marketers need to be aware of these drawbacks. Perhaps the major problem is the composition of the sample. Unlike the process used with most telephone and mail surveys, the population of responders is not usually selected but is a matter of convenience, consisting of whoever responds to the survey. This is a particular problem when respondents are recruited from other websites and click through to the survey. In these cases marketers may not even know who the responders are and whether they are in fact the right profile for answering the survey. To address this problem, companies are prequalifying respondents by telephone or e-mail, then asking for enough demographic information to ensure that the respondents meet the desired requirements.

Sources: A. Hogg, "Online Research Overview," MarketingPower.com, updated 2004; D. McCullough, "Web-Based Market Research Ushers in New Age," *Marketing News,* September 14, 1998, p. 28; R. Weible and J. Wallace, "Cyber Research: The Impact of the Internet on Data Collection," *Marketing Research,* Fall 1998, pp. 19–24; R. Nadilo, "On-Line Research Taps Consumers Who Spend," *Marketing News,* June 8, 1998, p. 12.

scores. Among the most important generic behavioral intentions are willingness to recommend the service to others and repurchase intent. These behavioral intentions can be viewed as positive and negative consequences of service quality. Positive behavioral intentions include saying positive things about the company, recommending the company to others, remaining loyal, spending more with the company, and paying a price premium. Negative behavioral intentions include saying negative things to others, doing less business with the company, switching to another company, and complaining to outside organizations such as the Better Business Bureau. Other more specific behaviors differ by service; for example, behaviors related to medical care include following instructions from the doctor, taking medications, and returning for follow-up. Tracking these areas can help a company estimate the relative value of service improvements to the company and can also identify customers who are in danger of defecting.

Summary

The research criteria discussed here should be incorporated into a services marketing research program. As we discuss the elements in an effective services marketing research program, we will indicate how these approaches satisfy the criteria. In addition to the types and techniques of research shown in Exhibit 6.1, the boxes in this chapter show how electronic and other technologies add to the information that managers can collect.

ELEMENTS IN AN EFFECTIVE SERVICES MARKETING RESEARCH PROGRAM

A good services marketing research program includes multiple types of research studies. The composite of studies and types of research will differ by company because the range of uses for service quality research—from employee performance assessment to advertising campaign development to strategic planning—requires a rich, multifaceted flow of information. If a company were to engage in virtually all types of service research, the portfolio would look like Exhibit 6.1, but few companies do all types of research. The particular portfolio for any company will match company resources and address the key areas needed to understand the customers of the business. So that it will be easier for you to identify the appropriate type of research for different research objectives, we list the objectives in column 2 of Exhibit 6.1. In the following sections we describe each major type of research and show the way each type addresses the criteria associated with it. The Technology Spotlight discusses research conducted online.

Complaint Solicitation

Many of you have complained to employees of service organizations, only to find that nothing happens with your complaint. No one rushes to solve it, and the next time you experience the service the same problem is present. How frustrating! Good service organizations take complaints seriously. Not only do they listen to complaints—they also seek complaints as communications about what can be done to improve their service and their service employees. Vail Resorts, which owns the Vail, Breckenridge, Heavenly, Keystone, and Beaver Creek resorts, has an innovative way to capture complaints and comments of its customers. The resort hires researchers to ride the lifts with skiers and ask and record into handheld computer devices customers' responses to questions about their perceptions of the resorts. Then the researchers ski down the mountain and ride up again with another customer. At the end of the day, the researchers download the results into a computer at the base. The researchers survey 200 skiers per week, looking for patterns of customer comments and complaints. For example, if the researchers receive a number of complaints about certain lift lines or service in one of the restaurants, they will alert managers in those areas so the problems can be resolved quickly. At the end of the week, the data are collected and reported at weekly meetings.

Firms that use complaints as research collect and document them, then use the information to identify dissatisfied customers, correct individual problems where possible, and identify common service failure points. Although this research is used for both goods and services, it has a critical real-time purpose in services—to improve

FIGURE 6.2
Participants in a focus group discuss services using the critical incidents technique.

Source: David Grossman/Photo Researchers, Inc.

failure points and to improve or correct the performance of contact personnel. Research on complaints is one of the easiest types of research for firms to conduct, leading many companies to depend solely on complaints to stay in touch with customers. Unfortunately, convincing research provides evidence that customer complaints alone are a woefully inadequate source of information: Only a small percentage of customers with problems actually complain to the company. The rest will stay dissatisfied, telling other people about their dissatisfaction.

To be effective, complaint solicitation requires rigorous recording of numbers and types of complaints through many channels, and then working to eliminate the most frequent problems. Complaint channels include employees at the front line, intermediary organizations like retailers who deliver service, managers, and complaints to third parties such as customer advocate groups. Companies must both solve individual customer problems and seek overall patterns to eliminate failure points. More sophisticated forms of complaint resolution define "complaint" broadly to include all comments—both negative and positive—as well as questions from customers. Firms should build depositories for this information and report results frequently, perhaps weekly or monthly.

Critical Incidents Studies

In Chapter 5, we discussed the critical incident technique (CIT), a qualitative interview procedure in which customers are asked to provide verbatim stories about satisfying and dissatisfying service encounters they have experienced (Figure 6.2). According to a recent summary of the use of the technique in services, CIT has been reported in hotels, restaurants, airlines, amusement parks, automotive repair, retailing, banking, cable television, public transportation, and education.[4] The studies have explored a wide range of service topics: consumer evaluation of services, service failure and recovery, employees, customer participation in service delivery, and service experience.

CIT has many benefits. First, data are collected from the respondent's perspective and are usually vivid because they are expressed in consumers' own words and reflect the way they think. Second, the method provides concrete information about the way the company and its employees behave and react, thereby making the research easy to translate into action. Third, like most qualitative methods, the research is particularly useful when the topic or service is new and very little other information exists. Finally, the method is well suited for assessing perceptions of customers from different cultures because it allows respondents to share their perceptions rather than answer researcher-defined questions.[5]

Requirements Research

Requirements research involves identifying the benefits and attributes that customers expect in a service. This type of research is very basic and essential because it determines the type of questions that will be asked in surveys and ultimately the improvements that will be attempted by the firm. Because these studies are so foundational, qualitative techniques are appropriate to begin them. Quantitative techniques may follow, usually during a pretest stage of survey development. Unfortunately, many companies do inadequate requirements research, often developing surveys on the basis of intuition or company direction rather than thorough customer probing.

An example of requirements research is *structured brainstorming,* a technique developed by researchers in IBM's Advanced Business Systems unit.[6] In this technique a sample of customers and potential customers is assembled. A facilitator leads the group through a series of exercises on creativity and then has the customers describe the ideal provider of the service—what they would want if they could have their ideal service. The facilitator asks "what" customers want (to elicit fundamental requirements), "why" they want it (to elicit the underlying need or benefit sought), and "how" they will know when they receive it (to elicit specific service features).

Another approach to requirements research that has been effective in services industries is to examine existing research about customer requirements in similar service industries. The five dimensions of quality service are generalizable across industries, and sometimes the way these dimensions are manifest is also remarkably similar. Hospital patients and customers of hotels, for example, expect many of the same features when using these two services. Besides expert medical care, patients in hospitals expect comfortable rooms, courteous staff, and food that tastes good—the same features that are salient to hotel customers. In these and other industries that share common customer expectations, managers may find it helpful to seek knowledge from existing research in the related service industry. Because hotels have used marketing and marketing research longer than hospitals have, insights about hotel guests' expectations can inform about patients' expectations. Hospital administrators at Albert Einstein Medical Center in Philadelphia, for example, asked a group of nine local hotel executives for advice in understanding and handling patients. Many improvements resulted, including better food, easier-to-read name tags, more prominent information desks, and radios in many rooms.[7]

Relationship and SERVQUAL Surveys

One category of surveys could appropriately be named *relationship surveys* because they pose questions about all elements in the customer's relationship with the company (including service, product, and price). This comprehensive approach can help a company diagnose its relationship strengths and weaknesses. These surveys typically monitor and track service performance annually with an initial survey providing a baseline. Relationship surveys are also effective in comparing company performance with that of competitors, often focusing on the best competitor's performance as a benchmark. When used for this purpose, the sponsor of the survey is not identified and questions are asked about both the focal company and one or more competitors.

A sound measure of service quality is necessary for identifying the aspects of service needing performance improvement, assessing how much improvement is needed on each aspect, and evaluating the impact of improvement efforts. Unlike goods quality, which can be measured objectively by such indicators as durability and number of defects, service quality is abstract and is best captured by surveys that measure customer evaluations of service. One of the first measures to be developed specifically to measure service quality was the SERVQUAL survey.

The SERVQUAL scale involves a survey containing 21 service attributes, grouped into the five service quality dimensions (discussed in Chapter 5) of reliability, responsiveness, assurance, empathy, and tangibles. The survey sometimes asks customers to provide two different ratings on each attribute—one reflecting the level of service they would expect from excellent companies in a sector and the other reflecting their perception of the service delivered by a specific company within that sector. The difference between the expectation and perception ratings constitutes a quantified measure of service quality. Exhibit 6.2 shows the items on the basic SERVQUAL scale as well as the phrasing of the expectations and perceptions portions of the scale.[8]

Data gathered through a SERVQUAL survey can be used for a variety of purposes:

- To determine the average gap score (between customers' perceptions and expectations) for each service attribute.

- To assess a company's service quality along each of the five SERVQUAL dimensions.

- To track customers' expectations and perceptions (on individual service attributes and/or on the SERVQUAL dimensions) over time.

- To compare a company's SERVQUAL scores against those of competitors.

- To identify and examine customer segments that differ significantly in their assessments of a company's service performance.

- To assess internal service quality (that is, the quality of service rendered by one department or division of a company to others within the same company).

This instrument spawned many studies focusing on service quality assessment and is used all over the world in service industries. Published studies have used SERVQUAL and adaptations of it in a variety of contexts: real estate brokers, physicians in private practice, public recreation programs, dental schools, business school placement centers, tire stores, motor carrier companies, accounting firms, discount and department stores, gas and electric utility companies, hospitals, banking, pest control, dry cleaning, fast food, and higher education.

SERVQUAL has been productively used in multiple contexts, cultures, and countries for measuring service quality in commercial as well as public-sector organizations. Many of the findings from these applications are unpublished and/or proprietary. However, based on our knowledge of some of these applications, two samples are briefly described here.

Consumer Service Context

A large Australian bank used SERVQUAL to measure its quality of service as evaluated by several segments of individual customers.[9] The bank analyzed the data to assess service quality deficiencies on individual attributes and on the five SERVQUAL dimensions as well as to compute gap scores. The bank also benchmarked its SERVQUAL scores against those of two similar U.S. banks that had participated in

Exhibit 6.2 SERVQUAL: A MULTIDIMENSIONAL SCALE TO CAPTURE CUSTOMER PERCEPTIONS AND EXPECTATIONS OF SERVICE QUALITY

The SERVQUAL scale was first published in 1988 and has undergone numerous improvements and revisions since then. The scale currently contains 21 perception items that are distributed throughout the five service quality dimensions. The scale also contains expectation items. Although many different formats of the SERVQUAL scale are now in use, we show here the basic 21 perception items as well as a sampling of ways the expectation items have been posed.

PERCEPTIONS

Perceptions Statements in the Reliability Dimension

	Strongly disagree					Strongly agree
1. When XYZ Company promises to do something by a certain time, it does so.	1	2	3	4	5	6 7
2. When you have a problem, XYZ Company shows a sincere interest in solving it.	1	2	3	4	5	6 7
3. XYZ Company performs the service right the first time.	1	2	3	4	5	6 7
4. XYZ Company provides its services at the time it promises to do so.	1	2	3	4	5	6 7
5. XYZ Company insists on error-free records.	1	2	3	4	5	6 7

Statements in the Responsiveness Dimension

1. XYZ Company keeps customers informed about when services will be performed.   1 2 3 4 5 6 7
2. Employees in XYZ Company give you prompt service.   1 2 3 4 5 6 7
3. Employees in XYZ Company are always willing to help you.   1 2 3 4 5 6 7
4. Employees in XYZ Company are never too busy to respond to your request.   1 2 3 4 5 6 7

Statements in the Assurance Dimension

1. The behavior of employees in XYZ Company instills confidence in you.   1 2 3 4 5 6 7
2. You feel safe in your transactions with XYZ Company.   1 2 3 4 5 6 7
3. Employees in XYZ Company are consistently courteous with you.   1 2 3 4 5 6 7
4. Employees in XYZ Company have the knowledge to answer your questions.   1 2 3 4 5 6 7

Statements in the Empathy Dimension

	Strongly disagree					Strongly agree
1. XYZ Company gives you individual attention.	1	2	3	4	5	6 7
2. XYZ Company has employees who give you personal attention.	1	2	3	4	5	6 7
3. XYZ Company has your best interests at heart.	1	2	3	4	5	6 7
4. Employees of XYZ Company understand your specific needs.	1	2	3	4	5	6 7
5. XYZ Company has operating hours that are convenient to all its customers	1	2	3	4	5	6 7

Statements in the Tangibles Dimension

1. XYZ Company has modern-looking equipment.   1 2 3 4 5 6 7
2. XYZ Company's physical facilities are visually appealing.   1 2 3 4 5 6 7
3. XYZ Company's employees appear neat.   1 2 3 4 5 6 7
4. Materials associated with the service (such as pamphlets or statements) are visually appealing at XYZ Company.   1 2 3 4 5 6 7

EXPECTATIONS: Several Formats for Measuring Customer Expectations Using Versions of SERVQUAL

Matching Expectations Statements (Paired with the Previous Perception Statements)

	Strongly disagree					Strongly agree

When customers have a problem, excellent firms will show a sincere interest in solving it.   1 2 3 4 5 6 7

Referent Expectations Formats

1. Considering a "world class" company to be a "7," how would you rate XYZ Company's performance on the following service features?

	Low						High
Sincere, interested employees	1	2	3	4	5	6	7
Service delivered right the first time	1	2	3	4	5	6	7

2. Compared with the level of service you expect from an excellent company, how would you rate XYZ Company's performance on the following?

	Low						High
Sincere, interested employees	1	2	3	4	5	6	7
Service delivered right the first time	1	2	3	4	5	6	7

Combined Expectations/Perceptions Statements

For each of the following statements, circle the number that indicates how XYZ Company's service compares with the level you expect:

	Lower than my desired service level			The same as my desired service level			Higher than my desired service level		
1. Prompt service	1	2	3	4	5	6	7	8	9
2. Courteous employees	1	2	3	4	5	6	7	8	9

Expectations Distinguishing between Desired Service and Adequate Service

For each of the following statements, circle the number that indicates how XYZ Company's performance compares with your *minimum service level* and with your *desired service level.*

When it comes to . . .	Compared with my *minimum* service level XYZ's service performance is:									Compared with my *desired* service level XYZ's service performance is:								
	Lower			Same			Higher			Lower			Same			Higher		
1. Prompt service	1	2	3	4	5	6	7	8	9	1	2	3	4	5	6	7	8	9
2. Employees who are consistently courteous	1	2	3	4	5	6	7	8	9	1	2	3	4	5	6	7	8	9

Source: A. Parasuraman, V.A. Zeithaml, and L.L. Berry, "SERVQUAL: A Multiple-Item Scale for Measuring Consumer Perceptions of Service Quality," Journal of Retailing 64, no. 1 (Spring 1988). Reprinted by permission of C. Samuel Craig.

previous studies. Although some differences between the results for the Australian and U.S. banks were found on specific service attributes, there were striking similarities in the overall pattern of results. For instance, the relative importance of the levels of the five dimensions (as measured by the point allocation question) were as follows:

	Points Allocated		
	Australian Bank	U.S. Bank 1	U.S. Bank 2
Tangibles	13	10	11
Reliability	28	31	32
Responsiveness	22	22	22
Assurance	19	20	19
Empathy	18	17	16

The Australian bank set up a measurement system to track service quality at regular intervals and to assess the impact of service improvement efforts.

Industrial Product Context

The Ceramic Products Division of Corning, Inc., a large U.S. manufacturing company, developed a systematic process for monitoring and improving its service quality as perceived by customer organizations to which it supplied its manufactured products. The SERVQUAL approach was an integral component of this process. Corning's Ceramic Products Division began its service improvement process by focusing on its largest client, a multinational company. This division modified the SERVQUAL instrument for assessing its service quality as perceived by multiple levels within this company. The SERVQUAL survey was re-administered a year later to assess the impact of the corrective actions. Results indicated significant improvements in most of the targeted attributes and also identified additional areas for further corrective action. The success of SERVQUAL in this pilot application prompted Corning to make this process an ongoing activity in the Ceramics Product Division and to expand its implementation to other divisions and customer groups.

Corning's use of SERVQUAL touches on virtually all the potential applications of the instrument listed earlier. It also illustrates the fact that SERVQUAL can be adapted for use in a variety of contexts, including industrial product and internal service contexts.

Trailer Calls or Posttransaction Surveys

Whereas the purpose of SERVQUAL surveys is usually to gauge the overall relationship with the customer, the purpose of transaction surveys is to capture information about one or all of the key service encounters with the customer. In this method, customers are asked a short list of questions immediately after a particular transaction (hence the name *trailer calls*) about their satisfaction with the transaction and contact personnel with whom they interacted. Because the surveys are administered continuously to a broad spectrum of customers, they are more effective than complaint solicitation (where the information comes only from dissatisfied customers).

At checkout, immediately after staying at Fairfield Inns, customers are asked to use a computer terminal to answer four or five questions about their stay in the hotel. This novel approach has obvious benefits over the ubiquitous comment cards left in rooms—the response rate is far higher because the process engages customers and takes only a few minutes. In other companies, transaction surveys are administered by telephone several days after a transaction such as installation of durable goods or claims adjustment in insurance. Because they are timed to occur close to service transactions, these surveys are useful in identifying sources of dissatisfaction and satisfaction. For example, Enterprise Rent-A-Car often calls customers a day after a car has been rented (and is still in the customer's possession) to ensure that customers are satisfied with the rental. If the customer has problems with the car (a broken window, a nonworking radio), a new car is provided at no charge to the customer.

A strong benefit of this type of research is that it often appears to customers that the call is following up to ensure that they are satisfied; consequently the call does double duty as a market research tool and as customer service. This type of research is simple and fresh and provides management with continuous information about interactions with customers. Further, the research allows management to associate service quality performance with individual contact personnel so that high performance can be rewarded and low performance corrected. It also serves as an incentive for employees to provide better service because they understand how and when they are being evaluated. One posttransaction study that you may be familiar with is the BizRate.Com study that follows online purchases. When a consumer makes a purchase at one of BizRate's online partners (which include many major companies), a message automatically pops up on the site and invites consumers to fill out a survey. Consumers who agree are asked questions about ease of ordering, product selection, website navigation, and customer support.

Service Expectation Meetings and Reviews

In business-to-business situations when large accounts are involved, a form of customer research that is highly effective involves eliciting the expectations of the client at a specified time of the year and then following up later (usually after a year) to determine whether the expectations were fulfilled. Even when the company produces a physical product, the meetings deal almost completely with the service expected and provided by an account or sales team assigned to the client. Unlike other forms of research we have discussed, these meetings are not conducted by objective and unbiased researchers but are instead initiated and facilitated by senior members of the account team so that they can listen carefully to the client's expectations. You may be surprised to find that such interaction does not come naturally to sales teams who are used to talking *to* clients rather than listening carefully to their needs. Consequently, teams have to be carefully trained not to defend or explain but instead to comprehend. One company found that the only way it could teach its salespeople not to talk on these interviews was to take a marketing researcher along to gently kick the salesperson under the table whenever he or she strayed from the format!

The format, when appropriate, consists of (1) asking clients what they expect in terms of 8 to 10 basic requirements determined from focus group research, (2) inquiring what particular aspects of these requirements the account team performed well in the past as well as what aspects need improvement, and (3) requesting that the client rank the relative importance of the requirements. After getting the input, senior account members go back to their teams and plan their goals for the year around client requirements. The next step is verifying with the client that the account plan will satisfy requirements or, when it will not, managing expectations to let the client know what cannot be accomplished. After executing the plan for the year, the senior account personnel then return to the client, determine whether the plan has been successfully executed and expectations met, then establish a new set of expectations for the coming year.

Process Checkpoint Evaluations

With professional services such as consulting, construction, and architecture, services are provided over a long period, and there are not obvious ways or times to collect customer information. Waiting until the entire project is complete—which could last years—is undesirable because myriad unresolvable problems could have occurred by then. But discrete service encounters to calibrate customer perceptions are also not usually available. In these situations, the smart service provider defines a process for delivering the services and then structures the feedback around the process, checking in at frequent points to ensure that the client's expectations are being met. For example, a management consulting firm might establish the following process for delivering its services to clients: (1) collect information, (2) diagnose problems, (3) recommend alternative solutions, (4) select alternatives, and (5) implement solutions. Next, it could agree with the client up front that it will communicate at major process checkpoints—after diagnosing the problem, before selecting the alternative, and so on—to make certain that the job is progressing as planned.

Market-Oriented Ethnography

Many of the types of research we discuss in this section are particularly relevant for the United States and cultures similar to it. Structured questionnaires, for example, make key assumptions about what people are conscious of or can recall about their behavior and what they are willing to explain to researchers about their opinions. These assumptions are based on American culture. Even focus group interviews are inherently culture based because they depend on norms of participation, or what people are willing to say in front of others and to researchers. To fully understand how customers of other cultures assess and use services, it is necessary and effective to use other approaches, such as market-oriented ethnography. This set of approaches allows researchers to observe consumption behavior in natural settings. The goal is to enter the consumer's world as much as possible—observing how and when a service is used in an actual home environment or consumption environment, such as watching consumers eat in restaurants or attend concerts. Among the techniques used are observation, interviews, documents, and examination of material possessions such as artifacts.

In professional services, evaluations are made at important checkpoints in the process.

Source: Jiang Jin/SuperStock

Observation involves entering the experience as a participant observer and watching what occurs rather than asking questions about it. One-on-one interviews, particularly with key informants in the culture rather than consumers themselves, can provide compelling insights about culture-based behavior. Studying existing documents and cultural artifacts can also provide valuable insights, especially about lifestyles and usage patterns.[10]

Best Western International used this technique to better understand its senior market. Rather than bringing participants into focus group facilities and asking them questions, the company paid 25 over-55 couples to videotape themselves on cross-country journeys. The firm was able to listen to how couples actually made decisions rather than the way they reported them. The insights they gained from this research were decidedly different from what they would have learned otherwise. Most noteworthy was the finding that seniors who talked hotel clerks into better deals on rooms did not need the lower price to afford staying at the hotel—they were simply after the thrill of the deal, as illustrated in this description:

> The 60-ish woman caught on the grainy videotape is sitting on her hotel bed, addressing her husband after a long day spent on the road. "Good job!" she exults. "We beat the s—t out of the front desk and got a terrific room."[11]

These customers then spent their discount money on better dinners elsewhere, contributing nothing to Best Western. "The degree of discount clearly isn't what it used to be in importance—and we got that right out of the research," claimed the manager of programs for Best Western.[12] This finding would be highly unlikely using traditional research and asking customers directly, for few customers would admit to being willing to pay a higher price for a service!

Mystery Shopping

In this form of research, which is unique to services,[13] companies hire outside research organizations to send people into service establishments and experience the service as if they were customers. These "mystery" shoppers are trained in the criteria important to customers of the establishment. They deliver objective assessments about service performance by completing questionnaires about service standards. Questionnaires contain items that represent important quality or service issues to customers. Au Bon Pain, for example, sends mystery shoppers to its stores to buy meals and then complete questionnaires about the servers, the restaurant, and the food. Servers are evaluated on standards that include the following:

Acknowledged within three seconds after reaching first place in line.

Acknowledged pleasantly.

Server suggested additional items.

Server requested payment prior to delivering order.

Received receipt.

Received correct change.

Correct order received.

Au Bon Pain motivates workers to perform to service standards by using the mystery shopper program as a key element in its compensation and reward system. Individual workers who receive positive scores have their names posted on the store's bulletin board and receive letters of congratulations as well as bonuses. Managers whose stores earn high scores can receive on-the-spot bonuses of "Club Excellence" dollars that can be traded like green stamps for items in a company catalog. Perhaps more important, the overall scores received by shift and district managers qualify them for monthly profit-sharing cash bonuses. A score lower than 78 percent removes them from consideration for a bonus, whereas high numbers lead to good bonuses.

Mystery shopping keeps workers on their toes because they know they may be evaluated at any time. They know they are being judged on the company's service standards and therefore carry out the standards more consistently than if they were not going to be judged. Mystery shopping can be a very effective way of reinforcing service standards.

Customer Panels

Customer panels are ongoing groups of customers assembled to provide attitudes and perceptions about a service over time. They offer a company regular and timely customer information—virtually a pulse on the market. Firms can use customer panels to represent large segments of end customers.

Customer panels are used in the entertainment industry to screen movies before they are released to the public. After a rough cut of a film has been created, the movie is viewed by a panel of consumers that matches the demographic target. In the most basic of these panels, consumers participate in postscreening interviews or focus groups in which they report on their responses to the movie. They may be asked questions as general as their reactions to the ending of the movie and as specific as whether they understood different aspects of the plot line. Based on these panels, movies are revised and edited to ensure that they are communicating the desired message and that they will succeed in the marketplace. In extreme situations, entire endings of movies have been changed to be more consistent with customer attitudes. In some of the most sophisticated consumer panel research on movies (also used for television shows and commercials) consumers have digital devices in their seats through which they indicate their responses as they watch films. This instantaneous response allows the producers, directors, and editors to make changes at the appropriate places in the film to ensure that the story line, characters, and scenery are "tracking."

Lost Customer Research

This type of research involves deliberately seeking customers who have dropped the company's service to inquire about their reasons for leaving. Some lost customer research is similar to exit interviews with employees in that it asks open-ended, in-depth questions to expose the reasons for defection and the particular events that led to dissatisfaction. It is also possible to use more standard surveys on lost customers. For example, a Midwestern manufacturer used a mail survey to ask former customers about its performance during different stages of the customer–vendor relationship. The survey also sought specific reasons for customers' defections and asked customers to describe problems that triggered their decreases in purchases.[14]

One benefit of this type of research is that it identifies failure points and common problems in the service and can help establish an early-warning system for future defectors. Another benefit is that the research can be used to calculate the cost of lost customers.

Future Expectations Research

Customer expectations are dynamic and can change very rapidly in markets that are highly competitive and volatile. As competition increases, as tastes change, and as consumers become more knowledgeable, companies must continue to update their information and strategies. One such "industry" is interactive video, representing the merger of computer, telecommunications, and cable television. The technologies available in this industry are revolutionary. In dynamic market situations, companies want to understand not just current customer expectations but also future expectations—the service features desired in the future. Future expectations research is new and includes different types. First, *features research* involves environmental scanning and querying of customers about desirable features of possible services. *Lead user research* brings in customers who are opinion leaders/innovators and asks them what requirements are not currently being met by existing products or services. Another form of this research is the *synectics approach*, which defines lead users more broadly than in standard lead user research.

The question of customer involvement in expectation studies is often debated. Designers and developers claim that consumers do not know what they might want, especially in industries or services that are new and rapidly changing. Consumers and marketing researchers, on the other hand, counter that services developed independent of customer input are likely to be targeted at needs that do not exist. To study this question, researchers assessed the contributions made by users compared with professional developers for end-user telecom services. Three groups were studied: users alone, developers alone, and users with a design expert present to provide information on feasibility. Findings showed that users created more original but less producible ideas. However, inviting users to test and explore possibilities once a prototype has been created can produce positive results.[15]

ANALYZING AND INTERPRETING MARKETING RESEARCH FINDINGS

One of the biggest challenges facing a marketing researcher is converting a complex set of data to a form that can be read and understood quickly by executives, managers, and other employees who will make decisions from the research. For example, database management is being adopted as a strategic initiative by many firms (see the Strategy Insight box), but merely having a sophisticated database does not ensure that the findings will be useful to managers. Many of the people who use marketing research findings have not been trained in statistics and have neither the time nor the expertise to analyze computer printouts and other technical research information. The goal in this stage of the marketing research process is to communicate information clearly to the right people in a timely fashion. Among considerations are the following: Who gets this information? Why do they need it? How will they use it? Does it mean the same thing across cultures? (See the Global Feature box.) When users feel confident that they understand the data, they are far more likely to apply it appropriately. When managers do not understand how to interpret the data, or when they lack confidence in the research, the investment of time, skill, and effort will be lost.

Depicting marketing research findings graphically is a powerful way to communicate research information. Here are a sample of graphic representations of the types of marketing research data we have discussed throughout this chapter.

Tracking of Performance, Gap Scores, and Competition

A simple way of tracking performance is shown in Figure 6.3. Both expectations and perceptions are plotted, and the gap between them shows the service quality shortfall.

Most of the marketing research approaches in this chapter study patterns of customers in groups. Surveys examine the service quality perceptions of the totality of a firm's customers to get a sense of how they feel as a group. Focus groups identify the needs of important service segments, and lost customer research pinpoints the primary reasons why exiting customers are dissatisfied enough to leave the company. However, an important and powerful form of research—called *database marketing* or *customer relationship management (CRM)*—studies customers one by one to develop profiles on their individual needs, behaviors, and responses to marketing. This approach allows a company to get very close to its customers and to tailor services uniquely to individuals.

Individual customer research is founded on a database, which allows a company to tell customers apart and remember them uniquely. You may be most familiar with this form of data collection in grocery store loyalty cards—like VIC for Harris Teeter or MVP for Food Lion—that capture information about your purchases and offer you tailored coupons and specials based on your buying patterns. One of the most familiar examples of using a technology database to remember customers is the Ritz-Carlton's frequent guest registry, which documents preferences of each frequent guest. (Does he like a smoking or nonsmoking room? Feather pillows? Does she read *USA Today* or *The Wall Street Journal*?) Each time a guest visits, new observations about preferences are entered so that the institution itself comes to "know" each guest.

Here are two of the most innovative examples of database marketing and how they are applied to understand and market to individual customers:

HALLMARK GOLD CROWN

Hallmark's database, capable of recognizing customers in all 5,000 Hallmark retail stores, tracks purchases, contacts, and communications so that it learns what each customer individually values about the relationship with the company. This information includes what core product or benefit has the most value to the customer and what differentiates Hallmark from its competition. The mechanism by which the company tracks this information is a Gold Crown Card that customers use to accumulate points for purchases. They receive personalized point statements, newsletters, reward certificates, and individualized news of products and events at local stores. The top 10 percent of customers—who buy more cards and ornaments than others—get special amenities such as longer bonus periods and their own private priority toll-free number, as well as very targeted communication about the specific products they value:

> We are using our data to learn more about our customers and give them what they want. Ornament lovers want to hear all about new products. They want to hear a lot of product info, and they want it as soon as possible. Knowing this, we are able to isolate them and give them just what they want. Other segments represent busy women who want the shortened version—tell me the short notes, the highlights of what I need to know for Valentine's Day, is there a bonus offer, where is my reward certificate? Our whole goal is to respond to what our customers are telling us with their purchases. It really is a dialogue.

Several times a year Hallmark executives sit down with preferred and regular members to hear how they feel about the program, what they would like to see added or changed, and how they react to product offerings. Results of the program have been impressive. The program has more than 25 million permanent cardholders, 10 million who have purchased in the last 6-month period, and over 12 million who have purchased in the last 12 months. Member sales represent 35 percent of total store transactions and 45 percent of total store sales.

HARRAH'S ENTERTAINMENT, INC.

The gambling industry has long recognized that certain customers are better than others and that encouraging the "high rollers" to spend time in one's casinos is a worthwhile and profitable strategy. One of the main ways they encourage increased patronage is "comping"—giving free drinks, hotel rooms, limousines, and sometimes chips to top customers. The strategy has been limited in most casinos to customers who could be identified and followed, making the approach spotty and missing many potential repeat patrons. Harrah's Entertainment, which owns and operates more than 20 gambling casinos in places such as Las Vegas and Atlantic City, found a more systematic way to extend the practice to a wider group of customers. Harrah's developed a customer relationship management system called the Total Rewards program, a loyalty program started several years ago that tracks the names and addresses of repeat visitors along with what slot machines they play, for how long, and how much money they gamble. The company's approach uses a Total Rewards card that any customer can obtain—often with the incentive of covering their slot losses for half an hour up to $100. To earn points toward drinks, rooms, and other benefits, customers allow their cards to be swiped on the casino floor to monitor the sums gambled and time spent at slot machines and card tables. The company is also working to automate table games such as blackjack by inserting radio frequency transmitters into gaming chips and installing an antenna under the table felt to record the amount of each wager. The reaction of gamblers to this kind of intense scrutiny of their habits is still unknown, but Harrah's is counting on customers wanting the points enough to agree to be tracked.

Although individual players can earn platinum or diamond status based on their gambling levels, the program is designed for mass markets. The average Harrah's customer gambles less than $3,000 annually and comes to Vegas just once or twice a year. This program allows Harrah's to determine how profitable all customers are as individuals and make special offers tailored to their casino behavior to keep them coming back. The newest initiative is to turn the program into immediate rewards. For example, Harrah's data can watch when a customer is losing, thereby providing the winner with an immediate credit toward future gambling. Printers placed at the gaming machines issue customers these real-time credits.

Database marketing has applications in virtually any service in which customers make repeat purchases. Underlying the approach is the necessity for the company to create customer information files that integrate different data sources on individual customers including demographics, segmentation, usage information, customer satisfaction data, and accounting and financial information. Although this approach raises privacy concerns with some customers, you can see the extent to which marketing research is enhanced under these conditions. A company no longer needs to depend on the customers' words on a

continued

survey about whether they intend to remain customers with a company—it can track their purchases and find out for certain. It no longer needs to guess which demographics are most related to psychographic segmentation information—the company can run an analysis to provide valid and reliable data on the topic.

Sources: F. Newell, *loyalty.com* (New York: McGraw-Hill, 2000), pp. 232–38; C. T. Heun, "Harrah's Bets on IT to Understand Its Customers," *Informationweek,* December 11, 2000; www.harrahs.com, 2004; www.hallmark.com, 2004.

Although any attribute or dimension of service can be tracked, Figure 6.3 shows the scores for service reliability. Competitor service performance is another frequently tracked service quality measurement. It allows managers to have a better grasp of service improvement priorities for their firm by comparing the firm's service strengths and weaknesses against those of key competitors.[16]

Zones of Tolerance Charts

When companies collect data on the dual expectation levels described in Chapter 4—desired service and adequate service—along with performance data, they can convey the information concisely on zones of tolerance charts. Figure 6.4 on page 167 plots customer service quality perceptions relative to customers' zones of tolerance. Perceptions of company performance are indicated by the circles, and the zones of tolerance boxes are bounded on the top by the desired service score and on the bottom by the adequate service score. When the perception scores are within the boxes, as in Figure 6.4, the company is delivering service that is above customers' minimum level of expectations. When the perception scores are below the boxes, the company's service performance is lower than the minimum level, and customers are dissatisfied with the company's service.[17]

FIGURE 6.3
Tracking of Customer Expectations and Perceptions of Service Reliability

Source: E. Sivadas, "Europeans Have a Different Take on CS [Customer Satisfaction] Programs," Marketing News, October 26, 1998, p. 39. Reprinted by permission of the American Marketing Association.

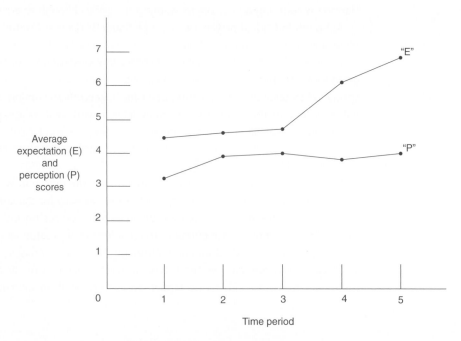

Marketing research practices that are developed in the United States are not always directly transferable to other cultures. Customer satisfaction measurement and CRM (Customer Relationship Management), both created in the United States, have relevance in other countries and geographies but must be adapted to key differences that require a deep understanding of culture. In this box, we discuss how customer research must be adapted in Europe and how CRM must be adapted in Asia.

CUSTOMER RESEARCH IN EUROPE

The industry of customer satisfaction measurement and research started in the United States and spread to Europe and other countries largely when U.S. companies moved their businesses into Europe. Although it would seem that the need for customer satisfaction measurement is universal and that importing practices for effective programs would be easy, key differences have surfaced between U.S. and European programs.

First, European companies are less likely than U.S. companies to have quality departments and therefore less likely to use customer satisfaction measurement as a way to make improvements across organizations. Instead, customer satisfaction is largely a marketing issue—a way to calibrate how effective the marketing mix for a service is—rather than a central issue from which all decisions about services stem. One negative result of this orientation is that nonmarketing problems identified in customer satisfaction research (such as operations and delivery issues) are often left unaddressed, frustrating the customer. Imagine how you would feel providing input about aspects of service that displease you, then having no changes take place! It is probably no surprise that response rates to surveys are also lower in Europe than in the United States; if nothing positive occurs as a result of filling out a survey, why should a customer do it?

Second, few European companies measure employee satisfaction or link employee compensation to customer satisfaction scores. Top management in U.S. companies, who have learned the value of customer service programs and their impact on front-line employees, buy into the idea of motivating employees with monetary incentives. European companies are less inclined to do so, perhaps resulting in the well-documented lower levels of motivation to provide service on the part of front-line personnel. European labor law also protects employees from employers who might penalize them for delivering poor customer service. One of the central causes of the early failure of Euro Disney was the unwillingness of French employees to adhere to service standards of dress, friendliness, and responsiveness.

Third, European attitudes toward service quality training are very different from those in the United States. Standardized employee training that results in consistent service delivery is viewed as artificial and uniquely American. European managers see this "one-size-fits-all" style of greeting and dealing with customers as a packaged approach to service delivery. The European approach is more individualistic—perhaps more genuine at times but also less predictable.

Fourth, and very problematic in developing effective customer satisfaction research in Europe, is that customers across countries are very different and respond inconsistently to the same research. Using the same survey across countries is not the most effective technique because respondents of different cultures require customized questions geared to their unique values and attitudes (as discussed in Chapter 3). Language, its structure, and conversational

continued

habits also differ, making results difficult to compare. Furthermore, researchers have documented that consumers differ in their levels of response to satisfaction questions. For example, respondents in southern Europe tend to claim that their satisfaction is higher than it is, while those in northern European countries tend to understate it. Comparing scores across countries is therefore very difficult—"a 90 percent satisfaction rate in Italy probably reflects less good performance than an 80 percent satisfaction score in Germany."

Any service company that plans to extend its offerings in Europe or elsewhere should be warned: merely taking U.S. research practices abroad will not gather valid information unless it takes into account these and other potential differences. Other international locations have their idiosyncrasies as well. What is a U.S. researcher to do? One of the best strategies is the same one found to work well in all international business: to involve managers and market research firms from host countries when conducting customer satisfaction studies abroad.

CUSTOMER RELATIONSHIP MANAGEMENT IN ASIA

Don Peppers and Martha Rogers, consultants in CRM and related areas, have noted the Western orientation of CRM and have emphasized that inherent values in the CRM literature do not reconcile with Asian values. Whereas CRM literature in the United States assumes that customers will "unerringly respond [on] the basis of self-interest and self-gratification," Asian values—such as delayed gratification, loyalty to family and clan, and *Guanxi* (networks of obligations and connections)—must be taken into account if CRM is to succeed in Asia. As the consultants point out, customer relationships are different in Asia in these ways:

- Language preferences are more complex in China than in the United States. Chinese/Malaysian customers may speak one Chinese dialect formally, transact business in Bahasa Malay, and complete legal documents in English. Knowing these differences customizes a relationship but very few CRM systems can accommodate this level of customization.

- Customer names are very different in societies that are racially diverse. Some names are very long and do not have surnames. Chinese names start with the last (family) names and then are followed by the first and second given names. As you probably are aware from your Chinese classmates, Chinese people also sometimes give themselves Western names. Recognizing all these differences is very difficult for a CRM system.

- Some Asian customers have more than one marriage, family, and address. Sending information, such as for life insurance or financial services, to the wrong address violates privacy and can create very difficult situations!

- Asians will rarely tell anyone their net worth because of a cultural bias against flaunting wealth. Therefore, it is difficult to find out which customers are most valuable based on their income.

For these and other reasons, CRM has been adopted much more slowly in Asia than in the United States.

Sources: E. Sivadas, "Europeans Have a Different Take on CS [Customer Satisfaction] Programs," *Marketing News,* October 26, 1998, p. 39; A. Berhad and T. Tyler, "Customer Relationship Management in Asia: A Cross Cultural Case Study Based on Aetna Universal Insurance," Peppers and Rogers Group, 2001.

FIGURE 6.4
Service Quality
Perceptions Relative
to Zones of Tolerance
by Dimensions

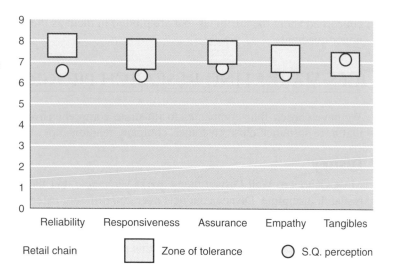

Importance/Performance Matrices

One of the most useful forms of analysis in marketing research is the importance/performance matrix. This chart combines information about customer perceptions and importance ratings. An example is shown in Figure 6.5. Attribute importance is represented on the vertical axis from high (top) to low (bottom). Performance is shown on the horizontal axis from low (left) to high (right). There are many variations of these matrices: Some companies define the horizontal axis as the gap between expectations and perceptions, or as performance relative to competition. The shading on the chart indicates the area of highest leverage for service quality improvements—where importance is high and performance is low. In this quadrant are the attributes that most need to be improved. In the adjacent upper quadrant are attributes to be maintained, ones that a company performs well and that are very important to customers. The lower two quadrants contain attributes that are less important, some of which are performed well and others poorly. Neither of these quadrants merit as much attention in terms of service improvements as the upper quadrants because customers are not as

FIGURE 6.5
Importance/
Performance Matrix

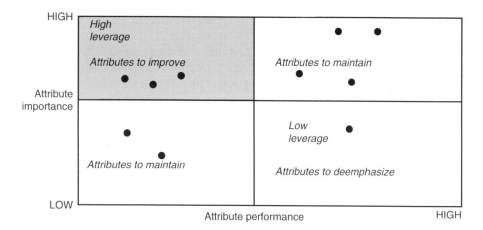

concerned about the attributes that are plotted in them as they are the attributes in the upper quadrants.

MODEL SERVICES MARKETING RESEARCH PROGRAMS

We have chosen four companies to illustrate comprehensive and effective programs that have sustained close customer–company relationships.

Disney

Most visitors to Walt Disney theme parks see magic, but the magic is based on solid research discipline. Disney conducts over 200 different external surveys a year, tracking satisfaction along with demographic profiles of its customers. The company also conducts price sensitivity analysis to determine the tolerance of guests for various levels of pricing. One recent outcome of this price sensitivity analysis was the FastPass, a premium-priced ticket to the park that allows its purchasers to avoid lines and expedite their access to rides and other attractions. The company also has guests evaluate its different attractions, noting the aspects that are pleasing or troublesome and changing aspects to ensure that the attractions run as smoothly as possible. In addition, the company monitors tens of thousands of letters and comment cards it receives and practices "management by walking around." By doing so, Disney gathers critical information that enables the design of a service experience that delights its guests.[18]

Intuit

Intuit, maker of the software *Quicken* and *Turbo Tax,* became successful in the extremely competitive software market by using a comprehensive marketing research strategy. The approach included focus groups of potential users, annual customer satisfaction surveys, new product feature testing, mystery shopping of dealers, intense listening to complaints, and a lifetime guarantee that served as a constant line of communication to find out what problems customers were having with their software. One of the more innovative approaches they used early in software development was a "follow me home" program, in which observers went to customers' homes and watched them install and use the program. The company involved customers in the design of its products, thereby opening a dialogue between customers and design engineers. Engineers also listened to technical support calls so that they fully understood problems in the words of the customer.

Federal Express

Federal Express, the first major service company to win the Malcolm Baldrige National Quality Award, has a strong and comprehensive program of marketing and customer satisfaction research.[19] Its program includes:

- Customer requirements and expectations, gleaned from multiple qualitative and quantitative research studies, feedback from sales professionals, and feedback from customer service professionals.

- Toll-free numbers for complaints, which are systematically captured and dispatched to responsible parties. Trends are also tracked and analyzed.

- Customer satisfaction studies, with objectives of assessing satisfaction, identifying reasons for dissatisfaction, and monitoring satisfaction over time. This involves

2,400 telephone interviews per quarter measuring 17 domestic service attributes, 22 export service attributes, eight drop-box attributes, and eight service center attributes.

- Ten targeted satisfaction studies on specialized business functions. These are direct-mail, self-administered surveys.

- Satisfaction monitoring at every point of interaction with the customer, some through transaction-based studies and others using operational measures driven by customer requirements.

- A comment card program, monitoring satisfaction with counter service.

- Customer satisfaction studies in world markets, focusing on understanding how service delivery must be adapted to global markets.

Continental Airlines

"Worst to first to favorite" is the way that Bonnie Reitz of Continental Airlines described the inside story of Continental Airline's business turnaround.[20] Key to the turnaround was the company's strategy of making Continental the best airline to fly by identifying the five most important attributes that customers expect:

- "I can ask any question and get a straight answer."

- "Continental employees deliver on their promises."

- "Continental employees appreciate my business."

- "Continental genuinely seeks and responds to suggestions and ideas."

- "Continental employees treat me like more than just another customer."

The company identified and focused on its most valuable customers, whom it called its Priority Elite. Using qualitative techniques, Continental identified what these customers wanted and how they felt when they were treated in special ways, such as when they were provided "eliteAccess" at the check-in line. Recognizing that employees were key to the change, the company used market research to identify the most critical attributes that created trust and then followed up the research with a program to motivate employees to deliver to customers. Every interaction with customers was identified, researched, and improved.

How well has the plan worked? Continental now gets consistent high ratings in the Department of Transportation metrics on on-time arrival and has been at or near the top in J. D. Power's customer satisfaction ratings in the airline industry.

USING MARKETING RESEARCH INFORMATION

Conducting research about customer expectations is only the first part of understanding the customer, even if the research is appropriately designed, executed, and presented. A service firm must also use the research findings in a meaningful way—to drive change or improvement in the way service is delivered. The misuse (or even nonuse) of research data can lead to a large gap in understanding customer expectations. When managers do not read research reports because they are too busy dealing with the day-to-day challenges of the business, companies fail to use the resources available to them. And when customers participate in marketing research studies but never see changes in the way the company does business, they feel frustrated and annoyed with the company. Understanding how to make the best use of research—to apply what has been learned to the business—is a key way to close the gap between customer expectations and management perceptions of customer expectations. Managers must learn to turn research information and insights into action, to recognize that the purpose of research is to drive improvement and customer satisfaction.

The research plan should specify the mechanism by which customer data will be used. The research should be actionable: timely, specific, and credible. It can also have a mechanism that allows a company to respond to dissatisfied customers immediately.

UPWARD COMMUNICATION

In some service firms, especially small and localized firms, owners or managers may be in constant contact with customers, thereby gaining firsthand knowledge of customer expectations and perceptions. But in large service organizations, managers do not always get the opportunity to experience firsthand what their customers want.

The larger a company is, the more difficult it will be for managers to interact directly with the customer and the less firsthand information they will have about customer expectations. Even when they read and digest research reports, managers can lose the reality of the customer if they never get the opportunity to experience the actual service. A theoretical view of how things are supposed to work cannot provide the richness of the service encounter. To truly understand customer needs, management benefits from hands-on knowledge of what really happens in stores, on customer service telephone lines, in service queues, and in face-to-face service encounters. If gap 1 is to be closed, managers in large firms need some form of customer contact.

Objectives for Upward Communication

Exhibit 6.3 shows the major research objectives for improving upward communication in an organization. These objectives include gaining firsthand knowledge about customers, improving internal service quality, gaining firsthand knowledge of employees, and obtaining ideas for service improvement. These objectives can be met by two types of interactive activities in the organization: one designed to improve the type and effectiveness of communications from customers to management, and the other designed to improve communications between employees and management.

Research for Upward Communication

Executive Visits to Customers

This approach is frequently used in business-to-business services marketing. In some visits, executives of the company make sales or service calls with customer contact personnel (salespeople). In other situations, executives of the selling company arrange meetings with executives at a similar level in client companies. When Lou Gerstner became CEO of IBM, one of his first actions was to arrange a meeting with 175 of the company's biggest customers for a discussion of how IBM can better meet their needs. The meeting was viewed as a signal that the new IBM would be more responsive and focused on the customer than it had become in the late 1980s and early 1990s.

Executive or Management Listening to Customers

The marketing director at Milliken, a U.S. textile and chemicals firm, called his experience working the swing shift "naive listening," and he described its benefits as follows:

Exhibit 6.3 ELEMENTS IN AN EFFECTIVE PROGRAM OF UPWARD COMMUNICATION

Type of Interaction or Research	Research Objective	Qualitative/ Quantitative	Cost of Information		
			Money	Time	Frequency
Executive visits to customers	To gain firsthand knowledge about customers	Qualitative	Moderate	Moderate	Continuous
Executive listenings	To gain firsthand knowledge about customers	Qualitative	Low	Low	Continuous
Research on intermediate customers	To gain in-depth information on end customers	Quantitative	Moderate	Moderate	Annual
Employee internal satisfaction surveys	To improve internal service quality	Quantitative	Moderate	Moderate	Annual
Employee visits or listenings	To gain firsthand knowledge about employees	Qualitative	Moderate	Moderate	Continuous
Employee suggestions	To obtain ideas for service improvements	Qualitative	Low	Low	Continuous

Getting close to the customer is a winner!…I worked the second shift (3:00 P.M. to midnight) and actually cleaned carpeting as well as hard-surface floors. I operated all the machinery they used daily, plus handled the same housekeeping problems.…Now I can put together my trade advertising as well as my entire merchandising program based directly upon the needs of my customers as I observed them.…I'm learning—from new-product introduction to maintenance of existing products—exactly what our health care customers require.[21]

As this example illustrates, direct interaction with customers adds clarity and depth to managers' understanding of customer expectations and needs.

Managers can also spend time on the line, interacting with customers and experiencing service delivery. A formal program for encouraging informal interaction is often the best way to ensure that the contact takes place. First National Bank of Chicago's survey process involves having senior managers, among them the senior vice president and his department heads, trained and certified to conduct survey interviews.

Research on Intermediate Customers

Intermediate customers (such as contact employees, dealers, distributors, agents, and brokers) are people the company serves who serve the end customer. Researching the needs and expectations of these customers *in serving the end customer* can be a useful and efficient way to both improve service to and obtain information about end users. The interaction with intermediate customers provides opportunities for understanding end customers' expectations and problems. It can also help the company learn about and satisfy the service expectations of intermediate customers, a process critical in their providing quality service to end customers.

Research on Internal Customers

Employees who perform services are themselves customers of internal services on which they depend heavily to do their jobs well. There is a strong and direct link between the quality of internal service that employees receive and the quality of service they provide to their own customers. For this reason it is important to conduct employee research that focuses on the service that internal customers give and receive. In many companies this focus requires adapting existing employee opinion research to focus on service satisfaction. Employee research complements customer research when service quality is the issue being investigated. Customer research provides insight into what is occurring, whereas employee research provides insight into why. The two types of research play unique and equally important roles in improving service quality. Companies that focus service quality research exclusively on external customers are missing a rich and vital source of information.[22]

Executive or Management Listening Approaches to Employees

Employees who actually perform the service have the best possible vantage point for observing the service and identifying impediments to its quality. Customer contact personnel are in regular contact with customers and thereby come to understand a great deal about customer expectations and perceptions.[23] If the information they know can be passed on to top management, top managers' understanding of the customer may improve. In fact, it could be said that in many companies, top management's understanding of the customer depends largely on the extent and types of communication received from customer contact personnel and from noncompany contact personnel (like independent insurance agents and retailers) who represent the company and its services. When these channels of communication are closed, management may not get feedback about problems encountered in service delivery and about how customer expectations are changing.

Sam Walton, the late founder of the highly successful discount retailer Wal-Mart, once remarked, "Our best ideas come from delivery and stock boys."[24] To stay in touch with the source of new ideas, Walton spent endless hours in stores working the floor, helping clerks, or approving personal checks, even showing up at the loading dock with a bag of doughnuts for a surprised crew of workers.[25] He was well known for having his plane drop him next to a wheat field where he would meet a Wal-Mart truck driver. Giving his pilot instructions to meet him at another landing strip 200 miles down the road, he would make the trip with the Wal-Mart driver, listening to what he had to say about the company.

Upward communication of this sort provides information to upper-level managers about activities and performances throughout the organization. Specific types of communication that may be relevant are formal (such as reports of problems and exceptions in service delivery) and informal (like discussions between contact personnel and upper-level managers). Managers who stay close to their contact people benefit not only by keeping their employees happy but also by learning more about their customers.[26] These companies encourage, appreciate, and reward upward communication from contact people. Through this important channel, management learns about customer expectations from employees in regular contact with customers and can thereby reduce the size of gap 1.

Employee Suggestions

Most companies have some form of employee suggestion program whereby contact personnel can communicate to management their ideas for improving work. Suggestion systems have come a long way from the traditional suggestion box. Effective suggestion systems are ones in which employees are empowered to see their suggestions through, where supervisors can implement proposals immediately, where employees participate for continuous improvement in their jobs, where supervisors respond quickly to ideas, and where coaching is provided in ways to handle suggestions. The National Association of Suggestion Systems (NASS) reports that U.S. companies receive fewer suggestions than do their counterparts in Japan and that the typical financial return for an idea in the United States is much higher than the return in Japan.[27] In today's companies, suggestions from employees are facilitated by self-directed work teams that encourage employees to identify problems and then work to develop solutions to those problems.

Summary

This chapter discussed the role of marketing research in understanding customer perceptions and expectations. After first describing criteria for effective services research, the chapter defined key forms of services research including critical incidents studies, mystery shopping, service expectation meetings and reviews, process checkpoint evaluations, and database research. Important topics in researching services—including developing research objectives and presenting data—were also described. Finally, upward communication, ways in which management obtains and uses information from customers and customer contact personnel, was discussed. These topics combine to close gap 1 between customer expectations and company understanding of customer expectations, the first of four provider gaps in the gaps model of service quality.

Discussion Questions

1. Give five reasons why research objectives must be established before marketing research is conducted.
2. Why are both qualitative and quantitative research methods needed in a services marketing research program?
3. Why does the frequency of research differ across the research methods shown in Exhibit 6.1?
4. Compare and contrast the types of research that help a company identify common failure points (see column 2 in Exhibit 6.1). Which of the types do you think produces better information? Why?
5. In what situations does a service company need requirements research?
6. What reasons can you give for companies' lack of use of research information? How might you motivate managers to use the information to a greater extent? How might you motivate front-line workers to use the information?
7. Given a specific marketing research budget, what would be your recommendations for the percentage to be spent on customer research versus upward communication? Why?
8. What kinds of information could be gleaned from research on intermediate customers? What would intermediate customers know that service providers might not?

9. For what types of products and services would research on the Internet be preferable to traditional research?

Exercises

1. Choose a local services organization to interview about marketing research. Find out what the firm's objectives are and the types of marketing research it currently uses. Using the information in this chapter, think about the effectiveness of its marketing research. What are the strengths? Weaknesses?

2. Choose one of the services you consume. If you were in charge of creating a survey for that service, what questions would you ask on the survey? Give several examples. What type of survey (relationship versus transaction based) would be most appropriate for the service? What recommendations would you give to management of the company about making such a survey actionable?

3. If you were the marketing director of your college or university, what types of research (see Exhibit 6.1) would be essential for understanding both external and internal customers? If you could choose only three types of research, which ones would you select? Why?

4. Using the SERVQUAL scale in this chapter, create a questionnaire for a service firm that you use. Give the questionnaire to 10 people, and describe what you learn.

5. To get an idea of the power of the critical incidents technique, try it yourself with reference to restaurant service. Think of a time when, as a customer, you had a particularly satisfying interaction with a restaurant. Follow the instructions here, which are identical to the instructions in an actual study, and observe the insights you obtain about your requirements in restaurant service:
   a. When did the incident happen?
   b. What specific circumstances led up to this situation?
   c. Exactly what did the employee (or firm) say or do?
   d. What resulted that made you feel the interaction was satisfying?
   e. What could or should have been done differently?

Notes

1. J. McGregor, "Customers First: 2004 Fast Company Customers First Awards," Fast Company, October 2004, 79–88.
2. Ibid.
3. A. Parasuraman, L. L. Berry, and V. A. Zeithaml, "Guidelines for Conducting Service Quality Research," *Marketing Research: A Magazine of Management and Applications,* December 1990, pp. 34–44.
4. This section is based on a comprehensive assessment of the critical incident technique in D. D. Gremler, "The Critical Incident Technique in Service Research," *Journal of Service Research* 7 (August 2004), pp. 65–89.
5. Ibid.
6. E. E. Lueke and T. W. Suther III, "Market-Driven Quality: A Market Research and Product Requirements Methodology," *IBM Technical Report* (June 1991).
7. J. Carey, J. Buckley, and J. Smith, "Hospital Hospitality," *Newsweek,* February 11, 1985, p. 78.
8. See V. A. Zeithaml and A. Parasuraman, *Service Quality,* MSI Relevant Knowledge Series (Cambridge, MA: Marketing Science Institute, 2004) for a complete review of this research, including the many publications by the original authors of SERVQUAL and the extensions by other authors.

9. J. M. Farley, C. F. Daniels, and D. H. Pearl, "Service Quality in a Multinational Environment," *Proceedings of the ASQC Quality Congress Transactios,* San Francisco, CA, 1990.

10. E. Day, "Researchers Must Enter Consumer's World," *Marketing News,* August 17, 1998, p. 17.

11. G. Khermouch, "Consumers in the Mist," *BusinessWeek,* February 26, 2001, pp. 92–93.

12. Ibid., p. 92.

13. For examples, see S. J. Grove and R. P. Fiske, "Observational Data Collection Methods for Services Marketing: An Overview," *Journal of the Academy of Marketing Science* 20 (Summer 1992), pp. 117–214.

14. "Knowing What It Takes to Keep (or Lose) Your Best Customers," *Executive Report on Customer Satisfaction* 5 (October 30, 1992).

15. P. R. Magnusson, J. Mathing, and P. Kristensson, "Managing User Involvement in Service Innovation: Experiments with Innovating End Users," *Journal of Service Research* 2003 6 (November 2003), pp. 111–24.

16. V. A. Zeithaml, A. Parasuraman, and L. L. Berry, *Delivering Quality Service: Balancing Customer Perceptions and Expectations* (New York: Free Press, 1990), p. 28.

17. A. Parasuraman, V. A. Zeithaml, and L. L. Berry, "Moving Forward in Service Quality Research," *Marketing Science Institute Report No. 94-114,* September 1994.

18. R. Johnson, "A Strategy for Service—Disney Style," *Journal of Business Strategy* (September–October 1991), pp. 38–43.

19. "Multiple Measures Give FedEx Its 'Good' Data," *The Service Edge,* June 1991, p. 6.

20. B. Reitz (presentation at Conference on Customer Management sponsored by the Marketing Science Institute, Durham, NC, March 4–5, 2004).

21. T. J. Peters and N. Austin, *A Passion for Excellence* (New York: Random House, 1985), p. 16.

22. "Baldridge Winner Co-Convenes Quality Summit," *Executive Report on Customer Satisfaction,* October 30, 1992.

23. M. J. Bitner, B. Booms, and L. Mohr, "Critical Service Encounters: The Employee's Viewpoint," *Journal of Marketing* 58 (October 1994), pp. 95–106.

24. S. Koepp, "Make That Sale, Mr. Sam," *Time,* May 18, 1987.

25. Ibid.

26. Zeithaml, Parasuraman, and Berry, *Delivering Quality Service,* p. 64.

27. "Empowerment Is the Strength of Effective Suggestion Systems," *Total Quality Newsletter,* August 1991.

7

Building Customer Relationships

This chapter's objectives are to

1. Explain relationship marketing, its goals, and the benefits of long-term relationships for firms and customers.

2. Explain why and how to estimate customer relationship value.

3. Introduce the concept of customer profitability segments as a strategy for focusing relationship marketing efforts.

4. Present relationship development strategies—including quality core service, switching barriers, and relationship bonds.

5. Identify challenges in relationship development, including the somewhat controversial idea that "the customer is not always right."

USAA Focuses on Long-Term Relationships

USAA is a preeminent example of a company focused on building long-term relationships with customers.[1] Customer retention has been a core value of the company since long before customer loyalty became a popular business concept. In business since 1922, USAA provides for the insurance needs of a highly targeted market segment: current and former U.S. military personnel and their families. Headquartered in San Antonio, Texas, USAA owns and manages more than $60 billion in assets. It consistently appears on *Fortune* magazine's list of the 100 best companies to work for in America, and customer retention figures approach 100 percent. In fact, the most likely reason for a customer to leave the company is death.

The goal of the company is to "think about the events in the life of a career officer and then work out ways to help him get through them." The company is intent on serving its current customer base and growing with them. To do this, USAA relies heavily on extensive customer research through surveys and a member advisory board that meets regularly with executives. The company also focuses on retaining the best employees and rewarding them for customer-oriented objectives such as percentage of customer questions or requests that are handled on the first call with no need for follow-up. USAA believes so strongly in the importance of customer retention that managers' and executives' own bonuses are based on this metric.

A striking example of how USAA gives priority to the needs of its existing customers occurred during the Gulf War. Anticipating the needs of those who were sent to the Gulf, the company encouraged them to *downgrade* their automobile insurance to save themselves money. For instance, if their cars were just going to sit in garages while they were gone, they would not need liability coverage. And when two-car families had one spouse in the Gulf, USAA gave them the rates for a single person with two cars. Although this approach obviously cost USAA immediate dollars, actions such as these clearly indicate USAA's commitment to its current members, serving to ensure their loyalty and grow their business over time.

The commitment to customer retention and employees is reflected in what USAA refers to as the *loyalty chain:*

> If you don't take care of the employees, they can't take care of the customers. We give employees all they need to be happy and absolutely enthralled to be here. If they are unhappy, we will not have satisfied customers in the long run. . . . We must have a passion for customers. If we don't, we are in the wrong business. Our members have served our country, and we want to serve them. We take them seriously. We always ask, "What is the impact on our members?"[2]

USAA provides a strong example of a company that has focused on keeping its customers and building long-term relationships with them. Unlike the USAA example, however, many companies fail to understand customers accurately because they fail to focus on customer relationships. They tend to fixate on acquiring new customers rather than viewing customers as assets that they need to nurture and retain. By concentrating on new customers, firms can easily fall into the traps of short-term promotions, price discounts, or catchy ads that bring customers in but are not enough to bring them back. By adopting a relationship philosophy, on the other hand, companies begin to understand customers over time and in great depth and are better able to meet their changing needs and expectations.

Marketing strategies for understanding customers over time and building long-term relationships are the subjects of this chapter.

RELATIONSHIP MARKETING

> There has been a shift from a transactions to a relationship focus in marketing. Customers become partners and the firm must make long-term commitments to maintaining those relationships with quality, service, and innovation.[3]

Relationship marketing essentially represents a paradigm shift within marketing—away from an acquisitions/transaction focus toward a retention/relationship focus.[4] Relationship marketing (or relationship management) is a philosophy of doing business, a strategic orientation, that focuses on *keeping and improving* relationships with current customers rather than on acquiring new customers. This philosophy assumes that many consumers and business customers prefer to have an ongoing relationship with one organization than to switch continually among providers in their search for value. Building on this assumption and the fact that it is usually much cheaper to keep a current customer than to attract a new one, successful marketers are working on effective strategies for retaining customers. Our opening example showed how USAA has built its business around a relationship philosophy.

It has been suggested that firms frequently focus on attracting customers (the "first act") but then pay little attention to what they should do to keep them (the "second act").[5] Ideas expressed in an interview with James L. Schorr, then executive vice president of marketing at Holiday Inns, illustrate this point.[6] In the interview he stated that he was famous at Holiday Inns for what is called the "bucket theory of marketing." By this he meant that marketing can be thought of as a big bucket: It is what the sales, advertising, and promotion programs do that pours business into the top of the bucket. As long as these programs are effective, the bucket stays full. However, "There's only one problem," he said, "there's a hole in the bucket." When the business is running well and the hotel is delivering on its promises, the hole is small and few customers are leaving. When the operation is weak and customers are not satisfied with what they get, however, people start falling out of the bucket through the holes faster than they can be poured in through the top.

The bucket theory illustrates why a relationship strategy that focuses on plugging the holes in the bucket makes so much sense. Historically, marketers have been more concerned with acquisition of customers, so a shift to a relationship strategy often represents changes in mind set, organizational culture, and employee reward systems. For example, the sales incentive systems in many organizations are set up to reward bringing in new customers. There are often fewer (or no) rewards for retaining current accounts. Thus, even when people see the logic of customer retention, the existing organizational systems may not support its implementation.

The Evolution of Customer Relationships

Firms' relationships with their customers, like other social relationships, tend to evolve over time. Scholars have suggested that marketing exchange relationships between providers and customers often have the potential to evolve from strangers to acquaintances to friends to partners. Exhibit 7.1 illustrates different issues at each successive level of the relationship.[7]

Customers as Strangers

Strangers are those customers who are not aware of or, perhaps, those who have not yet had any transactions (interactions) with a firm. At the industry level, strangers may be conceptualized as customers who have not yet entered the market; at the firm level, they may include customers of competitors. Clearly the firm has no relationship with the customer at this point. Consequently, the firm's primary goal with these potential customers ("strangers") is to initiate communication with them in order to *attract* them and *acquire* their business. Thus, the primary marketing efforts directed toward such customers deal with familiarizing those potential customers with the firm's offerings and, subsequently, encouraging them to give the firm a try.

Customers as Acquaintances

Once customer awareness and trial are achieved, familiarity is established and the customer and the firm become acquaintances, creating the basis for an exchange relationship. A primary goal for the firm at this stage of the relationship is *satisfying* the customer. In the acquaintance stage, firms are generally concerned about providing a value proposition to customers that is comparable with that of competitors. For a customer, an acquaintanceship is effective as long as the customer is relatively satisfied

Exhibit 7.1 A Typology of Exchange Relationships

Customers as...	Strangers	Acquaintances	Friends	Partners
Product offering	Attractive relative to competitive offerings or alternative purchases.	Parity product as a form of industry standard.	Differentiated product adapted to specific market segments.	Customized product and dedicated resources adapted to an individual customer or organization.
Source of competitive advantage	Attractiveness	Satisfaction	Satisfaction + trust	Satisfaction + trust + commitment
Buying activity	Interest, exploration, and trial.	Satisfaction facilitates and reinforces buying activity and reduces need to search for market information.	Trust in firm is needed to continue the buying activity without perfect information.	Commitment in the form of information sharing and idiosyncratic investments is needed to achieve customized product and to adjust product continuously to changing needs and situations.
Focus of selling activities	Awareness of firm's offerings (encouraging trial) facilitates initial selling.	Familiarity and general knowledge of customer (identification) facilitates selling.	Specific knowledge of customer's connection to segment need and situation facilitates selling.	Specific knowledge of customer's need and situation and idiosyncratic investments facilitates selling.
Relationship time horizon	None: Buyer may have had no previous interactions with or knowledge of the firm.	Short: Generally short because the buyer can often switch firms without much effort or cost.	Medium: Generally longer than acquaintance relationships because trust in a differentiated position takes a longer time to build and imitate.	Long: Generally long because it takes time to build and replace interconnected activities and to develop a detailed knowledge of a customer's needs and the unique resources of a supplier to commit resources to the relationship.

continued

179

Exhibit 7.1 A TYPOLOGY OF EXCHANGE RELATIONSHIPS—CONTINUED

Customers as...	Strangers	Acquaintances	Friends	Partners
Sustainability of competitive advantage	Low: Generally low, as firm must continually find ways to be attractive, in terms of the value offered, in order to induce trial.	Low: Generally low, but competitors can vary in how they build unique value into selling and serving even if the product is a form of industry standard.	Medium: Generally medium but depends on competitors' ability to understand heterogeneity of customer needs and situations and the ability to transform this knowledge into meaningful, differentiated products.	High: Generally high but depends on how unique and effective the interconnected activities between customer and supplier are organized.
Primary relationship marketing goal	*Acquire* customer's business.	*Satisfy* customer's needs and wants.	*Retain* customer's business.	*Enhance* relationship with customer.

Source: Adapted from M. D. Johnson and F. Seines, "Customer Portfolio Management: Toward a Dynamic Theory of Exchange Relationships," *Journal of Marketing* 68 (April 2004), p. 5. Reprinted by permission of the American Marketing Association.

and what is being received in the exchange is perceived as fair value. With repetitive interactions, the customer gains experience and becomes more familiar with the firm's product offerings. These encounters can help reduce uncertainty about the benefits expected in the exchange and, therefore, increase the attractiveness of the company relative to the competition. Repetitive interactions improve the firm's knowledge of the customer, helping to facilitate marketing, sales, and service efforts. Thus, an acquaintance relationship facilitates transactions primarily through the reduction of the customer's perceived risk and the provider's costs.

In acquaintance relationships, firms generally focus on providing value comparable to the competition, often through the repetitive provision of standardized offerings. As a result, for a firm in such a relationship with a customer, the potential to develop a sustainable competitive advantage through relationship activities is limited. However, firms that have many such relationships with their customers can create value for acquaintances by learning from all their transactions. For example, Amazon.com has created value for its acquaintances through a highly developed order processing system. By processing and organizing historical transaction data from a customer and comparing it with data from other customers demonstrating similar purchase behaviors, the system is able to identify additional products of potential interest to the acquaintance customer and to generate cross-selling opportunities.

Customers as Friends

As a customer continues to make purchases from a firm and to receive value in the exchange relationship, the firm begins to acquire specific knowledge of the customer's needs, allowing it to create an offering that directly addresses the customer's situation. The provision of a unique offering, and thus differential value, transforms the exchange relationship from acquaintance to friendship. This transition from acquaintanceship to friendship, particularly in service exchange relationships, requires the development of trust.[8] As discussed in an earlier chapter, customers may not be able to assess a service outcome prior to purchase and consumption, and for those services high in credence qualities, customers may not be able to discern service performance even after experiencing it. Therefore, customers must trust the provider to do what is promised. As customers become friends they not only become familiar with the company but also come to trust that it provides superior value.

A primary goal for firms at the friendship stage of the relationship is customer *retention*. Given their likelihood of past satisfying experiences and repeated purchases, these customers ("friends") are more likely to appreciate the firm's product offerings and are, perhaps, more open to other related services. A firm's potential to develop sustainable competitive advantage through friends should be higher than for acquaintances, because the offering is more unique (and more difficult for competition to imitate) and the customer comes to trust that uniqueness.[9]

Customers as Partners

As a customer continues to interact with a firm, the level of trust often deepens and the customer may receive more customized product offerings and interactions. The trust developed in the friendship stage is a necessary but not sufficient condition for a customer–firm partnership to develop.[10] That is, the creation of trust leads to (ideally) the creation of commitment—and that is the condition necessary for customers to extend the time perspective of a relationship.[11] The deepening of trust and the establishment of commitment reduce the customer's need to solve problems in the traditional sense of "finding a better alternative." Thus, in order to move the relationship into a partner relationship, a firm must use customer knowledge and information systems to deliver highly personalized and customized offerings.

The key to success in the partnership stage is the firm's ability to organize and use information about individual customers more effectively than competitors. Customers benefit from, and therefore desire to commit to, relationships with firms whose knowledge of their needs enables them to deliver highly personalized and customized offerings.[12] Over time, the customer–firm relationship may evolve through continuous adaptation and commitment, and the parties may become increasingly interdependent. At this point the relationship has advanced from having the purpose of merely meeting the customer's needs to a situation in which both parties sense a deep appreciation of each other. However, in order to continue to receive such benefits, customers generally must be willing to pay a price premium or to commit themselves to the firm for an extended period of time. For an annual membership fee of $50, Hertz #1 Club Gold customers have personal data and rental preferences stored in their database. Among the many benefits Hertz Gold customers receive are guaranteed availability of a car, separate counters where all they have to do is show their driver's license in order to receive the car keys, and paperwork that is already completed because their signature is on file.

At the partnership stage, the firm is concerned with *enhancing* the relationship. Customers are more likely to stay in the relationship if they feel that the company understands their changing needs and is willing to invest in the relationship by constantly improving and evolving its product and service mix. By enhancing these relationships, the firm expects such customers to be less likely to be lured away by competitors and more likely to buy additional products and services from the company over time. These loyal customers not only provide a solid base for the organization, they may represent growth potential. This is certainly true for USAA, our opening example in this chapter, whose officer members' needs for insurance increase over their lifetimes as well as the lifetimes of their children. Other examples abound. A bank checking account customer becomes a better customer when she sets up a savings account, takes out a loan, and/or uses the financial advising services of the bank. And a corporate account becomes a better customer when it chooses to do 75 percent of its business with a particular supplier rather than splitting the business equally among three suppliers. In recent years, in fact, many companies have aspired to be the "exclusive supplier" of a particular product or service for their customers. Over time these enhanced relationships can increase market share and profits for the organization. Our Technology Spotlight features two very different companies, NewsEdge and Ritz-Carlton, that are successfully using information technology to enhance relationships with their customers.

The Goal of Relationship Marketing

The discussion of the evolution of customer relationships demonstrates how a firm's relationship with its customers might be enhanced as customers move further along this relationship continuum. As the relationship value of a customer increases, the provider is more likely to pursue a closer relationship. Thus, the primary goal of relationship marketing is *to build and maintain a base of committed customers who are profitable for the organization.* Figure 7.1 graphically illustrates the goals of relationship marketing. The overriding goal is to move customers up the ladder (that is, along the relationship continuum) from the point at which they are strangers that need to be attracted through to the point at which they are highly valued, long-term customers whose relationship with the firm has been enhanced. From a customer's problem-solving perspective, the formation of satisfaction, trust, and commitment corresponds to the customer's willingness to engage in an exchange relationship as an acquaintance, friend, and partner, respectively. From a firm's resource-allocation perspective, the delivery of differential, and perhaps customized, value corresponds to the extent of its ability and/or desire to create an acquaintance, friend, or partner relationship with

FIGURE 7.1
Customer goals of relationship marketing: acquiring customers, satisfying customers, retaining customers, and enhancing customers.

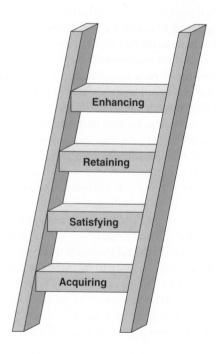

Technology Spotlight
Customer Information Systems Help Enhance the Customer Relationship

The potential of today's customer information systems far exceeds any traditional marketing information system that has gone before. These new systems differ from the old in their scale (thousands of bits of information on tens of millions of customers), the depth of information that can be captured on each individual or household, and the ways in which the information can be used. In many cases, access to this type of information about individual customers allows the organization to customize to the individual level what previously would have been undifferentiated services.

For example, the Ritz-Carlton Hotel Company, winner of the 1992 Malcolm Baldrige National Quality Award, targets its services to industry executives, meeting and corporate travel planners, and affluent travelers. Although there are many dimensions to the company's success, one of the keys is the quality of its customer database. By training each employee to note the likes and dislikes of regular guests and to enter this information immediately into the customer's file, employees at any Ritz-Carlton Hotel are able to personalize services to the Ritz-Carlton's 240,000 repeat customers. The employees can know in advance the guest's preferences and be prepared to provide individualized service even before the guest's arrival. For example, if a guest prefers a feather pillow, wants extra brown sugar with her oatmeal, or always orders a glass of sherry before retiring, this information can be entered into the database and these needs anticipated—often much to the guest's surprise.

In a very different realm, NewsEdge is a leader in an industry that gives business customers customized news and information based on individual client needs and preferences. NewsEdge is a $71 million company that provides real-time news and information products and services to approximately 1,500 corporations and professional service firms worldwide. This information can be provided to websites, company intranets, or directly to employees. The need addressed by this industry is the "information overload" that exists in our modern world, combined with corporations' desires for their people to be up-to-date on industry-specific news. (Note that whereas NewsEdge focuses on corporate clients, Dow Jones provides a similar service for individual consumers.) NewsEdge content is individually tailored to its corporate clients' specified needs as identified and tracked in its customer database. Using sophisticated technology as well as human content experts, NewsEdge sifts through hundreds of premier information sources in thousands of topic categories and then provides tailored real-time content to clients. Clients are corporations or professional service firms who want their employees to have access to particular types of breaking news. In addition to individual corporate clients, other customers of NewsEdge include online information providers, such as Lycos Small Business (a comprehensive online resource for small businesses), that purchase NewsEdge services to provide relevant news and information for small businesses that they could not afford to supply individually. In 2001 The Thomson Corporation acquired NewsEdge.

Sources: "1992 Award Winner," publication of the Ritz-Carlton Hotel Company; www.newsedge.com, 2001.

the customer. As customers make the transition from satisfaction-based acquaintanceships to trust-based friendships to commitment-based partnerships, increases are required in both the value received and the level of cooperation.

Benefits for Customers and Firms

Both parties in the customer–firm relationship can benefit from customer retention. That is, it is not only in the best interest of the organization to build and maintain a loyal customer base, but customers themselves also benefit from long-term associations.

Benefits for Customers

Assuming they have a choice, customers will remain loyal to a firm when they receive greater value relative to what they expect from competing firms. *Value* represents a trade-off for the consumer between the "give" and the "get" components. Consumers are more likely to stay in a relationship when the gets (quality, satisfaction, specific benefits) exceed the gives (monetary and nonmonetary costs). When firms can consistently deliver value from the customer's point of view, clearly the customer benefits and has an incentive to stay in the relationship.

Beyond the specific inherent benefits of receiving service value, customers also benefit in other ways from long-term associations with firms. Sometimes these relationship benefits keep customers loyal to a firm more than the attributes of the core service. Research has uncovered specific types of relational benefits that customers experience in long-term service relationships including confidence benefits, social benefits, and special treatment benefits.[13]

Confidence Benefits Confidence benefits comprise feelings of trust or confidence in the provider along with a sense of reduced anxiety and comfort in knowing what to expect. Across all the services studied in the research just cited, confidence benefits were the most important to customers.

Human nature is such that most consumers would prefer not to change service providers, particularly when there is a considerable investment in the relationship. The costs of switching are frequently high in terms of dollar costs of transferring business and the associated psychological and time-related costs. Most consumers (whether individuals or businesses) have many competing demands for their time and money and are continually searching for ways to balance and simplify decision making to improve the quality of their lives. When they can maintain a relationship with a service provider, they free up time for other concerns and priorities.

Social Benefits Over time, customers develop a sense of familiarity and even a social relationship with their service providers. These ties make it less likely that they will switch, even if they learn about a competitor that might have better quality or a lower price. This customer's description of her hair stylist in a quote from the research just cited illustrates the concept of social benefits: "I like him. . . . He's really funny and always has lots of good jokes. He's kind of like a friend now. . . . It's more fun to deal with somebody that you're used to. You enjoy doing business with them."

In some long-term customer–firm relationships, a service provider may actually become part of the consumer's social support system.[14] Hairdressers, as in the example just cited, often serve as personal confidants. Less common examples include proprietors of local retail stores who become central figures in neighborhood networks; the health club or restaurant manager who knows her customers personally; the private school principal who knows an entire family and its special needs; or the river guide who befriends patrons on a long rafting trip.[15]

These types of personal relationships can develop for business-to-business customers as well as for end consumers of services. The social support benefits resulting from these relationships are important to the consumer's quality of life (personal and/or work life) above and beyond the technical benefits of the service provided. Many times the close personal and professional relationships that develop between service providers and clients are the basis for the customer's loyalty. The flip side of this customer benefit is the risk to the firm of losing customers when a valued employee leaves the firm and takes customers with him or her.[16]

Special Treatment Benefits Special treatment includes getting the benefit of the doubt, being given a special deal or price, or getting preferential treatment as exemplified by the following quotes from the research:

I think you get special treatment [when you have established a relationship]. My pediatrician allowed me to use the back door to the office so my daughter could avoid contact with other sick children. Other times I have been in a hurry and they take me right back.

You should get the benefit of the doubt in many situations. For example, I always pay my VISA bill on time, before a service charge is assessed. One time my payment didn't quite arrive on time. When I called them, by looking at my past history, they realized that I always make an early payment. Therefore, they waived the service charge.

Interestingly, the special treatment benefits, while important, were less important than the other types of benefits received in service relationships. Although special treatment benefits can clearly be critical for customer loyalty in some industries (think of frequent flyer benefits in the airline industry), they seem to be less important to customers overall.

Benefits for Firms

The benefits to organizations of maintaining and developing a loyal customer base are numerous. In addition to the economic benefits that a firm receives from cultivating close relationships with its customers, a variety of customer behavior benefits and human resource management benefits are also often received.

Economic Benefits   Research based on information contained in the Compustat and Compact Disclosure databases reveals that over the long run, relationship-oriented service firms achieve higher overall returns on their investments than do transaction-oriented firms.[17] These bottom-line benefits come from a variety of sources, including increased revenues over time from the customer, reduced marketing and administrative costs, and the ability to maintain margins without reducing prices.

One of the most commonly cited economic benefits of customer retention is increased purchases over time, as illustrated in Figure 7.2. The figure summarizes results of studies showing that across industries customers generally spent more each year with a particular relationship partner than they did in the preceding period.[18] As customers get to know a firm and are satisfied with the quality of its services relative to that of its competitors, they tend to give more of their business to the firm.

Another economic benefit is lower costs. Some estimates suggest that repeat purchases by established customers require as much as 90 percent less marketing expenditure.[19] Many start-up costs are associated with attracting new customers, including advertising and other promotion costs, the operating costs of setting up new accounts, and time costs of getting to know the customers. Sometimes these initial costs can outweigh the revenue expected from the new customers in the short term, so it is to the firm's advantage to cultivate long-term relationships. Even ongoing relationship maintenance costs are likely to drop over time. For example, early in a relationship a customer is likely to have questions and encounter problems as he or she learns to use the service; an experienced customer will likely have fewer problems and questions, and the firm will incur fewer costs in serving the customer. In Chapter 18 we will provide more specifics on the financial impact of customer retention.

Customer Behavior Benefits   The contribution that loyal customers make to a service business can go well beyond their direct financial impact on the firm.[20] The first, and maybe the most easily recognized, customer behavior benefit that a firm receives from long-term customers is the free advertising provided through word-of-mouth communication. When a product is complex and difficult to evaluate and when risk is involved in the decision to buy it—as is the case with many services—consumers

FIGURE 7.2
Profit Generated by a Customer over Time

Source: Adapted and reprinted by permission of *Harvard Business Review*. An exhibit from "Zero Defection: Quality Comes to Services," by F. F. Reichheld and W. E. Sasser, Jr., September–October 1990. Copyright © 1990 by the Harvard Business School Publishing Corporation; all rights reserved.

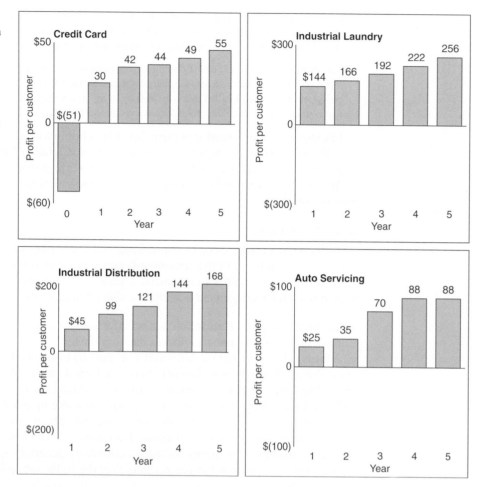

often look to others for advice on which providers to consider. Satisfied, loyal customers are likely to provide a firm with strong word-of-mouth endorsements. This form of advertising can be more effective than any paid advertising that the firm might use, and it has the added benefit of reducing the costs of attracting new customers. Indeed, loyal customers often talk a great deal about a company and may generate much new business over the years.

In addition to word-of-mouth communication, a second consumer behavior benefit is one that is sometimes labeled customer voluntary performance;[21] in a restaurant, such behavior might include customers busing their own tables, reporting messy restrooms to an employee, or picking up trash in the parking lot. Such behaviors support the firm's ability to deliver quality services. Although customer voluntary performance could be engaged in by anyone, those customers who have a long-term relationship with the firm are perhaps more likely to do so because they may want to see the provider do well. Third, for some services loyal customers may provide social benefits to other customers in the form of friendships or encouragement. At a physical therapy clinic, for example, a patient who is recovering from knee surgery is likely to think more highly of the clinic when fellow patients provide encouragement and emotional support to the patient during the rehabilitation process. Finally, loyal customers may serve as mentors and, because of their experience with the provider, help other customers understand the explicitly or implicitly stated rules of conduct.[22]

Human Resource Management Benefits   Loyal customers may also provide a firm with human resource management benefits. First, loyal customers may, because of their experience with and knowledge of the provider, be able to contribute to the co-production of the service by assisting in service delivery; often the more experienced customers can make the service employees' job easier. For example, a regular patient of a medical service provider is likely to know how the system works; she would know to bring her medication with her on a visit, to plan on paying by check (having previously learned that the office cannot process credit cards), and to schedule an annual mammogram without waiting for her doctor to prompt her. A second benefit relates to one of the benefits for customers that we have already discussed. We noted that loyal customers receive social benefits as a result of being in a relationship with a firm; employees who regularly interact with the same customers may also receive similar social benefits.[23] A third benefit of customer retention is employee retention. It is easier for a firm to retain employees when it has a stable base of satisfied customers. People like to work for companies whose customers are happy and loyal. Their jobs are more satisfying, and they are able to spend more of their time fostering relationships than scrambling for new customers. In turn, customers are more satisfied and become even better customers—a positive upward spiral. Because employees stay with the firm longer, service quality improves and costs of turnover are reduced, adding further to profits.

RELATIONSHIP VALUE OF CUSTOMERS

Relationship value of a customer is a concept or calculation that looks at customers from the point of view of their lifetime revenue and/or profitability contributions to a company. This type of calculation is obviously needed when companies start thinking of building long-term relationships with their customers. Just what is the potential financial value of those long-term relationships? And what are the financial implications of *losing* a customer? Here we will first summarize the factors that influence a customer's relationship value, and then show some ways it can be estimated. In Chapter 18 we provide more detail on lifetime value financial calculations.

Factors That Influence Relationship Value

The lifetime or relationship value of a customer is influenced by the length of an average "lifetime," the average revenues generated per relevant time period over the lifetime, sales of additional products and services over time, referrals generated by the customer over time, and costs associated with serving the customer. *Lifetime value* sometimes refers to lifetime revenue stream only; but most often when costs are considered, lifetime value truly means "lifetime profitability." Exhibit 7.2 provides an example of some factors that could be considered when calculating the potential relationship value of a Quicken (personal finance) software customer.

Estimating Customer Lifetime Value

If companies knew how much it really costs to lose a customer, they would be able to accurately evaluate investments designed to retain customers. One way of documenting the dollar value of loyal customers is to estimate the increased value or profits that

Exhibit 7.2 CALCULATING THE RELATIONSHIP VALUE OF A QUICKEN CUSTOMER

Intuit Corporation's Quicken Software for personal finance can be purchased for about $50.* However, the relationship value of a Quicken customer to Intuit is potentially much more. How can this be? First, consider the additional products available to Quicken customers. Once a customer gets hooked on using the software, there are several other Quicken products she might find appealing. For example, Quicken provides a bill-paying service for $10 per month. Quicken customers can print their own checks ($58 for a box of 250) and send them in envelopes that can also be purchased from Quicken ($38 for a box of 250). For about $40, Quicken customers can purchase TurboTax, a software product that can automatically use previously created Quicken data to prepare federal and state income tax returns. Quicken provides customers with the option to do an automatic backup of the customer's data files on Intuit's website, Quicken.com, for $8 per month. If a customer uses all these services, the revenue generated in just one year would be $402. (Intuit provides several other services, such as small business accounting software and home mortgages, that might be of interest to Quicken customers. Quicken also offers its customers a credit card; there is no annual fee, but the card has the potential to generate revenues from interest payments on outstanding balances.) After the first year, a satisfied Quicken customer is likely to continue to purchase annual software updates to acquire the latest product features and tax information. Over the course of five years, the revenue generated from this single customer would be more than $2,000. Finally, Quicken's satisfied customers are likely to refer new customers to Intuit, thus further enhancing the value of the initial customer relationship. Even one new customer referral per year can increase the relationship value potential of the first customer to several thousand dollars in just a few years!

*Figures in this example are based on 2004 prices as listed on http://www.intuit.com.

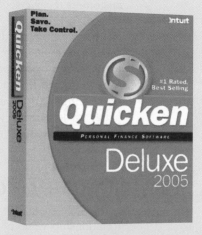

accrue for each additional customer who remains loyal to the company rather than defecting to the competition. This is what Bain & Co. has done for a number of industries, as shown in Figure 7.3.[24] The figure shows the percentage of increase in total firm profits when the retention or loyalty rate rises by 5 percentage points. The increases are dramatic, ranging from 35 to 95 percent. These increases were calculated by comparing the net present values of the profit streams for the average customer life at current retention rates with the net present values of the profit streams for the average customer life at 5 percent higher retention rates.

With sophisticated accounting systems to document actual costs and revenue streams over time, a firm can be quite precise in documenting the dollar value and costs of retaining customers. These systems attempt to estimate the dollar value of *all* the benefits and costs associated with a loyal customer, not just the long-term revenue stream. The value of word-of-mouth advertising, employee retention, and declining account maintenance costs can also enter into the calculation.[25]

For example, Table 7.1 shows how First Data Corporation estimates the lifetime value of an average business customer at its TeleCheck International subsidiary (prod-

FIGURE 7.3
Profit Impact of 5 Percent Increase in Retention Rate

Source: Reprinted with permission of the American Marketing Association. From F. F. Reichheld, "Loyalty and the Renaissance of Marketing," *Marketing Management,* vol. 2, no. 4 (1994), p. 15.

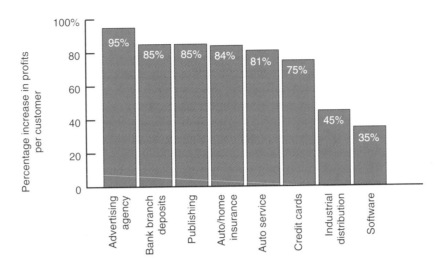

uct names and data are disguised in the table). TeleCheck is a large check acceptance company that provides a range of financial services for business customers related to check guarantees, verifications, and collection services. By including estimates over a five-year lifetime of increased revenues from its core product (QuickResponse), declining per-unit service costs, increasing revenues from a new product (FastTrack), and profit from referrals, the company estimated that an annual increase in revenue of 20 percent on its base product would result in a 33 percent annual increase in operating profit over a five-year customer life.[26]

TABLE 7.1 **Lifetime Value of an Average Business Customer at Telecheck International**

	Year 0	Year 1	Year 2	Year 3	Year 4	Year 5
Revenue:[a]						
QuickResponse	—	$33,000	$39,600	$47,520	$57,024	$68,429
FastTrack	—	—	5,500	6,600	7,920	9,504
Costs:						
QuickResponse	$6,600	$24,090	$28,908	$34,690	$41,627	$49,953
FastTrack	—	—	4,152	4,983	5,980	7,175
Lifetime customer value:						
QuickResponse profit	($6,600)	$8,910	$10,692	$12,830	$15,397	$18,476
FastTrack profit	—	—	1,348	1,617	1,940	2,329
Reduced overhead allocation[b]	—	—	1,155	1,486	1,663	1,995
Profit from referrals[c]	—	—	1,100	1,650	3,300	6,600
Total profit	($6,600)	$8,910	$14,295	$17,583	$22,300	$29,400

Note: Product names and data have been disguised. As a result, profit on these products is overstated.

[a]Assuming revenue increases on both products of 20 percent per year.

[b]Declining at the rate of 15 percent per year in relation to revenue, to reflect lower costs of customer relationship associated with both customer and supplier learning curve effects.

[c]Estimated, based on assumptions concerning (1) the importance of referrals to new customers from old customers, (2) the frequency with which satisfied customers refer new customers, (3) the size of customers referred, and (4) the lifetime value calculations for new customers.

Source: Reprinted with permission of The Free Press, a Division of Simon & Schuster, Inc., adapted from J. L. Heskett, W. E. Sasser, Jr., and L. A. Schlesinger, *The Service Profit Chain: How Leading Companies Link Profit and Growth to Loyalty* (New York: The Free Press, 1997), p. 201. Copyright © 1997 by J. L. Heskett, W. E. Sasser, and L. A. Schlesinger.

Linking Customer Relationship Value to Firm Value

The emphasis on estimating the relationship value of customers has increased substantially in the past decade. Part of this emphasis has resulted from an increased appreciation of the economic benefits that firms accrue with the retention of loyal customers. (Our Strategy Insight for this chapter describes ways that firms explicitly demonstrate this appreciation to customers.) Interestingly, recent research suggests that customer retention has a large impact on firm value and that relationship value calculations can also provide a useful proxy for assessing the value of a firm.[27] That is, a firm's market value can be roughly determined by carefully calculating customer lifetime value. The approach is straightforward: Estimate the relationship value of a customer, forecast the future growth of the number of customers, and use these figures to determine the value of a company's current and future base. To the extent that the customer base forms a large part of a company's overall value, such a calculation can provide an estimate of a firm's value—a particularly useful figure for young, high-growth firms for which traditional financial methods (e.g., discounted cash flow) do not work well.

CUSTOMER PROFITABILITY SEGMENTS

Companies may want to treat all customers with excellent service, but they generally find that customers differ in their relationship value and that it may be neither practical nor profitable to meet (and certainly not to exceed) *all* customers' expectations.[28] Federal Express Corporation, for example, has categorized its customers internally as the good, the bad, and the ugly—based on their profitability. Rather than treating all its customers the same, the company pays particular attention to enhancing their relationships with the good, tries to move the bad to the good, and discourages the ugly.[29] Other companies also try to identify segments—or, more appropriately, tiers of customers—that differ in current and/or future profitability to a firm. This approach goes beyond usage or volume segmentation because it tracks costs and revenues for segments of customers, thereby capturing their financial worth to companies. After identifying profitability bands, the firm offers services and service levels in line with the identified segments. Building a high-loyalty customer base of the right customers increases profits. At MBNA, a leading financial services firm, a 5 percent jump in retention of the right customers increased the company profits 60 percent by the fifth year.[30]

Profitability Tiers—The Customer Pyramid

Although some people may view the FedEx grouping of customers into "the good, the bad, and the ugly" as negative, descriptive labels of the tiers can be very useful internally. Labels are especially valuable if they help the company keep track of which customers are profitable.

Virtually all firms are aware at some level that their customers differ in profitability, in particular, that a minority of their customers accounts for the highest proportion of sales or profit. This finding has often been called the "80/20 rule"—20 percent of customers produce 80 percent of sales or profit.

In this version of tiering, 20 percent of the customers constitute the top tier, those who can be identified as the most profitable in the company. The rest are indistinguishable from each other but differ from the top tier in profitability. Most companies realize that there are differences among customers within this tier but do not possess the data or capabilities to analyze the distinctions. The 80/20 two-tier scheme assumes that consumers within the two tiers are similar, just as conventional market segmentation schemes typically assume that consumers within segments are similar.

One relatively obvious, but often neglected, way for firms to demonstrate that they value their customers is to show them appreciation for their business. Partnering relationships with customers, such as those provided by the Hertz #1 Gold Club or Northwest Airlines Elite program, implicitly demonstrate the value of such customers to firms. Guaranteed reservations; special counters, cues, or lounges; and occasional special deals all communicate to customers that a firm values them and wants to retain their business. In addition to providing the services as promised, a company that explicitly thanks customers for their business can go a long way toward retaining customers. Customers appreciate small gestures such as smiles, eye contact, and a genuine "thank you for your business." Customer appreciation events, such as golf days, barbecue luncheons, or evening dinner cruises, are ways to remind customers of their value to the firm. Occasional giveaways, such as a day of free greens fees for a golf course's customers, provide an opportunity for a firm to explicitly tell customers that their business is appreciated. One pizzeria has instituted an annual "free pizza" night in which, unannounced, customers who place an order are surprised to learn—via a letter, thanking them for their loyalty, handed to them as they prepare to pay for their order—that their entire meal is free that night.* One of us uses a dentist who always makes it a point to send a personal, hand-written note to each patient who recommends another to his practice; once a person recommends more than three new patients, the customer is often surprised with free tickets to the opera or an NBA basketball game.

The demonstration of customer appreciation is especially important in business-to-business situations, because customers would like their suppliers to extend appreciation either in person or over the telephone and not just take their business for granted. Letters addressed to "Dear Valued Customer" are not really the answer, especially for the organization's best customers. Such an impersonal approach may well communicate exactly the opposite of what was intended. Instead, a personal letter (addressed to the right person with correct spelling and current title) or a personal phone call will have greater impact. For example, at IBM Global Services, customers who take the time to recognize the special actions of an employee are themselves thanked personally for the recognition and for their business. Most firms have a business plan; if customers are indeed important assets to a firm, then perhaps a customer-appreciation plan is also needed. Firms who truly understand the relationship value of a customer should not find it difficult to demonstrate to customers that they are indeed valued.

*For more details on the free pizza customer appreciation night, see http://www.pmq.com/bigdave_winter-fall-1998.shtml (accessed December 29, 2004).

However, more than two tiers are likely and can be used if the company has sufficient data to analyze customer tiers more precisely. Different systems and labels can be helpful. One useful four-tier system, shown in Figure 7.4, includes the following:

1. The *platinum tier* describes the company's most profitable customers, typically those who are heavy users of the product, are not overly price sensitive, are willing to invest in and try new offerings, and are committed customers of the firm.

2. The *gold tier* differs from the platinum tier in that profitability levels are not as high, perhaps because the customers want price discounts that limit margins or are

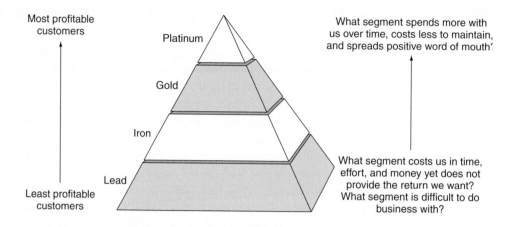

FIGURE 7.4
The Customer Pyramid

Most profitable customers

Least profitable customers

Platinum

Gold

Iron

Lead

What segment spends more with us over time, costs less to maintain, and spreads positive word of mouth?

What segment costs us in time, effort, and money yet does not provide the return we want? What segment is difficult to do business with?

not as loyal. They may be heavy users who minimize risk by working with multiple vendors rather than just the focal company.

3. The *iron tier* contains essential customers who provide the volume needed to utilize the firm's capacity, but their spending levels, loyalty, and profitability are not substantial enough for special treatment.

4. The *lead tier* consists of customers who are costing the company money. They demand more attention than they are due given their spending and profitability and are sometimes problem customers—complaining about the firm to others and tying up the firm's resources.

Note that this classification is superficially reminiscent of, but very different from, traditional usage segmentation performed by airlines such as American Airlines. Two differences are obvious. First, in the customer pyramid profitability rather than usage defines all levels. Second, the lower levels actually articulate classes of customers who require a different sort of attention. The firm must work either to change the customers' behavior—to make them more profitable through increases in revenue—or to change the firm's cost structure to make them more profitable through decreases in costs.

Examples of effective use of the customer pyramid approach exist in a number of business contexts. Financial services firms are leading the way, perhaps because of the vast amounts of data already housed in those firms. In 1994 Bank One realized that all financial institutions had grossly overcharged their best customers to subsidize others who were not paying their way. Determined to grow its top-profit customers, who were vulnerable because they were being underserved, Bank One implemented a set of measures to focus resources on their most productive use. Next it identified the profit drivers in this top segment and thereby stabilized its relationships with key customers.[31]

Once a system has been established for categorizing customers, the multiple levels can be identified, motivated, served, and expected to deliver differential levels of profit. Companies improve their opportunities for profit when they increase shares of purchases by customers who either have the greatest need for the services or show the greatest loyalty to a single provider. By strengthening relationships with the loyal customers, increasing sales with existing customers, and increasing the profitability on each sale opportunity, companies thereby increase the potential of each customer.

The Customer's View of Profitability Tiers

Whereas profitability tiers make sense from the company's point of view, customers are not always understanding, nor do they appreciate being categorized into a less desirable segment.[32] For example, at some companies the top clients have their own individual account representative whom they can contact personally. The next tier of clients may be handled by representatives who each have 100 clients. Meanwhile, most clients are served by an 800 number, an automated voice response system, or referral to a website. Customers are aware of this unequal treatment, and many resist and resent it. It makes perfect sense from a business perspective, but customers are often disappointed in the level of service they receive and give firms poor marks for quality as a result.

Therefore, it is increasingly important that firms communicate with customers so they understand the level of service they can expect and what they would need to do or pay to receive faster or more personalized service. The most significant issues result when customers do not understand, believe they have been singled out for poor service, or feel that the system is unfair. Although many customers refuse to pay for quality service, they react negatively if they believe it has been taken away from them unfairly.

The ability to segment customers narrowly based on profitability implications also raises questions of privacy for customers. In order to know who is profitable and who is not, companies must collect large amounts of individualized behavioral and personal data on consumers. Many consumers today resent what they perceive as an intrusion into their lives in this way, especially when it results in differential treatment that they perceive is unfair.

Making Business Decisions Using Profitability Tiers

Prudent business managers are well aware that past customer purchase behavior, although useful in making predictions, can be misleading.[33] What a customer spends today, or has spent in the past, may not necessarily be reflective of what he or she will do (or be worth) in the future. Banks serving college students know this well—a typical college student generally has minimal financial services needs (i.e., a checking account) and tends to not have a high level of deposits. However, within a few years that student may embark on a professional career, start a family, and/or purchase a house, and thus require several financial services and become a potentially very profitable customer to the bank. Generally speaking, a firm would like to keep its consistent big spenders and lose the erratic small spenders. But all too often a firm also has two other groups they must consider: erratic big spenders and consistent small spenders. So, in some situations where consistent cash flow is a concern, it may be helpful to a firm to have a portfolio of customers that includes steady customers, even if they have a history of being less profitable. Some service providers have actually been quite successful in targeting customers who were previously considered to be unworthy of another firm's marketing efforts.[34] Paychex, a payroll processing company, became very successful in serving small businesses that the major companies in this industry did not think were large enough to profitably serve. Similarly, Progressive Insurance became very successful in selling automobile insurance to undesirable customers—young drivers and those with poor driving records—that most of the competition did not feel had a sufficient relationship value. Firms, therefore, need to be cautious in blindly applying customer value calculations without thinking carefully about the implications.

RELATIONSHIP DEVELOPMENT STRATEGIES

To this point in the chapter, we have focused on the rationale for relationship marketing; the benefits (to both firms and customers) of the development of strong exchange relationships; and an understanding of the relationship value of a customer. In this section we examine a variety of factors that influence the development of strong customer relationships, including the customer's overall evaluation of a firm's offering, bonds created with customers by the firm, and barriers that the customer faces in leaving a relationship. These factors, illustrated in Figure 7.5, provide the rationale for specific strategies that firms often use to keep their current customers.

Core Service Provision

Retention strategies will have little long-term success unless the firm has a solid base of service quality and customer satisfaction on which to build. The firm does not necessarily have to be the very best among its competitors or be world-class in terms of quality and customer satisfaction. It must be competitive, however, and frequently better than that. All the retention strategies that we describe in this section are built on the assumption of competitive quality and value being offered. Clearly, a firm needs to begin the relationship development process by providing a good core service delivery that, at a minimum, meets customer expectations; it does no good to design relationship strategies for inferior services. Two earlier examples, Intuit and USAA, provide convincing support for the argument that excellence in the core service or product offered is essential to a successful relationship strategy. Both these companies have benefited tremendously from their loyal customer base; both offer excellent quality; both use relationship strategies to enhance their success.

FIGURE 7.5
**Relationship
Development Model**

Source: Adapted from D. D. Gremler and S. W. Brown, "Service Loyalty: Antecedents, Components, and Outcomes," in *1998 AMA Winter Educators' Conference: Marketing Theory and Applications,* Vol. 9, D. Grewal and C. Pechmann, eds. Chicago, IL: American Marketing Association, pp. 165–166.

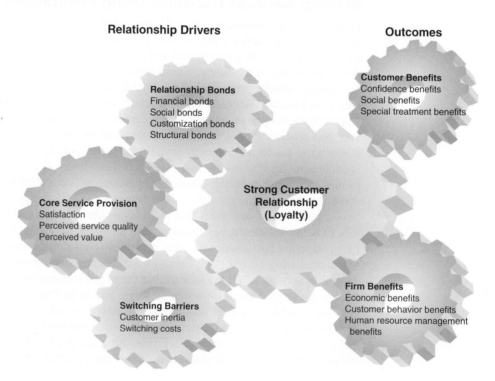

Relationship Drivers

Outcomes

Relationship Bonds
Financial bonds
Social bonds
Customization bonds
Structural bonds

Customer Benefits
Confidence benefits
Social benefits
Special treatment benefits

Core Service Provision
Satisfaction
Perceived service quality
Perceived value

**Strong Customer
Relationship
(Loyalty)**

Switching Barriers
Customer inertia
Switching costs

Firm Benefits
Economic benefits
Customer behavior benefits
Human resource management
  benefits

Switching Barriers

When considering a switch in service providers, a customer may face a number of barriers that make it difficult to leave one service provider and begin a relationship with another. Literature suggests that switching barriers influence consumers' decisions to exit from relationships with firms and, therefore, help to facilitate customer retention.[35]

Customer Inertia

One reason that customers commit to developing relationships with firms is that a certain amount of effort may be required to change firms. Sometimes consumers simplistically state that "it's just not worth it" to switch providers. Inertia may even explain why some dissatisfied customers stay with a provider. In discussing why people remain in relationships (in general) that they no longer find satisfying, scholars suggest that people may stay because breaking the relationship would require them to restructure their life—to develop new habits of living, to refashion old friendships, and to find new ones.[36] In other words, people do not like to change their behavior.

To retain customers, firms might consider increasing the perceived effort required on the part of the customer to switch service providers. If a customer believes that a great deal of effort is needed to change companies, the customer is more likely to stay put. For example, automobile repair facilities might keep a complete and detailed maintenance history of a customer's vehicle. These records remove from the customer the burden of having to remember all the services performed on the vehicle and would force the customer to expend considerable effort in providing a complete maintenance history if the vehicle is taken to a new mechanic. Conversely, if a firm is looking to attract a competitor's customers, it might automate the process for switching providers as much as possible in order to reduce the effort required to switch. Long-distance telephone companies generally make switching providers as simple as saying "yes" on the telephone to a company representative—thereby removing any action required of the customer.

Switching Costs

In many instances, customers develop loyalty to an organization in part because of costs involved in changing to and purchasing from a different firm. These costs, both real and perceived, monetary and nonmonetary, are termed *switching costs.* Switching costs include investments of time, money, or effort—such as setup costs, search costs, learning costs, and contractual costs—that make it challenging for the customer to move to another provider.[37] To illustrate, a patient may incur *setup costs* such as paying for a complete physical when changing doctors or for new X-rays when switching dentists. Because services often have characteristics that make them difficult to evaluate—including intangibility, nonstandardization, and inseparability of production and consumption as well as high experience and credence qualities—high *search costs* may be required to obtain suitable information about alternative services. *Learning costs* are those costs associated with learning the idiosyncrasies of how to use a product or service; in many situations, a customer who wishes to switch firms may need to accumulate new user skills or customer know-how. *Contractual costs* arise when the customer is required to pay a penalty to switch providers (e.g., prepayment charges for customer-initiated switching of mortgage companies or mobile telephone services), making it financially difficult, if not impossible, for the customer to initiate an early termination of the relationship.

In order to retain customers, firms might consider increasing their switching costs in order to make it difficult for customers to exit the relationship (or at least create the perception of difficulty). Indeed, many firms explicitly specify such costs in the contracts that they require their customers to sign (e.g., mobile telephone services, health clubs). In order to attract new customers, a service provider might consider implementing strategies designed to *lower* the switching costs of customers not currently using the provider. To reduce the setup costs involved when switching, providers could complete the paperwork required from the customer. Banks, for example, could offer to do all the paperwork to set up a checking account, including both automatic deposits and automatic payments.

Relationship Bonds

Switching barriers tend to serve as constraints that keep customers in relationships with firms because they "have to."[38] However, firms can engage in activities that encourage customers to remain in the relationship because they "want to." Leonard Berry and A. Parasuraman have developed a framework for understanding the types of retention strategies that focus on developing bonds with customers.[39] The framework suggests that relationship marketing can occur at different levels and that each successive level of strategy results in ties that bind the customer a little closer to the firm. At each successive level, the potential for sustained competitive advantage is also increased. Building on the levels of the retention strategy idea, Figure 7.6 illustrates four types of retention strategies, which are discussed in the following sections. Recall,

FIGURE 7.6
Levels of Relationship Strategies

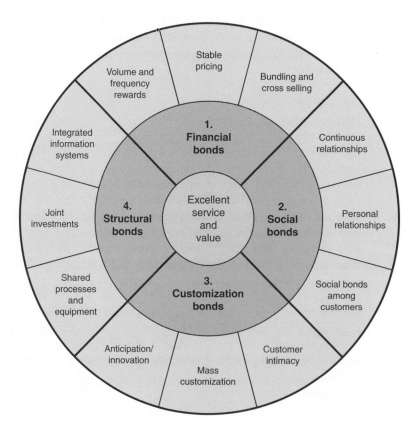

however, that the most successful retention strategies will be built on foundations of core service excellence.

Level 1—Financial Bonds

At level 1, the customer is tied to the firm primarily through financial incentives—lower prices for greater volume purchases or lower prices for customers who have been with the firm a long time. Examples of level 1 relationship marketing are not hard to find. Think about the airline industry and related travel service industries like hotels and car rental companies. Frequent flyer programs provide financial incentives and rewards for travelers who bring more of their business to a particular airline. Hotels and car rental companies do the same. Long-distance telephone companies in the United States have engaged in a similar battle, trying to provide volume discounts and other price incentives to retain market share and build a loyal customer base. One reason these financial incentive programs proliferate is that they are not difficult to initiate and frequently result in at least short-term profit gains. Unfortunately, financial incentives do not generally provide long-term advantages to a firm because, unless combined with another relationship strategy, they do not differentiate the firm from its competitors in the long run. Many travelers belong to several frequent flyer programs and do not hesitate to trade off among them. Although price and other financial incentives are important to customers, they are generally not difficult for competitors to imitate because the primary customized element of the marketing mix is price.

Other types of retention strategies that depend primarily on financial rewards are focused on bundling and cross-selling of services. Frequent flyer programs again provide a common example. Many airlines link their reward programs with hotel chains, auto rental, and in some cases, credit card usage. By linking airline mileage points earned to usage of other firms' services, customers can enjoy even greater financial benefits in exchange for their loyalty.

In other cases, firms aim to retain their customers by simply offering their most loyal customers the assurance of stable prices, or at least lower price increases than those paid by new customers. In this way firms reward their loyal customers by sharing with them some of the cost savings and increased revenue that the firm receives through serving them over time.

Although widely and increasingly used as retention tactics, loyalty programs based on financial rewards merit caution.[40] These programs are often easily imitated. Thus, any increased usage or loyalty from customers may be short-lived. Second, these strategies are not likely to be successful unless they are structured so that they truly lead to repeat or increased usage rather than serving as means to attract new customers and potentially causing endless switching among competitors.

Level 2—Social Bonds

Level 2 strategies bind customers to the firm through more than financial incentives. Although price is still assumed to be important, level 2 retention marketers build long-term relationships through social and interpersonal as well as financial bonds. Customers are viewed as "clients," not nameless faces, and become individuals whose needs and wants the firm seeks to understand.

Social, interpersonal bonds are common among professional service providers (lawyers, accountants, teachers) and their clients as well as among personal care providers (hairdressers, counselors, health care providers) and their clients. A dentist who takes a few minutes to review her patient's file before coming into the exam room is able to jog her memory on personal facts about the patient (occupation, family details, interests, dental health history). By bringing these personal details into the conversation, the dentist reveals her genuine interest in the patient as an individual and builds social bonds.

Interpersonal bonds are also common in business-to-business relationships in which customers develop relationships with salespeople and/or relationship managers working with their firms.[41] Recognizing the value of continuous relationships in building loyalty, Caterpillar Corporation credits its success to its extensive, stable distribution organization worldwide. Caterpillar is the world's largest manufacturer of mining, construction, and agriculture heavy equipment. Although its engineering and product quality are superior, the company attributes much of its success to its strong dealer network and product support services offered throughout the world. CEO David Fites contends that knowledge of the local market and the close relationships with customers that Caterpillar's dealers provide is invaluable: "Our dealers tend to be prominent business leaders in their service territories who are deeply involved in community activities and who are committed to living in the area. Their reputations and long-term relationships are important because selling our products is a personal business."[42]

Sometimes relationships are formed with the organization because of the social bonds that develop *among customers* rather than between customers and the provider of the service. Such bonds are often formed in health clubs, country clubs, educational settings, and other service environments where customers interact with each other. Over time the social relationships they have with other customers are important factors that keep them from switching to another organization. One company that has built a significant strategy around customer-to-customer bonds is Harley Davidson, with its local Harley Owners Groups, or HOGs. HOGs are involved in local rallies, tours, and parties as well as in national HOG events organized by the company. Through the HOGs, Harley customers come to know each other and develop a sense of community around their common interest—motorcycle riding—as illustrated in Figure 7.7.

Social bonds alone may not tie the customer permanently to the firm, but they are much more difficult for competitors to imitate than are price incentives. In the absence of strong reasons to shift to another provider, interpersonal bonds can encourage cus-

FIGURE 7.7
Harley Davidson riders develop customer-to-customer bonds through Harley Owners Group (HOG) activities.

Source: EyeWire Collection/Getty Images

tomers to stay in a relationship.[43] In combination with financial incentives, social bonding strategies may be very effective.

Level 3—Customization Bonds

Level 3 strategies involve more than social ties and financial incentives, although there are common elements of level 1 and 2 strategies encompassed within a customization strategy and vice versa. For example, Caterpillar dealers are relied on not just to form strong personal commitments to customers but also to feed information back into the system to help Caterpillar customize services to fit developing customer needs.[44]

Two commonly used terms fit within the customization bonds approach: *mass customization* and *customer intimacy.* Both these strategies suggest that customer loyalty can be encouraged through intimate knowledge of individual customers and through the development of one-to-one solutions that fit the individual customer's needs.

Mass customization has been defined as "the use of flexible processes and organizational structures to produce varied and often individually customized products and services at the price of standardized, mass-produced alternatives."[45] Mass customization does not mean providing customers with endless solutions or choices that only make them work harder for what they want; rather, it means providing them through little effort on their part with tailored services to fit their individual needs. The earlier Technology Spotlight provides examples of companies who are using technology to customize services to large numbers of individual customers. Our Global Feature illustrates how Boots The Chemists in the United Kingdom has used technology to understand its customers and build the world's largest smart card loyalty scheme.

Level 4—Structural Bonds

Level 4 strategies are the most difficult to imitate; they involve structural as well as financial, social, and customization bonds between the customer and the firm. Structural bonds are created by providing services to the client that are frequently designed right into the service delivery system for that client. Often, structural bonds are created by providing customized services to the client that are technology based and make the customer more productive.

An example of structural bonds can be seen in a business-to-business context with Allegiance Healthcare Corporation. By working closely with its hospital customers, Allegiance (a Cardinal Health company) has developed ways to improve hospital supply ordering, delivery, and billing that have greatly enhanced its value as a supplier. For example, Allegiance developed "hospital-specific pallet architecture," which meant that all items arriving at a particular hospital were shrink-wrapped with labels visible for easy identification. Separate pallets were assembled to reflect the individual hospital's storage system so that instead of miscellaneous supplies arriving in boxes sorted at the convenience of Allegiance's internal needs, they arrived on client-friendly pallets designed to suit the distribution needs of the individual hospital. By linking the hospital through its ValueLink service into a database ordering system and by providing enhanced value in the actual delivery, Allegiance has structurally tied itself to its more than 150 acute care hospitals in the United States. In addition to the enhanced service that ValueLink provides, Allegiance estimates that the system saves its customers an average of $500,000 or more each year.[46]

Another example of level 4 strategy can be seen in the long competitive battle between UPS and Federal Express.[47] In the mid 1990s, both firms attempted to tie their clients closer to them by providing them with free computers—Federal Express's PowerShips and UPS's MaxiShips—that stored addresses and shipping data, printed

Source: Newscast

Boots The Chemists is one of the best-known and trusted brands in the United Kingdom and is the United Kingdom's leading health and beauty retailer. The company was founded in 1887, spanning three centuries of successful operations. Currently offering its products through 1,400 retail stores as well as an online store at www.wellbeing.com, the company is deservedly called the "Chemist to the Nation." On its website, the Boots Company states that it intends to become the global leader in well-being products and services and is expanding globally through Boots Healthcare International.

A foundation for Boots's success in recent years is its increased focus on the customer and a desire to develop customer loyalty through a number of retention and relationship strategies. At the heart of the company's loyalty strategy is its Advantage Card, started in 1997. The Advantage Card is right now the world's largest smart card loyalty scheme, with close to 13 million members. Over 50 percent of Boots's current sales are now linked to the card. The card offers a number of benefits to customers and has helped the company increase sales, but more than that, it has been the foundation for building greater loyalty among Boots's best customers.

Using the card for purchases, Boots's customers receive 4 points for every pound spent. These points can be redeemed for selected products, aimed to treat customers to something special rather than simply to offer discounts off purchases. In fact the card is *not* about discounts; rather, it is about treating oneself. Customers can use their points to treat themselves to a simple lunch or to a full day of pampering at a spa. From a financial perspective, the company has seen increasing average transaction values among higher-spending customers. Boots managers say that they have increased loyalty and spending from people who were already good and profitable customers—a clear win for the company.

A number of initiatives are tied to the Advantage Card, taking it beyond a pure points reward program from the customer's perspective. For example, Boots now mails a first-class health and beauty magazine to the top spending 3 million Advantage Card holders. The magazine is Britain's biggest health and beauty magazine; it is not viewed as a "Boots" magazine but rather as a health and beauty magazine sent by Boots. Cardholders also have access to additional benefits and discounts using interactive kiosks in over 380 stores. The card can be used for purchases at the online store through the www.wellbeing.com site that was launched jointly with Granada Media in 2001. Many products are offered on the site that are not available in Boots stores. In addition, the site provides access to an online magazine, answers to questions, a chat room, and other features and services. A credit card version of the Advantage Card was launched in 2001. And Boots joined with the Department of Health to enable Advantage Card holders to register with the National Health Service Organ Donor program and to carry an Advantage Card featuring the program's logo.

From the company's perspective as well, the card is much more than a reward program. Data generated through the card is used to understand customers and to anticipate and identify individual needs in health and beauty care products. In fact, the goals with the Advantage Card program back in 1997 were to gain customer insight; build a database that would allow the company to tailor offerings to individual customers' needs; develop incremental sales by building customer loyalty; and use the customer knowledge to develop and introduce new products and services. A great deal of planning and testing went into developing the program, and this planning paid off in customer loyalty. Buy-in from the company's 60,000 staff members also aided in the rapid success of the program. All associates were signed up as members six months before the launch of the card. After experiencing the benefits of the card firsthand, they became enthusiastic advocates, encouraging customers to sign up.

Through the program, Boots has learned that the more broadly customers buy, in more categories over time, the more they increase visits to Boots stores. The result has been customization of product and service offerings and more sales and greater loyalty from its best customers.

Sources: Frederick Newell, *Loyalty.com,* New York: McGraw-Hill, 2000, Chapter 24, pp. 239–45; www.boots-plc.com, 2002; www.wellbeing.com, 2002.

mailing labels, and helped track packages. By tying into one of the systems, a company saved time overall and could better track daily shipping records. As technology has continued to advance, the two companies have tied their customers to them through the Web and now through wireless technology, as shown in the UPS ad in Figure 7.8.

But there is also a potential downside to this arrangement from the customer's perspective. Customers may fear that tying themselves too closely to one provider may not allow them to take advantage of potential price savings from other providers in the future.

RELATIONSHIP CHALLENGES

Given the many benefits of long-term customer relationships, it would seem that a company would not want to refuse or terminate a relationship with any customer. Yet, situations arise in which either the firm, the customer, or both want to end (or have to end) their relationship. This final section of the chapter discusses situations in which the firm might actually consider ending the relationship and how that might occur; in the next chapter we discuss situations in which the customer decides to terminate the relationship and switch providers.

FIGURE 7.8
**UPS uses technology
to build ties to
customers.**

Source: Courtesy of UPS;
Photo by William Howard ©
The Martin Agency

The Customer Is *Not* Always Right

The assumption that all customers are good customers is very compatible with the belief that "the customer is always right," an almost sacrosanct tenet of business. Yet any service worker can tell you that this statement is *not* always true, and in some cases it may be preferable for the firm and the customer to not continue their relationship. The following discussion presents a view of customer relationships that suggests that all relationships may not be beneficial and that every customer is not right all the time.

The Wrong Segment

A company cannot target its services to all customers; some segments will be more appropriate than others. It would not be beneficial to either the company or the customer for a company to establish a relationship with a customer whose needs the company cannot meet. For example, a school offering a lock-step, daytime MBA program would not encourage full-time working people to apply for its program, nor would a law firm specializing in government issues establish a relationship with individuals seeking advice on trusts and estates. These examples seem obvious. Yet firms frequently do give in to the temptation to make a sale by agreeing to serve a customer who would be better served by someone else.

Similarly, it would not be wise to forge relationships simultaneously with incompatible market segments. In many service businesses (such as restaurants, hotels, tour package operators, entertainment, and education), customers experience the service together and can influence each other's perceptions about value received. Thus, to maximize service to core segments, an organization may choose to turn away marginally profitable segments that would be incompatible. For example, a conference hotel may find that mixing executives in town for a serious educational program with students in town for a regional track meet may not be wise. If the executive group is a key long-term customer, the hotel may choose to pass up the sports group in the interest of retaining the executives.

Not Profitable in the Long Term

In the absence of ethical or legal mandates, organizations will prefer *not* to have long-term relationships with unprofitable customers. Some segments of customers will not be profitable for the company even if their needs can be met by the services offered. Some examples of this situation are when there are not enough customers in the segment to make it profitable to develop a marketing approach, when the segment cannot afford to pay the cost of the service, or when the projected revenue flows from the segment would not cover the costs incurred to originate and maintain the business. For example, in the banking industry it has been estimated that 40 to 70 percent of customers served in a typical bank are not profitable in the sense that the costs of serving these customers exceed the revenues generated.[48]

At the individual customer level, it may not be profitable for a firm to engage in a relationship with a particular customer who has bad credit or who is a poor risk for some other reason. Retailers, banks, mortgage companies, and credit card companies routinely refuse to do business with individuals whose credit histories are unreliable. Although the short-term sale may be beneficial, the long-term risk of nonpayment makes the relationship unwise from the company's point of view. Similarly, some car rental companies check into the driving records of customers and reject bad-risk drivers.[49] This practice, while controversial, is logical from the car rental companies' point of view because they can cut back on insurance costs and accident claims (thus reducing rental costs for good drivers) by not doing business with accident-prone drivers.

Beyond the monetary costs associated with serving the wrong customers, there can be substantial time investments in some customers that, if actually computed, would make them unprofitable for the organization. Everyone has had the experience of waiting in a bank, a retail store, or even in an education setting while a particularly demanding customer seems to use more than his share of the service provider's time. The dollar value of the time spent with a specific customer is typically not computed or calculated into the price of the service.

FIGURE 7.9
Some customers may be difficult, if not impossible, to serve.

Source: Masterfile.

In a business-to-business relationship, the variability in time commitment to customers is even more apparent. Some customers may use considerable resources of the supplier organization through inordinate numbers of phone calls, excessive requests for information, and other time-consuming activities. In the legal profession, clients are billed for every hour of the firm's time that they use in this way because time is essentially the only resource the firm has. Yet in other service businesses, all clients essentially pay the same regardless of the time demands they place on the organization.

Difficult Customers

Managers have repeated the phrase "the customer is always right" so often that you would expect it to be accepted by every employee in every service organization. So why isn't it? Perhaps because it simply is not true. The customer is not always right. No matter how frequently it is said, repeating that mantra does not make it become reality, and service employees know it.

In many situations, firms have service encounters that fail because of *dysfunctional customers*. Dysfunctional customer behavior refers to actions by customers who intentionally, or perhaps unintentionally, act in a manner that in some way disrupts otherwise functional service encounters.[50] Such customers have been described as "customers from hell," "problem customers," or "jay customers." One of us was awakened during a recent hotel stay at 4:00 A.M. by drunk customers who were arguing with each other in a room above; management eventually called the police and asked them to escort the customers off the property. An Enterprise Rent-A-Car customer demanded that she not be charged for any of the two weeks that she had a car because, near the end of the rental period, she found a small stain in the back seat.[51] These customers often have the objective of gaining faster, superior, or perhaps free service, but their behavior is considered dysfunctional from the perspective of the service provider and perhaps fellow customers.

Dysfunctional customer behavior can affect employees, other customers, and the organization. Research suggests that exposure to dysfunctional customer behavior can have psychological, emotional, behavioral, and physical effects on employees.[52] For example, customer-contact employees who are exposed to rude, threatening, obstructive, aggressive, or disruptive behavior by customers often have their mood or temper negatively affected as well as their motivation and morale. Such customers are difficult to work with and often create stress for employees. (See Figure 7.9 for one example.) Dysfunctional customers can also have an impact on other customers: Such behavior can spoil the service experience for other customers, and the dysfunctional customer behavior may become contagious for other customers witnessing it, particularly if it includes vociferous or illegitimate complaining. Finally, dysfunctional customer behavior can create both direct costs and indirect costs for the organization. Direct costs of such behavior can include the expense of restoring damaged property, increased insurance premiums, property loss by theft, costs incurred in compensating customers affected by the dysfunctional behavior of others, and the costs incurred through illegitimate claims by dysfunctional customers. Additionally, indirect costs might include increased workloads for staff required to deal with dysfunctional behavior as well as increased costs for attracting and retaining appropriate personnel and, perhaps, for absenteeism payments.

Although often these difficult customers will be accommodated and employees can be trained to recognize and deal with them appropriately, at times the best choice may be to not maintain the relationship at all—especially at the business-to-business level, where long-term costs to the firm can be substantial. Take, for example, the view of some of Madison Avenue's major ad agencies. "Some ad agencies say some accounts are so difficult to work with that they simply cannot—or will not—service them."[53] Difficult clients paralyze an ad agency for a variety of reasons. Some ask that a particular ad campaign work for all their diverse constituencies at the same time, which in some cases may be next to impossible. Others require so much up-front work and ad testing before selecting an agency that the work is essentially done for free by those agencies not selected. Other clients are stingy; require dozens of storyboards before settling on a concept; or require a lot of direct, frequently disruptive, involvement in the production process. As a result, agencies have become more wary of chasing every client that comes along. "As in a marriage, all agencies and all clients don't work well together."[54]

Ending Business Relationships

For the effective management of service relationships, managers should not only know how to establish a relationship but also how to end one. As suggested earlier in this chapter, firms may identify some customers who are not in their targeted segment, who are not profitable in the long run, or who are difficult to work with or dysfunctional. A company may *not* want to continue in a relationship with every customer. However, gracefully exiting a relationship may not be easy. Customers may end up feeling disappointed, confused, or hurt if a firm attempts to terminate the relationship.

Relationship Endings

Relationships end in different ways—depending on the type of relationship in place.[55] In some situations, a relationship is established for a certain purpose and/or time period and then dissolves when it has served its purpose or the time frame has elapsed. For example, a house painting service may be engaged with the customer for four days while painting the house exterior, but both parties understand that the end of the relationship is predetermined—the end occurs when the house has been painted and the customer has paid for the service. Sometimes a relationship has a natural ending. Piano lessons for children, for example, often cease as the child gets older and develops interests in other musical areas (such as singing or playing the clarinet); in such situations, the need for the relationship has diminished or become obsolete. In other situations, an event may occur that forces the relationship to end; a provider who relocates to the other side of town may force some customers to select a different company. Or an ending may occur because the customer is not fulfilling his or her obligations. For example, a bank may choose to end the relationship with a customer who regularly has insufficient funds in the checking account. Whatever the reason for ending the relationship, firms should clearly communicate their reasons for wanting (or needing) to terminate it so that customers understand what is occurring and why.

Should Firms Fire Their Customers?

A logical conclusion to be drawn from the discussion of the challenges firms face in customer relationships is that perhaps firms should seek to get rid of those customers who are not right for the company. More and more companies are making these types of decisions based on the belief that troublesome customers are usually less profitable and less loyal and that it may be counterproductive to attempt to retain their business.[56] Another reason for "firing" a customer is the negative effect that these customers can have on employee quality of life and morale.

One company came to this conclusion when a client, the CEO of an Internet start-up company, paged one of its employees at her home on the West Coast at 4 A.M. and asked her to order a limousine for him in New York City.[57] This incident was enough to push the employee over the edge and cause her boss to agree that the company should fire this client. It did so by directly telling him that the relationship was not working out and to take his business elsewhere.

Another company took reducing its customer base to the extreme. Nypro—a global, employee-owned company specializing in molded plastics applications for such clients as Gillette, Abbott Laboratories, Hewlett-Packard, and other large organizations.[58]—reduced its customer base in the 1980s from 800 to approximately 30 clients on the belief that it could better serve those clients and grow more effectively if it focused on fewer relationships. Nypro adopted a customer intimacy strategy and tied itself closely to this much smaller number of clients. Some of these clients have now been with Nypro for more than 40 years. Over time Nypro has selectively added clients to this base, and the company has enjoyed 18 consecutive years of record sales and profit growth.

Although it may sound like a good idea, firing customers is not that simple and needs to be done in a way that avoids negative publicity or negative word of mouth. Sometimes raising prices or charging for services that previously had been given away for free can move unprofitable customers out of the company. Helping a client find a new supplier who can better meet its needs is another way to gracefully exit a nonproductive relationship. If the customer has become too demanding, the relationship may be salvaged by negotiating expectations or finding more efficient ways to serve the client. If not, both parties may find an agreeable way to end the relationship.

Summary

In this chapter we focused on the rationale for, benefits of, and strategies for developing long-term relationships with customers. It should be obvious by now that organizations that focus only on acquiring new customers may well fail to understand their current customers; thus, while a company may be bringing customers in through the front door, equal or greater numbers may be exiting. Estimates of lifetime relationship value accentuate the importance of retaining current customers.

The particular strategy that an organization uses to retain its current customers can and should be customized to fit the industry, the culture, and the customer needs of the organization. However, in general, customer relationships are driven by a variety of factors that influence the development of strong customer relationships, including (1) the customer's overall evaluation of the quality of a firm's core service offering, (2) the switching barriers that the customer faces in leaving a relationship, and (3) the relationship bonds developed with that customer by the firm. By developing strong relationships with customers and by focusing on factors that influence customer relationships, the organization will accurately understand customer expectations over time and consequently will narrow service quality gap 1.

The chapter concluded with a discussion of the challenges that firms face in developing relationships with customers. Although long-term customer relationships are critical and can be very profitable, firms should not attempt to build relationships with just any customer. In other words, "the customer is not always right." Indeed, in some situations it may be best for firms to discontinue relationships with some customers—for the sake of the customer, the firm, or both.

Discussion Questions

1. Discuss how relationship marketing or retention marketing is different from the traditional emphasis in marketing.

2. Describe how a firm's relationships with customers may evolve over time. For each level of relationship discussed in the chapter, identify a firm with which you have that level of relationship and discuss how its marketing efforts differ from other firms.

3. Think about a service organization that retains you as a loyal customer. Why are you loyal to this provider? What are the benefits to you of staying loyal and not switching to another provider? What would it take for you to switch?

4. With regard to the same service organization, what are the benefits to the organization of keeping you as a customer? Calculate your "lifetime value" to the organization.

5. Describe the logic behind "customer profitability segmentation" from the company's point of view. Also discuss what customers may think of the practice.

6. Describe the various switching barriers discussed in the text. What switching barriers might you face in switching banks? Mobile telephone service providers? Universities?

7. Describe the four levels of retention strategies, and give examples of each type. Again, think of a service organization to which you are loyal. Can you describe the reason(s) you are loyal in terms of the different levels? In other words, what ties you to the organization?

8. Have you ever worked as a front-line service employee? Can you remember having to deal with difficult or "problem" customers? Discuss how you handled such situations. As a manager of front-line employees, how would you help your employees deal with difficult customers?

Exercises

1. Interview the manager of a local service organization. Discuss with the manager the target market(s) for the service. Estimate the lifetime value of a customer in one or more of the target segments. To do this estimate, you will need to get as

much information from the manager as you can. If the manager cannot answer your questions, make some assumptions.

2. In small groups in class, debate the question "Is the customer always right?" In other words, are there times when the customer may be the wrong customer for the organization?

3. Design a customer appreciation program for the organization with whom you currently work. Why would you have such a program, and to whom would it be directed toward?

4. Choose a specific company context (your class project company, the company you work for, or a company in an industry you are familiar with). Calculate the lifetime value of a customer for this company. You will need to make assumptions to do this calculation, so make your assumptions clear. Using ideas and concepts from this chapter, describe a relationship marketing strategy to increase the number of lifetime customers for this firm.

Notes

1. USAA is featured in the following two books, and material in this section is drawn from them: L. L. Berry, *Discovering the Soul of Service* (New York: The Free Press, 1999); F. F. Reichheld, *Loyalty Rules!* (Boston: Harvard Business School Press, 2001).

2. A quote from Bill Cooney, deputy CEO for USAA's Property and Casualty Insurance operations as it appeared in L. L. Berry, *Discovering the Soul of Service,* p. 32.

3. F. E. Webster Jr., "The Changing Role of Marketing in the Corporation," *Journal of Marketing,* October 1992, pp. 1–17.

4. For discussions of relationship marketing and its influence on the marketing of services, consumer goods, strategic alliances, distribution channels, and buyer–seller interactions, see *Journal of the Academy of Marketing Science,* Special Issue on Relationship Marketing (vol. 23, Fall 1995). Some of the early roots of this paradigm shift can be found in C. Gronroos, *Service Management and Marketing* (New York: Lexington Books, 1990); and E. Gummesson, "The New Marketing—Developing Long-Term Interactive Relationships," *Long Range Planning* 20 (1987), pp. 10–20. For current thinking and excellent reviews of relationship marketing across a spectrum of topics, see J. N. Sheth, *Handbook of Relationship Marketing* (Thousand Oaks, CA: Sage Publications, 2000).

5. L. L. Berry and A. Parasuraman, *Marketing Services* (New York: Free Press, 1991), chap. 8.

6. G. Knisely, "Comparing Marketing Management in Package Goods and Service Organizations," a series of interviews appearing in *Advertising Age,* January 15, February 19, March 19, and May 14, 1979.

7. This discussion is based on M. D. Johnson and F. Selnes, "Customer Portfolio Management: Toward a Dynamic Theory of Exchange Relationships," *Journal of Marketing* 68 (April 2004), pp. 1–17.

8. R. M. Morgan and S. D. Hunt, "The Commitment-Trust Theory of Relationship Marketing," *Journal of Marketing* 58 (July 1994), pp. 20–38; N. Bendapudi and L. L. Berry, "Customers' Motivations for Maintaining Relationships with Service Providers," *Journal of Retailing* 73 (Spring 1997), pp. 15–37.

9. Johnson and Selnes, "Customer Portfolio Management."

10. Ibid.

11. See also D. Siredeshmukh, J. Singh, and B. Sabol, "Customer Trust, Value, and Loyalty in Relational Exchanges," *Journal of Marketing* 66 (January 2002), pp. 15–37.

12. See C. Huffman and B. Kahn, "Variety for Sale: Mass Customization or Mass Confusion?" *Journal of Retailing* 74 (Winter 1998), pp. 491–513; B. J. Pine and J. H. Gilmore, "Welcome to the Experience Economy," *Harvard Business Review* 76 (July–August 1998), pp. 97–105; B. J. Pine, D. Peppers, and M. Rodgers, "Do You Want to Keep Your Customers Forever?" *Harvard Business Review* 73 (March–April 1995), pp. 103–14.

13. The three types of relational benefits discussed in this section are drawn from K. P. Gwinner, D. D. Gremler, and M. J. Bitner, "Relational Benefits in Service Industries: The Customer's Perspective," *Journal of the Academy of Marketing Science* 26 (Spring 1998), pp. 101–14.

14. See M. B. Adelman, A. Ahuvia, and C. Goodwin, "Beyond Smiling: Social Support and Service Quality," in *Service Quality: New Directions in Theory and Practice,* ed. R. T. Rust and R. L. Oliver (Thousand Oaks, CA: Sage Publications, 1994), pp. 139–72; and C. Goodwin, "Private Roles in Public Encounters: Communal Relationships in Service Exchanges," unpublished manuscript, University of Manitoba, 1993.

15. E. J. Arnould and L. L. Price, "River Magic: Extraordinary Experience and the Extended Service Encounter," *Journal of Consumer Research* 20 (June 1993), pp. 24–45.

16. N. Bendapudi and R. P. Leone, "How to Lose Your Star Performer without Losing Customers, Too," *Harvard Business Review,* November 2001, pp. 104–15.

17. P. Kumar, "The Impact of Long-Term Client Relationships on the Performance of Business Service Firms," *Journal of Service Research* 2 (August 1999), pp. 4–18.

18. F. F. Reichheld and W. E. Sasser Jr., "Zero Defections: Quality Comes to Services," *Harvard Business Review,* September–October 1990, pp. 105–11; and F. F. Reichheld, *The Loyalty Effect* (Boston: Harvard Business School Press, 1996).

19. R. Dhar and R. Glazer, "Hedging Customers," *Harvard Business Review* 81 (May 2003), pp. 86–92.

20. D. D. Gremler and S. W. Brown, "The Loyalty Ripple Effect: Appreciating the Full Value of Customers," *International Journal of Service Industry Management* 10, no. 3 (1999), pp. 271–91.

21. L. A. Bettencourt, "Customer Voluntary Performance: Customers as Partners in Service Delivery," *Journal of Retailing* 73 (Fall 1997), pp. 383–406.

22. S. J. Grove and R. P. Fisk, "The Impact of Other Customers on Service Experiences: A Critical Incident Examination of 'Getting Along'," *Journal of Retailing* 73 (Spring 1997), pp. 63–85.

23. L. L. Price, E. J. Arnould, and A. Hausman, "Commercial Friendships: Service Provider–Client Relationship Dynamics," in *Frontiers in Services,* ed. R. T. Rust and R. L. Oliver (Nashville: Vanderbilt University, 1996).

24. Reichheld and Sasser, "Zero Defections."

25. Additional frameworks for calculating lifetime customer value that include a variety of other variables can be found in W. J. Reinartz and V. Kumar, "The Impact of Customer Relationship Characteristics on Profitable Lifetime Duration," *Journal of Marketing* 67 (January 2003), pp. 77–99; Dhar and Glazer, "Hedging Customers"; H. K. Stahl, K. Matzler, and H. H. Hinterhuber, "Linking Customer Lifetime Value with Shareholder Value," *Industrial Marketing Management* 32, no. 4 (2003), pp. 267–79.

26. This example is cited in J. L. Heskett, W. E. Sasser Jr., and L. A. Schlesinger, *The Service Profit Chain* (New York: The Free Press, 1997), pp. 200–201.

27. S. Gupta, D. R. Helmann, and J. A. Stuart, "Valuing Customers," *Journal of Marketing Research* 41 (February 2004), pp. 7–18.

28. For more on customer profitability segments and related strategies, see V. A. Zeithaml, R. T. Rust, and K. N. Lemon, "The Customer Pyramid: Creating and Serving Profitable Customers," *California Management Review* 43 (Summer 2001), pp. 118–42.

29. R. Brooks, "Alienating Customers Isn't Always a Bad Idea, Many Firms Discover," *The Wall Street Journal*, January 7, 1999, p. A1.

30. F. Reichheld, "Loyalty-Based Management," *Harvard Business Review,* March–April 1993, pp. 64–74.

31. G. Hartfeil, "Bank One Measures Profitability of Customers, Not Just Products," *Journal of Retail Banking Services* 18, no. 2 (1996), pp. 24–31.

32. D. Brady, "Why Service Stinks," *BusinessWeek,* October 23, 2000, pp. 118–28.

33. Dhar and Glazer, "Hedging Customers."

34. D. Rosenblum, D. Tomlinson, and L. Scott, "Bottom-Feeding for Blockbuster Businesses," *Harvard Business Review* 81 (March 2003), pp. 52–59.

35. See T. A. Burnham, J. K. Frels, and V. Mahajan, "Consumer Switching Costs: A Typology, Antecedents, and Consequences," *Journal of the Academy of Marketing Science* 32 (Spring 2003), pp. 109–26; F. Selnes, "An Examination of the Effect of Product Performance on Brand Reputation, Satisfaction, and Loyalty," *European Journal of Marketing* 27, no. 9 (2003), 19–35; P. Klemperer, "The Competitiveness of Markets with Switching Costs," *Rand Journal of Economics* 18 (Spring 1987), pp. 138–50.

36. T. L. Huston and R. L. Burgess, "Social Exchange in Developing Relationships: An Overview," in *Social Exchange in Developing Relationships*, ed. R. L. Burgess and T. L. Huston (New York: Academic Press, 1979), pp. 3–28; L. White and V. Yanamandram, "Why Customers Stay: Reasons and Consequences of Inertia in Financial Services," *Managing Service Quality* 14, nos. 2/3 (2004), pp. 183–94.

37. See J. P. Guiltinan, "A Classification of Switching Costs with Implications for Relationship Marketing," in *Marketing Theory and Practice*, ed. Terry L. Childers et al. (Chicago: American Marketing Association, 1989), pp. 216–20; Klemperer, "The Competitiveness of Markets with Switching Costs"; C. Fornell, "A National Customer Satisfaction Barometer: The Swedish Experience," *Journal of Marketing* 56 (January 1992), pp. 6–21; P. G. Patterson and T. Smith, "A Cross-Cultural Study of Switching Barriers and Propensity to Stay with Service Providers," *Journal of Retailing* 79 (Summer 2003), pp. 107–20.

38. See Bendapudi and Berry, "Customers' Motivations for Maintaining Relationships with Service Providers"; H. S. Bansal, P. G. Irving, and S. F. Taylor, "A Three-Component Model of Customer Commitment to Service Providers," *Journal of the Academy of Marketing Science* 32 (Summer 2004), pp. 234–50.

39. Berry and Parasuraman, *Marketing Services,* pp. 136–42.

40. For more information on cautions to be considered in implementing rewards strategies, see L. O'Brien and C. Jones, "Do Rewards Really Create Loyalty?" *Harvard Business Review,* May–June 1995, pp. 75–82; and G. R. Dowling and M. Uncles, "Do Customer Loyalty Programs Really Work?" *Sloan Management Review,* Summer 1997, pp. 71–82.

41. Bendapudi and Leone, "How to Lose Your Star Performer without Losing Customers."

42. D. V. Fites, "Make Your Dealers Your Partners," *Harvard Business Review,* March–April 1996, pp. 84–95.

43. D. D. Gremler and S. W. Brown, "Service Loyalty: Its Nature, Importance, and Implications," in *Advancing Service Quality: A Global Perspective*, ed. Bo Edvardsson et al. (Jamaica, NY: International Service Quality Association, 1996), pp. 171–80; H. Hansen, K. Sandvik, and F. Selnes, "Direct and Indirect Effects of Commitment to a Service Employee on the Intention to Stay," *Journal of Service Research 5* (May 2003), pp. 356–68.

44. See J. Pine, *Mass Customization: The New Frontier in Business Competition* (Boston: Harvard Business School Press, 1993); and M. Treacy and F. Wiersema, "Customer Intimacy and Other Value Disciplines," *Harvard Business Review*, January–February 1993, pp. 84–93.

45. C. W. Hart, "Made to Order," *Marketing Management* 5 (Summer 1996), pp. 11–23.

46. Arthur Andersen, *Best Practices: Building Your Business with Customer-Focused Solutions* (New York: Simon & Schuster, 1998), pp. 125–27.

47. L. M. Grossman, "Federal Express, UPS Face Off on Computers," *The Wall Street Journal*, September 17, 1993, p. B1.

48. R. Brooks, "Alienating Customers Isn't Always a Bad Idea." P. Carroll and S. Rose, "Revisiting Customer Retention," *Journal of Retail Banking* 15, no. 1 (1993), pp. 5–13.

49. J. Dahl, "Rental Counters Reject Drivers without Good Records," *The Wall Street Journal*, October 23, 1992, p. B1.

50. See L. C. Harris and K. L. Reynolds, "The Consequences of Dysfunctional Customer Behavior," *Journal of Service Research* 6 (November 2003), p. 145 for cites; also, see A. A. Grandey, D. N. Dickter, and H. P. Sin, "The Customer Is *Not* Always Right: Customer Aggression and Emotion Regulation of Service Employees," *Journal of Organizational Behavior* 25 (2004), pp. 397–418.

51. K. Ohnezeit, recruiting supervisor for Enterprise Rent-A-Car, personal communication, February 12, 2004.

52. See Harris and Reynolds, "The Consequences of Dysfunctional Customer Behavior."

53. L. Bird, "The Clients That Exasperate Madison Avenue," *The Wall Street Journal*, November 2, 1993, p. B1.

54. Ibid.

55. For a detailed discussion on relationship ending, see A. Halinen and J. Tähtinen, "A Process Theory of Relationship Ending," *International Journal of Service Industry Management* 13, no. 2 (2002), 163–80.

56. M. Schrage, "Fire Your Customers," *The Wall Street Journal*, March 16, 1992, p. A8.

57. S. Shellenbarger, "More Firms, Siding with Employees, Bid Bad Clients Farewell," *The Wall Street Journal*, February 16, 2000, p. B1.

58. "Service with Soul" video, hosted by Tom Peters (Chicago: Video Publishing House, 1995); and http://www.nypro.com.

Chapter 8

SERVICE RECOVERY

This chapter's objectives are to

1. Illustrate the importance of recovery from service failures in keeping customers and building loyalty.

2. Discuss the nature of consumer complaints and why people do and do not complain.

3. Provide evidence of what customers expect and the kind of responses they want when they do complain.

4. Present strategies for effective service recovery, together with examples of what does and does not work.

5. Discuss service guarantees—what they are, the benefits of guarantees, and when to use them—as a particular type of service recovery strategy.

September 11, 2001: Rebuilding a Firm—The Ultimate Service Recovery

"As I watched TV on September 11, 2001, I was struck with horror along with the rest of the world at the sight of the World Trade Center towers in New York City collapsing. My immediate thoughts that morning were, as for many, of friends and loved ones who worked in those towers, wondering where they were and if they were all right. In my case, it was a friend of over 30 years who worked in the North Tower of the World Trade Center, on the 55th floor, in a law firm where he is a partner. Other friends and I immediately started to think of ways to reach him, and eventually one of us did, that afternoon. He was safe."

M.J.B.

The story of how Sidley Austin Brown & Wood was able to rebuild itself and serve its clients and employees was reported in *The New York Times* the following Sunday, September 16.[1] A remarkable story, it is the ultimate example of service recovery in its most monumental proportions. All but one of the firm's '600 employees who worked in the WTC survived the disaster, and they were back in business, able to serve their clients, within six days.

Sidley Austin Brown & Wood is the fourth largest law firm in the United States, employing 1,325 attorneys and serving large corporate, financial, and government clients. The firm is the result of a merger in 2001 of two firms with long histories—Sidley & Austin founded in 1866 in Chicago and Brown & Wood founded in 1914 in New York. The firm has primary offices in New York and Chicago and additional offices in San Francisco; Los Angeles; Washington, D.C.; Seattle; Dallas; Shanghai; Tokyo; Hong Kong; Beijing; Singapore; and London.

How did the firm achieve its remarkable recovery following September 11? Some of it had to do with careful planning as a result of surviving the WTC bombing in 1993. A lot of it had to do with courageous, focused employees as well as cooperative, helpful suppliers and understanding clients. We can capture here only a tiny bit of what happened.

The first and highest priority of the firm was, of course, its employees and their safety. All 13 offices of the firm around the world were shut down the day following the collapse of the twin towers, and three centers of activity were established to deal with the aftermath. Once it was learned that most employees were accounted for and out of the building, the firm's administrators and managing partners focused on reestablishing the New York office and began assessing what it needed to do to serve its employees and its corporate and government clients.[2]

Within three hours of the disaster, a partner in the firm had secured leases on four additional floors of a building in midtown New York where the firm already had some space. The cost of the space was not discussed, and a firm that was due to move into the space agreed to delay its move to give the space to Sidley, at least temporarily. By the end of the day, others had arranged for the delivery of 800 desks, 300 computers, and hundreds of cell phones. Contractors were hired that day to string cable and reestablish the firm's computer network. Normal rules of business were bypassed as suppliers and even competitors offered to help. Nightly backups of the firm's entire electronic network enabled everything up to the night before the attacks to be restored. The backup tapes were stored in New Jersey by two independent firms and needed to be shipped immediately to Chicago so they could be restored and readied for use. Because no planes were flying for several days, these companies offered to have their own employees drive the tapes to Chicago from New Jersey.

On September 12 a letter to "our colleagues, clients, and friends" appeared on the firm's website to assure clients of the progress being made to serve them without interruption, ending with the following statement: "We will not let down our predecessors, or our current colleagues, clients, and friends. From this tragedy, we have the opportunity to build something stronger and more energized than ever before, and we intend to do so. Thank you for your thoughts and prayers. We will keep you informed."[3] The firm was back in business, serving its clients, in its new midtown offices on September 17.

During and following all the hectic efforts to reopen the firm for business, people remained a primary concern. Once the safety of employees, friends, and loved ones was assured, the firm turned to providing counseling, to ensuring that employees' pay was not interrupted, to bringing people together to see each other and share their feelings, and to ensuring the security of the workplace. Heroic stories of employee actions and sad accounts of the things they felt and saw in those days in September have become part of the fabric and culture of the firm. Six hundred of its employees worked in the WTC and were displaced on that day in September. All but one of those employees survived the disaster.

The preceding two chapters have given you grounding in understanding customers through research as well as through knowing them as individuals and developing strong relationships with them. These strategies, matched with effective service design, delivery, and communication—treated in other parts of the text—form the foundations for service success. But, in all service contexts—whether customer service, consumer services, or business-to-business services—service failure is inevitable. Failure is inevitable even for the best of firms with the best of intentions, even for those with world-class service systems.

To fully understand and retain their customers, firms must know what customers expect when service failures occur, and must implement effective strategies for service recovery. Our chapter opening vignette illustrates how one firm was able to recover even under the most unexpected and dire circumstances.

THE IMPACT OF SERVICE FAILURE AND RECOVERY

Service recovery refers to the actions taken by an organization in response to a service failure. Failures occur for all kinds of reasons—the service may be unavailable when promised, it may be delivered late or too slowly, the outcome may be incorrect or poorly executed, or employees may be rude or uncaring.[4] All these types of failures bring about negative feelings and responses from customers. Left unfixed, they can result in customers leaving, telling other customers about their negative experiences, and even challenging the organization through consumer rights organizations or legal channels.

Service Recovery Effects

Research has shown that resolving customer problems effectively has a strong impact on customer satisfaction, loyalty, word-of-mouth communication, and bottom-line performance.[5] That is, customers who experience service failures but who are ultimately satisfied based on recovery efforts by the firm, will be more loyal than those whose problems are not resolved. That loyalty translates into profitability, as you learned in Chapter 7. Data from the Technical Assistance Research Program (TARP) verifies this relationship, as shown in Figure 8.1.[6] Customers who complain and have their problems resolved quickly are much more likely to repurchase than are those whose complaints are not resolved. Those who never complain are *least* likely to repurchase.

Similar results were reported in a study of 720 HMO members in which researchers found that those who were not satisfied with service recovery were much more likely to switch to a different health care provider than were those who were happy with how their problems were addressed.[7] The study also found that satisfaction with service recovery was the second most important factor out of 11 service attributes in predicting overall customer satisfaction. The most important factor, not surprisingly, was perceived medical outcome.

Hampton Inn® Hotels directly realized the benefits of effective service recovery through their service guarantee. They achieved $11 million in additional revenue and the highest customer retention rate in their industry after implementing the 100 percent customer satisfaction guarantee shown in Figure 8.2.[8] The guarantee reimburses customers who experience service failures in their hotels—and is part of an overall service recovery and customer retention strategy.

FIGURE 8.1
Unhappy Customers'
Repurchase
Intentions

Source: Adapted from data
reported by the Technical
Assistance Research Program.

Unhappy customers who
***DON'T* complain** 9%

Unhappy customers who
***DO* complain**

Complaints not resolved 19%

Complaints resolved 54%

Complaints resolved
quickly 82%

Percentage of customers who will buy again after a major complaint
(over $100 losses)

An effective service recovery strategy has multiple potential impacts. It can increase customer satisfaction and loyalty and generate positive word-of-mouth communication. A well-designed, well-documented service recovery strategy also provides information that can be used to improve service as part of a continuous improvement effort. By making adjustments to service processes, systems, and outcomes based on previous service recovery experiences, companies increase the likelihood of "doing it right the first time." In turn, this reduces costs of failures and increases initial customer satisfaction.

Unfortunately, many firms do not employ effective recovery strategies. A recent study suggests that 50 percent of customers who experienced a serious problem received no response from the firm.[9] There are tremendous downsides to having no service recovery or ineffective service recovery strategies. Poor recovery following a bad service experience can lead to customers who are so dissatisfied that they become "terrorists," actively pursuing opportunities to openly criticize the company.[10] When customers experience a service failure, they talk about it to others no matter what the outcome. That recent study also found that customers who were satisfied with a firm's recovery efforts talked to an

FIGURE 8.2
The 100 Percent
Hampton Inn®
Hotels Guarantee

Source: Courtesy of Hampton
Inn® Hotels.

Exhibit 8.1

THE INTERNET SPREADS THE STORY OF POOR SERVICE RECOVERY: "YOURS IS A VERY BAD HOTEL"

In November 2002, when Tom F. and Shane A. experienced poor service from a hotel in Houston, Texas, they decided to create a PowerPoint slide show as a way to vent their frustrations. Their intent was to chronicle the "shabby treatment" they received at a Doubletree Inn while on a business trip. The men sent the PowerPoint presentation to two managers at the hotel as well as to two clients from Houston and Shane's mother-in-law. Within a month this presentation, entitled "Yours is a Very Bad Hotel," had been circulated around the globe. As a result, the Seattle-based Web consultants received more than 9,000 e-mail messages from six continents, and their experience was written up in *USA Today*.

companion Shane did expect an apology and a prompt resolution from the employee they would later dub "Night Clerk Mike." Instead, as they noted in the slide show, they received "insolence plus insults" and, eventually, two smokers' rooms in a "dump" of a hotel several miles away (and 15 minutes further) from the downtown area where they were to have a meeting later that morning.

Once the disappointed travelers returned to Seattle, they detailed their frustrations via bar charts, graphs, and statistical analyses ("Lifetime chances of dying in a bathtub: 1 in 10,455. Chances of winning the U.K. Lottery: 7 in 13,983,816. Chance of us returning to the Doubletree Club Houston: Worse than any of those."). After the two had created and e-mailed the PowerPoint file to the hotel managers, they encouraged the three extra people to whom they sent the file to "share it with a few of your friends," anticipating that no more than a few dozen fellow travelers would ever see the PowerPoint slide show. Instead, the response "percolated beyond our wildest dreams," said Tom. At various points in time *The Wall Street Journal, Forbes, MSNBC,* and *Travel Weekly* ran short stories, without any direct input from the travelers, based on a Frequently Asked Questions web page the two businessmen had created in response to inquiries they received about their experience. Tom and Shane received hundreds of requests from business schools and hospitality companies to use the slide show as an example of "customer service gone horribly wrong." And in addition to the response from supportive well-wishers, the presentation generated an offer of a free two-night stay at any Hilton hotel. The two men declined the offer in lieu of a $1,000 charitable donation to Houston's Toys for Tots and encouraged their "fans" to do the same. Hotel management also provided the men with a list of actions taken to improve employee training and overbooking policies. All these changes occurred simply because two men documented their frustrations and made it available to a couple of friends via the Internet!

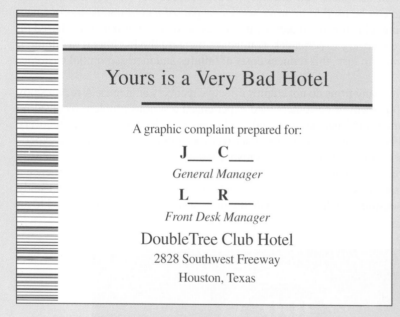

Yours is a Very Bad Hotel

A graphic complaint prepared for:

J___ C___

General Manager

L___ R___

Front Desk Manager

DoubleTree Club Hotel

2828 Southwest Freeway

Houston, Texas

The trouble began one early morning that November when the two businessmen, delayed in their arrival at Doubletree (owned by Hilton Hotels) because of a late-arriving plane, stepped up to the front desk at about 2:00 A.M. with a confirmation and credit card guarantee for late arrival. Unfortunately, the hotel was overbooked and their rooms had been given away hours earlier. Although disappointed, they understood. "These things happen, and we didn't expect miracles," recalled Tom. However, as a "card-carrying Hilton HHonors Gold VIP" who had logged 100,000 miles of business travel the previous year, Tom and his traveling

Source: L. Bly, "Online Complaint about Bad Hotel Service Scores Bull's-eye," *USA Today,* January 4, 2002, p. D6.

average of seven people, whereas those customers who were dissatisfied with the response talked to an average of 25 people.[11] With the ability to share such stories on the Internet, the potential reach of such dissatisfied customers is even greater. (See Exhibit 8.1 about the two dissatisfied Doubletree Inn customers.) Further, repeated service failures without an effective recovery strategy in place can aggravate even the best employees. The costs in employee morale and even lost employees can be huge but often overlooked costs of not having an effective service recovery strategy.

The Recovery Paradox

Occasionally some businesses have customers who are initially dissatisfied with a service experience and then experience a high level of excellent service recovery, seemingly leading them to be even more satisfied and more likely to repurchase than if no problem had occurred at all; that is, they appear to be more satisfied after they experience a service failure than they otherwise would have been![12] To illustrate, consider a hotel customer who arrives to check in and finds that no room is available. In an effort to recover, the hotel front desk person immediately upgrades this guest to a better room at the original price. The customer, thrilled with this compensation, reports that she is extremely satisfied with this experience, is even more impressed with the hotel than she was before, and vows to be loyal into the future. Although such extreme instances are relatively rare, this idea—that an initially disappointed customer who has experienced good service recovery might be even more satisfied and loyal as a result—has been labeled the *recovery paradox.*

So, should a firm "screw up" just a little so that it can "fix the problem" superbly? If doing so would actually lead to more satisfied customers, is this strategy worth pursuing? The logical, but not very rational, conclusion is that companies should *plan to disappoint customers* so they can recover well and (hopefully) gain even greater loyalty from them! What are the problems with such an approach? First, as we indicated earlier in this chapter, a vast majority of customers do not complain when they experience a problem. The possibility of a recovery exists only in situations in which the firm is aware of a problem and is able to recover well; if customers do not make the firm aware of the failure—and most do not—dissatisfaction is most likely to be the result. Second, it is expensive to fix mistakes; re-creating or reworking a service may be quite costly to a firm. Third, it would appear somewhat ludicrous to encourage service failures—after all, reliability ("doing it right the first time") is the most critical determinant of service quality across industries. Finally, although the recovery paradox suggests that a customer *may* end up more satisfied after experiencing excellent recovery, there is certainly *no* guarantee that the customer actually *will* end up more satisfied. The recovery paradox is highly dependent on the context and situation; although one customer may find it easy to forgive a restaurant who provides him with a gift certificate for a later date for having lost his dinner reservation, another customer who had planned to propose marriage to his date over dinner may not be all that happy with the same recovery scenario.

The intrigue stimulated by the recovery paradox has led to empirical research specifically on this issue. Although anecdotal evidence provides limited support for the recovery paradox, research seems to indicate that this phenomenon is not pervasive. In one study, researchers found that only the very highest levels of customers' service recovery ratings resulted in increased satisfaction and loyalty.[13] This research suggests that customers weigh their most recent experiences heavily in their determination of whether to buy again. If the most recent experience is negative, overall feelings about the company will decrease and repurchase intentions will also diminish significantly.

Unless the recovery effort is absolutely superlative, it cannot overcome the negative impression of the initial experience enough to build repurchase intentions beyond the point at which they would be if the service had been provided correctly in the first place. A second study found that overall satisfaction was consistently lower for those customers who had experienced a service failure than for those who had experienced no failure, no matter what the recovery effort.[14] An explanation for why no recovery paradox occurred is suggested by the magnitude of the service failure in this study— a three-hour airplane flight delay. Perhaps this type of failure may be too much to be overcome by any recovery effort. However, in this study, strong service recovery was able to mitigate, if not reverse, the effects of the failure by reducing overall dissatisfaction. Finally, a rather recent study suggests that the recovery paradox phenomenon *may* only exist after *one* service failure; however, if a customer experiences a second service failure, the likelihood of the customer's evaluations of the service being greater after the second failure is minimal.[15] That is, although satisfactory service recoveries might produce a recovery paradox after one failure, they do not trigger such paradoxical increases after two failures.

Given the mixed opinions on the extent to which the recovery paradox exists, "doing it right the first time" is still the best and safest strategy in the long run. However, when a failure does occur, then every effort at a superior recovery should be made to mitigate its negative effects. If the failure can be fully overcome, if the failure is less critical, or if the recovery effort is clearly superlative, it may be possible to observe evidence of the recovery paradox.

HOW CUSTOMERS RESPOND TO SERVICE FAILURES

Customers who experience service failures can respond in a variety of ways, as illustrated in Figure 8.3.[16] It is assumed that following a failure, dissatisfaction at some level will occur for the customer. In fact, research suggests that a variety of negative emotions can occur following a service failure, including such feelings as anger, discontent, disappointment, self-pity, and anxiety.[17] These initial negative responses will affect how customers evaluate the service recovery effort and presumably their ultimate decision to return to the provider or not.[18]

Many customers are very passive about their dissatisfaction, simply saying or doing nothing. Whether they take action or not, at some point the customers will decide whether to stay with that provider or switch to a competitor. As we already have pointed out, customers who do not complain are least likely to return. For companies, customer passivity in the face of dissatisfaction is a threat to future success.

Why People Do (and Do Not) Complain

Some customers are more likely to complain than others for a variety of reasons. These consumers believe that positive consequences may occur and that there are social benefits of complaining, and their personal norms support their complaining behavior. They believe they should and will be provided compensation for the service failure in some form. They believe that fair treatment and good service are their due, and that in cases of service failure, someone should make good. In some cases they feel a social obligation to complain—to help others avoid similar situations or to punish the service provider. A very small number of consumers have "complaining" personalities—they just like to complain or cause trouble.

FIGURE 8.3   **Customer Complaint Actions Following Service Failure**

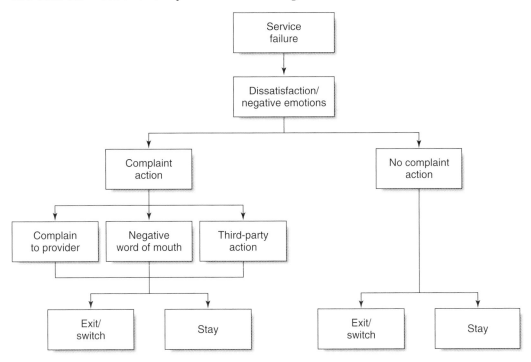

Consumers who are unlikely to take any action hold the opposite beliefs. They often see complaining as a waste of their time and effort. They do not believe anything positive will occur for them or others based on their actions. Sometimes they do not know how to complain—they do not understand the process or may not realize that avenues are open to them to voice their complaints. In some cases noncomplainers may engage in "emotion-focused coping" to deal with their negative experiences. This type of coping involves self-blame, denial, and possibly seeking social support.[19] They may feel that the failure was somehow their fault and that they do not deserve redress.

Personal relevance of the failure can also influence whether people complain.[20] If the service failure is really important, if the failure has critical consequences for the consumer, or if the consumer has much ego involvement in the service experience, then he or she is more likely to complain. The situation at Doubletree Inn, which is described in Exhibit 8.1, illustrates a failure for a service that had been considered especially important to two customers. Consumers are more likely to complain about services that are expensive, high risk, and ego involving (like vacation packages, airline travel, and medical services) than they are about less expensive, frequently purchased services (fast-food drive-through service, a cab ride, a call to a customer service help line). These latter services are simply not important enough to warrant the time to complain. Unfortunately, even though the experience may not be important to the consumer at the moment, a dissatisfying encounter can still drive him or her to a competitor next time the service is needed.

Types of Customer Complaint Actions

If customers initiate actions following service failure, the action can be of various types. A dissatisfied customer can choose to complain on the spot to the service provider, giving the company the opportunity to respond immediately. This reaction is often the best-case scenario for the company because it has a second chance right at that moment to satisfy the customer, keep his or her business in the future, and potentially avoid any negative word of mouth. Customers who do not complain immediately may choose to complain later to the provider by phone, in writing, or via the Internet. Again, the company has a chance to recover. Researchers refer to these proactive types of complaining behavior as *voice* responses or *seeking redress.*

Some customers choose not to complain directly to the provider but rather spread negative word of mouth about the company to friends, relatives, and coworkers. This negative word-of-mouth communication can be extremely detrimental because it can reinforce the customer's feelings of negativism and spread that negative impression to others as well. Further, the company has no chance to recover unless the negative word of mouth is accompanied by a complaint directly to the company. In recent years, customers have taken to complaining via the Internet. A variety of websites, including web-based consumer opinion platforms,[21] have been created to facilitate customer complaints and, in doing so, have provided customers with the possibility of spreading negative word-of-mouth communication to a much broader audience. Some customers become so dissatisfied with a product or service failure that they construct websites targeting the firm's current and prospective customers. On these sites,[22] angry customers convey their grievances against the firm in ways designed to convince other consumers of the firm's incompetence and evil.[23]

Finally, customers may choose to complain to third parties such as the Better Business Bureau, to consumer affairs arms of the government, to a licensing authority, to a professional association, or potentially to a private attorney. No matter the action (or inaction), ultimately the customers determine whether to patronize the service provider again or to switch to another provider.

Types of Complainers

Research suggests that people can be grouped into categories based on how they respond to failures. Four categories of response types were identified in a study that focused on grocery stores, automotive repair services, medical care, and banking and financial services[24]: *passives, voicers, irates,* and *activists.* Although the proportion of the types of complainers is likely to vary across industries and contexts, it is likely that these four types of complainers will be relatively consistent and that each type can be found in all companies and industries.

Passives

This group of customers is least likely to take any action. They are unlikely to say anything to the provider, less likely than others to spread negative word of mouth, and unlikely to complain to a third party. They often doubt the effectiveness of complaining, thinking that the consequences will not merit the time and effort they will expend. Sometimes their personal values or norms argue against complaining. These folks tend to feel less alienated from the marketplace than irates and activists.

Voicers

These customers actively complain to the service provider, but they are less likely to spread negative word of mouth, to switch patronage, or to go to third parties with their complaints. *These customers should be viewed as the service provider's best friends!* They actively complain and thus give the company a second chance. As with the passives, these customers are less alienated from the marketplace than those in the other two groups. They tend to believe complaining has social benefits and therefore do not hesitate to voice their opinions. They believe that the consequences of complaining to the provider can be very positive, and they believe less in other types of complaining such as spreading word of mouth or talking to third parties. Their personal norms are consistent with complaining.

Irates

These consumers are more likely than are others to engage in negative word-of-mouth communication with friends and relatives and to switch providers. They are about average in their propensity to complain to the provider. They are unlikely to complain to third parties. These folks tend to feel somewhat alienated from the marketplace. As their label suggests, they are more angry with the provider, although they do believe that complaining to the provider can have social benefits. They are less likely to give the service provider a second chance and instead will switch to a competitor, spreading the word to friends and relatives along the way.

Activists

These consumers are characterized by above average propensity to complain on all dimensions: they will complain to the provider, they will tell others, and they are more likely than any other group to complain to third parties. Complaining fits with their personal norms. As with the irates, these consumers are more alienated from the marketplace than the other groups. They have a very optimistic sense of the potential positive consequences of all types of complaining.

In extreme cases these consumers can become "terrorists," as in the Starbucks Coffee case described in Exhibit 8.2.

CUSTOMERS' RECOVERY EXPECTATIONS

When they take the time and effort to complain, customers generally have high expectations. They expect the firm to be accountable. They expect to be helped quickly. They expect to be compensated for their grief and for the hassle of being inconvenienced. And they expect to be treated nicely in the process. Our "Story of a Service Hero," Exhibit 8.3, epitomizes this kind of service recovery.

Understanding and Accountability

In many service failure situations, customers are not looking for extreme actions from the firm; however, they are looking to understand what happened and for firms to be accountable for their actions (or inactions).[25] One study identified the seven most common "remedies" that customers seek when they experience a serious problem[26]; three of these remedies were to have the product repaired or service fixed, to be reimbursed all their money, or to be reimbursed part of their money. Interestingly, however, the other four remedies—including an apology from the firm, an explanation by the firm as to what happened, an assurance that the problem would not be repeated, and an opportunity for the customer to vent his or her frustrations to the firm—cost the firm very little to provide.

These four non-monetary remedies consist primarily of providing employees the opportunity to communicate with customers. Understanding and accountability are very important to many customers after a service failure, for if they perceive an injustice has occurred, someone is to blame. Customers expect an apology when things go

Exhibit 8.2 THE STARBUCKS COFFEE TERRORIST

Starbucks Coffee has set the pace in its industry—from its humble beginnings in Seattle, Washington, in the early 1970s, this coffee retail giant has grown to approximately 4,000 outlets in the United States and over 1,000 in other parts of the world including the Middle East, Europe, and the Pacific Rim. The company and its legendary CEO, Howard Schulz, have a reputation for world-class service and outstanding employee relations and benefits. (Look ahead to Chapter 14, Exhibit 14.1, for a full description of the Starbucks success story.) But even giants like Starbucks can stumble—no one in the service industry can escape failures from time to time. And sometimes a seemingly innocent failure can escalate, as it did for Starbucks in the following story.

The story began when a Starbucks customer bought a defective cappuccino maker, which he returned for a replacement. While returning the machine, he bought another for a friend as a gift—however, he did not receive the 1/2-pound free coffee promised with the machine. And, the customer claims, the employee was rude besides. Unfortunately, the gift machine also turned out to be defective, so the customer demanded that Starbucks replace it with its top-of-the-line cappuccino machine, worth approximately $2,000 more than he had paid for the gift. The customer threatened to take out a full-page ad in *The Wall Street Journal* denouncing the company if his request were refused. The company refused. A full-page ad against Starbucks appeared in the *Journal,* with the customer soliciting others to complain through his own 800 number. When Starbucks apologized and attempted to replace both machines, the customer claimed that was not enough and placed even more demands on Starbucks. He demanded that the company place a full-page ad in the *Journal* apologizing to him and that it fund his favorite charity. Needless to say, the whole issue received national media attention.

Although these types of customer terrorism are rare indeed, the example points to what can happen and the lengths some customer terrorists are willing to go to.

Experts were asked at the time of the incident to comment on the situation at Starbucks. All experts noted how critical that first encounter with the Starbucks employee was in setting the stage and tone for the rest of the story. One expert believed Starbucks should have given the customer two pounds of coffee when he came to return the first defective machine, and then followed up with a call within a week to determine whether both machines were working. Another expert suggested that customers with problems be put on a VIP list to alert employees and management to treat subsequent transactions with extreme care and priority. Still another felt Starbucks should have replaced the defective machine with the $2,000+ machine immediately—no questions. This expert believes that the percentage of customers who are this demanding is so small that it is worth spending whatever is necessary to avoid potential acts of customer terrorism such as this one. Another expert felt that as soon as the *Journal* ad appeared the company should have flown someone out to talk to the customer face-to-face, apologize, listen to the customer, and find out what he wanted. Several of the experts acknowledged that past a certain point damage control is the only option, but escalation to that point can often be avoided.

This story illustrates how even world-class service providers can be caught in tough situations.

Sources: "Customers from Hell: Nightmare or Opportunity," *On Achieving Excellence,* December 1995, pp. 2–3; and A. Lucas, "Trouble Brews for Starbucks," *Sales and Marketing Management* 147, no. 8 (August 1995), p. 15; www.starbucks.com.

wrong, and a company that provides one demonstrates courtesy and respect; customers also want to know what the company is going to do to ensure that the problem does not recur.[27] Results from the study mentioned in the previous paragraph suggest that when a firm does nothing about a service failure, 86 percent of the customers are dissatisfied with the "response"; however, if a firm provides an apology to the customer, the percentage of dissatisfied customers drops to 20 percent.[28] Providing customers with an opportunity to vent their frustrations has a similar effect, because doing so reduces customer dissatisfaction with the response to about 33 percent.[29] Customer discontent can also be moderated if customers understand why the failure occurred and what specific actions were undertaken to recover.[30] Customers clearly value such communication, because these nonmonetary remedies were found to be positively

A good recovery can turn angry, frustrated customers into loyal ones. It can, in fact, create more goodwill than if things had gone smoothly in the first place. Consider how Club Med–Cancun, part of the Paris-based Club Mediterranèe, recovered from a service nightmare and won the loyalty of one group of vacationers.

The vacationers had nothing but trouble getting from New York to their Mexican destination. The flight took off 6 hours late, made two unexpected stops, and circled 30 minutes before it could land. Because of all the delays and mishaps, the plane was en route for 10 hours more than planned and ran out of food and drinks. It finally arrived at two o'clock in the morning, with a landing so rough that oxygen masks and luggage dropped from overhead. By the time the plane pulled up to the gate, the soured passengers were faint with hunger and convinced that their vacation was ruined before it had even started. One lawyer on board was already collecting names and addresses for a class-action lawsuit.

Silvio de Bortoli, the general manager of the Cancun resort and a legend throughout the organization for his ability to satisfy customers, got word of the horrendous flight and immediately created an antidote. He took half the staff

to the airport, where they laid out a table of snacks and drinks and set up a stereo system to play lively music. As the guests filed through the gate, they received personal greetings, help with their bags, a sympathetic ear, and a chauffeured ride to the resort. Waiting for them at Club Med was a lavish banquet, complete with mariachi band and champagne. Moreover, the staff had rallied other guests to wake up and greet the newcomers, and the partying continued until sunrise. Many guests said it was the most fun they'd had since college.

In the end, the vacationers had a better experience than if their flight from New York had gone like clockwork. Although the company probably couldn't measure it, Club Mediterranèe won market share that night. After all, the battle for market share is won not by analyzing demographic trends, ratings points, and other global measures, but rather by pleasing customers one at a time.

related to satisfaction with the complaint process, continued loyalty, and positive word-of-mouth communication.[31]

Fair Treatment

Customers also want justice and fairness in handling their complaints. Service recovery experts Steve Brown and Steve Tax have documented three specific types of justice that customers are looking for following their complaints: *outcome fairness, procedural fairness,* and *interactional fairness.*[32] Outcome fairness concerns the results that customers receive from their complaints; procedural fairness refers to the policies, rules, and timeliness of the complaint process; and interactional fairness focuses on the interpersonal treatment received during the complaint process.[33] Exhibit 8.4 shows examples of each type of fairness taken from Brown and Tax's study of consumers who reported on their experiences with complaint resolution.

Outcome Fairness

Customers expect outcomes, or compensation, that match the level of their dissatisfaction. This compensation can take the form of actual monetary compensation, an apology, future free services, reduced charges, repairs, and/or replacements. Customers expect equity in the exchange—that is, they want to feel that the company has "paid" for its mistakes in a manner at least equal to what the customer has suffered. The company's "punishment should fit the crime." Customers expect equality—that is, they want to be compensated no more or less than other customers who have experienced the same type of service failure. They also appreciate it when a company gives

Exhibit 8.4   Fairness Themes in Service Recovery

	Fair	Unfair
Outcome fairness: the results that customers receive from complaints	*"The waitress agreed that there was a problem. She took the sandwiches back to the kitchen and had them replaced. We were also given a free drink."* *"They were very thorough with my complaint. One week later I received a coupon for a free oil change and an apology from the shop owner."*	*"Their refusal to refund our money or make up for the inconvenience and cold food was inexcusable."* *"If I wanted a refund, I had to go back to the store the next day. It's a 20-minute drive; the refund was barely worth the trouble."* *"All I wanted was for the ticket agent to apologize for doubting my story. I never got the apology."*
Procedural fairness: the policies, rules, and timeliness of the complaint process	*"The hotel manager said that it didn't matter to her who was at fault, she would take responsibility for the problem immediately."* *"The sales manager called me back one week after my complaint to check if the problem was taken care of to my satisfaction."*	*"They should have assisted me with the problem instead of giving me a phone number to call. No one returned my calls, and I never had a chance to speak to a real person."* *"I had to tell my problem to too many people. I had to become irate in order to talk with the manager, who was apparently the only one who could provide a solution."*
Interactional fairness: the interpersonal treatment received during the complaint process	*"The loan officer was very courteous, knowledgeable, and considerate—he kept me informed about the progress of the complaint."* *"The teller explained that they had a power outage that morning so things were delayed. He went through a lot of files [effort] so that I would not have to come back the next day."*	*"The person who handled my complaint about the faulty air conditioner repair wasn't going to do anything about it and didn't seem to care."* *"The receptionist was very rude; she made it seem like the doctor's time was important but mine was not."*

Source: Reprinted from "Recovering and Learning from Service Failure," by S. S. Tax and S. W. Brown, MIT *Sloan Management Review,* Fall 1998, p. 79, by permission of the publisher. Copyright © 1998 by Massachusetts Institute of Technology. All rights reserved.

them choices in terms of compensation. For example, a hotel guest could be offered the choice of a refund or a free upgrade to a better room in compensation for a room not being available on arrival. Outcome fairness is especially important in settings in which customers have particularly negative emotional responses to the service failure; in such situations recovery efforts should focus on improving the outcome from the customer's point of view.[34]

In the Club Med example in Exhibit 8.3, customers were compensated by being met at the airport with snacks and drinks, being chauffeured to the resort, being served a lavish buffet, and being treated to an all-night party that was not part of the package initially. These guests had suffered a lot through the delay of their long-awaited vacation, and the compensation definitely was adequate. Note that in this case the service failure was not even Club Med's fault.

On the other hand, customers can be uncomfortable if they are overly compensated. Early in its experience with service guarantees, Domino's Pizza offered not to charge for the pizza if the driver arrived after the 30-minute guaranteed delivery time. Many customers were not comfortable asking for this level of compensation, especially if the driver was only a few minutes late. In this case "the punishment was greater than the crime." For a while Domino's changed the compensation to a more reasonable $3 off for late deliveries. Later the time guarantee was dropped altogether because of problems it caused with employees who were driving too fast in order to make their deliveries.

Procedural Fairness

In addition to fair compensation, customers expect fairness in terms of policies, rules, and timeliness of the complaint process. They want easy access to the complaint process, and they want things handled quickly, preferably by the first person they contact. They appreciate companies that can be adaptable in their procedures so that the recovery effort can match their individual circumstances. In some cases, particularly in business-to-business services, companies actually ask the customer, "What can we do to compensate you for our failure?" Many times what the customer asks for is actually less than the company might have expected.

Fair procedures are characterized by clarity, speed, and absence of hassles. Unfair procedures are those that customers perceive as slow, prolonged, and inconvenient. Customers also feel it is unfair if they have to prove their case—when the assumption seems to be they are wrong or lying until they can prove otherwise.

In the Club Med case in Exhibit 8.3, the recovery happened as quickly as possible when the passengers landed in Mexico. Even though the problems were not Club Med's fault, the company went out of its way to compensate the delayed guests immediately on arrival. The vacationers had no more hassles once they were on the ground.

Interactional Fairness

Above and beyond their expectations of fair compensation and hassle-free, quick procedures, customers expect to be treated politely, with care and honesty. This form of fairness can dominate the others if customers feel the company and its employees have uncaring attitudes and have done little to try to resolve the problem. This type of behavior on the part of employees may seem strange—why would they treat customers rudely or in an uncaring manner under these circumstances? Often it is due to lack of training and empowerment—a frustrated front-line employee who has no authority to compensate the customer may easily respond in an aloof or uncaring manner, especially if the customer is angry and/or rude.

In the Club Med case in Exhibit 8.3, Silvio de Bortoli and his staff were gracious, caring, and upbeat when they greeted the long-delayed passengers. They personally met them at the airport even though it was late at night. They even involved other guests already staying at the resort to greet the new arrivals and party with them, making them feel welcome and helping to give their vacation a jump start.

SWITCHING VERSUS STAYING FOLLOWING SERVICE RECOVERY

Ultimately, how a service failure is handled and the customer's reaction to the recovery effort can influence future decisions to remain loyal to the service provider or to switch to another provider. Whether customers switch to a new provider following service failure will depend in addition on a number of other factors. The magnitude and criticality of the failure will clearly be a factor in future repurchase decisions. The more serious the failure, the more likely the customer is to switch no matter what the recovery effort.[35]

The nature of the customer's relationship with the firm may also influence whether the customer stays or switches providers. Research suggests that customers who have "true relationships" with their service providers are more forgiving of poorly handled service failures and are less likely to switch than are those who have a "pseudo-relationship" or a "first-time encounter" type of relationship.[36] A true relationship is one in which the customer has had repeated contact over time with the same service provider. A first-time encounter relationship is one in which the customer has had only one contact, on a transaction basis, with the provider. And a pseudo-relationship is one in which the customer has interacted many times with the same company, but with different service providers each time.

Other research reveals that the individual customer's attitude toward switching will strongly influence whether he or she ultimately stays with the provider and that this attitude toward switching will be even more influential than basic satisfaction with the service.[37] This research suggests that certain customers will have a greater propensity to switch service providers no matter how their service failure situations are handled. Research in an online service context, for example, shows that demographic factors such as age and income as well as individual factors such as risk aversion will influence whether a customer continues to use an online service or switches to another provider.[38] The profile of an "online service switcher" emerged in the research as a person who was influenced to subscribe to the service through positive word-of-mouth communication; who used the service less; who was less satisfied and less involved with the service; who had a lower income and education level; and who also had a lower propensity for taking risks.

Finally, the decision to switch to a different service provider may not occur immediately following service failure or poor service recovery, but may follow an accumulation of events. That is, service switching can be viewed as a process resulting from a series of decisions and critical service encounters over time rather than one specific moment in time when a decision is made.[39] This process orientation suggests that companies could potentially track customer interactions and predict the likelihood of defection based on a series of events, intervening earlier in the process to head off the customer's decision to switch.

Although customers may decide to switch service providers for a variety of reasons, service failure and poor service recovery are often a cause of such behavior. A study of approximately 500 service-switching incidents identified eight broad themes underlying the decision to defect.[40] These themes (pricing, inconvenience, core service failure, service encounter failure, response to service failure, competition, ethical problems, and involuntary switching) are shown in Figure 8.4. In about 200 of the incidents, a single theme was identified as the cause for switching service providers, and the two largest categories were related to service failure. Core service failure was the cause of switching for 25 percent of the respondents, and service encounter failure was

FIGURE 8.4
**Causes Behind
Service Switching**

Source: Reprinted with
permission of the American
Marketing Association. From S.
Keaveney, "Customer
Switching Behavior in Service
Industries: An Exploratory
Study," *Journal of Marketing*
59 (April 1995), pp. 71–82.

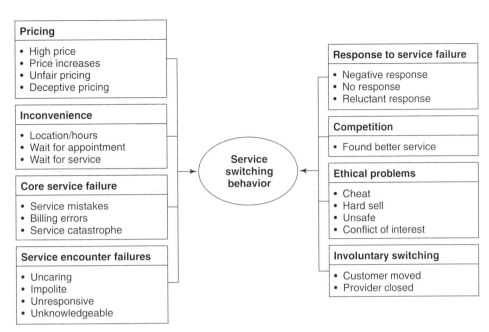

the reason for switching services for an additional 20 percent of the sample. In incidents that listed two themes, 29 percent listed core service failure and 18 percent service encounter failure as contributing to their desire to switch providers; poor response to failure was mentioned by an additional 11 percent of the respondents as the cause for switching. As these findings suggest, service failure can cause customers to switch companies. To minimize the impact of service failure, excellent service recovery is needed. In the next section we discuss several service recovery strategies that attempt to keep dissatisfied customers from defecting.

SERVICE RECOVERY STRATEGIES

Many companies have learned the importance of providing excellent recovery for disappointed customers. In this section we examine their strategies and share examples of benchmark companies and what they are doing. It will become clear that excellent service recovery is really a combination of a variety of strategies that need to work together, as illustrated in Figure 8.5. We discuss each of the strategies shown in the figure, starting with the basic "do it right the first time."

Make the Service Fail-Safe—Do It Right the First Time!

The first rule of service quality is to do it right the first time. In this way recovery is unnecessary, customers get what they expect, and the costs of redoing the service and compensating for errors can be avoided. As you have already learned, reliability, or doing it right the first time, is the most important dimension of service quality across industry contexts.[41]

What specific strategies do firms employ to achieve reliability? TQM, or total quality management, practices aimed at "zero defects" are commonly used. However, given the inherent differences between services and manufactured products, these

FIGURE 8.5
Service Recovery
Strategies

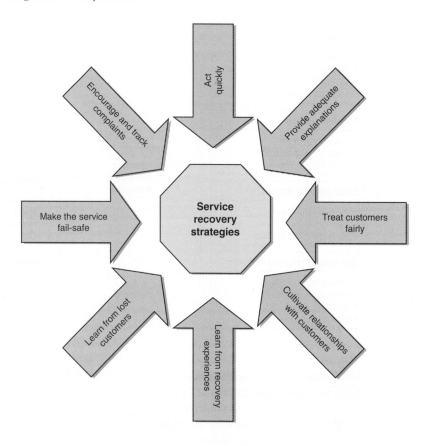

tools typically require considerable adaptation to work well in service contexts. Firms that blindly adopt TQM practices without considering services implications often fail in their efforts.

Dick Chase, noted service operations expert, suggests that services adopt the TQM notion of *poka yokes* to improve service reliability.[42] Poka yokes are automatic warnings or controls in place to ensure that mistakes are not made; essentially they are quality control mechanisms, typically used on assembly lines. Chase suggests that poka yokes can be devised in service settings to "mistakeproof" the service, to ensure that essential procedures are followed, and to ensure that service steps are carried out in the proper order and in a timely manner. In a hospital setting, numerous poka yokes ensure that procedures are followed to avoid potentially life-threatening mistakes. For example, trays for surgical instruments have indentations for specific instruments, and each instrument is nested in its appropriate spot. In this way surgeons and their staff know that all instruments are in their places prior to closing the patient's incision.[43]

Similarly, poka yokes can be devised to ensure that the tangibles associated with the service are clean and well maintained and that documents are accurate and up-to-date. Poka yokes can also be implemented for employee behaviors (checklists, role-playing and practice, reminder signs) and even for ensuring that customers perform effectively. Many of the strategies we discuss in Parts 4 and 5 of the text ("Aligning Service Design and Standards" and "Delivering and Performing Service") are aimed at ensuring service reliability and can be viewed as applications of the basic fail-safe notion of poka yokes.

Even more fundamentally, it is important for a firm to create a culture of zero defections to ensure doing it right the first time.[44] Within a zero defections culture, everyone understands the importance of reliability. Employees and managers aim to satisfy every customer and look for ways to improve service. Employees in a zero defections culture fully understand and appreciate the "relationship value of a customer" concept that was presented in Chapter 7. Thus they are motivated to provide quality service *every time* and to *every customer.*

Encourage and Track Complaints

Even in a zero defections organization that aims for 100 percent service quality, failures occur. A critical component of a service recovery strategy is thus to encourage and track complaints. Our Strategy Insight describes several ways in which customer complaints can be encouraged.

Firms can utilize a number of ways to encourage and track complaints. Customer research can be designed specifically for this purpose through satisfaction surveys, critical incidents studies, and lost customer research, as discussed in Chapter 6. Toll-free call centers, e-mail, and pagers are now used to facilitate, encourage, and track complaints. Software applications in a number of companies also allow complaints to be analyzed, sorted, responded to, and tracked automatically.[45] Our Global Feature shows how a world-class airline, British Airways, encourages, facilitates, and tracks customer complaints as a critical component of its effective service recovery process. It is apparent that British Airways is highly dependent on information technology to implement its strategy.

In some cases technology can anticipate problems and complaints before they happen, allowing service employees to diagnose problems before the customer recognizes they exist. At companies such as IBM and Caterpillar, information systems are being implemented to anticipate equipment failures and to send out an electronic alert to the local field technician with the nature of the problem as well as which parts and tools will be needed to make the repair—a repair the customer does not yet know is needed.[46]

Act Quickly

Complaining customers want quick responses.[47] Thus if the company welcomes, even encourages, complaints, it must be prepared to act on them quickly. Immediate response requires not only systems and procedures that allow quick action but also empowered employees.

Take Care of Problems on the Front Line

Customers want the persons who hear their complaints to solve their problems whether a complaint is registered in person, over the phone, or via the Internet. The Ritz-Carlton, for example, insists that the first person to hear a complaint from a customer "owns" that complaint until the employee is sure it is resolved. If a maintenance employee hears a complaint from a customer while the employee is in the middle of fixing a light in the hotel corridor, he owns that complaint and must be sure that it is handled appropriately before returning to his work.

Another obvious way to speed complaint handling is to call (or in some cases electronically respond to) customers rather then send responses in the mail. Even customers who take the time to write can be called back. Smith and Hawken, a garden supply mail-order company based in California, found that this strategy of phoning

Service failures can occur in a variety of ways and at numerous times throughout the service delivery process. However, in many cases it is difficult, if not impossible, for the firm to know that a service failure has occurred unless the customer informs the firm accordingly. Unfortunately, a relatively low percentage of customers (5–10 percent) will actually complain to the firm. Thus, a major challenge facing management is how to get customers to complain when they experience a service failure and/or they are not satisfied with service delivery. What can a firm do to elicit complaints? Here are some issues to consider.

- *Develop the mind-set that complaints are good.* Too often the complaining customer is looked on by employees in the organization as the *enemy*—someone to be conquered and subdued. The more prudent approach is to develop the mind-set that the complaining customer is the firm's *friend.* Complaints provide valuable feedback to the firm, giving it the opportunity not only to address the service failure for the complaining customer but also to identify problems that other (less vocal) customers may also be experiencing. One scholar suggests that "complainers ought to be treated with the dignity and respect afforded to the highest-priced analysts and consultants." One company puts all customers who have complained on a VIP list. Accepting complaints is truly reflective of firms who are close to their customers.

- *Make complaining easy.* If the firm truly wants to hear from customers who experience poor service, it needs to make it easy for them to share their experiences with the firm. Sometimes customers have no idea whom to speak to if they have a complaint, what the process is, or what will be involved. Complaining should be easy—the last thing customers want when they are dissatisfied is to face a complex, difficult-to-access process for complaining. Customers should know where to go and/or who to talk to when they encounter problems, and they should be made to feel confident that something positive will result from their efforts. Technological advances have made it possible to provide customers with multiple avenues to complain, including toll-free customer call centers, company e-mail addresses, and website feedback forms. The firm should regularly communicate to customers that complaining is easy and that it welcomes and appreciates such feedback.

- *Be an active listener.* Employees should be encouraged and trained to actively listen to customers, particularly to see if they can pick up on any cues to suggest less-than-ideal service. A restaurant customer might respond "fine" to the waiter's question "How is your meal?" However, the customer's body language and tone of voice, or the amount of food not eaten, might indicate that all is not fine. Some customers may not be assertive in voicing their displeasure, but they may drop clues to suggest that something is amiss. Employees as well as managers should be consistently listening not only to the customer's actual words but also to what he or she may really be trying or wanting to communicate.

- *Ask customers about specific service issues.* A very simple, informal way to find out about any service failure is simply to ask. Managers at one hotel with a high percentage of business travelers make it a point to be at the front desk between 7:45 and 8:45 A.M. every day, because approximately 80 percent of their business travelers check out at that time. During the checkout process, managers avoid questions that can be answered with a simple "yes," "OK," or "fine" (e.g., "How was your stay?") and instead ask questions that force customers to provide specific feedback (e.g., "How could we have improved the technology accommodations in your room?" or "What needs to be done to improve our recreation center?"). Asking customers very specific questions that cannot be answered with a simple "yes" or "no" may provide customers with an easy way to point out expectations that were not fulfilled.

- *Conduct short, trailer surveys.* A follow-up telephone call to a customer still in the midst of the service experience can help to identify problems in real time and thus enable real-time recovery. Enterprise Rent-A-Car Company, for example, regularly calls customers a day after they have picked up a rental car and asks the customer if everything is okay with the car. Customers who report problems, such as a broken window or a car that smells of smoke, are brought a replacement vehicle that day without any additional questions or hassle. Trailer surveys work especially well in business-to-business services in addressing problems early, before they become major issues.

Sources: S. S. Tax and S. W. Brown, "Recovering and Learning from Service Failure," *Sloan Management Review,* Fall 1998, pp. 75–88; O. Harari, "Thank Heaven for Complainers," *Management Review* 81 (January 1992), p. 59.

customers worked well for them—they were quicker to respond to their customers, and the costs of the phone calls were offset by the reduced costs and time involved with paperwork.[48]

Empower Employees

Employees must be trained and empowered to solve problems as they occur. A problem not solved can quickly escalate. Take, for example, a true story of a corporate vice president who sent an e-mail to his bank to register a complaint while he was attempting a transaction through its Internet banking service. The e-mail was never answered. The customer then sent an e-mail directly to the president of the bank. That e-mail was never answered either. Ultimately the customer withdrew his approximately $70,000 account because his complaint was not handled in a timely manner. In this case the technology was not effectively linked to other systems, nor ultimately to employees. The Internet access encouraged the complaint, but the response never occurred.

Sometimes employees can even anticipate problems before they arise and surprise customers with a solution. For example, flight attendants on a flight severely delayed because of weather anticipated everyone's hunger, particularly the young children's. Once in flight, they announced to the harried travelers, "Thank you for your extreme patience in waiting with us. Now that we're on our way, we'd like to offer you complimentary beverages and dinner. Because we have a number of very hungry children on board, we'd like to serve them first, if that's OK with all of you." The passengers nodded and applauded their efforts, knowing that hungry, crying children could make

Source: Newscast

Ads for British Airways (BA) reinforce the company's branding strategy as the "World's Favourite Airline." Indeed, British Airways is a favorite among world travelers—but it was not always so. The success in turning BA around from a bureaucratic institution that regarded itself as doing the public a favor by allowing them to fly on its planes to a customer-responsive, world-class service provider can be attributed to its CEO at the time, Sir Colin Marshall. Marshall (currently chairman of the board) was brought in to head up a major change for BA in the 1980s—and he did. His legacy has sustained and further propelled the airline to its current level of success.

A big part of this success was achieved in new ways of listening to customers and new approaches to dealing with customer complaints. One of the first things Marshall did was to install video booths at Heathrow airport so that upset customers could immediately go to the video booth while still at the airport and complain directly to him. In addition to this type of innovative action, Marshall instituted a series of systems and training changes to encourage and be responsive to customer complaints. To quote him directly, "I ardently believe that customer complaints are precious opportunities to hold on to customers who otherwise might take their business elsewhere and to learn about problems that need to be fixed."

Initially BA did research to understand the effect that dissatisfied or defecting customers had on the business. It learned that 50 percent of the dissatisfied customers who did *not* tell BA about their problems left the airline for a competitor. However, of those who *did* tell the company of their problems, 87 percent remained loyal to BA. It quickly became obvious that complaints should be encouraged! Considering that an average business class passenger has a lifetime value of $150,000, encouraging complaints and retaining their business was obviously critical.

BA responded by building a model for "Making Customers into Champions." Goals of the new system were to (1) use customer feedback more effectively to improve quality; (2) strive to prevent future service problems through teamwork; (3) compensate customers on their terms, not the company's; and (4) practice customer retention, not adjudication. The bottom-line objective: to prevent customer defections.

To accomplish this objective, BA set up a four-step process to guide development of its technical and human delivery systems. This process was based on knowledge of how customers would like their complaints handled. The first step in the process was to *apologize and own the customer's problem*—not to search for someone to blame but rather to become the customer's advocate. The second essential was to *respond quickly*—taking absolutely no longer than 72 hours, and preferably providing an immediate solution. The third step was to *assure the customer that the problem is being fixed*. Finally, as much as possible, *handle complaints by phone*. BA found that customers with problems were delighted to speak personally to a customer service representative who could solve their problems.

To facilitate the process just described required major investments in systems and people. First, BA invested in a computer system called *Caress* that eliminated all paper by scanning or manually entering all customer information relevant to a complaint into a customer complaint database. A particular customer's information was thus easily accessed, and the data could be analyzed for patterns as well. The process for dealing with a complaint was also shortened by eliminating a number of unnecessary and redundant steps: the number of steps required to deal with a complaint was reduced from 13 to 3. Further, customer service representatives were given the tools and authority—they were empowered—to use whatever resources were needed to retain the customer's business. New training on listening skills, how to handle anger, and how to negotiate win–win solutions were put in place for customer service representatives. Finally, customers were encouraged to complain. Previous to the new initiatives, BA knew that only about 10 percent of its customers ever communicated with the airline directly—whether for good or bad reasons. The airline thus worked hard to get customers to complain and provide input by establishing 12 different "listening posts" or ways of communicating, including postage-paid cards, customer forums, surveys, and a "Fly with Me" program, where customer service representatives flew with customers to experience and hear their responses firsthand.

Not only did BA use the information and systems it developed to directly retain dissatisfied customers, it also built systems to use the data and information to improve systems for the future. It used the information to design out common failure patterns and to design early-warning mechanisms to alert the company to potential future failures.

BA found that all its efforts toward complaint management paid off. For every £1 spent in customer retention efforts, BA found it had a £2 return. BA continues to take great pride in delivering the highest levels of customer service. In January 2000 the company unveiled £600,000,000 worth of new customer service initiatives to be rolled out over the following two years.

Sources: J. Barlow and C. Moller, *A Complaint Is a Gift* (San Francisco: Berrett-Koehler Publishers, 1996), pp. 16–18; C. R. Weiser, "Championing the Customer," *Harvard Business Review,* November–December 1995, pp. 113–15; S. E. Prokesch, "Competing on Service: An Interview with British Airways' Sir Colin Marshall," *Harvard Business Review,* November–December 1995, pp. 101–16; and www.BritishAirways.com, 2002.

the situation even worse. The flight attendants had anticipated a problem and solved it before it escalated.

Service employees have a specific and real need for recovery training. Because customers demand that service recovery take place on the spot and quickly, front-line employees need the skills, authority, and incentives to engage in effective recovery. Effective recovery skills include hearing the customer's problems, taking initiative, identifying solutions, improvising, and perhaps bending the rules from time to time.

Not only do employees need the authority to act (usually within certain defined limits), but they also should not be punished for taking action. In fact, incentives should exist that encourage employees to exercise their recovery authority. At the Ritz-Carlton, employees are authorized to spend $2,000 on behalf of the customer to solve a problem. This amount of money is rarely needed, but knowing that they have it encourages employees to be responsive without fear of retribution.

Allow Customers to Solve Their Own Problems

Another way that problems or complaints can be handled quickly is by building systems that allow customers to actually solve their own service needs and fix their own problems. Typically this approach is done through technology. Customers directly

Technology Spotlight
Cisco Systems—Customers Recover for Themselves

One of the challenges of 90 percent growth per year is learning how to handle customers' service needs quickly. This was the problem faced by Cisco Systems, a worldwide leader in the networking equipment business. Cisco provides the equipment, builds the factories, and produces networking devices that keep businesses running. If the network is not working, the business is not working. Failures in this environment become extremely costly very quickly. Customers want to know that their problems can be solved immediately, and they want a sense of control over the solution.

To address these issues—extremely high growth coupled with the critical nature of the business—Cisco Systems turned to the Internet. It built a world-class model of customer service using the Internet. The system described here has set Cisco apart in its industry and helped the company build customer loyalty in a highly competitive environment.

Essentially, Cisco has put customers in charge of their own service through the Internet. In many cases customers now solve their own service problems totally, with no intervention of Cisco personnel. Access to information is immediate, and solutions can be highly customized for the individual customer. Called "Cisco Connection Online," the system includes the following types of services:

- *Discussion forum*—A searchable database for answers to networking questions. If the question is too complex, the customer can escalate the request to a highly trained service representative. However, most questions can be answered without human intervention. Plus, the questions asked are used to further enhance and develop the information system to answer questions in the future.

- *Troubleshooting engine*—An expert system that takes the user through the problem identification and resolution process. Here customers actually solve problems and are instructed on how to fix their systems. This system saves time for customers and gives them

a much greater sense of control, particularly in critical situations in which every minute of downtime is extremely costly.

- *Bug toolkit*—A collection of interactive tools for identifying, tracking, and resolving software bugs.

- *Software center*—A comprehensive vending machine for Cisco software. This system provides one-stop shopping for Cisco software and helps customers upgrade in a timely manner and be sure that they have the right release of a particular software.

- *Service order agent*—A parts information, ordering, and tracking system that allows customers to conduct transactions online. This system provides fast service for orders and saves on administrative costs for both Cisco and its customers.

- *Service contract center*—A system that allows customers to view the contents and/or status of their contracts with Cisco.

Through its continual innovation in providing service to its customers through the Internet, Cisco has recognized tremendous benefits. Currently 80 percent of customer problems are handled via the Internet through information provided by Cisco and self-help tools that allow customers to diagnose and solve their own problems. Customer satisfaction increased with the introduction of Internet-based customer service, productivity increased at the rate of 200 percent, and the company saves over $500 million per year. This is truly a win–win situation for Cisco's bottom line, for its employees, and for its business customers.

Sources: www.cisco.com, 2004; "The Globally Networked Business," Cisco presentation at "Activating Your Firm's Service Culture" symposium, Arizona State University, 1997; R. L. Nolan, "Cisco Systems Architecture: ERP and Web-Enabled IT," Harvard Business School Case #9-301-099, 2001; "Ten Minutes with John Chambers," NASDAQ: *The International Magazine* 29, January 2001.

interface with the company's technology to perform their own customer service, which provides them with instant answers. FedEx uses this strategy for its package tracking services, for example. Our Technology Spotlight features a company that is a master at online customer service—Cisco Systems.

Provide Adequate Explanations

In many service failures, customers look to try to understand why the failure occurred. Research suggests that when the firm's ability to provide an adequate outcome is not successful, further dissatisfaction can be reduced if an adequate explanation is provided to the customer.[49] In order for an explanation to be perceived as adequate, it must possess two primary characteristics. First, the content of the explanation must be appropriate; relevant facts and pertinent information are important in helping the customer understand what occurred. Second, the style of the delivery of the explanation, or how the explanation is delivered, can also reduce customer dissatisfaction. Style includes the personal characteristics of the explanation givers, including their credibility and sincerity. Explanations perceived by customers as honest, sincere, and not manipulative are generally the most effective. Part of the frustration of the Doubletree Inn customers mentioned in Exhibit 8.1 was the result of not receiving an adequate explanation from the hotel; they never received an explanation as to why their confirmed, guaranteed reservations were not held, and the night clerk apparently interacted with them in a very apathetic manner.

Treat Customers Fairly

In responding quickly, it is also critical to treat each customer fairly. Customers expect to be treated fairly in terms of the outcome they receive, the process by which the service recovery takes place, and the interpersonal treatment they receive. In the section titled "Customers' Recovery Expectations," we discussed examples, strategies, and results of research that focused on fairness in service recovery. Here we remind you that fair treatment is an essential component of an effective service recovery strategy.

Cultivate Relationships with Customers

In Chapter 7 we discussed the importance of developing long-term relationships with customers. One additional benefit of relationship marketing is that if the firm fails in service delivery, those customers who have a strong relationship with the firm are often more forgiving of service failures and more open to the firm's service recovery efforts. Research suggests that strong customer–firm relationships can help shield the firm from the negative effects of failures on customer satisfaction.[50] To illustrate, one study demonstrated that the presence of rapport between customers and employees provided several service recovery benefits, including increased postfailure satisfaction, increased loyalty intentions, and decreased negative word-of-mouth communication.[51] Another study found that customers who expect the relationship to continue also tend to have lower service recovery expectations and may demand less immediate compensation for a failure because they consider the balance of equity across a longer time horizon.[52] Thus, cultivation of strong customer relationships can provide an important buffer to service firms when failures occur.

Learn from Recovery Experiences

"Problem-resolution situations are more than just opportunities to fix flawed services and strengthen ties with customers. They are also a valuable—but frequently ignored or underutilized—source of diagnostic, prescriptive information for improving customer service."[53] By tracking service recovery efforts and solutions, managers can often learn about systematic problems in the delivery system that need fixing. By conducting root-cause analysis, firms can identify the sources of the problems and modify processes, sometimes eliminating almost completely the need for recovery. At Ritz-Carlton Hotels, all employees carry service recovery forms called "instant action forms" with them at all times so that they can immediately record service failures and suggest actions to address them. Each individual employee "owns" any complaint that he or she receives and is responsible for seeing that service recovery occurs. In turn, the employees report to management these sources of service failure and the remedies. This information is then entered into the customer database and analyzed for patterns and systemic service issues that need to be fixed. If common themes are observed across a number of failure situations, changes are made to service processes or attributes. In addition, the information is entered into the customer's personal data file so when that customer stays at the Ritz-Carlton again (no matter what hotel), employees can be aware of the previous experience, ensuring that it does not happen again for that particular customer.

Learn from Lost Customers

Another key component of an effective service recovery strategy is to learn from the customers who defect or decide to leave. Formal market research to discover the reasons customers have left can assist in preventing failures in the future. This type of research is difficult, even painful for companies, however. No one really likes to examine their failures. Yet such examination is essential for preventing the same mistakes and losing more customers in the future.[54]

As presented in Chapter 6, lost customer research typically involves in-depth probing of customers to determine their true reasons for leaving. This information is most effectively obtained by depth interviews, administered by skilled interviewers who truly understand the business. It may be best to have this type of research done by senior people in the company, particularly in business-to-business contexts in which customers are large and the impact of even one lost customer is great. The type of depth analysis often requires a series of "why" questions or "tell me more about that" questions to get at the actual, core reason for the customer's defection.[55]

In conducting this kind of research, a firm must focus on important or profitable customers who have left—not just everyone who has left the company. An insurance company in Australia once began this type of research to learn about their lost customers, only to find that the customers they were losing tended to be their least profitable customers anyway. They quickly determined that depth research on how to keep these unprofitable customers would not be a good investment!

SERVICE GUARANTEES

A guarantee is a particular type of recovery tool. In a business context, a guarantee is a pledge or assurance that a product offered by a firm will perform as promised, and if not then some form of reparation will be undertaken by the firm. Although guarantees are relatively common for manufactured products, they have only recently been used for services. Traditionally, many people believed that services simply could not be guaranteed given their intangible and variable nature. What would be guaranteed? With a product, the customer is guaranteed that it will perform as promised and if not, that it can be returned. With services, it is generally not possible to take returns or to "undo" what has been performed. The skepticism about service guarantees is being dispelled, however, as more and more companies find they can guarantee their services and that there are tremendous benefits for doing so.

Companies are finding that effective service guarantees can complement the company's service recovery strategy—serving as one tool to help accomplish the service recovery strategies depicted in Figure 8.5. The Hampton Inn® Hotels guarantee shown at the beginning of the chapter is an example of such an effective guarantee.

Benefits of Service Guarantees

"Service organizations, in particular, are beginning to recognize that guarantees can serve not only as a marketing tool but as a means for defining, cultivating, and maintaining quality throughout an organization."[56] The benefits to the company of an effective service guarantee are numerous:[57]

- *A good guarantee forces the company to focus on its customers.* To develop a meaningful guarantee, the company must know what is important to its customers—what they expect and value. In many cases "satisfaction" is guaranteed, but in order for the guarantee to work effectively, the company must clearly understand what satisfaction means for its customers (what they value and expect).

- *An effective guarantee sets clear standards for the organization.* It prompts the company to clearly define what it expects of its employees and to communicate that expectation to them. The guarantee gives employees service-oriented goals that can quickly align employee behaviors around customer strategies. For example, Pizza Hut's guarantee that "If you're not satisfied with your pizza, let our restaurant know. We'll make it right or give you your money back" lets employees know exactly what they should do if a customer complains. It is also clear to employees that making it right for the customer is an important company goal.

- *A good guarantee generates immediate and relevant feedback from customers.* It provides an incentive for customers to complain and thereby provides more representative feedback to the company than simply relying on the relatively few customers who typically voice their concerns. The guarantee communicates to customers that they have the right to complain.

- *When the guarantee is invoked there is an instant opportunity to recover,* thus satisfying the customer and helping retain loyalty.

- *Information generated through the guarantee can be tracked and integrated into continuous improvement efforts.* A feedback link between customers and service operations decisions can be strengthened through the guarantee.

- *Studies of the impact of service guarantees suggest that employee morale and loyalty can be enhanced as a result.* A guarantee generates pride among employees. Through feedback from the guarantee, improvements can be made in the service that benefit customers and, indirectly, employees.

- *For customers, the guarantee reduces their sense of risk* and builds confidence in the organization. Because services are intangible and often highly personal or ego-involving, customers seek information and cues that will help reduce their sense of uncertainty. Guarantees have been shown to reduce risk and increase positive evaluation of the service prior to purchase.[58]

The bottom line for the company is that an effective guarantee can affect profitability through building customer awareness and loyalty, through positive word of mouth, and through reduction in costs as service improvements are made and service recovery expenses are reduced. Indirectly, the guarantee can reduce costs of employee turnover through creating a more positive service culture.

Exhibit 8.5 SERVICE GUARANTEE—DATAPRO SINGAPORE

Datapro Information Services provided IT and telecommunications information and consulting services around the world in the early 1990s. It employed over 400 analysts and consultants. Although having been in Asia for many years selling its prepackaged information services, only in 1993 did Datapro start offering consulting services throughout Southeast Asia via its Singapore office. Being confident about the high quality of its work, but at the same time somewhat lacking the brand equity that other providers of similar services enjoyed, Datapro decided to become Asia's first IT consulting firm that explicitly guaranteed its services. In 1994 the company developed and introduced the guarantee described here in collaboration with the author of this case. Every proposal contained this guarantee in this last section just before the acceptance form:

> Datapro guarantees to deliver the report on time, to high quality standards, and to the contents outlined in this proposal. Should we fail to deliver according to this guarantee, or should you be dissatisfied with any aspect of our work, you can deduct any amount from the final payment which you deem as fair, subject to a maximum of 30%.
>
> In the event Datapro should fail to deliver the commissioned report in its entirety at the end of the period, you will have the option to deduct 10% off the price of the study for each week the said study is overdue, subject to a maximum of 20%.
>
> We are able to offer this guarantee as we are confident about the good quality and professionalism of our work. We have secured a large number of blue-chip clients who have been completely satisfied with our services. Our clients in the last twelve months have included: Fujitsu, Hewlett-Packard, Intel, Northern Telecom, Philips, Sony, etc.

Datapro had ideally wanted to provide a 100 percent money-back guarantee, but at the same time wanted to limit the potential financial risks inherent in the introduction of such guarantees. These risks were considerable, with typical projects exceeding a value of well over $100,000. The guarantee contained a full satisfaction clause as well as concrete promises such as on-time delivery.

The marketing impact was dramatic. Clients were delighted that Datapro was willing to stand by its word and guarantee deadlines as well as content quality—especially because deadlines were a thorny issue in Asia's rapidly growing IT markets, and clients were often promised the sky during the proposal stage only to be confronted with late deliveries subsequently. The guarantee allowed Datapro to credibly promise delivery dates that otherwise might have been discounted by its clients. Datapro's management felt that the guarantee was an effective marketing tool that helped to sell a number of projects, and Datapro's consulting unit was extremely successful, with an annual revenue and profit growth of around 100 percent for a number of successive years.

On the operations side, the guarantee pushed Datapro to keep up its quality. For example, it did not have a single late delivery after the introduction of the guarantee, mainly for two reasons. First, case leaders were cautious not to promise delivery dates they knew they could not keep. Second, in the case of unforeseen problems or delays, case leaders would try to bring the case back on track. Similar pressure was on the case teams to keep their clients happy because a dissatisfied client could mean a significant reduction in revenue and profit for that case, resulting in a steep reduction in staff bonuses.

Datapro was very successful, especially in breaking into the high-growth telecommunications consulting market, and was taken over at the end of 1997 by the Gartner Group, the world's largest IT consulting firm.

Types of Service Guarantees

Satisfaction versus Service Attribute Guarantees

Service guarantees can be *unconditional satisfaction guarantees* or *service attribute guarantees.* Hampton Inn® Hotels' guarantee is an unconditional satisfaction guarantee. In another context, Bain & Company, a management consulting firm, has offered some clients an unconditional guarantee for its services.[59] If clients are unhappy, they do not pay for the services. Bank One Corporation offers an unconditional guarantee to return fees to any client dissatisfied with its trust services. Lands' End, a catalog retailer, has abbreviated its guarantee to "Guaranteed. Period."

In other cases, firms offer guarantees of particular aspects of the service that are important to customers. Wells Fargo, for example, guarantees that customers will not wait longer than five minutes in a teller line. If they do, they are given $5. FedEx guarantees package delivery by a certain time. In introducing a new seat design in first class, British Airways advertised "Comfort guaranteed or you get 25,000 miles." McDonald's advertised a guarantee that stated "Hot Food; Fast, Friendly Delivery; Double-Check Drive-Thru Accuracy…We'll make it right, or your next meal is on us." In all these cases, the companies have guaranteed elements of the service that they know are important to customers.

Another type of service guarantee, a *combined guarantee,* combines the wide scope of the total satisfaction guarantee with specific attribute performance standards. Research suggests that this type of guarantee can be more effective than either of the other two types.[60] Exhibit 8.5 provides an example of a successful combined service guarantee offered by Datapro in Singapore.

External versus Internal Guarantees

Interestingly, guarantees do not have to be just for external customers. Some companies are finding that internal service guarantees—one part of the organization guaranteeing its services to others—are effective ways of aligning internal service operations. For example, at Embassy Suites the housekeeping supplies department guarantees its internal customer, the housekeeping staff, that they can get supplies on the day requested. If not, the supply department pays $5 to the housekeeper. At one direct-mail firm, the sales force guarantees to give the production department all the specifications needed to provide service to the external customer, or the offending salesperson will take the production department to lunch, will sing a song at their next department meeting, or will personally input all the specs into the computer.[61]

Characteristics of Effective Guarantees

No matter the type of guarantee, certain characteristics make some guarantees more effective than others. Characteristics of effective guarantees are shown in Exhibit 8.6. The guarantee should be unconditional—no strings attached. Some guarantees can appear as if they were written by the legal department (and often are), with all kinds of restrictions, proof required, and limitations. These guarantees are generally not effective. The guarantee should be meaningful. Guaranteeing what is obvious or expected is not meaningful to customers. For example, a water delivery company offered a guarantee to deliver water on the day promised, or a free jug of water would be provided next time. In that industry, delivery on the day scheduled was an expectation nearly always met by every competitor—thus the guarantee was not meaningful to the customer. It was a bit like guaranteeing four wheels on an automobile! The payout should also be meaningful. Customers expect to be reimbursed in a manner that fully compensates them for their dissatisfaction, their time, and even for the hassle involved. One of us offered university students a guarantee in my classes; compensation for poor service, which included reimbursement for the cost of the three-credit course and the textbook, was perceived by students as quite meaningful.[62] A firm's guarantee should also be easy to understand and communicate to both customers and employees. Sometimes the wording is confusing, the guarantee language is verbose, or the guarantee contains so many restrictions and conditions that neither customers nor employees are certain what is being guaranteed. Similarly, the guarantee should be easy to invoke. Requiring customers to write a letter and/or provide documented proof of service failure are common pitfalls that make invoking the guarantee time-consuming and not worth it to the customer, particularly if the dollar value of the service is relatively low.

When to Use (or Not Use) a Guarantee

Service guarantees are not appropriate for every company and certainly not in every service situation. Before putting a guarantee strategy in place, a firm needs to address a number of important questions (see Exhibit 8.7). A guarantee is probably *not* the right strategy when:

- *Existing service quality in the company is poor.* Before instituting a guarantee, the company should fix any significant quality problems. Although a guarantee will certainly draw attention to these failures and the poor quality, the costs of implementing the guarantee could easily outweigh any benefits. These costs include actual monetary payouts to customers for poor service as well as costs associated with customer goodwill.

- *A guarantee does not fit the company's image.* If the company already has a reputation for very high quality, and in fact implicitly guarantees its service, then a formal guarantee is most likely unnecessary. For example, if the Four Seasons Hotel were to offer an explicit guarantee, it could potentially confuse customers who already expect the highest of quality, implicitly guaranteed, from this high-end hotel chain. Research suggests that the benefits of offering a guarantee for a high-end hotel like the Four Seasons or the Ritz-Carlton may be significantly less than the benefits that a hotel of lesser quality would enjoy, and in fact the benefits might not be justified by the costs.[63]

- *Service quality is truly uncontrollable.* Uncontrollable service quality is often an excuse for not employing a guarantee, but firms encounter few situations in which service quality is truly uncontrollable. Here are a couple of examples to illustrate

Exhibit 8.7 QUESTIONS TO CONSIDER IN IMPLEMENTING A SERVICE GUARANTEE

DECIDING WHO DECIDES

- Is there a guarantee champion in the company?
- Is senior management committed to a guarantee?
- Is the guarantee design a team effort?
- Are customers providing input?

WHEN DOES A GUARANTEE MAKE SENSE?

- How high are quality standards?
- Can we afford a guarantee?
- How high is customer risk?
- Are competitors offering a guarantee?
- Is the company's culture compatible with a guarantee?

WHAT TYPE OF GUARANTEE SHOULD WE OFFER?

- Should we offer an unconditional guarantee or a specific-outcome one?

- Is our service measurable?
- What should our specific guarantee be about?
- What are the uncontrollables?
- Is the company particularly susceptible to unreasonable triggerings?
- What should the payout be?
- Will a refund send the wrong message?
- Could a full refund make customers feel guilty?
- Is the guarantee easy to invoke?

Source: A. L. Ostrom and C. W. L. Hart, "Service Guarantees: Research and Practice," in *Handbook of Services Marketing and Management,* ed. D. Iacobucci and T. Swartz (Thousand Oaks, CA: Sage Publications, 2000). © 2000 by Sage Publications. Reprinted by permission of Sage Publications.

such situations. It would not be a good practice for a training organization to guarantee that all participants would pass a particular certification exam on completion of the training course if passing depends too much on the participants' own effort. The company could, however, guarantee satisfaction with the training or particular aspects of the training process. Similarly, an airline flying out of Chicago in the winter would probably not guarantee on-time departure because of the unpredictability and uncontrollability of the weather.

- *Potential exists for customer abuse of the guarantee.* Fear of opportunistic customer behavior, including customer cheating or fraudulent invocation of service guarantees, is a common reason that firms hesitate to offer guarantees.[64] For example, at one large pizza chain students occasionally "cheated" the company by invoking the service guarantee without cause in order to receive free food.[65] In those situations in which abuse of the service guarantee can easily occur, firms should carefully consider the consequences of offering a guarantee. A recent study found that guarantees are more likely to be abused when offered in situations in which a large percentage of customers are not regular (repeat) customers.[66] In general, customer abuse of service guarantees is fairly minimal and not at all widespread.[67]

- *Costs of the guarantee outweigh the benefits.* As it would with any quality investment, the company will want to carefully calculate expected costs (payouts for failures and costs of making improvements) against anticipated benefits (customer loyalty, quality improvements, attraction of new customers, word-of-mouth advertising).

• *Customers perceive little risk in the service.* Guarantees are usually most effective when customers are uncertain about the company and/or the quality of its services. The guarantee can allay uncertainties and help reduce risk.[68] If customers perceive little risk, if the service is relatively inexpensive with lots of potential alternative providers, and if quality is relatively invariable, then a guarantee will likely produce little effectiveness for the company other than perhaps some promotional value.

• *Customers perceive little variability in service quality among competitors.* Some industries exhibit extreme variability in quality among competitors. In these cases a guarantee may be quite effective, particularly for the first company to offer one. Guarantees may also be effective in industries in which quality is perceived to be low overall across competitors. The first firm with a guarantee can often distinguish itself from competitors. A study of guarantees offered by several service firms in Singapore found that companies that were the only competitor offering a guarantee in their industry attributed more of their success to the guarantee than did companies in industries in which guarantees were more common.[69]

Summary

Part 3 of this text (Chapters 6, 7, and 8) focused on the critical importance of understanding customer expectations as well as many of the strategies firms use to accomplish this goal. Part of understanding customer expectations is being prepared for and knowing what to do when things go wrong or when the service fails. In this chapter we focused on service recovery, the actions taken by an organization in response to a service failure.

You learned in this chapter the importance of an effective service recovery strategy for retaining customers and increasing positive word-of-mouth communication. Another major benefit of an effective service recovery strategy is that the information it provides can be useful for service improvement. The potential downsides of poor service recovery are tremendous—negative word of mouth, lost customers, and declining business when quality issues are not addressed.

In this chapter you learned how customers respond to service failures and why some complain while others do not. You learned that customers expect to be treated fairly when they complain—not just in terms of the actual outcome or compensation they receive, but also in terms of the procedures that are used and how they are treated interpersonally. We pointed out in this chapter that there is tremendous room for improvement in service recovery effectiveness across firms and industries.

The second half of the chapter focused on specific strategies that firms are using for service recovery: (1) making the service fail-safe, or doing it right the first time, (2) encouraging and tracking complaints, (3) acting quickly, (4) providing adequate explanations, (5) treating customers fairly, (6) cultivating relationships with customers, (7) learning from recovery experiences, and (8) learning from lost customers. The chapter ended with a discussion of service guarantees as a tool used by many firms to build a foundation for service recovery. You learned the benefits of service guarantees, the elements of a good guarantee, and the pros and cons of using guarantees under various circumstances.

Discussion Questions

1. Why is it important for a service firm to have a strong recovery strategy? Think of a time when you received less-than-desirable service from a particular service organization. Was any effort made to recover? What should/could have been done differently? Do you still buy services from the organization? Why or why not? Did you tell others about your experience?

2. Discuss the benefits to a company of having an effective service recovery strategy. Describe an instance in which you experienced (or delivered as an employee) an effective service recovery. In what ways did the company benefit in this particular situation?

3. Explain the recovery paradox, and discuss its implications for a service firm manager.

4. Discuss the types of actions that customers can take in response to a service failure. What type of complainer are you? Why? As a manager, would you want to encourage your customers to be voicers? If so, how?

5. Review Exhibits 8.1 and 8.2. What would you have done if you were on the management team at Doubletree Inn or Starbucks?

6. Explain the logic behind these two quotes: "a complaint is a gift" and "the customer who complains is your friend."

7. Choose a firm you are familiar with. Describe how you would design an ideal service recovery strategy for that organization.

8. What are the benefits to the company of an effective service guarantee? Should every service organization have one?

9. Describe three service guarantees that are currently offered by companies or organizations in addition to the ones already described in the chapter. (Examples are readily available on the Internet.) Are your examples good guarantees or poor guarantees based on the criteria presented in this chapter?

Exercises

1. Write a letter of complaint (or voice your complaint in person) to a service organization from which you have experienced less-than-desirable service. What do you expect the organization to do to recover? (Later, report to the class the results of your complaint, whether you were satisfied with the recovery, what could/should have been done differently, and whether you will continue using the service.)

2. Interview five people about their service recovery experiences. What happened, and what did they expect the firm to do? Were they treated fairly based on the definition of recovery fairness presented in the chapter? Will they return to the company in the future?

3. Interview a manager about service recovery strategies used in his or her firm. Use the strategies shown in Figure 8.5 to frame your questions.

4. Reread the Technology Spotlight in this chapter, featuring Cisco Systems. Visit Cisco System's website (www.cisco.com). Review what the company is currently doing to help its customers solve their own problems. Compare what Cisco is doing with the self-service efforts of another service provider of your choice.

5. Choose a service you are familiar with. Explain the service offered and develop a good service guarantee for it. Discuss why your guarantee is a good one, and list the benefits to the company of implementing it.

Notes

1. J. Schwartz, "Up from the Ashes, One Firm Rebuilds," *The New York Times,* September 16, 2001, section 3, p. 1. For a follow-up story see John Schwartz, "Rebuilding a Day at a Time; Law Firm Pushes Two Steps Forward for Every Step Back," *The New York Times,* December 14, 2001, p. C1.

2. "Our Test," a personal account of the events surrounding September 11, 2001, by Thomas Cole, chairman of the executive committee of Sidley Austin Brown & Wood, at www.sidley.com, news and events; accessed November 15, 2004.

3. Sidley Austin Brown & Wood website; www.sidley.com

4. For research that shows different types of service failures, see M. J. Bitner, B. H. Booms, and M. S. Tetreault, "The Service Encounter: Diagnosing Favorable and Unfavorable Incidents," *Journal of Marketing* 54 (January 1990), pp. 71–84; and S. M. Keaveney, "Customer Switching Behavior in Service Industries: An Exploratory Study," *Journal of Marketing* 59 (April 1995), pp. 71–82.

5. For research on important outcomes associated with service recovery, see S. S. Tax, S. W. Brown, and M. Chandrashekaran, "Customer Evaluations of Service Complaint Experiences: Implications for Relationship Marketing," *Journal of Marketing* 62 (April 1998), pp. 60–76; S. S. Tax and S. W. Brown, "Recovering and Learning from Service Failure," *Sloan Management Review,* Fall 1998, pp. 75–88; A. K. Smith and R. N. Bolton, "An Experimental Investigation of Customer Reactions to Service Failure and Recovery Encounters," *Journal of Service Research* 1 (August 1998), pp. 65–81; S. W. Kelley, K. D. Hoffman, and M. A. Davis, "A Typology of Retail Failures and Recoveries," *Journal of Retailing* 69 (Winter 1993), pp. 429–52; R. N. Bolton, "A Dynamic Model of the Customer's Relationship with a Continuous Service Provider: The Role of Satisfaction," *Marketing Science* 17, no. 1 (1998), pp. 45–65; A. K. Smith and R. N. Bolton, "The Effect of Customers' Emotional Responses to Service Failures on Their Recovery Effort Evaluations and Satisfaction Judgments," *Journal of the Academy of Marketing Science,* 30 (Winter 2002), pp. 5–23.

6. Technical Assistance Research Program, "Consumer Complaint Handling in America: An Update Study" (Washington, DC: Department of Consumer Affairs, 1986).

7. D. Sarel and H. Marmorstein, "The Role of Service Recovery in HMO Satisfaction," *Marketing Healthcare Services* 19 (Spring 1999), pp. 6–12.

8. B. Ettorre, "Phenomenal Promises That Mean Business," *Management Review,* March 1994, pp. 18–23.

9. M. Granier, J. Kemp, and A. Lawes, "Customer Complaint Handling—The Multimillion Pound Sinkhole: A Case of Customer Rage Unassuaged," study conducted by the Customer Care Alliance, 2004.

10. Tax and Brown, "Recovering and Learning from Service Failure."

11. Granier, Kemp, and Lawes, "Customer Complaint Handling—The Multimillion Pound Sinkhole."

12. See C. W. Hart, J. L. Heskett, and W. E. Sasser Jr., "The Profitable Art of Service Recovery," *Harvard Business Review* 68 (July–August 1990), pp. 148–56; M. A. McCollough and S. G. Bharadwaj, "The Recovery Paradox: An Examination of Consumer Satisfaction in Relation to Disconfirmation, Service Quality, and Attribution Based Theories," in *Marketing Theory and Applications,* ed. C. T. Allen et al. (Chicago: American Marketing Association, 1992), p. 119.

13. Smith and Bolton, "An Experimental Investigation of Customer Reactions to Service Failure and Recovery Encounters."

14. M. A. McCullough, L. L. Berry, and M. S. Yadav, "An Empirical Investigation of Customer Satisfaction after Service Failure and Recovery," *Journal of Service Research,* 3 (November 2000), pp. 121–37.

15. J. G. Maxham III and R. G. Netemeyer, "A Longitudinal Study of Complaining Customers' Evaluations of Multiple Service Failures and Recovery Efforts," *Journal of Marketing* 66 (October 2002), pp. 57–71.

16. For research foundations on typologies of customer responses to failures, see R. L. Day and E. L. Landon Jr., "Towards a Theory of Consumer Complaining Behavior," in *Consumer and Industrial Buying Behavior,* ed. A. Woodside, J. Sheth, and P. Bennett (Amsterdam: North-Holland Publishing Company, 1977); J. Singh, "Consumer Complaint Intentions and Behavior: Definitional and Taxonomical Issues," *Journal of Marketing* 52 (January 1988), pp. 93–107; and J. Singh, "Voice, Exit, and Negative Word-of-Mouth Behaviors: An Investigation across Three Service Categories," *Journal of the Academy of Marketing Science* 18 (Winter 1990), pp. 1–15.

17. Smith and Bolton, "The Effect of Customers' Emotional Responses to Service Failures."

18. Ibid.

19. N. Stephens and K. P. Gwinner, "Why Don't Some People Complain? A Cognitive–Emotive Process Model of Consumer Complaining Behavior," *Journal of the Academy of Marketing Science* 26 (Spring 1998), pp. 172–89.

20. Ibid.

21. T. Hennig-Thurau, K. P. Gwinner, G. Walsh, and D. D. Gremler, "Electronic Word-of-Mouth via Consumer-Opinion Platforms: What Motivates Consumers to Articulate Themselves on the Internet?" *Journal of Interactive Marketing* 18 (Winter 2004), pp. 38–52.

22. Many such Web sites exist; examples include www.untied.com (for United Airlines experiences), www.starbucked.com (for Starbucks), and www.walmartsucks.com (for Wal-Mart).

23. J. C. Ward and A. L. Ostrom, "Online Complaining via Customer-created Web Sites: A Protest Framing Perspective," working paper, W. P. Carey School of Business, Arizona State University, 2004.

24. J. Singh, " A Typology of Consumer Dissatisfaction Response Styles," *Journal of Retailing* 66 (Spring 1990), pp. 57–99.

25. J. R. McColl-Kennedy and B. A. Sparks, "Application of Fairness Theory to Service Failures and Service Recovery," *Journal of Service Research* 5 (February 2003), pp. 251–66; M. Davidow, "Organizational Responses to Customer Complaints: What Works and What Doesn't," *Journal of Service Research* 5 (February 2003), pp. 225–50.

26. Granier, Kemp, and Lawes, "Customer Complaint Handling—The Multimillion Pound Sinkhole."

27. Davidow, "Organizational Responses to Customer Complaints."

28. Granier, Kemp, and Lawes, "Customer Complaint Handling—The Multimillion Pound Sinkhole."

29. Ibid.

30. McColl-Kennedy and Sparks, "Application of Fairness Theory to Service Failures and Service Recovery"; A. S. Mattila and P. G. Patterson, "Service Recovery and Fairness Perceptions in Collectivist and Individualist Contexts," *Journal of Service Research* 6 (May 2004), pp. 336–46.

31. Granier, Kemp, and Lawes, "Customer Complaint Handling—The Multimillion Pound Sinkhole."

32. See Tax, Brown, and Chandrashekaran, "Customer Evaluations of Service Complaint Experiences"; Tax and Brown, "Recovering and Learning from Service Failure."

33. Tax and Brown, "Recovering and Learning from Service Failure."

34. Smith and Bolton, "The Effect of Customers' Emotional Responses to Service Failures."

35. McCullough, Berry, and Yadav, "An Empirical Investigation of Customer Satisfaction after Service Failure and Recovery."

36. A. S. Mattila, "The Impact of Relationship Type on Customer Loyalty in a Context of Service Failures," *Journal of Service Research,* 4 (November 2001), pp. 91–101; see also R. L. Hess Jr., S. Ganesan, and N. M. Klein, "Service Failure and Recovery: The Impact of Relationship Factors on Customer Satisfaction," *Journal of the Academy of Marketing Science* 31 (Spring 2003), pp. 127–45; R. Priluck, "Relationship Marketing Can Mitigate Product and Service Failures," *Journal of Services Marketing* 17, no. 1 (2003), pp. 37–52.

37. H. S. Bansal and S. F. Taylor, "The Service Provider Switching Model (SPSM)," *Journal of Service Research* 2 (November 1999), pp. 200–218.

38. S. M. Keaveney and M. Parthasarathy, "Customer Switching Behavior in Online Services: An Exploratory Study of the Role of Selected Attitudinal, Behavioral, and Demographic Factors," *Journal of the Academy of Marketing Science* 29, no. 4 (2001), pp. 374–90.

39. I. Roos, "Switching Processes in Customer Relationships," *Journal of Service Research* 2 (August 1999), pp. 68–85.

40. Keaveney, "Customer Switching Behavior in Service Industries."

41. A. Parasuraman, V. A. Zeithaml, and L. L. Berry, "SERVQUAL: A Multiple-Item Scale for Measuring Consumer Perceptions of Service Quality," *Journal of Retailing* 64 (Spring 1988), pp. 64–79.

42. R. B. Chase and D. M. Stewart, "Make Your Service Fail-Safe," *Sloan Management Review,* Spring 1994, pp. 35–44.

43. Ibid.

44. F. R. Reichheld and W. E. Sasser Jr., "Zero Defections: Quality Comes to Services," *Harvard Business Review,* September–October 1990, pp. 105–7.

45. L. M. Fisher, "Here Comes Front-Office Automation," *Strategy and Business* 13 (Fourth Quarter, 1999), pp. 53–65; and R. A. Shaffer, "Handling Customer Service on the Web," *Fortune,* March 1, 1999, pp. 204, 208.

46. S. W. Brown, "Service Recovery through IT," *Marketing Management,* Fall 1997, pp. 25–27.

47. Davidow, "Organizational Responses to Customer Complaints."

48. Hart, Heskett, and Sasser, "The Profitable Art of Service Recovery."

49. J. Dunning, A. Pecotich, and A. O'Cass, "What Happens When Things Go Wrong? Retail Sales Explanations and Their Effects," *Psychology and Marketing* 21, no. 7 (2004), pp. 553–72; McColl-Kennedy and Sparks, "Application of Fairness Theory to Service Failures and Service Recovery"; Davidow, "Organizational Responses to Customer Complaints."

50. Hess, Ganesan, and Klein, "Service Failure and Recovery: The Impact of Relationship Factors on Customer Satisfaction"; Priluck, "Relationship Marketing Can Mitigate Product and Service Failures."

51. T. DeWitt and M. K. Brady, "Rethinking Service Recovery Strategies: The Effect of Rapport on Consumer Responses to Service Failure," *Journal of Service Research* 6 (November 2003), pp. 193–207.

52. Hess, Ganesan, and Klein, "Service Failure and Recovery: The Impact of Relationship Factors on Customer Satisfaction."

53. L. L. Berry and A. Parasuraman, *Marketing Services* (New York: Free Press, 1991), p. 52.

54. F. F. Reichheld, "Learning from Customer Defections," *Harvard Business Review,* March–April 1996, pp. 56–69.

55. Ibid.

56. A. L. Ostrom and C. W. L. Hart, "Service Guarantees: Research and Practice," in *Handbook of Services Marketing and Management,* ed. D. Iacobucci and T. Swartz (Thousand Oaks, CA: Sage Publications, 2000), pp. 299–316.

57. See ibid.; C. W. L. Hart, "The Power of Unconditional Guarantees," *Harvard Business Review,* July–August 1988, pp. 54–62; and C. W. L. Hart, *Extraordinary Guarantees* (New York: AMACOM, 1993).

58. A. L. Ostrom and D. Iacobucci, "The Effect of Guarantees on Consumers' Evaluation of Services," *Journal of Services Marketing* 12, no. 5 (1998), pp. 362–78; S. B. Lidén and P. Skålén, "The Effect of Service Guarantees on Service Recovery," *International Journal of Service Industry Management* 14, no. 1 (2003), pp. 36–58.

59. Ostrom and Hart, "Service Guarantees."

60. J. Wirtz and D. Kum, "Designing Service Guarantees: Is Full Satisfaction the Best You Can Guarantee?" *Journal of Services Marketing,* 15, no. 4 (2001), pp. 282–99.

61. Example cited in Ostrom and Hart, "Service Guarantees."

62. For more information, see M. A. McCollough and D. D. Gremler, "Guaranteeing Student Satisfaction: An Exercise in Treating Students as Customers," *Journal of Marketing Education* 21 (August 1999), pp. 118–30; D. D. Gremler and M. A. McCollough, "Student Satisfaction Guarantees: An Empirical Examination of Attitudes, Antecedents, and Consequences," *Journal of Marketing Education* 24 (August 2002), pp. 150–60.

63. J. Wirtz, D. Kum, and K. S. Lee, "Should a Firm with a Reputation for Outstanding Service Quality Offer a Service Guarantee?" *Journal of Services Marketing,* 14, no. 6 (2000), pp. 502–12.

64. J. Wirtz, "Development of a Service Guarantee Model," *Asia Pacific Journal of Management* 15 (April 1998), pp. 51–75.

65. Ibid.

66. Wirtz and Kim, "Consumer Cheating on Service Guarantees," *Journal of the Academy of Marketing Science* 32 (Spring 2004), pp. 159–75.

67. Wirtz, "Development of a Service Guarantee Model."

68. Ostrom and Iacobucci, "The Effect of Guarantees."

69. Wirtz, "Development of a Service Guarantee Model."

Part 4

ALIGNING SERVICE DESIGN AND STANDARDS

Meeting customer expectations of service requires not only understanding what the expectations are, but also taking action on that knowledge. Action takes several forms: designing services based on customer requirements, setting service standards to ensure that employees perform as customers expect, and providing physical evidence that creates the appropriate cues and ambience for service. When action does not take place, there is a gap—service design and standards gap—as shown in the accompanying figure. In this section you will learn to identify the causes of gap 2 as well as effective strategies for closing this gap.

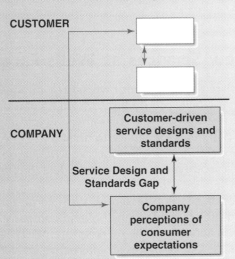

Provider Gap 2

Chapter 9 describes the tools that are most effective in service development and design, especially a tool called service blueprinting. Chapter 10 helps you differentiate between company-defined standards and customer-defined standards and to recognize how they can be developed. Chapter 11 explores the strategic importance of physical evidence, the variety of roles it plays, and strategies for effectively designing physical evidence and the servicescape to meet customer expectations.

Chapter 9

SERVICE DEVELOPMENT AND DESIGN

This chapter's objectives are to

1. Describe the challenges inherent in service design.

2. Present the stages and unique elements of the new-service development process.

3. Demonstrate the value of service blueprinting and how to develop and read service blueprints.

4. Present lessons learned in choosing and implementing high-performance service innovations.

Innovative New Services at Wells Fargo Bank

Have you ever considered starting your own service business? What type of service would it be? What would you do first? Assuming you understood your market and had a good feel for potential customers' needs and expectations, how would you go about designing the service to meet those needs? If you were starting a business to manufacture a new product, you would most likely begin by designing and building a prototype of your new product. But how could you do this for a service?

These are the types of questions asked by Wells Fargo Bank, fifth largest, and by many counts the most profitable, bank holding company in the United States, when it introduces new services to the marketplace. Wells Fargo is recognized as the industry leader in the United States for alternative delivery strategies of banking services. As such, it constantly introduces new services that allow customers to reach the bank when and where they want to—meeting expectations for speed and accessibility. Its strategy depends on a range of services, from a vast automated teller machine (ATM) system (it even has an ATM in Antarctica) to providing extensive banking services in supermarkets to highly accessible phone banking systems and call centers to online, Internet-based services. Wells was the first U.S. bank to offer online services (in 1989) and Internet banking (1995). Wireless banking was introduced in 2001. Wells has over 3 million Internet banking customers and leads U.S. banks in market share for Internet banking. In 2003, Wells was named the "Best Corporate/Institutional Internet Bank" in North America by *Global Finance.* To succeed in these pioneering efforts, Wells has had to anticipate its customers' needs, develop effective delivery systems, and be willing to constantly change.

For example, in 1998 Wells introduced WellsTrade, an online discount trading service. This service has evolved into WellsChoice online, a full-service brokerage account, combining high tech and high touch. The service is designed to combine the convenience of online trading with the guidance of a human financial consultant. In 2000 Wells had 178 Web-related projects under way in the bank, partnering with companies such as eBay to develop unique services for customers. To hold onto its position as the top-rated corporate Internet bank, Wells' current efforts revolve around redesigning their corporate online banking services to be even more responsive to customer needs. The focus is on customized service, speed, and convenience. New self-service tools for corporate clients are being introduced to save customers time and give them more control. In addition, new "CEO Portlets" are being introduced to provide customizable snapshots of key banking information for corporate clients. Through these improvements and other planned innovations, Wells intends to remain the leader in Internet banking.

All these efforts and new service introductions are initiated to support the company's vision of providing "every channel our customers want, every product our customers need, anytime our customers choose." Through developing new services and being a leader in its industry, Wells has learned some important lessons. According to one of Wells' executive vice presidents, the firm has learned (1) the importance of having integrated marketing, sales, and support infrastructure to support the new services and (2) that nothing ever happens as quickly as you would like it to—it is hard work being the one that blazes the trail.[1]

So what causes new products and services such as those offered by Wells Fargo to fail or succeed? If you decide to start your own business, what can you do to protect yourself as much as possible from failure?

A study of 11,000 new products launched by 77 manufacturing, service, and consumer products companies found that only 56 percent of new offerings are still on the market five years later.[2] Failures can be traced to a number of causes: no unique benefits offered, insufficient demand, unrealistic goals for the new product/service, poor fit between the new service and others within the organization's portfolio, poor location, insufficient financial backing, or failure to take the necessary time to develop and introduce the product.[3] An analysis of over 60 studies on new product and service success showed that the dominant and most reliable predictors of success for new introductions relate to *product/service characteristics* (product meeting customer needs, product advantage over competing products, technological sophistication); *strategy characteristics* (dedicated human resources to support the initiative, dedicated R&D focused on the new product initiative), *process characteristics* (marketing, predevelopment, technological, and launch proficiencies); and *marketplace characteristics* (market potential).[4]

Frequently a good service idea fails because of development, design, and specification flaws, topics that are emphasized in this chapter. As more firms, across industries, move into services as a growth strategy, the challenges and opportunities of developing and delivering service offerings become a reality. Our Strategy Insight highlights three firms that are looking to new services for their growth.

Firms in many industries are discovering the value of strategically focusing on new service offerings to provide value for their customers as well as profits and growth for the firm. Using this strategic approach, services are developed to enhance relationships with customers by providing them total packages of offerings, sometimes referred to as "solutions." By adding services to their traditional offerings, firms can differentiate themselves from their competitors and frequently earn higher profit margins on the new services compared to traditional manufactured or retail product offerings. IBM Global Services is perhaps the best known example of this type of solutions strategy (see opening to Chapter 1). Like IBM, many companies are attempting to "grow through services" in business-to-consumer as well as business-to-business markets. As they move in this direction, they quickly recognize the great opportunities as well as the complex challenges of introducing new services. Here we highlight three firms' growth-through-services strategies.

PETSMART's pet hotel concept
Source: Courtesy of PETsMART

PETSMART

The pet products market is booming, and services are a big part of the growth for the leading U.S. pet retailer, PETsMART. With over 675 pet stores in the United States and Canada, PETsMART's vision is to serve "pet parents" through "total lifetime care" of their pets. Although sales of pet food, toys, and pet accessories are part of this vision, total lifetime care means much more. The company also promotes comprehensive pet training, grooming, and upscale day and overnight care through its pet hotels. PETsHOTEL, its newest service, not only ensures pet safety and health but also promotes professional care and a total "pet experience" through daily "yappy hours" and a "bone booth," where pet parents can call in and speak to their pet. The company's success in the past several years can be directly traced to the expansion into services.

UNITED PARCEL SERVICE

In a totally different realm, UPS is also projecting growth through adding services for its business-to-business customers. The company has evolved from a simple messenger service and delivery business in the early 1900s to a common carrier competing with the U.S. Postal Service in the 1950s, to an airborne overnight delivery

CHALLENGES OF SERVICE DESIGN

Because services are largely intangible and process oriented (such as a hospital stay, a golf lesson, or an NBA basketball game), they are difficult to describe and communicate. When services are delivered over a long period—a week's resort vacation, a six-

service in the 1980s. In recent years, UPS has evolved even further into broad-based logistics services including freight forwarding, financing, warehousing and inventory management, and shipment coordination and tracking. Three years ago, for example, Ford Motor Company handed over its entire vehicle distribution network to UPS for a complete overhaul. The result has been a 40 percent reduction in the time it takes autos to arrive at dealers. As another example, UPS now manages a warehouse and also handles all Internet ordering for apparel company, Jockey International.

HOME DEPOT

As the world's largest home-improvement retailer, Home Depot sees strong potential growth through services. Its CEO, Robert Nardelli, came to the company from General Electric's Power Systems unit, where he had led that unit's successful growth, primarily through services, in the late 1990s. Nardelli brought the services philosophy with him to Home Depot, where traditionally the relationship with the customer had ended at the checkout counter. Now the company offers to install what customers buy as well as manage relationships between building and installation contractors and customers. This type of "solution" is exactly what many Home Depot customers are seeking. Because Home Depot screens and monitors the contractors it uses, customer risk is reduced and a high level of satisfaction is likely. The company has had some rough spots in moving from a pure retail mind-set to a services orientation. For example, store managers were initially reluctant to put much effort into promoting services, and important service project management software was slow in development. As these barriers have been overcome, the company is projecting continued and even more rapid success through its service solutions strategy, which is currently expanding at 40 percent per year.

Although the examples we provide here are all U.S.-based companies, the growth through services strategy is clearly a global phenomenon. Later in this chapter, our Global Feature focuses on an international Swedish-based company, Volvo Truck, and its business-to-business services strategy.

Sources: M. Sawhney, S. Balasubramanian, and V. V. Krishnan, "Creating Growth with Services," *Sloan Management Review*, Winter 2004, pp. 34–43; R. C. Morais, "Dog Days," *Forbes*, June 21, 2004, pp. 78–89;"Stock Highlight: PETsMART," *Value Line Selection and Opinion*, July 30, 2004, p. 2192; www.petsmart.com; D. Foust, "Big Brown's New Bag," *BusinessWeek*, July 19, 2004, pp. 54–56; C. R. Schoenberger, "House Call," *Forbes*, September 6, 2004, pp. 93–94.

month consulting engagement, 10 weeks on a Weight Watchers program—their complexity increases, and they become even more difficult to define and describe. Further, because services are delivered by employees to customers, they are variable. Rarely, are two services alike or experienced in the same way. These characteristics of services, which we explored in the first chapter of this book, are the heart of the challenge involved in designing services.

FIGURE 9.1
Risks of Relying on Words Alone to Describe Services

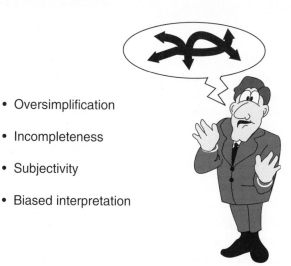

- Oversimplification

- Incompleteness

- Subjectivity

- Biased interpretation

Because services cannot be touched, examined, or tried out, people frequently resort to words in their efforts to describe them. Lynn Shostack, a pioneer in developing design concepts for services, has pointed out four risks of attempting to describe services in words alone (see Figure 9.1).[5] The first risk is *oversimplification.* Shostack points out that "to say that 'portfolio management' means 'buying and selling stocks' is like describing the space shuttle as 'something that flies.' Some people will picture a bird, some a helicopter, and some an angel" (p. 76). Words are simply inadequate to describe a complex service system.

The second risk is *incompleteness.* In describing services, people (employees, managers, customers) tend to omit details or elements of the service with which they are not familiar. A person might do a fairly credible job of describing how a discount stock brokerage service takes orders from customers. But would that person be able to describe fully how the monthly statements are created, how the interactive computer system works, and how these two elements of the service are integrated into the order-taking process?

The third risk is *subjectivity.* Any one person describing a service in words will be biased by personal experiences and degree of exposure to the service. There is a natural (and mistaken) tendency to assume that because all people have gone to a fast-food restaurant, they all understand what that service is. Persons working in different functional areas of the same service organization (a marketing person, an operations person, a finance person) are likely to describe the service very differently as well, biased by their own functional blinders.

A final risk of describing services using words alone is *biased interpretation.* No two people will define "responsive," "quick," or "flexible" in exactly the same way. For example, a supervisor or manager may suggest to a front-line service employee that the employee should try to be more flexible or responsive in providing service to the customer. Unless the term "flexibility" is further defined, the employee is likely to interpret the word differently from the manager.

All these risks become very apparent in the new service development process, when organizations may be attempting to design services never before experienced by customers. It is critical that all involved (managers, front-line employees, and behind-the-scenes support staff) be working with the same concepts of the new service, based on customer needs and expectations. For a service that already exists, any attempt to improve it will also suffer unless everyone has a shared vision of the service and associated issues.

In the following sections of this chapter, we present approaches for new service development and design to address these unique challenges.

NEW SERVICE DEVELOPMENT

Research suggests that products that are designed and introduced via the steps in a structured planning framework have a greater likelihood of ultimate success than those not developed within a framework.[6] The fact that services are intangible makes it even more imperative for a new service development system to have four basic characteristics. (1) It must be objective, not subjective. (2) It must be precise, not vague. (3) It must be fact driven, not opinion driven. (4) It must be methodological, not philosophical.[7] Although the process of developing new services should be structured and should follow a set of defined stages, it should not become overly rigid or bureaucratized. Such structure taken to an extreme can result in a rigid and plodding approach that could waste time and/or allow competitors to get out in front. Thus, common sense must dictate when flexibility and speed will override the structure.

Often new services are introduced on the basis of managers' and employees' subjective opinions about what the services should be and whether they will succeed, rather than on objective designs incorporating data about customer perceptions, market needs, and feasibility. A new service design process may be imprecise in defining the nature of the service concept because the people involved believe either that intangible processes cannot be defined precisely or that "everyone knows what we mean." Neither of these explanations or defenses for imprecision is justifiable, as we illustrate in this chapter's model for new service development.[8]

Because services are produced and consumed simultaneously and often involve interaction between employees and customers, it is also critical that the new service development process involve both employees and customers. Employees frequently *are* the service, or at least they perform or deliver the service, and thus their involvement in choosing which new services to develop and how these services should be designed and implemented can be very beneficial. Contact employees are psychologically and physically close to customers and can be very helpful in identifying customer needs for new services. Involving employees in the design and development process also increases the likelihood of new service success because employees can identify the organizational issues that need to be addressed to support the delivery of the service to customers.[9] For example, at Metropolitan Life Insurance Company, cross-functional teams comprising representatives from administration, claims, marketing, and information systems are included to ensure that all aspects of the service and delivery process are considered before full-scale development of a new insurance service concept begins.

Because customers often actively participate in service delivery, they too should be involved in the new service development process. Beyond just providing input on their own needs, customers can help design the service concept and the delivery process, particularly in situations in which the customer personally carries out part of the service process. Marriott Corporation is well known for involving its guests in the design of its hotel rooms to ensure that the features and placement of furnishings in the rooms will work for the guests and not just for the staff or the architects who design the rooms. Bank of America has also been very successful with developing new service innovations in branch banking by relying on results of a series of experiments in its Atlanta branches.[10] The experiments are designed to more rigorously test, in real time and with real customers, new service innovations that the bank is considering (see Exhibit 9.2 later in this chapter for details about Bank of America's experiments). In this way the bank gains actual customer feedback as well as employee reactions to new service ideas.

TYPES OF NEW SERVICES

As we describe the new service development process, remember that not all new services are "new" to the same degree. New service options can run the gamut from major innovations to minor style changes:[11]

- *Major or radical innovations* are new services for markets as yet undefined. Past examples include the first broadcast television services and Federal Express's introduction of nationwide, overnight small package delivery. Many innovations now and in the future will evolve from information, computer, and Internet-based technologies. Our Technology Spotlight features eBay, a company that epitomizes radical service innovations.

- *Start-up businesses* consist of new services for a market that is already served by existing products that meet the same generic needs. Service examples include the creation of health maintenance organizations to provide an alternative form of health care delivery, online banking for financial transactions, and door-to-door airport shuttle services that compete with traditional taxi and limousine services.

- *New services for the currently served market* represent attempts to offer existing customers of the organization a service not previously available from the company (although it may be available from other companies). Examples include Barnes and Noble offering coffee service, a health club offering nutrition classes, and airlines offering fax, phone, and Internet service during flights.

- *Service line extensions* represent augmentations of the existing service line, such as a restaurant adding new menu items, an airline offering new routes, a law firm offering additional legal services, and a university adding new courses or degrees.

- *Service improvements* represent perhaps the most common type of service innovation. Changes in features of services that are already offered might involve faster execution of an existing service process, extended hours of service, or augmentations such as added amenities in a hotel room (e.g., the addition of wireless Internet connections).

- *Style changes* represent the most modest service innovations, although they are often highly visible and can have significant effects on customer perceptions, emotions, and attitudes. Changing the color scheme of a restaurant, revising the logo for an organization, redesigning a website, or painting aircraft a different color all represent style changes. These innovations do not fundamentally change the service, only its appearance, similar to how packaging changes are used for consumer products.

Technology Spotlight
eBay: A Radical Service Innovation

When eBay was founded in 1995 it was not much more than an online flea market for individuals seeking to buy and sell old or unique items to other individuals. The original eBay concept was to provide the online service needed to facilitate these basic, simple trades among buyers and sellers. In the intervening years, the company has grown to a powerhouse of Internet retailing, with over 30 million active users and well over $20 billion in annual trade. Meg Whitman, the company's now-famous CEO, describes eBay as a "dynamic self-regulating economy."

Clearly, eBay is a radical service innovation. Nothing like it existed before, and its limits and bounds are yet unknown. From the original basic trading services, the company has evolved to a complex self-regulating system that is completely dependent on its community of members. Services offered by eBay now include PayPal, a safe and secure online payment system, education classes for those who want to learn to be successful on eBay, and a developer's program for members who want to create their own software solutions for making eBay transactions more efficient and effective. Going far beyond its original focus on individual members, eBay has introduced important services for small businesses as well. These services help small businesses address issues such as improving cash flow, hiring, and shipping. eBay offers equipment leasing and financing services by Direct Capital, employment services through Monster.com, integrated shipping solutions through the U.S. Postal Service, online postage through Pitney Bowes, and cost-effective online payment through Pay-Pal. More than 430,000 small business sellers are trading through eBay, and the number of business-related items for sale on eBay doubled to one million in just one year.

One of the most important aspects of eBay's success is its member community and the support and services they provide to each other. The company encourages open communication among members through discussion and chat boards that are actively used. These member-facilitated services and communications can be viewed as new service innovations in their own right. There are even "neighborhood watch" groups that ensure that everyone in the community learns and follows the etiquette and behavior norms that govern the community. Through an ongoing feedback system, members rate each other in terms of reliability and quality; this system provides a "self-policing" orientation for the community. (As the community has grown, more formalized fraud protection and policing services have been initiated by the company as well.) Extending the community aspect further, some members even interact with each other offline, going so far as to vacation together and buy special items for one another. One group even spent vacation time doing home repairs for an eBay member in need, and another group planned a Labor Day picnic together. eBay literally has become a part of many people's lives around the world.

Strategically, one of the most important elements of eBay's success has been its unrelenting devotion to its members and its willingness to listen. Being innovative in developing new services is dependent on listening to customers. One of eBay's most cherished institutions, according to Whitman, is the Voice of the Customer program. Every couple months, eBay brings in groups of customers to ask them specifically how they work and how eBay can change to make things better. At least twice a week the company holds hour-long teleconferences to poll members on new features or policies. eBay's listening ear encourages constant complaints and suggestions to the company. And unlike many companies, eBay responds. Change is constant on eBay's site and in its service features—almost to a fault, say some users. According to the company's senior vice president of international operations, "Some of the terms you learn in business school—drive, force, commit—don't apply...We're over here listening, adapting, enabling." The result is that eBay users feel like owners, and their voices have shaped the company, its practices, the site itself, and the community norms.

eBay is a growing, dynamic community that has evolved from a radical service innovation made possible through technology. Undoubtedly eBay will continue to evolve and play an important role in the world of retail and business trade.

Sources: R. D. Hof, "The eBay Economy," *BusinessWeek,* August 25, 2003, pp. 124–28; www.ebay.com, 2004; D. McDonald, "Meet eBay's New Postman," *Business 2.0,* September 2004, pp. 52–54.

FIGURE 9.2
New Service Development Process

Sources: Booz-Allen & Hamilton, *New Product Management for the 1980s* (New York: Booz-Allen & Hamilton, 1982); M. J. Bowers, "An Exploration into New Service Development: Organization, Process, and Structure," doctoral dissertation, Texas A&M University, 1985; A. Khurana and S. R. Rosenthal, "Integrating the Fuzzy Front End of New Product Development," *Sloan Management Review,* Winter 1997, pp. 103–20; and R. G. Cooper, *Winning at New Products,* 3rd ed. (Cambridge, MA: Perseus Publishing, 2001).

Front-end planning

Implementation

- **Business strategy development or review**

- **New service strategy development**

- **Idea generation**
  - Screen ideas against new service strategy

- **Concept development and evaluation**
  - Test concept with customers and employees

- **Business analysis**
  - Test for profitability and feasibility

- **Service development and testing**
  - Conduct service prototype test

- **Market testing**
  - Test service and other marketing mix elements

- **Commercialization**

- **Postintroduction evaluation**

STAGES IN NEW SERVICE DEVELOPMENT

In this section we focus on the actual steps to be followed in new service development. The steps can be applied to any type of new service. Much of what is presented in this section has direct parallels in the new product development process for manufactured goods. Because of the inherent characteristics of services, however, the development process for new services requires adaptations.[12] Figure 9.2 shows the basic principles and steps in new service development. Although these steps may be similar to those for manufactured goods, their implementation is significantly different.[13] The challenges typically lie in defining the concept in the early stages of the development process and again at the prototype development stage. Partially because of these challenges, service firms are generally less likely to carry out a structured development process for new innovations than are their manufacturing and consumer-goods counterparts.[14]

An underlying assumption of new product development process models is that new product ideas can be dropped at any stage of the process if they do not satisfy the criteria for success at that particular stage.[15] Figure 9.2 shows the checkpoints (represented by stop signs) that separate critical stages of the development process. The checkpoints specify requirements that a new service must meet before it can proceed to the next stage of development.

New service or product development is rarely a completely linear process. Many companies are finding that to speed up new service development, some steps can be worked on simultaneously, and in some instances a step may even be skipped. The overlapping of steps and simultaneous development of various pieces of the new service/product development process has been referred to as "flexible product development." This type of flexible, speedy process is particularly important in technology industries, in which products and services evolve extremely quickly. In these environments, computer technology lets companies monitor customer opinions and needs during development and change the final offering right up until it is launched. Often, the next version of the service is in planning stages at the same time that the current version is being launched.[16] Even if the stages are handled simultaneously, however, the important checkpoints noted in Figure 9.2 must be assessed to maximize chances of success.

The process shown in Figure 9.2 is divided into two sections: front-end planning and implementation. The front end determines what service concepts will be developed, whereas the back end executes or implements the service concept. When asked where the greatest weaknesses in product and service innovation occur, managers typically report problems with the "fuzzy front end."[17] The front end is called "fuzzy" because of its relative abstractness, which is even more apparent with intangible and variable services than with manufactured products.

Front-End Planning

Business Strategy Development or Review

It is assumed that an organization will have an overall strategic orientation, vision, and mission. Clearly a first step in new service development is to review that mission and vision. The new service strategy and specific new service ideas must fit within the larger strategic mission and vision of the organization. For example, Wells Fargo Bank's mission, presented in our opening vignette for this chapter, is to be the industry leader in alternative delivery channels for financial services and to offer customized services to its clientele when and where they need them. Its vast array of ATMs, in-supermarket branches, and Internet banking services support this strategy. PETsMART, one company featured in this chapter's Strategy Insight, has as its mission to serve "pet parents" through the "lifetime care of pets." This mission has led to the development of a host of new services, such as training, grooming, overnight care, and day care, in addition to traditional food, toys, and accessories offered in its stores. For both Wells Fargo Bank and PETsMART, the new services strategy clearly fits the mission of the company.

In addition to its strategic mission, the company's underlying orientation toward growth will affect how it defines its new services strategy. Becoming aware of the organization's overall strategic orientation is fundamental to plotting a direction for growth. Noted strategy researchers suggest four primary strategic orientations that are taken by companies:[18] (1) *Prospectors* seek to be innovative, searching out new opportunities and taking on risks; (2) *Defenders* are experts in their own areas and tend not to seek new opportunities outside their domain of expertise; (3) *Analyzers* maintain stability in certain areas of operation but are open to experimenting and seeking out opportunities on the margin; (4) *Reactors* seldom make adjustments unless forced to do so by environmental pressures. Another noted management strategist suggests that firms can be distinguished by whether they primarily pursue a cost-leadership strategy, a differentiation strategy, or a focused strategy.[19] An organization's strategic orientation will affect how it views growth through new service development.

New Service Strategy Development

Research suggests that without a clear new product or service strategy, a well-planned portfolio of new products and services, and an organizational structure that facilitates product development via ongoing communications and cross-functional sharing of responsibilities, front-end decisions become ineffective.[20] Thus a product portfolio strategy and a defined organizational structure for new product or service development are critical—and are the foundations—for success.

The types of new services that will be appropriate will depend on the organization's goals, vision, capabilities, and growth plans. By defining a new service strategy (possibly in terms of markets, types of services, time horizon for development, profit criteria, or other relevant factors), the organization will be in a better position to begin generating specific ideas. For example, it may focus its growth on new services at a particular level of the described continuum from major innovations to style changes. Or the organization may define its new service strategy even more specifically in terms of particular markets or market segments or in terms of specific profit generation goals.

One way to begin formulating a new service strategy is to use the framework shown in Figure 9.3 for identifying growth opportunities. The framework allows an organization to identify possible directions for growth and can be helpful as a catalyst for creative ideas. The framework may also later serve as an initial idea screen if, for example, the organization chooses to focus its growth efforts on one or two of the four cells in the matrix. The matrix suggests that companies can develop a growth strategy around current customers or for new customers, and can focus on current offerings or new service offerings. Figure 9.4 illustrates how Taco Bell has expanded its existing service to new locations such as universities and airports. Exhibit 9.1 further explains how Taco Bell has pursued growth in all four areas of the matrix.

Idea Generation

The next step in the process is the formal solicitation of new ideas. The ideas generated at this phase can be passed through the new service strategy screen described in the preceding step. Many methods and avenues are available for searching out new service ideas. Formal brainstorming, solicitation of ideas from employees and customers, lead user research, and learning about competitors' offerings are some of the most common approaches. Some companies are even collaborating with outsiders (e.g., competitors, vendors, alliance partners) or developing licensing agreements and joint ventures in an effort to exploit all possible sources of new ideas.[21]

FIGURE 9.3
New Service Strategy Matrix for Identifying Growth Opportunities

Source: Adapted from H. I. Ansoff, *Corporate Strategy* (New York: McGraw-Hill, 1965).

Offerings	Markets	
	Current Customers	New Customers
Existing Services	Share building	Market development
New Services	Service development	Diversification

FIGURE 9.4
Taco Bell Has Grown through Market Development on University Campuses

Source: Fritz Hoffman/Image Works/TimePix

Observing customers and how they use the firm's products and services can also generate creative ideas for new innovations. Sometimes referred to as *empathic design,* observation is particularly effective in situations in which customers may not be able to recognize or verbalize their needs.[22] In service businesses, contact personnel, who actually deliver the services and interact directly with consumers, can be particularly good sources of ideas for complementary services and ways to improve current offerings.

Whether the source of a new idea is inside or outside the organization, some established mechanism should exist for ensuring an ongoing stream of new service possibilities. This mechanism might include a formal new service development department or function with responsibility for generating new ideas, suggestion boxes for employees and customers, new service development teams that meet regularly, surveys and focus groups with customers and employees, or formal competitive analysis to identify new services. Although new service ideas may arise outside the formal mechanism, total dependence on luck is not a good strategy.

In listening to their customers, many firms around the world have discovered ideas for new *services* rather than product enhancements (see our Strategy Insight earlier in this chapter). These new services allow the firm to move in the direction of becoming a solutions provider, as is the case with Volvo Truck, discussed in our Global Feature.

Service Concept Development and Evaluation

Once an idea surfaces that is regarded as a good fit with both the business and the new service strategies, it is ready for initial development. In the case of a tangible product, this next step would mean formulating the basic product definition and then presenting consumers with descriptions and drawings to get their reactions.

The inherent characteristics of services, particularly intangibility and simultaneous production and consumption, place complex demands on this phase of the process. Drawing pictures and describing an intangible service in concrete terms are difficult. It is therefore important that agreement be reached at this stage on exactly what the concept is. By involving multiple parties in sharpening the concept definition, it often becomes apparent that individual views of the concept are not the same. For example,

Exhibit 9.1 TACO BELL EXPANDS MARKETS AND OFFERINGS

To illustrate how the matrix shown in Figure 9.3 might function as a catalyst for idea generation, consider growth strategies pursued by Taco Bell, one of the world's fastest-growing fast-food chains, specializing in Mexican food.

SHARE BUILDING (CURRENT CUSTOMERS, EXISTING SERVICES)

Share building is another term for market penetration—gaining a greater proportion of sales from existing markets. This strategy is pursued by Taco Bell in the expansion of Taco Bell outlets, resulting in 6,500 restaurants across the United States in 2004. In the late 1990s Taco Bell stepped up its efforts to gain market share among Hispanic consumers, another share-building strategy.

MARKET DEVELOPMENT (NEW CUSTOMERS, EXISTING SERVICES)

Taco Bell has expanded by offering its existing services in nontraditional locations, using creative formats to reach new customers. For example, Taco Bells can be found in airports, universities, and schools. Taco Bell has also opened Taco Bell Express units in gas stations around the United States. Often the outlets in these locations are scaled-back "express" versions with a limited menu and small space requirement. Another form of market development is expansion into international markets, taking existing services to other countries. In 2004, Taco Bell operated 280 restaurants outside the United States.

SERVICE DEVELOPMENT (CURRENT CUSTOMERS, NEW SERVICES)

Service growth is possible when current customers are offered additional new services or service improvements. Taco Bell has added new menu items—for example, its Gordita beef steak and its Baja Blast tropical Mountain Dew drink—better service delivery, value meals, and lower prices to better serve its current customers.

DIVERSIFICATION (NEW CUSTOMERS, NEW SERVICES)

Diversification, involving new services for consumers not currently served, is frequently the most challenging because it takes the organization into unfamiliar territories on both the product and market dimensions. Taco Bell has pursued this growth option by selling its branded products in grocery stores and by buying significant interests in other restaurant chains.

Sources: "It's No Longer Just 'Fill 'Er Up,'" *Franchise Times*, August 1997, pp. 27ff; "Taco Bell's Hispanic Strategy," *Advertising Age*, October 20, 1997, p. 12; "Taco Bell Takes Wraps Off Higher-End Items," *Brandweek*, March 30, 1998, p. 5; www.tacobell.com, 2004.

Lynn Shostack relates that the design and development of a new discount brokerage service was initially described by the bank as a way "to buy and sell stocks for customers at low prices."[23] Through the initial concept development phase it became clear that not everyone in the organization had the same idea about how this description would translate into an actual service and that there were a variety of ways the concept could be developed. Only through multiple iterations of the service—and the raising of hundreds of issues, large and small—was an agreement finally reached on the discount brokerage concept.

After clear definition of the concept, it is important to produce a description of the service that represents its specific features and characteristics and then to determine initial customer and employee responses to the concept. The service design document would describe the problem addressed by the service, discuss the reasons for offering the new service, itemize the service process and its benefits, and provide a rationale for purchasing the service.[24] The roles of customers and employees in the delivery process would also be described. The new service concept would then be evaluated by asking employees and customers whether they understand the idea of the proposed service, whether they are favorable to the concept, and whether they feel it satisfies an unmet need.

Volvo, headquartered in Sweden, is one of the world's largest producers of trucks. In fact, approximately two-thirds of Volvo's total sales come from its Global Trucks group. But, like many manufacturers worldwide, Volvo is much more than an equipment company. It views itself as a total customer solution company offering a variety of services to enhance the value of its products and to provide revenue growth.

By listening to its truck fleet customers, Volvo has identified ideas for new services that can enhance the value of its trucks. The physical product, the truck, has become a component of Volvo's service concept, and the company is moving in the direction of becoming a service company instead of purely a heavy truck manufacturer.

One of Volvo's recent service offerings, Dynafleet 2.0, provides a good example of how Volvo is enhancing the value it offers to its business customers. Dynafleet 2.0 is an extensive transportation information system that Volvo can customize for its truck transportation business customers. The system is composed of three separate modules that are installed in the company's fleet of trucks to provide exact information and direct communication resulting in more efficient operations and reduced costs for the company. One of the modules is the "logger tool" that gathers information on a vehicle and its driver. Some information is stored on the driver's smart card, and some information is logged in by the driver. The second module is the "communication tool," which transmits and receives text messages and also sends information about the vehicle's location, fuel consumption, and other details to the company's fleet office. Drivers can also communicate directly with the office or send messages to other drivers through this communication system. The third module is the "information tool," which provides maps and traffic information to the driver of the vehicle via a color display.

Back in the office, the fleet manager utilizes a "logger manager" that provides reports on vehicle fuel consumption, hour-by-hour information on workday activities of each vehicle and driver, and start and stop times. This information is useful for wage calculations and keeping track of work hours. The "transport manager," used to track exactly where each vehicle is at all times, generates reports that can be used in traffic planning and other operational decisions.

Volvo has expanded far beyond simply providing trucks for its business customers. Other services, such as maintenance agreements, training, and financing, further enhance Dynafleet's offering.

The services available through Dynafleet address more fully the total customer value chain, allowing Volvo to move toward its goal of being a customer solution provider rather than a truck manufacturer. The benefits accrue directly to the drivers of the trucks as well as the transportation companies that buy the trucks. Administrative work is simplified, and fleet managers and traffic planners become more efficient. Volvo aims to maintain its leadership and compete effectively through offering Dynafleet 2.0 and other services aimed at improving its customers' efficiency, service reliability, and economic returns.

Sources: "Volvo Dynafleet 2.0—Applying a Service Perspective," in B. Edvardsson, A. Gustafsson, M. D. Johnson, and B. Sanden, *New Service Development and Innovation in the New Economy* (Lund, Sweden: Studentlitteratur AB, 2000), pp. 52–55; www.volvo.com, 2002.

Business Analysis

Assuming that the service concept is favorably evaluated by customers and employees at the concept development stage, the next step is to estimate its economic feasibility and potential profit implications. Demand analysis, revenue projections, cost analyses, and operational feasibility are assessed at this stage. Because the development of service concepts is so closely tied to the operational system of the organization, this stage will involve preliminary assumptions about the costs of personnel hiring and training, delivery system enhancements, facility changes, and any other projected operations costs. The organization will pass the results of the business analysis through its profitability and feasibility screen to determine whether the new service idea meets the minimum requirements.

Implementation

Once the new service concept has passed all the front-end planning hurdles, it is ready for the implementation stages of the process.

Service Development and Testing

In the development of new tangible products, the development and testing stage involves construction of product prototypes and testing for consumer acceptance. Again, because services are intangible and largely produced and consumed simultaneously, this step presents unique challenges. To address these challenges, this stage of service development should involve all who have a stake in the new service: customers and contact employees as well as functional representatives from marketing, operations, and human resources. During this phase, the concept is refined to the point at which a detailed service blueprint representing the implementation plan for the service can be produced. The blueprint is likely to evolve over a series of iterations on the basis of input from all the involved parties. For example, when a large state hospital was planning a new computer-based information service for doctors throughout its state, it involved many groups in the service development and evaluation stage, including medical researchers, computer programmers and operators, librarians, telecommunications experts, and records clerks as well as the physician customers.[25]

A final step is for each area involved in rendering the service to translate the final blueprint into specific implementation plans for its part of the service delivery process. Because service development, design, and delivery are so intricately intertwined, all parties involved in any aspect of the new service must work together at this stage to delineate the details of the new service. If not, seemingly minor operational details can cause an otherwise good new service idea to fail. For example, careful service development and lots of testing are the rules at Expedia.com, the giant travel information and transportation-booking website. Customers who use Expedia's website potentially have a lot to lose—a $1,000 trip may be at stake, or it may be the only week of vacation the person has in a whole year. So before launching any new software onto the site or redesigning the site itself, Expedia holds dozens of meetings with the design team to consider customer requirements. It then builds and tests prototypes of the software or website changes, conducts usability tests, and gathers customer feedback on designs. Feedback is reviewed and integrated into the design constantly before, during, and after the launch.[26] Exhibit 9.2 illustrates how Bank of America generates ideas and uses experimental tests to evaluate new service concepts in its branches.

Market Testing

At the market testing stage of the development process, a tangible product might be test marketed in a limited number of trading areas to determine marketplace accep-

Exhibit 9.2   NEW SERVICE EXPERIMENTS AT BANK OF AMERICA

Through a series of mergers and acquisitions over the last three decades, Bank of America has become one of the largest banks in the United States, operating in 21 states and serving approximately 27 million households and 2 million businesses. In recent years, the opportunities for further growth by acquisition have become limited, and the bank has turned to other strategies for growth—particularly growth through new and improved services.

One major initiative at the Bank of America is its Innovation and Development (I&D) Team, a corporate unit charged with pioneering new services and service delivery approaches aimed at strengthening customer relationships and improving efficiencies. Instead of focusing on growth by acquisition, this group focuses on organic growth of the company through attracting more customers and fulfilling more of their needs. Recognizing that it did not have a formal new service development process in place, the bank looked to traditional and well-established prototype testing procedures in the manufacturing sector for guidance. Although these models were very helpful, bank strategists realized that they would need to fine-tune these formal research and development approaches to fit the intangible, simultaneous nature of service processes. Live experimentation was the approach that the bank chose to use in testing its new ideas.

To accomplish its objectives, the I&D team has created an "innovation market" in Atlanta, Georgia, where it has set up a series of experiments to test innovative services and approaches to branch banking. These "live experiments" are conducted in actual bank branches with real customers. The first step was to reconfigure the 20 Atlanta branches into three alternative branch models. The first model is an "express center" that is efficient, modern, and quick—and focused on getting customers in and out efficiently. Express centers are housed in modernistic facilities that reinforce the concept. The second model is a "financial center," spacious and relaxed, in which trained staff and advanced technologies offer high-end, sophisticated banking services such as stock trading and portfolio management. The rest of the banks in the innovation market were configured as "traditional centers," with familiar decor and conventional banking services.

Once the test branches were reconfigured, the I&D team followed a structured process to come up with experimental services and service improvements worthy of testing. Every potential idea was entered into a spreadsheet called an "idea portfolio" that included a description of the idea, the process or problem it addressed, and the customer segment affected by the idea. The I&D team then categorized and prioritized the ideas based on projected impact on customers and the fit with the bank's strategy.

By May 2002, more than 200 new ideas had been generated and 40 of them had been tested through formal experiments. For example, one experiment tested whether the presence of TV monitors set to CNN in the bank could reduce the perceived waiting time of patrons. Once the I&D team determined that, yes, the presence of TV monitors could reduce waiting time perceptions and thus increase customer satisfaction, the bank proceeded to evaluate the costs and benefits of installing TVs in all branches over a certain size. They also continued with testing of placement of monitors within the branches as well as the effects of programming beyond CNN.

By introducing formal idea generation processes and live experimentation into its innovation process, Bank of America and its customers have benefited. Within the innovation market, customer satisfaction has significantly improved and the experimental branches have drawn in new customers. In the process, the bank has also learned many lessons and overcome many of the challenges inherent in developing new services. Experimenting with real people (employees and customers) in actual service delivery settings is much different than running a highly controlled prototype test of a product in a laboratory. Bank of America's experience illustrates clearly that product testing approaches that are second nature to manufacturers and IT developers require adaptation and refinement in a services setting.

Source: S. Thomke, "R&D Comes to Services: Bank of America's Pathbreaking Experiments," *Harvard Business Review,* April 2003, pp. 70–79.

---

tance of the product as well as other marketing mix variables such as promotion, pricing, and distribution systems. Again, the standard approach for a new manufactured product is typically not possible for a new service because of its inherent characteristics. Because new service offerings are often intertwined with the delivery system for existing services, it is difficult to test new services in isolation. And in some cases, such as a one-site hospital, it may not be possible to introduce the service to an isolated market area because the organization has only one point of delivery. There are alternative ways of testing the response to marketing mix variables, however. The new service might be offered to employees of the organization and their families for a time to assess their responses to variations in the marketing mix. Or the organization might decide to test variations in pricing and promotion in less realistic contexts by presenting customers with hypothetical mixes and getting their responses in terms of intentions to try the service under varying circumstances. This approach certainly has limitations compared with an actual market test, but it is better than not assessing market response at all.

It is also extremely important at this stage in the development process to do a pilot run of the service to be sure that the operational details are functioning smoothly. Frequently this step is overlooked, and the actual market introduction may be the first test of whether the service system functions as planned. By this point, mistakes in design are harder to correct. As one noted service expert says, "There is simply no substitute for a proper rehearsal" when introducing a new service.[27] In the case of the discount brokerage service described earlier, the bank ran a pilot test by offering employees a special price for one month. The offer was marketed internally, allowing the bank to observe the service process in action before it was actually introduced to the external market.

Commercialization

During the commercialization stage, the service goes live and is introduced to the marketplace. This stage has two primary objectives. The first is to build and maintain acceptance of the new service among large numbers of service delivery personnel who will be responsible day to day for service quality. This task is made easier if acceptance has been built in by involving key groups in the design and development process all along. However, it will still be a challenge to maintain enthusiasm and communicate the new service throughout the system; excellent internal marketing will help.

The second objective is to monitor all aspects of the service during introduction and through the complete service cycle. If the customer needs six months to experience the entire service, then careful monitoring must be maintained through at least six months. Every detail of the service should be assessed—phone calls, face-to-face transactions, billing, complaints, and delivery problems. Operating efficiency and costs should also be tracked.

Postintroduction Evaluation

At this point, the information gathered during commercialization of the service can be reviewed and changes made to the delivery process, staffing, or marketing mix variables on the basis of actual market response to the offering. For example, Expedia.com, the travel website, realized that despite prelaunch testing, restrictions on Expedia bargain fares were confusing to customers. A "hot fix" team was called in to repair the problem.[28] Within a day, the project team redesigned the presentation of information so that the fare restrictions would be clear to customers.

No service will ever stay the same. Whether deliberate or unplanned, changes will always occur. Therefore, formalizing the review process to make those changes that enhance service quality from the customer's point of view is critical. The service blueprint serves a valuable purpose in providing a focal point for discussing and planning changes in the offering.

SERVICE BLUEPRINTING

A stumbling block in developing new services (and in improving existing services) is the difficulty of describing and depicting the service at the concept development, service development, and market test stages. One of the keys to matching service specifications to customer expectations is the ability to describe critical service process characteristics objectively and to depict them so that employees, customers, and managers alike know what the service is, can see their role in its delivery, and understand all the steps and flows involved in the service process. In this section of the chapter we look in depth at service blueprinting, a useful tool for designing and specifying intangible service processes.[29]

What Is a Service Blueprint?

The manufacturing and construction industries have a long tradition of engineering and design. Can you imagine a house being built without detailed specifications? Can you imagine a car, a computer, or even a simple product like a child's toy or a shampoo being produced without concrete and detailed plans, written specifications, and engineering drawings? Yet services commonly lack concrete specifications. A service, even a complex one, might be introduced without any formal, objective depiction of the process.

A service blueprint is a picture or map that accurately portrays the service system so that the different people involved in providing it can understand and deal with it objectively regardless of their roles or their individual points of view. Blueprints are particularly useful at the design stage of service development. A service blueprint visually displays the service by simultaneously depicting the process of service delivery, the points of customer contact, the roles of customers and employees, and the visible elements of the service (see Figure 9.5). It provides a way to break a service down into its logical components and to depict the steps or tasks in the process, the means by which the tasks are executed, and the evidence of service as the customer experiences it.

Blueprinting has its origins in a variety of fields and techniques, including logistics, industrial engineering, decision theory, and computer systems analysis—all of which deal with the definition and explanation of processes.[30] Because services are "experiences" rather than objects, blueprinting is a particularly useful tool for describing them.

Blueprint Components

The key components of service blueprints are shown in Figure 9.6.[31] They are customer actions, "onstage" contact employee actions, "backstage" contact employee actions, and support processes. The conventions for drawing service blueprints are not rigidly defined, and thus the particular symbols used, the number of horizontal lines in the blueprint, and the particular labels for each part of the blueprint may vary somewhat depending on what you read and the complexity of the blueprint being described.

FIGURE 9.5
Service Blueprinting

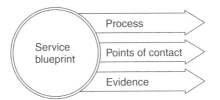

Service blueprinting
A tool for simultaneously depicting the service process, the points of customer contact, and the evidence of service from the customer's point of view.

FIGURE 9.6
Service Blueprint
Components

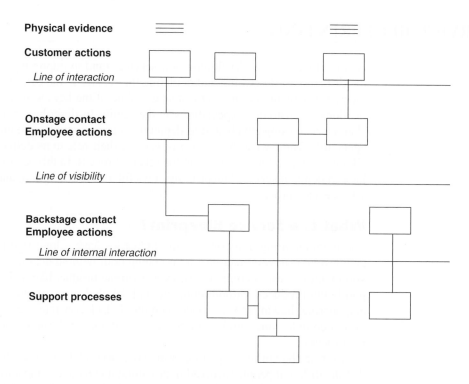

These variations are not a problem as long as you keep in mind the purpose of the blueprint and view it as a useful tool rather than as a set of rigid rules for designing services.

The *customer actions* area encompasses the steps, choices, activities, and interactions that the customer performs in the process of purchasing, consuming, and evaluating the service. The total customer experience is apparent in this area of the blueprint. In a legal services example, the customer actions might include a decision to contact an attorney, phone calls to the attorney, face-to-face meetings, receipt of documents, and receipt of a bill.

Paralleling the customer actions are two areas of contact employee actions. The steps and activities that the contact employee performs that are visible to the customer are the *onstage contact employee actions*. In the legal services setting, the actions of the attorney (the contact employee) that are visible to the client are, for example, the initial interview, intermediate meetings, and final delivery of legal documents.

Those contact employee actions that occur behind the scenes to support the onstage activities are the *backstage contact employee actions*. In the example, anything the attorney does behind the scenes to prepare for the meetings or to prepare the final documents will appear in this section of the blueprint, together with phone call contacts the customer has with the attorney or other front-line staff in the firm. All *non-visible* contact employee actions are shown in this area of the blueprint.

The *support processes* section of the blueprint covers the internal services, steps, and interactions that take place to support the contact employees in delivering the service. Again, in our legal example, any service support activities such as legal research by staff, preparation of documents, and secretarial support to set up meetings will be shown in the support processes area of the blueprint.

At the very top of the blueprint you see the *physical evidence* of the service. Typically, above each point of contact the actual physical evidence of the service is listed. In the legal example, the physical evidence of the face-to-face meeting with the attorney would be such items as office decor, written documents, lawyer's clothing, and so forth.

The four key action areas are separated by three horizontal lines. First is the *line of interaction,* representing direct interactions between the customer and the organization. Anytime a vertical line crosses the horizontal line of interaction, a direct contact between the customer and the organization, or a service encounter, has occurred. The next horizontal line is the critically important *line of visibility.* This line separates all service activities that are visible to the customer from those that are not visible. In reading blueprints it is immediately obvious whether the consumer is provided with much visible evidence of the service simply by analyzing how much of the service occurs above the line of visibility versus the activities carried out below the line. This line also separates what the contact employees do onstage from what they do backstage. For example, in a medical examination situation, the doctor would perform the actual exam and answer the patient's questions above the line of visibility, or onstage, whereas she might read the patient's chart in advance and dictate notes following the exam below the line of visibility, or backstage. The third line is the *line of internal interaction,* which separates contact employee activities from those of other service support activities and people. Vertical lines cutting across the line of internal interaction represent internal service encounters.

One of the most significant differences between service blueprints and other process flow diagrams is the inclusion of customers and their views of the service process. In fact, in designing effective service blueprints it is recommended that the diagramming start with the customer's view of the process and work backward into the delivery system. The boxes shown within each action area depict steps performed or experienced by the actors at that level.

Service Blueprint Examples

Figures 9.7 and 9.8 show service blueprints for two different services: express mail delivery and an overnight hotel stay.[32] These blueprints are deliberately kept very simple, showing only the most basic steps in the services. Complex diagrams could be developed for each step, and the internal processes could be much more fully developed. In addition to the four action areas separated by the three horizontal lines, these blueprints also show the physical evidence of the service from the customer's point of view at each step of the process.

Examine the express mail delivery blueprint in Figure 9.7. It is clear that from the customer's point of view there are only three steps in the service process: the phone call, the package pickup, and the package delivery. The process is relatively standardized; the people who perform the service are the phone order-taker and the delivery person; and the physical evidence is the document package, the transmittal forms, the truck, and the handheld computer. In some cases the customer may also engage the online or phone-based package tracking system. The complex process that occurs behind the line of visibility is of little interest or concern to the customer. However, for the three visible-to-the-customer steps to proceed effectively, invisible internal services are needed. What these steps are and the fact that they support the delivery of the service to the external customer are apparent from the blueprint.

Any of the steps in the blueprint could be exploded into a detailed blueprint if needed for a particular purpose. For example, if the delivery company learned that the

FIGURE 9.7 **Blueprint for Express Mail Delivery Service**

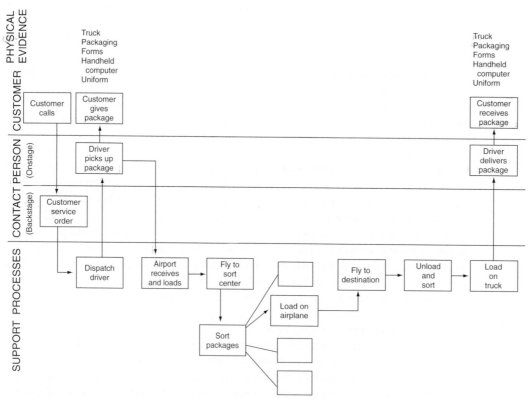

Source: Service Quality Handbook by Scheuing, Eberhard E./. Copyright 1993 by AM MGMT ASSN / AMACOM (B). Reproduced with permission of AM MGMT ASSN / AMACOM (B) in the format Textbook via Copyright Clearance Center.

"unload and sort" step was taking too long and causing unacceptable delays in delivery, that step could be blueprinted in much greater detail to isolate the problems.

In the case of the overnight hotel stay depicted in Figure 9.8, the customer obviously is more actively involved in the service than he or she is in the express mail service. The guest first checks in, then goes to the hotel room where a variety of steps take place (receiving bags, sleeping, showering, eating breakfast, and so on), and finally checks out. Imagine how much more complex this process could be and how many more interactions might occur if the service blueprint depicted a week-long vacation at the hotel, or even a three-day business conference. The service blueprint makes clear also (by reading across the line of interaction) those employees with whom the guest interacts and thus those employees who provide evidence of the service to the customer. Several interactions occur with a variety of hotel employees including the bellperson, the front desk clerk, the food service order-taker, and the food delivery person. Each step in the customer action area is also associated with various forms of physical evidence, from the hotel parking area and hotel exterior and interior to the forms used at guest registration, the lobby, the room, and the food. The hotel facility itself is critical in communicating the image of the hotel company, in providing satisfaction for the guest through the manner in which the hotel room is designed and maintained, and in facilitating the actions and interactions of both the guest and the employees of the hotel. In the hotel case, the process is relatively complex (although again somewhat standardized), the people providing the service are a variety of front-line employees, and the physical

FIGURE 9.8   Blueprint for Overnight Hotel Stay Service

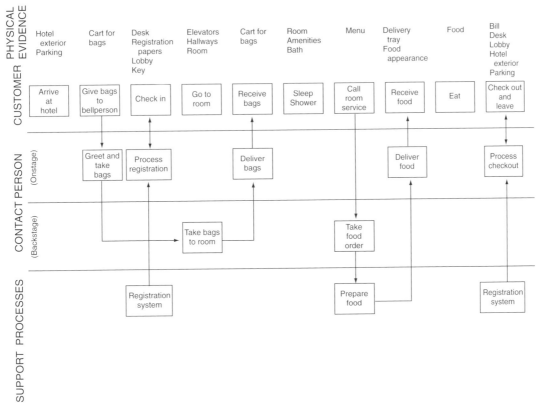

Source: Service Quality Handbook by ED. EE Scheuing and WF Christopher. Copyright 1993 by AM MGMT ASSN / AMACOM (B). Reproduced with permission of AM MGMT ASSN / AMACOM (B) in the format Textbook via Copyright Clearance Center.

evidence includes everything from the guest registration form to the design of the lobby and room to the uniforms worn by front-line employees.

Blueprints for Technology-Delivered Self-Service

To this point all our discussion of service blueprints has related to services that are delivered in person, services in which employees interact directly with customers at some point in the process. But what about technology-delivered services like self-service websites (Expedia's travel information site, Cisco Systems customer self-service site) and interactive kiosks (ATMs, airline self-check in machines)? Can service blueprinting be used effectively to design these types of services? Certainly it can, but the lines of demarcation change, and some blueprint labels may need to be adapted.

If no employees are involved in the service (except when there is a problem or the service does not function as planned), the contact person areas of the blueprint are not needed. Instead, the area above the line of visibility can be used to illustrate the interface between the customer and the computer website or the physical interaction with the kiosk. This area can be relabeled onstage technology. The backstage contact person actions area would be irrelevant in this case.

If the service involves a combination of human and technology interfaces, as with airline computerized check-in, the onstage area can be cut into two distinct spaces divided by an additional horizontal line. In the airline computerized check-in example, the human contact with the airline employee who takes the bags and checks identification would be shown in one area and the technology interactions with the check-in computer kiosk would be shown in the second area, both above the line of visibility.

Reading and Using Service Blueprints

A service blueprint can be read in a variety of ways, depending on the purpose. If the purpose is to understand the customer's view of the process or the customer experience, the blueprint can be read from left to right, tracking the events in the customer action area. Questions that might be asked include these: How is the service initiated by the customer? What choices does the customer make? Is the customer highly involved in creating the service, or are few actions required of the customer? What is the physical evidence of the service from the customer's point of view? Is the evidence consistent with the organization's strategy and positioning?

If the purpose is to understand contact employees' roles, the blueprint can also be read horizontally but this time focusing on the activities directly above and below the line of visibility. Questions that might be asked include these: How rational, efficient, and effective is the process? Who interacts with customers, when, and how often? Is one person responsible for the customer, or is the customer passed off from one contact employee to another? A hospital in Florida, recognizing that its patients were passed from one employee to another with little or no individual attention, reorganized itself so that each patient was assigned to a "care pair" (usually a nurse and an assistant) who served the patient's needs from check-in to discharge. The result was a reduction in operating costs of greater than 9 percent, along with higher patient satisfaction.[33]

If the purpose is to understand the integration of the various elements of the service process, or to identify where particular employees fit into the bigger picture, the blueprint can be analyzed vertically. In this analysis, it becomes clear what tasks and which employees are essential in the delivery of service to the customer. The linkages from internal actions deep within the organization to front-line effects on the customer can also be seen in the blueprint. Questions that might be asked include these: What actions are being performed backstage to support critical customer interaction points? What are the associated support actions? How are handoffs from one employee to another taking place?

If the purpose is service redesign, the blueprint can be looked at as a whole to assess the complexity of the process, how it might be changed, and how changes from the customer's point of view would impact the contact employee and other internal processes, and vice versa. Blueprints can also be used to assess the overall efficiency and productivity of the service system and to evaluate how potential changes will impact the system.[34] The blueprint can also be analyzed to determine likely failure points or bottlenecks in the process. When such points are discovered, a firm can introduce measures to track failures, or that part of the blueprint can be exploded so that the firm can focus in much greater detail on that piece of the system.

A blueprinting application in the design of a new rapid train service in Sweden illustrated a number of benefits (see Exhibit 9.3.)[35] Clearly, one of the greatest benefits of blueprinting is education.[36] When people begin to develop a blueprint, it quickly becomes apparent what is actually known about the service. Sometimes the shared knowledge is minimal. Biases and prejudices are made explicit, and agreements and compromises must be reached. The process itself promotes cross-functional integration and understanding. In the attempt to visualize the entire service system, people are forced to consider the service in new and more comprehensive ways.

Exhibit 9.3 BENEFITS OF SERVICE BLUEPRINTING

1. Provides an overview so employees can relate "what I do" to the service viewed as an integrated whole, thus reinforcing a customer-oriented focus among employees.

2. Identifies fail points—that is, weak links of the chain of service activities, which can be the target of continuous quality improvement.

3. Line of interaction between external customers and employees illuminates the customer's role and demonstrates where the customer experiences quality, thus contributing to informed service design.

4. Line of visibility promotes a conscious decision on what customers should see and which employees will be in contact with customers, thus facilitating rational service design.

5. Line of internal interaction clarifies interfaces across departmental lines, with their inherent interdependencies, thus strengthening continuous quality improvement.

6. Stimulates strategic discussions by illuminating the elements and connections that constitute the service. Those who participate in strategic sessions tend to exaggerate the significance of their own special function and perspective unless a common ground for an integrated view of the service is provided.

7. Provides a basis for identifying and assessing cost, revenue, and capital invested in each element of the service.

8. Constitutes a rational basis for both external and internal marketing. For example, the service map [blueprint] makes it easier for an advertising agency or an in-house promotion team to overview a service and select essential messages for communication.

9. Facilitates top-down, bottom-up approach to quality improvement. It enables managers to identify, channel, and support quality improvement efforts of grass-roots employees working on both front-line and support teams. Employee work teams can create service maps [blueprints] and thus more clearly apply and communicate their experience and suggestions for improvements.

Source: Reprinted with permission, from E. Gummesson and J. Kingman-Brundage, "Service Design and Quality: Applying Service Blueprinting and Service Mapping to Railroad Services," in *Quality Management in Services*, ed. P. Kunst and J. Lemmink (Assen/Maastricht, Netherlands: Van Gorcum, 1991).

Building a Blueprint

Recall that many of the benefits and purposes of building a blueprint evolve from the process of doing it. Thus the final product is not necessarily the only goal. Through the process of developing the blueprint, many intermediate goals can be achieved: clarification of the concept, development of a shared service vision, recognition of complexities and intricacies of the service that are not initially apparent, and delineation of roles and responsibilities, to name a few. The development of the blueprint needs to involve a variety of functional representatives as well as information from customers. Drawing or building a blueprint is not a task that should be assigned to one person or one functional area. Figure 9.9 identifies the basic steps in building a blueprint. Exhibit 9.4 provides answers to frequently asked questions about service blueprints.

FIGURE 9.9
Building a Service Blueprint

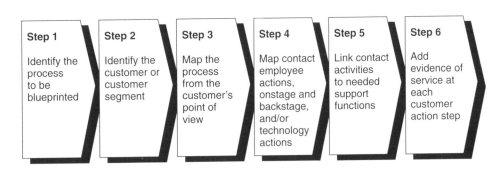

Step 1	Step 2	Step 3	Step 4	Step 5	Step 6
Identify the process to be blueprinted	Identify the customer or customer segment	Map the process from the customer's point of view	Map contact employee actions, onstage and backstage, and/or technology actions	Link contact activities to needed support functions	Add evidence of service at each customer action step

Exhibit 9.4 FREQUENTLY ASKED QUESTIONS ABOUT SERVICE BLUEPRINTING

What process should be blueprinted?

What process to map depends on the team or organization's objectives. If these are not clearly defined, then identifying the process can present a challenge. Questions to ask: Why are we blueprinting the service? What is our objective? Where does the service process begin and end? Are we focusing on the entire service, a component of the service, or a period of time?

Can multiple market segments be included on one blueprint?

Generally the answer to this question is no. Assuming that market segments require different service processes or attributes, the blueprint for one segment may look very different from the blueprint for another. Only at a very high level (sometimes called a *concept blueprint*) might it be relevant to map multiple segments simultaneously.

Who should "draw" the blueprint?

A blueprint is a team effort. It should not be assigned as an individual task, certainly not in the development stages. All relevant parties should be involved or represented in the development effort. The task might include employees across multiple functions in the organization (marketing, operations, human resources, facilities design) as well as customers in some cases.

Should the actual or desired service process be blueprinted?

If a new service is being designed, then clearly it is important to start with the desired service process. However, in cases of service improvement or service redesign, it is very important to map (at least at a conceptual level) the actual service process first. Once the group knows how the service is actually functioning, then the blueprint can be modified or used as a base for changes and improvements.

Should exceptions or recovery processes be incorporated within the blueprint?

It may be possible to map relatively simple, commonly occurring recovery processes onto a blueprint, assuming there are not a lot of these. However, this process can quickly become complex and cause the blueprint to be confusing or unreadable. Often a better strategy is to indicate common fail points on the blueprint and, if needed, develop sub-blueprints for the service recovery processes.

What is the appropriate level of detail?

The answer to this question depends again on the objective or purpose for doing the blueprint in the first place. If it is to be used primarily to communicate the general nature of the service, then a concept blueprint with few details is best. If it is being used to focus on diagnosing and improving the service process, then more detail is needed. Because some people are more detail oriented than others, this particular question will always arise and needs to be resolved in any team blueprinting effort.

What symbols should be used?

At this point in time, there is not a lexicon of blueprinting symbols that is commonly used or accepted across companies. What is most important is that the symbols be defined, be kept relatively simple, and be used consistently by the team and across the organization if blueprints are being shared internally.

Should time or dollar costs be included on the blueprint?

Blueprints are very versatile. If reducing the time taken for various parts of the service process is an objective of the blueprinting effort, then time can definitely be included. The same is true for dollar costs or anything else that is relevant as an objective. However, it is not advisable to put such information on the blueprint unless it is of central concern.

Step 1: Identify the Service Process to Be Blueprinted

Blueprints can be developed at a variety of levels, and there needs to be agreement on the starting point. For example, the express mail delivery blueprint shown in Figure 9.7 is at the basic service concept level. Little detail is shown, and variations based on market segment or specific services are not shown. Specific blueprints could be developed for two-day express mail, large accounts, Internet-facilitated services, and/or storefront drop-off centers. Each of these blueprints would share some features with the concept blueprint but would also include unique features. Or if the "sort packages" and "loading" elements of the process were found to be problem areas or bottlenecks that were slowing service to customers, a detailed blueprint of the subprocesses at work in those two steps could be developed. A firm can identify the process to be mapped once it has determined the underlying purpose for building the blueprint.

Step 2: Identify the Customer or Customer Segment Experiencing the Service

A common rationale for market segmentation is that each segment's needs are different and therefore will require variations in the service or product features. Thus, blueprints are most useful when developed for a particular customer or customer segment, assuming that the service process varies across segments. At a very abstract or conceptual level it may be possible to combine customer segments on one blueprint. However, once almost any level of detail is reached, separate blueprints should be developed to avoid confusion and maximize their usefulness.

Step 3: Map the Service Process from the Customer's Point of View

Step 3 involves charting the choices and actions that the customer performs or experiences in purchasing, consuming, and evaluating the service. Identifying the service from the customer's point of view first will help avoid focusing on processes and steps that have no customer impact. This step forces agreement on who the customer is (sometimes no small task) and may involve considerable research to determine exactly how the customer experiences the service. In mapping the Margaret River Masters surfing event in Australia, researchers used a team of participant observers who involved themselves in the event while recording details about each stage and encounter in the total experience. These detailed observations, combined with customer surveys, allowed the researchers to identify the important actions and activities of this unique event from a customer's point of view. The blueprint was then used to identify points for improvement in this competitive event that attracts the world's best surfers.[37]

Sometimes the beginning and ending of the service from the customer's point of view may not be obvious. For example, research in a hair-cutting context revealed that customers viewed the process as beginning with the phone call to the salon and setting of the appointment, whereas the hair stylists did not typically view the making of appointments as part of the service process.[38] Similarly, in a mammography screening service, patients viewed driving to the clinic, parking, and locating the screening office as part of the service experience. If the blueprint is being developed for an existing service, it may be helpful at this point in the process to videotape or photograph the service process from the customer's point of view. Often managers and others who are not on the front lines do not actually know what the customers are experiencing.

Step 4: Map Contact Employee Actions, Both Onstage and Backstage, and/or Technology Actions

First the lines of interaction and visibility are drawn, and then the process from the customer contact person's point of view is mapped, distinguishing visible or onstage activities from invisible backstage activities. For existing services this step involves questioning front-line operations employees to learn what they do and which activities are performed in full view of the customer versus which activities are carried out behind the scenes.

For technology-delivered services or those that combine technology and human delivery, the required actions of the technology interface will be mapped above the line of visibility as well. If no employees are involved in the service, the area can be relabeled "onstage technology actions." If both human and technology interactions are involved, an additional horizontal line can separate "onstage contact employee actions" from "onstage technology actions." Using the additional line will facilitate reading and interpretation of the service blueprint.

Step 5: Link Contact Activities to Needed Support Functions

The line of internal interaction can then be drawn and linkages from contact activities to internal support functions can be identified. In this process, the direct and indirect impact of internal actions on customers becomes apparent. Internal service processes take on added importance when viewed in connection with their link to the customer. Alternatively, certain steps in the process may be viewed as unnecessary if there is no clear link to the customer's experience or to an essential internal support service.

Step 6: Add Evidence of Service at Each Customer Action Step

Finally, the evidence of service can be added to the blueprint to illustrate what the customer sees and receives as tangible evidence of the service at each step in the customer experience. A photographic blueprint, including photos, slides, or video of the process, can be very useful at this stage to aid in analyzing the impact of tangible evidence and its consistency with the overall strategy and service positioning.

QUALITY FUNCTION DEPLOYMENT

In addition to service blueprinting, another approach that can be used to develop a service architecture is *quality function deployment (QFD)*. QFD has been defined as "a system for translating customer requirements into appropriate company requirements at every stage, from research through production design and development to manufacture; distribution; installation; and marketing, sales, and services."[39] Because QFD is used as a means of integrating marketing and engineering personnel in the development process, it has more applications in manufacturing than in services. Its ideas are also applicable to services, however. QFD is implemented via what is known as the "house of quality," which links customer requirements to design characteristics of the product or service.[40] These are then linked to internal processes such as product planning, process planning, production planning, and parts deployment. The house of quality is a diagrammatic representation of the service, its attributes, the customers' requirements, and the company's capabilities.

For services, the concept of service quality deployment has been suggested as a means of adapting QFD tools for service development and design.[41] The resulting house of service quality (see Figure 9.10 for an example) comprises three distinct sections: customer quality criteria (what customers perceive), service company facets (how these criteria are created by the firm), and the relationship grid (how the two are related). This matrix is extended to include quantitative information so that relative importance of relationships among different functions of the firm can be highlighted.

Figure 9.10 provides an example of QFD applied to Village Volvo, a Volvo service garage, to create a house of service quality.[42] The following paragraphs explain elements of the house of service quality shown in Figure 9.10:

1. *Customer expectations.* On the far left of the house are listed the customers' expectations of Village Volvo's customer service. In this case the customers' expectations correspond to the five service quality dimensions presented in Chapter 5.

2. *Importance of expectations.* Next to each expectation (on the chimney of the house) is listed the importance of that particular attribute to customers on a scale from 1

FIGURE 9.10
House of Service Quality for Village Volvo

Source: Reprinted from J. A. Fitzsimmons and M. J. Fitzsimmons, *Service Management,* 3rd ed. (New York: Irwin McGraw-Hill, 2000), p. 58. © 2000 by The McGraw-Hill Companies, Inc. Reprinted by permission of The McGraw-Hill Companies.

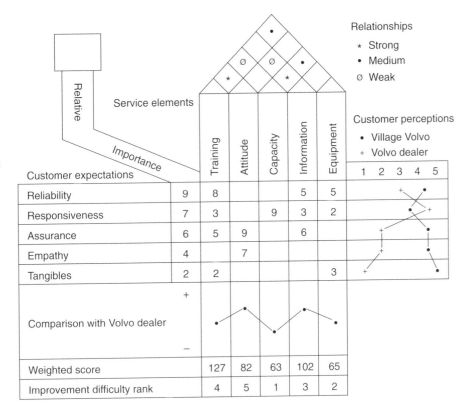

to 9, with 9 being the most important. These importance weights are determined by customer research.

3. *Controllable elements of service.* The columns of the house represent the elements of service that the company has control over, such as training, capacity, equipment, attitude, and information.

4. *Relationship among elements.* The relationships among the elements of service are shown in the roof of the house. The relationship among elements can be strong, medium, or weak. For example, the relationship between training and attitude is strong, whereas the relationship between training and capacity is weak.

5. *Association between expectations and service elements.* In the body of the matrix are numbers representing the strength of the relationship between each expectation and the related service element. The numbers reflect (from the service team's perspective) how various elements affect the company's ability to satisfy the particular customer expectation. A 0 suggests no effect, whereas a 9 suggest a very strong effect.

6. *Overall importance of service elements for meeting customer expectations.* The weighted score on the floor of the house represents the total points for each element, calculated by multiplying the importance weights by the element association ratings and adding all the scores for each element together [e.g., training = (9)(8) + (7)(3) + (6)(5) + (4)(0) + (2)(2) = 127]. These scores should be treated relatively, however, and not as absolutes because they are based on some subjectivity and judgment.

7. *Difficulty rankings.* In the basement of the house are listed the difficulty rankings assigned to each element in terms of how difficult it would be to make improvements in that element, with the ranking of 1 being the most difficult.

8. *Competitive assessment.* Two areas of the house suggest some comparisons of Village Volvo with the competing Volvo dealership. On the right are shown comparisons of the two on the dimensions of service quality. Just above the floor of the house are shown relative ratings comparing Village Volvo with the Volvo dealership on the elements of service.

The completed house of service quality in Figure 9.10 can be used to make preliminary service design decisions based on the relative importance of various attributes to customers, Village Volvo's relative competitive position, the weighting of the elements in terms of their contribution overall to customer satisfaction, and the difficulty of implementing change. In this example it would appear that training would be a good investment because it has the strongest weight, is rated relatively weak with respect to competition, and is relatively less difficult to change.

HIGH-PERFORMANCE SERVICE INNOVATIONS

To this point in the chapter, we have discussed approaches and tools for developing and designing new services. A dilemma in most companies is that there are too many new ideas from which to choose. New technologies, changing customer needs, deregulation, competitors' actions—all these areas result in myriad potential new offerings to consider. The question is which to pursue. How can a company decide which new offerings will likely be major successes, and which may be less successful or even fail?

In this section we summarize some of what has been learned about successful new services in terms of measures of success, key success drivers, and the importance of integrating new services.

Choose the Right Projects

Success with new services is going to be determined by two things: choosing the right projects and doing the projects right.[43] Researchers confirm that following the new service development process discussed earlier in the chapter and illustrated in Figure 9.2 will help with both these goals.[44] Service blueprinting and QFD, also presented in this chapter, will help as well, primarily with the second goal.

Another concept, *portfolio management for new products,* is very useful in helping companies choose the right projects in the first place.[45] Using this approach, companies manage their product portfolio like they manage their financial portfolio. The approach helps companies prioritize projects, choose which ones to accelerate, and determine the best balance between risk versus return, maintenance versus growth, and short-term versus long-term projects. Methods for portfolio management include financial models, scoring models and checklists, mapping approaches, and behavioral approaches.[46]

Integrate New Services

Because of the nature of services—they are processes, typically delivered at least in part by people, consumed and produced simultaneously—any new service introduction will affect the existing systems and services. Unlike when a manufacturer adds a new product to its production facility, new service introductions are frequently visible to customers and may even require their participation. Explicit recognition of these potential impacts, and planning for the integration of people, processes, and physical evidence, will facilitate success.[47] This recognition will help in both (1) deciding which projects to pursue—sometimes the disruptive effect on existing systems is too great to warrant the investment—and (2) knowing how to proceed with implementation—what elements of existing processes, people, and physical facilities will need to be adjusted, added, or changed.

Consider Multiple Measures of Success

In predicting the success of a new service, multiple performance measures may be considered.[48] First, and most commonly used, is near-term *financial performance* including revenue growth, profitability, market share, and return on investment (ROI). In other cases, *relationship enhancement* may be a more appropriate measure of success. This measurement might include (1) the new service's effect on customer loyalty, (2) image enhancement, and (3) the effect on the success of other products and services. Or success may be measured in terms of *market development*—the degree to which the new service opens up new markets or new customer segments. Successful projects will lead to increases in one, or perhaps more than one, of these measures.

Learn from Major Successes

In investing in new products and services, most companies are looking for big winners rather than modest improvements.[49] In a study of financial services, the following factors were found to distinguish major successes from moderate or small successes:[50]

Market synergy. A strong fit exists between the new service and the company's marketing, promotion, sales, and distribution expertise and resources.

Market-driven new product process. The company has a well-planned and executed new service development process including customer input, research and development, customer testing, and competitive analysis.

Effective marketing communications. The company has an effective strategy for raising customer awareness, explaining service benefits, and establishing a unique positioning and distinct brand image.

Customer service. The most successful new financial products were linked to excellent customer service support.

Managerial and financial synergy. A strong fit exists between the new project and the company's management and financial expertise and resources.

Launch preparation. The company provides extensive training and preparation of front-line personnel to support the product prior to launch.

Product responsiveness. Major successes are new services that truly offer improvements from the customers' point of view—better than competition, responsive to a new need, or offering greater flexibility.

Product advantage. Major successes are better than alternatives in terms of benefits, quality, and distinct branding.

Innovative technology. Technology is instrumental in providing a superior product, or it provides innovation for the delivery system, or the company uses hardware and software to develop significant new offerings. (This factor is particularly important for market development.)

Maintain Some Flexibility

New service success depends on (1) market-driven, customer-focused new product processes; (2) emphasis on planning for and executing the launch; (3) integration of services within existing processes (including staff training); and (4) strong marketing communications, both external and internal. Yet, firms must be cautioned about being too rigid in the new service development approach. Steps in the development process should be allowed some flexibility, and there will no doubt be overlapping processes. Initial service development, for example, can be occurring simultaneously with additional gathering of customer information. Because services, particularly business-to-business services, are often very complex, some creativity and "out of order" decisions will be needed. There must be some elements of improvisation, anarchy, and internal competition in the development of new services. "Consequently, the innovation and adoption of new services must be both a planned process and a happening!"[51]

Summary

Service providers must effectively match customer expectations to new service innovations and actual service process designs. However, because of the very nature of services—their intangibility and variability specifically—the design and development of service offerings are complex and challenging. Many services are only vaguely defined before their introduction to the marketplace. This chapter has outlined some of the challenges involved in designing services and some strategies for effectively overcoming the challenges.

Through adaptations of the new product development process that is commonplace in goods production and manufacturing companies, service providers can begin to not only make their offerings more explicit but also avoid failures. The new service development process presented in the chapter includes nine stages, beginning with the development of a business and new service strategy and ending with postintroduction evaluation of the new service. Between these initial and ending stages are a number of steps and checkpoints designed to maximize the likelihood of new service success. Carrying out the stages requires the inclusion of customers, contact employees, and anyone else who will affect or be affected by the new service. Because successful new service introduction is often highly dependent on service employees (often they are the service), integration of employees at each stage is critical.

Service blueprinting is a particularly useful tool in the new service development process. A blueprint can make a complex and intangible service concrete through its visual depiction of all the steps, actors, processes, and physical evidence of the service. The key feature of service blueprints is their focus on the customer—the customer's experience is documented first and is kept fully in view as the other features of the blueprint are developed. This chapter has provided the basic tools needed to build, use, and evaluate service blueprints. Quality function deployment (QFD) was introduced as another tool for linking customer requirements to internal elements of service design.

The final section of the chapter summarized some of the key factors driving successful new service innovations, including the need for portfolio planning and integration of new services with existing processes and systems. The need to consider multiple measures of success was highlighted as well as the importance of maintaining flexibility in the new service development process.

Discussion Questions

1. Why is it challenging to design and develop services?
2. What are the risks of attempting to describe services in words alone?
3. Compare and contrast the blueprints in Figures 9.7 and 9.8.
4. How might a service blueprint be used for marketing, human resource, and operations decisions? Focus on one of the blueprint examples shown in the text as a context for your answer.
5. Assume that you are a multiproduct service company that wants to grow through adding new services. Describe a logical process you might use to introduce a new service to the marketplace. What steps in the process might be most difficult and why? How might you incorporate service blueprinting into the process?
6. Discuss Figure 9.3 in terms of the four types of opportunities for growth represented there. Choose a company or service, and explain how it could grow by developing new services in each of the four cells (see the Taco Bell example in Exhibit 9.1).
7. Explain the house of service quality that is shown in Figure 9.10. Based on the information in that figure for Village Volvo, what might you do to improve service if you were the manager of that organization?

Exercises

1. Think of a new service you would like to develop if you were an entrepreneur. How would you go about it? Describe what you would do and where you would get your information.
2. Find a new and interesting service in your local area, or a service offered on your campus. Document the service process via a service blueprint. To do this exercise, you will probably need to interview one of the service employees. After you have documented the existing service, use blueprinting concepts to redesign the service or change it in some way.
3. Choose a service you are familiar with and document the customer action steps through a photographic blueprint. What is the "evidence of service" from your point of view as a customer?
4. Develop a service blueprint for a technology-delivered service (such as an Internet-based travel service). Compare and contrast this blueprint to one for the same service delivered via more traditional channels (such as a personal travel agent).
5. Interview customers and employees of a service of your choice. Construct a basic house of service quality. What would you recommend to the manager of the service based on your analysis?
6. Compare two services on the Internet. Discuss the design of each in terms of whether it meets your expectations. How could the design or the service process be changed? Which one is most effective, and why?

Notes

1. Wells Fargo website, 2004 (www.wellsfargo.com); G. Anders, "Power Partners," *Fast Company,* September 2000, pp. 146–48; "The World's Best Internet Banks 2003, *Global Finance,* December 2003, p. 29; B. Condon, "Banking on Brashness," *Forbes,* August 16, 2004, pp. 91–100.
2. "Flops, Too Many New Products Fail. Here's Why—and How to Do Better," cover story, *BusinessWeek,* August 16, 1993, pp. 76–82.

3. Ibid.; R. G. Cooper, *Winning at New Products,* 3rd ed. (Cambridge, MA: Perseus Publishing, 2001); R. G. Cooper and S. J. Edgett, *Product Development for the Service Sector* (Cambridge, MA: Perseus Books, 1999); C. M. Froehle, A. V. Roth, R. B. Chase, and C. A. Voss, "Antecedents of New Service Development Effectiveness," *Journal of Service Research* 3 (August 2000), pp. 3–17.

4. D. H. Henard and D. M. Szymanski, "Why Some New Products Are More Successful Than Others," *Journal of Marketing Research,* August 2001, pp. 362–75.

5. G. L. Shostack, "Understanding Services through Blueprinting," in *Advances in Services Marketing and Management,* vol. 1, ed. T. A. Swartz, D. E. Bowen, and S. W. Brown (Greenwich, CT: JAI Press, 1992), pp. 75–90.

6. Cooper, *Winning at New Products;* Cooper and Edgett, *Product Development for the Service Sector;* Henard and Szymanski, "Why Some New Products Are More Successful Than Others."

7. G. L. Shostack, "Service Design in the Operating Environment," in *Developing New Services,* ed. W. R. George and C. Marshall (Chicago: American Marketing Association, 1984), pp. 27–43.

8. For excellent reviews of research and issues in new services development see *Journal of Operations Management* 20 (2002), Special Issue on New Issues and Opportunities in Service Design Research; A. Johne and C. Story, "New Service Development: A Review of the Literature and Annotated Bibliography," *European Journal of Marketing* 32, no. 3–4 (1998), pp. 184–251; B. Edvardsson, A. Gustafsson, M. D. Johnson, and B. Sanden, *New Service Development and Innovation in the New Economy* (Lund, Sweden: Studentlitteratur AB, 2000).

9. B. Schneider and D. E. Bowen, "New Services Design, Development and Implementation and the Employee," in George and Marshall, *Developing New Services,* pp. 82–101.

10. S. Thomke, "R&D Comes to Services: Bank of America's Pathbreaking Experiments," *Harvard Business Review,* April 2003, pp. 70–79.

11. Adapted from D. F. Heany, "Degrees of Product Innovation," *Journal of Business Strategy,* Spring 1983, pp. 3–14, appearing in C. H. Lovelock, "Developing and Implementing New Services," in George and Marshall, *Developing New Services,* pp. 44–64.

12. For a discussion of these adaptations and related research issues, see M. V. Tatikonda and V. A. Zeithaml, "Managing the New Service Development Process: Synthesis of Multidisciplinary Literature and Directions for Future Research," in *New Directions in Supply Chain Management: Technology, Strategy, and Implementation,* ed. T. Boone and R. Ganeshan (New York: AMACOM, 2002), pp. 200–236; B. Edvardsson et al., *New Service Development and Innovation in the New Economy.*

13. The steps shown in Figure 9.2 and discussed in the text are based primarily on the model developed by M. J. Bowers, "An Exploration into New Service Development: Organization, Process, and Structure," doctoral dissertation, Texas A&M University, 1985. Bowers's model is adapted from Booz-Allen & Hamilton, *New Product Management for the 1980s* (New York: Booz-Allen & Hamilton, 1982).

14. A. Griffin, "PDMA Research on New Product Development Practices: Updating Trends and Benchmarking Best Practices," *Journal of Product Innovation Management* 14 (1997), pp. 429–58; Thomke, "R&D Comes to Services."

15. R. G. Cooper, "Stage Gate Systems for New Product Success," *Marketing Management* 1, no. 4 (1992), pp. 20–29.

16. M. Iansiti and A. MacCormack, "Developing Products on Internet Time," *Harvard Business Review,* September–October 1997, pp. 108–17.

17. A. Khurana and S. R. Rosenthal, "Integrating the Fuzzy Front End of New Product Development," *Sloan Management Review,* Winter 1997, pp. 103–20.

18. R. E. Miles and C. C. Snow, *Organizational Strategy, Structure, and Process* (New York: McGraw-Hill, 1978).

19. M. E. Porter, *Competitive Strategy* (New York: The Free Press, 1980).

20. Khurana and Rosenthal, "Integrating the Fuzzy Front End"; see also R. G. Cooper, S. J. Edgett, and E. J. Kleinschmidt, *Portfolio Management for New Products* (Reading, MA: Addison-Wesley, 1998).

21. D. Rigby and C. Zook, "Open-Market Innovation," *Harvard Business Review,* October 2002, pp. 80–89.

22. D. Leonard and J. F. Rayport, "Spark Innovation through Empathic Design," *Harvard Business Review,* November–December 1997, pp. 103–13.

23. Shostack, "Service Design."

24. E. E. Scheuing and E. M. Johnson, "A Proposed Model for New Service Development," *Journal of Services Marketing* 3, no. 2 (1989), pp. 25–34.

25. M. R. Bowers, "Developing New Services for Hospitals: A Suggested Model," *Journal of Health Care Marketing* 7, no. 2 (June 1987), pp. 35–44.

26. D. Maxey, "Testing, Testing, Testing," *The Wall Street Journal,* December 10, 2001, p. R8.

27. Shostack, "Service Design," p. 35.

28. Maxey, "Testing, Testing, Testing."

29. The service blueprinting section of the chapter draws from the pioneering works in this area: G. L. Shostack, "Designing Services That Deliver," *Harvard Business Review,* January–February 1984, pp. 133–39; G. L. Shostack, "Service Positioning through Structural Change," *Journal of Marketing* 51 (January 1987), pp. 34–43; J. Kingman-Brundage, "The ABC's of Service System Blueprinting," in *Designing a Winning Service Strategy,* ed. M. J. Bitner and L. A. Crosby (Chicago: American Marketing Association, 1989), pp. 30–33.

30. Shostack, "Understanding Services through Blueprinting," pp. 75–90.

31. These key components are drawn from Kingman-Brundage, "The ABC's."

32. The text explaining Figures 9.7 and 9.8 relies on M. J. Bitner, "Managing the Evidence of Service," in *The Service Quality Handbook,* ed. E. E. Scheuing and W. F. Christopher (New York: American Management Association, 1993), pp. 358–70.

33. "Hospital, Heal Thyself," *BusinessWeek,* August 27, 1990, pp. 66–68.

34. S. Flieb and M. Kleinaltenkamp, "Blueprinting the Service Company: Managing Service Processes Efficiently," *Journal of Business Research* 57 (2004), pp. 392–404.

35. E. Gummesson and J. Kingman-Brundage, "Service Design and Quality: Applying Service Blueprinting and Service Mapping to Railroad Services," in *Quality Management in Services,* ed. P. Kunst and J. Lemmink (Assen/Maastricht, Netherlands: Van Gorcum, 1991).

36. Shostack, "Understanding Services through Blueprinting."

37. D. Getz, M. O'Neill, and J. Carlsen, "Service Quality Evaluation at Events through Service Mapping," *Journal of Travel Research* 39 (May 2001), pp. 380–90.

38. A. R. Hubbert, A. Garcia Sehorn, and S. W. Brown, "Service Expectations: The Consumer vs. the Provider," *International Journal of Service Industry Management* 6, no. 1 (1995), pp. 6–21.

39. American Supplier Institute, 1987, as quoted in R. S. Behara and R. B. Chase, "Service Quality Deployment: Quality Service by Design," in *Perspectives in Operations Management: Essays in Honor of Elwood Buffa,* ed. R. V. Sarin (Norwell, MA: Kluwer Academic Publisher, 1993).

40. J. R. Hauser and D. Clausing, "The House of Quality," *Harvard Business Review,* May–June 1988, pp. 63–73.

41. Behara and Chase, "Service Quality Deployment." See also F. I. Stuart and S. S. Tax, "Planning for Service Quality: An Integrative Approach," *International Journal of Service Industry Management* 7, no. 4 (1996), pp. 58–77.

42. J. A. Fitzsimmons and M. J. Fitzsimmons, *Service Management,* 4th ed. (New York: McGraw-Hill/Irwin, 2004), pp. 144–46.

43. Cooper et al., *Portfolio Management for New Products.*

44. Froehle et al., "Antecedents of New Service Development Effectiveness"; Henard and Szymanski, "Why Some New Products Are More Successful Than Others"; Edvardsson et al., *New Service Development and Innovation in the New Economy.*

45. Cooper et al., *Portfolio Management for New Products.*

46. See ibid. for an excellent discussion and coverage of multiple methods for managing product and service portfolios.

47. S. S. Tax and I. Stuart, "Designing and Implementing New Services: The Challenges of Integrating Service Systems," *Journal of Retailing* 73 (Spring 1977), pp. 105–34.

48. R. G. Cooper, C. J. Easingwood, S. Edgett, E. J. Kleinschmidt, and C. Storey, "What Distinguishes the Top Performing New Products in Financial Services," *Journal of Product Innovation Management* 11(1994), pp. 281–99.

49. For information on success and failure of new services, see Cooper et al., "What Distinguishes the Top Performing New Products"; Ulrike de Brentani, "New Industrial Service Development: Scenarios for Success and Failure," *Journal of Business Research* 32 (1995), pp. 93–103; C. R. Martin Jr., and D. A. Horne, "Services Innovation: Successful versus Unsuccessful Firms," *International Journal of Service Industry Management* 4, no. 1 (1993), pp. 49–65; B. Edvardsson, L. Haglund, and J. Mattsson, "Analysis, Planning, Improvisation, and Control in the Development of New Services," *International Journal of Service Industry Management* 6, no. 2 (1995), pp. 24–35; Froele et al., "Antecedents of New Service Development Effectiveness"; Henard and Szymanski, "Why Some New Products Are More Successful Than Others"; Cooper and Edgett, *Product Development for the Service Sector.*

50. Cooper et al., "What Distinguishes the Top Performing New Products in Financial Services."

51. Edvardsson, Haglund, and Mattsson, "Analysis, Planning, Improvisation, and Control," p. 34.

10

CUSTOMER-DEFINED SERVICE STANDARDS

This chapter's objectives are to

1. Distinguish between company-defined and customer-defined service standards.

2. Differentiate among one-time service fixes and "hard" and "soft" customer-defined standards.

3. Explain the critical role of the service encounter sequence in developing customer-defined standards.

4. Illustrate how to translate customer expectations into behaviors and actions that are definable, repeatable, and actionable.

5. Explain the process of developing customer-defined service standards.

6. Emphasize the importance of service performance indexes in implementing strategy for service delivery.

FedEx Sets Standards through SQI

Marketing research data are not the only numbers that Federal Express tracks to run its business. The company drives its operations with the aid of the most comprehensive, customer-defined index of service standards and measures in the world. FedEx's service quality indicator (SQI) was designed as "unforgiving internal performance measurement" to ensure that the company delivered to its goal of "100 percent customer satisfaction after every interaction and transaction and 100 percent service performance on every package handled."[1] The development and implementation of SQI led to a Malcolm Baldrige National Quality Award.

What makes this service index different from those of other companies is its foundation in customer feedback. Since the 1980s, FedEx has documented customer complaints and used the information to improve internal processes. Its composite listing of the 12 most common customer complaints, called the "Hierarchy of Horrors," included wrong day delivery, right day late delivery, pickup not made, lost package, customer misinformed by Federal Express, billing and paperwork mistakes, employee performance failures, and damaged packages. Although this list was useful, it fell short of giving management the ability to anticipate and eliminate customer complaints before they occurred.

In 1988 the company developed the 12-item statistical SQI to be a more "comprehensive, pro-active, customer-oriented measure of customer satisfaction and service quality."[2] The SQI consists of the following components and weighting (based on relative importance of each component to customers):

Indicator	Weight
Right day late deliveries	1
Wrong day late deliveries	5
Traces not answered	1
Complaints reopened	5
Missing proofs of delivery	1
Invoice adjustments	1
Missed pickups	10
Damaged packages	10
Lost packages	10
Aircraft delay minutes	5
Overgoods	5
Abandoned calls	1

Another distinguishing feature of the SQI is its reporting in terms of *numbers* of errors rather than percentages. Management of the company strongly believes that percentages distance the company from the consumer: to report 1 percent of packages late diminished the reality of 20,000 unhappy customers (1 percent of the approximately 2 million packages shipped a day). The service quality indicator report is disseminated weekly to everyone in the company. On receipt of the report, root causes of service failures are investigated. With a senior officer assigned to each component, and with bonuses for everyone in the company tied to performance on the SQI, the company drives continuously closer to its goal of 100 percent satisfaction with every transaction.[3]

As we saw in Chapters 6, 7, and 8, understanding customer requirements is the first step in delivering high service quality. Once managers of service businesses accurately understand what customers expect, they face a second critical challenge: using this knowledge to set service quality standards and goals for the organization. Service companies often experience difficulty in setting standards to match or exceed customer expectations partly because doing so requires that the marketing and operations departments within a company work together. In most service companies, integrating the work of the marketing function and the operations function (appropriately called *functional integration*) is not a typical approach; more frequently these two functions operate separately—setting and achieving their own internal goals—rather than pursuing a joint goal of developing the operations standards that best meet customer expectations.

Creating service standards that address customer expectations is not a common practice in U.S. firms. Doing so often requires altering the very process by which work is accomplished, which is ingrained in tradition in most companies. Often change requires new equipment or technology. Change also necessitates aligning executives from different parts of the firm to understand collectively the comprehensive view of service quality from the customer's perspective. And almost always, change requires a willingness to be open to different ways of structuring, calibrating, and monitoring the way service is provided.

FACTORS NECESSARY FOR APPROPRIATE SERVICE STANDARDS

Standardization of Service Behaviors and Actions

The translation of customer expectations into specific service quality standards depends on the degree to which tasks and behaviors to be performed can be standardized or routinized (Figure 10.1). Some executives and managers believe that services cannot be standardized—that customization is essential for providing high-quality service. Managers also may feel that standardizing tasks is inconsistent with employee empowerment—that employees will feel controlled by the company if tasks are standardized. Further, they feel that services are too intangible to be measured. This view leads to vague and loose standard setting with little or no measurement or feedback.

In reality, many service tasks are routine (such as those needed for opening checking accounts or spraying lawns for pests), and for these, specific rules and standards can be fairly easily established and effectively executed. Employees may welcome knowing how to perform actions most efficiently: it frees them to use their ingenuity in the more personal and individual aspects of their jobs.

According to one long-term observer of service industries, standardization of service can take three forms: (1) substitution of technology for personal contact and human effort, (2) improvement in work methods, and (3) combinations of these two methods.[4] Examples of technology substitution include automatic teller machines, automatic car washes, and airport X-ray machines. Improvements in work methods are

FIGURE 10.1
Federal Express has standardized service behaviors and actions, resulting in superior employee performance.

Source: © 1995–2002 FedEx. All Rights Reserved.

illustrated by restaurant salad bars and routinized tax and accounting services developed by firms such as H&R Block and Comprehensive Accounting Corporation.

Technology and work improvement methods facilitate the standardization of service necessary to provide consistent delivery to customers. By breaking tasks down and providing them efficiently, technology also allows the firm to calibrate service standards such as the length of time a transaction takes, the accuracy with which operations are performed, and the number of problems that occur. In developing work improvements, the firm comes to understand completely the process by which the service is delivered. With this understanding, the firm more easily establishes appropriate service standards.

Standardization, whether accomplished by technology or by improvements in work processes, reduces gap 2. Standardization does not mean that service is performed in a rigid, mechanical way. Customer-defined standardization ensures that the most critical elements of a service are performed as expected by customers, not that every action in a service is executed in a uniform manner. Using customer-defined standardization can, in fact, allow for and be compatible with employee empowerment. One example of this compatibility involves the time limits many companies establish for customer service calls. If their customers' highest priorities involve feeling good about the call or resolving problems, then setting a limit for calls would be decidedly company defined and not in customers' best interests. Companies such as American Express and L. L. Bean, in using customer priorities rather than company priorities, have no set standard for the amount of time an employee spends on the telephone with a customer. Instead, they have standards that focus on making the customer satisfied and comfortable, allowing telephone representatives to use their own judgment about the time limits. Standardization of service is not appropriate in some situations. See the Strategy Insight for examples of these situations.

Formal Service Targets and Goals

Companies that have been successful in delivering consistently high service quality are noted for establishing formal standards to guide employees in providing service. These companies have an accurate sense of how well they are performing service that is critical to their customers—how long it takes to conduct transactions, how frequently service fails, how quickly they settle customer complaints—and strive to improve by defining goals that lead them to meet or exceed customer expectations.

One type of formal goal setting that is relevant in service businesses involves specific targets for individual behaviors or actions. As an example, consider the behavior "calls the customer back quickly," an action that signals responsiveness in contact employees. If the service goal for employee behavior is stated in such a general term as "call the customer back quickly," the standard provides little direction for service employees. Different employees will interpret this vague objective in their own ways, leading to inconsistent service: Some may call the customer back in 10 minutes whereas others may wait 2 to 4 days. And the firm itself will not be able to determine when or if individual employees meet the goal because its expression is not measurable—one could justify virtually any amount of time as "quickly." On the other hand, if the individual employee's service goal is to call each customer back within 4 hours, employees have a specific, unambiguous guideline about how quickly they should execute the action (4 hours). Whether the goal is met is also unequivocal: If the call occurs within 4 hours the company meets the goal; otherwise it does not.

Another type of formal goal setting involves the overall department or company target, most frequently expressed as a percentage, across all executions of the behavior or action. For example, a department might set as its overall goal "to call the customer

This chapter focuses on the benefits of customer-defined standards in the context of situations—hotels, retail stores, service outlets—in which it is important to provide the same service to all or most customers. In these situations, standards establish strong guidelines for technology and employees in order to ensure consistency and reliability. In other services, providing standardization is neither appropriate nor possible, and customization—providing unique types and levels of service to customers—is a deliberate strategy.

In most "expert" services—such as accounting, consulting, engineering, and dentistry, for example—professionals provide customized and individualized services; standardization of the tasks is perceived as being impersonal, inadequate, and not in the customer's best interests. Because patient and client needs differ, these professionals offer very customized services that address individual requirements. They must adapt their offerings to the particular needs of each customer because each situation is different. Even within a given medical specialty, few patients have the same illness with precisely the same symptoms and the same medical history. Therefore, standardizing the amount of time a doctor spends with a patient is rarely possible, one of the reasons why patients usually must wait before receiving medical services even though they have advance appointments. Because professionals such as accountants and lawyers cannot usually standardize what they provide, they often charge by the hour rather than by the job, which allows them to be compensated for the customized periods of time they spend with clients. It is important to recognize, however, that even in highly customized services, some aspects of service provision can be routinized. Physicians and dentists, for example, can and do standardize recurring and nontechnical aspects such as checking patients in, weighing patients, taking routine measurements, billing patients and collecting payment. In delegating these routine tasks to assistants, physicians and dentists can spend more of their time on the expert service of diagnosis or patient care.

Another situation in which customization is the chosen strategy is in business-to-business contexts, particularly with key accounts. When accounts are large and critical to a provider, most aspects of service provision are customized. At a very basic level, this customization takes the form of service contracts in which the client and the provider agree on issues such as response time when clients have equipment failures or delivery time and fulfillment when retail clients depend on items being in stock in their stores. At a higher level, customization involves creative problem solving and innovative ideas (as in consulting services).

Finally, many consumer services are designed to be (or appear) very customized. These services include spa and upscale hotel visits, rafting trips, exotic vacations such as safaris, and even haircuts from expensive salons. In these situations, the steps taken to ensure the successful delivery of service is often standardized behind the scenes but appears to the customer to be very individualized. Even Disney theme parks use this approach, employing hundreds of standards to ensure the delivery of "magic" to customers.

back within 4 hours 97 percent of the time" and collect data over a month's or year's time to evaluate the extent to which it meets the target.

Service firms that produce consistently excellent service—firms such as Walt Disney, Federal Express, and Merrill Lynch—have very specific, quantified, measurable service goals. Walt Disney calibrates employee performance on myriad behaviors and actions that contribute to guest perceptions of high service quality. Whether they are set and monitored using audits (such as timed actions) or customer perceptions (such as opinions about courtesy), service standards provide a means for formal goal setting.

Customer—Not Company—Defined Standards

Virtually all companies possess service standards and measures that are *company defined*—they are established to reach internal company goals for productivity, efficiency, cost, or technical quality. A current company-defined standard that does not meet customer expectations is the common practice of voice-activated telephone support systems that do not allow consumers to speak to humans. Because these systems save companies money (and actually provide faster service to some customers), many organizations have switched from the labor-intensive practice of having customer representatives to these system. To close gap 2, standards set by companies must be based on customer requirements and expectations rather than just on internal company goals. In this chapter we make the case that company-defined standards are not typically successful in driving behaviors that close provider gap 2. Instead, a company must set *customer-defined standards:* operational standards based on pivotal customer requirements that are visible to and measured by customers. These standards are deliberately chosen to match customer expectations and to be calibrated the way the customer views and expresses them. Because these goals are essential to the provision of excellent service, the rest of this chapter focuses on customer-defined standards.

Knowing customer requirements, priorities, and expectation levels can be both effective and efficient. Anchoring service standards on customers can save money by identifying what the customer values, thus eliminating activities and features that the customer either does not notice or will not pay for. Through precise measurement of expectations, the company often discovers that it has been overdelivering to many customer needs:

> a bank might add several extra tellers and reduce the average peak waiting time in line from 7 minutes to 5 minutes. If customers expect, however, to wait up to 8 minutes during peak time, the investment in extra tellers may not be effective. An opportunity thus exists to capture the value of this information through reduced teller costs and higher profits.[5]

On the other hand, many firms create standards and policies to suit their own needs that are so counter to the wishes of customers that the companies endanger their customer relationships. In late 1998, when the hotel industry was booming, many hotels initiated policies penalizing late arrivals and early departures as well as imposing minimum-stay requirements. The Hilton San Francisco and Towers Hotel began to charge guests $50 when they stayed fewer days than agreed to at check-in. The Peabody Orlando kept guests' one-night deposits unless they canceled at least three days prior to arrival. And a Chicago hotel required a business customer to buy four nights' lodging when all she needed was three, which cost the customer an extra $270.[6] Hotels defend these policies on the basis of self-protection, but they are clearly not customer oriented.

Although customer-defined standards need not conflict with productivity and efficiency, they are not developed for these reasons. Rather, they are anchored in and steered by customer perceptual measures of service quality or satisfaction. The service standards that evolve from a customer perspective are likely to be different from company-defined service standards.

Virtually all organizations have lists of actions that they measure regularly, most of which fall into the category of company-defined standards. Often these standards deal with activities or actions that reflect the history of the business rather than the reality of today's competitive marketplace or the needs of current customers.

TYPES OF CUSTOMER-DEFINED SERVICE STANDARDS

The type of standards that close provider gap 2 are *customer-defined standards:* operational goals and measures based on pivotal customer requirements that are visible to and measured by customers rather than on company concerns such as productivity or efficiency. Take a typical operations standard such as inventory control. Most firms control inventory from the company's point of view. However, the highly successful office supply retailer Office Depot captures every single service measurement related to inventory control *from the customer's point of view.* The company began with the question, "What does the customer see?" and answered, "The average number of stockouts per week." Office Depot then designed a customer-focused measurement system based on measures such as the number of complaints and compliments it received about inventory as well as a transaction-based survey with the customer about its performance in this area. These and other customer-defined standards allowed for the translation of customer requirements into goals and guidelines for employee performance. Two major types of customer-defined service standards can be distinguished: "hard" and "soft." These standards will be discussed in the following two sections.

Hard Customer-Defined Standards

All the Federal Express standards that comprise the SQI fall into the category of hard standards and measures: *things that can be counted, timed, or observed through audits.* Many of Federal Express's standards relate to on-time delivery and not making mistakes, and for good reason. As we stressed in Chapter 4, customer expectations of reliability—fulfillment of service promises—are high. A series of 35 studies across numerous industries from the Arthur D. Little management consulting firm found that the most frequently cited customer complaint was late product and service delivery (44 percent), followed by product and service quality mistakes (31 percent).[7]

To address the need for reliability, companies can institute a "do it right the first time" and an "honor your promises" value system by establishing reliability standards. An example of a generic reliability standard that would be relevant to virtually any service company is "right first time," which means that the service performed is done correctly the first time according to the customer's assessment. If the service involves delivery of products, "right first time" to the customer might mean that the shipment is accurate—that it contains all that the customer ordered and nothing that the customer did not order. If the service involves installation of equipment, "right first time" would likely mean that the equipment was installed correctly and was able to be used immediately by the customer. Another example of a reliability standard is "right on time," which means that the service is performed at the scheduled time. The company representative arrives when promised or the delivery is made at the time the customer expects it. In more complex services, such as disaster recovery or systems integration in computer service, "right on time" would likely mean that the service was completed by the promised date.

Reliability is the single most important concern of service customers. In electronic retailing, on-time and accurate fulfillment of orders is one of the most important aspects of reliability. One of the best examples of customer-defined hard standards in the Internet context is the set of summary metrics that Dell Computer uses for fulfillment.[8] They include

- *Ship to target (SSTT)*—the percentage of orders delivered on time with complete accuracy.

- *Initial field incident rate (IFIR)*—the frequency of customer problems.

- *On time first time fix (OTFTF)*—the percentage of problems fixed on the first visit by a service representative arriving at the time promised.

Dell tracks its performance to these standards and rewards employees on the basis of their "met promises" or reliability, which is often higher than 98 percent.

When it comes to providing service across cultures and continents, service providers need to recognize that customer-defined service standards often need to be adapted (see our Global Feature). In the United States we expect waiters to bring the check promptly. In fact, if we do not receive it shortly after the last course, and without our asking for it, we evaluate the service as slow and nonresponsive. In Spain, however, customers consider it rude for the waiter to bring the check to the table without being asked to do so. They feel rushed, a state they dislike during meals. Although bringing the check to the table (whether sooner or later, requested or not) is an activity that restaurants need to incorporate as a customer-defined service standard, the parameters of the standard must be adapted to the culture.

Hard service standards for responsiveness are set to ensure the speed or promptness with which companies deliver products (within two working days), handle complaints (by sundown each day), answer questions (within 2 hours), answer the telephone (see the Technology Spotlight), and arrive for repair calls (within 30 minutes of the estimated time). In addition to standard setting that specifies levels of response, companies must have well-staffed customer service departments. Responsiveness perceptions diminish when customers wait to get through to the company by telephone, are put on hold, or are dumped into a phone mail system.

Exhibit 10.1 shows a sampling of the hard standards that have been established by service companies. This list is a small subset of all these standards because we include only those that are customer defined—based on customers' requirements and perspectives. Because Federal Express has a relatively simple and standard set of services, it can translate most of its customers' requirements into hard standards and measures. Not all standards, however, are as easily quantifiable as those at FedEx.

Soft Customer-Defined Standards

Not all customer priorities can be counted, timed, or observed through audits. As Albert Einstein once said, "Not everything that counts can be counted, and not everything that can be counted, counts." For example, "understanding and knowing the customer" is not a customer priority that can be adequately captured by a standard that counts, times, or observes employees. In contrast to hard measures, soft measures are those that must be documented using perceptual data. We call the second category of customer-defined standards *soft standards and measures* because they are opinion-based measures and cannot be directly observed. They must be collected by talking to customers, employees, or others. Soft standards provide direction, guidance, and feedback to employees in ways to achieve customer satisfaction and can be quantified by measuring customer perceptions and beliefs. Soft standards are especially important for person-to-person interactions such as the selling process and the delivery process for professional services. Exhibit 10.2 shows examples of soft customer-defined standards.

Mini Maid Services, a firm that franchises home and office janitorial services, successfully built a business by developing a repertoire of 22 customer-defined soft standards for daily cleaning chores. The company sends out crews of four who perform these 22 tasks in an average time of 55 minutes for a fee ranging from approximately

As service companies expand their offerings to international stages, they face a critical question about service delivery: Do they provide the same level of service in other countries as they do in their home country? The answer to this question depends on the answers to several other questions. First, are customer expectations of service delivery uniform across international locations, or do cultural influences lead to different service delivery expectations? Second, what is the performance of competing firms in the countries in which expansion is to take place? Third, do personnel and infrastructure constraints exist in other countries that prevent meeting service performance expectations? All these questions are important, but we discuss the answer to the first most fully because it strongly influences the other two questions.

RESPONSIVENESS VARIES BY CULTURES

Customers from different cultures have different tolerances for service responsiveness and timeliness. Spanish and American customers, for example, have different expectations of the speed with which a check is brought to the table following a meal. Whereas Americans consider bringing the check to the table quickly to be good service, Spanish customers are insulted—believing that the service establishment is rushing them out the door.

Larry Crosby, a renowned marketing researcher who has focused on international customer expectations, has provided research evidence of differences in international customer expectations that lead directly to implications for service standards. In his work on customer

expectations of service perceptions across countries, he developed the accompanying graphs, which are helpful and revealing. Two of the graphs, one for mail delivery (A) and one for a supplier's follow-through on requests (B), provide evidence of how differently customers view levels of responsiveness. In Italy, more than 70 percent of customers rate receiving a letter mailed in their country within three days good, very good, or excellent. In contrast, in the United Kingdom or the Netherlands, more than 90 percent consider that level of responsiveness fair or poor. As business-to-business customers of suppliers (B), Italians consider 75 percent follow-through on requests to be quite good (nearly 50 percent rated that level good, very good, or excellent), whereas almost 60 percent of Australians consider that same service level fair or poor. As you can see, there is a great difference in tolerances for responsiveness across countries.

RELIABILITY VARIES BY CULTURES

Other cultural expectation differences have a major effect on the service standards set in different countries. Asians are more sensitive to reliability than many other cultural groups, making it important that service standards focus on this area and ensure that performance is as promised. This sensitivity is demonstrated in graph C. The ratings of a concert pianist who makes one noticeable mistake in a one-hour solo performance are shown for people from the United States, Canada, Italy, and Japan. Whereas 45 percent of Americans and 40 percent of Canadians still consider the performance to be good,

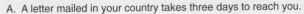

A. A letter mailed in your country takes three days to reach you.

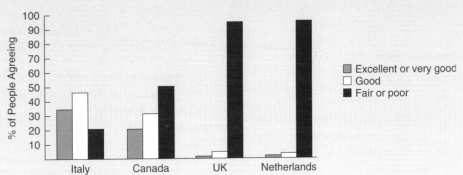

continued

B. A supplier's follow-through on requests you make is about
    75 percent without a reminder by you.

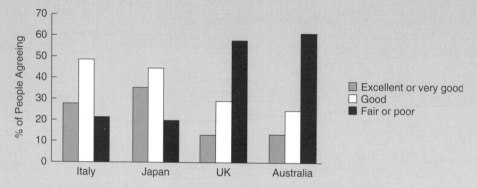

C. A concert pianist makes one noticeable mistake in a one-hour
    solo performance.

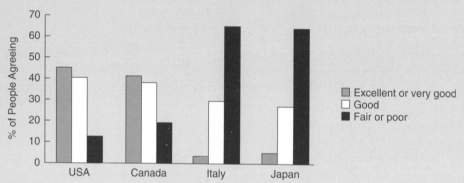

very good, or excellent, only 30 percent of the Japanese rate it that highly—in fact, around 65 percent devalue the performance to fair or poor based on one mistake! In this particular entertainment service, the ratings of Italians were similar to the ratings of the Japanese; however, in many other services Europeans are more forgiving than Asians of reliability problems.

IMPLICATIONS FOR SERVICE STANDARDS

Consider the implications of the data about responsiveness differences for services created in America and differentiated on the basis of speed and responsiveness—services such as overnight package delivery, immediate oil changes, fast food, "while you wait" shoe repair, and 15-minute haircuts. The lack of importance of responsiveness in some other cultures undermines the very positioning of these responsiveness-based services. Unless other aspects of the services make them competitive in other cultures, they may not be as successful as they are in the United States. On the other hand, if the services are well accepted in other countries, one implication may be that companies can relax U.S.-based responsiveness standards. In any case, companies from around the world need to recognize that universal service expectations are probably not the norm and that the best service offerings acknowledge differences across cultures and geographies.

Source: L. A. Crosby, "Factors Affecting the Comparability of Multicountry CSM Information," QUIS 3, Karlstad, Sweden, April 1994, pp. 273–86; figures reprinted with permission.

Technology Spotlight
The Power of a Good Telephone Responsiveness Standard

In 1993, at the National Performance Review's recommendation, President Clinton issued an executive order requiring all government agencies that deal directly with the public to survey their customers and establish customer service standards. By 1998 this order resulted in more than 4,000 customer service standards from 570 agencies. One of the most successful came from the Social Security Administration (SSA) and illustrates a customer-defined hard standard relating to a technology issue that all customers face in dealing with public and private companies alike: telephone responsiveness.

The SSA knew that access—getting through to the agency on its 800 number—was the single biggest driver of customer satisfaction and public perception of the agency's competency. Unfortunately, customers more often than not repeatedly encountered busy signals on the 60 million calls they placed to the SSA's high-volume 800 number. The National Performance Review suggested to the agency that its service standard ought to be that everyone who called its 800 number would get through on the first try: 100 percent access! The SSA balked, recognizing that its telephone technology, limited employee resources, and wide fluctuations in demand would prevent the standard from being met.

The agency ultimately settled on a more reasonable standard: 95 percent of all callers would be served within five minutes. This standard became a very clear and focused goal that "everybody knew and everybody was shooting for," according to an SSA manager. Early measurements indicated less-than-stellar performance; in 1995 only 73.5 percent of callers got through in five minutes.

What followed was an impressive effort of technology, people, and measurement. According to an expert,

"SSA endured tremendous expense, dislocation, pain—and even failure—to meet its standard." First, SSA officials developed a new phone system with AT&T that involved a sophisticated call-routing approach. Second, the organization trained virtually all technical people who held jobs other than in teleservices in those skills so that they could be shifted during peak hours to help with the volume. Third, the agency restricted leave for teleservice representatives at peak time, increased the use of overtime, and worked with employees to change processes and rules to improve performance.

The low point in performance to the standard was during the transition to the new system. In November 1995 only 57.2 percent of callers got through within five minutes. Even worse was that on the first day back to work in January 1996, the AT&T 800-number system crashed, leading to even more busy signals. By February, after AT&T fixed the system and the organization got used to its changes, performance improved significantly. The five-minute access rate was 92.1 percent in February, 95.9 percent in November, and above 95 percent ever since.

The SSA standard was successful because it was specific, measurable, and meaningful to customers. Because its results were documented and publicized both within and outside the agency, both employees and management were accountable for performance. Unlike many of the vague, meaningless standards that resulted from the National Performance Review's work with government agencies, this one was a winner.

Source: D. Osborne, "Higher Standards," *Government Executive,* July 2000, pp. 63–71.

$45 to $55. These standards are considered soft because they are measured by follow-up trailer calls that survey customer perceptions.

The Ritz-Carlton, winner of a Malcolm Baldrige Award, uses a set of "Gold Standards" to drive the service performance it wants. The soft standards established are included in Exhibit 10.2.

The differences between hard and soft standards are illustrated in Exhibit 10.3 using the customer care standards developed at Ford Motor Company.

One-Time Fixes

When customer research is undertaken to find out what aspects of service need to be changed, requirements can sometimes be met using one-time fixes. One-time fixes are

Exhibit 10.1 EXAMPLES OF HARD CUSTOMER-DEFINED STANDARDS

Company	Customer Priorities	Customer-Defined Standards
Federal Express	On-time delivery	Number of packages right day late Number of packages wrong day late Number of missed pickups
Dell Computer	On-time delivery Computer works properly Problems fixed right first time	Ship to target Initial field incident rate Missing, wrong, and damaged rate Service delivery on time first time fix
Social Security Administration	Telephone access	95 percent of calls served within five minutes (see Technology Spotlight)
Southwest Airlines	Reliability Responsiveness to complaints	On-time arrival Two-week reply to letters
Lenscrafters (optical retailer)	Quick turnaround on eyeglasses	Glasses ready in one hour
Fotomat (photograph-developing retailer)	Quick developing of photographs	Photographs developed within one hour
Honeywell Home and Building Division	Fast delivery On-time delivery Order accuracy	Orders entered same day received Orders delivered when promised Order 100 percent accurate
Southern Pacific	19 key customer-defined attributes	Operational measures to correspond with the 19 key attributes
Bank One Credit Card	Access	Calls answered within 20 seconds Abandon rate lower than 3 percent of incoming calls
Texas Instruments Defense System	Compliance with commitments More personal contact	On-time delivery Product compliance to requirements Increased number of personal visits

technology, policy, or procedure changes that, when instituted, address customer requirements (see Exhibit 10.4). We further define one-time fixes as those company standards that can be met by an outlet (a franchisee, for example) making a one-time change that does not involve employees and therefore does not require motivation and monitoring to ensure compliance. We include one-time fixes in our discussion of standards because organizations with multiple outlets often must clearly define these standards to ensure consistency. As an example, Hampton Inns' new "Make It Hampton" program requires that all inns institute 60 new product and service standards, many of which are one-time fixes. These include providing lap desks in rooms, outdoor planter gardens to hide trash containers, red carpet welcome mats, and new lobby artwork and music that celebrates travel.[9] Performance standards do not typically need to be developed for these dissatisfiers because the one-time change in technology, policy, or procedures accomplishes the desired change.

Examples of successful one-time fixes include Hertz and other rental car companies' express check-in, GM Saturn's one-price policy for automobiles, and Granite Rock's 24-hour express service. In each of these examples, customers expressed a

Exhibit 10.2   EXAMPLES OF SOFT CUSTOMER-DEFINED STANDARDS

Company	Customer Priorities	Customer-Defined Standards

General Electric	Interpersonal skills of operators:
	  Tone of voice
	  Problem solving
	  Summarizing actions
	  Closing
		Taking ownership of the call; following through with promises made; being courteous and knowledgeable; understanding the customer's question or request

Ritz-Carlton*	Being treated with respect	"Gold Standards"
		  Uniforms are to be immaculate
		  Wear proper and safe footwear
		  Wear name tag
		  Adhere to grooming standards
		  Notify supervisor immediately of hazards
		  Use proper telephone etiquette
		  Ask the caller, "May I place you on hold?"
		  Do not screen calls
		  Eliminate call transfers when possible

Nationwide Insurance	Responsiveness	Human voice on the line when customers report problems
L. L. Bean	Calming human voice; minimal customer anxiety	Tone of voice; other tasks (e.g., arranging gift boxes) not done while on the telephone with customers
BellSouth	Telephone responsiveness	Do not put customers on hold or transfer them; be able to answer questions; be courteous and professional; show caring and concern
American Express	Resolution of problems	Resolve problem at first contact (no transfers, other calls, or multiple contacts); communicate and give adequate instructions; take all the time necessary
	Treatment	Listen; do everything possible to help; be appropriately reassuring (open and honest)
	Courtesy of representative	Put card member at ease; be patient in explaining billing process; display sincere interest in helping card member; listen attentively; address card member by name; thank card member at end of call

*Source: "The Ritz-Carlton Basics," flyer distributed by the Ritz-Carlton to all employees.

desire to be served in ways different from the past. Hertz's customers had clearly indicated their frustration at waiting in long lines. Saturn customers disliked haggling over car prices in dealer showrooms. And Granite Rock, a Malcolm Baldrige National

Exhibit 10.3　Hard and Soft Standards at Ford Motor Company

In this chapter we discuss two types of customer-defined service standards. "Hard" standards and measures are operational measures that can be counted, timed, or observed through audits. The other category, "soft" standards, are opinion-based measures that cannot be obtained by counting or timing but instead must be asked of the customer. A real example of the difference between hard and soft standards might help distinguish between them. We use Ford Motor Company's Customer Care standards for service at their dealerships. Marketing research involving 2,400 customers asked them about specific expectations for automobile sales and service; the following seven specific service standards were established as most critical to customers in the service department of dealerships.

1. Appointment available within one day of customer's requested service day.

2. Write-up begins within 4 minutes or less.

3. Service needs are courteously identified, accurately recorded on repair order, and verified with customer.

4. Vehicle serviced right on the first visit.

5. Service status provided within one minute of inquiry.

6. Vehicle ready at agreed-upon time.

7. Thorough explanation given of work done, coverage, and charges.

HARD STANDARDS AND MEASURES

Several of these standards fall into the category of hard standards—they can be counted, timed, or observed through audits. Standards 2 and 5, for example, could be timed by an employee in the service establishment. The hard measure could be either (1) the frequency or percentage of times that the standard's time periods are met or (2) the average times themselves (e.g., average time that write-ups begin). Other standards could be counted or audited, such as standards 1, 4, and 6. The service clerk who answers the telephone could record the number of times that appointments were available within one day of the customer's request. The number of repeat visits could be counted to measure standard 4. And the number of vehicles ready at the agreed-upon time could be tallied as customers come in to pick up their cars.

SOFT STANDARDS AND MEASURES

Consider standards 3 and 7 and note how they differ from the ones we have just discussed. These standards represent desired behaviors that are soft and therefore cannot be counted or timed. Standard 7 requires a different type of measure—the customer's perception or opinion about whether this behavior was performed appropriately. It is not that soft standards cannot be measured; instead, they must be measured in different ways.

Soft standards provide direction, guidance, and feedback to employees in ways to achieve customer satisfaction and can be quantified by measuring customer perceptions and beliefs. Soft standards are especially important for person-to-person interactions such as the selling process and the delivery process for professional services. To be effective, companies must provide feedback to employees about customer perceptions of their performance.

Source: Benelux Press/Getty Images

Exhibit 10.4 ONE-TIME FIXES AND WAITING IN LINE

Few customers like to wait in line, and many of us measure the responsiveness and service of an organization by how long it takes us to get to the teller or the counter or our table in a restaurant. Because customers so often wait so long, it may surprise you to know that the subject is a source of constant study and one-time fixes in service companies! Take McDonald's, for example. In the late 1990s, an experiment conducted in 70 McDonald's restaurants in California tested whether it should change its age-old process of multiple waiting lines into a "serpentine-style" single line. Both Wendy's and Burger King already use the single-line system, as do airlines, banks, many hotels, and even the U.S. Postal Service. McDonald's research was conducted because the company was not certain that customers were served best by a single line. Let's visit the single-versus-multiple-line question to see which creates the better standard for customer service.

THE SINGLE LINE IS BETTER

Fairness, speed, and lack of stress and frustration top the reasons many companies and behavioral researchers favor a single line. Consider the following scenario:

> You fling open the door to a McDonald's, size up how fast the various lines are moving, trying to avoid any megaorders in the works. When you pick a line, you keep glancing from side to side to see if others are gaining on you. Inevitably, people who jump from line to line jostle one another. These queue hoppers also sometimes arrive at the register clueless about what they want to order.

Multiple lines have been found to create tremendous stress on customers because they require effort to be sure the "right" line is chosen. How many times have you been frustrated in lines and wondered how it is that you always choose the slow cashier/teller/order-taker?

MULTIPLE LINES ARE BETTER

Those who oppose a single line do so on three counts. First, some critics claim they are "dehumanizing, because [the] velvet ropes corral customers like cattle." Second, one line can appear to be much longer than several short ones, a perception that is incorrect based on actual time measurements but is nevertheless sufficient to drive customers away in search of an establishment with a shorter-appearing wait. Finally, many of them are difficult to use by the disabled.

Experts claim that most customers prefer the single line over the multiple lines, but innovative and customer-focused firms are going further than just making that decision. Some are managing customer perceptions in lines, giving them something to watch or read or otherwise focus on to get their minds off the waits. Others are removing lines altogether, as is the case with restaurants (and some doctor's offices) that give customers pagers so that they can shop or go elsewhere until it is time for them to be served. Still others are letting customers know how long the wait is. Digital signs in the lobby of First Chicago NBD Corporation tell customers the anticipated length of their wait, an up-to-date electronic version of the signs at Walt Disney theme parks that let little customers know how many minutes until they ride Space Mountain.

Source: R. Gibson, "Merchants Mull the Long and the Short of Lines," *The Wall Street Journal,* September 3, 1998, pp. B1ff. Republished by permission of Dow Jones, Inc. via Copyright Clearance Center, Inc., © 1998 Dow Jones and Company, Inc. All Rights Reserved Worldwide.

P.C. Vey

Quality Award winner with a "commodity" product, had customers who desired 24-hour availability of ground rock from its quarry.

Whereas most companies in these industries decided for various reasons not to address these customer requirements, Hertz, Saturn, and Granite Rock each responded with one-time fixes that virtually revolutionized the service quality delivered by their companies. Hertz used technology to create Express Checkout, a one-time fix that also resulted in productivity improvements and cost reductions. The company also pioneered a similar one-time fix for hotel Express Check-In, again in response to customers' expressed desires. Saturn countered industry tradition and offered customers a one-price policy that eliminated the haggling characteristics of automobile dealerships. And Granite Rock created an ATM-like system for 24-hour customer access to rock ground to the 14 most popular consistencies. The company created its own Granite Xpress Card that allowed customers to enter, select, and receive their supplies at any time of the day or night.

One-time fixes are often accomplished by technology. Technology can simplify and improve customer service, particularly when it frees company personnel by handling routine, repetitive tasks and transactions. Customer service employees can then spend more time on the personal and possibly more essential portions of the job. Some technology, in particular computer databases that contain information on individual needs and interests of customers, allows the company to standardize the essential elements of service delivery. These elements include information databases, automated transactions, and scheduling and delivery systems. Effective use of information databases is illustrated in this example from Pizza Hut:

> Pizza Hut centralized and computerized its home delivery operations. Rather than having the separate tasks of order taking, baking, and delivery all in the same location, the company developed a system that works more effectively for both the company and the customer. Operators in a customer service center (not a bakery) take requests for pizza. Working from a database that shows past orders, trained operators take an average of 17 seconds to verify directions to a caller's home and enter his or her request. Operators then route the orders to the closest bake shops, which are strategically located throughout cities to ensure fast deliveries. Cooks in the satellite bake shops prepare pizzas on instructions sent to bake shop printers from order-takers' computers. Drivers aim to complete their deliveries within a half hour of a customer's call, and usually succeed.[10]

One-time fixes also deal with the aspects of service that go beyond human performance: rules and policies, operating hours, product quality, and price. An example of a one-time fix involving a policy change is that of allowing front-line employees to refund money to dissatisfied customers. An example of operating hour changes is one allowing retail establishments to be open on Sundays.

DEVELOPMENT OF CUSTOMER-DEFINED SERVICE STANDARDS

Basing Standards on the Service Encounter Sequence

Performance requirements are rarely the same across all parts of a company; instead, they are associated with particular service processes and encounters. Consider Figure 10.2, a representation of AT&T General Business Systems' customer contact processes, which decomposes the relationship between the customer and AT&T across the entire business.[11] Except for the top branch, labeled "Product" (which reflects the tangible equipment the company sells), each of the business process branches represents a company process during which customers and the firm interact. The first

FIGURE 10.2
AT&T's Process Map for Measurements

Source: From R. E. Kordupleski, R. T. Rust, and A. J. Zaharik, "Why Improving Quality Doesn't Improve Quality (or Whatever Happened to Marketing?)," *California Management Review* 35, no. 3 (Spring 1993). Copyright © 1993 by The Regents of the University of California. By permission of The Regents.

Business Process	Customer Need		Internal Metric
30% Product	Reliability	(40%)	% Repair Call
	Easy to Use	(20%)	% Calls for Help
	Features / Functions	(40%)	Functional Performance Test
30% Sales	Knowledge	(30%)	Supervisor Observations
	Responsive	(25%)	% Proposal Made on Time
	Follow-Up	(10%)	% Follow-Up Made
10% Installation	Delivery Interval Meets Needs	(30%)	Average Order Interval
	Does Not Break	(25%)	% Repair Reports
	Installed When Promised	(10%)	% Installed on Due Date
15% Repair	No Repeat Trouble	(30%)	% Repeat Reports
	Fixed Fast	(25%)	Average Speed of Repair
	Kept Informed	(10%)	% Customers Informed
15% Billing	Accuracy, No Surprise	(45%)	% Billing Inquiries
	Resolve on First Call	(35%)	% Resolved First Call
	Easy to Understand	(10%)	% Billing Inquiries

Business processes are grouped under **Total Quality**.

customer–firm interaction point is sales, followed by installation, repair, and billing. AT&T recognized that its customers' requirements and priorities differed across these processes. Because of these differences, internal measurements chosen to drive behavior differ across the processes and correspond to customers' priorities in each individual encounter.

A customer's overall service quality evaluation is the accumulation of evaluations of multiple service experiences. Service encounters are the component pieces needed to establish service standards in a company. In establishing standards we are concerned with service encounter quality, because we want to understand for each service encounter the specific requirements and priorities of the customer. When we know these priorities we can focus on them as the aspects of service encounters for which standards should be established. Therefore, one of the first steps in establishing customer-defined standards is to delineate the service encounter sequence. Identifying the sequence can be done by listing the sequential steps and activities that the customer experiences in receiving the service. Alternatively, service blueprints (see Chapter 9) can be used to identify the sequence by noting all the customers' activities across the top of the blueprint. Vertical lines from customer activities into the lower levels of the blueprint signal the points at which service encounters take place. Standards that meet customer expectations can then be established.

Because many services have multiple encounters, companies and researchers have examined whether some encounters (for example, the first or the last) are more important than others. The Marriott Corporation identified the encounters that occur in the first 10 minutes of a hotel stay as the most critical, leading the hospitality company to focus on hotel front desk experiences (such as Express Check-In) when making improvements. As you can see from the AT&T data in Figure 10.2, the sales experience was considered by customers to be the most important service encounter for AT&T, which suggests that management should focus on the initial encounter. Although service practice and management literature have emphasized strong starts, recent research indicates that strong finishes in the final event of the encounter have a greater impact on overall satisfaction. Further, the research shows that consistent performance throughout the encounter—widely believed to produce the most favorable evaluations—is not as effective as a pattern of improving performance that culminates in a strong finish.[12] An implication of this research for hotels is that managers should focus on the "back end" of the hotel experience—checkout, parking, bellperson services—to leave a strong final impression.

Expressing Customer Requirements as Specific Behaviors and Actions

Setting a standard in broad conceptual terms, such as "improve skills in the company," is ineffective because the standard is difficult to interpret, measure, and achieve. When a company collects data, it often captures customer requirements in very abstract terms. In general, contact or field people often find that data are not diagnostic—they are too broad and general. Research neither tells them specifically what is wrong and right in their customer relationships nor helps them understand what activities can be eliminated so that the most important actions can be accomplished. In most cases, field people need help translating the data into specific actions to deliver better customer service.

Effective service standards are defined in very specific ways that enable employees to understand what they are being asked to deliver. At best, these standards are set and measured in terms of specific responses of human behaviors and actions.

Figure 10.3 shows different levels of abstraction/concreteness for standards in a service firm, arrayed from top (most abstract) to bottom (most concrete and specific). At the very abstract level are customer requirements that are too general to be useful to employees: customers want satisfaction, value, and relationships. One level under these very general requirements are abstract dimensions of service quality already discussed in this text: reliability, responsiveness, empathy, assurance, and tangibles. One level further are attributes more specific in describing requirements. If we dig still deeper beneath the attribute level, we get to specific behaviors and actions that are at the right level of specificity for setting standards.

FIGURE 10.3   **What Customers Expect: Getting to Actionable Steps**

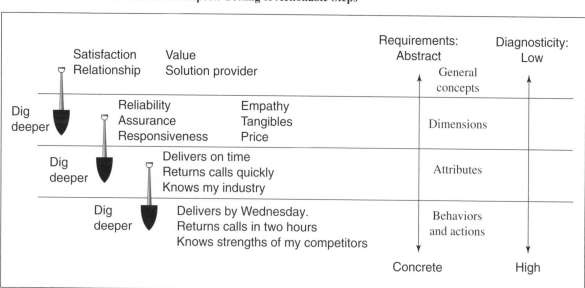

A real-world example of the difference in requirements across these levels will illustrate their practical significance. In a traditional measurement system for a major company's training division, only one aspect of the instructor was included in its class evaluation: ability of instructor. During qualitative research relating to the attributes that satisfy students, three somewhat more specific requirements were elicited: (1) instructor's style, (2) instructor's expertise, and (3) instructor's management of class. Although the articulation of the three attributes was more helpful to instructors than the broad "ability of instructor," management found that the attributes were still too broad to help instructors wanting to improve their course delivery. When the company invested in a customer-defined standards project, the resulting measurement system was far more useful in diagnosing student requirements because the research focused on *specific behaviors and actions* of instructors that met student requirements. Instead of a single broad requirement or three general attributes, the requirements of students were articulated in 14 specific behaviors and actions that related to the instructor and 11 specific behaviors and actions that related to the course content. These behaviors and actions were clearly more diagnostic for communicating what was good and bad in the courses. An additional benefit of this approach was that feedback on behaviors and actions was less personal than feedback on traits or personal characteristics. It was also easier for employees of the company to make changes that related to behaviors rather than to personality traits.

Measuring Behaviors and Actions

Hard Measurements

Hard measurements consist of counts or audits or timed actions that provide feedback about the operational performance of a service standard. What distinguishes these data from soft measurements is that they can be captured continuously and operationally without asking the customer's opinion about them. To demonstrate, here are some of the actual hard measurements for components of the FedEx SQI:

Missing proofs of delivery: the number of invoices that do not include proof-of-delivery paperwork.

Overgoods: lost and found packages that lack, or have lost, identifying labels for the sender and the addressee and are sent to the Overgoods Department.

Wrong day late deliveries: number of packages delivered after the commitment date.

Traces: the number of "proof of performance" requests from customers that cannot be answered through data contained in the computer system.[13]

In these and other hard measurements, the actual gauge involves a count of the number and type of actions or behaviors that are correct or incorrect. Somewhere in the operation system these actions and behaviors are tabulated, frequently through information technology. Other gauges of hard measures include service guarantee lapses (the number of times a service guarantee is invoked because the service did not meet the promise), amounts of time (as in the number of hours or days to respond to a question or complaint or minutes waited in line), and frequencies associated with relevant standards (such as the number of visits made to customers).

Computer information systems are often the basis for setting standards to improve customer service. L. L. Bean, the direct marketer, earned its reputation for outstanding customer service using a computer database that supplies moment-to-moment information about models, colors, and sizes of products in stock. With this system the company can set and achieve high standards of customer service. The database enables L. L. Bean to fill an incredible 99.8 percent of orders accurately.[14]

The appropriate hard measure to deliver to customer requirements is not always intuitive or obvious, and the potential for counting or tracking an irrelevant aspect of operations is high. For this reason it is desirable to link the measure of operational performance with soft measures (surveys or trailer calls) to be sure that they are strongly correlated.

Soft Measurements

Two types of perceptual measurement that were described in Chapter 6 can document customers' opinions about whether performance met the standards established: trailer calls and relationship surveys. Relationship and SERVQUAL surveys cover all aspects of the customer's relationship with the company, are typically expressed in attributes, and are usually completed once per year. Trailer calls are associated with specific service encounters, are short (approximately six or seven questions), and are administered as close in time to a specific service encounter as possible. Trailer calls can be administered in various ways: company-initiated telephone calls following the interactions, postcards to be mailed, letters requesting feedback, customer-initiated calls to a toll-free number, or online electronic surveys. For requirements that are longer term and at a higher level of abstraction (such as at the attribute level), annual relationship surveys can document customer perceptions on a periodic basis. Trailer calls are administered continuously, whenever a customer experiences a service encounter of the type being considered, and they provide data on a continuous basis. The company must decide on a survey strategy combining relationship surveys and trailer calls to provide soft measurement feedback.

Adapting Standards Globally or Locally

How do companies adjust for cultural or local differences in service standards if they recognize that these geographic differences are related to varying customer expectations? Companies with worldwide brands have much to lose if their service standards vary too much across countries, and therefore they must find ways to achieve universally high quality while still allowing for local differences.

As one of the world's leading operators of luxury hotels and resorts, the Four Seasons Hotel manages 63 properties in 29 countries, and successfully accomplishes this goal by balancing universal services standards with standards that vary by country.[15] The company, which has received more AAA Five Diamond awards than any other hotel company and was named top choice for travelers in the United States in the "Hotels, Resorts, and Spas" category, owes much of its success to its seven "service culture standards" expected of *all* staff *all* over the world at *all* times. The seven standards, which form the acrostic SERVICE, are:

1. **<u>S</u>mile:** Employees will actively greet guests, smile, and speak clearly in a friendly manner.

2. **<u>E</u>ye:** Employees will make eye contact, even in passing, with an acknowledgment.

3. **<u>R</u>ecognition:** All staff will create a sense of recognition by using the guest's name, when known, in a natural and discreet manner.

4. **<u>V</u>oice:** Staff will speak to guests in an attentive, natural, and courteous manner, avoiding pretension and in a clear voice.

5. **Informed:** All guest contact staff will be well informed about their hotel, their product, will take ownership of simple requests, and will not refer guests elsewhere.

6. **Clean:** Staff will always appear clean, crisp, well-groomed, and well-fitted.

7. **Everyone:** Everyone, everywhere, all the time, show their care for our guests.

In addition to these culture standards that are expected of all staff all over the world, the hotel has 270 core standards that apply to different aspects of service provision (examples include "the staff will be aware of arriving vehicles and will move toward them, opening doors within 30 seconds" and "unanswered guest room phones will be picked up within 5 rings, or 20 seconds"). Exceptions to these 270 standards are allowed if they make local or cultural sense. For example, in the United States, coffee pots are left on tables at breakfast; in many parts of Europe, including France, customers perceive this practice as a lack of service and servers personally refill coffee cups as needed. Standards for uniforms and decor differ across cultures, but minimum expectations must be met everywhere.

Even within a single country, some service standards are left to management's discretion once a basic high level of service has been achieved. For example, many hotel brands in the United States have recently changed their standards for breakfast to reflect the diet consciousness, speed of service, and varying expectations of consumers.[16] Hampton Inn and Suites has revamped its breakfast as part of its "Make It Hampton" program, which includes more than 60 new product and service standards. There are now eight different hot menu items that are changed periodically; individual Hampton properties can choose menus based on regional preferences of their guests. In its "Fit For You" program, Marriott International requires its hotels to include three menu items that fit into diets that are currently popular. Although the company has a standard requirement that all hotels offer three items, each hotel is encouraged to be creative in choosing the particular items and to include seasonal and local variations. One hotel in Wisconsin, for example, offers a Cheesehead Omelet using a Wisconsin cheese. As the vice president of lodging, food, and beverage stated, "We have given them guidelines, and we want the chefs to create something interesting."[17]

Developing Customer-Defined Standards

Figure 10.4 shows the general process for setting customer-defined service standards.

Step 1: Identify Existing or Desired Service Encounter Sequence

The first step involves delineating the service encounter sequence. Some companies will view this sequence like AT&T General Business Systems did in Figure 10.2. Other times a service blueprint may be used to identify the service encounter sequence. Ideally, the company would be open to discovering customers' desired service encounter sequences, exploring the ways customers want to do business with the firm.

Step 2: Translate Customer Expectations into Behaviors and Actions for Each Service Encounter

The input to step 2 is existing research on customer expectations. In this step, abstract customer requirements and expectations must be translated into concrete, specific behaviors and actions associated with each service encounter. Abstract requirements (like reliability) can call for a different behavior or action in each service encounter, and these differences must be probed. Eliciting these behaviors and actions is likely to

FIGURE 10.4
Process for Setting Customer-Defined Standards

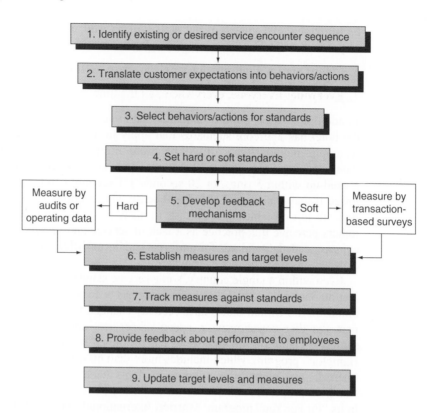

1. Identify existing or desired service encounter sequence

2. Translate customer expectations into behaviors/actions

3. Select behaviors/actions for standards

4. Set hard or soft standards

Measure by audits or operating data ← Hard ← 5. Develop feedback mechanisms → Soft → Measure by transaction-based surveys

6. Establish measures and target levels

7. Track measures against standards

8. Provide feedback about performance to employees

9. Update target levels and measures

require additional qualitative research because in most service companies, marketing information has not been collected for this purpose.

Information on behaviors and actions must be gathered and interpreted by an objective source such as a research firm or an inside department with no stake in the ultimate decisions. If the information is filtered through company managers or front-line people with an internal bias, the outcome would be company-defined rather than customer-defined standards.

Research techniques discussed in Chapter 6 that are relevant for eliciting behaviors and actions include in-depth interviewing of customers, focus group interviews, and other forms of research such as partnering.

Step 3: Select Behaviors and Actions for Standards

This stage involves prioritizing the behaviors and actions, of which there will be many, into those for which customer-defined standards will be established. The following are the most important criteria for creation of the standards.

1. *The standards are based on behaviors and actions that are very important to customers.* Customers have many requirements for the products and services that companies provide. Customer-defined standards need to focus on what is *very important* to customers. Unless very important behaviors/actions are chosen, a company could show improvement in delivering to standards with no impact on overall customer satisfaction or business goals.

2. *The standards cover performance that needs to be improved or maintained.* Customer-defined standards should be established for behavior that needs to be improved or maintained. The company gets the highest leverage or biggest impact from

FIGURE 10.5
Importance/
Performance Matrix:
Delivery, Installing,
Performing

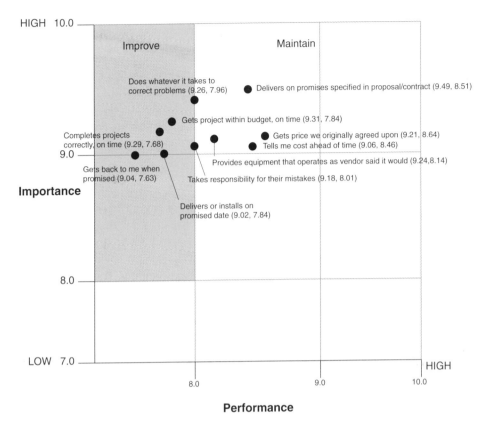

focusing on behaviors and actions that need to be improved. Figure 10.5 shows an importance/performance matrix for a computer manufacturer. It combines the importance and performance criteria and indicates them by the shading in the cell in the matrix where behaviors and actions should be selected to meet those criteria.

3. *The standards cover behaviors and actions employees can improve.* Employees perform according to standards consistently only if they understand, accept, and have control over the behaviors and actions specified in the standards. Holding contact people to standards that they cannot control (such as product quality or time lag in introduction of new products) does not result in improvement. For this reason, service standards should cover controllable aspects of employees' jobs.

4. *The standards are accepted by employees.* Employees will perform to standards consistently only if they understand and accept the standards. Imposing standards on unwilling employees often leads to resistance, resentment, absenteeism, even turnover. Many companies establish standards for the amount of time it should take (rather than for the time it does take) for each service job and gradually cut back on the time to reduce labor costs. This practice inevitably leads to increasing tensions among employees. In these situations, managers, financial personnel, and union employees can work together to determine new standards for the tasks.

5. *The standards are predictive rather than reactive.* Customer-defined standards should not be established on the basis of complaints or other forms of reactive feedback. Reactive feedback deals with past concerns of customers rather than with

Exhibit 10.6   CUSTOMER-DEFINED STANDARDS FOR COMPLAINT HANDLING BY SEGMENT

LARGE CUSTOMERS

Are assigned an individual to call with complaints.

Have a four-hour standard for resolving problems.

SMALL CUSTOMERS

Can call service center or individual.

Have an eight-hour standard for resolving problems.

ALL COMPLAINT-HANDLING PERSONNEL TRAINED TO

Paraphrase problems.

Ask customers what solution they prefer.

Verify that problem has been fixed.

current and future customer expectations. Rather than waiting for dissatisfied customers to complain, the company should actively seek both positive and negative perceptions of customers in advance of complaints.

6. *The standards are challenging but realistic.* A large number of studies on goal setting show that highest performance levels are obtained when standards are challenging but realistic. If standards are not challenging, employees get little reinforcement for mastering them. On the other hand, unrealistically high standards leave an employee feeling dissatisfied with performance and frustrated by not being able to attain the goal.

Exhibit 10.6 shows an example of the set of behaviors and actions selected by a company for its complaint-handling service encounter. Some of these are different across the two segments of customers for which standards were set (small and large customers). Three other behaviors were chosen for standards across all customers.

Step 4: Decide Whether Hard or Soft Standards Are Appropriate

The next step involves deciding whether hard or soft standards should be used to capture the behavior and action. One of the biggest mistakes companies make in this step is to choose a hard standard hastily. Companies are accustomed to operational measures and have a bias toward them. However, unless the hard standard adequately captures the expected behavior and action, it is not customer defined. The best way to decide whether a hard standard is appropriate is to first establish a soft standard by means of trailer calls and then determine over time which operational aspect most correlates to this soft measure. Figure 10.6 shows the linkage between speed of complaint handling (a hard measure) and satisfaction (a soft measure); the figure illustrates that satisfaction strongly depends on the number of hours it takes to resolve a complaint.

Step 5: Develop Feedback Mechanisms for Measurement to Standards

Once companies have determined whether hard or soft standards are appropriate and which specific standards best capture customer requirements, they must develop feedback mechanisms that adequately capture the standards. Hard standards typically involve mechanical counts or technology-enabled measurement of time or errors. Soft standards require perceptual measurements through the use of trailer surveys or employee monitoring. Employee monitoring is illustrated by the practice of supervisors

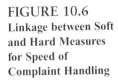

FIGURE 10.6
Linkage between Soft and Hard Measures for Speed of Complaint Handling

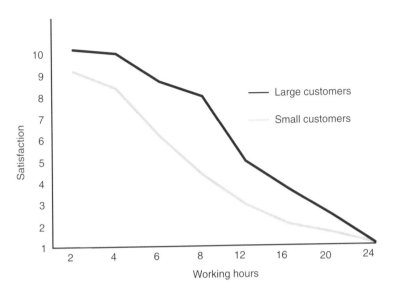

listening in on employee calls. You may have experienced this practice when you called customer service numbers for many organizations and noticed that the voice prompts tell you that calls may be monitored for quality purposes. The purpose of this monitoring is to provide feedback on employee performance to the standards set by the organization to meet customer needs. One critical aspect of developing feedback mechanisms is ensuring that performance captures the process from the customer's view rather than the company's perspective. A supervisor monitoring an employee's handling of a customer service call, for example, should focus not so much on how quickly the employee gets the customer off the phone as with how adequately she handles the customer's request.

Step 6: Establish Measures and Target Levels

The next step requires that companies establish target levels for the standards. Without this step the company lacks a way to quantify whether the standards have been met. Figure 10.6 provided a good example of the approach used to set standards for timeliness in a service company. Each time a complaint was made to the company, and each time one was resolved, employees logged in the times. They also asked each customer his or her satisfaction with the performance in resolving the complaint. The company was then able to plot the information from each complaint on the chart to determine how well the company was performing as well as where the company wished to be in the future. The vertical axis in the figure shows the satisfaction levels of customers, and the horizontal axis shows the number of hours it took the company to resolve customer problems. This technique is but one of several for determining the target level.

Another technique is a simple perception–action correlation study. When the service consists of repetitive processes, companies can relate levels of customer satisfaction with actual performance of a behavior or task. Consider, for example, a study to determine the standard for customers' wait time in a line. The information needed includes customer perceptions of their wait in line (soft perceptual measure) and the amount of time they actually stand in line (hard operations measure). The joint collection of these data over many transactions provides evidence of the sensitivity of customers to different wait times.

An airline conducted precisely this study by having a flight attendant intercept customers as they approached the ticket counter. As each customer entered the line, the attendant stamped the entry time on a ticket (using a machine like those in parking lots) and handed the customer the stamped ticket. As the customer exited the line at the end of the transaction, the flight attendant restamped the ticket with the exit time and asked the customer three or four questions about perceptions of the wait in line and satisfaction with the transaction. Aggregating the individual customer data provided a graph that allowed the company to evaluate the impact on perceptions of various levels of line waits.

Step 7: Track Measures against Standards

Roger Milliken, former head of Milliken Industries, is reported to have said, "In God we trust, all others bring data." Successful service businesses, such as Federal Express and Walt Disney, have careful and comprehensive fact-based systems about their operations. One company that lives and thrives through management by fact is Granite Rock in Watsonville, California. The 90-year-old, family-run business (concrete, asphalt, and crushed stone) that won a Baldrige Award in the small business category has been described as a "huge mechanism for gathering, analyzing, and acting on information." Statistical process control and other types of charts are everywhere, tracking characteristics of its concrete and crushed stone and processes such as the time it takes customers to fill their trucks. Customer complaints are also tracked through what the company calls "product-service discrepancy reports" and root-cause analysis, and updates are distributed to all plants. The reports show how long it takes to resolve complaints and provide detailed quarterly analyses of trends. Plants can track their trends for four years running. When it comes to product quality and customer service, Granite Rock leaves nothing to chance. According to Dave Franceschi, manager of quality support,

> We simply have to know how we're doing. And as soon as we see a dip in the numbers, we need to do some root-cause analysis. If something goes wrong, we have to figure out what happened and prevent it from happening again, so we can get back on that upward climb.[18]

Since the quality movement of the 1980s, many techniques have been developed to track measures against standards. W. Edwards Deming, one of the most influential leaders of the quality movement, developed an approach called the P-D-C-A cycle (Plan-Do-Check-Act) that is applied to processes to measure and continuously improve their performance. Joseph Juran, another founder of the quality movement, was one of the first to apply statistical methods to improvement, leading to the widespread use of statistical process control as a way to measure performance to standards.

Step 8: Provide Feedback about Performance to Employees

Federal Express communicates the performance on its service quality indicator daily so that everyone in the company knows how the company is performing. When problems occur, they can be identified and corrected. The SQI measurement gives everyone in the company immediate feedback on activity that is strongly related to customer perceptions. In a general sense, data and facts need to be analyzed and distributed to support evaluation and decision making at multiple levels within the company. The data also must be deployed quickly enough that the people who need it to make decisions about service or processes can do so. Responsibility for meeting service requirements must also be communicated throughout the organization. All parts of the organization must be measuring their services to internal customers and, ultimately, measuring how that performance relates to external customer requirements.[19]

Step 9: Periodically Update Target Levels and Measures

The final step involves revising the target levels, measures, and even customer requirements regularly enough to keep up with customer expectations.

Developing Service Performance Indexes

One outcome from following the process for developing customer-defined standards is a service performance index. *Service performance indexes* are comprehensive composites of the most critical performance standards. Development of an index begins by identifying the set of customer-defined standards that the company will use to drive behavior. Not all service performance indexes contain customer-defined standards, but the best ones, like FedEx's SQI, are based on them. Most companies build these indexes by (1) understanding the most important requirements of the customer, (2) linking these requirements to tangible and measurable aspects of service provision, and (3) using the feedback from these indexes to identify and improve service problems. The most progressive companies also use the feedback for reward and recognition systems within the company. Here are a few examples of service performance indexes in some U.S. companies.

Southern Pacific

At one time Southern Pacific was rated lowest in the railroad industry on customer satisfaction. Since then it has passed the competition in many areas because of a revised customer satisfaction measurement program and service performance index. It began by redesigning its survey around 19 key attributes that drove customer satisfaction. After gaining management commitment to these priorities, it linked these attributes to real operational measures and also to financial performance. It eliminated any operational measures that could not be directly linked to the 19 customer requirements. It now compares itself to the best railroad and trucking firms.

USAA's Family of Measures

The United Services Automobile Association tracks the quality of individual and unit performance to ensure that persons or groups are showing improvement in service delivery. The company focuses on continuous improvement—that people want an ongoing picture of how they are doing, that they want to be measured in accordance with standards they themselves have helped to set, and that they value the opportunity to improve performance without direct reference to compensation—and therefore it focuses on improvement over time rather than on giving grades. Every month USAA's Family of Measures (FOM) tracks five areas: quality, quantity of work completed, service timeliness, resource utilization, and customer satisfaction. The FOM is a flexible evaluation process that is developed by a representative group of employees from a work unit. To develop their index, each group asks itself four questions: (1) Is the activity under our control? (2) Is it significant? (3) Does it involve some form of data that we can collect? (4) Can we easily analyze the results? The groups decide which measures to include and the relative weight of each measure in the system. Two measures—quality and quantity—are weighted for each unit.[20]

The Ritz-Carlton Hotels

The Ritz-Carlton has created a Service Quality Indicator that is patterned on FedEx's SQI (discussed in this chapter's opening). The Ritz's SQI spells out the 12 most serious defects that can occur in the operation of a hotel and weights them by their seriousness. The defects and points associated with them include:

1. Missing guest preferences (10 points)
2. Unresolved difficulties (50 points)
3. Inadequate guestroom housekeeping (1 point)
4. Abandoned reservation calls (5 points)
5. Guestroom changes (5 points)
6. Inoperable guestroom equipment (5 points)
7. Unready guestroom (10 points)
8. Inappropriate hotel appearance (5 points)
9. Meeting event difficulties (5 points)
10. Inadequate food/beverage (1 point)
11. Missing/damaged guest property/accidents (50 points)
12. Invoice adjustment (3 points)

The hotel calculates the SQI by multiplying the total number of occurrences by their points, totals the points and divides by the number of working days to get an average daily point value. This value is communicated daily to employees.[21]

Airline Performance Index

This index (developed by the National Institute for Aviation Research, Wichita State University) identifies a comprehensive set of factors that influence airline service perceptions and rates all U.S. airlines annually on the index. These factors include the following:

1. On-time flights
2. Number of accidents
3. Flight problems
4. Pilot errors
5. Overbookings
6. Mishandled baggage
7. Fare complaints
8. Frequent flier awards
9. Other complaints
10. Refund complaints
11. Service complaints
12. Ticket complaints[22]

Among the issues that companies must tackle when developing service performance indexes are (1) the number of components to be contained, (2) what overall or summary measures will be included, (3) whether the index should be weighted or unweighted (to put greater emphasis on the performance of the attributes considered most important to customers), and (4) whether all parts of the business (departments, sectors, or business units) will be held to the same performance measures. One of the most important goals of an index is to simply and clearly communicate business performance in operational and perceptual terms. Companies must develop the rigor in these measurement areas that they have in financial performance.

Summary

This chapter discussed the discrepancy between company perceptions of customer expectations and the standards they set to deliver to these expectations. Among the major causes for provider gap 2 are inadequate standardization of service behaviors and actions, absence of formal processes for setting service quality goals, and lack of customer-defined standards. These problems were discussed and detailed, along with strategies to close the gap.

Customer-defined standards are at the heart of delivery of service that customers expect: They are the link between customers' expressed expectations and company actions to deliver to those expectations. Creating these service standards is not a common practice in U.S. firms. Doing so requires that companies' marketing and operations departments work together by using the marketing research as input for operations. Unless the operations standards are defined by customer priorities, they are not likely to have an impact on customer perceptions of service.

Discussion Questions

1. How does the service measurement that we describe in this chapter differ from the service measurement in Chapter 6? Which of the two types do you think is most important? Why?

2. In what types of service industries are standards most difficult to develop? Why? Recommend three standards that might be developed in one of the firms from the industries you specify. How would employees react to these standards? How could you gain buy-in for them?

3. Given the need for customer-defined service standards, do firms need company-defined standards at all? Could all standards in a company be customer defined? Why or why not? What functional departments in a firm would object to having all standards customer defined?

4. What is the difference between hard and soft standards? Which do you think would be more readily accepted by employees? By management? Why?

5. Consider the university or school you currently attend. What are examples of hard standards, soft standards, and one-time fixes that would address student requirements? Does the school currently use these standards for delivery of service to students? Why or why not? Do you think your reasons would apply to private-sector companies as well? To public or nonprofit companies?

6. Think about a service that you currently use, then map out the service encounter sequence for that service. What is your most important requirement in each interaction? Document these requirements, and make certain that they are expressed at the concrete level of behaviors and actions.

7. Which of the service performance indexes described at the end of this chapter is the most effective? Why? What distinguishes the one you selected from the others? How would you improve each of the others?

Exercises

1. Select a local service firm. Visit the firm and ascertain the service measurements that the company tracks. What hard measures does it monitor? Soft measures? On the basis of what you find, develop a service performance index.

2. Choose one of the peripheral services (such as computer, library, placement) provided by your school. What hard standards would be useful to track to meet

student expectations? What soft standards? What one-time fixes would improve service?

3. Think about a service company you have worked for or know about. Using Figure 10.3, write in customer requirements at each of the levels. How far down in the chart can you describe requirements? Is that far enough?

4. Look at three websites from which you can order products (such as amazon.com or llbean.com). What are the companies' delivery promises? What types of standards might they set for these promises? Are these customer- or company-defined standards?

Notes

1. "Taking the Measure of Quality," *Service Savvy,* March 1992, p. 3.

2. Ibid.

3. Speech by Federal Express Manager in Baltimore, Maryland, June 1993.

4. T. Levitt, "Industrialization of Service," *Harvard Business Review,* September–October 1976, pp. 63–74.

5. B. S. Lunde and S. L. Marr, "Customer Satisfaction Measurement: Does It Pay Off?" (Indianapolis: Walker Customer Satisfaction Measurements, 1990).

6. D. Reed, "Hotels Penalize Late Arrivals, Early Departures," *The Wall Street Journal,* August 18, 1998, p. B1.

7. "Fast, Reliable Delivery Processes Are Cheered by Time-Sensitive Customers," *The Service Edge* 4, no. 3 (1993): 1.

8. F. Reichhold, "e-loyalty," *Harvard Business Review,* July–August 2000, pp. 105–13.

9. J. Weinstein, "Redesigning the Box," *Hotels* 38, no. 3 (2004), p. 7.

10. "Fast, Reliable Delivery Processes," p. 21.

11. R. E. Kordupleski, R. T. Rust, and A. J. Zaharik, "Why Improving Quality Doesn't Improve Quality (or Whatever Happened to Marketing?)," *California Management Review* 35 (Spring 1993), p. 89.

12. D. E. Hansen and P. J. Danaher, "Inconsistent Performance during the Service Encounter: What's a Good Start Worth?" *Journal of Service Research* 1 (February 1999), pp. 227–35.

13. "Taking the Measure of Quality," p. 3.

14. G. Russell, "Where the Customer Is Still King," *Time,* February 2, 1987.

15. This discussion about the Four Seasons is based on R. Hallowell, D. Bowen, and C. Knoop, "Four Seasons Goes to Paris," *Academy of Management Executive* 16, no. 4 (2002), pp. 7–24.

16. R. Oliva, "Out with the Old Breakfast," *Hotels* no. 4 (April 2004), p. 46.

17. Ibid., p. 45.

18. "Managing by Fact: It's Exhaustive, Expensive, and Essential," *The Service Edge* 6, no. 5 (May 1993).

19. "Taking the Measure of Quality," p. 3.

20. T. Ehrenfeld, "Merit Evaluation and the Family of Measures," *Harvard Business Review,* September–October 1991, p. 122.

21. 1999 Application Summary for The Ritz-Carlton Hotel Company, Malcolm Baldrige National Quality Award, 2000.

22. D. Carroll, "Expert: Being on Time Isn't Everything for Airlines," *USA Today,* March 5, 1992, p. 6B.

11

PHYSICAL EVIDENCE AND THE SERVICESCAPE

This chapter's objectives are to

1. Explain the profound impact of physical evidence, particularly the servicescape, on customer perceptions and experiences.

2. Illustrate differences in types of servicescapes, the roles played by the servicescape, and the implications for strategy.

3. Explain *why* the servicescape affects customer and employee behavior, using a framework based in marketing, organizational behavior, and environmental psychology.

4. Present elements of an effective physical evidence strategy.

Using Physical Evidence to Position a New Service

When Speedi-Lube opened its doors in Seattle, Washington, it was one of the first 10-minute oil and lubrication services ever introduced. Now there are thousands of such outlets, but then the concept was totally new. The idea was to offer an alternative to corner gas stations for basic car lubrication service, quickly (within 10 minutes), with no appointment necessary. Because the concept was unknown to consumers at the time, the owners of Speedi-Lube needed to communicate and position the service clearly so that consumers would form accurate expectations. And because car maintenance is highly intangible and consumers often do not understand what is actually done to their cars, the owners relied heavily on tangible physical evidence to communicate the concept before, during, and after the sale.

To communicate an image of fast, efficient service, Speedi-Lube relied on straightforward, to-the-point advertising using clean, crisp letters. For example, a large billboard read in large blue and white letters: SPEEDI-LUBE, 10-MINUTE OIL CHANGE, NO APPOINTMENT, OPEN 7 DAYS, 9 TO 6. The very buildings in which the service was performed communicated the efficiency theme clearly. In fact, the exteriors of some of the first Speedi-Lube facilities had the look of a fast-food restaurant, not inconsistent with the intended image of speed, efficiency, and predictability. Entrance and exit signs were clearly displayed so that customers coming to Speedi-Lube for the first time would know exactly where to drive their cars.

On driving into the service bay the customer was greeted with additional physical evidence that clearly differentiated Speedi-Lube from its competitors at that time. The service bay was very neat and brightly painted, with a professional-appearing service counter in the bay where the customer filled out paperwork to get the service. Service personnel in professional uniforms helped with the paperwork, and the customer was invited to wait in a clean and functional waiting area where coffee and magazines were provided. (Alternatively, customers were welcome to stay in the service area to observe the work on their cars.) On one of the waiting room walls was displayed a large schematic that showed the underside of an automobile and identified all the lubrication points and exactly what was being done to the car (Figure 11.1). This form of evidence informed customers and gave them confidence in what was being done.

On completion, the customer was given a checklist itemizing the lubrication services provided. As a finishing touch, the employee would then lubricate the door locks on the car to indicate that nothing had been overlooked. Three months later Speedi-Lube would send a reminder suggesting that it was time for another oil change.

It is difficult to imagine a time when 10-minute oil and lubrication services did not exist. Yet when Speedi-Lube was established, the quick oil change concept was totally unknown to consumers. Speedi-Lube was dealing with both a totally new concept and an industry in which services are generally high in credence attributes. The company used physical evidence very effectively to communicate the new concept and to make elements of the process itself very concrete. The schematic on the waiting room wall detailing what the service entailed, as well as the checklist showing exactly what had been done, were ways the company tried to make credence attributes more tangible.

FIGURE 11.1
Speedi-Lube spells out the service offering.

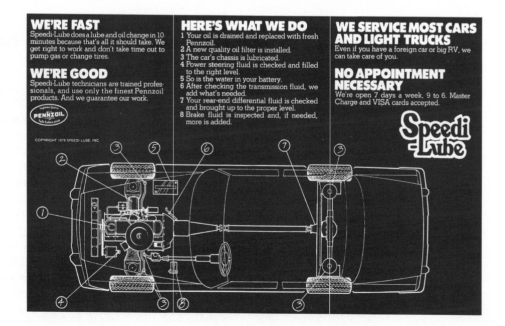

In this chapter we explore the importance of physical evidence for communicating service quality attributes, setting customer expectations, and creating the service experience. In Chapter 1, when we introduced the expanded marketing mix for services, we defined physical evidence as *the environment in which the service is delivered and in which the firm and the customer interact, and any tangible commodities that facilitate performance or communication of the service.* The first part of this definition encompasses the actual physical facility in which the service is performed, delivered, and consumed; throughout this chapter the physical facility is referred to as the *servicescape.*[1]

Physical evidence is particularly important for communicating about credence services (such as auto repair), but it is also important for services such as hotels, hospitals, and theme parks that are dominated by experience attributes. Think of how effectively Disney uses the physical evidence of its service to excite its customers. The brightly colored displays, the music, the fantastic rides, and the costumed characters all reinforce the feelings of fun and excitement that Disney seeks to generate in its customers. Think also of how effective Disney is in portraying consistent physical evidence that is compatible with its goals. The physical evidence and servicescape, or the "stage" in Disney's terms, is always stimulating to the extreme, is always clean, is always in top repair, and never fails to deliver what it has promised to consumers, and more. In this chapter we present many examples of how physical evidence communicates with customers and how it can play a role in creating the service experience, in satisfying customers, and in enhancing customers' perceptions of quality.

PHYSICAL EVIDENCE

What Is Physical Evidence?

Because services are intangible, customers often rely on tangible cues, or physical evidence, to evaluate the service before its purchase and to assess their satisfaction with the service during and after consumption. Effective design of physical, tangible evidence is important for closing gap 2.

General elements of physical evidence are shown in Table 11.1. They include all aspects of the organization's physical facility (the servicescape) as well as other forms of tangible communication. Elements of the servicescape that affect customers include

TABLE 11.1
Elements of Physical Evidence

Servicescape	Other Tangibles
Facility exterior	Business cards
Exterior design	Stationery
Signage	Billing statements
Parking	Reports
Landscape	Employee dress
Surrounding environment	Uniforms
Facility interior	Brochures
Interior design	Web pages
Equipment	Virtual servicescape
Signage	
Layout	
Air quality/temperature	

Technology Spotlight
Virtual Servicescapes: Experiencing Services on the Internet

Web pages and virtual service tours allow customers to preview service experiences through the Internet and see tangible evidence of the service without actually being there. This medium offers firms tremendous potential to communicate experiential aspects of their services in ways that were previously very difficult, if not impossible. Here we present several examples, across different industries.

TRAVEL

Travelers can now preview destinations, view hotels and their rooms, tour natural environments, and "experience" entertainment venues before booking their trips or even deciding where to travel. Before booking a trip to Great Britain, travelers can preview websites that show hotels, bed and breakfast inns, and other lodging all over the country. The exterior of the facilities as well as actual rooms can be examined in selecting accommodations. In planning a trip to visit the national parks of the United States, travelers can view full-length videos of the parks and various tours within the parks. For example, at the Yellowstone site (www.yellowstone.net/onlinetours/) video tours are available of driving loops within the park, complete with the sounds of the park's famous geysers. Detailed maps are also included, allowing a traveler to plan a route and choose among the many possible sights prior to even arriving at the park. Before the Internet, this kind of servicescape knowledge, available at a moment's notice, would have been impossible.

SPORTS AND LEISURE

Through sports and leisure websites, fans can now view much of the action and preview upcoming experiences online. For example, in 2004 fans of the 35th Ryder Cup Golf Match (www.rydercup.com) were able to view the actual course and other event-related information online at the Ryder Cup website. The event, an annual contest between the top U.S. and European golfers, took place at the Oakland Hills Country Club in Michigan. On the website, fans could view all 18 holes of the magnificent course by choosing to examine an illustration showing the topography of the hole or a color photo of the hole, or by zooming in on an aerial video that followed the green from the tee to the hole. A graphic of the entire course was also shown on the website. In addition, the site included video clips of event highlights, details on the players, and a complete history of the match. Spending time on the website allowed distant fans to more fully enjoy the event, almost as if they were there!

UNIQUE RETAIL EXPERIENCES

Many of today's unique retail experiences can be conveyed effectively via the Internet to give customers a preview of what they can expect. A great example is Build-A-Bear Workshop, where children "from 3 to 103" can create their own teddy bears and other furry friends during their visits to the store. The experience itself is memorable and fun, and the servicescape of the stores is a big part of creating the experience. For a preview of how it works and what the stores look like, the website of Build-A-Bear Workshops (www.buildabear.com) includes a step-by-step "virtual visit" that shows the various stations in the store and what happens at each one. In creating a furry friend, consumers go through the following steps: Choose Me; Hear Me; Stuff Me; Stitch Me; Fluff Me; Name Me; Dress Me; Take Me Home.® The virtual visit on the website shows each stage sequentially, detailing the activities at each step and providing a colorful photo that gives a real sense of the store en-

both exterior attributes (such as signage, parking, and the landscape) and interior attributes (such as design, layout, equipment, and decor). Note that web pages and virtual servicescapes conveyed over the Internet are more recent forms of physical evidence that companies can use to communicate about the service experience, making services more tangible for customers both before and after purchase (see our Technology Spotlight).

Physical evidence examples from different service contexts are given in Table 11.2. It is apparent that some services (like hospitals, resorts, and child care) rely heavily on physical evidence to communicate and create customer experiences. Others (insurance, express mail) provide limited physical evidence for customers. All the elements

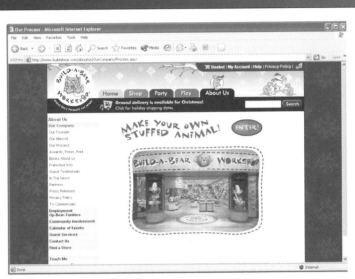

Build-A-Bear Workshop Website
Source: Courtesy Build-A-Bear Workshop.

vironment and the emotions of its patrons. Build-A-Bear Workshop began operations in 1997 and operates 170 of its stores, primarily in major mall locations, throughout the United States and Canada.

HIGHER EDUCATION

One of the most significant decisions that young people and their families make is the decision of what university to attend. For students lucky enough to have the means and intellectual abilities, the choices can be endless. The physical environment of the university—the campus itself as well as specific facilities—can play a major role in students' choices as well as their actual experiences. Some universities now offer virtual tours of their campuses online that allow students to preview the physical environment in advance. The University of Idaho in the United States has a particularly effective tour on their site that allows students to view almost everything on campus, including its recreation centers, student union, library, classroom buildings, administration buildings, and common areas (www.webs.uidaho.edu/vtour/). Selecting one of these options opens a window with a photo, a brief written description, and a panoramic video tour of the chosen place.

Internet technology clearly provides tremendous opportunities for firms to communicate about their services. Tangible images on the Web create expectations for customers that set standards for service delivery, and it is critical that the actual services live up to these expectations. Images and virtual service tours presented on the Internet also need to support the positioning of the service brand and be consistent with other marketing messages.

of evidence listed for each service communicate something about the service to consumers, facilitate performance of the service, and/or add to the customer's total experience. Although we focus in this chapter primarily on the servicescape and its effects, keep in mind that what is said applies to the other forms of evidence as well.

How Does Physical Evidence Affect the Customer Experience?

Physical evidence, particularly the servicescape, can have a profound effect on the customer experience. This is true whether the experience is mundane (e.g., a bus or

TABLE 11.2
Examples of Physical
Evidence from the
Customer's Point
of View

Physical Evidence		
Service	**Servicescape**	**Other Tangibles**
Insurance	Not applicable	Policy itself Billing statements Periodic updates Company brochure Letters/cards Website
Hospital	Building exterior Parking Signs Waiting areas Admissions office Patient care room Medical equipment Recovery room	Uniforms Reports/stationery Billing statements Website
Airline	Airline gate area Airplane exterior Airplane interior (decor, seats, air quality)	Tickets Food Uniforms Website
Express mail	Not applicable	Packaging Trucks Uniforms Computers Website
Sporting event	Parking Stadium exterior Ticketing area Entrance Seating Restrooms Concession areas Playing field	Signs Tickets Programs Uniforms Website

subway ride), personally meaningful (e.g., a church wedding experience, or a birthing room at a hospital), or spectacular (e.g., a week-long travel adventure). In all cases, the physical evidence of the service will influence the flow of the experience, the meaning customers attach to it, their satisfaction, and their emotional connections with the company delivering the experience.

As marketers and corporate strategists begin to pay more attention to experiences, they have recognized the impact of physical space and tangibles in creating those experiences. Lewis Carbone, a leading consultant on experience management, has developed an entire lexicon and management process around the basic idea of "experience engineering" through "clue management."[2] *Clue management* refers to the process of clearly identifying and managing *all* the various clues that customers use to form their impressions and feelings about the company. Included in this set of clues are what Carbone refers to as *mechanics clues,* or the physical and tangible clues that we focus on in this chapter. Other writers and consultants who focus on managing cus-

TABLE 11.3
Typology of Service Organizations Based on Variations in Form and Use of the Servicescape

	Complexity of the Servicescape	
Servicescape Usage	**Elaborate**	**Lean**
Self-service (customer only)	Golf course eBay	ATM Car wash Simple Internet services Express mail drop-off
Interpersonal services (both customer and employee)	Hotel Restaurant Health clinic Hospital Bank Airline School	Dry cleaner Retail cart Hair salon
Remote service (employee only)	Telephone company Insurance company Utility Many professional services	Telephone mail-order desk Automated voice messaging services

Source: From M. J. Bitner, "Servicescapes: The Impact of Physical Surroundings on Customers and Employees," *Journal of Marketing* 56 (April 1992), pp. 57–71. Reprinted with permission of the American Marketing Association.

tomer experiences also zero in on the importance of tangible evidence and physical facilities in shaping those experiences.[3] Throughout this chapter are numerous examples of how physical evidence communicates with customers and shapes their experiences.

TYPES OF SERVICESCAPES

In this chapter we explain the roles played by the servicescape and how it affects employees and customers and their interactions. The chapter relies heavily on ideas and concepts from environmental psychology, a field that encompasses the study of human beings and their relationships with built (man-made), natural, and social environments.[4] The physical setting may be more or less important in achieving the organization's marketing and other goals depending on certain factors. Table 11.3 is a framework for categorizing service organizations on two dimensions that capture some of the key differences that will impact the management of the servicescape. Organizations that share a cell in the matrix will face similar issues and decisions regarding their physical spaces.

Servicescape Usage

First, organizations differ in terms of *whom* the servicescape will actually affect. That is, who actually comes into the service facility and thus is potentially influenced by its design—customers, employees, or both groups? The first column of Table 11.3 suggests three types of service organizations that differ on this dimension. At one extreme is the *self-service* environment, in which the customer performs most of the activities and few if any employees are involved. Examples of self-service environments include ATMs, movie theaters, express mail drop-off facilities, self-service entertainment such as golf and theme parks, and online Internet services. In these primarily self-service environments the organization can plan the servicescape to focus exclusively on marketing goals such as attracting the right market segment, making the facility pleasing and easy to use, and creating the desired service experience.

At the other extreme of the use dimension is the *remote service,* which has little or no customer involvement with the servicescape. Telecommunications, utilities, financial consultants, editorial, and mail-order services are examples of services that can be provided without the customer ever seeing the service facility. In fact, the facility may be in a different state or a different country (see the Global Feature in Chapter 1). In remote services, the facility can be set up to keep employees motivated and to facilitate productivity, teamwork, operational efficiency, or whatever organizational behavior goal is desired without any consideration of customers because they will never need to see the servicescape.

In Table 11.3, *interpersonal services* are placed between the two extremes and represent situations in which both the customer and the employee are present and active in the servicescape. Examples abound, such as hotels, restaurants, hospitals, educational settings, and banks. In these situations the servicescape must be planned to attract, satisfy, and facilitate the activities of both customers and employees simultaneously. Special attention must also be given to how the servicescape affects the nature and quality of the social interactions between and among customers and employees. A cruise ship provides a good example of a setting in which the servicescape must support customers and the employees who work there and also facilitate interactions between the two groups.

Servicescape Complexity

The horizontal dimension of Table 11.3 suggests another factor that will influence servicescape management. Some service environments are very simple, with few elements, few spaces, and few pieces of equipment. Such environments are termed *lean*. Shopping mall information kiosks and FedEx drop-off facilities would be considered lean environments because both provide service from one simple structure. For lean servicescapes, design decisions are relatively straightforward, especially in self-service or remote service situations in which there is no interaction among employees and customers.

Other servicescapes are very complicated, with many elements and many forms. They are termed *elaborate* environments. An example is a hospital with its many floors and rooms, sophisticated equipment, and complex variability in functions performed within the physical facility. In such an elaborate environment, the full range of marketing and organizational objectives theoretically can be approached through careful management of the servicescape. For example, a patient's hospital room can be designed to enhance patient comfort and satisfaction while simultaneously facilitating employee productivity. Firms such as hospitals that are positioned in the elaborate interpersonal service cell face the most complex servicescape decisions. To illustrate, when the Mayo Clinic, probably the best-known name in U.S. health care, opened its hospital in Scottsdale, Arizona, the organization painstakingly considered the interrelated goals, needs, and feelings of its employees, doctors, patients, and visitors in designing its distinctive servicescape (see Exhibit 11.3 later in this chapter).

STRATEGIC ROLES OF THE SERVICESCAPE

Within the cells of the typology, the servicescape can play many strategic roles simultaneously. An examination of the variety of roles and how they interact makes clear

BusinessWeek and *Architectural Record,* both McGraw-Hill publications, together sponsor an annual international competition to identify the best use of architecture that solves strategic business challenges. Company winners clearly demonstrate the impact of design on people—customers, employees, the general public, or all three. Here we present four of the 2003 award-winners that illustrate the ways that architecture and servicescapes execute or reinforce strategic decisions and marketing positioning.

APPLE STORE, SOHO, NEW YORK

In designing its store in New York's Soho district, Apple Computers brought together architects, graphic designers, product developers, merchandising people, and CEO Steve Jobs to create a retail space that would both convey the company's philosophy and sell computers. The result is a clean, open, and spacious store that displays only a few computers to create the ambience of a museum. The company establishes a modern feel using a central glass staircase, white walls, and a large skylight. A second-floor area encourages children to play with software and offers a large conference room for Apple product demonstrations. As one judge put it, "the store, like Apple, is all about information, interaction, and access."

Apple Store, Soho, NY
Source: Mario Tama/Getty Images

THE IMAGE FACTORY, OKLAHOMA CITY

Architectural design played a major role in reconceptualizing and rebranding a copy business in Oklahoma City. What was once a small copy firm was repositioned as a large, high-tech scanning and imaging company that attracts upscale clients. Glass walls allow clients to view the company's sophisticated production processes, and a display of old typewriters conveys the history of the company dating back to its days as a typewriter repair business. Other displays show the evolution of reproduction services from typewriters to copying machines to digital scanning. The facility conveys a sense of history, quality, and pride in the work done as well as inventiveness, efficiency, and organization.

SEKII LADIES CLINIC, JAPAN

To reposition its childbirth clinic in stark contrast to traditional Japanese hospitals, the Sekii Ladies Clinic relied heavily on a novel servicescape design. The new childbirth delivery and recovery rooms are elegant, warm, and simple, and the building itself is modern, open, and light-filled. Combined with interior gardens, the spaces offer mothers a rich, warm experience for childbirth. Delivery rooms and all areas welcome fathers, a departure from the tradition in Japan in which women typically give birth in large public hospitals without family members present. The clinic brings women's health to the forefront rather than hiding it, another Japanese tradition.

continued

DARWIN CENTRE MUSEUM, LONDON

The Darwin Centre Museum needed more room to house its huge collection of 22 million zoological specimens and to provide additional laboratory space for its scientists. To meet these objectives, the museum designed a new building that provided both storage and public access to its collections. An atrium in the building allows visitors to view scientists at work, and open shelves display the specimens. Touch-screen terminals provide another means for exploring the collection. The caterpillar-like roof over the building provides a clue to what is inside! Visits to the museum increased sharply when the new building was opened.

Source: "The *BusinessWeek/Architectural Record* Awards," Special Report, *BusinessWeek,* November 3, 2003, pp. 57–64.

how strategically important it is to provide appropriate physical evidence of the service. In fact, the servicescape is frequently one of *the* most important elements used in positioning a service organization (see our Strategy Insight).

Package

Similar to a tangible product's package, the servicescape and other elements of physical evidence essentially "wrap" the service and convey to consumers an external image of what is "inside." Product packages are designed to portray a particular image as well as to evoke a particular sensory or emotional reaction. The physical setting of a service does the same thing through the interaction of many complex stimuli. The servicescape is the outward appearance of the organization and thus can be critical in forming initial impressions or setting up customer expectations—it is a visual metaphor for the intangible service. This packaging role is particularly important in creating expectations for new customers and for newly established service organizations that are trying to build a particular image (as noted in the chapter's opening vignette on Speedi-Lube). The physical surroundings offer an organization the opportunity to convey an image in a way not unlike the way an individual chooses to "dress for success." The packaging role extends to the appearance of contact personnel through their uniforms or dress and other elements of their outward appearance.[5]

Interestingly, the same care and resource expenditures given to package design in product marketing are often not provided for services, even though the service package serves a variety of important roles. There are many exceptions to this generality, however. Smart companies like Starbucks, FedEx, and Marriott spend a lot of time and money relating their servicescape design to their brand, providing their customers with strong visual metaphors and "service packaging" that conveys the brand positioning. FedEx, for example, embarked on a major overhaul of its image by rethinking and redesigning all its tangibles—everything from its drop boxes to its service centers to the bags carried by its couriers.[6] The idea was to convey a consistent look and feel of "things are simple here," and "here, give us your package; we'll take care of everything."

Facilitator

The servicescape can also serve as a facilitator in aiding the performances of persons in the environment. How the setting is designed can enhance or inhibit the efficient flow of activities in the service setting, making it easier or harder for customers and employees to accomplish their goals. A well-designed, functional facility can make the service a pleasure to experience from the customer's point of view and a pleasure to perform from the employee's. On the other hand, poor and inefficient design may frustrate both customers and employees. For example, an international air traveler who finds himself in a poorly designed airport with few signs, poor ventilation, and few places to sit or eat will find the experience quite dissatisfying, and employees who work there will probably be unmotivated as well. The same international traveler will appreciate seats on the airplane that are conducive to work and sleep. The seating itself, part of the physical surroundings of the service, has been improved over the years to better facilitate travelers' needs to sleep. In fact, the competition for better seat design continues as a major point of contention among the international airline carriers, and the results have translated into greater customer satisfaction for business travelers.[7] British Airways has even seen its market share increase on some routes as a direct result of its award-winning Club-World seat.[8] As hotels begin development of new prototype rooms in the early 2000s, they are focusing on making the rooms more useful to their guests who are spending more time in their hotel rooms than they used to. Rooms are being designed with colors, fabrics, and textures that have a homelike look, and the new hotels are putting in bigger desks, more high-speed Internet connections, and larger TVs.[9] All these examples emphasize the facilitator role of the servicescape.

Socializer

The design of the servicescape aids in the socialization of both employees and customers in the sense that it helps convey expected roles, behaviors, and relationships. For example, a new employee in a professional services firm would come to understand her position in the hierarchy partially through noting her office assignment, the quality of her office furnishings, and her location relative to others in the organization.

The design of the facility can also suggest to customers what their role is relative to employees, what parts of the servicescape they are welcome in and which are for employees only, how they should behave while in the environment, and what types of interactions are encouraged. For example, consider a Club Med vacation environment that is set up to facilitate customer–customer interactions as well as guest interactions with Club Med staff. The organization also recognizes the need for privacy, providing areas that encourage solitary activities. To illustrate further, in many Starbucks locations, the company has shifted to more of a traditional coffeehouse environment in which customers spend social time rather than coming in for a quick cup of coffee on the run. To encourage this type of socializing, these Starbucks locations have comfortable lounge chairs and tables set up to encourage customers to interact and to stay longer. In a new initiative, Starbucks is moving into the world of music with its innovative Hear Music Coffeehouses. The Hear Music servicescapes include CD burning stations at which customers can drink coffee, listen to music, and create and burn their own CDs. This environment encourages a totally different type of behavior and socializing among customers compared to the traditional coffee shop environment.[10]

Differentiator

The design of the physical facility can differentiate a firm from its competitors and signal the market segment that the service is intended for. Given its power as a differentiator, changes in the physical environment can be used to reposition a firm and/or to attract new market segments. In shopping malls the signage, colors used in decor and displays, and type of music wafting from a store signal the intended market segment.

Exhibit 11.1   WASHINGTON MUTUAL PATENTS ITS
BANK BRANCH DESIGN

Washington Mutual, a large retail bank in the United States, has been particularly effective in differentiating itself as a family-oriented, friendly, inviting retail bank through its innovative branch design. Drawing on what it learned from customer research, the bank has transformed approximately half of its 1,800 branches to the new design. Features range from oval or circular branch layouts to freestanding teller stations. The new design offers play areas for kids with toys, television, and child-size furniture. Bright colors are used for furnishings and walls, and attractive, colorful posters are displayed on the walls. A concierge guides customers to where they need to go—particularly on a first visit. In a somewhat unusual step, the company recently patented its innovative design. U.S. patent No. 6, 681,985 describes the bank as "welcoming and inviting," in contrast to traditional bank branches. The differentiation strategy and resulting branch design reflect the bank's desire to build relationships with its retail customers. Established in 1889, WaMu, as the bank is known, is based in Washington State. The corporation serves 11.6 million households and operates 2,400 banking branches and other types of outlets. It was recognized by *Fortune* magazine as a "most admired company," with the top ranking for innovation.

Source: R. Wiles, "Breaking the Bank—the Mold, That Is," *The Arizona Republic,* July 5, 2004, p. D1.

Washington Mutual Bank Branch
Source: AP/Worldwide

In then banking industry, Washington Mutual Bank clearly communicates through its servicescape its differentiation as a bank for consumers and families.[11] The bank has an area for children to play as well as a retail store offering financial books, software, and piggy banks, clearly differentiating this bank from those whose focus is commercial accounts or private, upscale banking (see Exhibit 11.1).

In another context, the servicescape has been used as a major point of differentiation for PETsMART in the introduction of its innovative PETsHotel concept.[12] The hotels, which offer overnight care as well as day care for pets, are designed very differently from typical kennels or veterinary facilities. They feature a lobby area, colorful play areas, comfortable sleeping rooms, television, a "bone booth" for calling in, and another amenities that give the facilities a more residential, homelike appeal than traditional kennels have.

The design of a physical setting can also differentiate one area of a service organization from another. For example, in the hotel industry, one large hotel may have several levels of dining possibilities, each signaled by differences in design. Price differentiation is also often partially achieved through variations in physical setting. Bigger rooms with more physical amenities cost more, just as larger seats with more leg room (generally in first class) are more expensive on an airplane. A development in movie theaters is the addition of luxury screening rooms with club chairs and waiters.[13] Taking advantage of this alternative, customers who are willing to pay a higher price to see the same film can experience the service in an entirely different environment.

FRAMEWORK FOR UNDERSTANDING SERVICESCAPE EFFECTS ON BEHAVIOR

Although it is useful from a strategic point of view to think about the multiple roles of the servicescape and how they interact, making actual decisions about servicescape design requires an understanding of why the effects occur and how to manage them. The next sections of the chapter present a framework or model of environment and behavior relationships in service settings.

The Underlying Framework

The framework for understanding servicescape effects on behavior follows from basic *stimulus–organism–response* theory. In the framework the multidimensional environment is the *stimulus,* consumers and employees are the *organisms* that respond to the stimuli, and behaviors directed at the environment are the *responses.* The assumptions are that dimensions of the servicescape will impact customers and employees and that they will behave in certain ways depending on their internal reactions to the servicescape.

A specific example will help illustrate the theory in action. Assume there is a cookie cart that is parked outside the student union on campus. The cart is colorful and playful in design, and an aroma of baking cookies wafts from it. The design and the aroma are two elements of the servicescape that will impact customers in some way. Now assume you are a hungry student, just out of class, strolling across campus. The fun design of the cart attracts your attention, and simultaneously you smell baking cookies. The fun design and the delicious smell cause you to feel happy, relaxed, and hungry at the same time. You are attracted to the cart and decide to buy a cookie because you have another class to attend before lunch. The movement toward the cart and the purchase of a cookie are behaviors directed at the servicescape. Depending on how much time you have, you may even choose to converse with the vendor or other customers standing around munching cookies, other forms of behavior directed at the servicescape.

The framework shown in Figure 11.2 is detailed in the next sections. It represents a comprehensive stimulus–organism–response model that recognizes complex dimensions of the environment, impacts on multiple parties (customers, employees, and their interactions), multiple types of internal responses (cognitive, emotional, and physiological), and a variety of individual and social behaviors that can result.

Our discussion of the framework will begin on the right side of the model with *behaviors.* Next we will explain and develop the *internal responses* portion of the model. Finally we will turn to the dimensions of the *environment* and the holistic perception of the environment.

Behaviors in the Servicescape

That human behavior is influenced by the physical setting in which it occurs is essentially a truism. Interestingly, however, until the 1960s psychologists largely ignored the effects of physical setting in their attempts to predict and explain behavior. Since that time, a large and steadily growing body of literature within the field of environmental psychology has addressed the relationships between human beings and their built environments. Recent marketing focus on the customer experience has also drawn attention to the effects of physical spaces and design on customer behavior.[14]

FIGURE 11.2   **A Framework for Understanding Environment–User Relationships in Service Organizations**

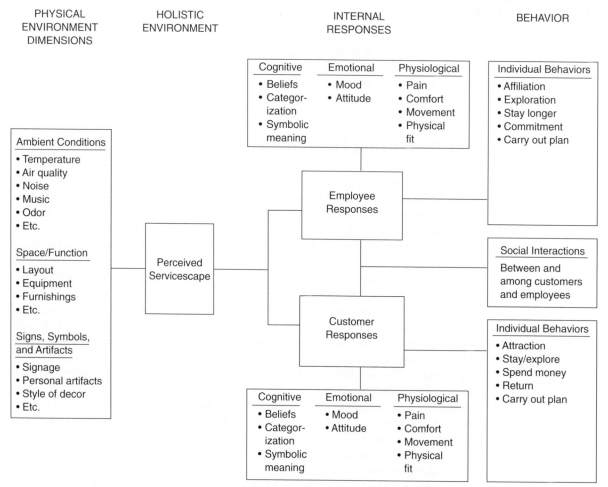

Source: Adapted from M. J. Bitner, "Servicescapes: The Impact of Physical Surroundings on Customers and Employees," *Journal of Marketing* 56 (April 1992), pp. 57–71. Reprinted with permission of the American Marketing Association.

Individual Behaviors

Environmental psychologists suggest that individuals react to places with two general, and opposite, forms of behavior: approach and avoidance. Approach behaviors include all positive behaviors that might be directed at a particular place, such as desire to stay, explore, work, and affiliate.[15] Avoidance behaviors reflect the opposite—a desire not to stay, to explore, to work, or to affiliate. In a study of consumers in retail environments, researchers found that approach behaviors (including shopping enjoyment, returning, attraction and friendliness toward others, spending money, time spent browsing, and exploration of the store) were influenced by perceptions of the environment.[16] At one 7-Eleven store the owners played "elevator music" to drive away the youthful market segment that was detracting from the store's image. And our cookie cart example is reminiscent of cinnamon roll bakeries in malls that attract patrons through the power of smell.

FIGURE 11.3
**Social interactions
are defined partially
by the configuration
of the servicescape.**

Source: Carnival Cruise Lines.

In addition to attracting or deterring entry, the servicescape can actually influence the degree of success that consumers and employees experience in executing their plans once inside. Each individual comes to a particular service organization with a goal or purpose that may be aided or hindered by the setting. NBA basketball fans are aided in their enjoyment of the game by adequate, easy-access parking; clear signage directing them to their seats; efficient food service; and clean restrooms. The ability of employees to do their jobs effectively is also influenced by the servicescape. Adequate space, proper equipment, and comfortable temperature and air quality all contribute to an employee's comfort and job satisfaction, causing him or her to be more productive, stay longer, and affiliate positively with coworkers.

Social Interactions

In addition to its effects on their individual behaviors, the servicescape influences the nature and quality of customer and employee interactions, most directly in interpersonal services. It has been stated that "all social interaction is affected by the physical container in which it occurs."[17] The "physical container" can affect the nature of social interaction in terms of the duration of interaction and the actual progression of events. In many service situations, a firm may want to ensure a particular progression of events (a "standard script") and limit the duration of the service. Environmental variables such as physical proximity, seating arrangements, size, and flexibility can define the possibilities and limits of social episodes such as those occurring between customers and employees, or customers and other customers. The Carnival Cruise Line photo shown in Figure 11.3 illustrates how the design of the servicescape can help define the social rules, conventions, and expectations in force in a given setting, thus serving to define the nature of social interaction.[18] The close physical proximity of passengers on the sunbathing deck will in and of itself prescribe certain patterns of behavior. This vacation is not designed for a social recluse! Some researchers have implied that recurring social behavior patterns are associated with particular physical settings and that when people encounter typical settings, their social behaviors can be predicted.[19]

Examples of how environments shape social interactions—and how these interactions in turn influence the environment—are abundant.[20] Even casual observation of the retail phenomenon "Nike Town Chicago" (Exhibit 11.2) shows how this form of "entertainment retail" shapes the behaviors of consumers but at the same time allows them to interpret and create their own realities and experiences.[21] In a river-rafting trip, the "wilderness servicescape" profoundly influences the behaviors, interactions, and total experiences of rafting consumers and their guides. In this case the natural, and for the most part uncontrollable, environment is the setting for the service.[22]

Internal Responses to the Servicescape

Employees and customers respond to dimensions of their physical surroundings cognitively, emotionally, and physiologically, and those responses are what influence their behaviors in the environment (as shown in the middle portion of Figure 11.2). In other words, the perceived servicescape does not directly *cause* people to behave in certain ways. Although the internal responses are discussed independently here, they are clearly interdependent: A person's beliefs about a place, a cognitive response, may well influence the person's emotional response, and vice versa. For example, patients who come into a dentist's office that is designed to calm and sooth their anxieties (emotional responses) may believe as a result that the dentist is caring and competent (cognitive responses).

Environment and Cognition

The perceived servicescape can have an effect on people's beliefs about a place and their beliefs about the people and products found in that place. In a sense the servicescape can be viewed as a form of nonverbal communication, imparting meaning through what is called "object language."[23] For example, particular environmental cues such as the type of office furniture and decor and the apparel worn by the lawyer may influence a potential client's beliefs about whether the lawyer is successful, expensive, and trustworthy. In a consumer study, variations in descriptions of store atmospheres were found to alter beliefs about a product (perfume) sold in the store.[24] Another study showed that a travel agent's office decor affected customer attributions and beliefs about the travel agent's behavior.[25] Travel agents whose facilities were more organized and professional were viewed more positively than were those whose facilities were disorganized and unprofessional.

In other cases, perceptions of the servicescape may simply help people distinguish a firm by influencing how it is categorized. The overall perception of the servicescape enables the consumer or employee to categorize the firm mentally. Research shows that in the restaurant industry a particular configuration of environmental cues suggests "fast food," whereas another configuration suggests "elegant sit-down restaurant."[26] In such situations, environmental cues serve as a shortcut device that enables customers to categorize and distinguish among types of restaurants.

Environment and Emotion

In addition to influencing beliefs, the perceived servicescape can directly elicit emotional responses that, in turn, influence behaviors. Just being in a particular place can make a person feel happy, lighthearted, and relaxed, whereas being in another place may make that person feel sad, depressed, and gloomy. The colors, decor, music, and other elements of the atmosphere can have an unexplainable and sometimes very

Exhibit 11.2 NIKE TOWN CHICAGO

"Nike Town Chicago is built as a theater, where our consumers are the audience participating in the production. Nike Town gives us the opportunity to explore and experiment with innovative ways to connect with our consumers." (Nike press release)

Nike Town Chicago (NTC) is the embodiment of Nike's corporate tagline "Just Do It." NTC and other Nike Towns around the United States epitomize the role of servicescape design in building the brand, providing customers with a way to interact with the brand, and making Nike come alive. NTC represents the height of retail theater.

So what is so special about NTC? What sets it apart from other retail environments? First, NTC is a showcase for the full range of Nike products. A common reaction of consumers is that they had no idea Nike made and carried all of the products displayed. And every designed element of the servicescape encourages impulsive behavior, inviting instant gratification. But the prices are very high—higher than prices on the same items in other stores. This is by design. Here the servicescape and the experience of NTC are meant to build the brand—not necessarily to sell the products and especially not to compete with other Nike stores and dealers.

When consumers enter NTC, they are struck by the extensive array of products. The first floor of the store has an open-air feel that gives the sense of a small-town shopping district, complete with cobblestone streets and manhole covers. Statues and framed photos of celebrities, large fish tanks, a video pond that projects the illusion of water and underwater scenes, and exhibit cases containing products and memorabilia greet the visiting customers. Visitors are also struck by the immensity of the store, which occupies three full stories.

As they enter through the vestibule, they are greeted by framed pictures of Nike sports celebrity endorsers and a unique display of athletic shoes with a banner over them proclaiming "There Is No Finish Line." The theme of "touching greatness" is echoed throughout the store in

Nike Town Elicits Emotional Responses from Customers
Source: Courtesy of Nike, Inc.

framed photos, statues of famous athletes, and background sounds of basketball and other sports.

On the third floor consumers are provided aerial views of the store and can view the Air Jordan Pavilion—a shrine to Michael Jordan. Kids' pavilions are also on the third floor, as well as cased exhibits showing the history of the Nike brand.

From the detail of door handles and railing supports cast in the shape of the distinctive Nike swoosh logo to the expansiveness of the multistory photograph of Jordan, NTC embodies the Nike brand. The space is the brand—the customers create their own relationship with it through experiencing the servicescape.

Source: J. F. Sherry Jr., "The Soul of the Company Store: Nike Town Chicago and the Emplaced Brandscape," in *Servicescapes: The Concept of Place in Contemporary Markets,* ed. J. F. Sherry Jr. (Chicago: NTC/Contemporary Publishing Company, 1998), pp. 109–46. Copyright © 1998 by NTC Business Books. Reprinted by permission of NTC Contemporary Books. The initial quotation is from "Nike Town Comes to Chicago," Nike press release, July 2, 1992, as quoted in ibid., p. 109.

subconsciousness effect on the moods of people in the place. For some people, certain environmental stimuli (noises, smells) common in a dental office can bring on immediate feelings of fear and anxiety. In very different contexts, the marble interior and grandeur of the Supreme Court buildings in Washington, D.C., call up feelings of pride and awe and respect; lively music and bright decor in a local night spot may cause people to feel excited and happy. In all these examples, the response from the consumer probably does not involve thinking but, rather, is just an unexplained feeling. Consumers' responses to Nike Town Chicago (Exhibit 11.2) are in large part emotional.

REI (Recreational Equipment, Inc.) provides another example of emotional connection through architectural design and the servicescape. At its flagship store in Seattle, the company has created an experience for consumers that includes a climbing mountain, a bicycle track, and walking trails. Its store in Minnesota has a cross-country ski trail around it. REI, through its servicescape design, is simulating the experiences and emotions that customers associate with its products, reinforcing a strong approach response to its stores.

Environmental psychologists have researched people's emotional responses to physical settings.[27] They have concluded that any environment, whether natural or engineered, will elicit emotions that can be captured by two basic dimensions: (1) pleasure/displeasure and (2) degree of arousal (amount of stimulation or excitement). Servicescapes that are both pleasant and arousing would be termed *exciting,* whereas those that are pleasant and nonarousing, or sleepy, would be termed *relaxing.* Unpleasant servicescapes that are arousing would be called *distressing,* whereas unpleasant, sleepy servicescapes would be *gloomy.* These basic emotional responses to environments can be used to begin predicting the expected behaviors of consumers and employees who find themselves in a particular type of place.

Environment and Physiology

The perceived servicescape may also affect people in purely physiological ways. Noise that is too loud may cause physical discomfort, the temperature of a room may cause people to shiver or perspire, the air quality may make it difficult to breathe, and the glare of lighting may decrease ability to see and may cause physical pain. All these physical responses may, in turn, directly influence whether people stay in and enjoy a particular environment. It is well known that the comfort of seating in a restaurant influences how long people stay. The hard seats in a fast-food restaurant cause most people to leave within a predictable period of time, whereas the soft, cozy chairs in some Starbucks coffee shops have the opposite effect, encouraging people to stay. Similarly, environmental design and related physiological responses affect whether employees can perform their job functions well.

A vast amount of research in engineering and design has addressed human physiological responses to ambient conditions as well as physiological responses to equipment design.[28] Such research fits under the rubric of *human factors design* or *ergonomics.* Human factors research systematically applies relevant information about human capabilities and limitations to the design of items and procedures that people use. For example, Choice Hotels International targeted empty-nester couples and senior citizens in the redesign of many of the rooms in its Rodeway and EconoLodge brands. A significant percentage of the rooms in these hotels were converted to senior-friendly suites with brighter lighting, larger-button telephones and TV remotes, and grab bars in the showers.[29] Wall switches have lights so they can be found easily at night. To help people with arthritis, doors have lever handles instead of knobs so that every door and every drawer in the room can be opened with a fist rather than requiring hand and wrist dexterity.

Variations in Individual Responses

In general, people respond to the environment in the ways just described—cognitively, emotionally, physiologically—and their responses influence how they behave in the environment. However, the response will not be the same for every individual, every time. Personality differences as well as temporary conditions such as moods or the purpose for being there can cause variations in how people respond to the servicescape.[30]

One personality trait that has been shown to affect how people respond to environments is *arousal seeking*. Arousal seekers enjoy and look for high levels of stimulation, whereas arousal avoiders prefer lower levels of stimulation. Thus an arousal avoider in a loud, bright disco with flashing neon might show strong dislike for the environment, whereas an arousal seeker would be very happy. In a related vein, it has been suggested that some people are better *screeners* of environmental stimuli than others.[31] Screeners of stimuli would be able to experience a high level of stimulation but not be affected by it. Nonscreeners would be highly affected and might exhibit extreme responses even to low levels of stimulation.

The particular purpose for being in a servicescape can also affect a person's response to it. A person who is on an airplane for a one-hour flight will likely be less affected by the atmosphere on the plane than will the traveler who is embarking on a 10-hour overseas flight. Similarly, a day-surgery hospital patient will likely be less sensitive and demanding of the hospital environment than would a patient who is spending two weeks in the hospital. And a person who is staying at a resort hotel for a business meeting will respond differently to the environment than will a couple on their honeymoon.

Temporary mood states can also cause people to respond differently to environmental stimuli. A person who is feeling frustrated and fatigued after a long day at work is likely to be affected differently by a highly arousing restaurant than the person would be after a relaxing three-day weekend.

Environmental Dimensions of the Servicescape

The preceding sections have described customer and employee behaviors in the servicescape and the three primary responses—cognitive, emotional, and physiological—that lead to those behaviors. In this section we turn to the complex mix of environmental features that influence these responses and behaviors (the left portion of Figure 11.2). Specifically, environmental dimensions of the physical surroundings can include all the objective physical factors that can be controlled by the firm to enhance (or constrain) employee and customer actions. There is an endless list of possibilities: lighting, color, signage, textures, quality of materials, style of furnishings, layout, wall decor, temperature, and so on. In Figure 11.2 and in the discussion that follows here, the hundreds of potential elements have been categorized into three composite dimensions: *ambient conditions; spatial layout and functionality;* and *signs, symbols, and artifacts.* Exhibit 11.3 illustrates how the Mayo Clinic took into consideration all these dimensions in designing its hospital to accommodate patients, doctors, employees, and visitors.

Although we discuss the three dimensions separately, environmental psychology explains that people respond to their environments holistically. That is, although individuals perceive discrete stimuli (for example, they can perceive noise level, color, and

Exhibit 11.3 DESIGNING THE MAYO CLINIC HOSPITAL

In 1998 Mayo opened the Mayo Clinic Hospital in Scotts-dale, Arizona, the first hospital planned, designed, and built by Mayo Clinic. Located on a 210-acre site, the hospital houses 178 hospital rooms on five floors. More than 250 physicians; 950 nursing, technical, and support staff; and 300 volunteers work at the facility.

What is unique about this hospital facility is the tremendous care that was taken in its design to serve the needs of patients, doctors, staff, and visitors. The hospital is designed as a "healing environment" focused on patient needs, and focus groups were held with all constituents to determine how the hospital should be designed to facilitate this overall goal. A quotation from the Mayo brothers (founders of the clinic) captures the underlying belief that supported the design of the hospital: "The best interest of the patient is the only interest to be considered." This statement lies at the foundation of all Mayo does, even today, more than 100 years after the Mayo brothers began their practice of medicine. To focus on the best interests of the patient also requires acknowledgment of the needs of the care providers and the patient's family and friend support system. All these interests were clearly considered in the design of the hospital.

A FIVE-STORY ATRIUM LOW-STRESS ENTRY

As patients and others enter the Mayo Hospital, they encounter a five-story enclosed atrium, reminiscent of a luxury hotel lobby. A grand piano sits in the lobby, and volunteers play beautiful, relaxing music throughout the day. An abundance of plants and glass gives the lobby a natural feel and provides a welcoming atmosphere. On entering, visitors see the elevator bank directly in front of them across the atrium, so there is no stress in figuring out where to go.

Mayo Hospital Lobby
Source: Photo courtesy of Mayo Clinic Scottsdale

ALL PATIENT AND VISITOR SERVICES ARE TOGETHER

All services needed by patients and their families (information desk, cafeteria, chapel, patient admissions, gift shop)

decor as distinct elements), it is the total configuration of stimuli that determines their reactions to a place. Hence, though the dimensions of the environment are defined independently in the following sections, it is important to recognize that they are perceived by employees and customers as a holistic pattern of interdependent stimuli. The holistic response is shown in Figure 11.2 as the "perceived servicescape."

Ambient Conditions

Ambient conditions include background characteristics of the environment such as temperature, lighting, noise, music, scent, and color. All these factors can profoundly affect how people feel, think, and respond to a particular service establishment. For example, a number of studies have documented the effects of music on consumers' perceptions of products, their perceptions of how long they have waited for service, and the amount of money they spend.[32] When there is music, shoppers tend to perceive

are located around the atrium, easily visible and accessible. A sense of peace and quiet permeates the lobby—all by deliberate design to reduce stress and promote caring and wellness. There is no confusion here and very little of the atmosphere of a typical hospital entry.

ROOMS ARE DESIGNED AROUND PATIENT NEEDS AND FEELINGS

On disembarking the elevators to go to patient rooms, people again sense relaxation and peace in the environment. As the doors open, patients and guests face a five-story wall of paned glass with views out to the desert and mountains that ring the hospital site. As one progresses left or right down well-marked corridors to the patient rooms, the atmosphere becomes even quieter. Rooms (all of them private) are arranged in 12-bed pods surrounding a nursing station. Nurses are within 20 steps of any patient room. Nurses and other attendants use cell phones—there is no paging system with constant announcements, as in many hospitals.

The rooms themselves have interesting features, some designed by patients. For example, rooms contain a multishelf display area on which patients can put cards, flowers, and other personal items. Fold-out, cushioned bed-chairs are in each room so family members can nap or even spend the night with their loved ones. Visitors are never told they must leave. The rooms are arranged with consideration to what patients see from the beds, where they spend the most time. For example, special attention is paid to the ceilings, which patients view while flat on their backs; all rooms have windows; and a white board on the wall at the foot of each bed displays important information that patients want to know (like the name of the nurse on duty, the date, the room phone number, and other information).

DEPARTMENTS THAT WORK TOGETHER ARE ADJACENT

Another interesting design feature in this hospital is that departments that work together are housed very close to each other to facilitate communication and to reduce walking time between areas. This important feature allows caregivers to spend more time with patients and also lessens employee fatigue.

MAXIMIZE NURSES' TIME WITH PATIENTS

A critical element in the recovery of patients is the quality of care they are given by nurses. Many of the Mayo Clinic Hospital design features facilitate the quality of nursing care. The pod design puts nurses close to their patients; the white boards in the rooms allow easy communication; and the accessible placement of supplies and relevant departments help maximize the time nurses spend with patients.

It is clear that the design of the Mayo Hospital takes into account the critical importance of the servicescape in facilitating Mayo's primary goal: patient healing. All parties' voices were heard, and the place itself provides an environment that promotes well-being for patients, visitors, doctors, nurses, and other staff.

Sources: *Teamwork at Mayo: An Experiment in Cooperative Individualism* (Rochester, MN: Mayo Press, 1998); http://www.mayo.edu; author's personal tour of the Mayo Clinic Hospital in Scottsdale.

that they spend less time shopping and in line than when there is no music. Slower music tempos at lower volumes tend to make people shop more leisurely, and in some cases, they spend more. In the Mayo Hospital lobby, piano music serves to reduce stress (see Exhibit 11.3). Shoppers also spend more time when the music "fits" the product or matches their musical tastes. Other studies have similarly shown the effects of scent on consumer responses.[33] Scent in bakeries, coffee shops, and tobacco shops, for example, can be used to draw people in, and pleasant scents can increase lingering time. The presence of a scent can reduce perceptions of time spent and improve store evaluations.

The effects of ambient conditions are especially noticeable when they are extreme. For example, people attending a symphony in a hall in which the air conditioning has failed and the air is hot and stuffy will be uncomfortable, and their discomfort will be reflected in how they feel about the concert. If the temperature and air quality were within a comfort tolerance zone, these ambient factors would probably go unnoticed. Ambient conditions also have a greater effect when the customer or employee spends considerable time in the servicescape. The impact of temperature, music, odors, and colors builds over time. Another instance in which ambient conditions will be particularly influential is when they conflict with what the customer or employee expects. As a general rule, ambient conditions affect the five senses. Sometimes such dimensions may be totally imperceptible (gases, chemicals, infrasound) yet have profound effects, particularly on employees who spend long hours in the environment.

Spatial Layout and Functionality

Because service environments generally exist to fulfill specific purposes or needs of customers, spatial layout and functionality of the physical surroundings are particularly important. *Spatial layout* refers to the ways in which machinery, equipment, and furnishings are arranged, the size and shape of those items, and the spatial relationships among them. *Functionality* refers to the ability of the same items to facilitate the accomplishment of customer and employee goals. Previous examples in this chapter illustrate the layout and functionality dimensions of the servicescape; for example the Carnival ad in Figure 11.3, and the design of the Mayo Hospital (Exhibit 11.3).

The spatial layout and functionality of the environment are particularly important for customers in self-service environments, where they must perform the service on their own and cannot rely on employees to assist them. Thus the functionality of an ATM machine and of self-serve restaurants, gasoline pumps, and Internet shopping are critical to success and customer satisfaction.

The importance of facility layout is particularly apparent in retail, hospitality, and leisure settings, where research shows it can influence customer satisfaction, store performance, and consumer search behavior.[34]

Signs, Symbols, and Artifacts

Many items in the physical environment serve as explicit or implicit signals that communicate about the place to its users. Signs displayed on the exterior and interior of a structure are examples of explicit communicators. They can be used as labels (name of company, name of department, and so on), for directional purposes (entrances, exits), and to communicate rules of behavior (no smoking, children must be accompanied by an adult). Adequate signs have even been shown to reduce perceived crowding and stress.

Other environmental symbols and artifacts may communicate less directly than signs, giving implicit cues to users about the meaning of the place and norms and expectations for behavior in the place. Quality construction materials, artwork, certificates and photographs, floor coverings, and personal objects displayed in the environment can all communicate symbolic meaning and create an overall aesthetic impression. The meanings attached to environmental symbols and artifacts are culturally embedded, as illustrated in this chapter's Global Feature. Restaurant managers in the United States, for example, know that white tablecloths and subdued lighting symbolically convey full service and relatively high prices, whereas counter service, plastic furnishings, and bright lighting symbolize the opposite. In U.S. office environments, certain cues such as desk size and placement symbolize status and may be used to reinforce professional image.[35]

Signs, symbols, and artifacts are particularly important in forming first impressions and for communicating service concepts. When customers are unfamiliar with a particular service establishment, they look for environmental cues to help them catego-

People's reactions to elements of the physical environment and design are shaped to a large degree by culture and expectations they have formed through their life experiences, dominated by the culture they live in. Just think of one design element—color—and the variety of uses it has across cultures. Consider the commonly used earth tones in the decor of Japanese restaurants around the world compared with the glossy reds that are so evident in Chinese restaurants. Other cultural differences—personal space requirements, social distance preferences, sensitivity to crowding—can affect how consumers experience servicescapes around the world.

McDonald's Corporation recognizes these culturally defined expectations in allowing its franchisees around the world tremendous freedom in designing their servicescapes. In most McDonald's franchises, a large percentage of the ownership is retained locally. Employees are nationals, and marketing strategies reflect local consumers' buying and preference patterns. In all cases, the restaurant is a "community institution," involved in social causes as well as local events.

McDonald's strategy is to have its restaurants worldwide reflect the cultures and communities in which they are found—to mirror the communities they serve. At the same time that it allows this creative energy to flourish in design and marketing strategies, McDonald's is extremely tight on its operating procedures and menu standards.

Although the golden arches are always present, a brief tour around the globe shows the wide variation in McDonald's face to the community:

- Bologna, Italy: In Bologna, known as the "City of Arches" for hundreds of years, McDonald's has taken on the weathered, crafted look of the neighboring historic arches. Even the floor in the restaurant was done by hand, using old-world techniques. The restaurant used local architects and artists to bring the local architectural feel to the golden arches.

- Paris, France: Near the Sorbonne in Paris, the local McDonald's reflects its studious neighbor. The servicescape there has the look of a leather-bound library with books, statues, and heavy wood furniture.

- Salen, Sweden: On the slopes of Lindvallen Resort in Salen, you can find the world's first "ski-thru" restaurant, named McSki, located next to the main ski lift. The building is different from any other McDonald's restaurant, built in a typical mountain style with wood panels and natural stone from the surroundings. Skiers can simply glide to the counter without taking off their skis, or they can be seated indoors or out.

Source: Bill Bachmann/The Image Works, Inc.

continued

- Beijing, China: McDonald's restaurants here have become a "place to hang out," very different from the truly "fast-food" role they play in the United States. They are part of the community, serving young and old, families and couples. Customers can be seen lingering for long periods of time, relaxing, chatting, reading, enjoying the music, or celebrating birthdays. Teenagers and young couples even find the restaurants to be very romantic environments. The emphasis on a Chinese-style family atmosphere is apparent from the interior walls of local restaurants, which are covered by posters emphasizing family values.

- Tokyo, Japan: Although some McDonald's restaurants in Japan are located in prime real-estate districts such as the Ginza in Tokyo, many others are situated near major train stations or other high-traffic locations. The emphasis at these locations is on convenience and speed, not on comfort or socializing. Many of these locations have little frontage space and limited seating. Customers frequently stand while eating, or they may sit on stools at narrow counters. Even the elite Ginza location has few seats. Some locations have a small ordering and service area on the first floor, with limited seating (still primarily stools rather than tables and chairs) on the second floor. Young people—from teenagers to schoolchildren—are a common sight in Japanese McDonald's.

Sources: *Golden Arches East: McDonald's in East Asia,* ed. J. L. Watson (Stanford, CA: Stanford University Press, 1997); "A Unique Peak," *Franchise Times* 3, no. 4 (1997), p. 46; "McDonald's Turns Up the Heat on Fast Food," Video Case Series accompanying C. L. Bovee, M. J. Houston, and J. V. Thill, *Marketing,* 2nd ed. (New York: McGraw-Hill, 1995).

rize the place and form their expectations. A study of dentists' offices found that consumers use the environment, in particular its style of decoration and level of quality, as a cue to the competence and manner of the service provider.[36] Another interesting study explored the roles of ethnicity and sexual orientation on consumers' interpretation of symbols within consumption environments. Specifically, the study found that people of Jewish descent observe particular symbols in places that encourage them to feel at home and approach those places.[37] The same study found that homosexuals were also drawn to environments that included particular symbols and artifacts that they identified with. In the presence of other symbols, these groups felt unwelcome or even discriminated against.

GUIDELINES FOR PHYSICAL EVIDENCE STRATEGY

To this point in the chapter we have presented ideas, frameworks, and psychological models for understanding the effects of physical evidence and most specifically the effects of the physical facility or servicescape. In this section we suggest some general guidelines for an effective physical evidence strategy.[38]

Recognize the Strategic Impact of Physical Evidence

Physical evidence can play a prominent role in determining service quality expectations and perceptions. For some organizations, just acknowledging the impact of physical evidence is a major first step. After this step they can take advantage of the potential of physical evidence and plan strategically.

For an evidence strategy to be effective, it must be linked clearly to the organization's overall goals and vision. Thus planners must know what those goals are and then determine how the physical evidence strategy can support them. At a minimum, the basic service concept must be defined, the target markets (both internal and external) identified, and the firm's broad vision of its future known. Because many evidence decisions are relatively permanent and costly (particularly servicescape decisions), they must be planned and executed deliberately.

Blueprint the Physical Evidence of Service

The next step is to map the service. Everyone should be able to see the service process and the existing elements of physical evidence. An effective way to depict service evidence is through the service blueprint. (Service blueprinting was presented in detail in Chapter 9.) Although service blueprints clearly have multiple purposes, they can be particularly useful in visually capturing physical evidence opportunities. People, process, and physical evidence can all be seen in the blueprint. Firms can read the actions involved in service delivery, the complexity of the process, the points of human interaction that provide evidence opportunities, and the tangible representations present at each step. To make the blueprint even more useful, photographs or videotape of the process can be added to develop a photographic blueprint that provides a vivid picture of physical evidence from the customer's point of view.

Clarify Strategic Roles of the Servicescape

Early in the chapter we discussed the varying roles played by the servicescape and how firms could locate themselves in the typology shown in Table 11.3 to begin to identify their roles. For example, a child care company would locate itself in the "elaborate, interpersonal" cell of the matrix and quickly see that its servicescape decisions would be relatively complex and that the servicescape strategy (1) would have to consider the needs of both the children and the service providers and (2) could impact marketing, organizational behavior, and consumer satisfaction goals.

Sometimes the servicescape may have no role in service delivery or marketing from the customer's point of view, such as in telecommunications services or utilities. Clarifying the roles played by the servicescape in a particular situation will aid in identifying opportunities and deciding who needs to be consulted in making facility design decisions. Clarifying the strategic role of the servicescape also forces recognition of the importance of the servicescape in creating customer experiences.

Assess and Identify Physical Evidence Opportunities

Once the current forms of evidence and the roles of the servicescape are understood, possible changes and improvements can be identified. One question to ask is, Are there missed opportunities to provide service evidence? The service blueprint of an insurance or utility service may show that little if any evidence of service is ever provided to the customer. A strategy might then be developed to provide more evidence of service to show customers exactly what they are paying for. Speedi-Lube, our opening example, effectively used this approach in providing multiple forms of evidence to make car maintenance service more tangible to the consumer.

Or it may be discovered that the evidence provided is sending messages that do not enhance the firm's image or goals or that do not match customer expectations. For example, a restaurant might find that its high-price menu cues are not consistent with the design of the restaurant, which suggests "family dining" to its intended market segment. Either the pricing or the facility design would need to be changed, depending on the restaurant's overall strategy.

Another set of questions addresses whether the current physical evidence of service suits the needs and preferences of the target market. To begin answering such questions, the framework for understanding environment–user relationships (Figure 11.2) and the research approaches suggested in this chapter could be employed. And finally, does the evidence strategy take into account the needs (sometimes incompatible) of both customers and employees? This question is particularly relevant in making decisions regarding the servicescape.

Be Prepared to Update and Modernize the Evidence

Some aspects of the evidence, particularly the servicescape, require frequent or at least periodic updating and modernizing. Even if the vision, goals, and objectives of the company do not change, time itself takes a toll on physical evidence, necessitating change and modernization. Clearly, an element of fashion is involved, and over time different colors, designs, and styles may come to communicate different messages. Organizations obviously understand this concept when it comes to advertising strategy, but sometimes they overlook other elements of physical evidence.

Work Cross-Functionally

In presenting itself to the consumer, a service firm is concerned with communicating a desired image, with sending consistent and compatible messages through all forms of evidence, and with providing the type of service evidence the target customers want and can understand. Frequently, however, physical evidence decisions are made over time and by various functions within the organization. For example, decisions regarding employee uniforms may be made by the human resources area, servicescape design decisions may be made by the facilities management group, process design decisions are most frequently made by operations managers, and advertising and pricing decisions may be made by the marketing department. Thus it is not surprising that the physical evidence of service may at times be less than consistent. Service blueprinting can be a valuable tool for communicating within the firm, identifying existing service evidence, and providing a springboard for changing or providing new forms of physical evidence.

A multifunction team approach to physical evidence strategy is often necessary, particularly for making decisions about the servicescape. It has been said that "Facility planning and management…is a problem-solving activity that lies on the boundaries between architecture, interior space planning and product design, organizational [and consumer] behavior, planning and environmental psychology."[39]

Summary

In this chapter we explored the roles of physical evidence in forming customer and employee perceptions and shaping customer experiences. Because services are intangible and because they are often produced and consumed at the same time, they can be difficult to comprehend or evaluate before their purchase. The physical evidence of the service thus serves as a primary cue for setting customer expectations before purchase. These tangible cues, particularly the servicescape, also influence customers' responses as they experience the service. Because customers and employees often interact in the servicescape, the physical surroundings also influence employees and the nature of employee–customer interactions.

The chapter focused primarily on the servicescape—the physical surroundings or the physical facility where the service is produced, delivered, and consumed. We presented typology of servicescapes that illustrated their range of complexity and usage. By locating itself in the appropriate cell of the typology, an organization can quickly see who needs to be consulted regarding servicescape decisions, what objectives might be achieved through careful design of the facility, and how complex the decisions are likely to be. General strategic roles of the servicescape were also described. The servicescape can serve as a package (a "visual metaphor" for the service itself), a facilitator in aiding the accomplishment of customer and employee goals, a socializer in prescribing behaviors in the environment, and a differentiator to distinguish the organization from its competitors.

With this grounding in the importance of physical evidence, in particular the servicescape, we presented a general framework for understanding servicescape effects on employee and customer behaviors. The servicescape can affect the approach and avoidance behaviors of individual customers and employees as well as their social interactions. These behavioral responses come about because the physical environment influences (1) people's beliefs or cognitions about the service organization, (2) their feelings or emotions in response to the place, and (3) their actual physiological reactions while in the physical facility. The chapter also pointed out that individuals may respond differently to the servicescape depending on their personality traits, the mood they are in, or the goals they are trying to accomplish.

Three categories of environmental dimensions capture the complex nature of the servicescape: ambient conditions; spatial layout and functionality; and signs, symbols, and artifacts. These dimensions affect people's beliefs, emotions, and physical responses, causing them to behave in certain ways while in the servicescape.

Given the importance of physical evidence and its potentially powerful influence on both customers and employees, it is important for firms to think strategically about the management of the tangible evidence of service. The impact of physical evidence and design decisions needs to be researched and planned as part of the marketing strategy. The chapter concluded with specific guidelines for physical evidence strategy. If physical evidence is researched, planned, and implemented effectively, key problems leading to service quality shortcomings can be avoided. Through careful thinking about physical evidence decisions, an organization can avoid miscommunicating to customers via incompatible or inconsistent evidence or overpromising and raising customer expectations unrealistically. Beyond its role in helping avoid these negative outcomes, an effective physical evidence strategy can play a critically important role in communicating to customers and in guiding them in understanding the firm's offerings and setting up accurate expectations. During the service experience, physical evidence plays a major role in creating memorable outcomes and emotional connections with customers.

Discussion Questions	1. What is physical evidence, and why have we devoted an entire chapter to it in a marketing text?
	2. Describe and give an example of how servicescapes play each of the following strategic roles: package, facilitator, socializer, and differentiator.
	3. Imagine that you own an independent copying and printing shop (similar to Kinko's). In which cell would you locate your business in the typology of

servicescapes shown in Table 11.3? What are the implications for designing your physical facility?

4. How can an effective physical evidence strategy help close provider gap 2? Explain.

5. Why are both customers and employees included in the framework for understanding servicescape effects on behavior (Figure 11.2)? What types of behaviors are influenced by the servicescape according to the framework? Think of examples.

6. Using your own experiences, give examples of times when you have been affected cognitively, emotionally, and physiologically by elements of the servicescape (in any service context).

7. Why is everyone not affected in exactly the same way by the servicescape?

8. Describe the physical environment of your favorite restaurant in terms of the three categories of servicescape dimensions: ambient conditions; spatial layout and functionality; and signs, symbols, and artifacts.

9. Imagine that you are serving as a consultant to a local health club. How would you advise the health club to begin the process of developing an effective physical evidence strategy?

Exercises

1. Choose two very different firms (different market segments or service levels) in the same industry. Observe both establishments. Describe the service "package" in both cases. How does the package help distinguish the two firms? Do you believe that the package sets accurate expectations for what the firm delivers? Is either firm overpromising through the manner in which its servicescape (or other types of physical evidence) communicates with customers?

2. Think of a particular service organization (it can be a class project company, the company you work for, or some other organization) for which you believe physical evidence is particularly important in communicating with and satisfying customers. Prepare the text of a presentation you would give to the manager of that organization to convince him or her of the importance of physical evidence in the organization's marketing strategy.

3. Create a photographic blueprint for a service of your choice.

4. Choose a service organization and collect all forms of physical evidence that the organization uses to communicate with its customers. If customers see the firm's facility, also take a photo of the servicescape. Analyze the evidence in terms of compatibility, consistency, and whether it overpromises or underpromises what the firm can deliver.

5. Visit the websites of several service providers. Does the physical evidence of the website portray an image consistent with other forms of evidence provided by the organizations?

Notes

1. The term *servicescape* used throughout this chapter, and much of the content of this chapter, are based, with permission, on M. J. Bitner, "Servicescapes: The Impact of Physical Surroundings on Customers and Employees," *Journal of Marketing* 56 (April 1992), pp. 57–71. For recent contributions to this topic, see *Servicescapes: The Concept of Place in Contemporary Markets,* ed. J. F. Sherry Jr. (Chicago: NTC/Contemporary Publishing Company, 1998); and M. J. Bitner, "The Servicescape," in *Handbook of Services Marketing and Management,* ed. T.

A. Swartz and D. Iacobucci (Thousand Oaks, CA: Sage Publications, 2000), pp. 37–50.

2. L. P. Carbone, *Clued In: How to Keep Customers Coming Back Again and Again* (Upper Saddle River, NJ: Prentice Hall, 2004). See also L. L. Berry and N. Bendapudi, "Clueing In Customers," *Harvard Business Review,* February 2003, pp. 100–106.

3. J. H. Gilmore and B. J. Pine II, "The Experience Is the Marketing," *Strategic Horizons,* 2002; B. J. Pine II and J. H. Gilmore, *The Experience Economy: Work Is Theater and Every Business Is a Stage* (Boston: Harvard Business School Press, 1999); B. H. Schmitt, *Experiential Marketing* (New York: The Free Press, 1999).

4. For reviews of environmental psychology, see D. Stokols and I. Altman, *Handbook of Environmental Psychology* (New York: John Wiley, 1987); S. Saegert and G. H. Winkel, "Environmental Psychology," *Annual Review of Psychology* 41 (1990), pp. 441–77; and E. Sundstrom, P. A. Bell, P. L. Busby, and C. Asmus, "Environmental Psychology 1989–1994," *Annual Review of Psychology* 47 (1996), pp. 485–512.

5. See M. R. Solomon, "Dressing for the Part: The Role of Costume in the Staging of the Servicescape," in Sherry, *Servicescapes: The Concept of Space in Contemporary Markets*; and A. Rafaeli, "Dress and Behavior of Customer Contact Employees: A Framework for Analysis," in *Advances in Services Marketing and Management,* vol. 2, ed. T. A. Swartz, D. E. Bowen, and S. W. Brown (Greenwich, CT: JAI Press, 1993), pp. 175–212.

6. S. Casey, "Federal Expressive," *www.ecompany.com,* May 2001, pp. 45–48.

7. D. Michaels, "Business-Class Warfare: Rival Airlines Scramble to Beat BA's Reclining Bed Seats," *The Wall Street Journal,* March 16, 2001, p. B1.

8. Ibid.; and British Airways' website, www.britishairways.com.

9. R. Chittum, "New Concepts in Lodging," *The Wall Street Journal,* October 8, 2003, p. B1.

10. A. Overholt, "Listening to Starbucks," *Fast Company,* July 2004, pp. 49–56.

11. E. Gately, "Washington Mutual Banking on Being Different," *Mesa Tribune,* March 25, 2001, p. B1.

12. www.petsmart.com, 2004.

13. "The New VIP Rooms," *The Wall Street Journal,* December 11, 1998, p. W1.

14. Carbone, *Clued In;* Berry and Bendapudi, "Clueing In Customers"; Gilmore and Pine, "Experience Is the Marketing"; Pine and Gilmore, *The Experience Economy;* Schmitt, *Experiential Marketing.*

15. A. Mehrabian and J. A. Russell, *An Approach to Environmental Psychology* (Cambridge, MA: Massachusetts Institute of Technology, 1974).

16. R. Donovan and J. Rossiter, "Store Atmosphere: An Environmental Psychology Approach," *Journal of Retailing* 58 (Spring 1982), pp. 34–57.

17. D. J. Bennett and J. D. Bennett, "Making the Scene," in *Social Psychology through Symbolic Interactionism,* ed. G. Stone and H. Farberman (Waltham, MA: Ginn-Blaisdell, 1970), pp. 190–96.

18. J. P. Forgas, *Social Episodes* (London: Academic Press, 1979).

19. R. G. Barker, *Ecological Psychology* (Stanford, CA: Stanford University Press, 1968).

20. For a number of excellent papers on this topic spanning a range from toy stores to bridal salons to cybermarketspaces to Japanese retail environments and others, see Sherry, *Servicescapes: The Concept of Place in Contemporary Markets.*

21. J. F. Sherry Jr., "The Soul of the Company Store: Nike Town Chicago and the Emplace Brandscape," in Sherry, *Servicescapes: The Concept of Place in Contemporary Markets,* pp. 81–108.

22. E. J. Arnould, L. L. Price, and P. Tierney, "The Wilderness Servicescape: An Ironic Commercial Landscape," in Sherry, *Servicescapes: The Concept of Place in Contemporary Markets,* pp. 403–38.

23. A. Rapoport, *The Meaning of the Built Environment* (Beverly Hills, CA: Sage Publications, 1982); R. G. Golledge, "Environmental Cognition," in Stokols and Altman, *Handbook of Environmental Psychology,* vol. 1, pp. 131–74.

24. M. P. Gardner and G. Siomkos, "Toward a Methodology for Assessing Effects of In-Store Atmospherics," in *Advances in Consumer Research,* vol. 13, ed. R. J. Lutz (Ann Arbor, MI: Association for Consumer Research, 1986), pp. 27–31.

25. M. J. Bitner, "Evaluating Service Encounters: The Effects of Physical Surroundings and Employee Responses," *Journal of Marketing* 54 (April 1990), pp. 69–82.

26. J. C. Ward, M. J. Bitner, and J. Barnes, "Measuring the Prototypicality and Meaning of Retail Environments," *Journal of Retailing* 68 (Summer 1992) pp. 194–220.

27. See, for example, Mehrabian and Russell, *An Approach to Environmental Psychology;* J. A. Russell and U. F. Lanius, "Adaptation Level and the Affective Appraisal of Environments," *Journal of Environmental Psychology* 4, no. 2 (1984), pp. 199–235; J. A. Russell and G. Pratt, "A Description of the Affective Quality Attributed to Environments," *Journal of Personality and Social Psychology* 38, no. 2 (1980), pp. 311–22; J. A. Russell and J. Snodgrass, "Emotion and the Environment," in Stokols and Altman, *Handbook of Environmental Psychology,* vol. 1, pp. 245–81; J. A. Russell, L. M. Ward, and G. Pratt, "Affective Quality Attributed to Environments," *Environment and Behavior* 13 (May 1981), pp. 259–88.

28. See, for example, M. S. Sanders and E. J. McCormick, *Human Factors in Engineering and Design,* 7th ed. (New York: McGraw-Hill, 1993); and D. J. Osborne, *Ergonomics at Work,* 2nd ed. (New York: John Wiley, 1987).

29. "Empty Nests, Full Pockets," *Brandweek,* September 23, 1996, pp. 36ff; and "Lodging Chain to Give Older Guests a Choice," *The Wall Street Journal,* February 19, 1993, p. B1.

30. Mehrabian and Russell, *An Approach to Environmental Psychology;* Russell and Snodgrass, "Emotion and the Environment."

31. A. Mehrabian, "Individual Differences in Stimulus Screening and Arousability," *Journal of Personality* 45, no. 2 (1977), pp. 237–50.

32. For recent research documenting the effects of music on consumers, see J. Baker, D. Grewal, and A. Parasuraman, "The Influence of Store Environment on Quality Inferences and Store Image," *Journal of the Academy of Marketing Science* 22 (Fall 1994), pp. 328–39; J. C. Chebat, C. Gelinas-Chebat, and P. Filliatrault, "Interactive Effects of Musical and Visual Cues on Time Perception: An Application to Waiting Lines in Banks," *Perceptual and Motor Skills* 77 (1993), pp. 995–1020; L. Dube, J. C. Chebat, and S. Morin, "The Effects of Background Music on Consumers' Desire to Affiliate in Buyer–Seller Interactions," *Psychology and Marketing* 12, no. 4 (1995), pp. 305–19; J. D. Herrington and L. M. Capella, "Effects of Music in Service Environments: A Field Study," *Journal of Services Marketing* 10, no. 2 (1996), pp. 26–41; J. D. Herrington and L. M. Capella, "Practical Applications of Music in Service Settings," *Journal of Services Marketing* 8, no. 3 (1994), pp. 50–65; M. K. Hui, L. Dube, and J. C. Chebat, "The Impact of Music on Consumers' Reactions to Waiting for Services," *Jour-*

nal of Retailing 73 (Spring 1997) pp. 87–104; A. S. Matila and J. Wirtz, "Congruency of Scent and Music as a Driver of In-Store Evaluations and Behavior," *Journal of Retailing* 77 (Summer 2001), pp. 273–89; L. Dube and S. Morin, "Background Music Pleasure and Store Evaluation: Intensity Effects and Psychological Mechanisms," *Journal of Business Research* 54 (November 2001), pp. 107–13; J. Bakec, A. Parasuraman, D. Grewal, and G. B. Voss, "The Influence of Multiple Store Environment Cues as Perceived Merchandise Value and Patronage Intentions," *Journal of Marketing* 66 (April 2002), pp. 120–41.

33. For recent research documenting the effects of scent on consumer responses, see D. J. Mitchell, B. E. Kahn, and S. C. Knasko, "There's Something in the Air: Effects of Congruent and Incongruent Ambient Odor on Consumer Decision Making," *Journal of Consumer Research* 22 (September 1995), pp. 229–38; and E. R. Spangenberg, A. E. Crowley, and P. W. Henderson, "Improving the Store Environment: Do Olfactory Cues Affect Evaluations and Behaviors?" *Journal of Marketing* 60 (April 1996), pp. 67–80.

34. See J. M. Sulek, M. R. Lind, and A. S. Marucheck, "The Impact of a Customer Service Intervention and Facility Design on Firm Performance," *Management Science* 41, no. 11 (1995), pp. 1763–73; P. A. Titus and P. B. Everett, "Consumer Wayfinding Tasks, Strategies, and Errors: An Exploratory Field Study," *Psychology and Marketing* 13, no. 3 (1996), pp. 265–90; C. Yoo, J. Park, and D. J. MacInnis, "Effects of Store Characteristics and In-Store Emotional Experiences on Store Attitude," *Journal of Business Research* 42 (1998), pp. 253–63; K. L. Wakefield and J. G. Blodgett, "The Effect of the Servicescape on Customers' Behavioral Intentions in Leisure Service Settings," *Journal of Services Marketing* 10, no. 6 (1996), pp. 45–61.

35. T. R. V. Davis, "The Influence of the Physical Environment in Offices," *Academy of Management Review* 9, no. 2 (1984), pp. 271–83.

36. J. C. Ward and J. P. Eaton, "Service Environments: The Effect of Quality and Decorative Style on Emotions, Expectations, and Attributions," in *Proceedings of the American Marketing Association Summer Educators' Conference,* eds. R. Achrol and A. Mitchell (Chicago: American Marketing Association 1994), pp. 333–34.

37. M. S. Rosenbaum, "The Symbolic Servicescape: Your Kind Is Welcomed Here," *Journal of Consumer Behaviour,* forthcoming.

38. This section is adapted from M. J. Bitner, "Managing the Evidence of Service," in *The Service Quality Handbook,* ed. E. E. Scheuing and W. F. Christopher (New York: AMACOM, 1993), pp. 358–70.

39. F. D. Becker, *Workspace* (New York: Praeger, 1981).

Part

5

DELIVERING AND PERFORMING SERVICE

In the gaps model of service quality, provider gap 3 (the Service Performance Gap) is the discrepancy between customer-driven service standards and actual service delivery (see the accompanying figure). Even when guidelines exist for performing service well and treating customers correctly, high-quality service performance is not a certainty. Part 5 deals with all the ways in which companies ensure that services are performed according to customer-defined designs and standards.

Provider Gap 3

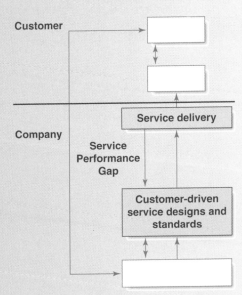

In Chapter 12, we focus on the key roles that employees play in service delivery and strategies that ensure they are effective in their roles. Issues of particular concern include employees who feel in conflict between customers and company management, the wrong employees, inadequate technology, inappropriate compensation and recognition, and lack of empowerment and teamwork.

In Chapter 13, we discuss the variability caused by customers. If customers do not perform appropriately—if they do not follow instructions or if they disturb other customers receiving service at the same time—service quality is jeopardized. Effective service organizations acknowledge the role of customer variability and develop strategies to teach customers to perform their roles appropriately.

Chapter 14 describes service delivery through intermediaries such as retailers, franchisees, agents and brokers, and electronic channels. Although some service companies have control over the delivery channel, many service companies depend on other organizations to provide service to the end customer. For this reason, firms must develop ways to either control or motivate these intermediaries to meet company goals and deliver consistent quality service.

Chapter 15 emphasizes the need to synchronize demand and capacity in service organizations in order to deliver consistent, high-quality service. Service organizations often face situations of over- or underdemand because they lack inventories to smooth demand. Marketing strategies for managing demand, such as price changes, advertising, promotion, and alternative service offerings, can help this challenge.

12

EMPLOYEES' ROLES IN SERVICE DELIVERY

This chapter's objectives are to

1. Demonstrate the importance of creating a service culture in which providing excellent service to both internal and external customers is a way of life.

2. Illustrate the critical importance of service employees in creating customer satisfaction and service quality.

3. Identify the challenges inherent in boundary-spanning roles.

4. Provide examples of strategies for creating customer-oriented service delivery through hiring the right people, developing employees to deliver service quality, providing needed support systems, and retaining the best service employees.

Employees Are the Service and the Brand

Noted service expert Leonard Berry has documented that investments in employee success are key drivers of sustained business success in companies as diverse as Charles Schwab, Midwest Express, USAA Insurance, Chick-fil-A, and Special Expeditions Travel.[1] Why is this true? Why do these companies choose to invest heavily in their employees?

For clues, consider the following true stories:

- On a long overseas Singapore Airlines flight, a restless toddler repeatedly dropped his pacifier. Every time the child would cry, and someone (the mother, another passenger, or a flight attendant) would retrieve the pacifier. Finally, one of the attendants picked up the pacifier, attached it to a ribbon, and sewed it to the child's shirt. The child and mother were happy, and passengers seated nearby gave the attendant a standing ovation.[2]

- A phone associate at Universal Card Services received a call from a husband whose wife, suffering from Alzheimer's disease, had vanished. The husband hoped that he could find his wife through tracing her use of her Universal Card. The phone associate placed a hold on the card and arranged to be called personally the moment there was any activity on the card. When it happened, about a week later, the associate contacted the husband, the doctor, and the police, who were then able to assist the missing woman and get her home.[3]

- At the Fairmont Hotel in San Francisco, a computer programmer made a room reservation for a discounted price. On arrival he discovered that all rooms were filled. The front desk clerk responded by sending him to the Sheraton and picking up his room charge, which was more than twice what he would have paid the Fairmont. He also paid for the guest's parking fee at the Fairmont and taxi fare to the new hotel, and threw in a free meal at the Fairmont as well.[4]

These stories illustrate the important roles played by service employees in creating satisfied customers and in building customer relationships. The frontline service providers in each example are enormously important to the success of the organizations they represent. They are responsible for understanding customer needs and for interpreting customer requirements in real time (as suggested by Figure 12.1). Leonard Berry has documented that in case after case, companies that represent sustained service success all recognize the critical importance of their employees.[5]

In this chapter we focus on service employees and human resource practices that facilitate delivery of quality services. The assumption is that even when customer expectations are well understood (gap 1) and services have been designed and specified to conform to those expectations (gap 2), there may still be discontinuities in service quality when the service is not delivered as specified. These discontinuities are labeled gap 3—the service performance gap—in the service quality framework. Because employees frequently deliver or perform the service, human resource issues are a major cause of this gap. By focusing on the critical role of service employees and by developing strategies that will lead to effective customer-oriented service, organizations can begin to close the service delivery gap.

The failure to deliver services as designed and specified can result from a number of employee and human performance factors: ineffective recruitment of service-oriented employees; role ambiguity and role conflict among contact employees; poor employee–technology–job fit; inappropriate evaluation and compensation systems; and lack of empowerment, perceived control, and teamwork. Prior to examining these factors and strategies for overcoming them, we begin the chapter with a discussion of service culture and its influence on employee behavior.

FIGURE 12.1
Service employees directly impact customers' satisfaction.

Source: John A. Rizzo/Getty Images.

SERVICE CULTURE

Before addressing the role of the employee in service delivery, we should look at the bigger picture. The behavior of employees in an organization will be heavily influenced by the culture of an organization, or the pervasive norms and values that shape individual and group behavior. *Corporate culture* has been defined as "the pattern of shared values and beliefs that give the members of an organization meaning, and provide them with the rules for behavior in the organization."[6] *Culture* has been defined more informally as "the way we do things around here."

Piglet in *Winnie the Pooh* might refer to culture as one of those things we sense "in an underneath sort of way." To understand at a personal level what corporate culture is, think of different places you have worked or organizations you have been a member of, such as churches, fraternities, schools, or associations. Your behavior and the behaviors of others were no doubt influenced by the underlying values, norms, and culture of the organization. Even when you first interview for a new job, you can begin to get a sense of the culture through talking to a number of employees and observing behavior. Once you are on the job, your formal training as well as informal observation of behavior will work together to give you a better picture of the organization's culture.

Experts have suggested that a customer-oriented, service-oriented organization will have at its heart a *service culture,* defined as "a culture where an appreciation for good service exists, and where giving good service to internal as well as ultimate, external customers is considered a natural way of life and one of the most important norms by everyone."[7] This very rich definition has many implications for employee behaviors. First, a service culture exists if there is an "appreciation for good service." This phrase does not mean that the company has an advertising campaign that stresses the importance of service, but "in that underneath sort of way" people know that good service is appreciated and valued. A second important point in this definition is that good service is given to internal as well as external customers.[8] It is not enough to promise excellent service to final customers; all people within the organization deserve the same kind of service. Finally, in a service culture good service is "a way of life" and it comes naturally because it is an important norm of the organization.

Service culture has been linked to competitive advantage in companies.[9] Why is it so important? No realistic amount of supervision would allow a firm to exercise sufficient control over *all* employee behavior. In many service settings, employees interact with customers with no management present. In such instances, the firm must rely on its service culture to influence employee thoughts, feelings, and behaviors.

Exhibiting Service Leadership

A strong service culture begins with leaders in the organization who demonstrate a passion for service excellence. Leonard Berry suggests that leaders of successful service firms tend to have similar core values, such as integrity, joy, and respect, and they "infuse those values into the fabric of the organization."[10] Leadership does not consist of bestowing a set of commands from a thick rulebook but, rather, the regular and consistent demonstration of one's values. Employees are more likely to embrace a service culture when they see management living out these values. Espoused values—what managers *say* the values are—tend to have less impact on employees than enacted values—what employees believe the values to be because of what they observe management actually *doing*.[11] That is, culture is what employees perceive that management *really* believes, and employees gain an understanding of what is important in the organization through the daily experiences they have with those people in key roles throughout the organization.

Developing a Service Culture

A service culture cannot be developed overnight, and there is no magic, easy way to sustain a service culture. The human resource and internal marketing practices discussed later in the chapter can help develop a service culture over time. If, however, an organization has a culture that is rooted in, product-, or operations-oriented government regulation–traditions, no single strategy will change it overnight. Hundreds of little (but significant) factors, not just one or two big factors, are required to build and sustain a service culture.[12] Successful companies such as Yellow Roadway Corporation and IBM Global Services have all found that it takes years of consistent, concerted effort to build a service culture and to shift the organization from its old patterns to new ways of doing business. Even for companies such as FedEx, Charles Schwab, Disney, and the Ritz-Carlton that started out with a strong service and customer focus, sustaining their established service cultures still takes constant attention to hundreds of details.

Transporting a Service Culture

Transporting a service culture through international business expansion is also very challenging. Attempting to "export" a corporate culture to another country creates additional issues. For instance, will the organization's service culture clash with a different *national* culture? If there is a clash, is it over *what* the actual values are, or over *how* they are to be enacted? If the issue is over what the values are, and they are core values critical to the firm's competitive advantage, then perhaps the company cannot be successful in that setting. If the issue is over how the values are enacted, then perhaps some service practices can be modified in the new setting. To illustrate, Four Seasons Hotels opened up a luxury hotel in Paris, France, in 1999.[13] As discussed in Chapter 10, Four Seasons has created seven globally uniform "SERVICE" standards that it expects of all its employees all over the world. The company has also identified several core values that they believe transcends national culture. One such value is to anticipate the guests' needs. This value has been enacted in the United States by leaving a coffeepot on the table in the hotel restaurant so that guests can help themselves whenever they like. However, at the Paris hotel restaurant, Four Seasons decided to never leave a coffeepot on the table; doing so would not be received favorably by French customers, who generally believe one should not have to pour coffee oneself. Four Seasons did not alter other practices; it continued, for example, its employee-of-the-month program as a way to provide recognition for exceptional service, even though such programs are not generally offered in France. These standards and values reflect Four Seasons's attempt to transport its service culture across national borders, but management is keenly aware that they need to carefully consider how these values are enacted in each hotel.

Although tremendous opportunities exist in the global marketplace, the many legal, cultural, and language barriers become particularly evident for services that depend on human interaction. Our Global Feature highlights some of the issues and experiences of several companies as they attempt to transport their service cultures.

THE CRITICAL IMPORTANCE OF SERVICE EMPLOYEES

An often-heard quotation about service organizations goes like this: "In a service organization, if you're not serving the customer, you'd better be serving someone who

Although international markets offer tremendous opportunities for growth, many companies find significant challenges when they attempt to transport their services to other countries. Services depend on people, are often delivered by people, and involve the interaction between employees and customers. Differences in values, norms of behavior, language, and even the definition of service become evident quickly and have implications for training, hiring, and incentives that can ultimately affect the success of the international expansion. Companies with strong service cultures are faced with the question of whether to try to replicate their culture and values in other countries or to adapt significantly. A few examples illustrate different approaches.

MCDONALD'S APPROACH

McDonald's has been very successful in its international expansion. In some ways it has remained very "American" in everything it does—people around the world want an American experience when they go to McDonald's. However, the company is sensitive to cultural differences as well. This subtle blending of the "McDonald's" way with adaptations to cultural nuances has resulted in great success. One way that McDonald's maintains its standards is through its Hamburger University, which is required training for *all* McDonald's employees worldwide before they can become managers. Each year approximately 3,000 employees from nearly 100 countries enroll and attend the Advanced Operations Course at HU, located in Oak Brook, Illinois. The curriculum is 80 percent devoted to communications and human relations skills. Because of the international scope of McDonald's, translators and electronic equipment enable professors to teach and communicate in 22 languages at one time. The result is that all managers in all countries have the same "ketchup in their veins," and the restaurant's basic human resources and operating philosophies remain fairly stable from operation to operation. Certain adaptations in decor, menu, and other areas of cultural differences are then allowed (see the Global Feature in Chapter 11 for some specific examples).

UPS'S EXPERIENCE

UPS has a strong culture built on employee productivity, highly standardized service delivery processes, and structured training. Their brown trucks and uniforms are instantly recognizable in the United States. In fact, in 2002 UPS launched the largest and most aggressive television and print advertising campaign in its nearly 100-year history around the tag line, "What Can Brown Do for You?" As it expanded into countries across Europe, UPS was surprised by some of the challenges of managing a global workforce. Here are some of the surprises: indignation in France, when drivers were told they could not have wine with lunch; protests in Britain, when drivers' dogs were banned from delivery trucks; and dismay in Spain, when it was found the brown UPS trucks resembled the local hearses.

DISNEY IN EUROPE

When Disney first expanded into Europe by opening EuroDisney near Paris, it also faced challenges and surprises. The highly structured, scripted, and customer-oriented approach that Disney used in the United States was not easily duplicated with European employees.

continued

In particular, the smiling, friendly, always customer-focused behaviors of Disney's U.S. workforce did not suit the experience and values of young French employees. In attempting to transport the Disney culture and experience to Europe, the company confronted clashing values and norms of behavior in the workplace that made the expansion difficult. Customers also needed to be "trained" in the Disney way—not all cultures are comfortable with waiting in long lines, for example. And not all cultures treat their children the same. For example, in the United States, families will spend lots of money at Disneyland on food, toys, and other things that their children "must" have. Some European cultures view this behavior as highly indulgent, so families will visit the park without buying much beyond the ticket for admission.

A U.S. LAW FIRM GOES TO THE UNITED KINGDOM

The professions such as law and medicine have well-established and quite unique practices across cultures. Pay rates, work styles, and business models can be quite different. So what happens when a law firm seeks to expand its services to another country? Unlike many U.S. law firms that tend to populate their international offices with American lawyers, Weil, Gotshal, and Manges, a New York firm, opened its offices in London by hiring primarily British solicitors who would function as a "firm within a firm." One of the biggest challenges was how to blend the very different American and British legal cultures. First, the U.S. lawyers at Weil, Gotshal, and Manges tend to be workaholics—commonly billing 2,500 hours a year, whereas in London a partner would bill a respectable 1,500 hours. Pay differences were also obvious—$650,000 on average for London partners, $900,000 for Americans. Conflict, rather than synergy, sometimes resulted from the deeply rooted cultural differences. Despite the challenges, the London office has done quite well; as of 2004, the office had more than 130 lawyers, became the second largest of the firm's worldwide offices, and received the "2004 U.S. Law Firm of the Year in London" award.

Sources: G. Flynn, "Can't Get This Big without HR Deluxe," *Personnel Journal* 75, no. 12 (December 1996), pp. 46–53; D. Milbank, "Can Europe Deliver?" *The Wall Street Journal,* September 30, 1994, pp. R15, R23; and P. M. Barrett, "Joining the Stampede to Europe, Law Firm Suffers a Few Bruises," *The Wall Street Journal,* April 27, 1999, p. A1.

is."[14] People—frontline employees and those supporting them from behind the scenes—are critical to the success of any service organization. The importance of people in the marketing of services is captured in the *people* element of the services marketing mix, which we described in Chapter 1 *as all the human actors who play a part in service delivery and thus influence the buyer's perceptions; namely, the firm's personnel, the customer, and other customers in the service environment.*

The key focus in this chapter is on customer-contact service employees because:

- They *are* the service.

- They *are* the organization in the customer's eyes.

- They *are* the brand.

- They *are* marketers.

In many cases, the contact employee *is the service*—there is nothing else. For example, in most personal and professional services (like haircutting, physical trainers, child care, cleaning/maintenance, limousine services, counseling, and legal services) the contact employee provides the entire service singlehandedly. The offering *is* the employee. Thus, investing in the employee to improve the service parallels making a direct investment in the improvement of a manufactured product.

Even if the contact employee doesn't perform the service entirely, he or she may still *personify the firm in the customer's eyes.* All the employees of a law firm or health clinic—from the professionals who provide the service to the receptionists and office staff—represent the firm to the client, and everything these individuals do or say can influence perceptions of the organization. Even off-duty employees, such as flight attendants or restaurant employees on a break, reflect on the organizations they represent. If they are unprofessional or make rude remarks about or to customers, customers' perceptions of the organization will suffer even though the employee is not on duty. The Disney Corporation insists that its employees maintain "onstage" attitudes and behaviors whenever they are in front of the public and that they relax these behaviors only when they are truly behind the scenes or "backstage" in underground tunnels where guests cannot see them in their off-duty times.

Service employees *are the brand.* An American Express financial advisor, a Nordstrom sales associate, a Southwest Airlines flight attendant—in each case, the primary image that a customer has of the firm is formed by the interactions the customer has with the employees of that firm. A customer sees American Express as a good provider of financial services if the employees she interacts with are knowledgeable, understanding, and concerned about her financial situation and goals. Similarly, a customer sees Nordstrom as a professional and empathetic company because of interactions he has with its sales associates. Even in a nonservice setting, Audi, an automobile manufacturer, recognizes the importance of its employees in representing and reinforcing the brand image of the company. As a result, Audi recruits service personnel at all levels whose psychological traits parallel and support the Audi image.[15] For example, Audi looks to hire employees who are not afraid to develop a personal relationship with customers. When looking for a technician, they are not just looking for someone who repairs cars well but also someone who is inclined to spend time interacting with customers and demonstrating empathy—characteristics that they want customers to associate with Audi. At Audi the brand image is not just built and maintained by the cars themselves and the advertising: It is a function of the people who work at Audi.

Because contact employees represent the organization and can directly influence customer satisfaction, they *perform the role of marketers.* They physically embody the product and are walking billboards from a promotional standpoint. Some service employees may also perform more traditional selling roles. For example, bank tellers are often called on to cross-sell bank products, a departure from the traditional teller role of operations function only. Whether acknowledged or not, whether actively selling or not, service employees perform marketing functions. They can perform these functions well, to the organization's advantage, or poorly, to the organization's detriment. In this chapter we examine frameworks, tools, and strategies for ensuring that service employees perform their marketing functions well.

The Services Triangle

Services marketing is about promises—promises made and promises kept to customers. A strategic framework known as the *services triangle* (illustrated in Figure 12.2) visually reinforces the importance of people in the ability of firms to keep their

FIGURE 12.2
The Services
Marketing Triangle

Source: Adapted from M. J. Bitner, "Building Service Relationships: It's All about Promises," *Journal of the Academy of Marketing Science* 23, 4 (1995), pp. 246–51; C. Gronroos, *Service Management and Marketing* (Lexington, MA: Lexington Books, 1990); and P. Kotler, *Marketing Management: Analysis, Planning, Implementation, and Control,* 8th ed. (Englewood Cliffs, NJ: Prentice Hall, 1994), p. 470.

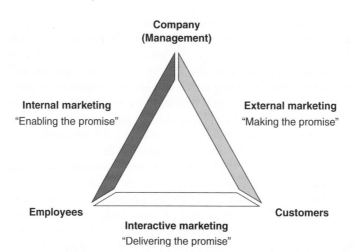

promises and succeed in building customer relationships.[16] The triangle shows the three interlinked groups that work together to develop, promote, and deliver services. These key players are labeled on the points of the triangle: the *company* (or SBU or department or "management"); the *customers;* and the *providers.* Providers can be the firm's employees, subcontractors, or outsourced entities who actually deliver the company's services. Between these three points on the triangle, three types of marketing must be successfully carried out for a service to succeed: external marketing, interactive marketing, and internal marketing.

On the right side of the triangle are the *external marketing* efforts that the firm engages in to set up its customers' expectations and make promises to customers regarding what is to be delivered. Anything or anyone that communicates to the customer before service delivery can be viewed as part of this external marketing function. But external marketing is just the beginning for services marketers: Promises made must be kept. On the bottom of the triangle is what has been termed *interactive marketing* or *real-time marketing.* Here is where promises are kept or broken by the firm's employees, subcontractors, or agents. People are critical at this juncture. If promises are not kept, customers become dissatisfied and eventually leave. The left side of the triangle suggests the critical role played by *internal marketing.* Management engages in these activities to aid the providers in their ability to deliver on the service promise: recruiting, training, motivating, rewarding, and providing equipment and technology. Unless service employees are able and willing to deliver on the promises made, the firm will not be successful, and the services triangle will collapse.

All three sides of the triangle are essential to complete the whole, and the sides of the triangle should be aligned. That is, what is promised through external marketing should be the same as what is delivered; and the enabling activities inside the organization should be aligned with what is expected of service providers. Strategies for aligning the triangle, particularly the strategies associated with internal marketing, are the subject of this chapter.

Employee Satisfaction, Customer Satisfaction, and Profits

Satisfied employees make for satisfied customers (and satisfied customers can, in turn, reinforce employees' sense of satisfaction in their jobs). Some researchers have even gone so far as to suggest that unless service employees are happy in their jobs, customer satisfaction will be difficult to achieve.[17]

Through their research with customers and employees in 28 different bank branches, Benjamin Schneider and David Bowen have shown that both a *climate for service* and a *climate for employee well-being* are highly correlated with overall customer perceptions of service quality.[18] That is, both service climate and human resource management experiences that *employees* have within their organizations are reflected in how *customers* experience the service. In a similar vein, Sears found customer satisfaction to be strongly related to employee turnover. In its stores with the highest customer satisfaction, employee turnover was 54 percent, whereas in stores with the lowest customer satisfaction, turnover was 83 percent.[19] Other research suggests that employees who feel they are treated fairly by their organizations will treat customers better, resulting in greater customer satisfaction.[20]

The underlying logic connecting employee satisfaction and loyalty to customer satisfaction and loyalty and ultimately profits is illustrated by the service profit chain shown in Figure 12.3.[21] In earlier chapters we focused on customer satisfaction and retention; here we focus on employee issues. The service profit chain suggests that there are critical linkages among internal service quality; employee satisfaction/productivity; the value of services provided to the customer; and ultimately customer satisfaction, retention, and profits.

Service profit chain researchers are careful to point out that the model does not suggest causality. That is, employee satisfaction does not *cause* customer satisfaction; rather the two are interrelated and feed off each other. The model does imply that companies that exhibit high levels of success on the elements of the model will be more successful and profitable than those that do not. This finding is borne out in other research, which reports that companies that manage people right will outperform by 30 to 40 percent companies that do not.[22] *Fortune* magazine also determined that the publicly traded companies making their list of the "100 Best Companies to Work for in America" delivered higher average annual returns to shareholders than did companies making up the Russell 3000, a general index of companies similar to the *Fortune* sample.[23]

The Effect of Employee Behaviors on Service Quality Dimensions

Customers' perceptions of service quality will be impacted by the customer-oriented behaviors of employees.[24] In fact, all of the five dimensions of service quality (reliability, responsiveness, assurance, empathy, and tangibles) can be influenced directly by service employees.

FIGURE 12.3   **The Service Profit Chain**

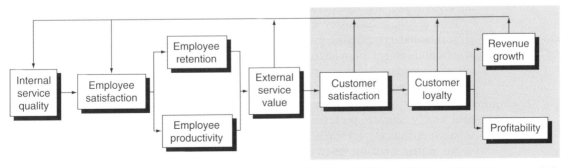

Delivering the service as promised—*reliability*—is often totally within the control of frontline employees. Even in the case of automated services (such as ATMs, automated ticketing machines, or self-serve and pay gasoline pumps), behind-the-scenes employees are critical for making sure all the systems are working properly. When services fail or errors are made, employees are essential for setting things right and using their judgment to determine the best course of action for service recovery.

Frontline employees directly influence customer perceptions of *responsiveness* through their personal willingness to help and their promptness in serving customers. Consider the range of responses you receive from different retail store clerks when you need help finding a particular item of clothing. One employee may ignore your presence, whereas another offers to help you search and calls other stores to locate the item. One may help you immediately and efficiently, whereas another may move slowly in accommodating even the simplest request.

The *assurance* dimension of service quality is highly dependent on employees' ability to communicate their credibility and to inspire trust and confidence. The reputation of the organization will help, but in the end, individual employees with whom the customer interacts confirm and build trust in the organization or detract from its reputation and ultimately destroy trust. For startup or relatively unknown organizations, credibility, trust, and confidence will be tied totally to employee actions.

It is difficult to imagine how an organization would deliver "caring, individualized attention" to customers independent of its employees. *Empathy* implies that employees will pay attention, listen, adapt, and be flexible in delivering what individual customers need.[25] For example, research documents that when employees are customer oriented, have good rapport with customers, and exhibit perceptive and attentive listening skills, customers will evaluate the service more highly and be more likely to return.[26] Employee appearance and dress are important aspects of the *tangibles* dimension of quality, along with many other factors that are independent of service employees (the service facility, decor, brochures, signage, and so on).

BOUNDARY-SPANNING ROLES

Our focus in this chapter is on frontline service employees who interact directly with customers, although much of what is described and recommended can be applied to internal service employees as well. The frontline service employees are referred to as *boundary spanners* because they operate at the organization's boundary. As indicated in Figure 12.4, boundary spanners provide a link between the external customer and environment and the internal operations of the organization. They serve a critical function in understanding, filtering, and interpreting information and resources to and from the organization and its external constituencies.

Who are these boundary spanners? What types of people and positions comprise critical boundary-spanning roles? Their skills and experience cover the full spectrum of jobs and careers. In industries such as fast food, hotels, telecommunication, and retail, the boundary spanners are the least skilled, lowest-paid employees in the organization. They are order-takers, front-desk employees, telephone operators, store clerks, truck drivers, and delivery people. In other industries, boundary spanners are well-paid, highly educated professionals—for example, doctors, lawyers, accountants, consultants, architects, and teachers.

No matter what the level of skill or pay, boundary-spanning positions are often high-stress jobs. In addition to mental and physical skills, these positions require ex-

FIGURE 12.4
Boundary spanners interact with and provide information to both internal and external constituents.

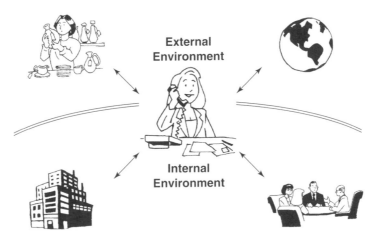

traordinary levels of emotional labor, frequently demand an ability to handle interpersonal and interorganizational conflict, and call on the employee to make real-time trade-offs between quality and productivity on the job. These stresses and trade-offs can result in failure to deliver services as specified, which widens gap 3.

Emotional Labor

The term *emotional labor* was coined by Arlie Hochschild to refer to the labor that goes beyond the physical or mental skills needed to deliver quality service.[27] It means delivering smiles, making eye contact, showing sincere interest, and engaging in friendly conversation with people who are essentially strangers and who may or may not ever be seen again. Friendliness, courtesy, empathy, and responsiveness directed toward customers all require huge amounts of emotional labor from the frontline employees who shoulder this responsibility for the organization. Emotional labor draws on people's feelings (often requiring them to suppress their true feelings) to be effective in their jobs. A frontline service employee who is having a bad day or is not feeling just right is still expected to put on the face of the organization when dealing with customers. One of the clearest examples of emotional labor is the story (probably apocryphal) of the flight attendant who was approached by a businessman who said, "Let's have a smile." "Okay," she replied, "I'll tell you what, first you smile and then I'll smile, okay?" He smiled. "Good," she said. "Now hold that for 15 hours," and walked away.[28]

Many of the strategies we will discuss later in the chapter can help organizations and employees deal with the realities of emotional labor on the job. For the organization, such strategies include carefully selecting people who can handle emotional stress, training them in needed skills (like listening and problem solving), and teaching or giving them coping abilities and strategies (via job rotation, scheduled breaks, teamwork, or other techniques).[29] Our Strategy Insight describes additional emotional labor strategies that service firms employ.

Customer contact employees in service positions are often required to display (or, conversely, to withhold display of) a variety of emotions. Such employees are increasingly being required to invest personal identity and expression into their work in many situations. The following description suggests how the experience of the service employee, even in the most routine of occupations, is markedly different from that of the traditional manufacturing worker:

> The assembly-line worker could openly hate his job, despise his supervisor, and even dislike his co-workers, and while this might be an unpleasant state of affairs, if he [completes] his assigned tasks efficiently, his attitude [is] his own problem. For the service worker, inhabiting the job means, at the very least, pretending to like it, and, at most, actually bringing his whole self into the job, liking it, and genuinely caring about the people with whom he interacts.*

Emotional labor occurs more often when the job requires frequent contact and long durations of voice contact or face-to-face contact with customers. These employees often need emotional management to deal with such situations. Later in this chapter we suggest many strategies for organizations to create an environment that helps employees deal with the realities of emotional labor on the job. Here we present some specific strategies that some firms are using to more directly support employee efforts to manage their emotions in the face of demanding, obnoxious, or unruly customers.

SCREENING FOR EMOTIONAL LABOR ABILITIES

Many firms look to hire employees who are well suited to meet the emotional labor requirements of the job. Dungarvin, an organization that provides a variety of services to people who have mental and physical disabilities, displays a realistic job preview on its website to indicate to prospective employees the emotional labor requirements. In doing so, Dungarvin's intent is to identify applicants who are comfortable with the emotional demands required of employees who must regularly interact with clients with special needs. Paychex, a provider of payroll services for small businesses, also provides a realistic job preview, in part, to gauge whether a prospective employee is well suited for the emotional labor required in various positions within the company. Delta Airlines puts prospective employees through simulated customer contact exercises to see the kind of friendliness and warmth they naturally communicate. Such practices help in identifying employees whose values, background, and personalities match the job's emotional labor requirements.

TEACHING EMOTIONAL MANAGEMENT SKILLS AND APPROPRIATE BEHAVIORS

Most customer contact employees are taught that they need to be courteous to customers. However, customers have no obligation to return empathy or courtesy. In situations in which customers exercise the privilege of "the customer is always right," employees face real challenges in suppressing their true feelings. Seldom do firms provide much training to assist employees in facing these challenges. Arlie Hochschild identifies two forms of emotional labor: *surface acting*, in which employees pretend to feel emotions that are not really present and, in doing so, deliberately and consciously create an outward appearance in order to deceive others; and *deep acting*, in which employees attempt to experience the real feelings they must express to the customer, including the active invocation of "thoughts, images, and memories to induce the associated emotion."** Hair salon stylists and airline flight attendants are often encouraged to engage in deep-acting strategies such as imagining that the client is a friend or that the passenger is a frightened little child flying for the first time. Often, in order to persuade clients to buy hair products or color their hair, stylists have to moderate their language or behavior; they may use deep acting to justify these behaviors to themselves. Companies may also train employees in how to avoid absorbing a customer's bad mood, perhaps by having employees spend hours role-playing to suppress their natural reaction to return negative customer emotions with their own negative emotions.

CAREFULLY CONSTRUCTING THE PHYSICAL WORK ENVIRONMENT

As we discussed in Chapter 11, the environment in which the service is delivered can have an impact on employee behaviors and emotions. MedAire, a company that provides telephone consultation to airlines when medical emergencies arise on flights, regularly has employees in the midst of life-threatening situations. To reduce the stress that MedAire employees face on a daily basis, the company designed its Tempe, Arizona, office with an open floor plan so that all employees are able to look through windows to see trees, grass, and cars driving by. In Seattle, Amazon.com employees are housed in a T-shaped building with many more windows than a traditional rectangular-shaped building has, which allows them to enjoy views of Puget Sound, the downtown Seattle skyline, and the calm blue surface of Lake Washington. Taking this idea one step further, JetBlue Airways, a low-fare airline based in New York City, allows its reservation agents to work from home rather than requiring them to sit all day in an office call center.

ALLOWING EMPLOYEES TO VENT

Employees who must exert emotional labor often need to have an outlet to let off steam. Allowing employees to vent lets them get rid of their frustrations. If such venting is done in a group setting, it can provide emotional support and encouragement as well as allowing employees to see that others are experiencing the same problems and that they are not alone. If part of the work day (or week) is explicitly set aside to allow employees to share their frustrations, it delivers a message to employees that the company is aware of and acknowledges the emotional contribution that they have made. RitzCarlton, Wal-Mart, and other companies regularly set aside time for such venting. In addition to the cathartic benefit this experience can provide, other employees may reveal coping strategies that they have found useful.

PUTTING MANAGEMENT ON THE FRONT LINE

Customer contact employees often feel that management does not truly understand or appreciate the emotional labor they must expend. Managers should regularly be required to interact with customers. JetBlue Airways has its management team work alongside its customer service representative in fielding customers' phone calls. In addition to understanding what the issues are, managers are truly able to empathize with employees. Managers

continued

who do so not only have an appreciation for the emotional labor requirements of their employees, but they are also in a better position to serve as role models and mentors in using emotional management skills.

GIVING EMPLOYEES A BREAK

In situations in which an employee has just handled a particularly tough customer, especially if the employee has frequent and long durations of voice or face-to-face contact with customers, a particularly helpful strategy is to allow the employee a short break to regroup. Many companies with toll-free call centers rotate employees into different positions throughout the day so that they do not spend the entire time on the telephone with customers. Customer contact employees can be reenergized and refreshed after spending a little time away from the situation, even if they take only a few minutes to finish paperwork or complete some other job responsibility.

HANDING OFF DEMANDING CUSTOMERS TO MANAGERS

Some customers may be too much for an employee to handle. In such situations, to alleviate pressure on the customer contact employee, firms may shift responsibility for the interaction to managers. Wing Zone, a restaurant chain specializing in chicken wings, understands the stress that angry customers can cause on employees, many of whom are college students. A majority of the company's orders are taken over the phone, and employees—particularly those with little experience—are trained to simply hand off demanding customers to the nearest manager. And a manager who is unsuccessful in handling the situation is encouraged to direct such customers to the corporate office via a toll-free number.

*Quoted from C. L. Macdonald and C. Sirianni, *Working in the Service Society* (Philadelphia: Temple University Press, 1996), p. 4.

**Quoted from B. F. Ashforth and R. H. Humphrey, "Emotional Labor in Service Roles: The Influence of Identity," *Academy of Management Review* 18 (1993), p. 93.

Sources: J. Solomon, "Trying to Be Nice Is No Labor of Love," *The Wall Street Journal*, November 29, 1990, p. B1; A. Hochschild, *The Managed Heart: Commercialization of Human Feeling* (Berkeley: University of California Press, 1983); B. F. Ashforth and R. H. Humphrey, "Emotional Labor in Service Roles: The Influence of Identity," *Academy of Management Review* 18 (1993), p. 88–115; S. D. Pugh, "Service with a Smile: Emotional Contagion in the Service Encounter," *Academy of Management Journal* 44, no. 5 (2001), pp. 1018–27; A. A. Grandey, "When 'The Show Must Go On': Surface Acting and Deep Acting as Determinants of Emotional Exhaustion and Peer-Rated Service Delivery," *Academy of Management Journal* 46, no. 1 (2003), pp. 86–96; C. Salter, "And Now the Hard Part," *Fast Company* 82 (May 2004), 66–74.

Sources of Conflict

Frontline employees often face interpersonal and interorganizational conflicts on the job. Their frustration and confusion can, if left unattended, lead to stress, job dissatisfaction, a diminished ability to serve customers, and burnout.[30] Because they represent the customer to the organization and often need to manage a number of customers simultaneously, frontline employees inevitably have to deal with conflicts, including person/role conflicts, organization/client conflicts, and interclient conflicts, as suggested by Figure 12.5 and discussed in the next sections.[31]

FIGURE 12.5
Boundary-Spanning Workers Juggle Many Issues

- Person versus role
- Organization versus client
- Client versus client

Person/Role Conflicts

In some situations, boundary spanners feel conflicts between what they are asked to do and their own personalities, orientations, or values. In a society such as the United States, where equality and individualism are highly valued, service workers may feel role conflict when they are required to subordinate their feelings or beliefs, as when they are asked to live by the motto "The customer is always right—even when he is wrong." Sometimes there is a conflict between role requirements and the self-image or self-esteem of the employee. An Israeli service expert tells an example from that culture:

> In Israel, for instance, most buses are operated by one man, the driver, who is also responsible for selling tickets. No trays are installed in buses for the transferring of bus fare from passenger to driver, and the money is transferred directly. Bus drivers often complain about the humiliating experience of having to stretch out their hands like beggars in order to collect the fare. Another typical case in Israeli buses is when money changes hands and a coin falls down accidentally onto the bus floor. The question, who will bend down to lift the coin, the driver or the passenger, clearly reflects the driver's role conflict.[32]

Whoever stoops to pick up the coin is indicating subservient status.

Person/role conflict also arises when employees are required to wear specific clothing or change some aspect of their appearance to conform to the job requirements. A young lawyer, just out of school, may feel an internal conflict with his new role when his employer requires him to cut his long hair and trade his casual clothes for a three-piece suit.

Organization/Client Conflict

A more common type of conflict for frontline service employees is the conflict between their two bosses, the organization and the individual customer. Service employees are typically rewarded for following certain standards, rules, and procedures. Ideally these rules and standards are customer based, as described in Chapter 10. When they are not, or when a customer makes excessive demands, the employee has to choose whether to follow the rules or satisfy the demands. The conflict is greatest when the employee believes the organization is wrong in its policies and must decide

Technology Spotlight
Quality versus Productivity: How CRM Systems Help Employees

Providing quality service to individual customers while also being productive and efficient is an ongoing challenge for sales and service providers—the front line of the organization. These are the people who produce revenue and build customer relationships for the company. In many leading companies these employees are challenged daily to satisfy increasing numbers of customers more effectively and efficiently.

In recent years, sophisticated customer relationship management (CRM) software has helped make quality service achievable and efficient. Also known as "front-office automation," this type of software represents the fastest-growing segment of the software industry. The large players include the industry leader, Siebel Systems, as well as PeopleSoft, Oracle, SAP, and Nortel Networks. These big companies bought some of the early leaders in this industry—for instance, Vantive was bought by PeopleSoft and Clarify by Nortel. Smaller companies also serving this niche include E.Piphany, Interact Commerce, Kana, Onyx, and Vignette. All these competitors focus on providing software tools for increasing employee productivity in sales, service, and customer management.

How exactly do these CRM systems support sales and service people to make them more productive? AT&T's customer sales and service centers provide one example. Through software applications, calls coming into AT&T's centers are identified (by phone number and market segment) and routed to the right customer segment personnel even before the calls are answered. Employees get the calls that they are trained for and best able to handle. The software also allows the employee to view the entire account history of the caller, and this information is available on the employee's computer screen simultaneously with the incoming call. Employees have at their fingertips information on the wide variety of calling plans and other options available to customers. The person who answers the call is empowered to make decisions, answer questions, and encourage sales in ways that were totally impractical prior to this technology. As AT&T's front door, the employees in the customer sales and service centers are equipped to build customer relationships and ultimately increase revenues for the company. Once viewed as an expense, these employees are now viewed as a key to the company's growth, thanks to front-office automation. The technology allows employees to take the time to customize service and satisfy individual customers.

CRM is also revolutionizing the sales function. By providing detailed customer histories and integrated

whether to accommodate the client and risk losing a job, or to follow the policies. These conflicts are especially severe when service employees depend directly on the customer for income. For example, employees who depend on tips or commissions are likely to face greater levels of organization/client conflict because they have even greater incentives to identify with the customer.

Interclient Conflict

Sometimes conflict occurs for boundary spanners when incompatible expectations and requirements arise from two or more customers. This situation occurs most often when the service provider is serving customers in turn (a bank teller, a ticketing agent, a doctor) or is serving many customers simultaneously (teachers, entertainers).

When serving customers in turn, the provider may satisfy one customer by spending additional time, customizing the service, and being very flexible in meeting the customer's needs. Meanwhile, waiting customers are becoming dissatisfied because their needs are not being met in a timely way. Beyond the timing issue, different clients may prefer different modes of service delivery. Having to serve one client who prefers personal recognition and a degree of familiarity in the presence of another client who

service and pricing information, these tools allow the salesperson to be much more consultative and to add more value than in the past. IBM, for example, is implementing the most comprehensive integrated CRM software system in the world for its sales and service people worldwide. Using Siebel's eBusiness Applications, IBM's goal is to integrate the whole company around its customers so that anyone in the company can respond to the customer in a consistent manner with the same basic account information. This goal is no small task in a company with over 80,000 internal system users, 30,000 business partners, and millions of customers.

Although front-office CRM systems hold great promise and have provided tremendous bottom-line benefits for companies already, they come with their own, often significant, challenges. They can require major monetary and human investments. They often mandate integration of incompatible information systems, significant internal training costs, and incentives to be sure they are used effectively. Frequently they fail, at least on the initial try, for a variety of reasons. Some companies do not anticipate the amount of work involved, and many do not realize how resistant their employees will be to making the necessary changes. CRM projects also fail when they do not have the support of top management.

Even giant Microsoft faced significant challenges when it attempted to integrate all of its 36 distinct customer information applications worldwide. Microsoft underestimated the internal demands of such a large deployment and cut back on end user training at the wrong time. It learned that training (of both employees and even customers sometimes) is critical to the success of the technology. Despite some bumps in the road, however, the system soon began to pay for itself, allowing Microsoft service staff and salespeople to make decisions better and in a more timely fashion, satisfying customers and building the business.

Many companies now see implementation of front-office CRM software as not only a potential competitive advantage but also, in some cases, a requirement for survival. As customers encounter world-class service from companies like AT&T, FedEx, IBM, or Cisco, they come to expect it from others—even in different industries.

Sources: M. Boslet, "CRM: The Promise, The Peril, The Eye-Popping Price," *The Industry Standard,* August 6–13, 2001, pp. 61–65; L. M. Fisher, "Here Comes Front-Office Automation," *Strategy and Business* 13 (4th quarter 1998), pp. 53–65; "Inside Big Blue's CRM Transformation," *The Siebel Journal: Best Practices,* www.siebel.com, 2002.

is all business and would prefer little interpersonal interaction can also create conflict for the employee.

When serving many customers at the same time, employees often find it difficult or impossible to simultaneously serve the full range of needs of a group of heterogeneous customers. This type of conflict is readily apparent in any college classroom in which the instructor must meet a multitude of expectations and different preferences for formats and style.

Quality/Productivity Trade-Offs

Frontline service workers are asked to be both effective and efficient: They are expected to deliver satisfying service to customers and at the same time to be cost-effective and productive in what they do. A physician in an HMO, for example, is expected to deliver caring, quality, individualized service to her patients but at the same time to serve a certain number of patients within a specified time frame. A checker at a grocery store is expected to know his customers and to be polite and courteous, yet also to process the groceries accurately and move people through the line quickly. An architectural draftsperson is expected to create quality drawings, yet to produce a required quantity of drawings in a given period of time. These essential trade-offs between quality and quantity and between maximum effectiveness and efficiency place real-time demands and pressures on service employees.

Research suggests that these trade-offs are more difficult for service businesses than for manufacturing and packaged goods businesses and that pursuing goals of customer satisfaction and productivity simultaneously is particularly challenging in situations in which service employees are required to customize service offerings to meet customer needs.[33]

Jagdip Singh, a noted services researcher, has studied productivity and quality as two types of performance inherent in frontline service jobs.[34] He explains the difficult trade-offs that employees face and has developed ways to measure these two types of performance together with a theoretical model to predict the causes and consequences of these trade-offs. He finds that quality of job performance is particularly susceptible to burnout and job stress. He also finds that internal support from understanding managers and control over the job tasks can help employees in making quality and productivity trade-offs, avoiding burnout, and maintaining their performance. Technology is being used to an ever-greater degree to balance the quality/quantity trade-off to increase productivity of service workers and at the same time free them to provide higher-quality service for the customer (see the Technology Spotlight).

STRATEGIES FOR DELIVERING SERVICE QUALITY THROUGH PEOPLE

A complex combination of strategies is needed to ensure that service employees are willing and able to deliver quality services and that they stay motivated to perform in customer-oriented, service-minded ways. These strategies for enabling service promises are often referred to as *internal marketing,* as shown on the left side of Figure 12.2.[35] Even during slow economic times, the importance of attracting, developing, and retaining good people in knowledge- and service-based industries cannot be overemphasized, as *Fast Company* magazine suggested:

> When it comes to building great companies, the most urgent business challenge is finding and keeping great people. Sure a Web strategy is important, and the stock market is scary, but still the best companies know that people are the foundation of greatness.[36]

By approaching human resource decisions and strategies from the point of view that the primary goal is to motivate and enable employees to deliver customer-oriented promises successfully, an organization will move toward delivering service quality through its people. The strategies presented here are organized around four basic themes. To build a customer-oriented, service-minded workforce, an organization must (1) hire the right people, (2) develop people to deliver service quality, (3) provide the needed support systems, and (4) retain the best people. Within each of these basic strategies are a number of specific substrategies for accomplishing the goal, as shown in Figure 12.6.

Hire the Right People

To effectively deliver service quality, considerable attention should be focused on hiring and recruiting service personnel. Such attention is contrary to traditional practices in many service industries, where service personnel are the lowest on the corporate ladder and work for minimum wage. At the other end of the spectrum, in the professional services, the most important recruiting criteria are typically technical training, certifi-

FIGURE 12.6
Human Resource Strategies for Delivering Service Quality through People

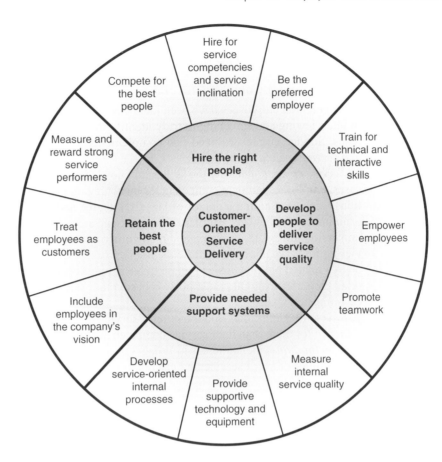

cations, and expertise. However, many organizations are now looking above and beyond the technical qualifications of applicants to assess their customer and service orientation as well. Figure 12.6 shows a number of ways to go about hiring the right people.

Compete for the Best People

To get the best people, an organization needs to identify them and compete with other organizations to hire them. Leonard Berry and A. Parasuraman refer to this approach as "competing for talent market share."[37] They suggest that firms act as marketers in their pursuit of the best employees, just as they use their marketing expertise to compete for customers. Firms that think of recruiting as a marketing activity will address issues of market (employee) segmentation, product (job) design, and promotion of job availability in ways that attract potential long-term employees. Washington Mutual, Cox Communication, the Limited, Time Warner, and other firms have changed the title of the head recruiting person to vice president of talent acquisition. Doing so recognizes the importance of the function and helps elevate the role to the strategic importance it deserves.[38]

A complementary strategy is to interview multiple employees for every position. At Southwest Airlines, the People Department (the name Southwest has given to what others call the human resources, or personnel, department) is relentless in its pursuit of talented employees. A quote from Southwest's long-time president, Herb Kelleher, illustrates the point: "The People Department came to me one day and said, 'We've interviewed 34 people for this ramp agent's position, and we're getting a little worried about the time and effort and cost that's going into it.' And I said if you have to interview 154 people to get the right person, do it."[39]

Hire for Service Competencies and Service Inclination

Once potential employees have been identified, organizations need to be conscientious in interviewing and screening to truly identify the best people from the pool of candidates. Service employees need two complementary capacities: *service competencies* and *service inclination*.[40]

Service competencies are the skills and knowledge necessary to do the job. In many cases, employees validate competencies by achieving particular degrees and certifications, such as attaining a doctor of law (JD) degree and passing the relevant state bar examination for lawyers. Similar rites of passage are required of doctors, airline pilots, university professors, teachers, and many other job seekers before they are ever interviewed for service jobs in their fields. In other cases, service competencies may not be degree related but may instead relate to basic intelligence or physical requirements. A retail clerk, for example, must possess basic math skills and the potential to operate a cash register.

Given the multidimensional nature of service quality, service employees should be screened for more than their service competencies. They must also be screened for *service inclination*—their interest in doing service-related work—which is reflected in their attitudes toward service and orientation toward serving customers and others on the job. Self-selection suggests that most service jobs will draw applicants with some level of service inclination and that most employees in service organizations are inclined toward service. However, some employees clearly have a greater service inclination than others. Research has shown that service effectiveness is correlated with service-oriented personality characteristics such as helpfulness, thoughtfulness, and sociability.[41] An ideal selection process for service employees assesses both service competencies and service inclination, resulting in employee hires who are high on both dimensions.[42]

In addition to traditional employment interviews, many firms use innovative approaches to assessing service inclination and other personal characteristics that fit the organization's needs. Southwest Airlines looks for people who are compassionate and who have common sense, a sense of humor, a "can do" attitude, and an egalitarian sense of themselves (they think in terms of "we" rather than "me"). One way the company assesses these service inclinations is by interviewing potential flight attendants in groups to see how they interact with each other. Pilots are also interviewed in groups to assess their teamwork skills, a critical factor above and beyond the essential technical skills they are required to possess.[43]

In many cases a component of the selection process will include a form of work simulation that allows employees to demonstrate how they would actually perform on the job. A simulation may take the form of role-playing or a series of exercises that parallel the demands of the actual job. In addition to being a good way to assess potential employee abilities, simulations can give the potential hire a better view of what the job is actually like. Those candidates who do not like what they experience can back out of the applicant pool before being hired and then finding out the job is not what they had expected.

Be the Preferred Employer

One way to attract the best people is to be known as the preferred employer in a particular industry or in a particular location. Rosenbluth International, headquartered in

Exhibit 12.1

SAS INSTITUTE IS A PREFERRED EMPLOYER IN ITS INDUSTRY

SAS Institute is the world's largest privately held software company, with revenue growing by double-digit percentages for the past 24 years. The hugely profitable company is known for its statistical software products that allow its more than 37,000 customers in over 111 countries to analyze huge amounts of data, searching for categories, patterns, and trends. Among its customers are the U.S. Census Bureau. Ninety percent of the *Fortune* 500 are SAS customers.

Although relatively unknown, SAS ranked number 8 in *Fortune*'s list of the 100 best companies to work for in America in 2004. SAS has also been on *Working Mothers* magazine's list of 100 best companies for which to work for 12 years, and it has earned numerous other awards for quality and excellence. Employee turnover is approximately 4 percent in an industry that averages more than 20 percent. SAS receives hundreds of applications for each job opening despite the current highly competitive environment in which most companies are scrambling to find qualified technical people. Here are some of the reasons employees love working for this company, and why it can be considered a preferred employer in its industry.

Founder, chairman, and majority owner of the company James H. Goodnight "likes happy people," and he believes strongly that happy employees are more productive, produce better quality for customers, and ultimately stay in their jobs longer, thus producing long-term benefits for the company.

A quote from the company's website captures SAS's philosophy about its people: "If you treat employees as if they make a difference to the company, they will make a difference to the company." The company invests heavily in its people, and the best performers at SAS seldom leave to work for competitors.

The wooded 200-acre campus outside Raleigh, North Carolina, is first of all a beautiful setting in which to work. Every employee has a private office, and much attention is given to flexible, family-oriented policies. A 35-hour schedule is promoted, flexible hours are available, and the company provides two top-quality day care centers with very reasonable prices on site. Employees get an extra week of paid vacation between Christmas and New Year's. Break rooms are stocked with free sodas, fresh fruit, candies, and pastries. Employees receive discounts on properties they purchase near SAS as well as discounts on country club memberships and tuition breaks at Cary Academy, a private school. Year-end bonuses and profit sharing are also valued perks.

Although SAS provides all these amenities, other types of perks are deliberately excluded. For example, stock options, common in the high-technology industry, are not offered at SAS; nor are tuition reimbursements or sales commissions. Mr. Goodnight's belief is that these types of benefits encourage autonomy, competition, and high-pressure tactics that are not compatible with the organization's culture. Neither are salaries notably high. Despite these absences, professional and technical people are clamoring to work for SAS because of the unique benefits and family-oriented culture it perpetuates.

Jeffrey Pfeffer, Stanford University business professor, says that his research on SAS leads him to conclude that the company has found an enormously effective business model. He figures that the approximately $50 million a year the company saves in low turnover pays for the family-friendly practices and corporate amenities.

Sources: T. D. Schellhardt, "An Idyllic Workplace under a Tycoon's Thumb," *The Wall Street Journal*, November 23, 1998, p. B1; R. Levering and M. Moskowitz, "The 100 Best Companies to Work For," *Fortune*, January 12, 2004, pp. 56–80; www.sasinstitute.com, 2002.

Philadelphia, enjoys a reputation as a preferred employer. With 56 offices in 15 countries around the world, Rosenbluth International provides corporate travel management for its clients. The company's president, Hal Rosenbluth, has gone so far as to say, "We don't believe that the customer can come first unless our people come first. If our people don't come first, then they're not free to focus on our clients; they're worrying about other kinds of things."[44]

Other strategies that support a goal of being the preferred employer include extensive training, career and advancement opportunities, excellent internal support, attractive incentives, and quality goods and services that employees are proud to be associated with. Exhibit 12.1 illustrates why SAS Institute is a preferred employer in the statistical software industry. Employees who work for SAS are, for the most part, professional or technical and well paid. In a very different industry, dominated by lower-paid workers, Marriott International has a stated company goal of being the "preferred employer" in its industry. Marriott uses employee stock options, a social services referral network, day care, welfare-to-work training classes, and English and reading classes to be the preferred employer in the highly competitive hospitality industry.[45] Both SAS Institute and Marriott International are consistently rated among *Fortune*'s list of the top 100 companies to work for, with rankings of 8 and 84, respectively, as recently as 2004.[46]

Develop People to Deliver Service Quality

To grow and maintain a workforce that is customer oriented and focused on delivering quality, an organization must develop its employees to deliver service quality. That is, once it has hired the right employees, the organization must train and work with these individuals to ensure service performance.

Train for Technical and Interactive Skills

To provide quality service, employees need ongoing training in the necessary technical skills and knowledge and in process or interactive skills.[47] Examples of technical skills and knowledge are working with accounting systems in hotels, cash machine procedures in a retail store, underwriting procedures in an insurance company, and any operational rules the company has for running its business. Most service organizations are quite conscious of and relatively effective at training employees in technical skills. These skills may be taught through formal education, as is the case at McDonald's Hamburger University, which trains McDonald's managers from all over the world. Additionally, technical skills are often taught through on-the-job training, as when education students work with experienced teachers in internship programs or when telephone service trainees listen in on the conversations of experienced employees. Recently, companies are increasing their use of information technology to train employees in the technical skills and knowledge needed on the job.

Service employees also need training in interactive skills that allow them to provide courteous, caring, responsive, and empathetic service. Exhibit 12.2 explains how the Tokyo Imperial Hotel in Japan effectively combines service employee training in both the technical and interactive skills needed to provide quality service.

Successful companies invest heavily in training and make sure that the training fits their business goals and strategies. For example, at Midwest Express—the company that takes pride in offering "the best care in the air"—all employees (pilots, baggage handlers, aircraft groomers) take part in a two-day orientation program. The focus revolves around the company values and customer service. In Zagat's regular international airline survey, Midwest Express consistently ranks as the top U.S. airline. At the Ritz-Carlton, all employees go through extensive initial training and are given pocket-sized, laminated credo cards to carry in their wallets. The credo card specifies the three steps of service, Ritz-Carlton's well-known motto "We are Ladies and Gentlemen Serving Ladies and Gentlemen," and the credo itself. Further, employees in every hotel attend a brief standing staff meeting each day to review one of Ritz-Carlton's "Gold Standards: The 20 Basics" so as to continually reinforce earlier training.

Empower Employees

Many organizations have discovered that to be truly responsive to customer needs, frontline providers need to be empowered to accommodate customer requests and to recover on the spot when things go wrong. *Empowerment* means giving employees the

Exhibit 12.2 TRAINING AT TOKYO'S IMPERIAL HOTEL

Tokyo's Imperial Hotel provides an excellent example of training for both knowledge and skills as well as interactive service quality. The hotel's "Capability Development Program" consists of training in "occupational abilities and knowledge" (technical skills) as well as "service manners training" (interactive skills). The first type of training involves on-the-job apprenticing, rotations through all the major departments within the hotel, visitations and inspection tours of comparable hotels in other countries, and focused study tours (for example, Imperial Hotel's senior waiters and sommeliers might tour famous wineries in California and France every three years). In addition, employees get specialized skills training through independent educational organizations on needed topics ranging from management strategy decision making to food hygiene to presentation know-how.

The "service manners training" focuses on the etiquette and psychology of guest contact and attitudes of service. Proper etiquette is taught via role playing and videotaping (to critique appearance, mannerisms, and personal idiosyncrasies). The way the staff should appear to hotel guests is stressed and demonstrated, with emphasis placed on cleanliness, a sense of understated elegance, and good taste. Guest psychology is discussed, emphasizing the following main points:

1. Imperial Hotel patrons, given the rank and reputation of the hotel, expect that you will consider them your most important priority, the center of your attention.

2. Guests do not want to suffer losses of any kind while in the hotel.

3. Guests expect to be received in a warm, welcoming fashion.

4. A guest does not want to be extended a level of treatment that is in any way inferior to that provided to other guests of the hotel.

5. Guests wish to experience an appropriate feeling of prestige or superiority, purely by virtue of their using what is commonly evaluated as a deluxe enterprise.

6. Guests enjoy feeling possessive about the hotel's facilities and services, and expect exclusive attention.

Finally, the basic principles of nonverbal communication and body language are discussed. Demonstrations and detailed explanations of appropriate behaviors are given, covering such points as facial expressions, appearance, and posture when standing; pleasing, attractive ways of talking and carriage; proper posture; and courtesy when escorting guests within the hotel premises. Because the bow is used regardless of the national origin of the guest, considerable time is spent on the intricacies of proper bowing. A bow of welcome involves a 15-degree angle, a bow of gratitude is 30 degrees, and a bow of apology is a full 45 degrees from the normal straight standing position. The remainder of the service manners training concentrates on the complexities of the Japanese language and the appropriate applications for hotel service. Trainees are instructed in some 25 common daily expressions, learning their politest forms as well as the English equivalents.

Ongoing training and service improvement programs at all levels are part of the hotel's total operations strategy.

Source: *Service Quality Handbook* by Scheuing, Ebert Copyright © 1993 by AM MGMT ASSN/AMACOM (A) Reproduced with permission of AM MGMT ASSN/AMACOM (B) in the format textbook via Copyright Clearance Center.

desire, skills, tools, and authority to serve the customer. Although the key to empowerment is giving employees authority to make decisions on the customer's behalf, authority alone is not enough. Employees need the knowledge and tools to be able to make these decisions, and they need incentives that encourage them to make the right decisions. Organizations do not succeed in empowering their employees if they simply tell them, "You now have the authority to do whatever it takes to satisfy the customer." First, employees often do not believe this statement, particularly if the organization has functioned hierarchically or bureaucratically in the past. Second, employees often do not know what it means to "do whatever it takes" if they have not received training, guidelines, and the tools needed to make such decisions.

Research suggests positive benefits to empowering frontline service workers. Some of these benefits include reduction in job-related stress, improved job satisfaction,

Exhibit 12.3 POTENTIAL COSTS AND BENEFITS OF EMPOWERMENT

BENEFITS

Quicker online responses to customer needs during service delivery. Employees who are allowed to make decisions on behalf of the customer can make decisions more quickly, bypassing what in the past might have meant a long chain of command, or at least a discussion with an immediate supervisor.

Quicker online responses to dissatisfied customers during service recovery. When failures occur in the delivery system, customers hope for an immediate recovery effort on the part of the organization. Empowered employees can recover on the spot, and a dissatisfied customer can potentially be turned into a satisfied, even loyal one.

Employees feel better about their jobs and themselves. Giving employees control and authority to make decisions makes them feel responsible and gives them ownership for the customer's satisfaction. Decades of job design research suggest that when employees have a sense of control and of doing meaningful work, they are more satisfied. The result is lower turnover and less absenteeism.

Employees will interact with customers with more warmth and enthusiasm. Employees feel better about themselves and their work, and these attitudes will spill over into their feelings about customers and will be reflected in their interactions.

Empowered employees are a great source of service ideas. When employees are empowered, they feel responsible for the service outcome and they will be excellent sources of ideas about new services or how to improve current offerings.

Great word-of-mouth advertising from customers. Empowered employees do special and unique things that customers will remember and tell their friends, family, and associates about.

COSTS

A potentially greater dollar investment in selection and training. To find employees who will work well in an empowered environment requires creative, potentially more costly selection procedures. Training will also be more expensive in general because employees need more knowledge about the company, its products, and how to work in flexible ways with customers.

Higher labor costs. The organization may not be able to use as many part-time or seasonal employees, and it may need to pay more for asking employees to assume responsibility.

Potentially slower or inconsistent service delivery. If empowered employees spend more time with all, or even some, customers, then service overall may take longer and may annoy customers who are waiting. Empowerment also means that customers will get what they need or request. When decisions regarding customer satisfaction are left to the discretion of employees, there may be inconsistency in the level of service delivered.

May violate customers' perceptions of fair play. Customers may perceive that sticking to procedures with every customer is fair. Thus, if they see that customers are receiving different levels of service or that employees are cutting special deals with some customers, they may believe that the organization is not fair.

Employees may "give away the store" or make bad decisions. Many people fear that empowered employees will make costly decisions that the organization cannot afford. Although this situation can happen, good training and appropriate guidelines will help.

Source: Reprinted from "The Empowerment of Service Workers: What, Why, How, and When," by DE Bowen and EE Lawler, *Sloan Management Review,* Spring 1992, pp. 31–39, by permission of the publisher. Copyright 1992 by Massachusetts Institute of Technology. All rights reserved.

greater adaptability, and better outcomes for customers.[48] But such success does not come easily. In fact, some experts have concluded that few organizations have truly taken advantage of, or properly implemented, successful empowerment strategies.[49] Nor is empowerment the answer for all organizations. Exhibit 12.3 enumerates both the costs and benefits of empowerment as documented by David Bowen and Edward Lawler, experts on this subject.[50] They suggest that organizations well suited to empowerment strategies are ones in which (1) the business strategy is one of differentiation and customization, (2) customers are long-term relationship customers, (3) technology is nonroutine or complex, (4) the business environment is unpredictable, and (5) managers and employees have high growth and social needs and strong interpersonal skills.

Promote Teamwork

The nature of many service jobs suggests that customer satisfaction will be enhanced when employees work as teams. Because service jobs are frequently frustrating, demanding, and challenging, a teamwork environment will help alleviate some of the stresses and strains. Employees who feel supported and feel that they have a team backing them up will be better able to maintain their enthusiasm and provide quality service.[51] "An interactive community of coworkers who help each other, commiserate, and achieve together is a powerful antidote to service burnout,"[52] and, we would add, an important ingredient for service quality. By promoting teamwork, an organization can enhance the employees' *abilities* to deliver excellent service while the camaraderie and support enhance their *inclination* to be excellent service providers.

One way of promoting teamwork is to encourage the attitude that "everyone has a customer." That is, even when employees are not directly responsible for or in direct interaction with the final customer, they need to know whom they serve directly and how the role they play in the total service picture is essential to the final delivery of quality service. If each employee can see how he or she is somehow integral in delivering quality to the final customer and if each employee knows whom to support to make service quality a reality, teamwork will be enhanced. Service blueprints, described in Chapter 9, can serve as useful tools to illustrate for employees their integral roles in delivering service quality to the ultimate customer.

Team goals and rewards also promote teamwork. When a firm rewards teams of individuals rather than basing all rewards on individual achievements and performance, team efforts and team spirit are encouraged.

Provide Needed Support Systems

To be efficient and effective in their jobs, service workers require internal support systems that are aligned with their need to be customer focused. This point cannot be overemphasized. In fact, without customer-focused internal support and customer-oriented systems, it is nearly impossible for employees to deliver quality service no matter how much they want to. For example, a bank teller who is rewarded for customer satisfaction as well as for accuracy in bank transactions needs easy access to up-to-date customer records, a well-staffed branch (so that he is not constantly facing a long line of impatient customers), and supportive customer-oriented supervisors and back-office staff. In examining customer service outcomes in Australian call centers, researchers found that internal support from supervisors, teammates, and other departments as well as evaluations of technology used on the job were all strongly related to employee satisfaction and ability to serve customers.[53] The following sections suggest strategies for ensuring customer-oriented internal support.

Measure Internal Service Quality

One way to encourage supportive internal service relationships is to measure and reward internal service. By first acknowledging that everyone in the organization has a customer and then measuring customer perceptions of internal service quality, an organization can begin to develop an internal quality culture. Internal customer service audits can be used to implement a culture of internal service quality. Through the audit, internal organizations identify their customers, determine their needs, measure how well they are doing, and make improvements. The process parallels market research practices used for external customers. Exhibit 12.4 outlines the steps in an internal service audit.

Exhibit 12.4 STEPS IN CONDUCTING AN INTERNAL CUSTOMER SERVICE AUDIT

1. *Define your customer.*
   a. List all the people or departments in the organization who need help from you or your department in any way. This list may include specific departments, particular staff people, the CEO, certain executives, or the board of directors.
   b. Prioritize the names on the list, placing the people or departments that rely on you the most at the top.

2. *Identify your contribution.*
   a. For each of these customers, specify the primary need you think they have to which you can contribute. Talk to your internal customers about what problems they are trying to solve and think about how you can help.

3. *Define service quality.*
   a. What are the critical moments of truth that really define the department–internal customer interface from your customer's point of view? Blueprint the process, and list the moments of truth.
   b. For each major internal customer, design a customer report card (based on customer input) and a set of evaluation criteria for your department's service package, as seen through the eyes of that customer. The criteria might include such dimensions as timeliness, reliability, and cost.

4. *Validate your criteria.*
   a. Talk to your customers. Allow them to revise, as necessary, how you saw their needs and the criteria they used in assessing your performance. This dialogue itself can go a long way toward building internal service teamwork.

5. *Measure service quality.*
   a. Evaluate your service (using internal measures and/or customer surveys) against the quality criteria you established in talking to your customers. See how you score. Identify opportunities for improvement. Set up a process and timetable for following through.

6. *Develop a mission statement based on what you contribute.*
   a. Consider drafting a brief, meaningful service mission statement for your operation. Be certain to frame it in terms of the value you *contribute*, not what you *do*. For example, the mission of the HR department should not be "to deliver training" (the action); it would be "to create competent people" (the contribution).

Source: Reprinted from K. Albrecht, *At America's Service* (Homewood, IL: Dow-Jones-Irwin, 1988), pp. 139–42, as discussed in B. Schneider and D. E. Bowen, *Winning at the Service Game* (Boston: The Harvard Business School Press, 1995), pp. 231–32. © 1988 by Dow-Jones-Irwin. Reprinted by permission of The McGraw-Hill Companies.

One risk of measuring and focusing on internal service quality and internal customers is that people can sometimes get so wrapped up in meeting the needs of internal customers that they forget they are in business to serve the ultimate, external customers.[54] In measuring internal service quality, therefore, it is important to constantly draw the linkages between what is being delivered internally and how it supports the delivery of the final service to customers. Service blueprinting, introduced in Chapter 9, can help to illustrate these critical linkages.

Provide Supportive Technology and Equipment

When employees do not have the right equipment or their equipment fails them, they can be easily frustrated in their desire to deliver quality service. To do their jobs effectively and efficiently, service employees need the right equipment and technology. Our Technology Spotlight earlier in this chapter highlights the role of front-office automation in providing technology support for employees.

Having the right technology and equipment can extend into strategies regarding workplace and workstation design. For example, in designing their corporate headquarters' offices, Scandinavian Airline Systems identified particular service-oriented goals that it wished to achieve, among them teamwork and open, frequent communication among managers. An office environment was designed with open spaces (to encourage meetings) and internal windows in offices (to encourage frequent interactions). In this way the work space facilitated the internal service orientation.

Develop Service-Oriented Internal Processes

To best support service personnel in their delivery of quality service on the front line, an organization's internal processes should be designed with customer value and customer satisfaction in mind. In other words, internal procedures must support quality service performance. In many companies internal processes are driven by bureaucratic rules, tradition, cost efficiencies, or the needs of internal employees. Providing service- and customer-oriented internal processes can therefore imply a need for total redesign of systems. This kind of wholesale redesign of systems and processes has become known as "process reengineering." Although developing service-oriented internal processes through reengineering sounds sensible, it is probably one of the most difficult strategies to implement, especially in organizations that are steeped in tradition. Refocusing internal processes and introducing large amounts of new, supportive technology were among the changes made by Yellow Roadway Corporation in its transition from a traditional, operations-driven company to a customer-focused one (see Exhibit 12.5).[55]

Retain the Best People

An organization that hires the right people, trains and develops them to deliver service quality, and provides the needed support must also work to retain them. Employee turnover, especially when the best service employees are the ones leaving, can be very detrimental to customer satisfaction, employee morale, and overall service quality. And, just as they do with customers, some firms spend a lot of time attracting employees but then tend to take them for granted (or even worse), causing these good employees to search for job alternatives. Although all the strategies depicted earlier in Figure 12.6 will support the retention of the best employees, here we will focus on some strategies that are particularly aimed at this goal.

Include Employees in the Company's Vision

For employees to remain motivated and interested in sticking with the organization and supporting its goals, they need to share an understanding of the organization's vision. People who deliver service day in and day out need to understand how their work fits into the big picture of the organization and its goals. They will be motivated to some extent by their paychecks and other benefits, but the best employees will be attracted away to other opportunities if they are not committed to the vision of the organization. And they cannot be committed to the vision if that vision is kept secret from them. What this strategy means in practice is that the vision is communicated to employees frequently and that it is communicated by top managers, often by the CEO.[56] Respected CEOs such as Herb Kelleher of Southwest Airlines, Howard Schulz of Starbucks, Fred Smith of FedEx, Bill Marriott of Marriott International, and Charles Schwab of Schwab are known for communicating their visions clearly and often to employees. Bill Zollars, CEO of Yellow Roadway Corporation, exemplifies this type of behavior, which was a critical ingredient to his success in turning the company around (see Exhibit 12.5).

Exhibit 12.5 YELLOW REINVENTS ITSELF

Yellow Transportation (now part of Yellow-Roadway Corporation) is one of the largest and oldest transportation companies in the United States. Over the last decade, Yellow Transportation (Yellow) has been transformed from a traditional, operations-driven trucking company to a service and transportation company with a customer-focused culture and innovative services. The transformation required a new vision for the company, feedback from customers and employees, investments in technology, and hundreds of small, detailed actions. Here is a summary of some of what took place over the ten years.

In 1996 Bill Zollars, a respected and experienced executive, was recruited to serve as president of Yellow. At the time, the company was recovering from its worst financial year in its over 70-year history and was still feeling the effects of a long Teamsters strike two years earlier. Zollars's challenge was to help the company start over and turn the negative trends around. His goal was to transform the tradition-bound, formerly regulated company into one that offered multiple services and unprecedented customer service—a customer-centered service business rather than an operations-driven trucking company.

SHARING THE VISION

The first thing Zollars did was share his vision of the new company with all company employees. He did this not through memos or videos but by visiting in person, over about a year and a half, almost every one of the company's U.S. terminals. He talked personally with dockworkers, office people, sales staff, and customers—sharing the same consistent message with each group. The company was going to change, and to do so required the involvement of all employees as well as feedback and ideas from customers.

Yellow's success depends on employees being motivated and having the tools to succeed.
Source: Courtesy of Yellow Roadway Corporation

Top management education was also an integral piece of the transformation. Zollars brought his two dozen top managers—across all functions of the company—to Arizona State University to build their team and to learn cutting-edge concepts of services marketing and management. He attended the program with them, and in future years sent smaller groups of new and continuing executives back for refreshers and continuing team building.

Tom Siebel of Siebel Systems, the industry leader in CRM software applications, is another good example (see this chapter's Technology Spotlight). He communicates clearly, through words and actions, that the company's mission is "customer first," no matter what the situation. He believes in putting customers ahead of technology and discipline ahead of inspiration; and he upholds these strong messages through his own actions—at every fork in the road, the decision rule is "customer first." In fact, he has several times turned down potentially lucrative business accounts if he felt that they would take away from current customer needs or that the company was not ready to provide 100 percent satisfaction to the potential customers. This type of action sends a strong message to employees, reinforcing the company vision.[57] When the vision and direction are clear and motivating, employees are more likely to remain with the company through the inevitable rough spots along the path to the vision.

INVESTING IN TECHNOLOGY SUPPORT

To become customer focused, Yellow invested in state-of-the-art technology, not for technology's sake but, rather, to allow every aspect of its business to focus on satisfying customer needs efficiently. Since 1994, about $80 million a year has been spent on technology infusion, affecting how orders get processed, how dispatchers assign drivers for pickups and deliveries, and how dockworkers load and unload the trucks. Each dockworker has a wireless mobile data terminal that speeds up the loading and unloading process. Employees who operate the customer service center (1-800-GO-YELLOW) have instant access to customers' account profiles, including customer location, type of loading dock, history of previous shipments, destinations, and delivery signatures. Investments in customer-facing technology allow customers to interact with the firm in whatever way they please—via phone, fax, e-mail, interactive voice response, or the Internet. The company is now considered a technology leader in its industry.

LISTENING TO CUSTOMERS

By initiating customer feedback processes, the company learned of new service needs of its customers and of service issues it needed to address. A major issue, addressed early on, was reliability. The most important concern for customers in the freight-handling business is that their shipments get picked up on time and delivered on time and that nothing is damaged. These simple rules of service reliability were ones that Yellow and many of its competitors were not performing well a decade ago. Now Yellow has fixed these basic issues through the infusion of technology and lots of employee communication, training, motivation, and incentive programs. Major investments in service recovery processes were also part of the solution.

Through the customer feedback process, Yellow also identified opportunities for new, innovative services that have taken it way beyond its roots in less-than-truckload freight distribution. One of its most innovative, popular, and profitable forays into the future is Exact Express—an expedited, time-definite, guaranteed service for large shipments. The service allows customers to specify exactly when they want their shipments picked up and delivered, and Yellow is on the mark 98 percent of the time. This new service has resulted in Yellow getting some unique jobs, such as shipping 10,000 pounds of air freshener to ground zero after the World Trade Center attack and carrying 40,000 flashlights from Los Angeles to Washington, D.C., for the 2001 presidential inauguration.

VIEWING RESULTS

During the transformation, employees and customers alike have responded with enthusiasm to the changes at Yellow. Financial results have been impressive; even during the downturn in 2001, Yellow continued to grow its newest services and receive recognition and awards. It has won awards for its innovative business practices, for its website, and for quality based on industry surveys. Nowhere is the excitement more apparent than at the company's annual employee and customer conference in Las Vegas (called "Transformation"), where each year 1,000 employees and 500 customers attend workshops and sessions together on change. Although much has been accomplished in the past decade, this transformation will surely continue for a long time into the future.

Sources: C. Salter, "On the Road Again," *Fast Company*, January 2002, pp. 50–58; www.yellowcorp.com, 2002; author's observations.

Treat Employees as Customers

If employees feel valued and their needs are taken care of, they are more likely to stay with the organization. Tom Siebel, for example, sees the CEO's primary job as cultivating a corporate culture that benefits all employees and customers. "If you build a company and a product or service that delivers high levels of customer satisfaction, and if you spend responsibly and manage your human capital assets well, the other external manifestations of success, like market valuation and revenue growth, will follow."[58] An extreme example of this view is provided by a quotation from Hal Rosenbluth, CEO of Rosenbluth International:

> As I watched people knocking themselves out for Rosenbluth...I suddenly realized that it was my responsibility to make their lives more pleasant. In simple terms, that meant giving

people the right working environment, the right tools, and the right leadership. It meant eliminating fear, frustration, bureaucracy, and politics. Of course, it meant decent compensation—and bonuses when the company did well—but it also meant helping people develop as human beings.[59]

Many companies have adopted the idea that employees are also customers of the organization and that basic marketing strategies can be directed at them.[60] The products that the organization has to offer its employees are a job (with assorted benefits) and quality of work life. To determine whether the job and work-life needs of employees are being met, organizations conduct periodic internal marketing research to assess employee satisfaction and needs. For example, within American Express Travel Related Services, the Travelers Check Group (TCG) had a goal of "Becoming the Best Place to Work" by treating employees as customers.[61]

On the basis of the research, TCG launched a number of initiatives to benefit employees: an expanded employee assistance program; child care resource and referral service; adoption assistance; health care and dependent care reimbursement plans; family leave; family sick days; flexible returns; sabbaticals; improved part-time employee benefits; flexible benefits; and workplace flexibility initiatives including job-sharing, flexplace, and flextime scheduling. What American Express and many other companies are finding is that to ensure employee satisfaction, productivity, and retention, companies are getting more and more involved in the private lives and family support of their workers.[62] And employees appreciate such efforts; American Express is regularly included in *Fortune*'s list of "Top 100 Companies to Work For"—making it every year between 2000 and 2004!

In addition to basic internal research, organizations can apply other marketing strategies to their management of employees. For example, segmentation of the employee population is apparent in many of the flexible benefit plans and career path choices now available to employees. Organizations that are set up to meet the needs of specific segments and to adjust as people proceed through their lives will benefit from increased employee loyalty. Advertising and other forms of communication directed at employees can also increase their sense of value and enhance their commitment to the organization.[63]

Measure and Reward Strong Service Performers

If a company wants the strongest service performers to stay with the organization, it must reward and promote them. This strategy may seem obvious, but often the reward systems in organizations are not set up to reward service excellence. Reward systems may value productivity, sales, or some other dimension that can potentially work *against* good service. Even those service workers who are intrinsically motivated to deliver high service quality will become discouraged at some point and start looking elsewhere if their efforts are not recognized and rewarded.

Reward systems need to be linked to the organization's vision and to outcomes that are truly important. For instance, if customer satisfaction and retention are viewed as critical outcomes, service behaviors that increase those outcomes need to be recognized and rewarded. At Siebel Systems all employees—the salespeople, the service people, the engineers, the product marketers, and everyone else—receive incentive compensation based on the company's customer satisfaction scores. For salespeople the bulk of their incentive compensation is paid only *after* the company knows the level of customer satisfaction—four quarters after the sales contract is signed.[64] At Intel, the "Vender of Choice" (VOC) customer retention measure is incorporated into all employees' incentive systems. For example, in January 2002 when VOC was 96 percent across the entire company, all employees received an extra day of pay, costing the company millions of dollars. The VOC score is calculated from customers' statements as to whether Intel is their first-choice vendor for a particular product or service. The measure itself, along with all the analyses and service improvement initiatives that are behind it, is intended to align employee behavior around retaining customers.

Companies with a goal of customer satisfaction in every service encounter often need to adjust the criteria by which employee performance is judged. Some companies will have to shift from a total emphasis on productivity data and hard numbers to other means of assessment. At AT&T's customer sales and service centers, part of the reward system for individual associates is based on customer satisfaction measured at the level of the employee. Ongoing "true moments" surveys are used whereby customers are called and asked to assess the level of service they received from the particular employee they interacted with over the phone. These measurements (multiple customers for each employee each quarter) are then integrated into the employee's performance evaluation and rewarded. Such measurement systems are challenging to effectively implement. The measures must be appropriate, the sampling of customers must be performed fairly, and the employees must buy in to the validity of the results. AT&T has been perfecting its process, with employee involvement, for many years.

Aligning reward systems with customer outcomes can be challenging. Reward systems are usually well entrenched, and employees have learned over time how they need to perform within the old structures. Change is difficult both for the managers who may have created and still may believe in the old systems and for employees who are not sure what they need to do to succeed under the new rules. In many organizations, however, reward and incentive systems are still not matched with customer satisfaction and loyalty goals.[65]

In developing new systems and structures to recognize customer focus and customer satisfaction, organizations have turned to a variety of rewards. Traditional approaches such as higher pay, promotions, and one-time monetary awards or prizes can be linked to service performance. In some organizations employees are encouraged to recognize each other by personally giving a "peer award" to an employee they believe has excelled in providing service to the customer. Other types of rewards include special organizational and team celebrations for achieving improved customer satisfaction or for attaining customer retention goals. In most service organizations it is not only the major accomplishments but the daily perseverance and attention to detail that move the organization forward, so recognition of the "small wins" is also important.

In many situations, a customer's relationship is with a specific employee and may be stronger with the *employee* than with the firm. If this employee leaves the firm and is no longer available to the customer, the firm's relationship with the customer may be jeopardized.[66] Clearly a firm should make great efforts to retain such employees; however, in spite of the firm's best efforts, some good employees are going to leave. If the firm is not successful at retaining a key customer contact employee, what can it do to reduce the impact on the customer? Employees could be rotated occasionally in order to ensure that the customer has exposure to and is comfortable with more than one employee. Firms might also form teams of employees who are responsible for interacting with each customer. In both cases, the idea is that the customer would have multiple contacts with several employees in the organization, thus reducing the firm's vulnerability to losing the customer should any one employee leave. Emphasis should also be placed on creating a positive firm image in the minds of its customers and in so doing convey that *all* its employees are capable.[67]

CUSTOMER-ORIENTED SERVICE DELIVERY

As indicated by the examples presented in this chapter, specific approaches for hiring and energizing frontline workers take on a different look and feel across companies, based on the organization's values, culture, history, and vision.[68] For example, "developing people to deliver service quality" is accomplished quite differently at Southwest Airlines than at Disney. At Disney the orientation and training process is highly structured, scripted, and standardized. At Southwest, the emphasis is more on developing needed skills but then empowering employees to be spontaneous and nonscripted in their approach to customers. Although the style and culture of the two organizations are different, both pay special attention to all four basic themes shown in Figure 12.6. Both have made significant investments in their people, recognizing the critical roles they play.

Throughout the book we have advocated a strong customer focus. Firms that have a strong service culture clearly put an emphasis on the customer and the customer's experience. In order to do so, firms must also create an environment that staunchly supports the customer contact employee, because this person in the organization is frequently the most responsible for ensuring that the customer's experience is delivered as designed. Historically, many firms have viewed senior management as the most important people in the firm, and indeed, organizational charts reflect this view in their structure. Such an approach, as suggested in Figure 12.7, places management at the top of the structure and (implicitly) the customer at the bottom, with customer contact employees just above them. If the organization's most important people are customers, they should be at the top of the chart, followed by those with whom they have contact. Such a view, illustrated in Figure 12.8, is more consistent with a customer-oriented focus. In effect, the role of top-level management changes from that of commanding employees to that of facilitating and supporting employees in the organization who are closest to the customer. The human resource strategies that we have offered in this chapter are suggested as a means to support the customer contact employee. A statement by Michel Bon, CEO of France Telecom, succinctly summarizes the philosophy behind this approach:

> If you sincerely believe that "the customer is king," the second most important person in this kingdom must be the one who has a direct interaction on a daily basis with the one who is king.[69]

FIGURE 12.7 **Traditional Organizational Chart**

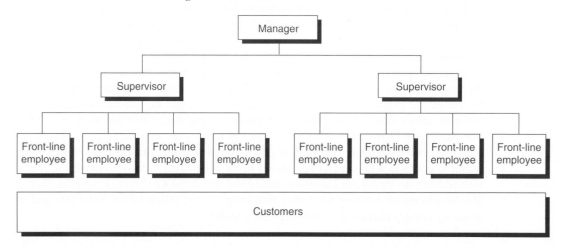

FIGURE 12.8 **Customer-Focused Organizational Chart**

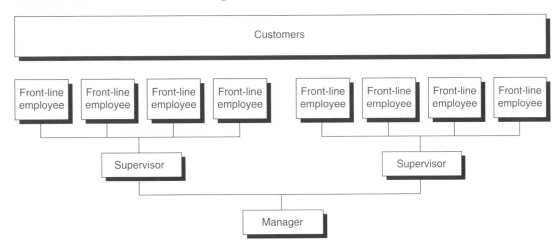

Summary

Because many services are delivered by people in real time, closing the service performance gap is heavily dependent on human resource strategies. The successful execution of such strategies begins with the development and nurturing of a true service culture in which "an appreciation for good service exists, and where giving good service to internal as well as ultimate, external customers is considered a natural way of life and one of the most important norms by everyone."[70]

Often, service employees are the service, and in all cases they represent the organization in customers' eyes. They affect service quality perceptions to a large degree through their influence on the five dimensions of service quality: reliability, responsiveness, empathy, assurance, and tangibles. It is essential to match what the customer wants and needs with service employees' abilities to deliver.

In this chapter we focused on service employees to provide you with an understanding of the critical nature of their roles and appreciation of the inherent stresses and conflicts they face. You learned that frontline service jobs demand significant investments of emotional labor and that employees confront a variety of on-the-job conflicts. Sometimes service employees are personally uncomfortable with the roles they are asked to play; other times the requirements of the organization may conflict with client expectations, and employees must resolve the dilemma on the spot. Sometimes there are conflicting needs among customers who are being served in turn (such as in a bank teller line) or among customers being served simultaneously (as in a college classroom). At other times a frontline employee may be faced with a decision about whether to satisfy a customer or meet productivity targets (such as an HMO physician who is required to see a certain number of patients in a defined period of time).

Grounded in this understanding of the importance of service employees and the nature of their roles in the organization, you learned strategies for integrating appropriate human resource practices into service firms. The strategies are aimed at allowing employees to effectively satisfy customers as well as be efficient and productive in their jobs. The strategies were organized around four major human resource goals in service organizations: to hire the right people, to develop people to deliver service quality, to provide needed support systems, and to retain the best people. A company that works toward implementing these strategies is well on its way to delivering service quality through its people, thereby diminishing gap 3.

Discussion Questions

1. Define *service culture.* Why is service culture so important? Can a manufacturing firm have a service culture? Why or why not?

2. Why are service employees critical to the success of any service organization? Why do we include an entire chapter on service employees in a marketing course?

3. What is emotional labor? How can it be differentiated from physical or mental labor?

4. Reflect on your own role as a frontline service provider, whether in a current job or in any full- or part-time service job you have had in the past. Did you experience the kinds of conflicts described in the boundary-spanning roles section of the chapter? Be prepared with some concrete examples for class discussion.

5. Select a service provider (your dentist, doctor, lawyer, hair stylist) with whom you are familiar, and discuss ways this person could positively influence the five dimensions of service quality in the context of delivering his or her services. Do the same for yourself (if you are currently a service provider).

6. Describe the four basic human resource strategy themes and why each plays an important role in building a customer-oriented organization.

7. What is the difference between technical and interactive service skills? Provide examples (preferably from your own work context or from another context with which you are familiar). Why do service employees need training in both?

8. Is empowerment always the best approach for effective service delivery? Why is employee empowerment so controversial?

Exercises

1. Visit the websites of companies with known world-class service cultures (such as Ritz-Carlton, FedEx, or Starbucks). How does the information conveyed on the website reinforce the company's service culture?

2. Review the section of the chapter on boundary-spanning roles. Interview at least two frontline service personnel regarding the stresses they experience in their jobs. How do the examples they provide relate to the sources of conflict and trade-offs described in the text?

3. Assume that you are the manager of a crew of frontline customer-service employees in a credit card company. Assume that these employees work over the phone and that they deal primarily with customer requests, questions, and complaints. In this specific context,

    a. Define what is meant by *boundary-spanning roles,* and discuss the basic purposes or functions performed by participants in these roles.

    b. Discuss two of the potential conflicts that your employees may face on the basis of their roles as boundary spanners.

    c. Discuss how you, as their supervisor, might deal with these conflicts based on what you have learned.

4. Choose one or more of the human resource strategy themes (hire the right people, develop people to deliver service quality, provide needed support systems, retain the best people). Interview a manager in a service organization of your choice regarding his or her current practices within the theme you have chosen. Describe the current practices and recommend any appropriate changes for improving them.

Notes

1. L. L. Berry, *Discovering the Soul of Service* (New York: The Free Press, 1999).
2. Interview with Singapore Airlines senior vice president of marketing services, included in "How May I Help You?" *Fast Company,* March 2000, pp. 93–126.
3. P. Gallagher, "Getting It Right from the Start," *Journal of Retail Banking* 15 (Spring 1993), pp. 39–41.
4. J. S. Hirsch, "Now Hotel Clerks Provide More Than Keys," *The Wall Street Journal,* March 5, 1993, p. B1.
5. Berry, *Discovering the Soul of Service.*
6. S. M. Davis, *Managing Corporate Culture* (Cambridge, MA: Ballinger, 1985).
7. C. Gronroos, *Service Management and Marketing* (Lexington, MA: Lexington Books, 1990), p. 244.
8. See K. N. Kennedy, F. G. Lassk, and J. R. Goolsby, "Customer Mind-Set of Employees throughout the Organization," *Journal of the Academy of Marketing Science*, 30 (Spring 2002), pp. 159–71.
9. R. Hallowell, D. Bowen, and C. Knoop, "Four Seasons Goes to Paris," *Academy of Management Executive* 16, no. 4 (2002), pp. 7–24; J. L. Heskett, L. A. Schlesinger, and E.W. Sasser Jr., *The Service Profit Chain* (New York: The Free Press, 1997); B. Schneider and D. E. Bowen, *Winning the Service Game* (Boston: Harvard Business School Press, 1995).
10. Berry, *Discovering the Soul of Service*, p. 40.
11. Hallowell, Bowen, and Knoop, "Four Seasons Goes to Paris."
12. For an excellent discussion of the complexities involved in creating and sustaining a service culture, see Schneider and Bowen, *Winning the Service Game,* chap. 9. See also Michael D. Hartline, James G. Maxham III, and Daryl O. McKee, "Corridors of Influence in the Dissemination of Customer-Oriented Strategy to Customer-Contact Service Employees," *Journal of Marketing* 64 (April 2000), pp. 35–50.
13. This discussion is based on Hallowell, Bowen, and Knoop, "Four Seasons Goes to Paris."
14. This quote is most frequently attributed to J. Carlzon of Scandinavian Airline Systems.
15. J. Garrett, "The Human Side of Brand: Why Audi Hires Workers with the Same Traits as Its Luxury Cars," *Gallup Management Journal,* Summer 2001, pp. 4–5.
16. The conceptualization of the services triangle presented in Figure 12.2 and the related text discussion are based on M. J. Bitner, "Building Service Relationships: It's All about Promises," *Journal of the Academy of Marketing Science* 23 (Fall 1995), pp. 246–51; P. Kotler, *Marketing Management: Analysis, Planning, Implementation, and Control,* 8th ed. (Englewood Cliffs, NJ: Prentice Hall, 1994); and Gronroos, *Service Management and Marketing.*
17. See, for example, H. Rosenbluth, "Tales from a Nonconformist Company," *Harvard Business Review,* July–August 1991, pp. 26–36; and L. A. Schlesinger and J. L. Heskett, "The Service-Driven Service Company," *Harvard Business Review,* September–October 1991, pp. 71–81.
18. B. Schneider and D. E. Bowen, "The Service Organization: Human Resources Management Is Crucial," *Organizational Dynamics* 21, (Spring 1993), pp. 39–52.
19. Ibid.
20. D. E. Bowen, S. W. Gilliland, and R. Folger, "How Being Fair with Employees Spills Over to Customers," *Organizational Dynamics* 27 (Winter 1999), pp. 7–23.
21. See J. L. Heskett, T. O. Jones, G. W. Loveman, W. E. Sasser Jr., and L. A. Schlesinger, "Putting the Service–Profit Chain to Work," *Harvard Business*

Review, March–April 1994, pp. 164–74; G. W. Loveman, "Employee Satisfaction, Customer Loyalty, and Financial Performance," *Journal of Service Research* 1 (August 1998), pp. 18–31; A. Rucci, S. P. Kirn, and R. T. Quinn, "The Employee–Customer Profit Chain at Sears," *Harvard Business Review,* January–February 1998, pp. 82–97; and R. Hallowell and L. L. Schlesinger, "The Service–Profit Chain," in *The Handbook for Services Marketing and Management,* ed. T. A. Swartz and D. Iacobucci (Thousand Oaks, CA: Sage Publications, 2000), pp. 203–22.

22. J. Pfeffer, *The Human Equation* (Boston: Harvard Business School Press, 1998); and A. M. Webber, "Danger: Toxic Company," *Fast Company,* November 1998, pp. 152–62.

23. S. Branch, "The 100 Best Companies to Work for in America," *Fortune,* January 11, 1999, pp. 118–44.

24. M. K. Brady and J. J. Cronin Jr., "Customer Orientation: Effects on Customer Service Perceptions and Outcome Behaviors," *Journal of Service Research* 3 (February 2001), pp. 241–51.

25. L. A. Bettencourt and K. Gwinner, "Customization of the Service Experience: The Role of the Frontline Employee," *International Journal of Service Industry Management* 7, no. 2 (1996), pp. 3–20.

26. For research on the influence of frontline employee behaviors on customers, see D. D. Gremler and K. P. Gwinner, "Customer–Employee Rapport in Service Relationships," *Journal of Service Research* 3 (August 2000), pp. 82–104; K. de Ruyter and M. G. M. Wetzels, "The Impact of Perceived Listening Behavior in Voice-to-Voice Service Encounters," *Journal of Service Research* 2 (February 2000), pp. 276–84; Tom J. Brown, John C. Mowen, D. Todd Donavan and Jane W. Licata, "The Customer Orientation of Service Workers: Personality Trait Effects of Self- and Supervisor Performance Ratings," *Journal of Marketing Research* 39 (February 2002), pp. 110–19.

27. A. Hochschild, *The Managed Heart: Commercialization of Human Feeling* (Berkeley: University of California Press, 1983).

28. A. Hochschild, "Emotional Labor in the Friendly Skies," *Psychology Today,* June 1982, pp. 13–15.

29. For additional discussion on emotional labor strategies, see R. Leidner, "Emotional Labor in Service Work," *Annals of the American Academy of Political and Social Science* 561, no. 1 (1999), pp. 81–95.

30. M. D. Hartline and O. C. Ferrell, "The Management of Customer-Contact Service Employees: An Empirical Investigation," *Journal of Marketing* 60 (October 1996), pp. 52–70; J. Singh, J. R. Goolsby, and G. K. Rhoads, "Burnout and Customer Service Representatives," *Journal of Marketing Research* 31 (November 1994), pp. 558–69; L. A. Bettencourt and S. W. Brown, "Role Stressors and Customer-Oriented Boundary-Spanning Behaviors in Service Organizations," *Journal of the Academy of Marketing Science* 31 (Fall 2003), pp. 394–408.

31. B. Shamir, "Between Service and Servility: Role Conflict in Subordinate Service Roles," *Human Relations* 33, no. 10 (1980), pp. 741–56.

32. Ibid., pp. 744–45.

33. E. W. Anderson, C. Fornell, and R. T. Rust, "Customer Satisfaction, Productivity, and Profitability: Differences between Goods and Services," *Marketing Science* 16, no. 2 (1997), pp. 129–45.

34. J. Singh, "Performance Productivity and Quality of Frontline Employees in Service Organizations," *Journal of Marketing* 64 (April 2000), pp. 15–34.

35. For discussions of internal marketing, see L. L. Berry and A. Parasuraman, "Marketing to Employees," chap. 9 in *Marketing Services* (New York: The Free Press, 1991); C. Gronroos, "Managing Internal Marketing: A Prerequisite for Successful External Marketing," chap. 10 in *Service Management and Marketing* (Lexington, MA: Lexington Books, 1990).

36. B. Breen and A. Muoio, "PeoplePalooza 2001," *Fast Company,* January 2001, cover and feature article.

37. Berry and Parasuraman, "Marketing to Employees," p. 153.

38. K. J. Dunham, "The Jungle: Focus on Recruitment, Pay, and Getting Ahead," *The Wall Street Journal,* April 10, 2001, p. B14.

39. T. W. Ferguson, "Airline Asks Government for Room to Keep Rising," *The Wall Street Journal,* March 9, 1993, p. A17.

40. This section on hiring for service competencies and service inclination draws from work by B. Schneider and colleagues, specifically, B. Schneider and D. Schechter, "Development of a Personnel Selection System for Service Jobs," in *Service Quality: Multidisciplinary and Multinational Perspectives,* ed. S. W. Brown, E. Gummesson, B. Edvardsson, and B. Gustavsson (Lexington, MA: Lexington Books, 1991), pp. 217–36.

41. J. Hogan, R. Hogan, and C. M. Busch, "How to Measure Service Orientation," *Journal of Applied Psychology* 69, no. 1 (1984), pp. 167–73. See also Brown et al., "The Customer Orientation of Service Workers" and D. T. Donovan, T. J. Brown, and J. C. Mowen, "Internal Benefits of Service-Worker Customer Orientation: Job Satisfaction, Commitment, and Organizational Citizenship Behaviors," *Journal of Marketing* 68 (January 2004), pp. 128–46.

42. For a detailed description of a model selection system for telephone sales and service people, see Schneider and Schechter, "Development of a Personnel Selection System."

43. For additional information on Southwest Airlines hiring practices, see C. Mitchell, "Selling the Brand Inside," *Harvard Business Review* 80 (January 2002), pp. 99–105.

44. R. Levering and M. Moskowitz, *100 Best Companies to Work for in America* (New York: Penguin Group, 1994), p. 457.

45. "Low Wage Lessons: How Marriott Keeps Good Help Even at $7.40 an Hour," *BusinessWeek,* cover story, November 11, 1996, pp. 108–16.

46. R. Levering and M. Moskowitz, "The 100 Best Companies to Work For," *Fortune,* January 12, 2004, pp. 56–80.

47. R. Normann, "Getting People to Grow," *Service Management* (New York: John Wiley, 1984), pp. 44–50.

48. J. C. Chebat and P. Kollias, "The Impact of Empowerment on Customer Contact Employees' Roles in Service Organizations," *Journal of Service Research* 3 (August 2000), pp. 66–81.

49. C. Argyris, "Empowerment: The Emperor's New Clothes," *Harvard Business Review* 76 (May–June 1998), pp. 98–105.

50. D. E. Bowen and E. E. Lawler III, "The Empowerment of Service Workers: What, Why, How, and When," *Sloan Management Review,* Spring 1992, pp. 31–39.

51. J. H. Gittell, "Relationships between Service Providers and Their Impact on Customers," *Journal of Service Research* 4 (May 2002), pp. 299–311.

52. Berry and Parasuraman, "Marketing to Employees," p. 162.

53. A. Sergeant and S. Frenkel, "When Do Customer-Contact Employees Satisfy Customers?" *Journal of Service Research* 3 (August 2000), pp. 18–34.

54. Scheider and Bowen, *Winning the Service Game,* pp. 230–34.

55. C. Salter, "On the Road Again," *Fast Company,* January 2002, pp. 50–58.

56. O. Gadiesh and J. L. Gilbert, "Transforming Corner-Office Strategy into Front-line Action," *Harvard Business Review,* May 2001, pp. 73–79.

57. B. Fryer, "High Tech the Old Fashioned Way," *Harvard Business Review,* March 2001, pp. 119–25; C. Hawn, "The Man Who Sees around Corners," *Forbes,* January 21, 2002, pp. 72–78.

58. B. Fryer, "High Tech the Old-Fashioned Way."

59. H. Rosenbluth, "Tales from a Nonconformist Company," *Harvard Business Review,* July–August 1991, p. 33.

60. L. L. Berry, "The Employee as Customer," *Journal of Retail Banking* 3 (March 1981), pp. 33–40.

61. C. Hegge-Kleiser, "American Express Travel-Related Services: A Human Resources Approach to Managing Quality," in *Managing Quality in America's Most Admired Companies,* ed. J. W. Spechler (San Francisco: Berrett-Koehler Publishers, 1993), pp. 205–12.

62. "Balancing Work and Family," *BusinessWeek,* cover story, September 16, 1996, pp. 74–84.

63. M. C. Gilly and M. Wolfinbarger, "Advertising's Internal Audience," *Journal of Marketing* 62 (January 1998), pp. 69–88.

64. B. Fryer, "High Tech the Old-Fashioned Way."

65. See Schneider and Bowen, *Winning the Service Game,* chap. 6, for an excellent discussion of the complexities and issues involved in creating effective reward systems for service employees.

66. N. Bendapudi and R. P. Leone, "Managing Business-to-Business Customer Relationships Following Key Contact Employee Turnover in a Vendor Firm," *Journal of Marketing* 66 (April 2002), pp. 83–101.

67. Ibid.

68. J. R. Katzenbach and J. A. Santamaria, "Firing Up the Front Line," *Harvard Business Review,* May–June 1999, pp. 107–17.

69. Quoted in D. Stauffer, "The Art of Delivering Great Customer Service," *Harvard Management Update* 4, no. 9 (September 1999), pp. 1–3.

70. Gronroos, *Service Management and Marketing,* p. 244.

Chapter

13

CUSTOMERS' ROLES IN SERVICE DELIVERY

This chapter's objectives are to

1. Illustrate the importance of customers in successful service delivery and cocreation of service experiences.

2. Discuss the variety of roles that service customers play: productive resources for the organization; contributors to quality and satisfaction; competitors.

3. Explain strategies for involving service customers effectively to increase both quality and productivity.

iPrint = Self-Service Printing Online

In the current environment of online and Internet-based services, customers can produce services for themselves with little or no personal interaction with the provider. One company, iPrint, has changed the way home office and small business customers interact with commercial printers. iPrint.com, a Web-based custom printing service, describes itself as a "complete, fully automated, self-service online creation, ordering, and commercial printing environment."[1]

iPrint opened its Internet storefront in January 1997 and successfully survived the dramatic downturn in Internet-based businesses in 2000, earning many industry awards for e-commerce innovation, website design, and customer service in the years that followed. Much of the company's success can be attributed to its business model, which provides customers an easy, continually accessible way to independently create and order customized print jobs, sometimes at half the cost of traditional commercial printers. A quote from a satisfied customer is indicative: "Not only is it fun to design everything myself, but the quality is fabulous! You're my favorite company on the Internet!"

Customers of iPrint create their own value through participation in the production of customized printing services. Customers with little or no knowledge of graphic design can easily, quickly, and from the convenience of their own homes or offices create their own designs for a wide range of products. iPrint offers business cards, notepads, stationery, various gift items, and promotional products.

Although creating graphic designs is a complex process with hundreds of variables to consider, iPrint developed a simple step-by-step process to create personalized products. Customers adapt existing designs to meet their specifications and then view the finished products, selecting from a wide range of options such as paper, font, size, and color as well as clip art or business logos.

Completed designs can be purchased over the Internet and are typically received in a few days. Designs are also automatically saved to allow for easy reordering. Although iPrint notifies customers via e-mail when the order is placed and when it has been printed, customers are also able to actively participate after the order has been placed by tracking the order throughout processing, printing, and shipping.

In addition to extensive customer education through detailed step-by-step instructions, iPrint provides access to frequently asked questions, and contact with service providers is available through e-mail, phone, or fax if necessary. Customers participating in the design of their own products are rewarded with prices significantly lower than what they would normally pay. iPrint also offers a 30-day complete satisfaction guarantee, removing some of the risk customers may feel in ordering customized printed materials online.

iPrint has transformed a people-intensive, manual service business into an electronically automated, self-service function in which customers are empowered to create their own value and satisfaction. Because they do so much of the work, customers essentially become "coproducers" of the service, enhancing iPrint's productivity, which allows the company to charge lower prices.

So, will traditional providers of commercial printing services be driven out of business by companies like iPrint? Probably not. Some customers will always want personal advice and the direct involvement of professional designers. However, some segments of customers in the marketplace will respond to new choices and are willing to coproduce services, cocreating value and satisfaction for themselves.

In this chapter we examine the unique roles played by customers in service delivery situations. Service customers are often present in the "factory" (the place the service is produced and/or consumed), interacting with employees and with other customers. For example, in a classroom or training situation, students (the customers) are sitting in the factory interacting with the instructor and other students as they consume and cocreate the educational services. Because they are present during service production, customers can contribute to or detract from the successful delivery of the service and to their own satisfaction. In a manufacturing context, rarely does the production facility contend with customer presence on the factory floor, nor does it rely on the customer's immediate real-time input to manufacture the product. As our opening vignette illustrates, service customers can actually produce the service themselves and to some extent are responsible for their own satisfaction. Using iPrint's online services, customers cocreate value for themselves and in the process also reduce the prices they pay for printing services.

Because customers are participants in service production and delivery, they can potentially contribute to the widening of gap 3. That is, customers themselves can influence whether the delivered service meets customer-defined specifications. Sometimes customers contribute to gap 3 because they lack understanding of their roles and exactly what they should do in a given situation, particularly if the customer is confronting a service concept for the first time. Customers using the services of iPrint for the first time need detailed, but simple, instructions to help them understand how to use the service effectively and get the greatest value.

At other times customers may understand their roles but be unwilling or unable to perform for some reason. In a health club context, members may understand that to get into good physical shape they must follow the workout guidelines set up by the trainers. If work schedule or illness keeps members from living up to their part of the guidelines, the service will not be successful because of customer inaction. In a different service situation, customers may choose not to perform the roles defined for them because they are not rewarded in any way for contributing their effort. When service customers are enticed through price reductions, greater convenience, or some other tangible benefit, they are more likely to perform their roles willingly, as in the case of our opening vignette about iPrint.

Finally, gap 3 may be widened not through actions or inactions on the part of the customer, but because of what *other* customers do. Other customers who are in the service factory either receiving the service simultaneously (passengers on an airplane flight) or waiting their turn to receive the service sequentially (bank customers waiting in line, Disneyland customers waiting for one of the rides) can influence whether the service is effectively and efficiently delivered.

This chapter focuses on the roles of customers in service delivery and cocreation of service experiences as well as strategies to effectively manage them.

THE IMPORTANCE OF CUSTOMERS IN SERVICE DELIVERY

Customer participation at some level is inevitable in service delivery and cocreation. Services are actions or performances, typically produced and consumed simultaneously. In many situations employees, customers, and even others in the service environment interact to produce the ultimate service outcome. Because they participate, customers are indispensable to the production process of service organizations, and they can actually control or contribute to their own satisfaction.[2] Our Strategy Insight illustrates how a broadened view of customers as cocreators of value can lead to innovative strategies.

The importance of customers in successful service delivery is obvious if service performances are looked at as a form of drama. The drama metaphor for services (discussed in Chapter 3) suggests the reciprocal, interactive roles of employees (actors) and customers (audience) in creating the service experience. The service actors and audience are surrounded by the service setting or the servicescape (discussed in Chapter 11). The drama metaphor argues that the development and maintenance of an interaction (a service experience) relies on the audience's input as well as the actors' presentation. Through this metaphor, service performances or service delivery situations are viewed as tenuous, fragile processes that can be influenced by behaviors of customers as well as by employees.[3] Service performance results from actions and interactions among individuals in both groups.

Consider the services provided by a cruise ship company. The actors (ship's personnel) provide the service through interactions with their audience (the passengers) and among each other. The audience also produces elements of the service through interactions with the actors and other audience members. Both actors and audience are surrounded by an elaborate setting (the cruise ship itself) that provides a context to facilitate the service performance. The drama metaphor provides a compelling frame of reference for recognizing the interdependent roles of actors and audience in service delivery.[4]

Consultants, researchers, and strategists are urging companies to think about their customers in new ways. Instead of viewing customers as end recipients of predesigned goods and services, they encourage a view of customers as active cocreators of value. This view goes beyond thinking of customer involvement in idea development or design of new products, and it is more than customer participation in service delivery. Instead, this view suggests that the value customers receive is in the *cocreated experience* they have as a result of choosing and combining elements of the company's offerings to create their own "total experience." This box contains some examples to help make the cocreation idea more concrete and the strategic possibilities apparent.

Starbuck's customers create their own CDs at new Hear Music Coffee Houses.
Source: Courtesy Starbucks.

STARBUCK'S HEAR MUSIC COFFEE HOUSES

Starbuck's, the international coffee mega-success story, is venturing into music in a big way in an effort to strategically reinvent its brand. Its new Hear Music Coffee Houses allow customers to create a total experience around coffee, socializing, and music that Howard Schultz, Starbuck's chairman and chief global strategist, hopes will eventually turn the entire music business upside down. The Hear Music Coffee Houses include individual music listening stations with CD-burning capabilities so that customers can drink coffee, listen to their favorite music, and burn a personal CD of just about any music they can imagine. Customers can simply listen (with no restrictions on what they listen to or how long), or they can create a personalized CD by choosing their own cover art, creating an album title, and selecting their own songs. The personalized CD costs just $6.99 for the first five tracks on the CD and $1 for each additional song, plus about a 5-minute wait while it is produced. Schultz sees CD burning as just the first step in evolving Starbuck's to an international "music services" company where customers can someday use its enormous Wi-Fi footprint to access, buy, and store music on just about any device they wish. All the while, customers can also drink coffee and socialize (or not)—cocreating their own music experiences. Starbucks plans to have 1,000 Hear Music Coffee House locations up and running by the end of 2005.

ONSTAR

OnStar is a service launched by General Motors Corporation (GM) to provide safety and emergency services for its automobile customers. The system can unlock a customer's door remotely when the customer is locked out of the car, assess the severity of damage to the car following an accident, and help police track down a stolen vehicle. Over time the service has been expanded to include information and entertainment. For example, the system allows customers to access location-based information on restaurants such as, "find me the nearest Italian restaurant to my current location and make a reservation." Many providers, services, and experiences can be linked via the OnStar service, which is sensitive to time and location. Each customer thus has the opportunity to create a total and unique experience by combining elements of the system. To be successful with OnStar, GM needed to view the customer as a cocreator of value, understand the interconnected services that could be desirable within a vehicle, and have the foresight to connect the relevant suppliers and information within its system. In thinking of potential services desired within a "vehicle experience space," GM went beyond OnStar's core security offerings into a broad range of additional services that consumers can access in creating their travel experiences.

HOME DEPOT

Another example of customer cocreation can be seen in Home Depot's full range of home remodeling solutions. Historically the company simply provided a vast "do-it-yourself" product selection, coupled with in-store advice provided by sales associates, allowing customers to complete their own home projects. Its customers did all the work themselves. More recently, the company has expanded into complete remodeling services—from design assistance to product selection, delivery, contracting, and installation. Through actively involving the customer in all stages and even recommending alternative sources for products it does not carry, the company allows the customer to cocreate a constellation of value and a total remodeling experience. Home Depot's strategic role has been to recognize the components of the total remodeling experience from the customer's perspective and to provide customers easy access to information, prescreened services, and resources to cocreate value for themselves. Each customer can thereby create an individual experience with as much or as little participation as desired. Some customers will choose to "do it themselves," whereas others will turn the entire job over to Home Depot. Still other customers will pick and choose the services they desire, resulting in a level of participation somewhere between these two extremes.

As companies begin to think about the "experience space" their customers are in and start to view the world from their customers' perspective, the possibilities for strategic innovation are endless. This approach contrasts with a traditional perspective that sees companies as producers of standardized value and customers as receivers. Instead, this view begins to look at customers as cocreators of value and companies as facilitators of this process.

Sources: C. K. Prahalad and V. Ramaswamy, "The New Frontier of Experience Innovation, *MIT Sloan Management Review* (Summer 2003), pp. 12–18; S. L. Vargo and R. F. Lusch, "Evolving to a New Dominant Logic for Marketing," *Journal of Marketing* 68, no. 1 (January 2004), pp. 1–17; A. Overholt, "Listening to Starbuck's," *Fast Company* (July 2004), pp. 50–56;C. R. Schoenberger, "House Call," *Forbes* (September 6, 2004), pp. 93–94.

Recognition of the role of customers is also reflected in the definition of the *people* element of the services marketing mix given in Chapter 1: *all human actors who play a part in service delivery and thus influence the buyer's perceptions; namely, the firm's personnel, the customer, and other customers in the service environment.* Chapter 12 thoroughly examined the role of the firm's employees in delivering service quality. In this chapter we focus on the customer receiving the service and on fellow customers in the service environment.

Customer Receiving the Service

Because the customer receiving the service participates in the delivery process, he or she can contribute to narrowing or widening gap 3 through behaviors that are appropriate or inappropriate, effective or ineffective, productive or unproductive. Even in a relatively simple service such as retail mail order, customers' actions and preparation can have an effect on service delivery. Customers who are unprepared in terms of what they want to order can soak up the customer service representative's time as they seek advice. Similarly, shoppers who are not prepared with their credit card numbers can put the representative on hold while they search for their cards or retrieve them from another room or their cars. Meanwhile, other customers and calls are left unattended, causing longer wait times and potential dissatisfaction.

The level of customer participation—low, medium, high—varies across services, as shown in Table 13.1. In some cases, all that is required is the customer's physical pres-

TABLE 13.1   Levels of Customer Participation across Different Services

Low: Consumer Presence Required during Service Delivery	*Moderate:* Consumer Inputs Required for Service Creation	*High:* Customer Cocreates the Service Product
Products are standardized.	Client inputs (information, materials) customize a standard service.	Active client participation guides the customized service.
Service is provided regardless of any individual purchase.	Provision of service requires customer purchase.	Service cannot be created apart from the customer's purchase and active participation.
Payment may be the only required customer input.	Customer inputs are necessary for an adequate outcome, but the service firm provides the service.	Customer inputs are mandatory and cocreate the outcome.
End Consumer Examples		
Airline travel	Haircut	Marriage counseling
Motel stay	Annual physical exam	Personal training
Fast-food restaurant	Full-service restaurant	Weight reduction program
		Major illness or surgery
Business-to-Business Customer Examples		
Uniform cleaning service	Agency-created advertising campaign	Management consulting
Pest control	Payroll service	Executive management seminar
Interior greenery maintenance service	Freight transportation	Installation of computer network

Source: Adapted from A. R. Hubbert, "Customer Co-Creation of Service Outcomes: Effects of Locus of Causality Attributions," doctoral dissertation, Arizona State University, Tempe, Arizona, 1995.

ence (*low level of participation*), with the employees of the firm doing all the service production work, as in the example of a symphony concert. Symphony-goers must be present to receive the entertainment service, but little else is required once they are seated. In other situations, consumer inputs are required to aid the service organization in creating the service (*moderate level of participation*). Inputs can include *information, effort,* or *physical possessions.* All three of these are required for a CPA to prepare a client's tax return effectively: information in the form of tax history, marital status, and number of dependents; effort in putting the information together in a useful fashion; and physical possessions such as receipts and past tax returns. In some situations, customers are truly cocreators of the service (*high level of participation*). For these services, customers have mandatory production roles that, if not fulfilled, will affect the nature of the service outcome. In a complex or long-term business-to-business consulting engagement, the client can be involved in activities such as identification of issues, shared problem solving, ongoing communication, provision of equipment and work space, and implementation of solutions.[5] Facilitating this type of positive customer participation can help ensure a successful outcome, as described in Exhibit 13.1.

Table 13.1 provides several examples of each level of participation for both consumer and business-to-business services. The effectiveness of customer involvement at all the levels will impact organizational productivity and, ultimately, quality and customer satisfaction.

Fellow Customers

In many service contexts, customers receive the service simultaneously with other customers or must wait their turn while other customers are being served. In both cases, "fellow customers" are present in the service environment and can affect the nature of the service outcome or process. Fellow customers can either *enhance* or *detract* from customer satisfaction and perceptions of quality.[6]

Some of the ways fellow customers can negatively affect the service experience are by exhibiting disruptive behaviors, causing delays, excessively crowding, and manifesting incompatible needs. In restaurants, hotels, airplanes, and other environments in which customers are cheek to jowl as they receive the service, crying babies, smoking patrons, and loud, unruly groups can be disruptive and detract from the experiences of their fellow customers. The customer is disappointed through no direct fault of the provider. In other cases, overly demanding customers (even customers with legitimate problems) can cause a delay for others while their needs are met. This occurrence is common in banks, post offices, and customer service counters in retail stores. Excessive crowding or overuse of a service can also affect the nature of the customer's experience. Visiting Sea World in San Diego on the Fourth of July is a very different experience from visiting the same park midweek in February. Similarly, the quality of telecommunication services can suffer on special holidays such as Christmas and Mother's Day when large numbers of customers all try to use the service at once.

Finally, customers who are being served simultaneously but who have incompatible needs can negatively affect each other. This situation can occur in restaurants, college classrooms, hospitals, and any service establishment in which multiple segments are served simultaneously. In a study of critical service encounters occurring in tourist attractions across central Florida, researchers found that customers negatively affected each other when they failed to follow either explicit or implicit "rules of conduct." Customers reported such negative behaviors as pushing, shoving, smoking, drinking alcohol, being verbally abusive, or cutting in line. Other times, dissatisfaction resulted when other customers were impersonal, rude, unfriendly, or even spiteful.[7]

Exhibit 13.1   CLIENT COPRODUCTION IN BUSINESS-TO-BUSINESS SERVICES

What do firms like IBM, McKinsey, Accenture, and neoIT have in common? All can be described as knowledge-intensive business services (KIBS) whose value-added activities provide their business clients with highly customized services (e.g., technical engineering, consulting, software development, business process outsourcing). To develop and deliver optimal service solutions, KIBS rely on inputs and cooperation from their clients as integral coproducers of the services. The KIBS provider needs accurate and detailed information from the client, access to people and resources, and cooperation in terms of deadlines and contingencies that inevitably arise.

Depth interviews and research conducted with clients of employees of an IT services provider ("TechCo") identified a number of *client* characteristics that can enhance the quality of the client's participation and the ultimate service outcome in these types of KIBS relationships. The characteristics are listed here with an illustrative quote from or about one of TechCo's clients, using disguised names. Clients who display these types of coproduction behaviors will contribute to the success of their projects and are likely to get better outcomes and be more satisfied.

- **Communication openness:** The client is forthcoming and honest in sharing pertinent information for project success.

  PharmCo actually did the up-front work to understand what it is we have to do, when we have to do it, and how it fits into our overall scheme of things . . . We [spent] the first days doing nothing but teaching them about what we're trying to accomplish.—TechCo, about PharmCo Client

- **Shared problem solving:** The client takes individual initiative and shared responsibility for developing solutions to problems that arise in the relationship.

  I think, as a customer, I have a responsibility to bring some critical thinking to what they've brought to the table. Not just to accept it . . . [You need to be able to say,] "I don't know if that's going to work for our environment" or technically, "Why did you do that?" So a lot of it's just asking questions and saying, "Why are we doing it that way? Is that the best way to do it?"—GovCo Client

- **Tolerance:** The client responds in an understanding and patient manner in the face of minor project encumbrances.

  That certainly was our goal—not to have roadblocks, not to have problems . . . And even at that, it took us longer than we had hoped. Again, not anybody's fault, it's just one of those things. It's a process, and sometimes those processes take a little longer than you initially had planned for.—EduCo Client

- **Accommodation:** The client demonstrates a willingness to accommodate the desires, approaches, and expert judgment of the service provider.

  [If we saw something that didn't fit with our goals,] we'd call them and ask them . . . If they could do it, they would simply say, "Oh, you bet, no problem" . . . If it was something that we really couldn't monkey with too much, they'd come out and say, "No, you probably don't want to change that because of this reason and that reason" and we'd say,

We can offer just as many examples of other customers enhancing satisfaction and quality for their fellow customers as detracting from them. Sometimes the mere presence of other customers enhances the experience, for example, at sporting events, in movie theaters, and in other entertainment venues. The presence of other patrons is essential for true enjoyment of these experiences. In other situations, fellow customers provide a positive social dimension to the service experience. At health clubs, churches, and resorts such as Club Med, other customers provide opportunities to socialize and build friendships, as suggested in Figure 13.1.

In some situations, customers may actually help each other achieve service goals and outcomes. The success of the Weight Watchers organization, for example, depends significantly on the camaraderie and support that group members provide each other. The study of central Florida tourist attractions mentioned earlier found that customers increased the satisfaction of others by having friendly conversations while waiting in

"Okay, that's fine" and we'd go on to the next one.—EduCo Client

- **Advocacy:** The client firm provides a vocal advocate and salesperson for the project.

  [The scope of the project] was cumbersome. Had we not had involvement and not had a group of people who had ownership, who really wanted to succeed, we might have been inclined to say…"I don't really care how this turns out because the boss told me I need to do it. I don't care if it's ugly because I'm never going to use it." So, I think it was a combination of things. One is having people who have a vested interest in making sure it worked and knew why they were doing it and [second] continuous involvement.—AgCo Client

- **Involvement in project governance:** The client takes an active role in monitoring project progress toward the stated goal.

  We would have our meetings and we'd set these action items. We would say when they're supposed to be done, and we would set the next meeting before we ended that meeting so everybody knew what their expectations were.—DonorCo Client

- **Personal dedication:** The client demonstrates a sense of personal obligation for project success by performing individual responsibilities in a conscientious manner.

  I think that was one of the things that I probably did right—was staying that involved. But it was hard, from my perspective, because it took time away from other things that I had

to do. But I think I brought some things to the project that, if I hadn't been as involved, I don't know that we would have had as successful an implementation of the three systems as I think we did.—GovCo Client

The challenge for KIBS firms is to develop processes, systems, and practices that will ensure that clients engage in these ways. The research suggests that these positive coproduction behaviors will be most likely when KIBS provider firms engage in (1) *client selectivity* (carefully screening clients in advance to ensure a good fit between provider and client); (2) *client training, education, and socialization* (making clients feel that they are part of the team by kicking off the relationship with a cooperative spirit, perhaps including events and expectations-setting workshops); and (3) *project leadership and client performance evaluation* (selecting the right project leaders on both sides and evaluating both on their relationship management skills as well as technical capabilities).

This research illustrates the importance of business clients as coproducers of the service and the value to both provider and client that can result from quality coproduction behaviors and associated business practices.

line, by taking photos, by assisting with children, and by returning dropped or lost items.[8] An ethnographic study that observed hundreds of hours of customer interactions among travelers on the U.K. rail system found that customers often helped each other by (1) providing important service-related information (e.g., schedules, interesting features en route) that can reduce trip-related anxiety; (2) engaging in enjoyable conversation, thus making the trip more pleasant; and (3) serving as someone to complain to when mishaps and service failures occurred.[9]

Customers helping each other is not limited to consumer services. An interesting example occurs at networking giant Cisco. By giving business customers open access to its information and systems through its online self-service, Cisco enables customers to engage in dialogue with each other, helping themselves and other customers who may be experiencing similar challenges. PeopleSoft, the enterprise software provider, assists its customers in helping each other through its annual user meetings, during which customers share their experiences using PeopleSoft products.

FIGURE 13.1
Social interactions with others can influence health club members' satisfaction with the service.

Source: David Madison/Getty Images

CUSTOMERS' ROLES

The following sections examine in more detail three major roles played by customers in service delivery: customers as productive resources; customers as contributors to quality and satisfaction; and customers as competitors.

Customers as Productive Resources

Service customers have been referred to as "partial employees" of the organization—human resources who contribute to the organization's productive capacity.[10] Some management experts have suggested that the organization's boundaries be expanded to consider the customer as part of the service system. In other words, if customers contribute effort, time, or other resources to the service production process, they should be considered as part of the organization. (Later in the chapter we devote a section to defining customers' jobs and strategies for managing them effectively.)

Customer inputs can affect the organization's productivity through both the quality of what they contribute and the resulting quality and quantity of output generated. In a business-to-business services context (see Exhibit 13.1), the contributions of the client can enhance the overall productivity of the firm in both quality and quantity of service.[11] In a very different context, Southwest Airlines depends on customers to perform critical service roles for themselves, thus increasing the overall productivity of the airline. Passengers are asked to carry their own bags when transferring to other airlines, get their own food, and seat themselves.

Customer participation in service production raises a number of issues for organizations. Because customers can influence both the quality and quantity of production, some experts believe the delivery system should be isolated as much as possible from customer inputs in order to reduce the uncertainty they can bring into the production process. This view sees customers as a major source of uncertainty—in the timing of their demands and the uncontrollability of their attitudes and actions. The logical conclusion is that any service activities that do not require customer contact or involvement should be performed away from customers: The less direct contact there is between the customer and the service production system, the greater the potential for the system to operate at peak efficiency.[12]

Other experts believe that services can be delivered most efficiently if customers are truly viewed as partial employees and their coproduction roles are designed to maximize their contributions to the service creation process. The logic behind this view is that organizational productivity can be increased if customers learn to perform service-related activities they currently are not doing or are educated to perform more effectively the tasks they are already doing.[13]

For example, when self-service gasoline stations first came into being, customers were asked to pump their own gas. With customers performing this task, fewer employees were needed and the overall productivity of gas stations improved. Now many gas stations offer customers the option of paying for their gas at the pump by popping their credit cards into a slot on the pump or using a wireless device and leaving the station without dealing directly with a cashier. Similarly, the introduction of many automated airline services such as baggage check-in and self-ticketing are intended to speed up the process for customers while freeing employees for other tasks.[14] Organizational productivity is increased by using customers as a resource to perform tasks previously completed by employees. In both business-to-business and business-to-consumer contexts, organizations are turning to automated and online customer service, as we noted in our Technology Spotlight in Chapter 1. One prominent goal with online customer service is to increase organizational productivity by using the customer as a partial employee, performing his or her own service.

Although organizations derive obvious productivity benefits by involving customers as coproducers, customers do not always like or accept their new roles, especially when they perceive the purpose to be bottom-line cost savings for the company. If customers see no clear benefit to being involved in coproduction (e.g., lower prices, quicker access, better quality outcome), then they are likely to resent and resist their coproduction roles.

Customers as Contributors to Service Quality and Satisfaction

Another role customers can play in services cocreation and delivery is that of contributor to their own satisfaction and the ultimate quality of the services they receive. Customers may care little that they have increased the productivity of the organization through their participation, but they likely care a great deal about whether their needs are fulfilled. Effective customer participation can increase the likelihood that needs are met and that the benefits the customer seeks are actually attained. Think about services such as health care, education, personal fitness, and weight loss in which the service outcome is highly dependent on customer participation. In these services, unless the customers perform their roles effectively, the desired service outcomes are not possible.

Research has shown that in education, active participation by students—as opposed to passive listening—increases learning (the desired service outcome) significantly.[15] The same is true in health care; patient compliance, in terms of taking prescribed medications or changing diet or other habits, can be critical to whether patients regain their health (the desired service outcome).[16] In both these examples, the customers contribute directly to the quality of the outcome and to their own satisfaction with the service. In a business-to-business context, Yellow Roadway Corporation and others in the industry have found that in many situations customers cause their own *dissatisfaction* with the service by failing to pack shipments appropriately, resulting in breakage or delays while items are repacked.

Research suggests that customers who believe they have done their part to be effective in service interactions are more satisfied with the service. In a study of the banking industry, bank customers were asked to rate themselves (on a scale from "strongly agree" to "strongly disagree") on questions related to their contributions to service delivery, as follows:

What They Did—Outcome Quality of Customer Inputs

I clearly explained what I wanted the bank employee to do.

I gave the bank employee proper information.

I tried to cooperate with the bank employee.

I understand the procedures associated with this service.

How They Did It—Interaction Quality of Customer Inputs

I was friendly to the bank employee.

I have a good relationship with the bank employee.

I was courteous to the bank employee.

Receiving this service was a pleasant experience.

Results of the study indicated that the customers' perceptions of both what they did and how they did it were significantly related to customers' satisfaction with the service they received from the bank.[17] That is, those customers who responded more positively to the questions listed above were also more satisfied with the bank. Research in another context showed that customers' perceptions of service quality increased with greater levels of participation. Specifically, customers (in this case members of a YMCA) who participated more in the club gave the club higher ratings on aspects of service quality than did those who participated less.[18]

Customers contribute to quality service delivery when they ask questions, take responsibility for their own satisfaction, and complain when there is a service failure. Consider the service scenarios shown in Exhibit 13.2.[19] The four scenarios illustrate the wide variations in customer participation that can result in equally wide variations in service quality and customer satisfaction. Customers who take responsibility and providers who encourage their customers to become their partners in identifying and satisfying their own needs will together produce higher levels of service quality. Our Global Feature shows how Sweden's IKEA, the world's largest retailer of home furnishings, has creatively engaged its customers in a new role: "IKEA wants its customers to understand that their role is not to *consume* value but to *create* it."[20]

In addition to contributing to their own satisfaction by improving the quality of service delivered to them, some customers simply enjoy participating in service delivery. These customers find the act of participating to be intrinsically attractive.[21] They enjoy using the Internet to attain airline tickets, or doing all their banking via ATMs and automated phone systems, or pumping their own gas. Often customers who like self-service in one setting are predisposed to serving themselves in other settings as well.

Interestingly, because service customers must participate in service delivery, they frequently blame themselves (at least partially) when things go wrong. Why did it take so long to reach an accurate diagnosis of my health problem? Why was the service contract for our company's cafeteria food full of errors? Why was the room we reserved for our meeting unavailable when we arrived? If customers believe they are partially (or totally) to blame for the failure, they may be less dissatisfied with the service provider than when they believe the provider is responsible.[22] A recent series of stud-

For each scenario, ask "Which customer (A or B) will be most satisfied and receive the greatest quality and value, and why?"

SCENARIO 1: A MAJOR INTERNATIONAL HOTEL

Guest A called the desk right after check-in to report that his TV was not working and that the light over the bed was burned out; both problems were fixed immediately. The hotel staff exchanged his TV for one that worked and fixed the light bulb. Later they brought him a fruit plate to make up for the inconvenience. Guest B did not communicate to management until checkout time that his TV did not work and he could not read in his bed. His complaints were over-heard by guests checking in, who wondered whether they had chosen the right place to stay.

SCENARIO 2: OFFICE OF A PROFESSIONAL TAX PREPARER

Client A has organized into categories the information necessary to do her taxes and has provided all documents requested by the accountant. Client B has a box full of papers and receipts, many of which are not relevant to her taxes but which she brought along "just in case."

SCENARIO 3: AN AIRLINE FLIGHT FROM LONDON TO NEW YORK

Passenger A arrives for the flight with a portable tape player and reading material and wearing warm clothes; passenger A also called ahead to order a special meal. Passenger B, who arrives empty-handed, becomes annoyed when the crew runs out of blankets, complains about the magazine selection and the meal, and starts fidgeting after the movie.

SCENARIO 4: ARCHITECTURAL CONSULTATION FOR REMODELING AN OFFICE BUILDING

Client A has invited the architects to meet with its remodeling and design committee made up of managers, staff, and customers in order to lay the groundwork for a major remodeling job that will affect everyone who works in the building as well as customers. The committee has already formulated initial ideas and surveyed staff and customers for input. Client B has invited architects in following a decision the week previously to remodel the building; the design committee is two managers who are preoccupied with other, more immediate tasks and have little idea what they need or what customers and staff would prefer in terms of a redesign of the office space.

ies suggests the existence of this "self-serving bias." That is, when services go better than expected, customers who have participated tend to take credit for the outcome and are less satisfied with the firm than are those customers who have not participated. However, when the outcome is worse than expected, customers who have chosen to participate in service production are less dissatisfied with the service than are those who choose not to participate—presumably because the participating customers have taken on some of the blame themselves.[23]

Customers as Competitors

A final role played by service customers is that of potential competitor. If self-service customers can be viewed as resources of the firm, or as "partial employees," they could in some cases partially perform the service or perform the entire service for themselves and not need the provider at all. Thus customers in a sense are competitors of the companies that supply the service. Whether to produce a service for themselves (*internal exchange*)—for example, child care, home maintenance, car repair—or have someone else provide the service for them (*external exchange*) is a common dilemma for consumers.[24]

Similar internal versus external exchange decisions are made by organizations. Firms frequently choose to outsource service activities such as payroll, data processing,

IKEA of Sweden has managed to transform itself from a small mail-order furniture company in the 1950s into the world's largest retailer of home furnishings. In 2004 over 200 stores in 30 countries around the world generated more than $13 billion in revenues. The company sells simple Scandinavian design furnishings, charging 25 to 50 percent less than its competitors.

A key to IKEA's success is the company's relationship with its customers. IKEA has drawn the customer into its production system: "If customers agree to take on certain key tasks traditionally done by manufacturers and retailers—the assembly of products and their delivery to customers' homes—then IKEA promises to deliver well-designed products at substantially lower prices." In effect IKEA's customers become essential contributors to value—they create value for themselves through participating in the manufacturing, design, and delivery processes.

IKEA has made being part of the value creation process an easy, fun, and pleasant experience for customers. The company's stores are a pleasure to shop in. The stores are set up with "inspirational displays," including realistic room settings and real-life homes that allow customers to get comfortable with the furnishings, try them out, and visualize the possibilities in their own homes. To make shopping easy, free strollers and supervised child care are provided as well as wheelchairs for those who need them.

When customers enter the store they are given catalogs, tape measures, pens, and notepaper to use as they shop, allowing them to perform functions commonly done by sales and service staff. After payment, customers take their purchases to their cars on carts; if necessary they can rent or buy a roof rack to carry larger purchases. Thus customers also provide furniture loading and delivery services for themselves. At home, IKEA customers then take on the role of manufacturer in assembling the new furnishings following carefully written, simple, and direct instructions.

research, accounting, maintenance, and facilities management. They find that it is advantageous to focus on their core businesses and leave these essential support services to others with greater expertise. Alternatively, a firm may decide to stop purchasing services externally and bring the service production process in-house.

Whether a household or a firm chooses to produce a particular service for itself or contract externally for the service depends on a variety of factors. A proposed model of internal/external exchange suggests that such decisions depend on the following:[25]

Expertise capacity: The likelihood of producing the service internally is increased if the household or firm possesses the specific skills and knowledge needed to produce it. Having the expertise will not necessarily result in internal service production, however, because other factors (available resources and time) will also influence the decision. (For firms, making the decision to outsource is often based on recognizing that although they may have the expertise, someone else can do it better.)

Resource capacity: To decide to produce a service internally, the household or firm must have the needed resources including people, space, money, equipment, and materials. If the resources are not available internally, external exchange is more likely.

IKEA prints catalogs in 17 different languages, making its products and instructions for their use accessible worldwide. In addition to tailoring its catalogs, another key to IKEA's successful global expansion has been the company's policy of allowing each store to tailor its mix according to the local market needs and budgets. For example, in its China stores, layouts reflect the design of many Chinese apartments. Because many of the apartments have balconies, the stores have a selection of balcony furnishings and displays. And because Chinese kitchens are generally small, few kitchen items and furnishings are shown. Even IKEA's famous "do it yourself" (DIY) assembly concept has also been adapted to some extent in China. Because fewer people have cars and therefore use public transportation, IKEA has more extensive delivery service in China than in most countries. And because labor is cheaper in China, many customers choose to have their furniture assembled for them rather than doing it themselves. Although IKEA has not abandoned its DIY strategy, it has been somewhat more flexible in China to suit customer realities in that country.

IKEA's success is attributable in part to recognizing that customers can be part of the business system, performing roles they have never performed before. The company's flexible implementation of this idea through clearly defining customers' new roles and making it fun to perform these roles is the genius of its strategy. Through the process, customers cocreate their own experiences and contribute to their own satisfaction.

Sources: http://www.ikea.com; R. Normann and R. Ramirez, "From Value Chain to Value Constellation: Designing Interactive Strategy," *Harvard Business Review,* July–August 1993, pp. 65–77; B. Edvardsson and B. Enquist, "The IKEA Saga: How Service Culture Drives Service Strategy," *The Service Industries Journal* 22 (October 2002), pp. 153–86; P. M. Miller, "IKEA with Chinese Characteristics," *The China Business Review* (July/August 2004), pp. 36–38; www.ikea.com, 2004.

Time capacity: Time is a critical factor in internal/external exchange decisions. Households and firms with adequate time capacity are more likely to produce services internally than are groups with time constraints.

Economic rewards: The economic advantages or disadvantages of a particular exchange decision will be influential in choosing between internal and external options. The actual monetary costs of the two options will sway the decision.

Psychic rewards: Rewards of a noneconomic nature have a potentially strong influence on exchange decisions. Psychic rewards include the degree of satisfaction, enjoyment, gratification, or happiness that is associated with the external or internal exchange.

Trust: In this context *trust* means the degree of confidence or certainty the household or firm has in the various exchange options. The decision will depend to some extent on the level of self-trust in producing the service versus trust of others.

Control: The household or firm's desire for control over the process and outcome of the exchange will also influence the internal/external choice. Entities that desire and can implement a high degree of control over the task are more likely to engage in internal exchange.

The important thing to remember from this section is that in many service scenarios customers can and often do choose to fully or partially produce the service themselves. Thus, in addition to recognizing that customers can be productive resources and cocreators of quality and value, organizations also need to recognize the customer's role as a potential competitor.

SELF-SERVICE TECHNOLOGIES—THE ULTIMATE IN CUSTOMER PARTICIPATION

Self-service technologies (SSTs) are services produced entirely by the customer without any direct involvement or interaction with the firm's employees. As such SSTs represent the ultimate form of customer participation along a continuum from services that are produced entirely by the firm to those that are produced entirely by the customer. This continuum is depicted in Figure 13.2, using the example of retail gasoline service to illustrate the various ways the same service could be delivered along all points on the continuum. At the far right end of the continuum, the gas station attendant does everything from pumping the gas to taking payment. On the other end of the spectrum, the customer does everything; in between are various forms and levels of customer participation. Many service delivery options, across industries, could be laid out on this type of continuum from total customer production through total firm production.

A Proliferation of New SSTs

Advances in technology, particularly the Internet, have allowed the introduction of a wide range of self-service technologies that occupy the far left end of the customer participation continuum in Figure 13.2. These technologies have proliferated as companies see the potential cost savings and efficiencies that can be achieved, potential sales growth, increased customer satisfaction, and competitive advantage. A partial list of some of the self-service technologies available to consumers includes

- ATMs.
- Pay at the pump.
- Airline check-in.
- Hotel check-in and checkout.
- Automated car rental.
- Automated filing of legal claims.
- Online driver's license testing.
- Automated betting machines.
- Electronic blood pressure machines.
- Various vending services.
- Tax preparation software.
- Self-scanning at retail stores.

- Internet banking.
- Vehicle registration online.
- Online auctions.
- Home and car buying online.
- Automated investment transactions.
- Insurance online.
- Package tracking.
- Internet shopping.
- Internet information search.
- Interactive voice response phone systems.
- Distance education.

FIGURE 13.2
Services Production Continuum

Source: Adapted from M. L. Meuter and M. J. Bitner, "Self-Service Technologies: Extending Service Frameworks and Identifying Issues for Research," in *Marketing Theory and Applications*, ed. D. Grewal and C. Pechmann (American Marketing Association Winter Educators' Conference, 1998), pp. 12–19. Reprinted by permission of the American Marketing Association.

Gas station illustration
1. Customer pumps gas and pays at the pump with automation.
2. Customer pumps gas and goes inside to pay attendant.
3. Customer pumps gas and attendant takes payment at the pump.
4. Attendant pumps gas and customer pays at the pump with automation.
5. Attendant pumps gas and customer goes inside to pay attendant.
6. Attendant pumps gas and takes payment from customer at the pump.

The rapid proliferation of new SSTs is occurring for several reasons.[26] Many times firms are tempted by the cost savings that they anticipate by shifting customers to technology-based, automated systems and away from expensive personal service. If cost savings is the only reason for introducing an SST and if customers see no apparent benefits, the SST is likely to fail. Customers quickly see through this strategy and are not likely to adopt the SST if they have alternative options for service. Other times, firms introduce new SSTs based on customer demand. More and more, customers are expecting to find access to information, services, and delivery options online. When they do not find what they want from a particular firm online, they are likely to choose a competitor. Thus, customer demand in some industries is forcing firms to develop and offer their services via technology. Other companies are developing SSTs in order to open up new geographic, socioeconomic, and lifestyle markets that were not available to them through traditional channels.

Customer Usage of SSTs

Some of the SSTs listed above—ATMs, pay-at-the-pump gas, Internet information search—have been very successful, embraced by customers for the benefits they provide in terms of convenience, accessibility, and ease of use.[27] Benefits to firms, including cost savings and revenue growth, can also result for those SSTs that succeed. Others—airline ticket kiosks, online hotel bookings, grocery self-scanning—have been less quickly embraced by customers.

Failure results when customers see no personal benefit in the new technology or when they do not have the ability to use it or know what they are supposed to do. Often, adopting a new SST requires customers to change their traditional behaviors significantly, and many are reluctant to make those changes. Research looking at customer adoption of SSTs found that "customer readiness" was a major factor in determining whether customers would even try a new self-service option.[28] Customer readiness results from a combination of personal motivation (What is in it for me?), ability (Do I have the ability to use this SST?), and role clarity (Do I understand what I am supposed to do?). Other times customers see no value in using the technology when compared to the alternative interpersonal mode of delivery; or the SSTs may be so poorly designed that customers may prefer not to use them, as we noted in the Technology Spotlight in Chapter 3.[29]

Success with SSTs

Throughout the text we have highlighted some of the most successful self-service technologies in the marketplace today: Cisco Systems (Chapter 8), Wells Fargo (Chapter 9),

Amazon.com (Chapter 5), and iPrint (the opening vignette in this chapter). These companies have been successful because they offer clear benefits to customers, the benefits are well understood and appreciated compared to the alternative delivery modes, and the technology is user-friendly and reliable. In addition, customers understand their roles and have the capability to use the technology.

From a strategic perspective, research suggests that as firms move into SSTs as a mode of delivery, these questions are important to ask:[30]

- What is our strategy? What do we hope to achieve through the SST (cost savings, revenue growth, competitive advantage)?

- What are the benefits to customers of producing the service on their own through the SST? Do they know and understand these benefits?

- How can customers be motivated to try the SST? Do they understand their role? Do they have the capability to perform this role?

- How "technology ready" are our customers?[31] Are some segments of customers more ready to use the technology than others?

- How can customers be involved in the design of the service technology system and processes so that they will be more likely to adopt and use the SST?

- What forms of customer education will be needed to encourage adoption? Will other incentives be needed?

- How will inevitable SST failures be handled to regain customer confidence?

STRATEGIES FOR ENHANCING CUSTOMER PARTICIPATION

The level and the nature of customer participation in the service process are strategic decisions that can impact an organization's productivity, its positioning relative to competitors, its service quality, and its customers' satisfaction. In the following sections we will examine the strategies captured in Figure 13.3 for involving customers effectively in the service delivery process. The overall goals of a customer participation strategy will typically be to increase organizational productivity and customer satisfaction while simultaneously decreasing uncertainty due to unpredictable customer actions.

Define Customers' Jobs

In developing strategies for addressing customer involvement in service delivery, the organization first determines what type of participation it wants from customers, thus beginning to define the customer's "job." Identifying the current level of customer participation can serve as a starting point. Customers' roles may be partially predetermined by the nature of the service, as suggested in Table 13.1. The service may require only the customer's presence (a concert, airline travel), or it may require moderate levels of input from the customer in the form of effort or information (a haircut, tax preparation), or it may require the customer to actually cocreate the service outcome (fitness training, consulting self-service offerings).

The organization may decide that it is satisfied with the existing level of participation it requires from customers but wants to make the participation more effective. For example, Charles Schwab has always positioned itself as a company whose customers are highly involved in their personal investment decisions. Over time this position has

FIGURE 13.3
Strategies for Enhancing Customer Participation

Source: Adapted from M.L. Meuter and M.J. Bitner, "Self Service Technologies: Extending Service Frameworks and Identifying Issues for Research," in Marketing Theory and Applications, ed. D. Grewal and C. Pechmann (American Marketing Association Winter Educators' Conference, 1998), pp. 12-19. Reprinted by permission of the American Marketing Association.

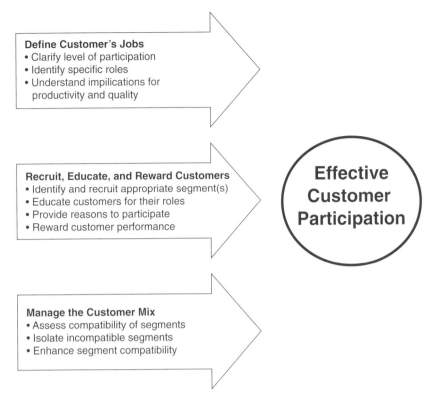

been implemented in different ways. Advances in technology have allowed Charles Schwab to solidify its position as a leading investment company for independent investors.

Alternatively, the organization may choose to increase the level of customer participation, which may reposition the service in the customers' eyes. Experts have suggested that higher levels of customer participation are strategically advisable when service production and delivery are inseparable; marketing benefits (cross-selling, building loyalty) can be enhanced by on-site contact with the customer; and customers can supplement for the labor and information provided by employees.[32]

In health care, researchers and providers are working on ways to gain more active customer participation in treatment decisions. The Internet and other technology advances have helped propel customers into this role in taking responsibility for their own health and well-being, as illustrated in our Technology Spotlight.

Finally, the organization may decide it wants to reduce customer participation due to all the uncertainties it causes. In such situations the strategy may be to isolate all but the essential tasks, keeping customers away from the service facility and employees as much as possible.[33] Mail order is an extreme example of this form of service. Customers are in contact with the organization via telephone or the Internet, never see the organization's facility, and have limited employee interactions. The customer's role is thus extremely limited and can interfere very little with the service delivery process.

Once the desired level of participation is clear, the organization can define more specifically what the customer's "job" entails.[34] The customer's "job description" will vary with the type of service and the organization's desired position within its industry. The job might entail helping oneself, helping others, or promoting the company.

Technology Spotlight
Technology Facilitates Customer Participation in Health Care

Customer participation is facilitated by technology in many industries. For example, in education, technology allows students to interact with each other and their professors via e-mail and discussion boards. In real estate, technology allows buyers to preview homes and develop lists of places they would like to visit without having to rely totally on a real estate agent to find all available properties. And in high-technology industries, business customers often interact with each other on the Web, helping each other solve problems, answering each other's questions, and so forth. All these examples show how technology—particularly the Internet—has facilitated customer participation and increased customer satisfaction.

Nowhere is this result more apparent than in health care. There is probably no greater, higher-participation service context than health care, where the customer must participate and where the provider and customer clearly cocreate the service. Patient participation is required at multiple levels. To achieve optimal health outcomes, patients must

- Provide accurate information about symptoms and health background.

- Answer detailed questions.

- Help to decide on a course of treatment.

- Carry out the prescribed regimen leading to recovery.

Technology is clearly influencing how customers perform these roles and shifting in some senses the power of information into the hands of consumers. Two studies by the Pew Internet and American Life Project, funded by the Pew Charitable Trusts, illuminate the trends in online health care as well as some of the challenging issues. This research showed that as of March 2002, 62 percent of U.S. Internet users, or over 73 million people, had gone online in search of health information. Of these "health seekers," a significant percentage go online for health care information at least once per month, and about half say the advice found there has helped improve the way they take care of themselves. They seek information about specific diseases, mental health, nutrition and fitness, drugs and drug interactions, and specific doctors and hospitals. Over 40 percent seek information for themselves and their own medical conditions, and over 50 percent seek information on behalf of a friend or family member. People like getting health information this way because of the convenience, the wealth of information that is available, and the fact that research can be done anonymously.

Thousands of Internet sites provide some type of health-related information. Some belong to health care providers like Mayo Clinic (www.mayo.edu) or pharmacy benefits providers like Caremark (www.caremark.com). Others are operated totally online—like WebMD (www.webmdhealth.com) or Drugstore.com (www.drugstore.com)—without affiliation to a specific health care provider. Some respected sites are sponsored by governmental entities such as the U.S. Department of Health and Human Services site (www.healthfinder.gov) and a site developed by the Na-

Helping Oneself

In many cases the organization may decide to increase the level of customer involvement in service delivery through active participation, as shown in Figure 13.4. In such situations the customer becomes a productive resource, performing aspects of the service heretofore performed by employees or others. Many of the examples presented in this chapter are illustrations of customers "helping themselves" (IKEA of Sweden, Charles Schwab, the Technology Spotlight). The result may be increased productivity for the firm and/or increased value, quality, and satisfaction for the customer.

Helping Others

Sometimes the customer may be called on to help others who are experiencing the service. A child at a day care center might be appointed "buddy of the day" to help a new child acclimate into the environment. Long-time residents of retirement communities often assume comparable roles to welcome new residents. Many universities have es-

tional Library of Medicine and the National Institutes of Health (www.medlineplus.gov). Yet other sites provide information for specific health conditions such as AIDS, depression, diabetes, breast cancer, and so on.

All this readily available medical information has the potential to change the role of the health care consumer to one of active participant in diagnosing illnesses, assessing treatment options, and determining overall well-being. Armed with information, patients gain confidence in asking questions and seeking appropriate diagnoses. In some cases they can e-mail questions to their doctors or other providers or find support in chat groups, bulletin boards, and e-mail lists on the Internet.

Despite this growth and popularity, patients and doctors share concerns regarding health information online. The two primary concerns are privacy of patient data and reliability of health information provided online. The Pew study of Internet health care usage found that 63 percent of those who sought health information on the Internet felt that putting their own private medical records and information on the Web would be a bad idea; 89 percent were concerned that their information could be sold to a third party; 85 percent were concerned that their insurance company might raise their rates or deny coverage based on sites they visited; and 52 percent were concerned about employers finding out which sites they visited. Many (86 percent) were also concerned about the reliability of the information they found on the Web.

Although health laws being implemented in the United States are intended to protect patient informa-

tion privacy, it appears that many websites may fall between the cracks in terms of being required to follow the new laws unless they are owned or operated by a health care provider, a health plan, or a health care clearinghouse. Thus consumers will continue to be wary of putting their personal health information on the Web.

As for information reliability, many sites are now making very apparent the sources of their information. For example, Aetna Intelihealth (www.Intelihealth.com) is closely linked with Harvard's medical school. National and international associations are also developing standards and "seal of approval" programs to address privacy, security, and quality of information on the Internet.

Despite the concerns and issues, the usage of health care information on the Web continues to increase and will forever change the way patients participate in health care.

Sources: "The Online Health Care Revolution: How the Web Helps Americans Take Better Care of Themselves," The Pew Internet and American Life Project, November 2000, www.pewinternet.org; "Exposed Online: Why the New Federal Health Privacy Regulation Doesn't Offer Much Protection to Internet Users," The Pew Internet and American Life Project, November 2001, www.pewinternet.org; "Vital Decisions," The Pew Internet and American Life Project, May 2002, www.pewinternet.org.

tablished mentoring programs, particularly for students from minority groups, in which experienced students with similar backgrounds help newcomers adjust and learn the system. Many membership organizations (like health clubs, churches, and social organizations) also rely heavily, although often informally, on current members to help orient new members and make them feel welcome. In engaging in these types of roles, customers are again performing productive functions for the organization, increasing customer satisfaction and retention. Acting as a mentor or facilitator can have very positive effects on the person performing the role and is likely to increase his or her loyalty as well.

Promoting the Company

In some cases the customer's job may include a sales or promotional element. As you know from previous chapters, service customers rely heavily on word-of-mouth endorsements in deciding which providers to try. They are more comfortable getting a

FIGURE 13.4
Customers help produce the service for themselves through scanning their own groceries.

Source: NCR FastLane™ self checkout from NCR Corporation

recommendation from someone who has actually experienced the service than from advertising alone. A positive recommendation from a friend, relative, colleague, or even an acquaintance can pave the way for a positive service experience. Many service organizations have been very imaginative in getting their current customers to work as promoters or salespeople, as shown in Exhibit 13.3.

Individual Differences: Not Everyone Wants to Participate

In defining customers' jobs it is important to remember that not everyone will want to participate.[35] Some customer segments enjoy self-service, whereas others prefer to have the service performed entirely for them. Companies that provide education and training services to organizations know that some customers want to be involved in designing the training and perhaps in delivering it to their employees. Other companies want to hand over the entire training design and delivery to the consulting organization, staying at arms length with little of their own time and energy invested in the service. In health care, it is clear that some patients want lots of information and want to be involved in their own diagnosis and treatment decisions. Others simply want the doctor to tell them what to do. Despite all the customer service and purchase options now available via the Internet, many customers still prefer human, high-contact service delivery rather than self-service. Research has shown, for example, that customers with a high "need for human interaction" are less likely to try new self-service options offered via the Internet and automated phone systems.[36] Because of these differences in preferences, most companies find they need to provide service delivery choices for different market segments.

Often an organization can customize its services to fit the needs of these different segments—those who want to participate and those who prefer little involvement. Banks typically customize their services by offering both automated self-service options and high-touch, human delivery options. At other times, organizations such as Charles Schwab or IKEA (see the Global Feature) can effectively position themselves to specifically serve segments of customers who want a high level of participation.

Recruit, Educate, and Reward Customers

Once the customer's role is clearly defined, the organization can think in terms of facilitating that role. In a sense, the customer becomes a "partial employee" of the organization at some level, and strategies for managing customer behavior in service production and delivery can mimic to some degree the efforts aimed at service employees discussed in Chapter 12. As with employees, customer participation in service production and delivery will be facilitated when (1) customers understand their roles and how they are expected to perform, (2) customers are able to perform as expected, and (3) customers receive valued rewards for performing as expected.[37] Through these means, the organization will also reduce the inherent uncertainty associated with the unpredictable quality and timing of customer participation.

Recruit the Right Customers

Before the company begins the process of educating and socializing customers for their roles, it must attract the right customers to fill those roles. The expected roles and responsibilities of customers should be clearly communicated in advertising, personal selling, and other company messages. By previewing their roles and what is required of them in the service process, customers can self-select into (or out of) the relationship. Self-selection should result in enhanced perceptions of service quality from the customer's point of view and reduced uncertainty for the organization.

To illustrate, a child care center that requires parent participation on the site at least one-half day per week needs to communicate that expectation before it enrolls any child in its program. For some families, this level of participation will not be possible or desirable, thus precluding them from enrolling in the center. The expected level of participation needs to be communicated clearly in order to attract customers who are ready and willing to perform their roles. In a sense this situation is similar to a manufacturing firm exercising control over the quality of inputs into the production process.[38]

Educate and Train Customers to Perform Effectively

Customers need to be educated, or in essence "socialized," so that they can perform their roles effectively. Through the socialization process, service customers gain an

Exhibit 13.4   WEIGHT WATCHERS EDUCATES AND
ORIENTS NEW MEMBERS

When new members first join Weight Watchers, one of the largest and most successful commercial weight loss organizations in the world, they are thoroughly educated regarding the program and their responsibilities. For example, when a new member attends her first meeting at a local chapter of Weight Watchers of Arizona, she watches a video that tells about the program and reviews how the food plan works. New members are also given a booklet called "Welcome to Weight Watchers" that covers various introductory topics.

In addition to the video, the booklet, and a discussion of all topics led by the group leader, the new member also receives a "Program Planner and Tracker." This form is used by the member to record daily food selections and physical activity. Weight Watchers knows that its business can succeed only if members do their part in following the weight loss plan. Through the orientation, the booklets, and the food and activity forms, the organization clearly defines the member's responsibilities and makes the plan as easy as possible to follow.

appreciation of specific organizational values, develop the abilities necessary to function within a specific context, understand what is expected of them, and acquire the skills and knowledge to interact with employees and other customers.[39] Customer education programs can take the form of formal orientation programs, written literature provided to customers, directional cues and signage in the service environment, and information obtained from employees and other customers.

Many services offer "customer orientation" programs to assist customers in understanding their roles and what to expect from the process before experiencing it. When customers begin the Weight Watchers program, their first group meeting includes a thorough orientation to the program and their responsibilities, as described in Exhibit 13.4. In a mammography screening context, research has found that orientation and formal education of customers can relieve customer fears and perceptions of risk and ultimately increase customer satisfaction (see Exhibit 13.5).

Customer education can also be partially accomplished through written literature and customer "handbooks." Many hospitals have developed patient handbooks, very similar in appearance to employee handbooks, to describe what the patient should do in preparation for arrival at the hospital, what will happen when he or she arrives, and policies regarding visiting hours and billing procedures. The handbook may even describe the roles and responsibilities of family members.

Although formal training and written information are usually provided in advance of the service experience, other strategies can continue customer socialization during the experience itself. On site, customers require two kinds of orientation: *place orientation* (Where am I? How do I get from here to there?) and *function orientation* (How does this organization work? What am I supposed to do?).[40] Signage, the layout of the service facility, and other orientation aids can help customers answer these questions, allowing them to perform their roles more effectively. Orientation aids can also take the form of rules that define customer behavior for safety (airlines, health clubs), appropriate dress (restaurants, entertainment venues), and noise levels (hotels, classrooms, theaters).

Customers may also be socialized to their expected roles through information provided by employees and by observing other customers. It has been said that when McDonald's first went to England, the British customers were not accustomed to busing their own trays. They quickly learned, however, by observing the customers that McDonald's had hired to "demonstrate" appropriate busing behavior. These customers

Exhibit 13.5 **REALISTIC SERVICE PREVIEWS REDUCE CUSTOMER ANXIETY AND IMPROVE SATISFACTION**

Research in a mammography screening context found that if potential patients are oriented through a realistic preview of the process, patient anxiety is reduced and ultimate satisfaction is increased. Researchers conducted a study that involved 134 women who had never experienced a mammogram and who had little knowledge about the procedure. Half the women were given a realistic preview of the process, and the others received no preview. The preview consisted of written information about mammography, including sections on how the procedure works, instructions to follow before mammography, what happens during mammography, after the examination, the role of mammography, and some common misconceptions. The realistic preview also included a seven-minute videotape illustrating the entire procedure. The written materials and the videotape helped to both dispel overly pessimistic expectations and guard against overly positive ideas the potential patients may have had.

After the preview (or no preview), women in the experiment answered questions that assessed the accuracy of their expectations, their sense of control, and their level of anxiety relative to mammography. The women then read one of three versions of an actual mammography experience and were asked to imagine themselves as the woman in the story. One version of the story followed the realistic preview exactly; another version included several blunders on the part of the fictitious provider; and the final version enhanced the service experience, making it even better than the realistic preview. After reading the story and imagining that the events had actually happened to them, the women responded to questions regarding their satisfaction with the mammography screening process.

Results of the study showed that those women who had been oriented through the realistic preview did indeed have more realistic and accurate expectations for the mammography experience than did those who had no preview. Second, the women who saw the preview reported significantly less anxiety and significantly greater perceptions of control over the process than did women who had no preview. Finally, across all the different scenarios, women who received the preview were more satisfied with the actual service experience. The realistic preview thus affected potential mammography patients' preservice feelings (anxiety and control) as well as their satisfaction with the service.

Source: W. T. Faranda, "Customer Participation in Service Production: An Empirical Assessment of the Influence of Realistic Service Previews," doctoral dissertation, Arizona State University, Tempe, Arizona, 1994.

were paid to sit in the restaurants and at predictable intervals carry a dirty tray over to the trash can and dispose of it.

Reward Customers for Their Contributions

Customers are more likely to perform their roles effectively, or to participate actively, if they are rewarded for doing so. Rewards are likely to come in the form of increased control over the delivery process, time savings, monetary savings, and psychological or physical benefits. For instance, some CPA firms have clients complete extensive forms before they meet with their accountants. If the forms are completed, the CPAs will have less work to do and the clients will be rewarded with fewer billable hours. Those clients who choose not to perform the requested role will pay a higher price for the service. ATM customers who perform banking services for themselves are also rewarded through greater access to the bank, in terms of both locations and times. In some situations, ATM customers are also rewarded because they avoid fees that are assessed for interpersonal transactions with tellers. In health care contexts, patients who perform their roles effectively are likely to be rewarded with better health or quicker recovery. For a long time airlines have offered price discounts for passengers who ordered tickets online, providing a monetary incentive for customer participation.

Customers may not realize the benefits or rewards of effective participation unless the organization makes the benefits apparent to them. In other words, the organization needs to clarify the performance-contingent benefits that can accrue to customers just as it defines these types of benefits to employees. The organization also should recognize that not all customers are motivated by the same types of rewards. Some may value the increased access and time savings they can gain by performing their service roles effectively. Others may value the monetary savings. Still others may be looking for greater personal control over the service outcome.

Avoid Negative Outcomes of Inappropriate Customer Participation

If customers are not effectively socialized, the organization runs the risk that inappropriate customer behaviors will result in negative outcomes for customers, employees, and the organization itself:[41]

1. Customers who do not understand the service system or the process of delivery may slow down the service process and negatively affect their own as well as other customers' outcomes. In a rental car context, customers who do not understand the reservation process, the information needed from them, insurance coverage issues, and the pickup and drop-off procedures can slow the flow for employees and other customers, lowering both productivity and quality of service.

2. If customers do not perform their roles effectively, it may not be possible for employees to provide the levels of technical and process quality promised by the organization. For example, in a management consulting practice, clients who do not provide the information and cooperation needed by the consultants will likely receive inferior service in terms of both the usefulness of the management report and the timeliness of the delivery.

3. If customers are frustrated because of their own inadequacies and incompetencies, employees are likely to suffer emotionally and be less able to deliver quality service. For example, if customers routinely enter the service delivery process with little knowledge of how the system works and their role in it, they are likely to take out their frustrations on frontline employees. This negative impact on individual employees can take its toll on the organization in the form of turnover and decreased motivation to serve.

Manage the Customer Mix

Because customers frequently interact with each other in the process of service delivery and consumption, another important strategic objective is the effective management of the mix of customers who simultaneously experience the service. If a restaurant chooses to serve two segments during the dinner hour that are incompatible with each other—for example, single college students who want to party and families with small children who want quiet—it may find that the two groups do not merge well. Of course it is possible to manage these segments so that they do not interact with each other by seating them in separate sections or by attracting the two segments at different times of day. Major tourism attractions around the world face the challenge of accommodating visitors who differ in the languages they speak, the foods they want to eat, their values, and their perceptions of appropriate behaviors. Sometimes these visitors can clash when they do not understand and appreciate each other.

The process of managing multiple and sometimes conflicting segments is known as *compatibility management,* broadly defined as "a process of first attracting homogeneous consumers to the service environment, then actively managing both the physical environment and customer-to-customer encounters in such a way as to enhance satisfying encounters and minimize dissatisfying encounters."[42] Compatibility management will be critically important for some businesses (such as health clubs, public transportation, and hospitals) and less important for others. Table 13.2 lists seven interrelated characteristics of service businesses that will increase the importance of compatibility management.

TABLE 13.2 **Characteristics of Service that Increase the Importance of Compatible Segments**

Characteristic	Explanation	Examples
Customers are in close physical proximity to each other.	Customers will more often notice each other and be influenced by each other's behavior when they are in close physical proximity.	Airplane flights Entertainment events Sports events
Verbal interaction takes place among customers.	Conversation (or lack thereof) can be a component of both satisfying and dissatisfying encounters with fellow patrons.	Full-service restaurants Cocktail lounges Educational settings
Customers are engaged in numerous and varied activities.	When a service facility supports varied activities all going on at the same time, the activities themselves may not be compatible.	Libraries Health clubs Resort hotels
The service environment attracts a heterogeneous customer mix.	Many service environments, particularly those open to the public, will attract a variety of customer segments.	Public parks Public transportation Open-enrollment colleges
The core service is compatibility.	The core service is to arrange and nurture compatible relationships between customers.	Big Brothers/Big Sisters Weight loss group programs Mental health support groups
Customers must occasionally wait for the service.	Waiting in line for service can be monotonous or anxiety producing. The boredom or stress can be magnified or lessened by other customers, depending on their compatibility.	Medical clinics Tourist attractions Restaurants
Customers are expected to share time, space, or service utensils with each other.	The need to share space, time, and other service factors is common in many services but may become a problem if segments are not comfortable with sharing with each other or if the need to share is intensified because of capacity constraints.	Golf courses Hospitals Retirement communities Airplanes

Source: Adapted from C. I. Martin and C. A. Pranter, "Compatibility Management: Customer-to-Customer Relationships in Service Environments," *Journal of Services Marketing* 3, no. 3 (Summer 1989), pp. 5–15. Reprinted with the permission of MCB University Press.

To manage multiple (and sometimes conflicting) segments, organizations rely on a variety of strategies. Attracting maximally homogeneous groups of customers through careful positioning and segmentation strategies is one approach. This strategy is used by the Ritz-Carlton Hotel Company, for which upscale travelers are the primary target segment. The Ritz-Carlton is positioned to communicate that message to the marketplace, and customers self-select into the hotel. However, even in that context there are potential conflicts—for example, when the hotel is simultaneously hosting a large business convention and serving individual leisure travelers. A second strategy is often used in such cases. Compatible customers are grouped together physically so that the segments are less likely to interact directly with each other. The Ritz-Carlton keeps meetings and large group events separated from the areas of the hotel used by individual businesspeople.

Other strategies for enhancing customer compatibility include customer "codes of conduct" such as the regulation of smoking behavior and dress codes. Clearly such codes of conduct may vary from one service establishment to another. Finally, training employees to observe customer-to-customer interactions and to be sensitive to potential conflicts is another strategy for increasing compatibility among segments. Employees can also be trained to recognize opportunities to foster positive encounters among customers in certain types of service environments.

Summary

This chapter focused on the role of customers in service creation and delivery. The customer receiving the service and the fellow customers in the service environment can all potentially cause a widening of gap 3 if they fail to perform their roles effectively. A number of reasons why customers may widen the service delivery gap were suggested: customers lack understanding of their roles; customers are unwilling or unable to perform their roles; customers are not rewarded for good performance; other customers interfere; or market segments are incompatible.

Managing customers in the process of service delivery is a critical challenge for service firms. Whereas manufacturers are not concerned with customer participation in the manufacturing process, service managers constantly face this issue because their customers are often present and active partners in service production. As participants in service creation, production, and delivery, customers can perform three primary roles, discussed and illustrated in the chapter: *productive resources* for the organization, *contributors* to service quality and satisfaction, and *competitors* in performing the service for themselves.

Through understanding the importance of customers in service delivery and identifying the roles played by the customer in a particular context, managers can develop strategies to enhance customer participation. Strategies discussed in the text include defining the customers' roles and jobs, recruiting customers who match the customer profile in terms of desired level of participation, educating customers so they can perform their roles effectively, rewarding customers for their contributions, and managing the customer mix to enhance the experiences of all segments. By implementing these strategies, organizations should see a reduction in gap 3 due to effective, efficient customer contributions to service delivery.

Discussion Questions

1. Using your own personal examples, discuss the general importance of customers in the successful creation and delivery of service experiences.

2. Why might customer actions and attitudes cause gap 3 to occur? Use your own examples to illustrate your understanding.

3. Using Table 13.1, think of specific services you have experienced that fall within each of the three levels of customer participation: low, medium, high. Describe specifically what you did as a customer in each case. How did your involvement vary across the three types of service situations?

4. Describe a time when your satisfaction in a particular situation was *increased* because of something another customer did. Could (or does) the organization do anything to ensure that this experience happens routinely? What does it do? Should it try to make this situation a routine occurrence?

5. Describe a time when your satisfaction in a particular situation was *decreased* because of something another customer did. Could the organization have done anything to manage this situation more effectively? What?

6. Discuss the customer's role as a *productive resource* for the firm. Describe a time when you played this role. What did you do and how did you feel? Did the firm help you perform your role effectively? How?

7. Discuss the customer's role as a *contributor to service quality and satisfaction.* Describe a time when you played this role. What did you do and how did you feel? Did the firm help you perform your role effectively? How?

8. Discuss the customer's role as a potential *competitor.* Describe a time when you chose to provide a service for yourself rather than pay someone to provide the service for you. Why did you decide to perform the service yourself? What could have changed your mind, causing you to contract with someone else to provide the service?

Exercises

1. Visit a service establishment where customers can influence each other (such as a theme park, entertainment establishment, resort, shopping mall, restaurant, airline, school, or hospital). Observe (or interview) customers and record cases of positive and negative customer influence. Discuss how you would manage the situation to increase overall customer satisfaction.

2. Interview someone regarding his or her decision to outsource a service—for example, legal services, payroll, or maintenance in a company; or cleaning, child care, or pet care in a household. Use the criteria for internal versus external exchange described in the text to analyze the decision to outsource.

3. Think of a service in which a high level of customer participation is necessary for the service to be successful (health club, weight loss, educational setting, health care, golf lessons, or the like). Interview a service provider in such an organization to find out what strategies the provider uses to encourage effective customer participation.

4. Visit a service setting in which multiple types of customer segments use the service at the same time (such as a theater, golf course, resort, or theme park). Observe (or interview the manager about) the organization's strategies to manage these segments effectively. Would you do anything differently if you were in charge?

5. Visit iPrint's website (http://www.iPrint.com). Compare its printing service process to similar onsite services offered by Kinko's. Compare and contrast the customer's role in each situation.

Notes

1. P. B. Seybold, *Customers.com: How to Create a Profitable Business Strategy for the Internet and Beyond* (New York: Random House, 1998), pp. 235–44; www.iPrint.com, 2004.

2. See B. Schneider and D. E. Bowen, *Winning the Service Game* (Boston: Harvard Business School Press, 1995), chap. 4; L. A. Bettencourt, "Customer Voluntary Performance: Customers as Partners in Service Delivery," *Journal of Retailing* 73, no. 3 (1997), pp. 383–406; P. K. Mills and J. H. Morris, "Clients as 'Partial' Employees: Role Development in Client Participation," *Academy of Management Review* 11, no. 4 (1986), pp. 726–35; C. H. Lovelock and R. F. Young, "Look to Customers to Increase Productivity," *Harvard Business Review,* Summer 1979, pp. 9–20; A. R. Rodie and S. S. Kleine, "Customer Participation in Services Production and Delivery," in *Handbook of Services Marketing and Management,* ed. T. A. Swartz and D. Iacobucci (Thousand Oaks, CA: Sage Publications, 2000), pp. 111–26; C. K. Prahalad and V. Ramaswamy, "Co-opting Customer Competence," *Harvard Business Review,* January–February 2000, p. 7; N. Bendapudi and R. P. Leone, "Psychological Implications of Customer Participation in Co-Production," *Journal of Marketing* 67 (January 2003), pp. 14–28.

3. S. J. Grove, R. P. Fisk, and M. J. Bitner, "Dramatizing the Service Experience: A Managerial Approach," in *Advances in Services Marketing and Management,* ed. T. A. Swartz, D. E. Bowen, and S. W. Brown, vol. 1 (Greenwich, CT: JAI Press, 1992), pp. 91–122.

4. For an interesting view of work and business as theater, see B. Joseph Pine II and J. H. Gilmore, *The Experience Economy: Work Is Theatre and Every Business a Stage* (Boston: Harvard Business School Press, 1999).

5. L. A. Bettencourt, S. W. Brown, A. L. Ostrom, and R. I. Roundtree, "Client Co-Production in Knowledge-Intensive Business Services," *California Management Review* 44 (Summer 2002), pp. 100–28.

6. See S. J. Grove and R. P. Fisk, "The Impact of Other Customers on Service Experiences: A Critical Incident Examination of 'Getting Along,'" *Journal of Retailing* 73, no. 1 (1997), pp. 63–85; C. I. Martin and C. A. Pranter, "Compatibility Management: Customer-to-Customer Relationships in Service Environments," *Journal of Services Marketing* 3 (Summer 1989), pp. 5–15.

7. Grove and Fisk, "The Impact of Other Customers on Service Experiences."

8. Ibid.

9. K. Harris and S. Baron, "Consumer-to-Consumer Conversations in Service Settings," *Journal of Service Research* 6 (February 2004), pp. 287–303.

10. See P. K. Mills, R. B. Chase, and N. Margulies, "Motivating the Client/Employee System as a Service Production Strategy," *Academy of Management Review* 8, no. 2 (1983), pp. 301–10; D. E. Bowen, "Managing Customers as Human Resources in Service Organizations," *Human Resource Management* 25, no. 3 (1986), pp. 371–83; and Mills and Morris, "Clients as 'Partial' Employees."

11. Bettencourt et al, "Client Co-Production in Knowledge-Intensive Business Services."

12. R. B. Chase, "Where Does the Customer Fit in a Service Operation?" *Harvard Business Review,* November–December 1978, pp. 137–42.

13. Mills, Chase, and Margulies, "Motivating the Client/Employee System."
14. Marilyn Adams, "Tech Takes Bigger Role in Air Services," *USA Today,* July 18, 2001, p. 1.
15. See D. W. Johnson, R. T. Johnson, and K. A. Smith, *Active Learning: Cooperation in the College Classroom* (Edina, MN: Interaction Book Company, 1991).
16. S. Dellande, M. C. Gilly, and J. L. Graham, "Gaining Compliance and Losing Weight: The Role of the Service Provider in Health Care Services," *Journal of Marketing* 68 (July 2004), pp. 78–91.
17. S. W. Kelley, S. J. Skinner, and J. H. Donnelly Jr., "Organizational Socialization of Service Customers," *Journal of Business Research* 25 (1992), pp. 197–214.
18. C. Claycomb, C. A. Lengnick-Hall, and L. W. Inks, "The Customer As a Productive Resource: A Pilot Study and Strategic Implications," *Journal of Business Strategies* 18 (Spring 2001), pp. 47–69.
19. Several of the scenarios are adapted from C. Goodwin, "'I Can Do It Myself': Training the Service Consumer to Contribute to Service Productivity," *Journal of Services Marketing* 2, no. 4 (Fall 1988), pp. 71–78.
20. R. Normann and R. Ramirez, "From Value Chain to Value Constellation: Designing Interactive Strategy," *Harvard Business Review,* July–August 1993, pp. 65–77; www.ikea.com, 2002.
21. J. E. G. Bateson, "The Self-Service Customer—Empirical Findings," in *Emerging Perspectives in Services Marketing,* eds. L. L. Berry, G. L. Shostack, and G. D. Upah (Chicago: American Marketing Association, 1983), pp. 50–53.
22. V. S. Folkes, "Recent Attribution Research in Consumer Behavior: A Review and New Directions," *Journal of Consumer Research* 14 (March 1988), pp. 548–65; and M. J. Bitner, "Evaluating Service Encounters: The Effects of Physical Surroundings and Employee Responses," *Journal of Marketing* 54 (April 1990), pp. 69–82.
23. Bendapudi and Leone, "Psychological Implications of Customer Participation in Co-Production."
24. R. F. Lusch, S. W. Brown, and G. J. Brunswick, "A General Framework for Explaining Internal vs. External Exchange," *Journal of the Academy of Marketing Science* 10 (Spring 1992), pp. 119–34.
25. Ibid.
26. See M. J. Bitner, A. L. Ostrom, and M. L. Meuter, "Implementing Successful Self-Service Technologies," *Academy of Management Executive* 16 (November 2002), pp. 96–109.
27. See P. Dabholkar, "Consumer Evaluations of New Technology-Based Self-Service Options: An Investigation of Alternative Models of Service Quality," *International Journal of Research in Marketing* 13 (1), pp. 29–51; F. Davis, "User Acceptance of Information Technology: System Characteristics, User Perceptions and Behavioral Impact," *International Journal of Man-Machine Studies* 38 (1993), pp. 475–87; L. M. Bobbitt and P. A. Dabholkar, "Integrating Attitudinal Theories to Understand and Predict Use of Technology-Based Self-Service," *International Journal of Service Industry Management* 12, no. 5 (2001), pp. 423–50; J. M. Curran, M. L. Meuter, and C. F. Surprenant, "Intentions to Use Self-Service Technologies: A Confluence of Multiple Attitudes," *Journal of Service Research* 5, no. 3 (2003), pp. 209–24.
28. M. L. Meuter, M. J. Bitner, A. L. Ostrom, and S. W. Brown, "Choosing among Alternative Service Delivery Modes: An Investigation of Customer Trial of Self-Service Technologies," *Journal of Marketing,* forthcoming, April 2005.

29. M. L. Meuter, A. L. Ostrom, R. I. Roundtree, and M. J. Bitner, "Self-Service Technologies: Understanding Customer Satisfaction with Technology-Based Service Encounters," *Journal of Marketing* 64 (July 2000), pp. 50–64.

30. Meuter et al., "Choosing among Alternative Service Delivery Modes"; see also Y. Moon and F. X. Frei, "Exploding the Self-Service Myth," *Harvard Business Review,* May–June 2000; M. J. Bitner, A. L. Ostrom, and M. L. Meuter, "Implementing Successful Self-Service Technologies."

31. A. Parasuraman and C. L. Colby, *Techno-Ready Marketing: How and Why Your Customers Adopt Technology* (New York: The Free Press, 2001).

32. Bowen, "Managing Customers as Human Resources."

33. Chase, "Where Does the Customer Fit in a Service Operation?"

34. See Schneider and Bowen, *Winning the Service Game,* chap. 4. The four job descriptions in this section are adapted from M. R. Bowers, C. L. Martin, and A. Luker, "Trading Places, Employees as Customers, Customers as Employees," *Journal of Services Marketing* 4 (Spring 1990), pp. 56–69.

35. Bateson, "The Self-Service Customer."

36. Meuter et al., "Choosing among Alternative Service Delivery Modes."

37. Bowen, "Managing Customers as Human Resources"; and Schneider and Bowen, *Winning the Service Game,* chap. 4; Meuter et al., "Choosing among Alternative Service Delivery Modes"; Dellande et al., "Gaining Compliance and Losing Weight."

38. C. Goodwin and R. Radford, "Models of Service Delivery: An Integrative Perspective," in *Advances in Services Marketing and Management,* ed. T. A. Swartz, D. E. Bowen, and S. W. Brown, pp. 231–52.

39. S. W. Kelley, J. H. Donnelly Jr., and S. J. Skinner, "Customer Participation in Service Production and Delivery," *Journal of Retailing* 66 (Fall 1990), pp. 315–35; and Schneider and Bowen, *Winning the Service Game,* chap. 4.

40. Bowen, "Managing Customers as Human Resources."

41. Ibid; see also L. C. Harris and K. L. Reynolds, "The Consequences of Dysfunctional Customer Behavior," *Journal of Service Research* 6 (November 2003), pp. 144–61.

42. Martin and Pranter, "Compatibility Management."

14

DELIVERING SERVICE THROUGH INTERMEDIARIES AND ELECTRONIC CHANNELS

This chapter's objectives are to

1. Identify the primary channels through which services are delivered to end customers.

2. Provide examples of each of the key service intermediaries.

3. View delivery of service from two perspectives—the service provider and the service deliverer.

4. Discuss the benefits and challenges of each method of service delivery.

5. Outline the strategies that are used to manage service delivery through intermediaries.

Distance Learning: Delivering Education Electronically

Distance learning is education that is accessible at a time, place, location, and pace that is convenient to the user. It can come in many forms: over phone lines, on CD-ROM, over the Internet, or through a video camera. It can be an instructor in Omaha videoconferencing with managers in Mobile, Lexington, and Minneapolis on the fundamentals of risk analysis. It can be an engineer taking a motor repair certification course online at home. It can be a lineman on a laptop during his lunch break brushing up on the latest pole maintenance techniques via CD-ROM. It can be a customer learning about the features of a product online before making a purchase. Distance learning breaks down the boundaries of the classroom and makes education more accessible than ever.[1]

Source: Dick Blume/The Image Works

Perhaps the widest application of distance learning is on-the-job training. But did you realize that more than three-quarters of all U.S. colleges and universities now offer "virtual" courses—delivered electronically at a distance—and many offer complete degrees that a student can earn without ever setting foot on a campus? Whereas total college enrollments are rising 1 to 2 percent a year, distance education enrollments are increasing 30 percent annually.[2] Over 350,000 people annually seek to complete undergraduate degrees or a master's degree online; these people are pure degree seekers, not people taking a course here and there.[3] Even if you never earn a degree electronically, you are almost certainly going to take at least one distance learning course in your life—if not in college, then at work. In the future, the number one vehicle for company training will be distance education: training delivered where it is needed, when it is needed, and to whom it is needed.

Although not new, the concept of distance learning has evolved in technology and scope. At its best, distance learning involves a rich interactive environment with multimedia including slides, video, text, e-mail, chat rooms, and two-way communication. The most effective environments also involve some ability to interact with the professor. In fact, an expert in distance learning found that successful programs had in common one factor: a minimum of 30 percent airtime dedicated to student interaction in which the learner is actively asking questions, talking with experts in the field, working in small groups, or putting answers into the keypad.[4]

At both Arizona State University and the University of North Carolina, where two of us are professors, business courses and degree programs are now offered online via the Internet to serve a wider market. The coursework is a combination of onsite, in-person instruction; online self-paced modules; and active learning assignments. Technology makes it possible for students to take courses when and where they wish, frequently time zones and continents away from other students and their professors.

Although most universities, and specifically business schools, are involved in distance education in various forms (see the Internet site www.edsurf.net/-edshack/virtualu.htm for the full list and www.lifelonglearning.com for an evaluation of different programs), one stands out as a unique entrant into this marketplace. UNext's Cardean University is a high-profile, private online university designed to deliver business and professional education and training at the MBA level. Launched in 2000, UNext has partnered with leading universities including Columbia Business School, Stanford University, University of Chicago, Carnegie Mellon, and London School of Economics. Three Nobel laureates are on Cardean's faculty, and its president, Geoffrey Cox, left Stanford University to join UNext, believing in its value and potential. The goal of UNext is to provide high-quality education to students around the globe who cannot afford either the expense or the time to attend top institutions, or who already have degrees but desire ongoing education and lifelong learning opportunities. The courses offered by UNext are problem focused and provide the students with activity-based assignments through the Internet that form the core of the educational experience. Technology allows the students to access courses when and where they wish, an attractive feature for students and companies alike. This feature is what attracted General Motors to contract with UNext to offer business courses to 88,000 white-collar workers in its company. Estimates suggest that the distance education sector is worth over $6 billion annually.[5]

Distance learning has its critics, among them the director of accreditation at the American Assembly of Collegiate Schools of Business, who said, "It's kind of like McEducation. I can't imagine that they could convince one of our committees that their faculty have the appropriate qualifications."[6] Despite this cynicism, in March 1999 Jones International University near Denver became the first U.S. university operating entirely online to earn regional accreditation from the North Central Association of Colleges and Schools.

Here are some of the most frequently asked questions about distance learning and the answers we have to date:

Who are the biggest consumers of distance learning? High-tech companies use more distance learning than any other industry because of the fast pace of product change. Higher education statistics show that 90 percent of all higher education institutions with more than 10,000 students and 85 percent of those with enrollments of 3,000 to 10,000 offer distance education courses.[7]

How effective is distance learning? "Some skeptics overlook the fact that learning is not a place; it's a process," claims Vicky Phillips, author of *The Best Distance Learning Graduate Schools.* Current research is sketchy, but one study supports her point. A researcher analyzed studies from 248 separate sources on the effectiveness of online degree programs and concluded that people learn just as well with a personal computer as they do by spending hours sitting in lecture halls.[8] Much remains to be learned about the effectiveness of distance learning as a whole as well as the types of distance learning that are most successful. People who read a lot adapt best, because they consider distance learning the same as a book but with more interaction and hands-on activity.[9]

How effective is distance learning in other cultures and countries? Thomas Cooper, an expert on mass communications, emphasizes that trust is a critical component of communications. Trust in many cultures involves either touch or direct vision, something that is not achieved with technology. The United States is one of the few cultures in which most consumers trust technologies such as ATMs. Videoconferencing seems to be culturally insensitive if not inappropriate for cultures in which surrogate or substitute people are either offensive or not acceptable. Also, some cultures accept distance learning but still feel "reduced, trivialized, muzzled, or as in the work, distanced from the educational process."[10] One success story in distance education is the 50-year-old, 30-campus ITESM (Technological Institute of Monterrey) in Mexico, which has online MBA courses, computer programs for the blind, online doctorates taught by top experts from Carnegie-Mellon University, and seminars for Latin American journalists. One of the most innovative seminars was a professional-level course for 150 mayors and municipal officers on how to run honest and open governments.[11]

Only time will tell how far the distance learning revolution will go, but many prognosticators expect it to completely alter the way learning is achieved. According to one expert:

Education will change from a place-centered enterprise to "education where you need it." A decade from now, it wouldn't surprise me if the majority of education took place in people's homes, in people's offices, on the production line, wherever it is needed.[12]

Although experts tend to agree that great value exists in an on-campus educational experience, the truth is that for much of the world's population on-campus education is not a realistic alternative.

Except for situations such as distance learning, where electronic channels can distribute services, providers and consumers come into direct contact in service provision. Because of the inseparability of production and consumption in service, providers must either be present themselves when customers receive service or find ways to involve others in distribution. Involving others can be problematic because quality in service occurs in the service encounter between company and customer. Unless the service distributor is willing and able to perform in the service encounter as the service principal would, the value of the offering decreases and the reputation of the original service may be damaged. Chapter 12 pointed out the challenges of controlling encounters within service organizations themselves, but most service (and many manufacturing) companies face an even more formidable task: attaining service excellence and consistency when intermediaries represent them to customers. This chapter discusses both the challenges of delivering service through intermediaries and approaches that engender alignment with the goals of the service provider.

Two distinct services marketers are involved in delivering service through intermediaries: the *service principal,* or originator, and the *service deliverer,* or intermediary. The service principal is the entity that creates the service concept (whose counterpart is the manufacturer of physical goods), and the service deliverer is the entity that interacts with the customer in the actual execution of the service (whose counterpart is the distributor or wholesaler of physical goods). In this chapter, we examine the issues surrounding distribution of services from both perspectives.

SERVICE DISTRIBUTION

Direct Delivery of Service

As we have indicated throughout this textbook, services are generally intangible and experiential in nature. Thus, service distribution does not typically involve moving items through a chain of firms that begins with a manufacturer and ends with a consumer, as is the case for goods distribution. In fact, many services are delivered directly from the service producer to the consumer. That is, in contrast to channels for goods, channels for services are often *direct*—with the creator of the service (i.e., the service principal) selling directly to and interacting directly with the customer. Examples include air travel (Southwest Airlines), health care (Mayo Clinic), and consulting services (IBM Global Services). Because services cannot be owned, there are no titles or rights to most services that can be passed along a delivery channel. Because services are intangible and perishable, inventories cannot exist, making warehousing a dispensable function. In general, because services cannot be produced, warehoused, and then retailed, as goods can, many channels available to goods producers are not feasible for service firms. Thus, many of the primary functions that distribution channels serve—inventorying, securing, and taking title to goods—have no meaning in services, allowing the service principal to deliver the service directly to the customer.

Delivery of Service through Intermediaries

Even though many of the functions that intermediaries provide for goods manufacturers are not relevant for service firms, intermediaries often deliver services and perform several important functions for service principals. First, they may coproduce the service, fulfilling service principals' promises to customers. Franchise services such as haircutting, key making, and dry cleaning are produced by the intermediary (the franchisee) using a process developed by the service principal. Service intermediaries also make services locally available, providing time and place convenience for the customer. Because they represent multiple service principals, such intermediaries as travel and insurance agents provide a retailing function for customers, gathering together in one place a variety of choices. And in many financial or professional services, intermediaries function as the glue between the brand or company name and the customer by building the trusting relationship required in these complex and expert offerings.

The primary types of intermediaries used in service delivery are franchisees, agents, brokers, and electronic channels. *Franchisees* are service outlets licensed by a principal to deliver a unique service concept it has created or popularized. Examples include fast-food chains (McDonald's, Burger King), video stores (Blockbuster), automobile repair services (Jiffy Lube, Midas), and hotels (Holiday Inn, Hampton Inn). *Agents and brokers* are representatives who distribute and sell the services of one or more service suppliers. Examples include insurance (Paul Revere Insurance Company), financial services (Oppenheimer mutual funds), and travel services (American Express). *Electronic channels* include all forms of service provision through television, telephone, interactive multimedia, and computers. Many financial and information services are currently distributed through electronic media: banking, bill paying, education.

We do not include retailers in our short list of service intermediaries because most retailers—from department stores to discount stores—are channels for delivering physical goods rather than services. Retailers that sell only services (movie theaters, film-processing kiosks, restaurants) or retail services that support physical products (automobile dealers, gas stations) can also be described as dealers or franchises. For our purposes in this chapter, such retailers are grouped into the franchise category because they possess the same characteristics, strengths, and weaknesses as franchises.

Goods retailers, by the way, are service organizations themselves; they are intermediaries for goods and perhaps services. Manufacturing companies depend on retailers to represent, explain, promote, and ensure their products—all of which are presale services. Manufacturers also need retailers to return, exchange, support, and service products—all of which are postsale services. These roles are increasingly critical as products become more complex, technical, and expensive. For example, camera and computer firms rely on retailers carrying their products to understand and communicate highly technical information so that customers choose products that fit their needs. A retailer that leads the customer to the wrong product choice or that inadequately instructs the customer on how to use the product creates service problems that strongly influence the manufacturer's reputation.

Service principals depend on their intermediaries to deliver service to their specifications. Service intermediaries determine how the customer evaluates the quality of the company. When a McDonald's franchisee cooks the McNuggets too short a time, the customer's perception of the company—and of other McDonald's franchisees—is tarnished. When one Holiday Inn franchisee has unsanitary conditions, it reflects on all other Holiday Inns and on the Holiday Inn brand itself. Unless service providers ensure that the intermediary's goals, incentives, and motives are consistent with their own, they lose control over the service encounters between the customer and the intermediary. When someone other than the service principal is critical to the fulfillment of quality service, a firm must develop ways to either control or motivate these intermediaries to meet company goals and standards. In the sections that follow, we discuss both direct delivery of service by the service principal and indirect delivery of the service through intermediaries.

DIRECT OR COMPANY-OWNED CHANNELS

Although we call this chapter "Delivering Service through Intermediaries and Electronic Channels," it is important to acknowledge that many services are distributed directly from provider to customer. Some of these are local services—doctors, dry cleaners, and hairstylists—whose area of distribution is limited. Others are national chains with multiple outlets but are considered direct channels because the provider owns all the outlets. Starbucks, the popular chain of coffee shops, is an example of a service provider with all company-owned outlets. Its 6,000 coffee shops in the United States are completely run and managed by the company. Exhibit 14.1, which describes some of the reasons for the success of the chain, illustrates the general benefits of company-owned outlets: control, consistency, and maintenance of image.

Perhaps the major benefit of distributing through company-owned channels is that the company has complete *control* over the outlets. One of the most critical implications of this type of control is that the owner can maintain consistency in service provision. Standards can be established and will be carried out as planned because the company itself monitors and rewards proper execution of the service. Control over hiring, firing, and motivating employees is also a benefit of company-owned channels. As demonstrated in Exhibit 14.1, one of the keys to Starbucks's success is hiring the right baristas, or coffee makers, something the company is far more likely to do than a

Exhibit 14.1 STARBUCKS SHOWS SUCCESS OF COMPANY-OWNED SERVICE CHANNELS

One of the biggest marketing success stories of the last decade is Starbucks Coffee Company, although it has been in business for more than 30 years. Twenty years ago, its owner began to think of coffee not as something to retail in a store but instead as something to experience in a coffeehouse. At that point, he created the Starbucks that we know today, the Starbucks that "successfully replicates a perfectly creamy cafè latte in stores from Seattle to St. Paul." Consistency of service and product are two of the most important reasons that Starbucks has grown to more than 6,000 U.S.-based outlets and expanded internationally, and that it annually reports profit growth of more than 50 percent a year. (Even a world-class service provider such as Starbucks can have a "bad day," as we saw in Chapter 8!) Starbucks owns more than 4,000 of the stores and maintains control over all that takes place in those stores. Here are some of the efforts it undertakes to ensure that the Starbucks experience is always the same, always positive.

EMPLOYEE TRAINING: LEARNING TO BE A BARISTA

All employees are called partners, and those who prepare coffee are called "baristas," the Italian name for one who prepares and serves coffee. As many as 400 to 500 employees per month nationally are carefully trained to "call" ("triple-tall nonfat mocha"), make drinks, clean espresso machines, and deliver quality customer service. Baristas are taught "coffee knowledge," so that among other things they know how everything tastes, and "customer service," so that they can explain the Italian drink names to customers.

ENSURING PRODUCT QUALITY

"Retail skills" are another portion of the training. Employees are taught such specifics as how to wipe oil from the coffee bin, open a giant bag of beans, and clean the milk wand on the espresso machine, all of which ensures that the coffee drinks taste just right. Another part, "brewing the perfect cup at home," helps baristas teach customers how to use the espresso machines and coffee they buy at Starbucks to replicate the product they get in the coffeehouse.

SERVICE STANDARDS

No pot of Starbucks coffee sits on a burner for more than 20 minutes. An espresso machine with unused coffee must be purged regularly. And no one goes home at night until everything is completed, cleaned, and polished according to the service standards in the manual. Using such standards ensures that both service and quality are maintained.

Source: Reprinted with permission of Starbucks Coffee Company

STAR SKILLS

To hire, keep, and motivate the very best employees, Starbucks has three guidelines for on-the-job interpersonal relations: (1) maintain and enhance self-esteem, (2) listen and acknowledge, and (3) ask for help. These and other human resource practices, including higher-than-average pay, health insurance, and stock options, lower barista turnover to 60 percent compared with 140 percent for hourly workers in the fast-food business in general.

STARBUCKS AND THE INTERNET

Starbucks had high hopes for the Internet, given that its shops tend to attract young, affluent, tech-savvy customers, 70 percent of whom are Internet users. However, it overestimated its ability to transition off-line success to the online environment. Several of its online initiatives failed, including Starbucks X, which was a quasi-separate division built around the Internet, and its online retail store, which once sold coffee beans, mugs, and brewing machines. Now, customers who wish to purchase Starbucks products must physically visit a store; no purchases can be made via the Internet. Starbucks originally refused to offer Internet connections in the coffee shops themselves, not wanting to

continued

create dimly lit cybercafés with people hunched over machines. The company has since changed its stance and has partnered with T-Mobile to create Wireless HotSpot Stores. At the time this book went to press, Starbucks provided high-speed wireless Internet connections in about 40 percent of its stores.

LICENSE SITES

If you have any doubt about whether all these steps pay off in terms of quality product and service, check out Starbucks at airports or on the turnpike. You will notice a difference. While the company does not franchise domestically, it does license sites to companies with contracts from public agen-

cies to run those facilities. No highly trained baristas work at these outlets, and no service quality standards are enforced in them. The result is a less consistent, less pleasant, and less flavorful experience. And, if you need further evidence, compare a coffee shop cup of Starbucks coffee to one offered on any United Airlines flight. It is the same coffee, but a harried flight attendant with 65 passengers needing meals and drinks just cannot provide the same consistency and attention to every cup.

Sources: J. Reese, "Starbucks: Inside the Coffee Cult," *Fortune,* December 9, 1996, pp. 190–200; G. Anders, "Starbucks Brews a New Strategy," *Fast Company,* August 2001, pp. 144–46; "Starbucks Keeps Pace," *Beverage Industry,* October 200l, p. 11; www.starbucks.com.

franchisee. Using company-owned channels also allows the company to expand or contract sites without being bound by contractual agreements with other entities.

A final benefit of company-owned channels is that the company owns the customer relationship. In service industries in which skilled or professional workers have individual relationships with customers, a major concern is whether the loyalty the customer feels is for the company or for the individual service employee. It is well known, for example, that most people are loyal to individual hairstylists and will follow them from one place of business to another. Therefore, one of the important issues in service delivery is who owns the customer relationship—the store or the employee. With company-owned channels, the company owns both the store and the employee and therefore has complete control over the customer relationship.

However, several disadvantages exist with company-owned channels. First, and probably the largest impediment to most service chains, the company must bear all the financial risk. When expanding, the firm must find all the capital, sometimes using it for store proliferation rather than for other uses (such as advertising, service quality, or new service development) that would be more profitable. Second, large companies are rarely experts in local markets—they know their businesses but not all markets. When adjustments are needed in business formats for different markets, they may be unaware of what these adjustments should be. This disadvantage is especially evident when companies expand into other cultures and other countries. Partnering or joint venturing is almost always preferred to company-owned channels in these situations.

When two or more service companies want to offer a service and neither has the full financial capability or expertise, they often undertake service partnerships. These partnerships operate very much like company-owned channels except that they involve multiple owners. The benefit is that risk and effort are shared, but the disadvantage is that control and returns are also distributed among the partners. Several areas in which partnerships are common are telecommunications, high-technology services, Internet-based services, and entrepreneurial services. Service partnerships also proliferate when companies expand beyond their country boundaries—typically one partner provides the business format and the other provides knowledge of the local market.

FRANCHISING

Franchising is the most common type of distribution in services, with more than 2,500 U.S. franchisers licensing their brand names, business processes or formats, unique products, services, or reputations in return for fees and royalties. Franchising works well with services that can be standardized and duplicated through the delivery process, service policies, warranties, guarantees, promotion, and branding. Jiffy Lube, H&R Block, McDonald's, and Red Roof Inns are examples of companies that are ideal for franchise operations. At its best, franchising is a relationship or partnership in which the service provider—the franchiser—develops and optimizes a service format that it licenses for delivery by other parties—the franchisees. There are benefits and disadvantages for both the franchiser and the franchisee in this relationship (see Table 14.1).

The Franchiser's Perspective

A franchiser typically begins by developing a business concept that is unique in some way. Perhaps it is a fast-food concept (such as McDonald's) with unique cooking or delivery processes. Perhaps it is a health and fitness center (such as Gold's Gym) with established formats for marketing to customers, pricing, and hiring employees. Or maybe it is a video store (such as Blockbuster) with unique store environments, employee training, purchasing, and computer systems. A franchiser typically expands business through this method because it expects the following benefits:

- *A leveraged business format for greater expansion and revenues.* Most franchisers want wider distribution—and increased revenues, market share, brand name recog-

TABLE 14.1
Benefits and Challenges in Franchising

Benefits	Challenges
For Franchisers	
Leveraged business format for greater expansion and revenues	Difficulty in maintaining and motivating franchisees
Consistency in outlets	Highly publicized disputes and conflict
Knowledge of local markets	Inconsistent quality
Shared financial risk and more working capital	Control of customer relationship by intermediary
For Franchisees	
An established business format	Encroachment
National or regional brand marketing	Disappointing profits and revenues
Minimized risk of starting a business	Lack of perceived control over operations
	High fees

nition, and economies of scale—for their concepts and practices than they can support in company outlets.

- *Consistency in outlets.* When franchisers have strong contracts and unique formats, they can require that service be delivered according to their specifications. This chapter's Global Feature, for example, shows how Starbucks is maintaining consistency across cultures and countries through franchising.

- *Knowledge of local markets.* National chains are unlikely to understand local markets as well as the businesspeople who live in the geographic areas. With franchising, the company obtains a connection to the local market.

- *Shared financial risk and more working capital.* Franchisees must contribute their own capital for equipment and personnel, thereby bearing part of the risk of doing business.

Franchising is not without its challenges, however. Most franchisers encounter the following disadvantages:

- *Difficulty in maintaining and motivating franchisees.* Motivating independent operators to price, promote, deliver, and hire according to standards the principal establishes is a difficult job, particularly when business is down.

- *Highly publicized disputes between franchisees and franchisers.* Franchisees are organizing and hiring lobbyists and lawyers to gain more economic clout. Many states and even the federal government have implemented legislation boosting franchisee rights.

- *Inconsistent quality.* Although some franchisees deliver the service in the manner in which the franchiser intended, other franchisees do not perform the service as well as desired. This inconsistency can undermine the company's image, reputation, and brand name.

- *Customer relationships controlled by the franchisee rather than the franchiser.* The closer a company is to the customer, the better able it is to listen to that customer's concerns and ideas. When franchisees are involved, a relationship forms between the customer and the franchisee rather than between the customer and the franchiser. All customer information, including demographics, purchase history, and preferences, is in the hands of the intermediary rather than the principal.

The Franchisee's Perspective

From the perspective of the franchisee, one of the main benefits of franchising is obtaining an established business format on which to base a business, something one expert has defined as an "entrepreneur in a prepackaged box, a super-efficient distributor of services and goods through a decentralized web."[13] A second benefit is receiving national or regional brand marketing. Franchisees obtain advertising and other marketing expertise as well as an established reputation. Finally, franchising minimizes the risks of starting a business. The U.S. Small Business Administration estimates that whereas 63 percent of new businesses fail within six years, only 5 percent of new franchises fail.[14]

Disadvantages for franchisees also exist. One of the most problematic is *encroachment*—the opening of new units near existing ones without compensation to the existing franchisee. When encroachment occurs, potential revenues are diminished and

Even in [China's] Forbidden City—where emperors and empresses, concubines and eunuchs, palanquins and peons roamed for five centuries—there could not have been a more striking contraposition in the only store I found in the palace interior: a Starbucks!

—Michael Shermer in *Scientific American*

Earlier in this chapter we talked about Starbucks coffeehouses as an example of a very successful company-owned service organization with 6,000 outlets in the United States. The company now has more than 1,500 outlets abroad in 31 countries outside North America. When the company chose to go international, management realized that its best route was not to own but instead to franchise or form other types of alliances with organizations within each country. This approach would allow Starbucks to understand the individual markets better and would limit the capital investment necessary to expand. In an unusual twist, the company began its expansion in Asia rather than in Europe. In each country Starbucks has entered, it has met different scenarios and challenges, as illustrated by its experiences in Japan, China, and Canada.

JAPAN

Joining with Sazaby, a Japanese retailer and restaurateur, Starbucks opened more than a dozen stores in Japan beginning in 1997. The company chose Japan as its first expansion outside North America because it is the third largest coffee-consuming country in the world (6.1 million bags per year compared with 18.1 million bags in the United States). Possibly the most compelling result of the announcement of the entry of Starbucks was intense fear on the part of existing coffee-bar owners in Japan. Even though Starbucks was introducing a mere dozen outlets, the owners of the mega-chains were filled with anxiety. A manager of Doutor Coffee Company, Japan's number one coffee-bar chain (453 shops at the time), exclaimed, "They're a big threat and could take customers away from us." Many coffee bars imitated Starbucks in design and started offering "Seattle coffee." Executives such as Seiji Homma, president of Pronto Corporation (94 stores), traveled to the United States to gather intelligence from more than 20 Starbucks locations on the West Coast. He, like others, worried that the Japanese outlets lacked the sophistication of Starbucks, the ability to "(package) the store: (mesh) such elements as store design, package design, and other merchandising techniques into a compelling entity." Starbucks had so successfully created and distributed its service in the United States that the Japanese were afraid they could not compete. But as Starbucks opened more stores (it now has more than 500 in Japan), the Japanese competitors were ready. Rather than entering quietly and gaining a toehold before having to compete, Starbucks was targeted before it opened its first Japanese store.

CHINA

After selling Starbucks coffee to Beijing hotels for four years, the company decided to open franchise outlets there in 1998. Challenges abounded. "There (was) of course, the challenge of persuading members of a tea-drinking nation to switch to java. But more immediate has been the challenge of establishing local managers to run shops that can convey the spirit of Seattle in Beijing." The problem was hiring, motivating, and training both baristas who could deliver the consistent service and coffee drinks that made the chain so successful in the United States and managers who would uphold the high standards of the company. The company approached the hiring problem for managers by targeting young people who had experience in running successful American-style restaurants such as the Hard Rock Café.

They recruited baristas through job fairs and ads and focused on aspects such as career and personal development as well as the "cool" factor of being associated with the pop-culture scene in Seattle. Starbucks dealt with the motivation issue by sending the best manager recruits to Seattle for three months to absorb the culture and lifestyle of Starbucks and the West Coast. The structured training, as it turns out, helped motivate and keep employees because they felt confident in the company. The informality and culture of listening at Starbucks also help because they inculcate trust in employees and thereby generate loyalty.

Starbucks' first outlet in China opened in January 1999 at the China World Trade Centre in Beijing. The company now has more than 100 stores, mainly in Beijing and Shanghai. According to David Sun, president of Beijing Mei Da Coffee Company, which owns the Starbucks franchise for northern China, expansion is going well: "When we first started, people didn't know who we were and it was rough finding sites. Now landlords are coming to us."

CANADA

When Starbucks considered opening stores in Canada, the firm realized that it was dealing with an area unique enough to require firsthand knowledge. Rather than open its own shops, the company decided to license Interaction Restaurants to lead the firm into Montreal. Interaction Restaurants plans to expand the handful of Starbucks stores to 50 to 70 outlets in Quebec, most of them in the Montreal area.

Moving the firm into the Montreal culture while maintaining the Starbucks identity was a concern. Starbucks wanted to maintain the essence of its image, so it was very careful about the company it chose to become its ambassador. Starbucks had dealt with different cultures—such as the U.S. Hispanic community, Japan, and China—but there were important differences in Quebec. One involves the language, which is mandated by government and is a very emotional issue. In 2000, three coffee shops belonging to Second Cup Ltd., a rival of Starbucks, were bombed by an anti-English group because the company retained its English name. To prevent such problems yet remain consistent, Starbucks agreed to be called Café Starbucks Coffee, which combines French and English. Over time, the Starbucks brand became recognizable and accepted in Canada. Today, more than 400 stores in Canada are known as Starbucks Coffee Canada.

Perhaps a larger issue was that Montreal residents had a firmly entrenched, sophisticated coffee culture with a history of small coffee shops and Van Houtte (the dominant firm in the market) serving dark, rich coffee. Unlike in the United States, where Starbucks popularized the latte and the coffee tradition that went with it, "[t]here already is a café paradigm there, so Starbucks [did not] have quite the free rein to invent café culture in Quebec." Fortunately, Starbucks' darkly roasted taste was consistent with the preferences in Montreal. Even so, the firm created a special blend called Melange Mont-Royal to recognize the new market and acknowledge that it was special.

The Canadian outlets are also different in that they contain a kitchen for preparing sandwiches and simple meals and an oven for breads and muffins. Freshly prepared food is not typical of Starbucks, and it will be an interesting experiment to see if the outlets can operate the kitchens as efficiently as they do their coffee machines.

Sources: N. Shirouzu, "Japan's Staid Coffee Bars Wake Up and Smell the Starbucks," *The Wall Street Journal,* July 25, 1996, pp. B1ff; J. Lee-Young, "Starbucks' Expansion in China Is Slated; Coffee-Shop Managers Face Cultural Challenges," *The Wall Street Journal,* October 5, 1998, pp. A27Lff; "Business: Coffee with Your Tea? Starbucks in China," *The Economist,* October 6, 200l, p. 62; Z. Olijnyk, "Latte, s'il Vous Plait," *Canadian Business,* September 3, 2001, pp. 50–52; M. Shermer, "Starbucks in the Forbidden City," *Scientific American,* July 2001, pp. 34–35; Starbucks Annual Report (2003).

competition is increased. Another frequent disadvantage involves disappointing profits and revenues: "Most people think of franchising as some kind of bonanza…the reality is you get a solid operation, work damn hard, and if you're making $40,000 a year after four years, that's good."[15] Other disadvantages include lack of perceived control over operations and high fees. Many of these problems are due to overpromising by the franchiser, but others are caused by unrealistic expectations about what will be achieved in a franchise agreement.

AGENTS AND BROKERS

An *agent* is an intermediary who acts on behalf of a service principal (such as a real estate agent) or a customer and is authorized to make agreements between the principal and the customer. Some agents, called selling agents, work with the principal and have contractual authority to sell a principal's output (such as travel, insurance, or financial services), usually because the principal lacks the resources or desire to do so. Other agents, called purchasing agents, often have long-term relationships with buyers and help them in evaluating and making purchases. Such agents are frequently hired by companies and individuals to find art, antiques, and rare jewelry. A *broker* is an intermediary who brings buyers and sellers together while assisting in negotiation. Brokers are paid by the party who hired them, rarely become involved in financing or assuming risk, and are not long-term representatives of buyers or sellers. The most familiar examples are real estate brokers, insurance brokers, and security brokers.

Agents and brokers do not take title to services but instead deliver the rights to them. They have legal authority to market services as well as to perform other marketing functions on behalf of producers. The benefits and challenges in using agents and brokers are summarized in Table 14.2.

Benefits of Agents and Brokers

The travel industry provides an example of both agents and brokers. Three main categories of travel intermediaries exist: tour packagers, retail travel agents, and specialty channelers (including incentive travel firms, meeting and convention planners, hotel representatives, association executives, and corporate travel offices). You are likely to be most familiar with traditional retail travel agents. Industry convention terms the travel companies as brokers and the individuals who work for them as travel agents or sales associates. We use this industry to illustrate some of the benefits and challenges of delivering service through agents and brokers. This traditional industry is changing rapidly because of electronic channels, and we illustrate these new entrants and their impact later in the chapter.

TABLE 14.2
Benefits and Challenges in Distributing Services through Agents and Brokers

Benefits	Challenges
Reduced selling and distribution costs	Loss of control over pricing
Intermediary's possession of special skills and knowledge	Representation of multiple service principals
Wide representation	
Knowledge of local markets	
Customer choice	

Reduced Selling and Distribution Costs

If an airline or resort hotel needed to contact every potential traveler to promote its offerings, costs would be exorbitant. Because most travel services are transactional rather than long term, travelers would need to expend tremendous effort to find services that meet their needs. Travel agents and brokers accomplish the intermediary role by assembling information from travel suppliers and offering it to travelers.

Possession of Special Skills and Knowledge

Agents and brokers have special knowledge and skills in their areas. For example, retail travel agents know the industry well and know how to access the information they do not possess, often through reference materials and online services. Tour packagers have a more specialized role—they assemble, promote, and price bundles of travel services from travel suppliers, then offer these bundles either to travelers themselves or to retail travel agents. Specialty channelers have even more specialized roles. Some work in corporate travel offices to lend their skills to an entire corporation; others are business meeting and convention planners who act almost as tour packagers for whole companies or associations; and some are incentive travel firms that focus on travel recognition programs in corporations or associations.

Wide Representation

Because agents and brokers are paid by commission rather than by salary, there is little risk or disadvantage to the service principal in extending the service offerings to a wide geography. Thus companies have representatives in many places, far more than if fixed costs such as buildings, equipment, and salaries were required.

Knowledge of Local Markets

Another key benefit of agents and brokers is that they become experts in the local markets they serve. They know or learn the unique needs of different markets, including international markets. They understand what their clients' preferences are and how to adapt the principal's services to match the needs of clients. This benefit is particularly needed and appreciated when clients are dispersed internationally. Knowing the culture and taboos of a country is critical for successful selling. Most companies find that obtaining local representation by experts with this knowledge is necessary.

Customer Choice

Travel and insurance agents provide a retailing service for customers—they represent the services of multiple suppliers. If a traveler needed to visit six or eight different travel agencies, each of which carried the services of a single supplier, imagine the effort a customer would need to make to plan a trip! Similarly, independent insurance agents have the right to sell a wide variety of insurance, which allows them to offer customers a choice. These types of agents also are able to compare prices across suppliers and get the best prices for their clients.

Challenges of Delivering Service through Agents and Brokers

Loss of Control over Pricing

As representatives of service principals and experts on customer markets, agents and brokers are typically empowered to negotiate price, configure services, and otherwise alter the marketing of a principal's service. This issue could be particularly important—and possibly detrimental—when a service provider depends on a particular (high) price to convey a level of service quality. If the price can be changed, it might drop to a level that undermines the quality image. In addition, the agent often has the flexibility to give different prices to different customers. As long as the customers are geographically dispersed, this variation will not create a problem for the service principal; however, if buyers compare prices and realize they are being given different prices, they may perceive the service principal as unfair or unethical.

Representation of Multiple Service Principals

When independent agents represent multiple suppliers, they offer customer choice. From the perspective of the service principal, however, customer choice means that the agent represents—and in many cases advocates—a competitive service offering. This is the same challenge a manufacturer confronts when distributing products in a retail store. Only in rare cases are its products the only ones in a given category on the retail floor. In a service context, consider the use of independent insurance agents. These agents carry a range of insurance products from different companies, serving as a surrogate service retail store for customers. When they find a customer who needs insurance, they sell from their portfolio the offerings that best match the customer's requirements.

ELECTRONIC CHANNELS

Electronic channels are the only service distributors that do not require direct human interaction. What they do require is some predesigned service (almost always information, education, or entertainment) and an electronic vehicle to deliver it. You are all familiar with telephone and television channels and the Internet and Web and may be aware of the other electronic vehicles that are currently under development. The consumer and business services that are made possible through these vehicles include movies on demand, interactive news and music, banking and financial services, multimedia libraries and databases, distance learning, desktop videoconferencing, remote health services, and interactive, network-based games.

The more a service relies on technology and/or equipment for service production and the less it relies on face-to-face contact with service providers, the less the service is characterized by inseparability and nonstandardization. As you will see in the following section, using electronic channels overcomes some of the problems associated with service inseparability and allows a form of standardization not previously possible in most services. Table 14.3 summarizes the benefits and challenges of electronic distribution.

Benefits of Electronic Channels

Consistent Delivery for Standardized Services

Electronic channels such as television and telecommunication do not alter the service, as channels with human interaction tend to do. Unlike delivery from a personal provider, electronic delivery does not interpret the service and execute it according to that interpretation. Its delivery is likely to be the same in all transmissions.

Distribution of television programming from networks through affiliate television and radio stations illustrates standardized electronic distribution. Networks create and finance programming including shows, news, and sports and distribute them through

TABLE 14.3
**Benefits and
Challenges in
Electronic
Distribution of
Services**

Benefits	Challenges
Consistent delivery for standardized services	Price competition
Low cost	Inability to customize with highly standardized services
Customer convenience	Lack of consistency due to customer involvement
Wide distribution	
Customer choice and ability to customize	Changes in consumer behavior
	Security concerns
Quick customer feedback	Competition from widening geographies

local stations in return for fees and advertising dollars. In most cases, the local stations deliver what is fed to them through the networks. Local stations can elect not to carry a particular show because of low ratings or lack of fit with the local market. They can also refuse to carry advertising spots that are judged in bad taste or too controversial. Except for these situations, which are not common, what is distributed through electronic channels is what the service creator sends.

Low Cost

Electronic media offer more efficient means of delivery than does interpersonal distribution. For example, the cost of reaching buyers using a direct sales force has been estimated to exceed $150 per interaction, whereas the use of electronic media such as television or radio often costs less than $30 per *thousand* interactions. Critics could rightly claim that the personal sales interaction is more powerful and effective, but with interactive media service, advertisers are able to gain some of the credibility benefits of personal interaction (such as being able to answer individual questions or tailor the service for individuals).

Customer Convenience

With electronic channels, customers are able to access a firm's services when and where they want. "Retailers still tell customers, You have to come to us. But online consumers are saying, No way—*you* have to come to *us*. My place, my time is the new mantra of consumers everywhere."[16] Just as catalog shopping freed working women from the perceived drudgeries of having to go to the mall—and fattened the purses of forward-thinking companies that recognized an underserved market—e-commerce is changing the way people shop. Many mail-order companies still limit their hours of availability, a real mistake if they are going to match the customer convenience of being able to order online 24 hours a day, seven days a week. For the marketer, electronic channels allow access to a large group of customers who would otherwise be unavailable to them because of busy schedules that do not allow them to shop in other ways.

Wide Distribution

Electronic channels do more than allow the service provider to interact with a large number of consumers. They also allow the service provider to interact (often simultaneously) with a large number of intermediaries. The costs and effort to inform, select, and motivate nonelectronic channels are higher than the costs to accomplish the same activities with electronic channels. Many franchisers have found that prospecting through the Internet provides better-qualified franchisees than the traditional methods of mainstream advertising and trade shows. Seattle-based World Inspection Network, a franchiser of home inspection operators, increased its franchisee pool fivefold using evaluation and prequalification on the Internet.[17]

Customer Choice and Ability to Customize

Consider the options available in movies and videos to customers who use video-on-demand services. Just as Dell Computer allows customers to configure entire products to their own particular needs and desires, the Internet allows many companies to design services from the beginning. Individuals who want to renovate their kitchen may now go to many Internet sites, specify their requirements, and order what they wish. Whether the supplier is a large retailer such as Home Depot or a small start-up company, customers get exactly what they want. Our Strategy Insight discusses how H&R Block uses the Internet to provide its customers with a wide range of options for receiving tax preparation services.

Quick Customer Feedback

Rapid customer feedback is without doubt one of the major strengths of e-commerce. Companies can find out immediately what customers think of services and can gain far higher participation from customers in surveys. With quick customer feedback, changes can be made rapidly to service assortments, problems can be addressed immediately, and the learning cycles of companies can speed up dramatically.

Challenges in Distributing Services through Electronic Channels

Price Competition

One of the traditional differences between goods and services has been the difficulty of directly comparing features and prices of services with each other. Whereas goods can typically be compared in retail settings, few retail settings exist that offer services from multiple sources. The Internet has changed all that. Services such as travelocity.com and Priceline.com make it simple for customers to compare prices for a wide variety of services. Priceline.com allows customers to name their price for a service such as an airline ticket, wait until Priceline.com finds an airline willing to accept it, then purchase the ticket. Never has the customer had such ability to bid on prices for services. In Chapter 17 we describe another type of price competition spawned by the Internet: the Internet auction as presented by such companies as eBay, which sells millions of products and services in more than 1,000 categories.

Inability to Customize with Highly Standardized Electronic Services

Some of you have learned college basics through video-transmitted courses. If you consider what you missed in learning that way compared with learning directly from a professor, you will understand this challenge. In mass sections, you cannot interact directly with the professor, ask questions, raise points for clarification, or experience the connection that you receive in person. In electronic classes—as in videoconferences that are springing up in many businesses—the quality of the service can also be impeded by the way the audience reacts (or does not react) in those situations. People talk among themselves, leave, laugh, and criticize, among other behaviors.

H&R Block, the world's largest tax services company, served nearly 22 million clients in the United States and 11 other countries in 2004. With so many customers, H&R Block delivers its services through a variety of channels. H&R Block's approach, referred to as a "blended channel" approach, is a multichannel strategy delivered through various types of intermediaries that creates tremendous flexibility for its clients and the means by which they receive services. This approach allows H&R Block to offer what it describes as services with "solutions for every taxpayer." Customers may receive H&R Block's services through retail offices, through the Internet, through software programs, or through some combination of these channels. Each method of service delivery is described in the following paragraphs.

SERVICE DELIVERY VIA COMPANY-OWNED AND FRANCHISED RETAIL OFFICES

H&R Block has approximately 11,000 offices worldwide, including more than 9,000 in the United States. Nearly 7,000 offices are company owned and the remaining 4,200 are franchises. Customers wanting to purchase H&R Block's services through an office have three options. The Face to Face option, in which customers can either call an H&R Block office for an appointment or just walk right in, provides an opportunity for the customer to be interviewed in person and to have the company completely prepare the tax return document. Here customers are paying for a H&R Block representative to spend time with them to understand their unique situation and to do everything possible to help reduce their tax liability. Those customers wanting to use the Office Drop-off option complete a questionnaire that captures key information and informs customers of what forms and documents to bring to the H&R Block office in order to have the company prepare a tax return; the customer is then called when the return has been completed. The third option, Online Drop-off, allows the customer to conduct a tax interview interactively via the Internet or via telephone, fax, or e-mail. Necessary tax data is then provided either via the Internet or fax, and the customer's tax return is prepared by the local H&R Block office.

SERVICE DELIVERY VIA THE INTERNET (ONLINE)

When it comes to preparing tax returns, a relatively large percentage of all taxpayers prefer the "Do It Yourself" method. Traditionally these people have completed their tax returns using pen-and-paper means. However, H&R Block offers these customers an alternative means of doing it themselves by providing its services through the Internet. Customers who prefer to complete the entire process online can purchase the Standard option (for $34.95), which allows them to use H&R Block's website to completely prepare and then electronically file their tax return. The Premium service option (for $49.95) provides, in addition to the Standard option's features, virtual assistance via the Internet (additional information for more complex topics such as rental property, home offices, or depreciation), audit alerts (pointing out areas that often trigger government audits), and one free (face-to-face) consultation with a tax advisor. In addition to the Standard and Premium service option features, the Signature service option (for $99.95) also includes having a tax advisor check the customer's tax return for errors, correct any problems on the return, and then sign and electronically file the return for the customer. This option also allows the customer year-round access to an H&R Block tax advisor for advice.

SERVICE DELIVERY VIA SOFTWARE

Another alternative for the tax preparation do-it-yourselfer is to purchase H&R Block tax services through its software offering, TaxCut. This program provides most of the same services that are available online but does not require the customer to be connected to the Internet. That is, the TaxCut program also provides a customized tax interview (asking only the questions that pertain to each customer's tax situation), checks for errors that could draw the attention of an auditor, imports financial data from other personal finance programs and/or the previous year's tax data, and electronically files tax returns. Because the software is installed on the customer's personal computer, customers do not have to worry about their financial data being stored somewhere other than on their own computer. Indeed, the software do-it-yourself customer tends to be older, more mature, more affluent, and more concerned with privacy than those who purchase H&R Block's online services. As with the other channels of service delivery, customers can select from three TaxCut options—Standard, Deluxe, or Premium—with differing levels of service provided.

SERVICE DELIVERY VIA THE TELEPHONE

Some customers do not wish to use H&R Block's services to prepare tax returns, but they do have tax questions that they would like answered. H&R Block's Ask a Tax Advisor program allows customers to submit a tax question online and have someone contact them however they wish (via e-mail or phone) within 48 hours. Customers are charged on a per-question basis for this service. H&R Block also provides customer service support for its other products through telephone, e-mail, and live chat vehicles.

H&R Block's blended channel strategy provides clients with many choices as to how they would like their service to be delivered and how much of the work they would like to do themselves. At one extreme, the customer can have the task of tax preparation completed entirely by H&R Block by visiting one of its offices. Alternatively, customers can pursue a do-it-yourself option by purchasing the TaxCut software and completing their tax returns without any assistance from H&R Block. And those customers who would like to coproduce the service by doing some of the work themselves may look to H&R Block for assistance with specific issues or questions. H&R Block provides clients with the ability to choose what method, channel, and products are best for them, at the time that meets their needs, and in the stage of the tax preparation experience that is relevant to them—in effect, allowing customers much flexibility by providing many choices to blend the channels of service delivery in a customized service. Thus, H&R Block has, through its blended channel strategy approach, created value for its customers by providing as much of the service as customers desire and through the channel in which the customer feels the most comfortable.

continued

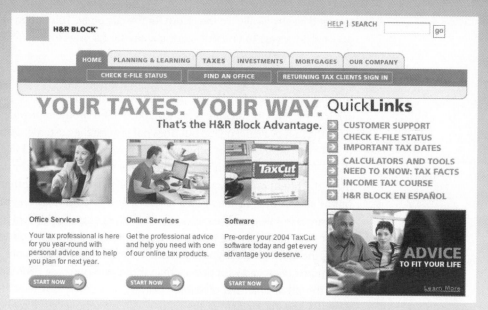

Sources: *2004 H&R Block Annual Report;* H&R Block website, www.hrblock.com (accessed November 12, 2004).

Lack of Consistency Because of Customer Involvement

Although electronic channels are very effective in minimizing the inconsistency from employees or providers of service, customer variability still presents a problem. Many times customers use the technology themselves to produce the service and can lead to errors or frustration unless the technology is highly user friendly. Maneuvering online can sometimes be overwhelming, and not all websites are easy to use. Furthermore, many customers may not have computers and, even if they do, may be reluctant to use this medium.

Changes in Consumer Behavior

A consumer purchasing a service through electronic channels engages in very different behavior than a consumer entering a retail store and talking to a salesperson. Considerable changes—in the willingness to search for information, in the willingness to perform some aspects of the services themselves, in the acceptance of different levels of service—are necessary when customers use electronic channels. Behavior change is difficult, even for a consumer wanting to make a change; therefore, marketers wishing to motivate consumers to alter long-established patterns will be challenged.

Security Concerns

One issue confronting marketers using electronic channels is concern about the security of information, particularly health and financial information. Many customers are still hesitant about giving credit-card numbers on the Internet. These problems can undermine consumers' trust in the Internet as a safe place to do business. Companies doing business through the Internet must continually devise ways to protect their systems from penetration, vandalism, eavesdropping, and impersonation.[18] With penetration, intruders steal passwords and exploit unprotected modems and connections, actually taking over the sites. With vandalism, hackers crash corporate and other computers. To combat these problems, firewalls and other software scan for unusual activity. With eavesdropping, hackers snoop on information as it passes through multiple computers to the Internet. The typical solution is encryption software that scrambles electronic mail and other data to make it unintelligible to eavesdroppers. Finally, with impersonation, criminals steal consumers' identities in order to buy goods and services. A form of encryption technology is often used to deal with this problem, and special service companies confirm signature holders.[19]

Competition from Widening Geographies

Historically, many services were somewhat protected from competition because customers had limited choice among the providers they could physically drive to. Banks, for example, supplied all local customers with checking accounts, savings accounts, and mortgages. In fact, it used to be said that because services could not be transported they were limited in their scope. Not any longer—and not with electronic channels. Through the Internet, many services, including financial services, can be purchased from service providers far from the local area. See this chapter's Technology Spotlight for several examples.

COMMON ISSUES INVOLVING INTERMEDIARIES

Key problems with intermediaries include conflict over objectives and performance, difficulty controlling quality and consistency across outlets, tension between empowerment and control, and channel ambiguity.

Channel Conflict over Objectives and Performance

The parties involved in delivering services do not always agree about how the channel should operate. Channel conflict can occur between the service provider and the service intermediary, among intermediaries in a given area, and between different types of channels used by a service provider (such as when a service principal has its own outlets as well as franchised outlets). The conflict most often centers on the parties having different goals, competing roles and rights, and conflicting views of the way the channel is performing. Sometimes the conflict occurs because the service principal and its intermediaries are too dependent on each other.

Difficulty Controlling Quality and Consistency across Outlets

One of the biggest difficulties for both principals and their intermediaries involves the inconsistency and lack of uniform quality that result when multiple outlets deliver services. When shoddy performance occurs, even at a single outlet, the service principal suffers because the entire brand and reputation are jeopardized, and other intermediaries endure negative attributions to their outlets. The problem is particularly acute in highly specialized services such as management consulting or architecture, in which execution of the complex offering may be difficult to deliver to the standards of the principal.

Tension between Empowerment and Control

McDonald's and other successful service businesses were founded on the principle of performance consistency. Both they and their intermediaries have attained profits and

Technology Spotlight
Electronic Channels in Action

The possibilities for selling and servicing on the Internet and other electronic channels are virtually limitless. Some baseball teams let you see the view of the field from any seat before you buy your ticket. At Lands' End you can create an onscreen model with your figure, then try clothes on the model to find out how they will look on you. Progressive real estate firms let you tour homes as if you were walking through them. Some interesting and innovative applications of the Internet and other electronic channels are illustrated here.

SUPER ATMS

Move over, standard banking ATMs. Enter multipurpose ATMs: ATMs that allow you to purchase discount lift tickets and ski lessons for Lake Tahoe resorts at no fee (Wells Fargo ATMs); ATMs that show movie clips and commercials while you wait for your money (EDS ATMs in San Diego); ATMs that convert currencies on international flights using satellites to send card information to your bank (Inflight ATI in Irvine, California); ATMs that let you book flights and print tickets for any airline for $4 to $7 (Docunet in San Francisco). Other companies are experimenting with machines that sell stamps and are customizing ATM screens to make your electronic banking even easier.

ONLINE TRAVEL

Online travel has been one of the biggest success stories in electronic channels. The industry expected to have more than $50 billion in travel revenues resulting from transactions completed online in 2004. The Internet has been an extremely effective channel for travel for three key reasons:

1. Prices are more competitive than offline prices, and the technology can conjure up literally thousands of providers in an instant.

2. Online travel companies have no inventory costs and therefore low cost of goods sold.

3. Sites obtain significant advertising revenue due to focused clientele, with advertisers knowing that all users are potential buyers of their travel services.

One of the most successful, profitable online travel sites is Travelocity.com. Like other online travel sites, it sells airline tickets, hotel rooms, and car rentals directly to consumers, avoiding travel agents. It has been one of the top online travel sites since its inception in 1996 by Sabre Holdings. In 2004 it had record revenues (more than $2 billion). The site earned the loyalty of its users by being very customer focused in an industry that is all too

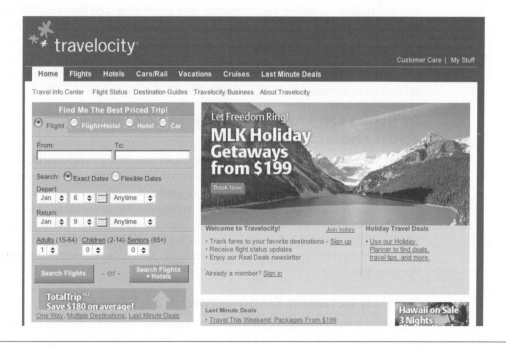

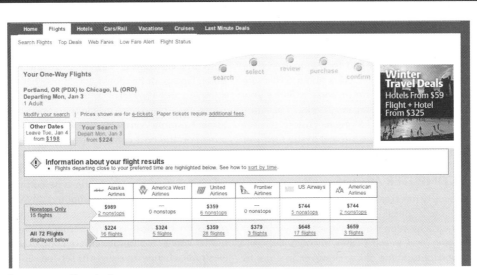

Source: www.Travelocity.com

often technology focused. Based on focus groups and surveys to assess site design and ease of use, the company created excellent customer service, carefully detailed explanations, and guarantees of its credit card security and privacy policies. The company has a special help desk that focuses on taking credit card numbers over the telephone for those afraid to input them online. The site also offers instantaneous price quotes and the ability to track prices to cities that customers plan to visit.

BILL PAYING ONLINE

In recent years many financial institutions have provided an online banking mechanism for customers to pay bills via the Internet. Once customers have made arrangements with their bank and supplied information about each of the companies that send them bills, customers can make payments to those companies using the Internet. This process is generally triggered when customers receive a bill (or bills). Then, accessing their bank account through the Internet, customers identify the company (or companies) to which they owe money and click through a couple of screens and options to initiate payments.

Paytrust, an online bill management company founded in 1998, takes this process several steps further. For a monthly fee of about $11, customers can have all their bills sent directly to Paytrust, where the bills are scanned and electronic imagines are created and made

available to customers via the Internet. Paytrust provides several service options to the customer for paying the bill, including: (1) the customer can peruse the bill before paying it, (2) the customer can have Paytrust pay the bill automatically, or (3) the customer can have Paytrust pay it automatically if the total amount due is less than a prespecified amount (set by the customer). These options allow customers to have as much (or little) control over the bill-paying process as they want and to eliminate the paper flow associated with bills coming and going. Paytrust can also receive electronic presentation of bills. Once customers have provided the appropriate user IDs and passwords to Paytrust, they do not have to log on to the website of each company. Instead, they can merely log onto the Paytrust website and access each biller's website from there—thereby eliminating the need to remember multiple user IDs, passwords, and URLs. For a small additional fee, Paytrust will provide a CD with a complete set of electronic images of all bills received and payments made during the year. Paytrust's services are particularly appealing to consumers who are time constrained or who are frequently away from home.

OPPORTUNITIES TO BE YOUR OWN SHOEMAKER

Companies that mass-market consumer items such as packaged goods have been challenged to use the Inter-

continued

Technology Spotlight
Electronic Channels in Action—continued

net as a channel to increase loyalty and create customer excitement. Nike.com found success when the company launched an Internet service allowing its website shoppers to create personalized shoes. Users can select shoes, color them to fit their tastes, and then emblazon their own names on the shoes. This costs about $10 more than off-the-rack shoes in the stores, and customers now buy thousands of such custom pairs per day. The initiative was just one step toward far greater custom services on the Web, including using the Internet to size their feet and custom fit shoes to unique foot sizes.

REMOTE COMPUTER ACCESS

Our mobile society has created a desire by many people to have access to a specific computer without being in the same physical location. For example, many companies are allowing (and, in some cases, encouraging) employees to work outside the office. However, in order to work effectively, these employees often need access to the same computer resources they would expect if they were in their office. GoToMyPC.com provides a service that allows access to a host computer from any other computer connected to the Internet. Travelers, telecommuters, or anyone desiring to access their computer

from a location other than where it is physically located simply need to install GoToMyPC software on a select (host) computer and leave that computer running and connected to the Internet. These customers then log onto the GoToMyPC website with any remote computer, laptop, or handheld device that has access to the Internet, and they can connect directly to that host computer. This service provides a window on the customer's remote computer that looks just like the video screen on the host computer; once connected, the service allows customers to work as if they were sitting in front of their (host) computer. Any files that the customer has access to from the host computer can be transferred to the remote computer; any software programs on the host computer can be run; and, documents on the host computer can be printed on any printer connected to the remote computer. In using an electronic channel to deliver its service, GoToMyPC provides time savings and convenience to its customers.

Sources: K. K. Choquette, "Super ATMs Sell Lift Tickets, Exchange Currencies," *USA Today,* January 19, 1998, p. B1; D. Coleman, "Internet Success Stories: Travelocity," australia.internet.com, November 12, 2001, p. 1.

longevity because the company controls virtually every aspect of their intermediaries' businesses. McDonald's, for example, is famous for its demanding and rigid service standards (such as "turn, never flip, hamburgers on the grill"), carefully specified supplies, and performance monitoring. The strategy makes sense: Unless an intermediary delivers service exactly the same way the successful company outlets provide it, the service may not be as desirable to customers. From the principal's point of view, its name and reputation are on the line in each outlet, making careful control a necessity.

Control, however, can have negative ramifications within intermediaries. Many service franchisees, for example, are entrepreneurial by nature and select service franchising because they can own and operate their own businesses. If they are to deliver according to consistent standards, their independent ideas must be integrated into and often subsumed by the practices and policies of the service principal. In these situations they often feel like automatons with less freedom than they have anticipated as owners of their own businesses.

Channel Ambiguity

When control is not the chosen strategy, doubt exists about the roles of the company and the intermediary. Who will undertake market research to identify customer requirements, the company or an intermediary? Who owns the results and in what way are they to be used? Who determines the standards for service delivery, the franchiser or the franchisee? Who should train a dealer's customer service representatives, the company or the dealer? In these and other situations, the roles of the principal and its intermediaries are unclear, leading to confusion and conflict.

STRATEGIES FOR EFFECTIVE SERVICE DELIVERY THROUGH INTERMEDIARIES

Service principals, of course, want to manage their service intermediaries to improve service performance, solidify their images, and increase profits and revenues. The principal has a variety of choices, which range from strict contractual and measurement control to partnering with intermediaries in a joint effort to improve service to the customer. One of the biggest issues a principal faces is whether to view intermediaries as extensions of its company, as customers, or as partners. We discuss three categories of intermediary management strategies: control strategies, empowerment strategies, and partnering strategies.

Control Strategies

In the control strategies category, the service principal believes that intermediaries will perform best when it creates standards both for revenues and service performance, measures results, and compensates or rewards on the basis of performance level. To use these strategies the principal must be the most powerful participant in the channel, possessing unique services with strong consumer demand or loyalty, or other forms of economic power.

Measurement

Some franchisers maintain control of the service quality delivered by their franchisees by ongoing measurement programs that feed data back to the principal. Virtually all automobile dealers' sales and service performance is monitored regularly by the manufacturer, which creates the measurement program, administers it, and maintains control of the information. The company surveys customers at key points in the service encounter sequence: after sale, 30 days out, 90 days out, and after a year. The manufacturer designs the survey instruments (some of them with the assistance of dealer councils) and obtains the customer feedback directly. On the basis of this information, the manufacturer rewards and recognizes both individuals and dealerships that perform well and can potentially punish those that perform poorly. The obvious advantage to this approach is that the manufacturer retains control; however, the trust and goodwill between manufacturers and dealers can easily be eroded if dealers feel that the measurement is used to control and punish.

Review

Some franchisers control through terminations, nonrenewals, quotas, and restrictive supplier sources. Expansion and encroachment are two of the tactics being used today. Another means by which franchisers exert control over franchisees is through quotas and sales goals, typically by offering price breaks after a certain volume is attained.

Empowerment Strategies

Empowerment strategies—in which the service principal allows greater flexibility to intermediaries based on the belief that their talents are best revealed in participation rather than acquiescence—are useful when the service principal is new or lacks sufficient power to govern the channel using control strategies. In empowerment strategies, the principal provides information, research, or processes to help intermediaries perform well in service.

Help the Intermediary Develop Customer-Oriented Service Processes

Individual intermediaries rarely have the funds to sponsor their own customer research studies or training programs. One way for a company to improve intermediary performance is to conduct research or standard-setting studies relating to service performance, then provide the results as a service to intermediaries. As an example, H&R Block amassed its customer information and codified it in a set of 10 "Ultimate Client Service" standards, which were displayed in each office. The standards, which tend to change over time, have included:

- No client will wait more than 30 minutes in the waiting area.

- Phone calls will be answered by the fourth ring, and no caller will be on hold for more than one minute.

- Every tax preparation client will receive a thorough interview to determine the client's lowest legal tax liability.

- Accurately prepared and checked returns will be delivered in 4 days or fewer.

Rather than administer this customer program from the home office, which could cause it to be perceived as a measurement "hammer," the company asks each franchisee to devise a way to measure the standards in its own offices, then report this information to H&R Block.

Provide Needed Support Systems

After Ford Motor Company conducted customer research and identified six sales standards and six service standards that address the most important customer expectations, it found that dealers and service centers did not know how to implement, measure, and improve service with these standards. For example, one sales standard specified that customers be approached within the first minute they enter the dealership and be offered help when and if the customer needs it. Although dealers could see that this standard was desirable, they did not immediately know how to make it happen. Ford stepped in and provided the research and process support to help the dealers. As another form of support, the company created national advertising featuring dealers discussing the quality care standards.

In airlines and hotels as well as other travel and ticketing services, the service principal's reservation system is an important support system. Holiday Inn has a franchise service delivery system that adds value to the Holiday Inn franchise and differentiates it from competitors.

Develop Intermediaries to Deliver Service Quality

Service originators can invest in training or other forms of development to improve the skills and knowledge of intermediaries and their employees. Prudential Real Estate Associates, a national franchiser of real estate brokers, engaged in a companywide program of service excellence. To teach sales associates (real estate agents) about what buyers and sellers expect, the company first conducted focus group interviews with end customers, then created a half-day training program to communicate what the research revealed. To teach brokers (the companies that employ the sales associates), the company created a highly successful operations review that examined the operational and financial aspects of the brokers, assessed their levels of effectiveness, then communicated individually with each broker about the specific issues that needed to be addressed and the approaches that would be successful in improving performance.

Change to a Cooperative Management Structure

Companies such as Taco Bell use the technique of empowerment to manage and motivate franchisees. They develop worker teams in their outlets to hire, discipline, and handle financial tasks such as deposits and audits. Taco Bell deliberately reduced levels of management (regional managers used to oversee 5 stores; now they oversee 50 stores) and reported improvements in revenue, employee morale, and profits.

Partnering Strategies

The group of strategies with the highest potential for effectiveness involves partnering with intermediaries to learn together about end customers, set specifications, improve delivery, and communicate honestly. This approach capitalizes on the skills and strengths of both principal and intermediary and engenders a sense of trust that improves the relationship.

Alignment of Goals

One of the most successful approaches to partnering involves aligning company and intermediary goals early in the process. Both the service principal and the intermediary have individual goals that they strive to achieve. If channel members can see that they benefit the ultimate consumer of services and in the process optimize their own revenues and profit, they begin the relationship with a target in mind. Sonic Corp, a drive-in hamburger chain, attempts to retain open relationships with its franchisees, continually adapting to changing customer needs and franchisee suggestions.

Consultation and Cooperation

A strategy of consultation and cooperation is not as dramatic as setting joint goals, but it does result in intermediaries participating in decisions. In this approach, which could involve virtually any issue, from compensation to service quality to the service environment, the principal makes a point of consulting intermediaries and asking for their opinions and views before establishing policy. Alpha Graphics, a franchiser of rapid printing services based in Tucson, Arizona, habitually consults its franchisees to hear how they think the operation should be run. For example, when the franchiser found that the outlets needed greater support in promotion, the company began to make customer mailings for franchisees. When the franchiser found that many franchisees were dissatisfied with the one-sided contracts they received, Alpha Graphics revised contracts to make it easier for franchisees to leave the system, changed fees to reflect a sliding scale linked to volume, and allowed franchisees to select the ways they use their royalty fees. This approach makes the franchisees feel that they have some control over the way they do business and also generates a steady stream of improvement ideas. Taco John's, one of the largest Mexican fast-food chains, is known for its cooperative relationships with franchisees.

Summary

This chapter discussed the benefits and challenges of delivering service through intermediaries. Service intermediaries perform many important functions for the service principal—coproducing the service, making services locally available, and functioning as the link between the principal and the customer. The focus in service distribution is on identifying ways to bring the customer and principal or its representatives together.

In contrast to channels for products, channels for services are almost always direct, if not to the customer then to the intermediary that sells to the customer. Many of the primary functions that distribution channels serve—inventorying, securing, and taking title to goods—have no meaning in services because of services' intangibility. Because services cannot be owned, most have no titles or rights that can be passed along a delivery channel. Because services are intangible and perishable, inventories cannot exist, making warehousing dispensable. In general, because services cannot be produced, warehoused, and then retailed as goods can, many channels available to goods producers are not feasible for service firms.

Four forms of distribution in service were described in the chapter: franchisees, agents/brokers, and direct and electronic channels. The benefits and challenges of each type of intermediary were discussed, and examples of firms successful in delivering services through each type were detailed. Discussion centered on strategies that could be used by service principals to improve management of intermediaries.

Discussion Questions

1. In what specific ways does the distribution of services differ from the distribution of goods?

2. Identify other service firms that are company owned and see whether the services they provide are more consistent than ones provided by the franchisees mentioned in this chapter.

3. List five services that could be distributed on the Internet that are not mentioned in this chapter. Why are these particular services appropriate for electronic distribution? Choose two that you particularly advocate. How would you address the challenges to electronic media discussed in this chapter?

4. List services that are sold through selling agents. Why is the use of agents the chosen method of distribution for these services? Could any be distributed in the other ways described in this chapter?

5. What are the main differences between agents and brokers?

6. What types of services are bought through purchasing agents? What qualifies a purchasing agent to represent a buyer in these transactions? Why do buyers themselves not engage in the purchase, rather than hiring someone to do so?

7. Which of the reasons for channel conflict described at in this chapter is the most problematic? Why? Based on the chapter, and in particular the strategies discussed at the end of the chapter, what can be done to address the problem you selected? Rank the possible strategies from most effective to least effective.

8. Which of the three categories of strategies for effective service delivery through intermediaries do you believe is most successful? Why? Why are the other two categories less successful?

Exercises

1. Develop a brief franchising plan for a service concept or idea that you believe could be successful.

2. Visit a franchisee and discuss the pros and cons of the arrangement from his or her perspective. How closely does this list of benefits and challenges fit the one

provided in this chapter? What would you add to the chapter's list to reflect the experience of the franchisee you interviewed?

3. Select a service industry with which you are familiar. How do service principals in that industry distribute their services? Develop possible approaches to manage intermediaries using the three categories of strategies in the last section of this chapter. Which approach do you believe would be most effective? Why? Which approaches are currently used by service principals in the industry?

4. On the Internet, locate three services that you believe are interesting. What benefits does buying on the Internet have over buying those services elsewhere?

Notes

1. P. Mangan, "What Is Distance Learning?" *Management Quarterly,* Fall 2001, pp. 30–35.
2. L. Bertagnoli, "Education Reservation," *Marketing News,* February 12, 2001, p. 4.
3. R. Hoffman, "Quality at a Distance," *The Greentree Gazette,* March 4, 2003, p. 16.
4. A. E. Hancock, "The Evolving Terrain of Distance Learning," *Satellite Communications,* March 1999, pp. 24ff.
5. J. McCormick, "The New School," *Newsweek,* April 24, 2000; www.unext.com.
6. S. Stecklow, "At Phoenix University, Class Can Be Anywhere—Even in Cyberspace," *The Wall Street Journal,* September 12, 1994, p. A1.
7. Hancock, "The Evolving Terrain of Distance Learning," p. 24.
8. A. Fisher, "Getting a BA Online," *Fortune,* February 1, 1999, p. 144.
9. L. J. Goff, "E-Learning Evangelists," *Computerworld,* September 10, 2001, pp. 40–41.
10. Hancock, "The Evolving Terrain of Distance Learning," p. 25.
11. A. Senzek, "Surfing for Credit," *Business Mexico,* July 2001, pp. 46–47.
12. R. Cwiklik, "Pieces of the Puzzle—A Different Course: For Many People, College Will No Longer Be a Specific Place, or a Specific Time," *The Wall Street Journal,* November 6, 1998, p. R31.
13. A. E. Serwer, "Trouble in Franchise Nation," *Fortune,* March 6, 1995, pp. 115–129.
14. L. Bongiorno, "Franchise Fracas," *Business Week,* March 22, 1993, pp. 68–72.
15. Serwer, "Trouble in Franchise Nation," p. 116.
16. G. Hamel and J. Sampler, "The e-Corporation," *Fortune,* December 7, 1998, pp. 80–92.
17. C. A. Laurie, "Franchisers Meet Challenges of Growth, Change," *Franchising World,* March/April 1999, pp. 11–14.
18. D. Clark, "Safety First," *The Wall Street Journal,* December 7, 1998, p. R14.
19. Ibid.

Chapter

15

MANAGING DEMAND AND CAPACITY

This chapter's objectives are to

1. Explain the underlying issue for capacity-constrained services: lack of inventory capability.

2. Present the implications of time, labor, equipment, and facilities constraints combined with variations in demand patterns.

3. Lay out strategies for matching supply and demand through (a) shifting demand to match capacity or (b) adjusting capacity to meet demand.

4. Demonstrate the benefits and risks of yield management strategies in forging a balance among capacity utilization, pricing, market segmentation, and financial return.

5. Provide strategies for managing waiting lines for times when capacity and demand cannot be aligned.

How to Fill 281 Rooms 365 Days of the Year

The Ritz-Carlton Hotel in Phoenix, Arizona, is an upscale hotel in the center of a metropolitan area of approximately 3 million people, the fifth largest metropolitan area in the United States. The hotel was named the number one business hotel in Arizona by *Travel and Leisure* magazine in 2004.[1] It has 281 luxury rooms, two restaurants, beautiful pools, and spacious meeting and conference facilities. These restaurants and meeting facilities are available to guests 365 days and nights of the year. Yet natural demand for them varies tremendously. During the tourist season from November through mid-April, demand for rooms is high, often exceeding available space. From mid-May through September, however, when temperatures regularly exceed 100 degrees Fahrenheit, demand for rooms drops considerably. Because the hotel caters to business travelers and business meetings, demand has a weekly cycle in addition to the seasonal fluctuations. Business travelers do not stay over weekends. Thus, demand for rooms from the hotel's primary market segment drops on Friday and Saturday nights.

To smooth the peaks and valleys of demand for its facilities, the Ritz-Carlton in Phoenix has employed a number of strategies. Group business (primarily business conferences) is pursued throughout the year to fill the lower demand periods. A variety of special events, sports, weddings, and getaway packages are offered year-round to increase weekend demand for rooms. During the hot summer months the hotel encourages local Phoenix and nearby Tucson residents to experience the luxury of the hotel. One creative package included an attractively priced hotel stay combined with a "progressive dinner" at nearby restaurants. The progressive dinner started with a reception in the hotel, a walk to one restaurant for appetizers, followed by dinner at a second restaurant. The evening finished with champagne and dessert in the guests' room. By encouraging local people to use the hotel, the hotel increases its occupancy during slow demand times while residents of the community get a chance to enjoy an experience they probably wouldn't be able to afford during the high season.

Most downtown hotels in urban areas face the same weekly demand fluctuations that the Phoenix Ritz-Carlton deals with, and many have found a partial solution by catering to families and children on the weekends.[2] For many dual-career couples, weekend getaways are a primary form of relaxation and vacation. The downtown hotels cater to these couples and families by offering discounted room rates, child-oriented activities and amenities, and an environment in which families feel comfortable. For example, at the Costa Mesa Marriott Suites in Orange County, California, employees dress casually on the weekend and toasters are put on the breakfast buffet just for kids. The Hyatt Regency Reston in Reston, Virginia, rented its 21 executive suites for kids' slumber parties on the weekend. The Chicago Hilton initiated a "Vacation Station" program that included gifts and games for kids, plenty of cribs in inventory, and gummi bears in the minibars.

For the Ritz-Carlton Hotel in Phoenix and the other hotels just mentioned, managing demand and utilizing the hotel's fixed capacity of rooms, restaurants, and meeting facilities can be a seasonal, weekly, and even daily challenge. Although the hotel industry epitomizes the challenges of demand and capacity management, many service providers face similar problems. For example, tax accountants and air-conditioning maintenance services face seasonal demand fluctuations, whereas services such as commuter trains and restaurants face weekly and even hourly variations in customer demand. For some businesses, demand is predictable, as for a tax accountant. For others, such as management or technology consultants, demand may be less predictable, fluctuating based on customer needs and business cycles. Sometimes firms experience too much demand for the existing capacity and sometimes capacity sits idle.

Overuse or underuse of a service can directly contribute to gap 3: failure to deliver what was designed and specified. For example, when demand for services exceeds maximum capacity, the quality of service may drop because staff and facilities are overtaxed. And some customers may be turned away, not receiving the service at all. During periods of slow demand it may be necessary to reduce prices or cut service amenities, changing the makeup of the clientele and the nature of the service and thus running the risk of not delivering what customers expect. At the Chicago Hilton mentioned in our vignette, older travelers or business groups who are in the hotel on a weekend may resent the invasion of families and children because it changes the nature of the service they expected. At the pool, for example, collisions can occur between adults trying to swim laps and children playing water games.[3]

In this chapter we focus on the challenges of matching supply and demand in capacity-constrained services. Gap 3 can occur when organizations fail to smooth the peaks and valleys of demand, overuse their capacities, attract an inappropriate customer mix in their efforts to build demand, or rely too much on price in smoothing demand. The chapter gives you an understanding of these issues and strategies for addressing them. The effective use of capacity is frequently a key success factor for service organizations.

THE UNDERLYING ISSUE: LACK OF INVENTORY CAPABILITY

The fundamental issue underlying supply and demand management in services is the lack of inventory capability. Unlike manufacturing firms, service firms cannot build up inventories during periods of slow demand to use later when demand increases. This lack of inventory capability is due to the perishability of services and their simultaneous production and consumption. An airline seat that is not sold on a given flight cannot be resold the following day. The productive capacity of that seat has perished. Similarly, an hour of a lawyer's billable time cannot be saved from one day to the next. Services also cannot be transported from one place to another or transferred from person to person. Thus the Phoenix Ritz-Carlton's services cannot be moved to an alternative location in the summer months—say, to the Pacific Coast where summers are ideal for tourists and demand for hotel rooms is high.

The lack of inventory capability combined with fluctuating demand leads to a variety of potential outcomes, as illustrated in Figure 15.1.[4] The horizontal lines in Figure 15.1 indicate service capacity, and the curved line indicates customer demand for the

FIGURE 15.1 **Variations in Demand Relative to Capacity**

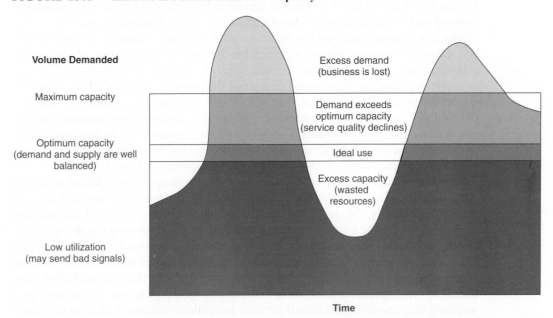

service. In many services, capacity is fixed; thus capacity can be designated by a flat horizontal line over a certain time period. Demand for service frequently fluctuates, however, as indicated by the curved line. The topmost horizontal line in Figure 15.1 represents maximum capacity. For example, in our opening vignette, the horizontal line would represent the Phoenix Ritz-Carlton's 281 rooms, or it could represent the approximately 70,000 seats in a large university football stadium. The rooms and the seats remain constant, but demand for them fluctuates. The band between the second and third horizontal lines represents optimum capacity—the best use of the capacity from the perspective of both customers and the company (the difference between optimal and maximum capacity utilization is discussed later in the chapter). The areas in the middle of Figure 15.1 are labeled to represent four basic scenarios that can result from different combinations of capacity and demand:

1. *Excess demand.* The level of demand exceeds maximum capacity. In this situation some customers will be turned away, resulting in lost business opportunities. For the customers who do receive the service, its quality may not match what was promised because of crowding or overtaxing of staff and facilities.

2. *Demand exceeds optimum capacity.* No one is being turned away, but the quality of service may still suffer because of overuse, crowding, or staff being pushed beyond their abilities to deliver consistent quality.

3. *Demand and supply are balanced at the level of optimum capacity.* Staff and facilities are occupied at an ideal level. No one is overworked, facilities can be maintained, and customers are receiving quality service without undesirable delays.

4. *Excess capacity.* Demand is below optimum capacity. Productive resources in the form of labor, equipment, and facilities are underutilized, resulting in lost productivity and lower profits. Customers may receive excellent quality on an individual level because they have the full use of the facilities, no waiting, and complete attention from the staff. If, however, service quality depends on the presence of other customers, customers may be disappointed or may worry that they have chosen an inferior service provider.

Not all firms will be challenged equally in terms of managing supply and demand. The seriousness of the problem will depend on the *extent of demand fluctuations over time,* and the *extent to which supply is constrained* (Table 15.1).[5] Some types of organizations will experience wide fluctuations in demand (telecommunications, hospitals, transportation, restaurants), whereas others will have narrower fluctuations (insurance, laundry, banking). For some, peak demand can usually be met even when demand fluctuates (electricity, natural gas), but for others peak demand may frequently exceed capacity (hospital emergency rooms, restaurants, hotels). Those firms with wide variations in demand (cells 1 and 4 in Table 15.1), and particularly those with wide fluctuations in demand that regularly exceed capacity (cell 4), will find the issues and strategies in this chapter particularly important to their success. Those firms that find themselves in cell 3 need a "one-time-fix" to expand their capacity to match regular patterns of excessive demand. The example industries in Table 15.1 are provided to illustrate where *most* firms in those industries would likely be classified. In reality, an individual firm from any industry could find itself in any of the four cells, depending on its immediate circumstances.

To identify effective strategies for managing supply and demand fluctuations, an organization needs a clear understanding of the constraints on its capacity and the underlying demand patterns.

TABLE 15.1
Demand versus Supply

Extent to Which Supply Is Constrained	Extent of Demand Fluctuations over Time	
	Wide 1	**Narrow** 2
Peak demand can usually be met without a major delay.	Electricity Natural gas Hospital maternity unit Police and fire emergencies	Insurance Legal services Banking Laundry and dry cleaning
	4	3
Peak demand regularly exceeds capacity.	Accounting and tax preparation Passenger transportation Hotels Restaurants Hospital emergency rooms	Services similar to those in 2 that have insufficient capacity for their base level of business

Source: C. H. Lovelock, "Classifying Services to Gain Strategic Marketing Insights," *Journal of Marketing* 47, (Summer 1983): 17. Reprinted by permission from the American Marketing Association.

CAPACITY CONSTRAINTS

Later in the chapter, we present some creative ways to expand and contract capacity in the short and long term, but for our discussion now, you can assume that service capacity is fixed. Depending on the type of service, critical fixed-capacity factors can be time, labor, equipment, facilities, or (in many cases) a combination of these.

Time, Labor, Equipment, Facilities

For some service businesses, the primary constraint on service production is *time*. For example, a lawyer, a consultant, a hairdresser, a plumber, and a psychological counselor all primarily sell their time. If their time is not used productively, profits are lost. If there is excess demand, time cannot be created to satisfy it. From the point of view of the individual service provider, time is the constraint.

From the point of view of a firm that employs a large number of service providers, *labor* or staffing levels can be the primary capacity constraint. A law firm, a university department, a consulting firm, a tax accounting firm, and a repair and maintenance contractor may all face the reality that at certain times demand for their organizations' services cannot be met because the staff is already operating at peak capacity. However, it does not always make sense (nor may it be possible in a competitive labor market) to hire additional service providers if low demand is a reality at other times.

In other cases, *equipment* may be the critical constraint. For trucking or air-freight delivery services, the trucks or airplanes needed to service demand may be the capacity limitation. During the Christmas holidays, UPS, FedEx, and other delivery service providers face this issue. Health clubs also deal with this limitation, particularly at certain times of the day (before work, during lunch hours, after work) and in certain months of the year. For network service providers, bandwidth, servers, and switches represent their perishable capacity.

Finally, many firms face restrictions brought about by their limited *facilities*. Hotels have only a certain number of rooms to sell, airlines are limited by the number of seats on the aircraft, educational institutions are constrained by the number of rooms and the number of seats in each classroom, and restaurant capacity is restricted to the number of tables and seats available.

TABLE 15.2
Constraints on
Capacity

Nature of the Constraint	Type of Service*
Time	Legal
	Consulting
	Accounting
	Medical
Labor	Law firm
	Accounting firm
	Consulting firm
	Health clinic
Equipment	Delivery services
	Telecommunications
	Network services
	Utilities
	Health club
Facilities	Hotels
	Restaurants
	Hospitals
	Airlines
	Schools
	Theaters
	Churches

*The examples illustrate the most common capacity constraint for each type of service. In reality, any of the service organizations listed can be operating under multiple constraints. For example, a law firm may be operating under constrained labor capacity (too few attorneys) and facilities constraints (not enough office space) at the same time.

Understanding the primary capacity constraint, or the combination of factors that restricts capacity, is a first step in designing strategies to deal with supply and demand issues (Table 15.2).

Optimal versus Maximum Use of Capacity

To fully understand capacity issues, it is important to know the difference between optimal and maximum use of capacity. As suggested in Figure 15.1, optimum and maximum capacity may not be the same. Using capacity at an optimum level means that resources are fully employed but not overused and that customers are receiving quality service in a timely manner. Maximum capacity, on the other hand, represents the absolute limit of service availability. In the case of a football game, optimum and maximum capacity may be the same. The entertainment value of the game is enhanced for customers when every single seat is filled, and obviously the profitability for the team is greatest under these circumstances (Figure 15.2). On the other hand, in a university classroom it is usually not desirable for students or faculty to have every seat filled. In this case, optimal use of capacity is less than the maximum. In some cases, maximum use of capacity may result in excessive waiting by customers, as in a popular restaurant. From the perspective of customer satisfaction, optimum use of the restaurant's capacity will again be less than maximum use.

In the case of equipment or facilities constraints, the maximum capacity at any given time is obvious. There are only a certain number of weight machines in the health club, a certain number of seats in the airplane, and a limited amount of space in a cargo carrier. In the case of a bottling plant, when maximum capacity on the assembly line is exceeded, bottles begin to break and the system shuts down. Thus it is relatively easy to observe the effects of exceeding maximum equipment capacity.

FIGURE 15.2
For sports and other entertainment venues, maximal and optimal capacity use are close to the same.

Source: Robert Brenner/PhotoEdit

When the limitation is people's time or labor, maximum capacity is harder to specify because people are in a sense more flexible than facilities and equipment. When an individual service provider's maximum capacity has been exceeded, the result is likely to cause decreased service quality, customer dissatisfaction, and employee burnout and turnover, but these outcomes may not be immediately observable even to the employee herself. It is often easy for a consulting firm to take on one more assignment, taxing its employees beyond their maximum capacity, or for an HMO clinic to schedule a few more appointments in a day, stretching its staff and physicians beyond their maximum capacity. Given the potential costs in terms of reduced quality and customer and employee dissatisfaction, it is critical for the firm to understand optimum and maximum human capacity limits.

Professional services and consulting firms face this dilemma all the time—whether to stretch their human capacity beyond what might be optimal for employees and for customers. An interview with Thomas Siebel, chairman and CEO of Siebel Systems, provides an example of the difficulty in making these types of trade-offs when human capacity and firm resources are constrained.

> We had an opportunity (in 1994) to sell MCI a call center system. I had a contract on my desk for $250,000 with the opportunity to expand the system to 11,000 users, which could have turned into millions in revenue for us—an unimaginable amount of money to us back then. . . . We could have signed the contract and received the revenue. But we did not have the resources at that time to make MCI happy *and* keep our other customers happy. So I sent their contract back. . . . This was a strategic decision. It communicated the values and culture for our company to key people at both MCI and Siebel Systems—and it was the right thing to do. Today, MCI-WorldCom is one of our largest and happiest customers.[6]

DEMAND PATTERNS

To manage fluctuating demand in a service business, it is necessary to have a clear understanding of demand patterns, why they vary, and the market segments that comprise demand at different points in time.[7] A number of questions need to be answered regarding the predictability and underlying causes of demand.

The Charting of Demand Patterns

First, the organization needs to chart the level of demand over relevant time periods. Organizations that have good computerized customer information systems can chart this information very accurately. Others may need to chart demand patterns more informally. Daily, weekly, and monthly demand levels should be followed, and if seasonality is a suspected problem, graphing should be done for data from at least the past year. In some services, such as restaurants or health care, hourly fluctuations within a day may also be relevant. Sometimes demand patterns are intuitively obvious; in other cases patterns may not reveal themselves until the data are charted.

Predictable Cycles

In looking at the graphic representation of demand levels, is there a predictable cycle daily (variations occur by hours), weekly (variations occur by day), monthly (variations occur by day or week), and/or yearly (variations occur according to months or seasons)? In some cases, predictable patterns may occur at all periods. For example, in the restaurant industry, especially in seasonal tourist locations, demand can vary predictably by month, by week, by day, and by hour.

If a predictable cycle is detected, what are its underlying causes? The Ritz-Carlton in Phoenix knows that demand cycles are based on seasonal weather patterns and that weekly variations are based on the workweek (business travelers do not stay at the hotel over the weekend). Tax accountants can predict demand based on when taxes are due, quarterly and annually. Services catering to children and families respond to variations in school hours and vacations. Retail and telecommunications services have peak periods at certain holidays and times of the week and day. When predictable patterns exist, generally one or more causes can be identified.

Random Demand Fluctuations

Sometimes the patterns of demand appear to be random—there is no apparent predictable cycle. Yet even in this case, causes can often be identified. For example, day-to-day changes in the weather may affect use of recreational, shopping, or entertainment facilities. Although the weather cannot be predicted far in advance, it may be possible to anticipate demand a day or two ahead. Health-related events also cannot be predicted. Accidents, heart attacks, and births all increase demand for hospital services, but the level of demand cannot generally be determined in advance. Natural disasters such as floods, fires, and hurricanes can dramatically increase the need for such services as insurance, telecommunications, and health care. Acts of war and terrorism such as that experienced in the United States on September 11, 2001, generate instantaneous need for services that cannot be predicted.

AT&T was faced with a sudden increase in demand for services to the military during the Gulf War. During this period, 500,000 U.S. troops were deployed to the Middle East, many without advance warning. Before their deployment these men and women had little time to attend to personal business, and all of them left behind concerned family and friends. With mail delivery between the United States and the Middle East taking more than six weeks, troops needed a quick way to communicate with their families and to handle personal business. Communications with home were determined by the military to be essential to troop morale. AT&T's ingenuity, responsiveness, and capacities were challenged to meet this unanticipated communication need. During and after the Gulf War crisis more than 2.5 million calls were placed over temporary public phone installations, and AT&T sent more than 1.2 million free faxes to family and friends of service men and women.[8]

Imagine a business in which customers' orders are unpredictable, where more than half of all customer orders are changed, often repeatedly and at the last minute, and where the product being delivered is never more than 90 minutes from spoiling. Welcome to the concrete delivery business. Cemex, based in Monterrey, Mexico, and founded in 1906, is a highly successful global player in this industry. The company operates in 30 countries with nearly 26,000 employees and annual net sales in excess of $7.1 billion.

Yet, when two internal consultants examined the business several years ago, they were amazed at the chaos that ruled the industry. Wild weather, unpredictable traffic, spontaneous labor disruptions, and sporadic government inspections of construction sites all combined with ever-changing customer orders to create a sense of chaos and uncontrollability in the business. Combine this chaos with 8,000 grades of concrete available through a half-dozen regional mixing plants, and you have an extremely complex system to manage.

Historically, Cemex had attempted to run the business through controlling its customers to stick with their orders and by imposing fines for changed orders. Efficiency ruled, not customers—in order to conquer the natural randomness of demand and the customers' needs to change orders at the last minute.

The company began searching for new ways to do business. It turned to FedEx and to the 911 emergency dispatch center in Houston, Texas, for ideas. What it found were organizations that, instead of trying to control demand for their services, had developed people and technology to be flexible in meeting customers' seemingly random demand patterns. Instead of penalizing customers for changing their orders, FedEx does not restrict its customers and, in fact, guarantees delivery at a certain time to any and all locations. This ability to serve customers is made possible by sophisticated information systems that track demand and schedule pickups and deliveries, customer-focused frontline employees, and a customer-centric corporate culture that supports it all. From the 911 center in Houston, Cemex learned that even seemingly random occurrences such as emergency health needs and accidents occur in sufficient number to allow patterns of demand to be discerned and

Our Global Feature illustrates how one company with seemingly random and chaotic demand for its services was able to change its business to serve customers. The feature is also a good example of organizational learning across cultures.

Demand Patterns by Market Segment

An organization that has detailed records on customer transactions may be able to disaggregate demand by market segment, revealing patterns within patterns. Or the analysis may reveal that demand from one segment is predictable whereas demand from another segment is relatively random. For example, for a bank, the visits from its commercial accounts may occur daily at a predictable time, whereas personal account holders may visit the bank at seemingly random intervals. Health clinics often notice that walk-in or "care needed today" patients tend to concentrate their arrivals on Monday, with fewer needing immediate attention on other days of the week. Knowing that this pattern exists, some clinics schedule more future appointments (which they can control) for later days of the week, leaving more of Monday available for same-day appointments and walk-ins.

planned for. In terms of Figure 15.1, what FedEx and the 911 emergency center did was adjust their capacity to meet the peaks and valleys of customer demand rather than insisting that the customers adjust their demand to fit the company's constrained capacity.

The experiences at FedEx and in Houston at the 911 center were a revelation to Cemex's team. The company went back to Mexico determined to embrace the complexity of its marketplace and to do business on the customers' terms. The company launched a project called Sincronizacion Dinamica de Operaciones: the dynamic synchronization of operations. It unleashed trucks from previous zone assignments, allowing them to roam the city. It outfitted the trucks with transmitters and receivers connected to a GPS system so that locations, direction, and speed of every vehicle could be tracked. It enrolled its drivers in secondary education classes over a period of two years so they would be more service oriented and able to deal with customers.

Impressed with FedEx's guaranteed service, Cemex worked toward being able to offer "same-day service, with free, unlimited order changes." Now, if a load fails to arrive within 20 minutes of its scheduled delivery time, the buyer gets back 20 pesos per cubic meter—"guarantia 20 × 20"—amounting to roughly 5 percent of the total cost.

Cemex embraced the chaos of its industry instead of trying to adjust and change it. By using technology, people, and systems, it was able to match its capacity constraints with its customers' wildly fluctuating demands. And the company came out a winner. Cemex can afford to offer its 20 × 20 guarantee now that its reliability exceeds 98 percent!

Today, the company's focus on the customer is clearly stated in the slogan across the top of its website: "By connecting with customer needs, we deliver value worldwide."

Sources: T. Petzinger Jr., "This Promise Is Set in Concrete," *Fast Company,* April 1999, pp. 216–18; see also T. Petzinger Jr., *The New Pioneers* (New York: Simon & Schuster, Inc., 1999), pp. 91–93. Reprinted with the permission of Simon & Schuster, Inc. Copyright © 1999 by Thomas Petzinger Jr.; updated with company information from the Cemex website, www.cemex.com, 2004.

STRATEGIES FOR MATCHING CAPACITY AND DEMAND

When an organization has a clear grasp of its capacity constraints and an understanding of demand patterns, it is in a good position to develop strategies for matching supply and demand. There are two general approaches for accomplishing this match. The first is to smooth the demand fluctuations themselves by shifting demand to match existing supply. This approach implies that the peaks and valleys of the demand curve (Figure 15.1) will be flattened to match as closely as possible the horizontal optimum capacity line. The second general strategy is to adjust capacity to match fluctuations in demand. This implies moving the horizontal capacity lines shown in Figure 15.1 to match the ups and downs of the demand curve. Each of these two basic strategies is described next with specific examples.

Shifting Demand to Match Capacity

With this strategy an organization seeks to shift customers away from periods in which demand exceeds capacity, perhaps by convincing them to use the service during periods

FIGURE 15.3 **Strategies for Shifting Demand to Match Capacity**

| **DEMAND TOO HIGH** | **SHIFT DEMAND** → | **DEMAND TOO LOW** |

- Use signage to communicate busy days and times.
- Offer incentives to customers for usage during nonpeak times.
- Take care of loyal or "regular" customers first.
- Advertise peak usage times and benefits of nonpeak use.
- Charge full price for the service—no discounts.

- Use sales and advertising to increase business from current market segments.
- Modify the service offering to appeal to new market segments.
- Offer discounts or price reductions.
- Modify hours of operation.
- Bring the service to the customer.

of slow demand. This change may be possible for some customers but not for others. For example, many business travelers are not able to shift their needs for airline, car rental, and hotel services; pleasure travelers, on the other hand, can often shift the timing of their trips. Customers who cannot shift and cannot be accommodated will represent lost business for the firm.

During periods of slow demand, the organization seeks to attract more and/or different customers to utilize its productive capacity. A variety of approaches, detailed in the following sections, can be used to shift or increase demand to match capacity. Frequently a firm uses a combination of approaches. Ideas for how to shift demand during both slow and peak periods are shown in Figure 15.3.

Vary the Service Offering

One approach is to change the nature of the service offering, depending on the season of the year, day of the week, or time of day. For example, Whistler Mountain, a ski resort in Vancouver, Canada, offers its facilities for executive development and training programs during the summer when snow skiing is not possible. A hospital in the Los Angeles area rents use of its facilities to film production crews who need realistic hospital settings for movies or television shows. Accounting firms focus on tax preparation late in the year and until April 15, when federal taxes are due in the United States. During other times of the year they can focus on audits and general tax consulting activities. Airlines even change the configuration of their plane seating to match the demand from different market segments. Some planes may have no first-class section at all. On routes with a large demand for first-class seating, a significant proportion of seats may be placed in first class. Our opening vignette featured ways in which downtown hotels have changed their offerings to appeal to the family market segment on weekends. In all these examples, the service offering and associated benefits are changed to smooth customer demand for the organization's resources.

Care should be exercised in implementing strategies to change the service offering, because such changes may easily imply and require alterations in other marketing mix variables—such as promotion, pricing, and staffing—to match the new offering. Unless these additional mix variables are altered effectively to support the offering, the strategy may not work. Even when done well, the downside of such changes can be a confusion in the organization's image from the customers' perspective, or a loss of strategic focus for the organization and its employees.

Communicate with Customers

Another approach for shifting demand is to communicate with customers, letting them know the times of peak demand so they can choose to use the service at alternative times and avoid crowding or delays. For example, signs in banks and post offices that let customers know their busiest hours and busiest days of the week can serve as a warning, allowing customers to shift their demand to another time if possible. Fore-warning customers about busy times and possible waits can have added benefits. Many customer service phone lines provide a similar warning by informing waiting customers of approximately how long it will be until they are served. Those who do not want to wait may choose to call back later when the lines are less busy or to visit the company's website for faster service. Research in a bank context found that customers who were forewarned about the bank's busiest hours were more satisfied even when they had to wait than were customers who were not forewarned.[9]

In addition to signage that communicates peak demand times to customers, advertising and other forms of promotion can emphasize different service benefits during peak and slow periods. Advertising and sales messages can also remind customers about peak demand times.

Modify Timing and Location of Service Delivery

Some firms adjust their hours and days of service delivery to more directly reflect customer demand. Historically, U.S. banks were open only during "bankers' hours" from 10 A.M. to 3 P.M. every weekday. Obviously these hours did not match the times when most people preferred to do their personal banking. Now U.S. banks open early, stay open until 6 P.M. many days, and are open on Saturdays, better reflecting customer demand patterns. Online banking has also shifted demand from branches to "anytime, anywhere" websites. Theaters accommodate customer schedules by offering matinees on weekends and holidays when people are free during the day for entertainment. Movie theaters are sometimes rented during weekdays by business groups—an example of varying the service offering during a period of low demand.

Differentiate on Price

A common response during slow demand is to discount the price of the service. This strategy relies on basic economics of supply and demand. To be effective, however, a price differentiation strategy depends on solid understanding of customer price sensitivity and demand curves. For example, business travelers are far less price sensitive than are families traveling for pleasure. For the Ritz-Carlton in Phoenix (our opening vignette), lowering prices during the slow summer months is not likely to increase bookings from business travelers dramatically. However, the lower summer prices attract considerable numbers of families and local guests who want an opportunity to experience a luxury hotel but are not able to afford the rooms during peak season.

The maximum capacity of any hotel, airline, restaurant, or other service establishment could be reached if the price were low enough. But the goal is always to ensure the highest level of capacity utilization without sacrificing profits. We explore this complex relationship among price, market segments, capacity utilization, and profitability later in the chapter in the section on yield management.

Heavy use of price differentiation to smooth demand can be a risky strategy. Over-reliance on price can result in price wars in an industry in which eventually all competitors suffer. Price wars are well known in the airline industry, and total industry

FIGURE 15.4 **Strategies for Adjusting Capacity to Match Demand**

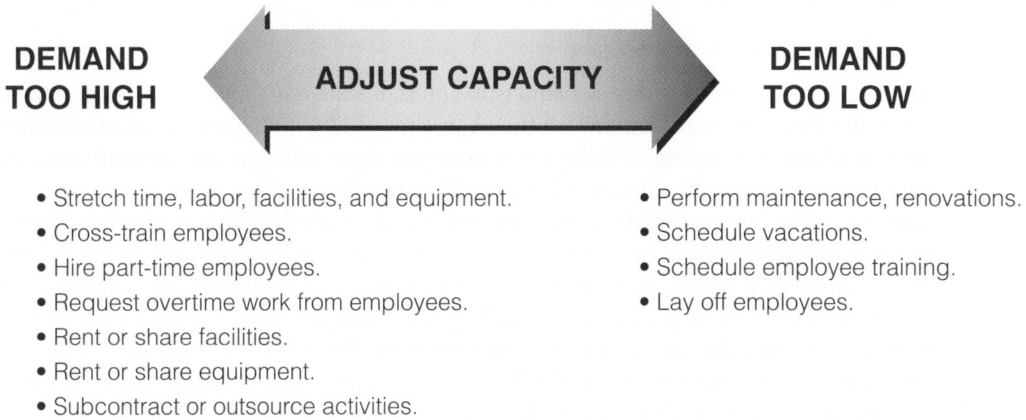

DEMAND TOO HIGH ⟵ ADJUST CAPACITY ⟶ **DEMAND TOO LOW**

- Stretch time, labor, facilities, and equipment.
- Cross-train employees.
- Hire part-time employees.
- Request overtime work from employees.
- Rent or share facilities.
- Rent or share equipment.
- Subcontract or outsource activities.

- Perform maintenance, renovations.
- Schedule vacations.
- Schedule employee training.
- Lay off employees.

profits often suffer as a result of airlines simultaneously trying to attract customers through price discounting. Another risk of relying on price is that customers grow accustomed to the lower price and expect to get the same deal the next time they use the service. If communications with customers are unclear, customers may not understand the reasons for the discounts and will expect to pay the same during peak demand periods. Overuse or exclusive use of price as a strategy for smoothing demand is also risky because of the potential impact on the organization's image, the potential for attracting undesired market segments, and the possibility that higher paying customers will feel they have been treated unfairly.

Adjusting Capacity to Meet Demand

A second strategic approach to matching supply and demand focuses on adjusting capacity. The fundamental idea here is to adjust, stretch, and align capacity to match customer demand (rather than working on shifting demand to match capacity, as just described). During periods of peak demand the organization seeks to stretch or expand its capacity as much as possible. During periods of slow demand it tries to shrink capacity so as not to waste resources. General strategies for adjusting the four primary service resources (time, people, equipment, and facilities) are discussed throughout the rest of this section. In Figure 15.4, we summarize specific ideas for adjusting capacity during periods of peak and slow demand. Often, a number of different strategies are used simultaneously.

Stretch Existing Capacity

The existing capacity of service resources can often be expanded temporarily to match demand. In such cases no new resources are added; rather the people, facilities, and equipment are asked to work harder and longer to meet demand.

Stretch Time It may be possible to extend the hours of service temporarily to accommodate demand. A health clinic might stay open longer during flu season, retailers are open longer hours during the holiday shopping season, and accountants have extended appointment hours (evenings and Saturdays) before tax deadlines.

Stretch Labor In many service organizations, employees are asked to work longer and harder during periods of peak demand. For example, consulting organizations face extensive peaks and valleys with respect to demand for their services. During peak demand, associates are asked to take on additional projects and work longer hours. And frontline service personnel in banks, tourist attractions, restaurants, and telecommunications companies are asked to serve more customers per hour during busy times than during hours or days when demand is low.

Stretch Facilities   Theaters, restaurants, meeting facilities, and classrooms can sometimes be expanded temporarily by the addition of tables, chairs, or other equipment needed by customers. Or, as in the case of a commuter train, a car that holds a fixed number of people seated comfortably can "expand" by accommodating standing passengers.

Stretch Equipment   Computers, power lines, and maintenance equipment can often be stretched beyond what would be considered the maximum capacity for short periods to accommodate peak demand.

In using these types of "stretch" strategies, the organization needs to recognize the wear and tear on resources and the potential for inferior quality of service that may go with the use. These strategies should thus be used for relatively short periods in order to allow for later maintenance of the facilities and equipment and refreshment of the people who are asked to exceed their usual capacity. Sometimes it is difficult to know in advance, particularly in the case of human resources, when capacity has been stretched too far.

Align Capacity with Demand Fluctuations

This basic strategy is sometimes known as a "chase demand" strategy. By adjusting service resources creatively, organizations can in effect chase the demand curves to match capacity with customer demand patterns. Time, labor, facilities, and equipment are again the focus, this time with an eye toward adjusting the basic mix and use of these resources. Specific actions might include the following.[10]

Use Part-Time Employees   In this situation the organization's labor resource is being aligned with demand. Retailers hire part-time employees during the holiday rush, tax accountants engage temporary help during tax season, tourist resorts bring in extra workers during peak season. Restaurants often ask employees to work split shifts (work the lunch shift, leave for a few hours, and come back for the dinner rush) during peak mealtime hours.

Outsourcing   Firms that find they have a temporary peak in demand for a service that they cannot perform themselves may choose to outsource the entire service. For example, in recent years, many firms have found they do not have the capacity to fulfill their own needs for technology support, Web design, and software-related services. Rather than try to hire and train additional employees, these companies look to firms that specialize in outsourcing these types of functions as a temporary (or sometimes long-term) solution.

Rent or Share Facilities or Equipment   For some organizations it is best to rent additional equipment or facilities during periods of peak demand. For example, express mail delivery services rent or lease trucks during the peak holiday delivery season. It would not make sense to buy trucks that would sit idle during the rest of the year. Sometimes organizations with complementary demand patterns can share facilities. An example is a church that shares its facilities during the week with a Montessori preschool. The school needs the facilities Monday through Friday during the day; the church needs the facilities evenings and on the weekend. There are whole businesses that have been created to satisfy other businesses' fluctuating demand. For example, a firm may offer temporary office suites and clerical support to individuals who do not need such facilities and support on a continuous basis.

Schedule Downtime during Periods of Low Demand   If people, equipment, and facilities are being used at maximum capacity during peak periods, then it is imperative to schedule repair, maintenance, and renovations during off-peak periods. This schedule ensures that the resources are in top condition when they are most needed. Vacations and training are also scheduled during slow demand periods.

Cross-Train Employees   If employees are cross-trained, they can shift among tasks, filling in where they are most needed. Cross-training increases the efficiency of the whole system and avoids underutilizing employees in some areas while others are being overtaxed. Many airlines cross-train their employees to move from ticketing to working the gate counters to assisting with baggage if needed. In some fast-food restaurants, employees specialize in one task (like making french fries) during busy hours, and the team of specialists may number 10 people. During slow hours the team may shrink to three, with each person performing a variety of functions. Grocery stores also use this strategy, with most employees able to move as needed from cashiering to stocking shelves to bagging groceries.

Modify or Move Facilities and Equipment   Sometimes it is possible to adjust, move, or creatively modify existing capacity to meet demand fluctuations. Hotels utilize this strategy by reconfiguring rooms—two rooms with a locked door between can be rented to two different parties in high demand times or turned into a suite during slow demand. The airline industry offers dramatic examples of this strategy. Using an approach known as "demand-driven dispatch," airlines have begun to experiment with methods that assign airplanes to flight schedules on the basis of fluctuating market needs.[11] The method depends on accurate knowledge of demand and the ability to quickly move airplanes with different seating capacities to flight assignments that match their capacity. The Boeing 777 aircraft is so flexible that it can be reconfigured within hours to vary the number of seats allocated to one, two, or three classes.[12] The plane can thus be quickly modified to match demand from different market segments, essentially molding capacity to fit demand. Another strategy may involve moving the service to a new location to meet customer demand or even bringing the service to customers. Mobile training facilities, libraries, and blood donation facilities are examples of services that physically follow customers.

Combining Demand and Capacity Strategies

Many firms use multiple strategies, combining marketing-driven demand management approaches with operations-driven capacity management strategies. Figuring out which is the best set of strategies for maximizing capacity utilization, customer satisfaction, and profitability can be challenging, particularly when the service offering is a constellation of offerings within one service setting, for example, theme parks with rides, restaurants, shopping; hotel vacation villages with hotels, shopping, spas, pools, restaurants; or ski resorts with ski slopes, spas, restaurants, and entertainment. Firms face complex problems in trying to balance demand across all the different offerings with an eye to quality and profitability. In our Strategy Insight, researchers create a ski resort simulation using operations and marketing solutions to determine the optimal combination of demand and capacity management strategies across the resort's various offerings and activities.

In many situations, firms use multiple demand and capacity management strategies simultaneously to obtain optimal usage and maximize profits. Because each strategy involves costs as well as potential service quality, customer loyalty, and revenue outcomes, determining the appropriate mix can be a complex decision.

Research done for a ski resort illustrates how operations and marketing data can be combined into a sophisticated model that attempts to predict the right mix of strategies. The ski industry presents particularly interesting challenges for capacity management because the industry sees typically large fluctuations in demand based on seasonal, weekly, and even daily usage patterns, unpredictable weather and snowfall, a variety of skiing ability segments that use the resort in different ways, and demographic shifts over time. In addition, most resorts face constraints on their capacity due to environmental regulations that limit acreage and parking as well as the large capital investment required for facility expansion and/or improvement. Furthermore, as ticket prices at ski resorts have continued to escalate, customers expectations have risen.

Powder Valley (PV, a disguised name), a ski resort in Northern Utah, had consistently lost market share for five years to its rivals. Lack of facility improvements and increased marketing efforts by its competitors were cited as likely reasons for declining market share. To improve the situation, PV managers had proposed several marketing strategies to increase demand on slow days and increase revenue per customer. Operations strategies to improve the skiing experience and reduce waiting during peak demand periods that relied on acquisition of new terrain and new, faster ski lifts were also proposed. Each of these strategies had its associated costs and less than totally predictable outcomes. Adding to the complexity of the inherent trade-offs in the various strategies was the fact that the resort offered multiple activities (e.g., restaurants, skiing, shopping) for customers to choose.

The researchers working with PV proposed that the optimal profit strategy would require an integrated set of approaches representing both demand and supply perspectives. Using data from the resort, they built a sophisticated simulation model to assess the impact on customer usage, waiting times, and profits of several different strategies that were being considered including:

Price variations. Strategies aimed at leveling demand by charging lower prices for off-peak skiing.

Promotions of underutilized services. Promotions to attract new customer segments or shift existing customers to underutilized services.

Information provision on waiting times. Strategies that provide information about less crowded periods or shorter waiting times to move customers temporarily to underutilized services.

Capacity expansion. Investments in additional fixed capacity for skiing such as adding new terrain or expanding the number of lifts.

Capacity upgrades. Improving or replacing existing lifts to carry more skiers and/or run faster.

continued

As input to their model the researchers used historic data on daily demand, demand smoothing and capacity expansion options, service times for each lift, flow patterns across various lifts within the resort, travel time between lifts, customer perceptions, and customer choice data. By combining these marketing and operations data, the researchers showed that retaining the current customer mix, installing two new chairs, and providing waiting time information would maximize profits for the resort. Adding new chair lifts by replacing old ones within the existing terrain was a more profitable approach than expanding to new terrain. The simulation model showed that contrary to management predictions, smoothing demand across the day through differential pricing would actually decrease profits significantly. The model results were also useful in suggesting a priority order for the investments. The wait time signage investment was the least expensive and offered the largest single improvement for customers as well as the largest single profit impact. Upgrading at least one chair lift was the next priority.

Balancing demand and capacity can involve a complex set of decisions, and sometimes the outcomes are not obvious, especially when strategies seem to have contradictory objectives. For example in the PV simulation, a marketing objective of increased revenues through attracting more customers was contradicted by an operations objective of providing optimal wait times for lifts. As illustrated in the ski resort research, firms can combine marketing and operations data into one overall model and run simulated experiments to determine the best set of combined strategies. Of course, the quality of the decisions based on the model are highly dependent on the accuracy of the assumptions in the model and the quality of the input data.

Managing demand and capacity in ski resorts can be very challenging.
Source: Photodisc Blue/Getty Images

Source: M. E. Pullman and G. Thompson, "Strategies for Integrating Capacity with Demand in Service Networks," *Journal of Service Research* 5 (February 2003), pp. 169–83.

YIELD MANAGEMENT: BALANCING CAPACITY UTILIZATION, PRICING, MARKET SEGMENTATION, AND FINANCIAL RETURN

Yield management is a term that has become attached to a variety of methods, some very sophisticated, matching demand and supply in capacity-constrained services. Using yield management models, organizations find the best balance at a particular point in time among the prices charged, the segments sold to, and the capacity used. The goal of yield management is to produce the best possible financial return from a limited available capacity. Specifically, yield management (also referred to as revenue management) has been defined as "the process of allocating the right type of capacity to the right kind of customer at the right price so as to maximize revenue or yield."[13]

Although the implementation of yield management can involve complex mathematical models and computer programs, the underlying effectiveness measure is the ratio of actual revenue to potential revenue for a particular measurement period:

$$Yield = \frac{Actual\ revenue}{Potential\ revenue}$$

where

$$Actual\ revenue = actual\ capacity\ used \times average\ actual\ price$$

$$Potential\ revenue = total\ capacity \times maximum\ price$$

The equations indicate that yield is a function of price and capacity used. Recall that capacity constraints can be in the form of time, labor, equipment, or facilities. Yield is essentially a measure of the extent to which an organization's resources (or capacities) are achieving their full revenue-generating potential. Assuming that total capacity and maximum price cannot be changed, yield approaches 1 as actual capacity utilization increases or when a higher actual price can be charged for a given capacity used. For example, in an airline context, a manager could focus on increasing yield by finding ways to bring in more passengers to fill the capacity, or by finding higher-paying passengers to fill a more limited capacity. In reality, expert yield managers work on capacity and pricing issues simultaneously to maximize revenue across different customer segments. Exhibit 15.1 shows simple yield calculations and the inherent trade-offs for two types of services: hotel and legal.

Implementing a Yield Management System

Our Technology Spotlight illustrates several examples of how information technology supports effective yield management applications. To implement a yield management system, an organization needs detailed data on past demand patterns by market segment as well as methods of projecting current market demand. The data can be combined through mathematical programming models, threshold analysis, or use of expert systems to project the best allocation of limited capacity at a particular point in time.[14] Allocations of capacity for specific market segments can then be communicated to sales representatives or reservations staff as targets for selling rooms, seats, time, or other limited resources. Sometimes the allocations, once determined, remain fixed. At other times allocations change weekly, or even daily or hourly, in response to new information.

Recent research indicates that traditional yield management approaches are most profitable when (1) a service provider faces different market segments or customers, who arrive or make their reservations at different times and (2) customers who arrive or reserve early are more price sensitive than those who arrive or reserve late.[15] These criteria exactly fit the situation for airlines and many hotels—industries that have effectively and extensively used yield management techniques to allocate capacity. In other services (entertainment, sports, fashion), those customers willing to pay the higher prices are the ones who buy early rather than late. People who really want to see a particular performance reserve their seats at the earliest possible moment. Discounting for early purchases would reduce profits. In these situations, the price generally starts out high and is reduced later to fill capacity if needed.

Exhibit 15.1   SIMPLE YIELD CALCULATIONS: EXAMPLES FROM HOTEL AND LEGAL SERVICES

You can do basic yield calculations for any capacity constrained service assuming you know the actual capacity, average price charged for different market segments, and maximum price that could be charged. Ideally, yield will approach the number 1, or 100 percent, where:

Yield = Actual Revenue/Potential Revenue

In this box we describe yield calculations for two simple examples—a 200-room hotel and a lawyer with a 40-hour work week—under different assumed pricing and usage situations. Although companies use much more complex mathematical models to determine yield, the underlying ideas are the same. The goal is to maximize the revenue-generating capability of the organization's capacity.

200-ROOM HOTEL WITH MAXIMUM ROOM RATE OF $100 PER ROOM PER NIGHT

Potential Revenue = $100 × 200 rooms = $20,000 per night

1. Assume: the hotel rents all its rooms at a discounted rate of $50 per night.

Yield = $50 × 200 rooms/$20,000 = 50%

At this rate, the hotel is maximizing capacity utilization, but not getting a very good price.

2. Assume: the hotel charges its full rate, but can only rent 40 percent of its rooms at that price, due to price sensitivity.

Yield = $100 × 80 rooms/$20,000 = 40%

In this situation the hotel has maximized the per-room price, but the yield is even lower than in the first situation because so few rooms were rented at that relatively high rate.

3. Assume: the hotel charges its full rate of $100 for 40 percent of its rooms and then gives a discount of $50 for the remaining 120 rooms.

Yield = [($100 × 80) + ($50 × 120)]/$20,000 = $14,000/$20,000 = 70%

Clearly, the final alternative, which takes into account price sensitivity and charges different prices for different rooms or market segments, will result in the highest yield.

40 HOURS OF A LAWYER'S TIME ACROSS A TYPICAL WORK WEEK AT $200 PER HOUR MAXIMUM (PRIVATE CLIENT RATE)

Potential Revenue = 40 hours × $200 per hour = $8000 per week

1. Assume: the lawyer is able to bill out 30 percent of her billable time at $200 per hour.

Yield = $200 × 12 hours/$8,000 = 30%

In this case the lawyer has maximized her hourly rate, but has only enough work to occupy 12 billable hours.

2. Assume: the lawyer decides to charge $100 for nonprofit or government clients and is able to bill out all 40 hours at this rate for these types of clients.

Yield = $100 × 40 hours/$8,000 = 50%

In this case, although she has worked a full week, yield is still not very good given the relatively low rate per hour.

3. Assume: the lawyer uses a combined strategy in which she works 12 hours for private clients and fills the rest of her time with nonprofit clients at $100 per hour.

Yield = [($200 × 12) + ($100 × 28)]/$8,000 = $5,200/$8,000 = 65%

Again, catering to two different market segments with different price sensitivities, is the best overall strategy in terms of maximizing revenue-generating capacity of the lawyer's time.

Interestingly, some airlines now use both these strategies effectively. They start with discounted seats for customers who are willing to buy early, usually leisure and discretionary travelers. They charge a higher fare for those who want a seat at the last minute, typically the less price-sensitive business travelers whose destinations and schedules are inflexible. However, in some cases a bargain fare can be found at the last minute as

Technology Spotlight
Information and Technology Drive Yield Management Systems

Yield management is not a new concept. In fact, the basic idea behind yield management—achieving maximum profits through the most effective use of capacity—has been around forever. It is easy to find examples of capacity-constrained businesses using price to shift demand: theaters that charge different prices for matinees versus evening performances, intercity trains with different prices on weekdays than on weekends, ski resorts with cheaper prices for night skiing, and restaurants with "twilight" dinner specials. All these strategies illustrate attempts to smooth the peaks and valleys of demand using price as the primary motivator.

The difference in these basic pricing strategies and more sophisticated yield management approaches currently in use by airlines, car rental companies, hotels, shippers, and others is the reliance of these latter strategies on massive databases, sophisticated mathematical algorithms, and complex analyses. These forms of yield management consider not only price but also market segments, price sensitivity among segments, timing of demand, and potential profitability of customer segments—all simultaneously. What makes new forms of yield management possible are the technology and systems underlying them. Here we provide a few examples of what some companies and industries have done.

AMERICAN AIRLINES

American Airlines is the original pioneer and still the king of yield management. Beginning with Super Saver Fares in the mid-1970s, American depends on systems developed by Sabre (the oldest and leading provider of technology for the travel industry) to support an exceedingly complex system of fares. Using a system of models containing algorithms that optimize prices, manage wait lists, and handle traffic management, American allocates seats on every one of its flights. The number of seats sold on each of American's flights is continuously compared with a sales forecast for that flight. Blocks of seats are moved from higher to lower fares if sales are below projections. If sales are at or above the forecast, no changes are made. The objective is to "sell the right seats to the right customers at the right price." To do this requires massive amounts of data! The typical yield management database for a large airline can exceed 300 gigabytes of data, equivalent to a 6,350-meter stack of paper. A person scanning this data would need to work 43 years, 40 hours per week, and spend only five seconds per page.

AUSTRIAN AIRLINES

Austrian Airlines has been one of the most consistently profitable airlines in Europe. Prior to deregulation of airlines in Europe, Austrian foresaw the need to develop a competitive advantage that would carry it into the deregulated future. The airline invested in a revenue management computer system to build a two-year historical database of booking data that would monitor flights up to 250 days into the future. Using the system, Austrian saw significant improvements in both number of passengers carried and revenue. By being more selective in its discounting practices than were its competitors, Austrian achieved excellent results.

MARRIOTT HOTELS

The hotel industry has also embraced the concepts of yield management, and Marriott Hotels has been a leader. The systems at Marriott, for example, maximize profits for a hotel across full weeks rather than by day. In their hotels that target business travelers, Marriott has peak days during the middle of the week. Rather than simply sell the hotel out on those nights on a first-come, first-served basis with no discounts, the revenue management system (which is reviewed and revised daily) now projects guest demand both by price and length of stay, providing discounts in some cases to guests who will stay longer, even on a peak demand night. One early test of the system was at the Munich Marriott during Oktoberfest. Typically no discounts would be offered during this peak period. However, the yield management system recommended that the hotel offer some rooms at a discount, but only for those guests who stayed an extended period before or after the peak days. Although the average daily rate was down 11.7 percent for the period, occupancy was up over 20 percent, and overall revenues were up 12.3 percent. Using yield management practices, Marriott Hotels estimates an additional $400 million per year in revenue.

YELLOW TRANSPORTATION

Pricing in the freight industry still seems to be stuck in a regulated mind-set in which costs dominate and discounts from class rates are determined by complex formulas. However, companies such as Yellow Transportation (part of Yellow Roadway Corporation) are moving toward market-driven models that price services

continued

Technology Spotlight
Information and Technology Drive Yield Management Systems—continued

consistent with the value as perceived by the customer. New pricing structures recognize the customers' and freight providers' desires for simplification while combining this with sophisticated use of yield management models that take into account the most profitable use of resources. Yield management systems encourage more rational scheduling of trucks and drivers by considering such subtle factors as equipment type and skills of a particular driver. The systems can match hundreds of drivers with loads in fractions of seconds to make the best dispatch and driver decisions. By analyzing its services, prices, and demand patterns in this way, Yellow was able to project the success of its time-definite delivery ser-

vice—Exact Express. This service targets a particular segment of customers who are willing to pay for guaranteed, time-definite delivery.

Sources: The primary source for this Technology Spotlight is R. G. Cross, *Revenue Management* (New York: Broadway Books, 1997). Other sources include "Dynamic Pricing at American Airlines," *Business Quarterly* 61 (Autumn 1996), p. 45; N. Templin, "Your Room Costs $250 . . . No! $200 . . . No," *The Wall Street Journal,* May 5, 1999, p. B1; H. Richardson, "Simplify! Simplify! Simplify!," *Transportation and Distribution* 39 (October 1998), pp. 111–17; and C. Salter "On the Road Again," *Fast Company,* January 2002, pp. 50–58.

well, commonly via Internet sales, to fill seats that would otherwise go unoccupied. Online auctions and services offered by companies like Internet-based Priceline.com serve a purpose in filling capacity at the last minute, often charging much lower fares. (See the Technology Spotlight in Chapter 17 for examples of dynamic pricing via the Internet.)

Challenges and Risks in Using Yield Management

Yield management programs can significantly improve revenues. However, although yield management may appear to be an ideal solution to the problem of matching supply and demand, it is not without risks. By becoming focused on maximizing financial returns through differential capacity allocation and pricing, an organization may encounter these problems:[16]

- *Loss of competitive focus.* Yield management may cause a firm to overfocus on profit maximization and inadvertently neglect aspects of the service that provide long-term competitive success.

- *Customer alienation.* If customers learn that they are paying a higher price for service than someone else, they may perceive the pricing as unfair, particularly if they do not understand the reasons. However, a study done in the restaurant industry found that when customers were informed of different prices being charged by time of day, week, or table location, they generally felt the practice was fair, particularly if the price difference was framed as a discount for less desirable times rather than a premium for peak times or table locations.[17] Customer education is thus essential in an effective yield management program. Customers can be further alienated if they fall victim (and are not compensated adequately) to overbooking practices that are often necessary to make yield management systems work effectively.

- *Employee morale problems.* Yield management systems take much guesswork and judgment in setting prices away from sales and reservations people. Although some employees may appreciate the guidance, others may resent the rules and restrictions on their own discretion.

- *Incompatible incentive and reward systems.* Employees may resent yield management systems that do not match incentive structures. For example, many managers are rewarded on the basis of capacity utilization *or* average rate charged, whereas yield management balances the two factors.

- *Lack of employee training.* Extensive training is required to make a yield management system work. Employees need to understand its purpose, how it works, how they should make decisions, and how the system will affect their jobs.

- *Inappropriate organization of the yield management function.* To be most effective with yield management, an organization must have centralized reservations. Although airlines and some large hotel chains and shipping companies do have such centralization, smaller organizations may have decentralized reservations systems and thus find it difficult to operate a yield management system effectively.

WAITING LINE STRATEGIES: WHEN DEMAND AND CAPACITY CANNOT BE MATCHED

Sometimes it is not possible to manage capacity to match demand, or vice versa. It may be too costly—for example, most health clinics would not find it economically feasible to add additional facilities or physicians to handle peaks in demand during the winter flu season; patients usually simply have to wait to be seen. Or demand may be very unpredictable and the service capacity very inflexible (it cannot be easily stretched to match unpredictable peaks in demand). Sometimes waits may occur when demand backs up because of the variability in length of time for service. For example, even though patients are scheduled by appointments in a physician's office, frequently there is a wait because some patients take longer to serve than the time allotted to them. According to many sources, the misalignment in capacity and demand has reached crisis proportions in the emergency health care context, as is described in Exhibit 15.2.

For most service organizations, waiting customers are a fact of life at some point (see Figure 15.5). Waiting can occur on the telephone (customers put on hold when they call in to ask for information, order something, or make a complaint) and in person (customers waiting in line at the bank, post office, Disneyland, or a physician's office). Waiting can occur even with service transactions through the mail—delays in mail-order delivery, or backlogs of correspondence on a manager's desk.

In today's fast-paced society, waiting is not something most people tolerate well. As people work longer hours, as individuals have less leisure, and as families have fewer hours together, the pressure on people's time is greater than ever. In this environment, customers are looking for efficient, quick service with no wait. Organizations that make customers wait take the chance that they will lose business or at the very least that customers will be dissatisfied.[18] To deal effectively with the inevitability of waits, organizations can utilize a variety of strategies, described next.

Employ Operational Logic

If customer waits are common, a first step is to analyze the operational processes to remove any inefficiencies. It may be possible to redesign the system to move customers

Exhibit 15.2 **OVERFLOW IN THE ER: HOW TO MANAGE CAPACITY CONSTRAINTS AND EXCESS DEMAND IN HOSPITAL EMERGENCY DEPARTMENTS**

Nowhere is there a more vivid example of demand and capacity issues than in the nearly 5,000 emergency departments (EDs) in hospitals across the United States (*emergency department* is the preferred term within the medical community for what has traditionally been called the ER). In a typical ED, rooms are filled, the corridors may be clogged with waiting patients, wait time may be anywhere from 15 minutes to 8 or 10 hours, and ambulances are routinely turned away to seek other hospitals on what is called "reroute" or "diversion." Many experts have referred to these issues as a national crisis in health care. The emergency department is the front door of hospitals and is also the treatment of last resort for many. Why has this overcrowding issue reached national proportions? Many factors come into play, including increased demand and severe capacity constraints.

INCREASED DEMAND FOR SERVICES

Emergency departments are to some extent victims of their own success. Decades of public health campaigns urging people to call 911 in case of medical emergency have been successful in educating people to do just that—and they end up in the ED. Many do indeed have life-threatening emergencies that belong in the ED. Others waiting in the ED are uninsured—43 million people in the United States. The ED is their only option, and legally the ED must care for them. But it is not only the uninsured and those with life-threatening emergencies that crowd the ED. It is also insured patients who cannot get appointments with their doctors in a timely manner, or who learn that it may be their fastest entry into a hospital bed. Patients and their doctors are becoming aware that they can get sophisticated care in the ED relatively quickly. Thus the demand for ED services has increased.

CAPACITY CONSTRAINTS

It is not just an increase in demand that is causing the overcrowding. It is also a shrinkage or unavailability of critical capacity at the same time. Doctors are overbooked in private practices, so patients who don't want to wait turn to the ED. Also, a shortage of specialists who are willing to take patients on call from the ED results in increased waiting times because these patients waiting for specialized care occupy beds in the ED longer than necessary. Another very critical capacity constraint is the number of beds in hospitals. Over the years many hospitals across the country have closed for financial reasons, reducing the number of beds available. So ED patients often cannot get beds right away even if they need one, again increasing waiting time for themselves and others. There is a critical shortage of nurses as well, and a hospital bed requires a nurse to attend it before it can be occupied. In the 1990s enrollment in nursing programs slumped as people turned to more lucrative careers, and the average age of a registered nurse is now 45. Many hospitals have 20 percent of their nursing slots empty. Staffing shortages in housekeeping also play a roll. A bed may be empty, but until it is cleaned and remade, it is not available for a waiting patient. In some communities, patients may find that emergency room facilities are simply not available. Some hospitals have actually closed their emergency departments after determining that it is unprofitable to run them at current reimbursement rates. In other areas, population growth is outpacing hospital and ED construction.

To address this complex set of issues, a few changes are being made or considered.

Technology and Systems Improvements

A partial solution is to turn to technology to smooth the process of admitting patients into the ED and to track the

along more quickly. Modifications in the operational system were part of the solution employed by the First National Bank of Chicago in its efforts to reduce customer waiting and improve service. The bank developed a computer-based customer information system to allow tellers to answer questions more quickly, implemented an electronic queuing system, hired "peak-time" tellers, expanded its hours, and provided customers with alternative delivery channels. Collectively these efforts reduced customer wait time, increased productivity, and improved customer satisfaction.[19]

availability of hospital beds. Some Web-based systems are used to reroute ambulances to hospitals that have capacity. Other systems help EDs track the availability of rooms in their own hospitals in terms of knowing exactly when a bed is vacant and when it has been cleaned and is available—similar to what hotels have done for decades. Wireless systems for registering patients at bedside and "radar screens" that track everything going on in the ED are other partial solutions. These screens can track patients, staff, carts, and equipment, making the service delivery process more efficient and quicker.

Other hospitals have segmented their patients and have developed parallel "fast track" processes for dealing with minor emergency patients that can account for 30 to 50 percent of total visits. This process can be separated from the major-emergency situations that may require more time and special equipment. Quicker admitting processes, sometimes done on wireless devices, are also being implemented. Instead of having a patient fill out long forms with detailed questions, the quicker process asks just three to four questions initially, saving the longer admitting forms for after treatment.

Yet another innovation is to have staff administer routine tests while the patient is waiting so that the doctor who finally sees the patient has information at hand. This solution also satisfies the patient's need for "something to happen" during the waiting time. Giving patients pagers so they can do something else while waiting is another way that EDs are helping patients cope with the long waits.

Increasing Capacity

Another set of partial solutions relates directly to hospital and staff capacity issues. Some hospitals have already begun adding rooms and other facilities. More urgent care centers are being built to take some of the pressure off EDs. For patients who need to be admitted to the hospital, however, increasing capacity is not a total solution. The nursing shortage, one of the most critical problems, is very difficult to solve. Individual hospital systems have gotten creative in their efforts to steal nurses away from other hospitals, even recruiting heavily overseas. However, in the long term the solution rests more in making the occupation attractive in salaries and working conditions, thus increasing the number of people entering nursing programs.

Insuring the Uninsured

A major political and social issue is how to handle the growing numbers of uninsured in the United States. Finding a way to provide coverage to these millions of Americans—many of whom are employed, but whose employers do not provide health insurance—has been a focus of political debate for decades.

It is obvious that this classic dilemma of matching supply and demand in a service context has multiple, deeply rooted causes when examined in the context of emergency care. The solutions to the issues are also multifaceted—some can be undertaken by individual hospitals, whereas others need to be addressed by the entire health care industry. Some, however, are societal issues with only long-term solutions. Yet all these issues play out daily in the very immediate environment of hospital emergency departments.

Sources: L. Landro, "ERs Now Turn to Technology to Help Deal with Overcapacity," *The Wall Street Journal,* July 13, 2001, p. B1; J. Snyder, "Curing the ER," *The Arizona Republic,* December 9, 2001, p. D1+; N. Shute and M. B. Marcus, "Crisis in the ER," *US News & World Report,* September 10, 2001.

In introducing its express check-in, Marriott Hotels used an operations-based modification to eliminate much of the waiting previously experienced by its guests. Guests who use a credit card and preregister can avoid waiting in line at the hotel front desk altogether. The guest can make it from the curb outside the hotel to his or her room in as little as three minutes when escorted by a "guest service associate" who checks the guest into the hotel, picks up keys and paperwork from a rack in the lobby, and then escorts the guest directly to the room.[20] Recently, the U.S. Department of Transportation

FIGURE 15.5
Waiting is common in many service industries.

Source: Photodisc Green/Getty Images.

Security Administration (TSA) has been experimenting with similar preferential treatment for selected frequent travelers through its "Registered Traveler Program."[21] Only U.S. citizens or permanent legal residents who meet certain flying criteria may apply. After registering with the system and clearing an extensive background check, travelers who qualify for this program are allowed to bypass the usual security checkpoint in their designated airport and instead be screened through a security system that reads either their fingerprints or irises in their eyes. They must still go through a metal detector and their bags are still passed through an X-ray scanner, but they get their own special line and are not randomly selected for additional screening.

When queues are inevitable, the organization faces the operational decision of what kind of queuing system to use, or how to configure the queue. Queue configuration refers to the number of queues, their locations, their spatial requirement, and their effect on customer behavior.[22] Several possibilities exist, as shown in Figure 15.6. In the multiple-queue alternative, the customer arrives at the service facility and must decide which queue to join and whether to switch later if the wait appears to be shorter in another line. In the single-queue alternative, fairness of waiting time is ensured in that the first-come, first-served rule applies to everyone; the system can also reduce the average time customers spend waiting overall. However, customers may leave if they perceive that the line is too long or if they have no opportunity to select a particular service provider. The last option shown in Figure 15.6 is the take-a-number option in which arriving customers take a number to indicate line position. Advantages are similar to the single-queue alternative with the additional benefit that customers are able to mill about, browse, and talk to each other. The disadvantage is that customers must be on the alert to hear their numbers when they are called. Recent research suggests that length of the queue and perceived cost of waiting are not the only influences on customers' likelihood of staying in line. In a series of experiments and field tests, researchers showed that the larger the number of customers waiting in line *behind* a consumer, the more likely that consumer is to stay in line and wait for the service.[23]

Many service businesses have become experts at handling queues effectively in terms of minimizing customer dissatisfaction. Some of the benchmarks include Dis-

FIGURE 15.6
**Waiting Line
Configurations**

Source: J. A. Fitzsimmons and
M. J. Fitzsimmons, *Service
Management,* 4th ed. (New
York: Irwin/McGraw-Hill,
2004), chap. 11, p. 296. © 2004
by The McGraw-Hill
Companies, Inc. Reprinted by
permission of The McGraw-Hill
Companies.

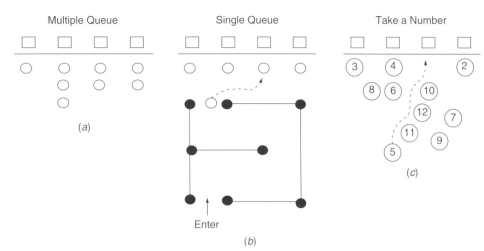

ney, Marriott, and FedEx. In fact, in its effort to plan and implement an effective, efficient, service-oriented security process at U.S. airports, the U.S. government consulted these benchmark companies for advice.[24]

Establish a Reservation Process

When waiting cannot be avoided, a reservation system can help to spread demand. Restaurants, transportation companies, theaters, physicians, and many other service providers use reservation systems to alleviate long waits. The idea behind a reservation system is to guarantee that the service will be available when the customer arrives. Beyond simply reducing waiting time, a reservation system has the added benefit of potentially shifting demand to less desirable time periods. A challenge inherent in reservation systems, however, is what to do about "no shows." Inevitably there will be customers who reserve a time but do not show up. Some organizations deal with this problem by overbooking their service capacity on the basis of past records of no-show percentages. If the predictions are accurate, overbooking is a good solution. When predictions are inaccurate, however, customers may still have to wait and sometimes may not be served at all, as when airlines overbook the number of seats available on a flight. Victims of overbooking may be compensated for their inconvenience in such cases. To minimize the no-show problem, some organizations (such as hotels, airlines, conferences/training programs, and theaters) charge customers who fail to show up or cancel their reservations within a certain time frame.

Differentiate Waiting Customers

Not all customers necessarily need to wait the same length of time for service. On the basis of need or customer priority, some organizations differentiate among customers, allowing some to experience shorter waits for service than others. Known as "queue discipline," such differentiation reflects management policies regarding whom to select next for service.[25] The most popular discipline is first-come, first-served. However, other rules may apply. Differentiation can be based on factors such as[26]

- *Importance of the customer.* Frequent customers or customers who spend large amounts with the organization can be given priority in service by providing them with a special waiting area or segregated lines.

- *Urgency of the job.* Those customers with the most urgent need may be served first. This strategy is used in emergency health care. It is also used by maintenance services such as air-conditioning repair that give priority to customers whose air conditioning is not functioning over those who call for routine maintenance.

- *Duration of the service transaction.* In many situations, shorter service jobs get priority through "express lanes." At other times, when a service provider sees that a transaction is going to require extra time, the customer is referred to a designated provider who deals only with these special-needs customers.

- *Payment of a premium price.* Customers who pay extra (first class on an airline, for example) are often given priority via separate check-in lines or express systems.

Make Waiting Fun, or at Least Tolerable

Even when they have to wait, customers can be more or less satisfied depending on how the wait is handled by the organization. Of course the actual length of the wait will affect how customers feel about their service experience. But it is not just the actual time spent waiting that has an impact on customer satisfaction—it is how customers feel about the wait and their perceptions during it. The type of wait (for example, a standard queue versus a wait due to a delay of service) can also influence how customers will react.[27] In a classic article entitled "The Psychology of Waiting Lines," David Maister proposes several principles about waiting, each of which has implications for how organizations can make waiting more pleasurable or at least tolerable.[28]

Unoccupied Time Feels Longer Than Occupied Time

When customers are unoccupied they will likely be bored and will notice the passage of time more than when they have something to do. Providing something for waiting customers to do, particularly if the activity offers a benefit in and of itself or is related in some way to the service, can improve the customer's experience and may benefit the organization as well.[29] Examples include giving customers menus to look at while waiting in a restaurant, providing interesting information to read in a dentist's office, or playing entertaining programs over the phone while customers are on hold. At Macy's in New York, children waiting to see Santa Claus wind their way through displays of dancing teddy bears, elves, and electric trains that become part of the total service adventure.[30]

Preprocess Waits Feel Longer Than In-Process Waits

If wait time is occupied with activities that relate to the upcoming service, customers may perceive that the service has started and they are no longer actually waiting. This in-process activity will make the length of the wait seem shorter and will also benefit the service provider by making the customer better prepared when the service actually does begin. Filling out medical information while waiting to see the physician, reading a menu while waiting to be seated in a restaurant, and watching a videotape of the upcoming service event are all activities that can both educate the customer and reduce perceptions of waiting.

Research in a restaurant context found that customers reacted less negatively to in-process waits than to either preprocess or postprocess waits.[31] Other researchers have found the same for waits due to routine slowness of the process. However, if the wait is due to a service failure, then the in-process wait is viewed more negatively than the preprocess wait.[32] Thus, how customers perceive preprocess, in-process, and post-process waits may depend to some extent on the cause of the wait.

Anxiety Makes Waits Seem Longer

When customers fear that they have been forgotten or do not know how long they will have to wait, they become anxious, and this anxiety can increase the negative impact of waiting. Anxiety also results when customers are forced to choose in a multiple-line situation and they discover they have chosen the "wrong line." To combat waiting line anxiety, organizations can provide information on the length of the wait. At its theme parks, Disney uses signs at intervals along the line that let customers know how long the wait will be from that point on. Using a single line also alleviates customer anxiety over having chosen the wrong line. Explanations and reassurances that no one has forgotten them alleviate customer anxiety by taking away their cause for worry. At the Omni Park Central Hotel in New York, when the line exceeds a certain length assistant managers bring orange and grapefruit juice to serve those waiting.[33] The customers know they have not been forgotten.

Uncertain Waits Are Longer Than Known, Finite Waits

Anxiety is intensified when customers do not know how long they will have to wait. Health care providers combat this problem by letting customers know when they check in how far behind the physician is that day. Some patients resolve this uncertainty themselves by calling ahead to ask. Maister provides an interesting example of the role of uncertainty, which he terms the "appointment syndrome." Customers who arrive early for an appointment will wait patiently until the scheduled time, even if they arrive very early. However, once the expected appointment time has passed, customers grow increasingly anxious. Before the appointment time the wait time is known; after that, the length of the wait is not known.

Research in an airline context has suggested that as uncertainty about the wait increases, customers become more angry, and their anger in turn results in greater dissatisfaction.[34] Research also shows that giving customers information on the length of the anticipated wait and/or their relative position in the queue can result in more positive feelings and acceptance of the wait and ultimately more positive evaluation of the service.[35]

Unexplained Waits Are Longer Than Explained Waits

When people understand the causes for waiting, they frequently have greater patience and are less anxious, particularly when the wait is justifiable. An explanation can reduce customer uncertainty and may help customers estimate how long they will be delayed. Customers who do not know the reason for a wait begin to feel powerless and irritated.

Unfair Waits Are Longer Than Equitable Waits

When customers perceive that they are waiting while others who arrived after them have already been served, the apparent inequity will make the wait seem even longer. This situation can easily occur when there is no apparent order in the waiting area and many customers are trying to be served. Queuing systems that work on a first-come, first-served rule are best at combating perceived unfairness. However, other approaches may be required to determine who will be served next. For example, in an emergency medical care situation, the most seriously ill or injured patients would be seen first.

When customers understand the priorities and the rules are clearly communicated and enforced, fairness of waiting time should not be an issue.

The More Valuable the Service, the Longer the Customer Will Wait

Customers who have substantial purchases or who are waiting for a high-value service will be more tolerant of long wait times and may even expect to wait longer. For example, in a supermarket, customers who have a full cart of groceries will generally wait longer than customers who have only a few items and expect to be checked through quickly. And diners expect to wait longer for service in an expensive restaurant than they do when eating at a "greasy spoon."

Solo Waits Feel Longer Than Group Waits

People will wait longer when they are in a group than when they are alone because of the distractions provided by other members of the group. People also feel comfort in waiting with a group rather than alone.[36] In some group waiting situations, such as at Disneyland or when patrons are waiting in long lines to purchase concert tickets, customers who are strangers begin to talk to each other and the waiting experience can actually become fun and a part of the total service experience.

Summary

Because service organizations lack the ability to inventory their products, the effective use of capacity can be critical to success. Idle capacity in the form of unused time, labor, facilities, or equipment represents a direct drain on bottom-line profitability. When the capacity represents a major investment (for example, airplanes, expensive medical imaging equipment, or lawyers and physicians paid on a salary), the losses associated with underuse of capacity are even more accentuated. Overused capacity is also a problem. People, facilities, and equipment can become worn out over time when used beyond optimum capacity constraints. People can quit, facilities become run down, and equipment can break. From the customer's perspective, service quality also deteriorates. Organizations focused on delivering quality service, therefore, have a natural drive to balance capacity utilization and demand at an optimum level in order to meet customer expectations.

This chapter has provided you with an understanding of the underlying issues of managing supply and demand in capacity-constrained services by exploring the lack of inventory capability, the nature of service constraints (time, labor, equipment, facilities), the differences in optimal versus maximum use of capacity, and the causes of fluctuating demand.

Based on grounding in the fundamental issues, the chapter presented a variety of strategies for matching supply and demand. The basic strategies fall under two headings: *demand strategies* (shifting demand to match capacity) and *supply strategies* (adjusting capacity to meet demand). Demand strategies seek to flatten the peaks and valleys of demand to match the flat capacity constraint, whereas supply strategies seek to align, flex, or stretch capacity to match the peaks and valleys of demand. Organizations frequently employ several strategies simultaneously to solve the complex problem of balancing supply and demand.

Yield management was presented as a sophisticated form of supply and demand management that balances capacity utilization, pricing, market segmentation, and financial return. Long practiced by the passenger airline industry, this strategy is growing in use by hotel, shipping, car rental, and other capacity-constrained industries in which bookings are made in advance. Essentially, yield management allows organizations to decide on a monthly, weekly, daily, or even hourly basis to whom they want to sell their service capacity at what price.

All strategies for aligning capacity and demand need to be approached with caution. Any one of the strategies is likely to imply changes in multiple marketing mix elements to support the strategy. Such changes, even if done well, carry a risk that the firm will lose focus or inadvertently alter its image in pursuit of increased revenues. Although a different focus or image is not necessarily bad, the potential strategic impact on the total organization should be considered.

In the last section of the chapter, we discussed situations in which it is not possible to align supply and demand. In these unresolved capacity utilization situations, the inevitable result is customer waiting. We described strategies for effectively managing waiting lines, such as employing operational logic, establishing a reservation process, differentiating waiting customers, and making waiting fun or at least tolerable.

Discussion Questions

1. Why do service organizations lack the capability to inventory their services? Compare a car repair and maintenance service with an automobile manufacturer/dealer in terms of inventory capability.

2. Discuss the four scenarios illustrated in Figure 15.1 and presented in the text (excess demand, demand exceeds optimum capacity, demand and supply are balanced, excess capacity) in the context of a professional basketball team selling seats for its games. What are the challenges for management under each scenario?

3. Discuss the four common types of constraints (time, labor, equipment, facilities) facing service businesses and give an example of each (real or hypothetical).

4. How does optimal capacity utilization differ from maximum capacity utilization? Give an example of a situation in which the two might be the same and one in which they are different.

5. Choose a local restaurant or some other type of service with fluctuating demand. What is the likely underlying pattern of demand? What causes the pattern? Is it predictable or random?

6. Describe the two basic strategies for matching supply and demand, and give at least two specific examples of each.

7. What is yield management? Discuss the risks in adopting a yield management strategy.

8. How might yield management apply in the management of the following: a Broadway theater? A consulting firm? A commuter train?

9. Describe the four basic waiting line strategies, and give an example of each one, preferably based on your own experiences as a consumer.

Exercises

1. Choose a local service organization that is challenged by fixed capacity and fluctuating demand. Interview the marketing manager (or other knowledgeable person) to learn (*a*) in what ways capacity is constrained, (*b*) the basic patterns of demand, and (*c*) strategies the organization has used to align supply and demand. Write up the answers to these questions, and make your own recommendations regarding other strategies the organization might use.

2. Assume you manage a winter ski resort in Colorado or Banff, Canada. (*a*) Ex-

plain the underlying pattern of demand fluctuation that is likely to occur at your resort and the challenges it would present to you as a manager. Is the pattern of demand predictable or random? (b) Explain and give examples of how you might use both demand-oriented and supply-oriented strategies to smooth the peaks and valleys of demand during peak and slow periods.

3. Choose a local organization in which people have to wait in line for service. Design a waiting line strategy for the organization.

4. Visit the website of Wells Fargo Bank (www.wellsfargo.com), a leader in online banking. What online services does the bank currently offer? How do these online services help Wells Fargo manage the peaks and valleys of customer demand? How do its strategies to use more ATMs, in-store bank branches, and other alternative delivery strategies complement the online strategies?

Notes

1. www.ritzcarlton.com, 2004.
2. J. S. Hirsch, "Vacationing Families Head Downtown to Welcoming Arms of Business Hotels," *The Wall Street Journal,* June 13, 1994, p. B1.
3. Ibid.
4. C. Lovelock, "Getting the Most Out of Your Productive Capacity," in *Product Plus* (Boston: McGraw-Hill, 1994), chap. 16.
5. C. H. Lovelock, "Classifying Services to Gain Strategic Marketing Insights," *Journal of Marketing* 47 (Summer 1983), pp. 9–20.
6. B. Fryer, "High Tech the Old-Fashioned Way: An Interview with Tom Siebel of Siebel Systems," *Harvard Business Review,* March 2001, p. 123.
7. Portions of this section are based on C. H. Lovelock, "Strategies for Managing Capacity-Constrained Service Organizations," in *Managing Services: Marketing, Operations, and Human Resources,* 2nd ed. (Englewood Cliffs, NJ: Prentice Hall, 1992), pp. 154–68.
8. D. Kenny, H. McGrath, T. J. Olsen, B. Sullivan, M. R. Tutton, and S. Yusko, "Service Quality under Crisis . . . AT&T Serving the Service—a Case Study," in *Advances in Services Marketing and Management,* vol. 1, ed. T. A. Swartz, D. E. Bowen, and S. W. Brown (Greenwich, CT: JAI Press, 1992), pp. 229–46.
9. E. C. Clemmer and B. Schneider, "Toward Understanding and Controlling Customer Dissatisfaction with Waiting during Peak Demand Times," in *Designing a Winning Service Strategy,* ed. M. J. Bitner and L. A. Crosby (Chicago: American Marketing Association, 1989), pp. 87–91.
10. Lovelock, "Getting the Most Out of Your Productive Capacity."
11. M. E. Berge and C. A. Hopperstad, "Demand Driven Dispatch: A Method for Dynamic Aircraft Capacity Assignment, Models, and Algorithms," *Operations Research* 41 (January–February 1993), pp. 153–68.
12. Lovelock, "Getting the Most Out of Your Productive Capacity."
13. See S. E. Kimes, "Yield Management: A Tool for Capacity-Constrained Service Firms," *Journal of Operations Management* 8 (October 1989), pp. 348–63; S. E. Kimes and R. B. Chase, "The Strategic Levers of Yield Management," *Journal of Service Research* 1 (November 1998), pp. 156–66; S. E. Kimes, "Revenue Management: A Retrospective," *Cornell Hotel and Restaurant Administration Quarterly* 44, no. 5/6 (2003), pp. 131–38.
14. Kimes, "Yield Management."
15. R. Desiraji and S. M. Shugan, "Strategic Service Pricing and Yield Management," *Journal of Marketing* 63 (January 1999), pp. 44–56.

16. Kimes, "Yield Management."

17. S. E. Kimes and J. Wirtz, "Has Revenue Management Become Acceptable? Findings From an International Study on the Perceived Fairness of Rate Fences," *Journal of Service Research* 6 (November 2003), pp. 125–35.

18. For research supporting the relationship between longer waits and decreased satisfaction, quality evaluations, and patronage intentions see Clemmer and Schneider, "Toward Understanding and Controlling Customer Dissatisfaction"; A. Th. H. Pruyn and A. Smidts, "Customer Evaluation of Queues: Three Exploratory Studies," *European Advances in Consumer Research* 1 (1993), pp. 371–82; S. Taylor, "Waiting for Service: The Relationship between Delays and Evaluations of Service," *Journal of Marketing* 58 (April 1994), pp. 56–69; K. L. Katz, B. M. Larson, and R. C. Larson, "Prescription for the Waiting-in-Line Blues: Entertain, Enlighten, and Engage," *Sloan Management Review,* Winter 1991, pp. 44–53; S. Taylor and J. D. Claxton, "Delays and the Dynamics of Service Evaluations," *Journal of the Academy of Marketing Science* 22 (Summer 1994), pp. 254–64; D. Grewal, J. Baker, M. Levy, and G. B. Voss, "The Effects of Wait Expectations and Store Atmosphere on Patronage Intentions in Service-Intensive Retail Stores," *Journal of Retailing* 79 (Winter 2003), pp. 259–68.

19. L. L. Berry and L. R. Cooper, "Competing with Time-Saving Service," *Business,* April–June 1990, pp. 3–7.

20. R. Henkoff, "Finding, Training, and Keeping the Best Service Workers," *Fortune,* October 3, 1994, pp. 110–22.

21. K. Murphy, "Zipping Through Airport Security," *BusinessWeek,* September 6, 2004, p. 106.

22. J. A. Fitzsimmons and M. J. Fitzsimmons, *Service Management,* 3rd ed. (New York: Irwin/McGraw-Hill, 2000), chap. 11.

23. R. Zhou and D. Soman, "Looking Back: Exploring the Psychology of Queuing and the Effect of the Number of People Behind," *Journal of Consumer Research* 29 (March 2003), pp. 517–30.

24. S. Power, "Mickey Mouse, Nike Give Advice on Air Security," *The Wall Street Journal,* January 24, 2002, p. B1.

25. Fitzsimmons and Fitzsimmons, *Service Management,* chap. 11.

26. Lovelock, "Getting the Most Out of Your Productive Capacity."

27. For an excellent review of the literature on customer perceptions of and reactions to various aspects of waiting time, see S. Taylor and G. Fullerton, "Waiting for Services: Perceptions Management of the Wait Experience," in *Handbook of Services Marketing and Management,* ed. T. A. Swartz and D. Iacobucci (Thousands Oaks, CA: Sage Publications), 2000, pp. 171–89.

28. D. A. Maister, "The Psychology of Waiting Lines," in *The Service Encounter,* ed. J. A. Czepiel, M. R. Solomon, and C. F. Surprenant (Lexington, MA: Lexington Books, 1985), pp. 113–23.

29. S. Taylor, "The Effects of Filled Waiting Time and Service Provider Control over the Delay on Evaluations of Service," *Journal of the Academy of Marketing Science* 23 (Summer 1995), pp. 38–48.

30. A. Bennett, "Their Business Is on the Line," *The Wall Street Journal,* December 7, 1990, p. B1.

31. L. Dube-Rioux, B. H. Schmitt, and F. Leclerc, "Consumer's Reactions to Waiting: When Delays Affect the Perception of Service Quality," in *Advances in Consumer Research,* vol. 16, ed. T. Srull (Provo, UT: Association for Consumer Research, 1988), pp. 59–63.

32. M. K. Hui, M. V. Thakor, and R. Gill, "The Effect of Delay Type and Service Stage on Consumers' Reactions to Waiting," *Journal of Consumer Research* 24 (March 1998), pp. 469–79.

33. Dube-Rioux, Schmitt, and Leclerc, "Consumer's Reactions to Waiting."

34. Taylor and Fullerton, "Waiting for Services."

35. M. K. Hui and D. K. Tse, "What to Tell Consumers in Waits of Different Lengths: An Integrative Model of Service Evaluation," *Journal of Marketing* 60 (April 1996), pp. 81–90.

36. J. Baker and M. Cameron, "The Effects of the Service Environment on Affect and Consumer Perception of Waiting Time: An Integrative Review and Research Propositions," *Journal of the Academy of Marketing Science* 24 (Fall 1996), pp. 338–49.

Part 6

MANAGING SERVICE PROMISES

The fourth provider gap, shown in the accompanying figure, illustrates the difference between service delivery and the service provider's external communications. Promises made by a service company through its media advertising, sales force, and other communications may potentially raise customer expectations that serve as the standard against which customers assess service quality. Broken promises can occur for many reasons: ineffective marketing communications, overpromising in advertising or personal selling, inadequate coordination between operations and marketing, and differences in policies and procedures across service outlets.

In service companies, a fit between communications about service and actual service delivery is necessary. Chapter 16 is devoted to the topic of integrated services

Provider Gap 4

Customer

Company

Service Delivery ⟷ The Communication Gap ⟷ External Communications to Customers

marketing communications—careful integration and organization of all of a service marketing organization's external and internal communications channels. The chapter describes why this communication is necessary and how companies can do it well. Successful company communications are the responsibility of both marketing and operations: marketing must accurately but beguilingly reflect what happens in actual service encounters, and operations must deliver what is promised in advertising. If communications set up unrealistic expectations for customers, the actual encounter will disappoint the customer.

Chapter 17 deals with another issue related to managing promises, the pricing of services. In packaged goods (and even in durable goods), many customers possess enough price knowledge before purchase to be able to judge whether a price is fair or in line with competition. With services, customers often have no internal reference point for prices before purchase and consumption. Techniques for developing prices for services are more complicated than those for pricing tangible goods, and all the approaches for setting prices must be adapted for the special characteristics of services.

In summary, external communications—whether from marketing communications or pricing—can create a larger customer gap by raising expectations about service delivery. In addition to improving service delivery, companies must also manage all communications to customers so that inflated promises do not lead to higher expectations. Companies must also manage the messages conveyed by pricing so that customer expectations are in line with what they perceive that they receive.

16

INTEGRATED SERVICES MARKETING COMMUNICATIONS

This chapter's objectives are to

1. Discuss the key reasons for service communication challenges.

2. Introduce the concept of integrated service marketing communications.

3. Present four ways to integrate marketing communications in service organizations.

4. Present specific strategies for managing promises, managing customer expectations, educating customers, and managing internal communications.

"Competition. Bad for them. Great for You."

DHL Integrates Marketing Communications

For decades, industry giants Federal Express and United Parcel Service together owned 70 percent of the U.S. market for express and package delivery services. DHL, the 34-year-old acknowledged leader in the global market, serving 220 countries, was little known to U.S. customers; it had only a 6 percent market share. When DHL acquired Airborne in 2003, the company knew it needed an all-out effort to compete head-on with the domestic behemoths. The company budgeted $1.2 billion for new initiatives to boost its presence in the U.S. market, starting with the addition of seven regional sorting centers to increase ground delivery capacity by 60 percent.[1] To support its ambitious goal of becoming number one in the U.S. parcel-delivery market, the company created an innovative new red logo and spent $150 million on an integrated six-month marketing communications campaign—including broadcast, print, interactive, and outdoor advertising as well as sponsorships, public relations, and a new website—that focused on brand awareness and brand value. As Dick Metzler, DHL Americas executive vice president of marketing, explained, "Using a full 360 degree arsenal of marketing channels, we are showcasing the DHL brand's value message to current and potential customers across all points of contact."[2]

The DHL marketing campaign, developed by advertising agency Ogilvy and Mather New York, opened with a June 2004 television ad showing drivers for FedEx and UPS watching in wonder as a freight train rolls by carrying brand-new yellow trucks with the red DHL logo. Three-page spreads in major newspapers supported the broadcast advertising with the headline, "The merger with Airborne has made DHL strong in the following areas:" followed by two full pages of ZIP codes. Billboards trumpeted: "Competition. Bad for them. Great for You." Impossible-to-ignore outdoor advertising spanning the full height of the Reuters building in New York's Times Square presented five different fully-animated video messages carrying the same theme and colors. Not only did the company completely renovate its own website (see http://www.dhl-usa.com), but it also placed full-motion interactive advertising on other websites. The company's website allows customers to download all its television, interactive, print, and outdoor advertising, as well as a computer screensaver with DHL trucks continuously streaming across a red background and interspersed with the campaign's catchy headlines. A public relations campaign by Ogilvy PR Worldwide that was aimed at core constituents and opinion leaders complemented the paid advertising. And the company's tangibles became an integral part of the marketing communications plan, with the new red logo and bright yellow background on every DHL building, vehicle, courier uniform, packaging unit, and drop box in North America.

DHL used sponsorship as a key element of the campaign, highlighted by its role as the "Official Express Delivery and Logistics Provider of the 2004 U.S. Olympics Team." According to *B to B* magazine, DHL "grabbed the gold" among business-to-business companies that advertised during the televised Olympics coverage. Ten-second television spots included one with two Olympic cyclists spinning their wheels on the ramp of a DHL truck while the driver tossed water bottles, another with a long jumper soaring into a landing pit of packing peanuts as DHL employees prepared to rake more packing peanuts into the pit, and a third with a pole vaulter landing on a bed of bubble wrap as DHL employees stood by to make sure everything went smoothly.[3] The narrator announced, "DHL is proud to support the U.S. Olympic team any way we can." According to *B to B* magazine, "No other b-to-b advertiser came close to DHL's Olympic work."[4]

Targeting small- and medium-sized businesses, which have larger revenue per shipment and are more profitable, DHL created one of the most coordinated services marketing communication campaigns in history.[5] The advertising agency achieved integration through color (yellow and red), theme (choice, competition, and innovation), tagline ("Competition. Bad for them. Great for You."), and design. Metzler claimed at the beginning of the campaign, "As our red and bright yellow trucks begin rolling through the streets, advertising increases and customers see our expanded product offering, the realization will set in that DHL is an even more powerful force in the American marketplace."[6] As this textbook goes to press, the outcome is unknown, but if the company's operational strategy matches its marketing strategy, all bets are on success.

A major cause of poorly perceived service is the difference between what a firm promises about a service and what it actually delivers. Customer expectations are shaped by both uncontrollable and company-controlled factors. Although word-of-mouth communication, customer experiences with other service providers, and customer needs are key factors that influence customer expectations, they are rarely controllable by the firm. However, controllable factors such as company advertising, personal selling, and promises made by service personnel also influence customer expectations. In this chapter we focus on these controllable factors. Accurate, coordinated, and appropriate company communication—advertising, personal selling, and online and other messages that do not overpromise or misrepresent—is essential to delivering services that customers perceive as high in quality.

Because company communications about services promise what people do and because people's behavior cannot be standardized like physical goods produced by machines, the potential for a mismatch between what is communicated and perceptions of actual service delivery (provider gap 4) is high. By coordinating communication within and outside the organization, companies can minimize the size of this gap.

THE NEED FOR COORDINATION IN MARKETING COMMUNICATION

Marketing communication is more complex today than it used to be. In the past, customers received marketing information about goods and services from a limited number of sources, usually mass communication sources such as network television and newspapers. With a limited number of sources, marketers could easily convey a uniform brand image and coordinate promises. However, today's consumers of both goods and services receive communications from a far richer variety of advertising vehicles—targeted magazines, websites, direct mail, movie theater advertising, e-mail solicitation, and a host of sales promotions. Consumers of services receive additional communication from servicescapes, customer service departments, and everyday service encounters with employees. These service interactions add to the variety, volume, and complexity of information that a customer receives. Ensuring that messages from all these company sources are consistent is a major challenge for marketers of services.

Any company that disseminates information through multiple channels needs to be certain that customers receive unified messages and promises. These channels include not only advertising messages that flow directly from the company but also personal messages that employees send to customers. Figure 16.1 shows an enhanced version of the services marketing triangle that we presented in Chapter 12, emphasizing that the customer of services is the target of two types of communication. First, external marketing communication includes traditional channels such as advertising, sales promotion, and public relations. Second, interactive marketing communication involves the messages that employees give to customers through such channels as personal selling, customer service interactions, service encounter interactions, and servicescapes (discussed in Chapter 11). A service company must be sure that these interactive messages are consistent both among themselves and with those sent through external communications. To do so, the third side of the triangle, internal marketing communications, must be managed so that information from the company to employees is accurate, complete, and consistent with what customers are hearing or seeing.

The need for integrated marketing campaigns is evident in both business-to-business situations (as discussed in Exhibit 16.1) and business-to-consumer instances. Consider

FIGURE 16.1
**Communications and
the Services
Marketing Triangle**

Source: Kotler, Philip,
*Marketing Management:
Analysis, Planning,
Implementation, and Control,*
9th Edition, © 1997. Reprinted
by permission of Pearson
Education, Inc., Upper Saddle
River.

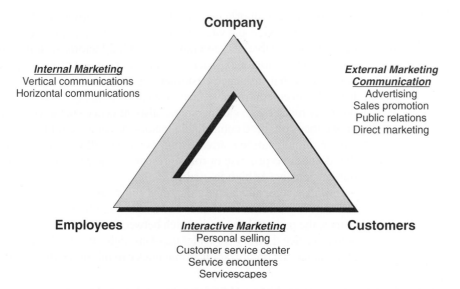

Company

Internal Marketing
Vertical communications
Horizontal communications

*External Marketing
Communication*
Advertising
Sales promotion
Public relations
Direct marketing

Employees

Interactive Marketing
Personal selling
Customer service center
Service encounters
Servicescapes

Customers

an example from your own experience that may illustrate what happens when services marketing communications are not integrated. Have you ever seen an advertisement for a service, such as a new sandwich from McDonald's, then gone to your local McDonald's and not found it available? Did the employee behind the counter offer a reason the sandwich was not available? Did he or she even realize that it was advertised and for sale elsewhere? One of us consulted for a bank on the West Coast in which both customers and employees constantly faced this situation. Bank advertising was changed frequently and quickly to meet competitive offerings, but the bank tellers' training in the new offerings did not keep pace with the changes in advertising. As a result, customers came in expecting new accounts and rates to be available, and employees were embarrassed because they had not been informed.

This example demonstrates one of the main reasons that integrated marketing communications have not been the norm in many companies. All too often, various parts of the company are responsible for different aspects of communication. The sales department develops and executes sales communication. The marketing department prepares and disseminates advertising. A public relations firm is responsible for publicity. Functional specialists handle sales promotions, direct marketing, and company websites. The human resources department trains frontline employees for service interactions, and still another area is responsible for the customer service department. Rarely is one person responsible for the overall communications strategy in a company, and all too often people responsible for the different communication components do not coordinate their efforts.

Today, however, more companies are adopting the concept of *integrated marketing communications (IMC),* where the company carefully integrates and organizes all of its external communications channels. As a marketing executive explained it,

> Integrated marketing communications build a strong brand identity in the marketplace by tying together and reinforcing all your images and messages. IMC means that all your corporate messages, positioning and images, and identity are coordinated across all venues. It means that your PR materials say the same things as your direct mail campaign, and your advertising has the same 'look and feel' as your website.[7]

B to B magazine annually selects the best business-to-business advertising in four categories: integrated campaign, single TV spot, single print ad, and single interactive advertisement. Winners are chosen on the following criteria: shows a high degree of visual magnetism; selects the right audience; invites the reader into the scene; promises a reward and backs up the promise; presents the selling proposition in a logical sequence; speaks to the reader as an individual; emphasizes the service, not the source; and reflects the company's character. Winners and runners-up in the integrated campaign category from 2001 to 2003 illustrate effective coordination of advertising that facilitates delivery to promises.

The 2003 winner was General Electric Company's branding makeover to "Imagination at Work," which combined television spots, print ads, and an imaginative interactive promotion. The product and service company's goal was to overhaul its brand and long-time tagline, "We bring good things to life," after research showed that investors equated GE with appliances and lightbulbs. Because these products were only 6 percent of GE's business and because the company's strategy was to be perceived as a broad brand and strong service provider, the campaign highlighted GE's strengths in medical systems, jet engines, security systems, and wind turbines. The campaign, created by BBDO Advertising, contained eight print ads with powerfully stark images, such as a GE wind turbine set against a field of white space. In one of the television spots designed to illustrate the breadth of the GE product line, the late Johnny Cash sang while GE employees humorously attached one of its jet engines to the Wright brothers' aircraft. Online advertising took visitors to a GE landing site to sketch illustrations of their imaginative ideas using a virtual felt-tip marker. The online interactive exercise reinforced the "Imagination at Work" tagline and generated both positive word of mouth and viral marketing (visitors to the site were urged to share their illustrations by e-mail). Results of the integrated campaign were positive, according to the company: "Research indicates GE is now being associated with attributes such as being high-tech, leading-edge, innovative, contemporary and creative."

The runner-up in 2002 was package delivery company UPS. Spending $46 million on a six-month marketing campaign launched during the 2002 Winter Olympics, UPS corrected the public's misperception that the company was only a ground carrier for small packages. The theme line, "What can Brown do for you?" and accompanying advertising "underscored the breadth of UPS's capabilities, including advanced supply chain management solutions, inventory warehousing, e-mail notification and financial services," according to Steve Holmes, spokesman for UPS advertising in Atlanta. The campaign was coordinated from the color of the uniforms and the trucks to the communications vehicles, including print, television, interactive, and direct advertising. Cliff Sorah, senior vice president and associate creative director of The Martin Agency, Richmond, Virginia, wanted to make Brown "cool." By using Brown as the creative center, the campaign gave UPS a more contemporary image. "You think about that color differently. You think of all the capabilities of Brown," Sorah said.

In 2001, Accenture won the top award for the best integrated marketing campaign while it was facing an unusual challenge: It was ordered by a judge to change its name from Andersen Consulting, and it had less than four months to launch its new name and position. Accenture and its agency created a $175 million rebranding campaign including television, print, and outdoor ads showing a ripped-through signature of its former name with the date 01-01-01 as its "rebirth" and the tagline "Now it gets interesting." To support the advertising, the company also sponsored a pro golf tournament and devised unusual and creative tactics such as putting its name on hang gliders. Because the company was repositioning itself as a consultant that focused not just on business but also on technology, it used images of virtual surgery and bacteria in computer chip technology. In the words of the judges, "The campaign is stellar work, encompassing original ideas, beautiful photography and clear messaging." After six months, it was clear that the campaign had succeeded: Accenture achieved an increase of 75 to 100% awareness.

Sources: Edmund O. Lawler, Sean Callahan, "2003 B to B Best Awards," *B to B* 88, no. 14 (Dec 8, 2003) ,p. 22; Ed Lawler, "19th Annual Sawyer Awards: Integrated Campaign Runner-up: United Parcel Service of America," *B to B* (December 9, 2002), **p. 21**; John Even Frook, "Cisco Scores with Its Latest Generation of Empowering Ads," *B to B*, August 20, 2001, p. 20; Kate Maddox, "Sawyer Awards," *B to B*, December 10, 2001, pp. 19–21.

In this chapter we propose that a more complex type of integrated marketing communication is needed for services than for goods. External communications channels must be coordinated, as with physical goods, but both external communications and

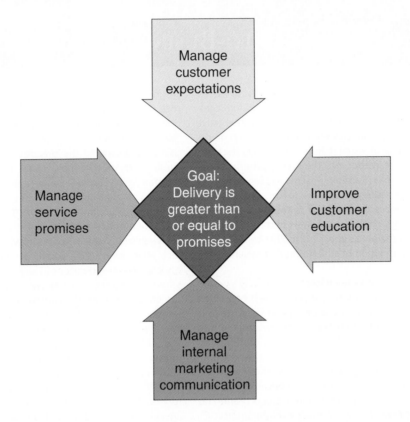

interactive communication channels must be integrated to create consistent service promises. To do that, internal marketing communications channels must be managed so that employees and the company are in agreement about what is communicated to the customer. As Figure 16.2 shows, this coordination requires both vertical communications—typically called *internal marketing communications*—and horizontal communications across departments and areas of the firm. We call this more complicated version of IMC *integrated services marketing communications (ISMC)*. ISMC requires that everyone involved with communication clearly understand both the company's marketing strategy and its promises to consumers.

KEY REASONS FOR SERVICE COMMUNICATION CHALLENGES

Discrepancies between service delivery and external communications, in the form of exaggerated promises and/or the absence of information about service delivery aspects intended to serve customers well, can powerfully affect consumer perceptions of service quality. The factors that contribute to these communication problems include (1) inadequate management of service promises, (2) elevated customer expectations, (3) insufficient customer education, and (4) inadequate internal communications. In this chapter, we first describe the challenges stemming from these factors and then detail strategies that firms have found useful in dealing with them.

Inadequate Management of Service Promises

A discrepancy between service delivery and promises occurs when companies fail to manage service promises—the vows made by salespeople, advertising, and service personnel. One of the primary reasons for this discrepancy is that the company lacks the information and integration needed to make fulfillable promises. Salespeople often sell services, particularly new business services, before their actual availability and without having an exact date of when they will be ready for market. Demand and supply variations make service provision possible at some times, improbable at others, and difficult to predict. The traditional functional structure in many companies also makes communication about promises and delivery difficult.

Inadequate Management of Customer Expectations

Appropriate and accurate communication about services is the responsibility of both marketing and operations. Marketing must accurately (if compellingly) reflect what happens in actual service encounters; operations must deliver what is promised in communications. For example, when a management consulting firm introduces a new offering, the marketing and sales departments must make the offering appealing enough to be viewed as superior to competing services. In promoting and differentiating the service, however, the company cannot afford to raise expectations above the level at which its consultants can consistently perform. If advertising, personal selling, or any other external communication sets up unrealistic expectations, actual encounters will disappoint customers.

Because of increasing deregulation and intensifying competition in the services sector, many service firms feel pressure to acquire new business and to meet or beat competition. To accomplish these ends, service firms often overpromise in selling, advertising, and other company communications. In the airline industry, advertising is a constant battlefield of competing offers and price reductions to gain the patronage of customers. The greater the extent to which a service firm feels pressured to generate new customers, and perceives that the industry norm is to overpromise ("everyone else in our industry overpromises"), the greater is the firm's propensity to overpromise.

If advertising shows a smiling young worker at the counter in a McDonald's commercial, the customer expects that, at least most of the time, there will be a smiling young worker in the local McDonald's. If advertising claims that a customer's wake-up call will always be on time at a Ramada Inn, the customer expects no mistakes. Raising expectations to unrealistic levels may lead to more initial business but invariably fosters customer disappointment and discourages repeat business.

Inadequate Customer Education

Differences between service delivery and promises also occur when companies do not sufficiently educate their customers. If customers are unclear about how service will be provided, what their role in delivery involves, and how to evaluate services they have never used before, they will be disappointed. When disappointed, they will often hold the service company, not themselves, responsible. Research by a leading service research firm reveals that one-third of all customer complaints are related to problems caused by customers themselves. These errors or problems in service—even when they are "caused" by the customer—still lead customers to defect. For this reason the firm must assume responsibility for educating customers.

For services high in credence properties—expert services that are difficult for customers to evaluate even after they have received the services—many customers do not know the criteria by which they should judge the service. For high-involvement services, such as long-term medical treatment or purchase of a first home, customers are also unlikely to comprehend and anticipate the service process. First-time home buyers rarely understand the complex set of services (inspection, title services, insurance) and processes (securing a mortgage, offers and counteroffers, escrow) that will be involved in their purchases. Professionals and other providers of high-involvement services often forget that customers are novices who must be educated about each step in the process. They assume that an overview at the beginning of the service, or a manual or set of instructions, will equip the customer. Unfortunately these steps are rarely sufficient, and customers defect because they can neither understand the process nor appreciate the value received from the service.

A final condition under which customer education can be beneficial involves services in which demand and supply are not synchronized, as discussed in Chapter 15. If the customer is not informed about peaks and valleys in demand, service overloads and failures, not to mention underutilized capacity, are likely to result.

Inadequate Internal Marketing Communications

Multiple functions in the organization, such as marketing and operations, must be coordinated to achieve the goal of service provision. Because service advertising and personal selling promise what *people* do, frequent and effective communication across functions—horizontal communication—is critical. If internal communication is poor, perceived service quality is at risk. If company advertising and other promises are developed without input from operations, contact personnel may not be able to deliver service that matches the image portrayed in marketing efforts.

Not all service organizations advertise, but all need coordination or integration across departments or functions to deliver quality service. All need internal communication between the sales force and service providers. Horizontal communication also must occur between the human resource and marketing departments. To deliver excellent customer service, firms must be certain to inform and motivate employees to deliver what their customers expect. If marketing and sales personnel who understand customer expectations do not communicate this information to contact employees, the lack of knowledge for these employees will affect the quality of service that they deliver.

A final form of internal coordination central to providing service excellence is consistency in policies and procedures across departments and branches. If a service organization operates many outlets under the same name, whether franchised or company owned, customers expect similar performance across those outlets. If managers of individual branches or outlets have significant autonomy in procedures and policies, customers may not receive the same level of service quality across the branches.

FOUR CATEGORIES OF STRATEGIES TO MATCH SERVICE PROMISES WITH DELIVERY

Figure 16.2 shows four categories of strategies to match service delivery with promises: (1) manage service promises, (2) manage customer expectations, (3) improve customer education, and (4) manage internal marketing communication. "Managing service promises" involves coordinating the vows made by all external and interactive marketing sources to ensure that they are consistent and feasible. "Managing customer expectations" incorporates strategies that tell customers that the firm cannot or may not always provide the level of service they expect. "Educating customers" means providing customers with information about the service process or evaluative criteria about important aspects of the service. Finally, "managing internal marketing communication" means transmitting information across organizational boundaries—upward, downward, and across—to align all functions with customer expectations. Strategies in each of these categories are discussed in detail in the following sections.

FIGURE 16.3
Approaches for
Managing Service
Promises

Manage Service Promises

In manufacturing physical goods, the departments that make promises and those that deliver them can operate independently. Goods can be fully designed and produced and then turned over to marketing for promotion and sale. In services, however, the sales and marketing departments make promises about what other employees in the organization will fulfill. Because what employees do cannot be standardized like physical goods produced mechanically, greater coordination and management of promises are required. Successful services advertising and personal selling become the responsibility of both marketing and operations.

Figure 16.3 shows specific strategies that are effective in managing promises.

Create Effective Services Advertising

One of the most critical ways that services promises are communicated is through advertising. Intangibility makes services advertising different from product advertising and difficult for marketers. The intangible nature of services creates problems for consumers both before and after purchase. Before buying services, consumers have difficulty understanding them and coming up with sets of services to consider.[8] After buying services, consumers have trouble evaluating their service experiences. Various authors have suggested strategies to overcome these problems, but before we turn to them, we will discuss intangibility in greater depth.

Banwari Mittal described the difficulties associated with intangibility by dividing it into five properties, each of which has implications for services advertising. In his view, intangibility involves incorporeal existence, abstractness, generality, nonsearchability, and mental impalpability:[9]

- *Incorporeal existence.* The service product is neither made out of physical matter nor occupies physical space. Although the delivery mechanism (such as a Jiffy Lube outlet) may occupy space, the service itself (car servicing and oil change) does not. This lack of form makes showing the service difficult compared to showing a product.

- *Abstractness.* Services are considered apart from any particular instances or material objects.[10] Service benefits such as financial security, fun, or health do not correspond directly with objects, making them difficult to visualize and understand. The Ad Council and the U.S. State Department worked together to create a media campaign to promote American goodwill at home and abroad and to help fight the war against terrorism. This abstract concept was challenging to portray, and at this writing the Ad Council has not arrived at a sufficiently concrete and effective approach.[11]

- *Generality versus specificity. Generality* refers to a class of things, persons, events, or properties, whereas *specificity* refers to particular objects, people, or events. Many services and service promises are described in generalities (wonderful experience, superior education, completely satisfied customers), making them difficult to differentiate from those of competitors.

- *Nonsearchability.* Because service is a performance, it often cannot be previewed or inspected in advance of purchase. As we discussed in Chapter 3, nonsearchability is particularly true of services that are classified as either experience or credence services.

- *Mental impalpability.* Services are often too complex, multidimensional, and difficult to grasp mentally. Impalpability is the absence of prior exposure, familiarity, or knowledge, which makes services difficult to interpret.

According to Mittal, only incorporeal existence is an inevitable property of services. The other four properties often tend to be present but are not intrinsic to intangibility. By following the strategies shown in Exhibit 16.2, service advertising can overcome these challenging properties. The abstract can be made concrete, the general can be made specific, the nonsearchable can be made searchable, and the mentally impalpable can be made palpable.

Service marketers have developed guidelines for service advertising effectiveness. These guidelines include the following:

- *Use narratives to demonstrate the service experience.* Many services are experiential, and a uniquely effective approach to communicating them involves story-based appeals. Research has concluded that consumers with relatively low familiarity with a service category prefer appeals based on stories to appeals based on lists of service attributes. Furthermore, the relative advantage of the story is intensified when the novice consumer is in a happy mood rather than a sad one.[12]

- *Present vivid information.* Effective service advertising creates a strong or clear impression on the senses and produces a distinct mental picture. One way to use vivid information is to evoke strong emotion, such as in AT&T's classic "Reach Out and Touch Someone" campaign. Vividness can also be achieved by concrete language and dramatization. One of the most effective examples of vividness was an Ad Council advertisement called "I am an American," created after the September 11, 2001, attacks. The spot featured people of different races and cultures who were all American citizens. The ad was simple and powerful, and TV stations picked it up immediately. Using vivid information cues is particularly desirable when services are highly intangible and complex. A print example of vividness is shown in an ad for the United Negro College Fund. The abstract themes of "limitless potential" and "chance to achieve" are made vivid by a photograph of a mind filled with books.

- *Use interactive imagery.* One type of vividness involves what is called *interactive imagery.*[13] Imagery (defined as a mental event that involves the visualization of a concept or relationship) can enhance recall of names and facts about service. Interactive imagery integrates two or more items in some mutual action, resulting in improved recall. Some service companies effectively integrate their logos or symbols with an expression of what they do, such as the Prudential rock—the image of the rock is solid, and that impression is designed to carry over to the services company.

- *Focus on the tangibles.*[14] Another way that advertisers can increase the effectiveness of services communications is to feature the tangibles associated with the service, such as showing a bank's marble columns or gold credit card. Showing the tangibles provides clues about the nature and quality of the service. Figure 16.4, an advertisement for the Sierra Club, features the tangible benefits of the club in saving the gray wolf from extinction. Showing the wolf itself communicates the benefits of the organization emphatically, far more clearly than if words alone were used.

Property of Intangibility	Advertising Strategy	Description
Incorporeal existence	Physical representation	Show physical components of service that are unique, indicate high quality, and create the right association.
Generality	System documentation	Objectively document physical system capacity by showing facts and figures.
	Performance documentation	Document and cite past positive performance statistics.
	Service performance episode	Present a vivid story of an actual service delivery incident that relates to the important service attribute.
Abstractness	Service consumption episode	Capture and display typical customers benefiting from the service, evoking particular incidents.
Nonsearchability	Performance documentation	Cite independently audited performance.
	Consumption documentation	Obtain and present customer testimonials.
Impalpability	Service process episode	Present a vivid documentary on the step-by-step service process.
	Case history episode	Present an actual case history of what the firm did for a specific client

Source: Adapted from B. Mittal, "The Advertising of Services: Meeting the Challenge of Intangibility," *Journal of Service Research* 2, no. 1, August 1999, pp. 98–116.

- Berry and Clark propose four strategies of tangibilization: association, physical representation, documentation, and visualization.[15] *Association* means linking the service to a tangible person, place, or object, such as "being in good hands with Allstate." *Physical representation* means showing tangibles that are directly or indirectly part of the service, such as employees, buildings, or equipment. *Documentation* means featuring objective data and factual information. *Visualization* is a vivid mental picture of a service's benefits or qualities, such as showing people on vacation having fun. Our Strategy Insight shows how advertising icons can be used as tangibles.

FIGURE 16.4
This advertisement for the Sierra Club features the gray wolf as a way to communicate the organization's efforts in a tangible and concrete way.

Source: Courtesy of the Sierra Club.

BACK BY POPULAR DEMAND.

It took a public outcry and an act of Congress to save the gray wolf from literally vanishing off the face of the earth. But we did it. Today, a lot of other creatures face similar extinction. And unless we step up our efforts to protect their habitats, they may not be so lucky. At the Sierra Club, we've mounted a major campaign to defend the Endangered Species Act and preserve threatened habitats before their inhabitants are gone forever. Please, contact us to find out how you can help protect threatened and endangered animals. Because no amount of popular demand can bring an extinct species back to life.

Protect America's Environment: For Our Families, For Our Future.

85 Second Street, San Francisco, CA 94105 • (415) 977-5653
Or visit our website at: www.sierraclub.org
Email us at: information@sierraclub.org

- *Feature service employees in communication.* Customer contact personnel are an important second audience for services advertising.[16] Featuring actual employees doing their jobs or explaining their services in advertising is effective for both the primary audience (customers) and the secondary audience (employees) because it communicates to employees that they are important. Furthermore, when employees who perform a service well are featured in advertising, they become standards for

How does an advertiser of services gain competitive differentiation and strong brand awareness in a highly competitive market? In the fast-food and insurance industries, one answer is to create a recognizable brand icon that represents the company and generates brand visibility. One of the most enduring service brand icons is Ronald McDonald, the red-and-yellow clown that represents McDonald's and its children's charity, the Ronald McDonald House. Originally played by the Today Show's meteorologist Willard Scott, Ronald is now played by a real Ringling Brothers' clown.

McDonald's competitor, Jack in the Box, has its own mascot named Jack, a ball-shaped head with a pointed hat. In television advertising, he appears as the "founder" of the chain—part clown and part businessman in a suit with the head of the icon. He is always part fun and part serious, such as in one television spot introducing the Chipotle Chicken Sandwich. While searching for new ingredients in a produce market, Jack encounters a woman who tells him about chipotle peppers. Jack, who cannot say the word—using mispronunciations such as "chi-poddle"—contorts his blue smile into squiggly lines. The company's advertising agency, Secret Weapon, introduced Jack more than five years ago and creates 18 to 25 spots for Jack in the Box each year, all featuring Jack.

Advertising icons are even more critical in industries in which the service is complex and difficult to understand. Insurance is an example. Aflac, a company that sells supplemental insurance on a voluntary basis in U.S. and Japanese worksites, faced a difficult challenge: getting potential customers to ask for its service by name. Enter the Aflac duck, an insistent and vocal character who screams "Aflac!" in commercials in which actors are trying to solve their insurance problems. The comic Gilbert Gottfried is responsible for the waterfowl's unrelenting honk. During the 2004 Summer Olympics, the Aflac duck was featured in a memorable television ad with a team of performing synchronized swimmers, one of which proclaimed, "You know, some people don't think what we do is a sport because you can't get hurt doing it." Another swimmer goes on to say that if injuries would occur, they would need insurance, whereupon the Aflac duck rises out of the circle of swimmers. At the peak of his ascent, he cries "Aflac!" after which he tries to follow the swimmers into the ladies' locker room. The humorous ending, where he is kicked out by a female swimmer, closes with "Aflac, ask for it at work." The duck, introduced in 2000, has generated such visibility that he has been featured on CNBC, *The Tonight Show With Jay Leno*, and *Saturday Night Live.*

Geico, an insurance company that specializes in automobile insurance, features a wisecracking gecko that is constantly forced to correct unfortunates who confuse the words "gecko" and "Geico." The mascot helps customers remember the company's difficult brand name and provides a tangible that unifies the company's humorous advertising. One 2004 television commercial features a young driver in sunglasses on a mountain road moving his head to rock music. The camera pans to the passenger's seat where the gecko, wearing sunglasses and a seatbelt, is also keeping time to the music. The company's video and print messages motivate potential customers to call or go to the Web for more information. One of the most memorable of the 2004 commercials is called "Robot" and opens with an executive of the firm reading a customer's letter. The letter reads, "Yo, I think that your Website would be da bomb if you had the gecko do the robot," after which the gecko enters dancing "the robot" to an upbeat song. The spot ends with the executive doing a bad imitation of the gecko's dancing.

continued

Don't take high car insurance rates lying down.

GEICO®
geico.com

Get a FREE rate quote today.

1-800-555-9128

Source: Courtesy of GEICO Insurance

Not all advertising icons are successful and lovable. Bob Garfield of AdAge.com roundly criticized Burger King's new 2004 King icon, describing him as "one of the creepiest characters we've ever seen on television." He further describes the monarch: "His face is frozen in a sickly grin. His head is far out of proportion to his body, like Tyrannosaurus Rex or Jay Leno." At this writing, we do not know if the King will survive, but we feel confident he won't be as revered as the gecko, the Aflac duck, Jack, or Ronald McDonald.

Sources: www.geico.com; www.Aflac.com; "Who's Your Favorite Advertising Icon?" advertising insert, *The New York Times*, Monday, September 20, 2004, p. 6; Bob Garfield, "Burger King's Dreadful New 'King' Commercial: Waking Up with a Truly Creepy Bed Partner," AdAge.com, October 18, 2004, QuikFIND ID:AAQ04V.

other employees' behaviors. An advertisement for GM's Mr. Goodwrench points out to both consumers and employees that the company hires females.

- *Promise what is possible.*[17] Many companies hope to create good service by leading with good advertising, but this strategy can backfire when the actual service does not live up to the promises in advertising. In line with the strategies we discuss in the next section, all service communications should promise only what is possible and not attempt to make services more attractive than they actually are.

- *Encourage word-of-mouth communication.* Because services are usually high in experience and credence properties, people frequently turn to others for information rather than to traditional marketing channels. Services advertising and other external messages can generate word-of-mouth communication that extends the investment in paid communication and improves the credibility of the messages. Advertising that generates talk because it is humorous, compelling, or unique can be particularly effective.

- *Feature service customers.* One way to generate positive word of mouth is to feature satisfied customers in the communications. Advertising testimonials featuring actual service customers simulate personal communications between people and are thereby a credible way to communicate the benefits of service. A 2004 advertising campaign for Blue Cross/Blue Shield of North Carolina featured real customers whose family members suffered medical crises that were handled successfully by the health insurance company. The testimonials were powerful and believable, particularly one featuring two parents and their cancer-surviving son, Davis. The campaign helped restore faith in the health insurance and generated positive word of mouth.

- *Use transformational advertising.*[18] Transformational advertising is image advertising that changes the experience of buying and consuming the product. Most advertising for vacation destinations is transformational: It invites the consumer to escape into a world that is necessarily subjective and perceptual. This approach involves making the ad vivid or rich in detail, realistic, and rewarding.

Coordinate External Communication

For any organization, one of the most important yet challenging aspects of managing brand image involves coordinating all the external communication vehicles that send information to customers. These communication vehicles include advertising, websites, sales promotion, public relations, direct marketing, and personal selling.

Advertising is any paid form of nonpersonal presentation and promotion of a company's offerings by an identified sponsor. Dominant advertising vehicles include television, radio, newspapers, magazines, outdoor signage, and the Internet. Because advertising is paid, marketers control the creative appeals, placement, and timing. Internet advertising is becoming a more important and larger portion of companies' advertising budgets (see the Technology Spotlight) and should be synchronized with traditional advertising vehicles. MasterCard's highly successful "Priceless" advertising campaign, which launched in 1997, lists three or four tangible items and their prices followed by a key customer benefit that is "priceless." The campaign is an example of solid synchronization because it is "extraordinarily flexible, and carries a brand message that is not only relevant globally but also adapts well to different media, different payment channels, different markets."[19] The campaign, now seen in 96 countries and 47 languages, has generated strong brand recall and has received the advertising industry's prestigious Gold Effie, Addy, and Cresta awards.

Websites are the company's own online communication to customers. Often a disconnect exists between the look, feel, and content of a company's website and its advertising, usually because different parts of the company (or different advertising vendors) are responsible for creating these vehicles. When websites are coordinated in theme, content, and promises—as they are in the DHL advertising in this chapter's opening vignette—a company is better able to match service delivery with promises because the promises themselves are consistent.

Sales promotion includes short-term incentives such as coupons, premiums, discounts, and other activities that stimulate customer purchases and stretch media spending. The fast-food industry, including McDonald's, Burger King, and Wendy's, offers premiums such as action figures that link the chains' offerings to current movies and television shows. A particularly successful version of joint promotions between service advertisers and entertainment was created by CKE Restaurants' Carl's Jr. The restaurant incorporated footage of television season premieres, finales, and other television shows into the company's advertising, "[deliver]ing upwards of 30% of a stretch in media spending."[20]

Technology Spotlight
Internet Advertising Surges

Since 1994, when the first Internet banner ad went online, advertisers have spent billions of dollars to catch the attention of online users. Today, Web ads are a $9 billion per year business, surpassing the previous high of $8 billion at the 2000 peak of the dot-com boom. Internet advertising spending is also growing at the highest rate of increase ever—25 percent in 2004, reports the digital market research firm eMarketer. David Hallerman, eMarketer's senior analyst, claims that the factors leading to the surge in online advertising include growing numbers of large companies that are shifting larger parts of their ad budgets to online. A major industry study from the Interactive Advertising Bureau and Pricewaterhouse-Coopers showed that online advertising revenue for the first six months of 2004 increased to $4.6 billion—a 40 percent rise over the first half of 2003. The study, which represents data from all companies that report meaningful online ad information, showed that consumer advertisers, computing, financial services, media, and health advertisers were the biggest spenders.

The increase in online advertising is due in large part to consumers' changing preferences in media. Although television and newspapers used to be the media of choice, consumers in all age groups up to age 54 currently select the Internet as their top medium, according to the Generational Media Study released by the Online Publishers Association. A full 70 percent use the Internet for entertainment, and 67 percent of the high-spending 25- to 34-year-old and 35- to 54-year-old groups said content on the Internet provides them with useful information about products and services. Another study, the Internet Deprivation Study conducted by Yahoo! and OMD, a media-buying organization, found that the Internet is indispensable to consumers. When 28 people received $150 each to stay off the Internet for two weeks, they were lost in figuring out how to pay bills, make vacation plans, take breaks from work, keep up with the news, and stay in touch with friends. With the Internet so pervasive in people's lives, advertisers recognize that reaching consumers through this vehicle is worth more now than ever.

Another major factor contributing to the success of Internet advertising is the availability of advertising approaches that are more popular than the banner ad, which dominated the medium for years.

BANNER ADS: THE PAST
Banner ads still account for the largest category of Internet ads, but their effectiveness as a marketing tool is being seriously questioned. Click-through rates, the most common measure of effectiveness, have dropped from 10 percent to .025 percent over the years. Analysts suggest the following reasons for the drop:

- *Banner clutter* As spending increased, so did the number of ads, which reduced the novelty and created sites filled with banners that often led to no value. Just as with other advertising clutter, users learned to stop paying attention.

- *Boring banners* Although the potential to create fun and interactive banner ads existed, many advertisers simply created me-too banners that were low on content and creativity.

- *Built-in banners* Once advertisers started using animation and other colorful attention-getting devices, the ads became intrusive, interfering with the users' surfing stream and with the time they spent on sites.

Public relations include activities that build a favorable company image with a firm's publics through publicity, relations with the news media, and community events. Richard Branson, founder of Virgin Atlantic Airways (see our Global Feature) is a master at obtaining publicity for his airline. When launching the airline, he claimed, "I knew that the only way of competing with British Airways and the others was to get out there and use myself to promote it."[21] In the years since the airline's launch, his publicity-winning stunts included recording the fastest time across the Atlantic Ocean in a speedboat, flying a hot-air balloon across the Atlantic Ocean and from Japan to Canada, dressing up in everything from a stewardess's uniform to a bikini on Virgin flights, and being photographed in his bath.

Some ads took so long to download that they delayed and derailed users' interactions on the Web.

Advertisers had to face the fact that their hopes for banner ads were not being fulfilled, at least as measured simply by click-through rates.

PAID SEARCH ADVERTISING: THE PRESENT

Improved advertising approaches have been developed in the last three years, with the most significant being search-based advertising, or paid search advertising. In this form of advertising, which currently represents the largest share of online spending among all online ad formats, advertisers pay only when qualified leads are delivered to their websites. With AdWords, a pay-per-click advertising service offered by Google, advertisers buy the rights to words and terms related to their business. When a consumer searches Google using one of those keywords, the advertiser's URL, along with its name and description, appears in a colored box beside the search results. The advertiser pays only when a user clicks on the ad, and the going rate is as little as 5 cents per click.

RICH MEDIA AND FLASH ANIMATIONS: THE FUTURE

Rich media—the use of flash animations and streaming video—rose by 65 percent in 2004 and is predicted to grow faster than search marketing. More than 42 percent of all online ads include some form of rich media, according to DoubleClick's second quarter 2004 Ad Serving Trends report. Rich media can easily be coordinated with television advertising because it can contain moving images. Using the same creative approach in interactive rich media, as DHL does (see the website mentioned in this chapter's opening vignette), creates synergies that extend the advertising impact. Rich media ads stand out more than banner ads, and innovations are constantly being developed. Point Roll is a promising approach that enables advertisers to simultaneously deliver multiple ad messages within a single banner ad when users point and roll their mouse across the banner. LiquidImage ads allow a user to reveal hidden layers of editorial content, streaming audio and video, advertising information, and e-commerce capabilities.

COMBINING CLICKS AND BRICKS

Marketers recognize that managing their media planning and buying strategy as a whole, rather than as segregated channels, maximizes campaign effectiveness. For this reason, more and more advertisers are adding online advertising to their traditional advertising buys. Today, online advertising accounts for a small percentage of total advertising expenditures, largely because the medium is not as costly as television or print. In the future, as consumers spend more time on the Web, Internet advertising will become even more important than before.

Sources: Kris Oser, "Internet Ad Revenue Grew 43% in Second Quarter: Search Advertising Continues to Show Strongest Growth," *AdAge.com*, September 21, 2004, QwikFIND ID: AAP98U; Kris Oser, "More Marketing Budgets Shift Money Online: Advertising Week Buzzes about Growing Impact of Internet," *AdAge.com*, September 27, 2004, QwikFIND ID: AAP99T; Kris Oser, "Ad Spending Returns to Good Old Days: 2004 Total Will Top Pre-Dot-Com-Crash High by $1 Billion," *AdAge.com*, August 10, 2004, QwikFIND ID: AAP87R; Karen J. Bannan, "Seven Ways to Make Online Advertising Work for You," *Advertising Age*, Oct 11, 2004, p. 11; Roby Bayani, "Banner Ads—Still Working After All These Years?" *Link-up*, November/December 2001, p. 2, 6.

Direct marketing involves the use of mail, telephone, fax, e-mail, and other tools to communicate directly with specific consumers to obtain a direct response. American Express is a service company that uses direct marketing extensively and ensures that it integrates well with all other messages, including interactive messages from employees. As the executive vice president of global advertising at American Express clearly states,

> Service brands are not created solely in advertising. In fact, much of a brand's equity stems from the direct consumer experiences with the brand. We partner with Bronner [Bronner, Slosberg Humphrey, a relationship marketing company] to help us manage consumer experiences with our brand across all products and services—Card, Travel, Financial Services, and Relationship Services—via all direct channels, including phone, Internet, and mail.[22]

Michael Bronner, the founder of the relationship marketing company that American Express uses, emphasizes the need for coordinating external and interactive marketing communications: "The client [such as American Express] may spend millions on network advertising but lose when the customer is working his way through layer upon layer of voice response options on the customer service line."[23]

Personal selling is face-to-face presentation by a representative from the firm to make sales and build customer relationships. One way that personal selling and advertising are integrated in business-to-business companies is through the development of advertising materials that salespeople distribute to customers. This approach not only creates an integrated message to customers but also keeps salespeople fully informed of the promises the company is making.

Our Global Feature shows an international campaign for Virgin Atlantic Airways that uses many elements of the advertising mix.

Make Realistic Promises

The expectations that customers bring to the service affect their evaluations of its quality: The higher the expectation, the higher the delivered service must be to be perceived as high quality. Therefore, promising reliability in advertising is appropriate only when reliability is actually delivered. It is essential for a firm's marketing or sales department to understand the actual levels of service delivery (percentage of times the service is provided correctly, or percentage and number of problems that arise) before making promises about reliability. To be appropriate and effective, communications about service quality must accurately reflect what customers will actually receive in service encounters.

Offer Service Guarantees

As discussed in Chapter 8, service guarantees are formal promises made to customers about aspects of the service they will receive. Although many services carry implicit service satisfaction guarantees, the true benefits from them—an increase in the likelihood of a customer choosing or remaining with the company—come only when the customer knows that guarantees exist and trusts that the company will stand behind them.

Manage Customer Expectations

Many service companies find themselves in the position of having to tell customers that service previously provided will be discontinued or available only at a higher price. In the 1990s, service from large computer companies such as IBM typically included salespeople who interacted with customers in person. This level of service attention was deemed necessary (because without it customers comprehended neither the options nor their needs adequately) and worthwhile (because almost all customers were perceived to be potentially large customers for computers). When demand for computers shifted from mainframes to PCs, the personal attention provided by direct salespeople was no longer necessary or cost-effective. Instead of the traditional face-to-face service, the companies shifted to telephone interaction alone, a distinct—and for many customers disappointing—departure from the past. Credit card companies that offer multiple value-added services when interest rates are high also find that they need to withdraw these services when interest rates drop.

Service delivery has been cut back in many service industries, but few as dramatically as in the health care industry. Hospital patients now experience far shorter stays and fewer diagnostic procedures. Patients requiring psychotherapy are limited to six

"A brand name that is known internationally for innovation, quality and a sense of fun—this is what we have always aspired to with Virgin." Richard Branson

Richard Branson, first known for Virgin Records, the legendary record label that signed the Rolling Stones, Janet Jackson, and The Human League, surprised the world in 1984 when he launched an upstart airline called Virgin Atlantic Airways. His vision was to create a high-quality, value-for-the-money airline to challenge the UK's market leader, British Airways. Twenty years later, Virgin Atlantic is the third-largest European carrier over the North Atlantic and includes destinations in the United States, Caribbean, Far East, India, China, Hong Kong, and Africa.

Parent company Virgin Group, with combined sales exceeding $2 billion, is known worldwide as an innovative global brand with megastore music retailing, book and software publishing, film and video editing facilities, clubs, trains, and financial advising through more than 100 companies in 15 countries. Virgin Atlantic Airways' brand and marketing campaign epitomizes successful global communication, with universal marketing components that are integrated in theme and design across the world as well as individual advertisements that adapt to geographies.

Source: Courtesy Virgin Atlantic Airways

Source: Red Advertising & Marketing, Barbados, W.I./Courtesy Virgin Atlantic Airways.

Virgin Atlantic Airways' common global marketing elements include its brand values, logo, and distinctive airplanes. The airlines' brand values—"caring, honest, value, fun, innovative"—are executed in all communications and strategies. Virgin focuses on customer service and low cost while also being the first to offer up unique services. For example, Virgin was the first airline to install television screens in every seat, offer massages and beauty services in first class, and mount a gambling casino right in the plane! The red and white logo, in the shape of an airline tail fin, appears in all worldwide advertising media including television, press, magazines, price promotions, outdoor posters, and taxi sides. Another common image is the company's Flying Lady, a Vargas painting of a red-headed, scantily-dressed woman holding a scarf. Distinctive airplanes feature the Flying Lady on the fuselage and Union Jacks on their wings in three core colors of red, purple and silver metallic. Even the paint technology—based on mica, a hard mineral that produces a pearl-like shine—is unique. When the iridescent gleam combines with the plane's vibrant colors, the aircraft stirs up memories of the 1930s, when flying was glamorous and romantic.

As shown in the accompanying international advertisement, Virgin Atlantic Airways manages to translate its brand themes in culturally specific ways while retaining its global image. The Caribbean ad draws in readers with its bananas. Although the text and appeal change to suit the culture, all international advertisements contain the same Virgin Atlantic Airways logo and the same company colors.

Source: www.virgin-atlantic.com

FIGURE 16.5
**Approaches for
Managing Customer
Expectations**

visits unless their doctors can substantiate in writing the need for more. Alcohol treatment is handled on an outpatient rather than inpatient basis.

How can a company gracefully give the customer news that service will not be as expected? Figure 16.5 summarizes four strategies.

Offer Choices

One way to reset expectations is to give customers options for aspects of service that are meaningful, such as time and cost. A clinical psychologist charging $100 per hour, for example, might offer clients the choice between a price increase of $10 per hour or a reduction in the number of minutes comprising the hour (such as 50 minutes). With the choice, clients can select the aspect of the trade-off (time or money) that is most meaningful to them. Making the choice solidifies the client's expectations of service.

This strategy is effective in business-to-business situations, particularly in terms of speed versus quality. Customers who are time conscious often want reports, proposals, or other written documents quickly. When asked to provide a 10-page proposal for a project within three days, an architectural firm responded that it could provide either a 2-page proposal in three days or a 10-page proposal in a week. Its customer selected the latter option, recognizing that the deadline could be extended. In most business-to-business services, speed is often essential but threatens performance. If customers understand the trade-off and are asked to make a choice, they are likely to be more satisfied because their service expectations for each option become more realistic.

Create Tiered-Value Service Offerings

Product companies are accustomed to offering different versions of their products with prices commensurate with the value customers perceive. Automobiles with different configurations of features carry price tags that match not their cost but instead their perceived value to the customer. This same type of formal bundling and pricing can be accomplished in services, with the extra benefit of managing expectations.

Credit card companies offer tiered-value offerings. American Express has multiple levels of credit card services based on the type of service provided: the traditional green card offers basic service features, the gold card additional benefits, and the platinum card still more. Two advantages of tiered offerings are (1) the practice puts the burden of choosing the service level on the customer, thereby familiarizing the customer with specific service expectations and (2) the company can identify which customers are willing to pay higher prices for higher service levels.

The opportunity to set expectations accurately is present when the customer makes the decision at the time of purchase when customers can be reminded of the terms of the agreement if they request support that is above the level in the contract.

Communicate the Criteria and Levels of Service Effectiveness

At times companies can establish the criteria by which customers assess service. Consider a business customer who is purchasing market research services for the first time. Because market research is an expert service, it is high in credence properties that are hard for customers to judge. Moreover, the effectiveness of this type of service differs depending on the objectives the client brings to the service. In this situation, a service provider can teach the customer the criteria by which to evaluate the service. The provider that teaches the customer in a credible manner will have an advantage in shaping the evaluation process.

As an example, consider research company A, which communicates the following criteria to the customer: (1) a low price signals low quality, (2) reputation of the firm is critical, and (3) person-to-person interviews are the only type of customer feedback that will provide accurate information. A customer who accepts these criteria will evaluate all other suppliers using them. If research company B had talked to the customer first, consider these (very different!) criteria and their impact on the buyer: (1) market research companies with good reputations are charging for their reputation, not their skill, (2) telephone interviews have been found to work as well as person-to-person interviews, and (3) price does not indicate quality level.

The same approach can be used with service *levels* rather than evaluative criteria. If research company B provides four-day turnaround on the results of the data analysis, the company has just set the customer's expectation level for all other suppliers.

Negotiate Unrealistic Expectations

Sometimes customers express service requests as they would their lowest bid at a garage sale. The service they request for the price they are willing to pay is unrealistic; they know it and the firm knows it. It is, in effect, a starting point for discussion, not the expected end point. In these situations successful service providers present their offerings in terms of value and not price alone. They also negotiate more realistic expectations.

Improve Customer Education

As discussed in Chapter 13, customers must perform their roles properly for many services to be effective. If customers forget to perform their roles, or perform them improperly, disappointment may result. For this reason, communication to customers can take the form of customer education. Figure 16.6 shows several types of customer education approaches that can help match promises with delivery.

Prepare Customers for the Service Process

One of us, on a return trip from Singapore on Singapore Airlines, neglected to heed the airline's warning that return flights to the United States must be confirmed 24 hours in advance. On my arrival at the airport to return home, my seat had been given to another customer who had conformed to the airline's request for confirmation. Depending on the perspective taken, you could argue that either the company or the customer was

FIGURE 16.6
**Approaches for
Improving Customer
Education**

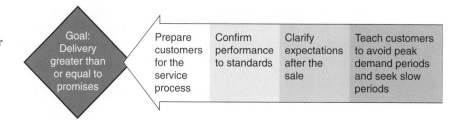

right in this situation. Whose responsibility is it to make sure that customers perform their roles properly?

Companies can avoid such situations by preparing customers for the service process. And companies may need to prepare the customer often, even every step of the way, for the subsequent actions the customer needs to take. A business-to-business example will help illustrate this strategy.

Customers of management consulting services purchase intangible benefits: marketing effectiveness, motivated workforces, culture change. The very fact that companies purchase these services usually indicates that they do not know how to perform them alone. Many clients will also not know what to look for along the way to judge progress. In management consulting and other complex service situations, the effective provider prepares the customer for the service process and creates structure for the customer. At the beginning of the engagement, the management consulting firm establishes checkpoints throughout the process, at which times progress will be evaluated, and also leads the customer to establish objectives for project completion. Because customers do not know what that progress will look like, the consulting firm takes the lead in setting goals or criteria to be examined at those times.

A similar approach is effective with individual service customers. Do you remember registration at the beginning of your first college semester or quarter? How aware were you of the steps in the process and where to go after each step? It is unlikely that directions, even in great detail, made you feel confident and competent in the new service experience. You may have required step-by-step—"next call this telephone number or go to page B"—guidance.

As these examples show, any time a customer is inexperienced or a service process is new or unique, education about what to expect is essential.

Confirm Performance to Standards and Expectations

Service providers sometimes provide service, even explicitly requested service, yet fail to communicate to the customer that it has been accomplished. These providers stop short of getting credit for their actions when they do not reinforce actions with communication about their fulfillment of the request. This situation may happen under one or more of the following conditions:

- The customer cannot evaluate the effectiveness of a service.

- The decision maker in the service purchase is a person different from the users of the service.

- The service is invisible.

- The provider depends on others to perform some of the actions to fulfill customer expectations.

When customers cannot evaluate service effectiveness, usually because they are inexperienced or the service is technical, the provider may fail to communicate specific actions that address client concerns because the actions seem too complex for the customer to comprehend. In this situation, the service provider can improve perceptions by translating the actions into customer-friendly terms. A personal injury lawyer who aids a client with the medical and financial implications of an accident needs to be able to tell the client in language the client can understand that the lawyer has performed the necessary actions.

When the decision maker in service purchases is different from the users of the service, a wide discrepancy in satisfaction may exist between decision makers and users. An example is in the purchase of information technology products and services in a company. The decision maker—the manager of information technology or someone in a similar position—makes the purchase decisions and understands the service promises. If users are not involved in the purchase process, they may not know what has been promised and may be dissatisfied.

Customers are not always aware of everything done behind the scenes to serve them well. Most services have invisible support processes. For instance, physicians frequently request diagnostic tests to rule out possible causes for illness. When these tests come back negative, doctors may neglect to inform patients. Many hairstyling firms have guarantees that ensure customer satisfaction with haircuts, permanents, and color treatments. However, only a few of them actively communicate these guarantees in advertising because they assume customers know about them. The firm that explicitly communicates the guarantee may be selected over others by a customer who is uncertain about the quality of the service. Making customers aware of standards or efforts to improve service that are not readily apparent can improve service quality perceptions.

Clarify Expectations after the Sale

When service involves a hand-off between sales and operations, as it does in most companies, clarifying expectations with customers helps the service delivery arm of the company to align with customer expectations. Salespeople are motivated and compensated to raise customer expectations—at least to the point of making the sale—rather than to communicate realistically what the company can provide. In these situations, service providers can avoid future disappointment by clarifying what was promised as soon as the hand-off is made.

Teach Customers to Avoid Peak Demand Periods and Seek Slow Demand Periods

Few customers want to face lines or delays in receiving services. In the words of two researchers, "At best, waiting takes their time, and at worst, they may experience a range of unpleasant reactions—feeling trapped, tired, bored, angry, or demeaned."[24] In a bank setting, researchers tested three strategies for dealing with customer waits: (1) giving customers prior notice of busy times, (2) having employees apologize for the delays, and (3) assigning all visible employees to serving customers. Only the first strategy focuses on educating customers; the other two involve managing employees. Researchers expected—and confirmed—that customers warned of a wait in line tended to minimize the negative effects of waiting to justify their decision to seek service at peak times. In general, customers given a card listing the branch's busiest and slowest times were more satisfied with the banking service. The other two strategies, apology and all-tellers-serving, showed no effects on satisfaction.[25] Educating customers to avoid peak times benefits both customers (through faster service) and companies (by easing the problem of overdemand).

Manage Internal Marketing Communication

The fourth major category of strategies necessary to match service delivery with promises involves managing internal marketing communications (see Figure 16.7). Internal marketing communications can be both vertical and horizontal. *Vertical communications* are either downward, from management to employees, or upward, from employees to management. *Horizontal communications* are those across functional boundaries in an organization.

Create Effective Vertical Communications

Companies that give customer contact employees adequate information, tools, and skills allow them to perform successful interactive marketing. Some of these skills come through training and other human resource efforts discussed in Chapter 12, but some are provided through downward communication. Among the most important forms of downward communication are company newsletters and magazines, corporate television networks, e-mail, briefings, videotapes and internal promotional campaigns, and recognition programs. One of the keys to successful downward communication is keeping employees informed of everything that is being conveyed to customers through external marketing. Employees should see company advertising before it is aired or published and should be familiar with the website, mailings, and direct selling approaches used. If these vertical communications are not present, both customers and employees suffer—customers will not receive the same messages from employees that they hear in company external marketing, and employees will feel uninformed and not be aware of what their company is doing. Customers come to them asking for services that have been marketed externally but not internally, making the employees feel uninformed, left out, and helpless.[26]

FIGURE 16.7
Approaches for Managing Internal Marketing Communications

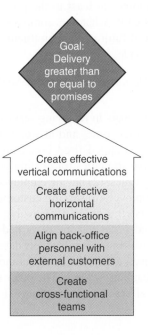

Upward communication is also necessary in closing the gap between service promises and service delivery. Employees are at the front line of service, and they know—more than anyone else in the organization—what can and cannot be delivered. They know when service breakdowns are occurring and, very often, why they are happening. Having open communication channels from employees to management can prevent service problems before they occur and minimize them when they do take place.

Create Effective Horizontal Communications

Horizontal communication—communication across functional boundaries in an organization—facilitates coordinated efforts for service delivery. This task is difficult because functions typically differ in goals, philosophies, outlooks, and views of the customer, but the payoff is high. Coordination between marketing and operations can result in communication that accurately reflects service delivery, thus reducing the gap between customer expectations and actual service delivery. Integration of effort between marketing and human resources can improve the ability of each employee to become a better marketer. Coordination between finance and marketing can create prices that accurately reflect the customer's evaluation of a service. In service firms, all these functions need to be integrated to produce consistent messages and to narrow the service gaps.

One important strategy for effective horizontal communications is to open channels of communication between the marketing department and operations personnel. For example, when a company creates advertising that depicts the service encounter, it is essential that the advertising accurately reflect what customers will experience in actual service encounters. Puffery or exaggeration puts service quality perceptions at risk, especially when the firm is consistently unable to deliver to the level of service portrayed in the advertising. Coordination and communication between advertising and service providers are pivotal in delivering service that meets expectations.

Featuring actual employees doing their jobs or explaining the services they provide, a strategy we mentioned earlier in this chapter, is one way to coordinate advertising portrayals and the reality of the service encounter. To create this type of advertising, the advertising department or agency interacts directly with service employees, facilitating horizontal communications. Similar benefits can be achieved if employees are included in the advertising process in other ways, such as by being shown advertising in its pretest forms.

Another important strategy for horizontal communications involves opening channels of communication between sales and operations. Mechanisms for achieving this goal can be formal or informal and can include annual planning meetings, retreats, team meetings, or workshops in which departments clarify service issues. In these sessions, the departments can interact to understand the goals, capabilities, and constraints of the other. Some companies hold "gap workshops" at which employees from both functions meet for a day or two to try to understand the difficulties in matching promises made through selling with delivery accomplished by operations personnel.[27]

Involving the operations staff in face-to-face meetings with external customers is also a strategy that allows operations personnel to more readily understand the salesperson's role and the needs and desires of customers. Rather than filtering customers' needs through the sales force, operations employees can witness firsthand the pressures and demands of customers. A frequent and desirable result is better service to the internal customer—the salesperson—from the operations staff as they become aware of their own roles in satisfying both external and internal customers.

Align Back-Office and Support Personnel with External Customers through Interaction or Measurement

As companies become increasingly customer focused, frontline personnel develop improved skills in discerning what customers require. As they become more knowledgeable about and empathetic toward external customers, they also experience intrinsic rewards for satisfying customers. Back-office or support personnel, who typically do not interact directly with external customers, miss out on this bonding and, as a consequence, fail to gain the skills and rewards associated with it.

Interaction   Companies are creating ways to facilitate the interaction between back-office and support personnel and external customers. Weyerhaeuser, for example, sends hourly employees to customers' plants to better understand their needs. When actual interaction is difficult or impossible, some companies videotape customers in their service facilities during the purchase and consumption process to vividly portray needs and requirements of customers and to show personnel the support that frontline people need to deliver to those expectations.

Measurement   When company measurement systems are established, employees are sometimes judged on the basis of how they perform for the next internal customer in the chain. Although this approach provides feedback in terms of how well the employees are serving the internal customer, it lacks the motivation and reward that come from seeing their efforts affect the end customer. Federal Express has aligned internal personnel with the external customer using measurement. As we discussed in Chapter 10, FedEx's service quality indicator (SQI) computes daily the number of company-wide service failures. To clearly communicate customer fail points to internal employees, the company created linking measures to trace the causes to each internal department. For example, the company's information technology department affects 8 of the 12 SQI measurements and therefore has submeasures that provide feedback on how the department's work is affecting the SQI.

Create Cross-Functional Teams

Another approach to improving horizontal communications to better serve customers is to involve employees in cross-functional teams to align their jobs with end customer requirements. For example, if a team of telecommunications service representatives is working to improve interaction with customers, back-office people such as computer technicians or training personnel can become part of the team. The team then learns requirements and sets goals for achieving them together, an approach that directly creates communications across the functions.

The cross-functional team approach can best be explained by the examples of an advertising agency. The individual in an advertising agency who typically interacts directly with the client is the account executive (often called a "suit" by the creative staff). In the traditional agency, the account executive visits the client, elicits client expectations, and then interacts with the various departments in the agency (art, copywriting, production, traffic, and media buying) that will perform the work. All functions are specialized and, in the extreme case, get direction for their portion of the work right from the account executive. A cross-functional team approach has representatives from all the areas meet with the account executive, even the client, and collectively discuss the account and approaches to address client needs. Each team member brings his or her function's perspectives and opens communication. All members can then understand the constraints and schedules of the other groups.

Summary

Discrepancies between service delivery and external communications have a strong effect on customer perceptions of service quality. In this chapter we discussed the role of and need for integrated services marketing communications in minimizing these discrepancies. We described external, interactive, and internal marketing communications using the service triangle and emphasized the need to coordinate all three forms to deliver service that meets customer expectations. We also discussed the factors that lead to problems in marketing communications and four sets of strategies to deal with them. These strategies include (1) managing service promises, (2) managing customer expectations, (3) improving customer education, and (4) managing internal marketing communications.

Discussion Questions

1. Think of another services company that provides integrated services marketing communications. Is it as comprehensive as DHL's campaign, as described in the opening vignette? Why or why not?

2. Which of the key reasons for provider gap 4 discussed in the beginning of this chapter is the easiest to address in a company? Which is the hardest to address? Why?

3. Review the four general strategies for achieving integrated services marketing communications. Would all these strategies be relevant in goods firms? Which would be most critical in goods firms? Which would be most critical in services firms? Are there any differences between those most critical in goods firms and those most critical in services firms?

4. What are the most effective Internet advertisements you have seen? Why are they effective?

5. Using the section on managing customer expectations, put yourself in the position of your professor, who must reduce the amount of "service" provided to the students in your class. Give an example of each strategy in this context. Which of the strategies would work best with you (the student) in managing your expectations? Why?

6. Why is internal marketing communication so important in service firms? Is it important in product firms?

7. Which form of internal marketing communication—vertical or horizontal—would you invest in if you had to select between them as an organization's CEO? Why?

8. What other strategies can you add to the four offered in the section on customer education? What types of education do you expect from service firms? Give an example of a firm from which you have received adequate education. What firm has not provided you with adequate education?

Exercises

1. Go to the DHL website referred to in the opening vignette. Explore each area of the site, and make a list of the types of information you can find based on the three categories of marketing communication (external, interactive, internal) discussed in this chapter. What additional information do you find useful on the site?

2. Find five effective service advertisements in newspapers and magazines. According to the criteria given in this chapter, identify why they are effective. Critique them using the list of criteria, and discuss ways they could be improved.

Notes

1. Ian Putzger, "Shifting Gears," *Journal of Commerce*, August 2, 2004, p. l.
2. Robin Londner, "Ads Will Tell What's Yellow, Red, and Brings Packages," *South Florida Business Journal*, June 18, 2004, p. A13.
3. "Going for Gold in B-to-B Marketing," *B to B*, September 13, 2004, p. 38.
4. Ibid.
5. Matthew Creamer, "DHL Bets on Flexibility as It Moves on FedEx, UPS in U.S.," *Advertising Age*, September 6, 2004, p. 8.
6. Londner, "Ads Will Tell."
7. P. G. Lindell, "You Need Integrated Attitude to Develop IMC," *Marketing News*, May 26, 1997, p. 5.
8. D. Legg and J. Baker, "Advertising Strategies for Service Firms," in *Add Value to Your Service,* ed. C. Suprenant (Chicago: American Marketing Association, 1987), pp. 163–68.
9. B. Mittal, "The Advertising of Services: Meeting the Challenge of Intangibility," *Journal of Service Research* 2 (August 1999), pp. 98–116.
10. E. Breivik and S. V. Troye, "Dimensions of Intangibility and Their Impact on Product Evaluations," *Developments in Marketing Science* 19, ed. E. Wilson and J. Hair (Miami, FL: Academy of Marketing Science, 1996), pp. 56–59.
11. P. Albiniak, "Promoting the United States," *Broadcasting and Cable,* October 29, 2001, p. 26.
12. A. S. Mattila, "The Role of Narratives in the Advertising of Experiential Services," *Journal of Service Research* 3 (August 2000), pp. 35–45.
13. K. L. Alesandri, "Strategies That Influence Memory for Advertising Communications," in *Information Processing Research in Advertising,* ed. R. J. Harris (Hillsdale, NJ: Erlbaum, 1983).
14. L. L. Berry and T. Clark, "Four Ways to Make Services More Tangible," *Business,* October–December 1986, pp. 53–54.
15. Ibid.
16. W. R. George and L. L. Berry, "Guidelines for the Advertising of Services," *Business Horizons,* May–June 1981, pp. 52–56.
17. Ibid.
18. B. Mittal, "The Advertising of Services."
19. www.mastercardinternational.com
20. Alice Z. Cuneo, "Sue Johenning," *Advertising Age*, September 27, 2004.
21. Pantea Denoyelle and Jean-Claude Larreche, "Virgin Atlantic Airways—Ten Years Later," INSEAD Case, 1995.
22. D. E. Bell and D. M. Leavitt, "Bronner Slosberg Humphrey," *Harvard Business School Case 9-598-136,* 1998, p. 5.
23. Ibid., p. 4.
24. E. C. Clemmer and B. Schneider, "Managing Customer Dissatisfaction with Waiting: Applying Social-Psychological Theory in a Service Setting," in *Advances in Services Marketing and Management,* vol. 2, ed. T. Schwartz, D. E. Bowen, and S. W. Brown (Greenwich, CT: JAI Press, 1993), pp. 213–29.
25. Ibid.
26. L. L. Berry, V. A. Zeithaml, and A. Parasuraman, "Quality Counts in Services, Too," *Business Horizons,* May–June 1985, pp. 44–52.
27. V. A. Zeithaml, A. Parasuraman, and L. L. Berry, *Delivering Quality Service: Balancing Customer Perceptions and Expectations* (New York: The Free Press, 1990), p. 120.

Chapter 17

PRICING OF SERVICES

This chapter's objectives are to

1. Discuss three major ways that service prices are perceived differently from goods prices by customers.

2. Articulate the key ways that pricing of services differs from pricing of goods from a company's perspective.

3. Demonstrate what value means to customers and the role that price plays in value.

4. Describe strategies that companies use to price services.

5. Give examples of pricing strategy in action.

What Do Consumers Pay for Music Online?

Welcome to the post-Napster era of rent-a-tune when music is leased instead of bought, and when every recording, from electric guitars to chamber ensembles, comes with strings attached.[1]

In their heyday, free online music exchange services such as Napster, FastTrack, and the Dutch firm KaZaA allowed more than 60 million Internet fans to download music free with virtually unrestricted availability of artists and selections. These companies were stopped from doing business by the major record companies and their artists, and "pay-for-play" services have taken over. Napster initially defined customer expectations for online music services—any time, anywhere, for free. Today most online music services, such as Apple Computer's iTunes Music Store and Roxio's relaunched Napster, charge a flat 99 cents per track for downloads. Wal-Mart recently cut that price to 88 cents per track, but other services have pricing strategies that are more difficult to compare.

Digital download music sales were estimated to be $250 million in 2004. Apple's iTunes, built as an extension of its overwhelmingly successful iPod music player, has a 70 percent share of that market.[2] Apple reports that an average of 4 million songs are downloaded a week, and it sold its 150 millionth song in October 2004. The price that the company established, 99 cents per song, set a standard for industry pricing, although competitors attempt to use pricing variations as part of

Internet Music Services:
What You Get, How Much It Costs

	Cost	Competitive Advantages	Competitive Disadvantages	Content
iTunes	99 cents per song	Only music store that is iPod compatible; AirPort Express lets you play downloads through stereo; has exclusive tracks; offers music videos; music can be shared with up to 5 Macs and PCs	None	Over one million tracks; 100,000 new tracks from independent artists; 5,000 audiobooks
MSN Music	99 cents per song; $9.90 per album	Higher sound quality level than other stores; Links to lyrics and tickets; Search engine corrects typos	Not iPod compatible; none of the CD and DVD players that read off data CDs can play downloads	600,000 tracks
Musicmatch	99 cents per song; $9.99 per album	Winner of PC Magazine Editor's Choice Award for Best Music Player; albums come with high-resolution album art; personalized recommendations	Not iPod compatible;	700,000 tracks and 40,000 albums
iMusic Search	$1 per month ($24.95 for two years; $37.95 lifetime membership)	Unlimited computer and MP3 downloads; unlimited CD burns; instant access to lyrics database	Not iPod compatible	Over 12 million songs and movies
KaZaA	Free with ads; $29.95 with no ads	Unlimited downloads; huge selection; unlimited burning; free	Not iPod compatible; artists do not get paid	Some content is limited (gold icons)
Napster	$9.95 per month; 80 cents per track to burn	Month-by-month subscription; music discovery and sharing through Napster community; Napster custom compilations	Downloads expire if subscription lapses	Over 700,000 tracks, 65,000 albums, 45,000 artists
Napster Light	99 cents a song; albums start at $9.95	Music discovery and sharing through Napster community	Downloads expire if subscription lapses	Over 700,000 tracks, 65,000 albums, 45,000 artists

their strategy to gain customers. Napster, for example, charges a monthly fee of $9.95, after which each download is only 80 cents. The accompanying table shows several top competitors along with the prices and benefits they offer.[3]

Which service offers the best deal? As the table shows, service prices are neither straightforward nor consistent. iMusic Search seems to cost the least: for $24.95, consumers get two years of unlimited computer and MP3 downloads as well as unlimited CD burns. The company also seems to have the largest library, with over 12 million tracks. On services such as the Napster, users obtain an unlimited number of streaming audios and downloads for $9.95 per month but must pay 80 cents for every song they burn to a CD. Users who discontinue their subscription wipe out their downloaded library, so the service is more similar to renting or leasing than owning. And services differ in whether CDs can be burned to play only on home, car, or portable stereos or on portable MP3 players. Only iTunes songs can be downloaded to iPods. Some services, such as MSN Music, offer higher sound quality downloads. Companies have added value to their offerings by making it easy to organize tunes into playlists, offering high-resolution album art, giving biographical notes on artists, creating music communities, and providing access to lyrics.

These differences in offerings illustrate an important issue about pricing that will be made clear in this chapter: Price is not only about monetary cost. Price also involves time, convenience, and psychic payments. In each of these offerings from online music companies, consumers are constrained in what they receive. How valuable is music if you must sit in front of your computer to hear it? How much is it worth to be able to burn a CD or transfer online music to an MP3 player? Is it enough to rent or license music, or will users want to own it as they have in the past?

In perhaps the most unique pricing strategy, online music retailer MusicRebellion. com introduced a dynamic-pricing system for downloading music from its limited library of approximately 300,000 songs. Each song was initially available at 10 cents per download. After that, consumer demand set prices for each song, with the highest cost expected to be around $1.[4]

According to one of the leading experts on pricing, most service organizations use a "naive and unsophisticated approach to pricing without regard to underlying shifts in demand, the rate that supply can be expanded, prices of available substitutes, consideration of the price–volume relationship, or the availability of future substitutes."[5] What makes the pricing of services more difficult than pricing of goods? What approaches work well in the context of services?

This chapter builds on three key differences between customer evaluation of pricing for services and goods: (1) customers often have inaccurate or limited reference prices for services, (2) price is a key signal of quality in services, and (3) monetary price is not the only price relevant to service customers. As we demonstrate, these three differences can have profound impact on the strategies companies use to set and administer prices for services.

The chapter also discusses common pricing structures including (1) cost-based, (2) competition-based, and (3) demand-based pricing. One of the most important aspects of demand-based pricing is perceived value, which must be understood by service providers so that they price in line with offerings and customer expectations. For that reason we also describe how customers define value and discuss pricing strategies in the context of value.

THREE KEY WAYS THAT SERVICE PRICES ARE DIFFERENT FOR CONSUMERS

What role does price play in consumer decisions about services? How important is price to potential buyers compared with other factors and service features? Service companies must understand how pricing works, but first they must understand how customers perceive prices and price changes. The three sections that follow describe what we know about the ways that customers perceive services, and each is central to effective pricing.

Customer Knowledge of Service Prices

To what extent do customers use price as a criterion in selecting services? How much do consumers know about the costs of services? Before you answer these questions, take the services pricing quiz in Exhibit 17.1. Were you able to fill in a price for each of the services listed? If you were able to answer the questions on the basis of memory, you have internal *reference prices* for the services. A reference price is *a price point in memory for a good or a service,* and can consist of the price last paid, the price most frequently paid, or the average of all prices customers have paid for similar offerings.[6]

To see how accurate your reference prices for services are, you can compare them with the actual price of these services from the providers in your hometown. If you are like many consumers, you feel quite uncertain about your knowledge of the prices of services, and the reference prices you hold in memory for services are not generally as accurate as those you hold for goods. There are many reasons for this difference.

- *Service variability limits knowledge.* Because services are not created on a factory assembly line, service firms have great flexibility in the configurations of services they offer. Firms can conceivably offer an infinite variety of combinations and permutations, leading to complex and complicated pricing structures. As an example, consider how difficult it is to get comparable price quotes when buying life insurance. With the multitude of types (such as whole life versus term), features (different deductibles), variations associated with customers (age, health risk, smoking or nonsmoking), few insurance companies offer exactly the same features and the same prices. Only an expert customer, one who knows enough about insurance to completely specify the options across providers, is likely to find prices that are directly comparable.

How did you answer the questions about prices for a medical checkup? If you are like most consumers, you probably wanted more information before you offered a reference price. You probably wanted to know what type of checkup the physician is providing. Does it include X-rays and other diagnostic tests? What types of tests? How long does it take? What is its purpose? If the checkup is undertaken simply to get a signature on a health form or a marriage certificate, the doctor may take a brief medical history, listen for a heartbeat, and measure blood pressure. If, however, the checkup is to monitor a chronic ailment such as diabetes or high blood pressure, the doctor may be more thorough. The point we want to illustrate here is that a high degree of variability often exists across providers of services. Not every physician defines a checkup the same way. You may have found it easier to estimate dental services than medical services. Dental checkups are likely to be more standardized than medical services, consisting of two basic types: with X-rays and without.

- *Providers are unwilling to estimate prices.* Another reason customers lack accurate reference prices for services is that many providers are unable or unwilling to estimate price in advance. For example, legal and medical service providers are rarely willing—or even able—to estimate a price in advance. The fundamental reason is that they do not know themselves what the services will involve until they have fully examined the patient or the client's situation or until the process of service delivery (such as an operation in a hospital or a trial) unfolds. In a business-to-business context, companies will obtain bids or estimates for complex services such as consulting or construction, but this type of price estimation is typically not undertaken with end consumers; therefore, they often buy without advance knowledge about the final price of the service.

• *Individual customer needs vary.* Another factor that results in the inaccuracy of reference prices is that individual customer needs vary. Some hairstylists' service prices vary across customers on the basis of length of hair, type of haircut, and whether a conditioning treatment and style are included. Therefore, if you were to ask a friend what a cut costs from a particular stylist, chances are that your cut from the same stylist may be a different price. In a similar vein, a service as simple as a hotel room will have prices that vary greatly: by size of room, time of year, type of room availability, and individual versus group rate. These two examples are for very simple services. Now consider a service purchase as idiosyncratic as braces from a dentist or help from a lawyer. In these and many other services, customer differences in need will play a strong role in the price of the service.

• *Collection of Price information is overwhelming in services.* Still another reason customers lack accurate reference prices for services is that customers feel overwhelmed with the information they need to gather. With most goods, retail stores display the products by category to allow customers to compare and contrast the prices of different brands and sizes. Rarely is there a similar display of services in a single outlet. If customers want to compare prices (such as for dry cleaning), they must drive to or call individual outlets.

In Chapter 3, we discussed several novel services being offered to help the time-deficient customer cope. See if you have reference prices for the unusual services of these providers: wedding adviser, pet nutritionist and therapist, baby-proofing expert, and executive organizer. We expect that your reference prices—if you can even come up with some—are even more uncertain and less accurate than for the services in the price quiz in Exhibit 17.1. Here are estimates from actual consultants: $3,500 for a wedding adviser's attention to all details, $75 to $125 a visit for depressed pets, $200 to $300 to protect a house for and from a baby, and $1,000 for four hours of executive organization.[7]

Here's one final test about reference prices. Suppose you were having a birthday party and wanted a celebrity—say, Chris Rock or Rod Stewart—to perform. Do you know what celebrities charge for a performance? Steve Einzig, who runs a celebrity-booking firm, reports these going rates for private performances.[8]

Bette Midler	$750,000 to $1,000,000
Rod Stewart	$500,000
Harry Connick Jr.	$350,000
Chris Rock	$200,000
Lionel Richie	$200,000
Bill Cosby	$150,000

The fact that consumers often possess inaccurate reference prices for services has several important managerial implications. Promotional pricing (as in couponing or special pricing) may be less meaningful for services, for which price anchors typically do not exist. Perhaps that is why price is not featured in service advertising as much as it is featured in advertising for goods. Promotional pricing may also create problems if the promotional price (such as a $50 permanent wave special from a salon) is the only one customers see in advertising, for it could become the customer's anchor price, making the regular price of $75 for a future purchase seem high by comparison.

The absence of accurate reference prices also suggests that advertising actual prices for services the customer is not used to purchasing may reduce uncertainty and overcome a customer's inflated price expectations for some services. For example, a marketing research firm's advertisements citing the price for a simple study (such as $10,000) would be informative to business customers who are not familiar with the costs of research studies and therefore would be guessing at the cost. By featuring price in advertising, the company overcomes the fear of high cost by giving readers a price anchor.

• *Prices are not visible.* One requirement for the existence of customer reference prices is *price visibility*—the price cannot be hidden or implicit. In many services, particularly financial services, most customers know about only the rate of return and not the costs they pay in the form of fund and insurance fees. American Express Financial Services discovered through research how little customers know about prices of the company's services.[9] After being told by the independent agents who sell its services to customers that its services were priced too high, the company did research to find out how much customers knew about what they pay for financial services and how much customers factor price into their value assessments.

The study surprised the company by revealing that customers knew even less than expected: Not only did they not understand *what* they were paying for many of their services, very few consumers understood *how* they pay for financial services in general. Only for financial products in which price was visible—such as with securities and term life insurance—were customers aware of fees. When price was invisible, such as in certificates, whole-life insurance, and annuities (which have rear-load charges), customers did not know how they were charged and what they paid. Further, when customers were asked to indicate how important 10 factors (including price) were, price ranked seventh. Finally, the company found that shopping behavior in the category of financial services was extremely limited. Between 50 and 60 percent of customers bought financial products from the very first person they talked to.

For all the reasons just listed, many customers do not see the price at all until *after* they receive certain services. Of course in situations of urgency, such as in accident or illness, customers must make the decision to purchase without respect to cost. And if cost is not known to the customer before purchase, it cannot be used as a key criterion for purchase, as it often is for goods. Price is likely to be an important criterion in *repurchase,* however. Furthermore, monetary price in repurchase may be an even more important criterion than in initial purchase.

The Role of Nonmonetary Costs

Economists have long recognized that monetary price is not the only sacrifice consumers make to obtain products and services. Demand, therefore, is not just a function of monetary price but is influenced by other costs as well. Nonmonetary costs represent other sources of sacrifice perceived by consumers when buying and using a service. Time costs, search costs, and psychological costs often enter into the evaluation of whether to buy or rebuy a service and may at times be more important concerns than monetary price. Customers will trade money for these other costs.

• *Time costs.* Most services require direct participation of the consumer and thus consume real time: time waiting as well as time when the customer interacts with the service provider. Consider the investment you make to exercise, see a physician, or get through the crowds to watch a concert or baseball game. Not only are you paying money to receive these services, but you are also expending time. Time becomes a sacrifice made to receive service in multiple ways. First, because service providers cannot completely control the number of customers or the length of time it will take for each customer to be served, customers are likely to expend time waiting to receive the service. The average waiting time in physicians' offices is 20.6 minutes, according to the American Medical Association, with 22 minutes for family practice doctors and 23 minutes for pediatricians, orthopedic surgeons, and gynecologists.[10] Waiting time for a service is frequently longer and less predictable than waiting time to buy goods. Second, customers often wait for an available appointment from a service provider (in

Customers will trade money for time savings. Customers who purchase lawn care, housekeeping, and other services often do so because the value of their time is higher than the value of money.

Source: © John Connell/Index Stock Imagery/PictureQuest

the price quiz, dentist A required a three-week wait whereas dentist D required only one week). Virtually everyone has expended waiting time to receive services.

• *Search costs.* Search costs—the effort invested to identify and select among services you desire—are often higher for services than for physical goods. Prices for services are rarely displayed on shelves of service establishments for customers to examine as they shop, so these prices are often known only when a customer has decided to experience the service. As an example, how well did you estimate the costs of an hour of housecleaning in the price quiz? As a student, it is unlikely that you regularly purchase housecleaning, and you probably have not seen the price of an hour of cleaning displayed in any retail store. Another factor that increases search costs is that each service establishment typically offers only one "brand" of a service (with the exception of brokers in insurance or financial services), so a customer must initiate contact with several different companies to get information across sellers. Price comparisons for some services (travel and hotels, for example) has been facilitated through the Internet.

• *Convenience costs.* There are also convenience (or, perhaps more accurately, inconvenience) costs of services. If customers have to travel to a service, they incur a cost, and the cost becomes greater when travel is difficult, as it is for elderly persons. Further, if service hours do not coincide with customers' available time, they must arrange their schedules to correspond to the company's schedule. And if consumers have to expend effort and time to prepare to receive a service (such as removing all food from kitchen cabinets in preparation for an exterminator's spraying), they make additional sacrifices.

• *Psychological costs.* Often the most painful nonmonetary costs are the psychological costs incurred in receiving some services. Fear of not understanding (insurance), fear of rejection (bank loans), fear of outcomes (medical treatment or surgery)—all these fears constitute psychological costs that customers experience as sacrifices when purchasing and using services. New services, even those that create positive change, bring about psychological costs that consumers factor into the purchase of services. When banks first introduced ATMs, customer resistance was significant, particularly to the idea of putting money into a machine: customers felt uncomfortable with the idea of letting go of their checks and bank cards. Direct deposit, a clear improvement in banking service for the elderly with limited mobility, was viewed with suspicion until the level of comfort improved. And most customers rejected voice mail when it was first developed.

Nonmonetary Cost Priorities

You can assess your own priorities on these nonmonetary cost components—time, effort, search, psychological—by thinking about your answer to question 2 in the price quiz. If you chose dentist A, you are probably most concerned about monetary costs—you are willing to wait for an appointment and in the waiting room of the dentist's office. If you chose dentist B over dentist A, your time and convenience costs are slightly more important than your monetary costs, because you are willing to pay $25 more to reduce the waiting time. If you chose dentist C, you are much more sensitive to time and convenience costs, including travel time, than to monetary costs—you are willing to pay $125 more than what you would pay for dentist A to avoid the other nonmonetary costs. And if you chose dentist D, you want to minimize psychological costs as well, in this case fear and pain.

Reducing Nonmonetary Costs

The managerial implications of these other sources of sacrifice are compelling. First, a firm may be able to increase monetary price by reducing time and other costs. For example, a services marketer can reduce the perceptions of time and convenience costs when use of the service is embedded in other activities (such as when a convenience store cashes checks, sells stamps, and serves coffee along with selling products). Second, customers may be willing to pay to avoid the other costs. Many customers willingly pay extra to have items delivered to their home—including restaurant meals—rather than transporting the services and products themselves. Some customers also pay a premium for fast check-in and checkout (as in joining the Hertz #1 club), for reduced waiting time in a professional's office (as in so-called executive appointments where, for a premium price, a busy executive comes early in the morning and does not have to wait), and to avoid doing the work themselves (such as paying one and one-half times the price per gallon to avoid having to put gas in a rental car before returning it). If time or other costs are pivotal for a given service, the company's advertising can emphasize these savings rather than monetary savings.

Many other services save time, thus actually allowing the customer to "buy" time. Household cleaning services, lawn care, babysitting, interactive cable shopping, personal shopper service, home banking, home delivery of groceries, painting, and carpet cleaning—all these services represent net gains in the discretionary time of consumers and can be marketed that way. Services that allow the customer to buy time are likely to have monetary value for busy consumers.

Price as an Indicator of Service Quality

One of the intriguing aspects of pricing is that buyers are likely to use price as an indicator of both service costs and service quality—price is at once an attraction variable and a repellent.[11] Customers' use of price as an indicator of quality depends on several factors, one of which is the other information available to them. When service cues to quality are readily accessible, when brand names provide evidence of a company's reputation, or when the level of advertising communicates the company's belief in the brand, customers may prefer to use those cues instead of price. In other situations, however, such as when quality is hard to detect or when quality or price varies a great deal within a class of services, consumers may believe that price is the best indicator of quality. Many of these conditions typify situations that face consumers when purchasing services.[12] Another factor that increases the dependence on price as a quality indicator is the risk associated with the service purchase. In high-risk situations, many of which involve credence services such as medical treatment or management consulting, the customer will look to price as a surrogate for quality.

Because customers depend on price as a cue to quality and because price sets expectations of quality, service prices must be determined carefully. In addition to being chosen to cover costs or match competitors, prices must be selected to convey the appropriate quality signal. Pricing too low can lead to inaccurate inferences about the quality of the service. Pricing too high can set expectations that may be difficult to match in service delivery.

APPROACHES TO PRICING SERVICES

This chapter's Strategy Insight briefly reviews key strategic concepts about pricing that apply equally to goods and services. Rather than repeat what you learned about pricing

Many of the strategic aspects of pricing of services are the same as pricing of goods. A summary of the basics is provided here. For more details, return to your basic marketing textbook or to *Marketing Management* by Philip Kotler, the text from which we excerpted these fundamental points about pricing.

1. The firm must consider many factors in setting its pricing policy: selecting the pricing objective, determining demand, estimating costs, analyzing competitors' prices and offers, selecting a pricing method, and selecting the final price.
2. Companies do not always seek to maximize profits through pricing. Other objectives they may have include survival, maximizing current revenue, maximizing sales growth, maximizing market skimming, and product/quality leadership.
3. Marketers need to understand how responsive demand would be to a change in price. To evaluate this important criterion of price sensitivity, marketers can calculate the price elasticity of demand, which is expressed as

$$\text{Elasticity} = \frac{\text{Percentage change in quantity purchased}}{\text{Percentage change in price}}$$

4. Various types of costs must be considered in setting prices, including direct and indirect costs, fixed and variable costs, indirect traceable costs, and allocated costs. If a product or service is to be profitable for a company, price must cover all costs and include a markup as well.
5. Competitors' prices will affect the desirability of a company's offerings and must be considered in establishing prices.
6. A variety of pricing methods exist including markup, target return, perceived-value, going-rate, sealed-bid, and psychological.
7. After setting a price structure, companies adapt prices using geographic pricing, price discounts and allowances, promotional pricing, discriminatory pricing, and product-mix pricing.

Source: Kotler, Philip, *Marketing Management,* 11th Edition, © 2003. Reprinted by permission of Pearson Education, Inc., Upper Saddle River, NJ.

in your marketing principles class, we want to emphasize in this chapter the way that services prices and pricing differ from both the customer's and the company's perspective. We discuss these differences in the context of the three pricing structures typically used to set prices: (1) cost-based, (2) competition-based, and (3) demand-based pricing. These categories, as shown in Figure 17.1, are the same bases on which goods prices are set, but adaptations must be made in services. The figure shows the three structures interrelating, because companies need to consider each of the three to some extent in setting prices. In the following sections we describe in general each basis for pricing and discuss challenges that occur when the approach is used in services pricing. Figure 17.1 summarizes those challenges.

FIGURE 17.1
Three Basic Marketing Price Structures and Challenges Associated with Their Use for Services

Challenges:
1. Small firms may charge too little to be viable.
2. Heterogeneity of services limits comparability.
3. Prices may not reflect customer value.

Challenges:
1. Costs are difficult to trace.
2. Labor is more difficult to price than materials.
3. Costs may not equal the value that customers perceive the services are worth.

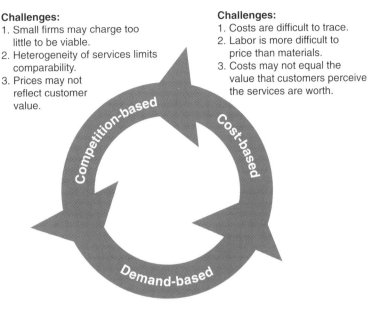

Challenges:
1. Monetary price must be adjusted to reflect the value of nonmonetary costs.
2. Information on service costs is less available to customers; hence, price may not be a central factor.

Cost-Based Pricing

In cost-based pricing, a company determines expenses from raw materials and labor, adds amounts or percentages for overhead and profit, and thereby arrives at the price. This method is widely used by industries such as utilities, contracting, wholesaling, and advertising. The basic formula for cost-based pricing is

$$\text{Price} = \text{Direct costs} + \text{Overhead costs} + \text{Profit margin}$$

Direct costs involve materials and labor that are associated with delivering the service, overhead costs are a share of fixed costs, and the profit margin is a percentage of full costs (direct + overhead).

Special Challenges in Cost-Based Pricing for Services

One of the major difficulties in cost-based pricing involves defining the units in which a service is purchased. Thus the price per unit—a well-understood concept in pricing of manufactured goods—is a vague entity. For this reason many services are sold in terms of input units rather than units of measured output. For example, most professional services (such as consulting, engineering, architecture, psychotherapy, and tutoring) are sold by the hour.

What is unique about services when using cost-based approaches to pricing? First, costs are difficult to trace or calculate in services businesses, particularly where multiple services are provided by the firm.[13] Consider how difficult it must be for a bank to allocate teller time accurately across its checking, savings, and money market accounts in order to decide what to charge for the services. Second, a major component of cost is employee time rather than materials, and the value of people's time, particularly non-professional time, is not easy to calculate or estimate.

An added difficulty is that actual service costs may underrepresent the value of the service to the customer. A local tailor charges $10 for taking in a seam on a $350 ladies' suit jacket and an equal $10 for taking in a seam on a pair of $14 sweat shorts. The tailor's rationale is that both jobs require the same amount of time. What she neglects to see is that the customer would pay a higher price—and might even be happier about the alterations—for the expensive suit jacket, and that $10 is too high a price for the sweat shorts.

Examples of Cost-Based Pricing Strategies Used in Services

Cost-plus pricing is a commonly used approach in which component costs are calculated and a markup added. In product pricing, this approach is quite simple; in service industries, however, it is complicated because the tracking and identification of costs are difficult. The approach is typically used in industries in which cost must be estimated in advance, such as construction, engineering, and advertising. In construction or engineering, bids are solicited by clients on the basis of the description of the service desired. Using their knowledge of the costs of the components of the service (including the raw materials such as masonry and lumber), labor (including both professional and unskilled), and margin, the company estimates and presents to the client a price for the finished service. A contingency amount—to cover the possibility that costs may be higher than estimated—is also stated because in large projects specifications can change as the service is provided.

Fee for service is the pricing strategy used by professionals; it represents the cost of the time involved in providing the service. Consultants, psychologists, accountants, and lawyers, among other professionals, charge for their services on an hourly basis. Virtually all psychologists and social workers have a set hourly rate they charge to their clients, and most structure their time in increments of an hour.

In the early 1900s, lawyers typically billed clients a certain fee for services rendered regardless of the amount of time they spent delivering them. Then in the 1970s, law firms began to bill on an hourly rate, in part because this approach offered accountability to clients and an internal budgeting system for the firm. One of the most difficult aspects of this approach is that recordkeeping is tedious for professionals. Lawyers and accountants must keep track of the time they spend for a given client, often down to 10-minute increments. For this reason the method has been criticized because it does not promote efficiency and sometimes ignores the expertise of the lawyers (those who are very experienced can accomplish much more than novices in a given time period, yet billings do not always reflect this). Clients also feared padding of their legal bills, and began to audit them. Despite these concerns, the hourly bill dominates the industry, with the majority of revenues billed this way.[14]

Competition-Based Pricing

The competition-based pricing approach focuses on the prices charged by other firms in the same industry or market. Competition-based pricing does not always imply charging the identical rate others charge but rather using others' prices as an anchor for the firm's price. This approach is used predominantly in two situations: (1) when services are standard across providers, such as in the dry cleaning industry, and (2) in oligopolies with a few large service providers, such as in the airline or rental car industry. Difficulties involved in provision of services sometimes make competition-based pricing less simple than it is in goods industries.

Special Challenges in Competition-Based Pricing for Services

Small firms may charge too little and not make margins high enough to remain in business. Many mom-and-pop service establishments—dry cleaning, retail, and tax accounting, among others—cannot deliver services at the low prices charged by chain operations.

Further, the heterogeneity of services across and within providers makes this approach complicated. Bank services illustrate the wide disparity in service prices. Customers buying checking accounts, money orders, or foreign currency, to name a few services, find that prices are rarely similar across providers. For example, at one point NationsBank charged $5 for a money order when the Postal Service charged $0.75 and 7-Eleven stores charged $1.09.[15] Compare these prices for having a check drawn on foreign currency: Bank of America, $20; Thomas Cook, $7; and Citibank, $15. And fees for cashier's checks ranged from $10 to no charge, with a nationwide average of $2.69.[16] Banks claim that they set fees high enough to cover the costs of these services. The wide disparity in prices probably reflects the bank's difficulty in determining prices as well as their belief that financial customers do not shop around nor discern the differences (if any) among offerings from different providers. A banking expert makes the point that "It's not like buying a quart of milk.... Prices aren't standardized."[17] Only in very standardized services (such as dry cleaning) are prices likely to be remembered and compared.

Examples of Competition-Based Pricing in Services Industries

Price signaling occurs in markets with a high concentration of sellers. In this type of market, any price offered by one company will be matched by competitors to avoid giving a low-cost seller a distinct advantage. The airline industry exemplifies price signaling in services. When any competitor drops the price of routes, others match the lowered price almost immediately.

Going-rate pricing involves charging the most prevalent price in the market. Rental car pricing is an illustration of this technique (and also an illustration of price signaling, because the rental car market is dominated by a small number of large companies). For years, the prices set by one company (Hertz) have been followed by the other companies. When Hertz instituted a new pricing plan that involved "no mileage charges, ever," other rental car companies imitated the policy. They then had to raise other factors such as base rates, size and type of car, daily or weekly rates, and drop-off charges to continue to make profits. Prices in different geographic markets, even cities, depend on the going rate in that location, and customers often pay different rates in contiguous cities in the same state. The newsletter *Consumer Reports Travel Letter* advises customers that the national toll-free reservation lines offer better rates than are obtained calling local rental car companies in cities, perhaps because those rates are less influenced by the going rates in a particular area.[18]

The Global Feature in this chapter illustrates some of the practices in pricing that differ across countries.

Demand-Based Pricing

The two approaches to pricing just described are based on the company and its competitors rather than on customers. Neither approach takes into consideration that customers may lack reference prices, may be sensitive to nonmonetary prices, and may judge quality on the basis of price. All these factors can be accounted for in a company's pricing decisions. The third major approach to pricing, *demand-based pricing,*

TIPPING

A Cornell University study revealed an interesting fact about tipping: The custom of tipping is more prevalent in countries where citizens value status and prestige than in countries where they do not. Michael Lynn found that the number of service professionals tipped is relatively small in countries where citizens value recognition and esteem less. "Tipping is really a form of conspicuous consumption. We tip more people in this country because we value status. Americans value recognition and esteem, and we receive that when we tip these service professionals."

One measure of the differences in tipping is the number of service professionals who are given tips in different countries. The United States leads the list with about 35 different professions. Other countries that place a high value on recognition and esteem also tip a large number of professionals. These include Spain (29), Canada (25), India (25), and Italy (24). In contrast, in Denmark and Sweden, the number of tipped professionals is under 10, reflecting the lower value placed on recognition and esteem in these countries.

SERVICE FEES

In Europe, Asia, and Latin America, fixed services charges rather than tips are added to customers' bills in restaurants. Except for large parties, this service charge had been an unusual practice in U.S. restaurants, perhaps for the reason cited in the previous paragraph. However, some U.S. establishments—such as the Chateaulin and Monet restaurants in Ashland, Oregon—are exchanging tips for service charges in spite of the preference of guests to choose what to tip. The reason is that the IRS has been leaning on restaurants to have their waiters and waitresses report tips. If reported tip income is less than 8 percent of gross receipts, the IRS has now made restaurant owners liable for back taxes on unreported income unless they participate in a program to track their employee's tips. Service personnel do not like the change, partly because they make less money (the restaurant shares the service fee with kitchen personnel) and partly because they do not receive the instant gratification that tips provide. Guests are typically unfavorable as well: "We surveyed our guests and they seem to feel that they have a constitutional right to reward and punish waiters."

involves setting prices consistent with customer perceptions of value: Prices are based on what customers will pay for the services provided.

Special Challenges in Demand-Based Pricing for Services

One of the major ways that pricing of services differs from pricing of goods in demand-based pricing is that nonmonetary costs and benefits must be factored into the calculation of perceived value to the customer. When services require time, inconvenience, and psychological and search costs, the monetary price must be adjusted to compensate. And when services save time, inconvenience, and psychological and search costs, the customer is willing to pay a higher monetary price. The challenge is to determine the value to customers of each of the nonmonetary aspects involved.

Another way services and goods differ with respect to this form of pricing is that information on service costs may be less available to customers, making monetary price not as salient a factor in initial service selection as it is in goods purchasing.

PRICELESS

A London restaurant called Just Around the Corner has an extraordinary demand-oriented pricing policy: It lets customers pay whatever they think the meal is worth. The policy has been extremely successful since it was started in 1986, with most customers paying more for their meals than the restaurant would charge if it set the prices. Customers average 25 pounds ($41) for a three-course dinner, but some are especially careful to pay enough. "One night, four American government officials handed over nearly $1,000 for a meal worth less than $200. They asked if they had left enough." The owner, Michael Vasos, claims, "I make more money from this restaurant than from any of my other [four] establishments." He thinks his customers' generosity accounts for the success of the restaurant and its pricing policies, although others state that the fear of embarrassment common to the English prevents patrons from paying too little.

PAY BY THE MINUTE IN TOKYO

Some restaurants in Japan are charging for dinner according to how quickly customers eat. At Dai-ichi Hotel Tokyo Seafort, diners punch a time clock when they start their meals, then pay 25 cents per minute until they clock out. Fast diners—like two young girls who gulped down platefuls of cake in 10 minutes and paid only $3—can get bargain meals. Perhaps that is why the restaurant is popular among college students! Other franchise restaurants throughout Japan put time limits on their all-you-can-eat buffets. Prices range from $10 an hour to $100 for 90 minutes. During that time, diners can consume unlimited quantities of top-quality sushi or shabu shabu, a Japanese specialty consisting of thin slices of beef cooked in boiling broth. At one restaurant, Mo Mo Paradise in Tokyo, for example, diners can pay $13.50 to eat for 90 minutes or $30 to eat as much as they want for as long as they want.

Sources: Andrea Sachs, "Eat All You Want; Pay by the Minute," *Washington Post,* September 26, 1999, p. H3; © 1999, *The Washington Post,* Reprinted with permission. "Study Examines Tipping," *Hotel and Motel Management,* March 17, 1997, p. 14; B. Ortega, "No Tips, Please—Just Pay the Service Fee," *The Wall Street Journal,* September 4, 1998, p. B1; "Priceless," *People,* February 15, 1999, p. 114; and I. Wall, "It May Be a Dog-Eat-Dog World, But This Restaurant Won't Prove It," *The Wall Street Journal,* December 11, 1998, p. B1.

Four Meanings of Perceived Value

One of the most appropriate ways that companies price their services is basing the price on the perceived value of the service to customers. Among the questions a services marketer needs to ask are the following: What do consumers mean by *value?* How can we quantify perceived value in dollars so that we can set appropriate prices for our services? Is the meaning of value similar across consumers and services? How can value perceptions be influenced? To understand demand-based pricing approaches, we must fully understand what value means to customers.

This is not a simple task. When consumers discuss value, they use the term in many different ways and talk about myriad attributes or components. What constitutes value, even in a single service category, appears to be highly personal and idiosyncratic. Customers define value in four ways: (1) Value is low price. (2) Value is whatever I want in a product or service. (3) Value is the quality I get for the price I pay. (4) Value is what

FIGURE 17.2
Four Customer Definitions of Value

Source: N.C. Mohn, "Pricing Research for Decision Making," Marketing Research: A Magazine of Management and Applications 7, no. 1 (Winter 1995), pp. 10–19. Reprinted by permission of the American Marketing Association.

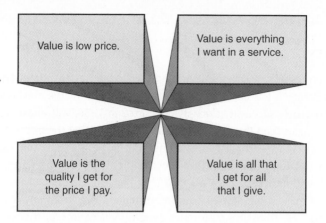

I get for what I give (Figure 17.2).[19] Let us take a look at each of these definitions more carefully.

Value Is Low Price　Some consumers equate value with low price, indicating that what they have to give up in terms of money is most salient in their perceptions of value, as typified in these representative comments from customers:

> *For dry cleaning:* "Value means the lowest price."

> *For carpet steam cleaning:* "Value is price—which one is on sale."

> *For a fast-food restaurant:* "When I can use coupons, I feel that the service is a value."

> *For airline travel:* "Value is when airline tickets are discounted."[20]

Value Is Whatever I Want in a Product or Service　Rather than focusing on the money given up, some consumers emphasize the benefits they receive from a service or product as the most important component of value. In this value definition, price is far less important than the quality or features that match what the consumer wants. In the telecommunications industry, for example, business customers strongly value the reliability of the systems and are willing to pay for the safety and confidentiality of the connections. Service customers describe this definition of value as follows:

> *For an MBA degree:* "Value is the very best education I can get."

> *For medical services:* "Value is high quality."

> *For a social club:* "Value is what makes me look good to my friends and family."

> *For a rock or country music concert:* "Value is the best performance."

Value Is the Quality I Get for the Price I Pay　Other consumers see value as a trade-off between the money they give up and the quality they receive.

> *For a hotel for vacation:* "Value is price first and quality second."

> *For a hotel for business travel:* "Value is the lowest price for a quality brand."

> *For a computer services contract:* "Value is the same as quality. No—value is affordable quality."

Value Is What I Get for What I Give   Finally, some consumers consider all the benefits they receive as well as all sacrifice components (money, time, effort) when describing value.

> *For a housekeeping service:* "Value is how many rooms I can get cleaned for what the price is."

> *For a hairstylist:* "Value is what I pay in cost and time for the look I get."

> *For executive education:* "Value is getting a good educational experience in the shortest time possible."

The four consumer expressions of value can be captured in one overall definition consistent with the concept of utility in economics: *Perceived value is the consumer's overall assessment of the utility of a service based on perceptions of what is received and what is given.* Although what is received varies across consumers (some may want volume, others high quality, still others convenience), as does what is given (some are concerned only with money expended, others with time and effort), value represents a trade-off of the give and get components. Customers will make a purchase decision on the basis of perceived value, not solely to minimize the price paid. These definitions are the first step in identifying the elements that must be quantified in setting prices for services.

Incorporating Perceived Value into Service Pricing

The buyer's perception of total value prompts the willingness to pay a particular price for a service. To translate the customer's value perceptions into an appropriate price for a specific service offering, the marketer must answer a number of questions. What benefits does the service provide? How important is each of these benefits? How much is it worth to the customer to receive a particular benefit from a service? At what price will the service be economically acceptable to potential buyers? In what context is the customer purchasing the service?

The most important thing a company must do—and often a difficult thing—is to estimate the value to customers of the company's services. Value may be perceived differently by consumers because of idiosyncratic tastes, knowledge about the service, buying power, and ability to pay. In this type of pricing, what the consumers value—not what they pay—forms the basis for pricing. Therefore its effectiveness rests solely on accurately determining what the market perceives the service to be worth.

When the services are for the end consumer, most often service providers will decide that they cannot afford to give each individual exactly the bundle of attributes he or she values. They will, however, attempt to find one or more bundles that address segments of the market. On the other hand, when services are sold to businesses (or to end customers in the case of high-end services), the company can understand and deliver different bundles to each customer.

An interesting manifestation of demand-oriented pricing is shown in the Technology Spotlight.

One of the most complex and difficult tasks of services marketers is setting prices internationally. If services marketers price on the basis of perceived value and if perceived value and willingness to pay differ across countries (which they often do), then service firms may provide essentially the same service but charge different prices in different countries. Here, as in pricing domestically, the challenge is to determine the perceived value not just to different customers but to customers in different parts of the

Technology Spotlight
Dynamic Pricing on the Internet Allows Price Adjustments Based on Supply and Demand

When shopping for an airline ticket on the Internet, have you ever found a low-priced ticket that you did not purchase immediately, then returned four hours later to find the same ticket had increased $100 in price? This experience is dynamic pricing in action—the buying and selling of goods in markets in which prices move quickly in response to supply and demand fluctuations. In the case of your airline ticket, chances are that other travelers had purchased tickets at the original low price, reducing the airlines' inventory and allowing the airline to gamble on getting customers to buy the remaining seats at higher prices.

Dynamic pricing is estimated to account for 40 percent of $1.4 trillion in total online transactions in 2004. The approach—often incorporating auctions and other forms of online bidding—is typically used at the end of the supply chain to eliminate surplus inventory or perishable service capacity, as with airline seats. Dynamic pricing has allowed companies to generate significant revenue from excess supply or discontinued products, which they used to turn over to intermediaries. In the past, liquidators would receive unsold services, getting five cents on the dollar in liquidation fees in addition to whatever they could get from reselling the products. Not only did the firm not receive revenue from the sale of the services, but it would also have to pay for liquidation services.

AUCTIONS: EBAY AND 1,500 RIVALS

Online auctions represent dynamic pricing because customers pay what they are willing and they compete with each other on the goods they desire. In 1995, eBay pioneered the Internet auction, but more than 1,500 websites now offer person-to-person online trading. Market leader eBay offers thousands of new items for auction each day and reported net income of $182 million in the third quarter of 2004, up from $103 million for the third quarter of the previous year. Revenue increased 52 percent in 2004 to more than $805 million, and international revenue grew 88 percent compared with 33 percent for the United States. Whereas eBay focuses on consumer-to-consumer transactions, uBid.com acts as a consignment house for manufacturers selling directly to customers. Founded in 1997, uBid offers leading manu-

facturers' merchandise to consumers and businesses at prices lower than wholesale. Most uBid auctions begin at $1 and allow market dynamics to set the price.

DUTCH AUCTIONS: KLIK-KLOK.COM, WRHAMBRECHT.COM

Dutch auctions, which originated in Netherlands for selling services such as insurance or perishable items such as tulips, reverse the typical auction in that the prices go down as the auction progresses. Also unlike in typical auctions, in which one of a particular type of product is sold at a given time, in Dutch auctions multiple—albeit limited—quantities of the same services are sold at the same time. The duration of the auction is very short, and the price drops rapidly over this time. At any given time (or price point), a bidder can stop the clock by bidding at the instantaneous price. The bid with time, price, and quantity is then recorded. This bidding continues until all bids have been received. At that point all winning bidders pay the same price, which is the lowest "successful" bid. The catch here is that there is a limited supply of each product. As the clock progresses and the remaining available inventory decreases, the nonbidders (those waiting for the lowest selling price) risk not getting their desired quantities.

REVERSE AUCTIONS: HOTWIRE.COM AND PRICELINE.COM

Reverse auctions are used on the buy-side, allowing buyers to see the lowest bid, but not identify the buyer or the seller. The brand or identity of the seller is revealed only if the seller decides to accept the bid offered by the buyer. An advantage for buyers is that they do not need to guess at the price and can receive the same products and services offered elsewhere with static prices at significant discounts. A disadvantage is that although buyers see a rating of the seller, they cannot be sure who the seller is and what the service outcome will be. The brand is eliminated as a communicator of quality. Furthermore, the buyer has to sacrifice controls over some aspects of the service that is being consumed. For instance, on Priceline.com, the buyer does not have full control over time of the flights.

GROUP BUYING: ONLINECHOICE.COM, HAPPYMANY.COM

Group buying sites such as OnlineChoice.com in the United States and HappyMany.com in other parts of the world, aggregate demand for sellers. The sites offer group rates on long distance and cell phone service, automobile and term life insurance, and mortgages. The concept behind this form of dynamic pricing is that the greater the number of people who want to buy products, the lower the price will be for everyone. Sellers generally bucket the prices of the product being sold based on the number of buyers. For example, for 0 to 10 buyers, the price for each buyer is $100; for 10 to 20 buyers, the price for each buyer is $95, and so on. Word-of-mouth is critical, because interested buyers are encouraged to enlist their friends and relatives to get a cheaper price for the whole group. Sellers motivate this action by placing an "Invite Your Friend" icon right next to the service or price information. Advantages of this form of dynamic pricing are that the price decreases as a greater number of people bid and the exact service and its specifications are known to buyers when bidding.

FINDING THE LOWEST PRICE ACROSS INTERNET SITES: BUY.COM

Buy.com's slogan is "lowest prices on Earth." The Internet allows consumers to do quick price comparisons, and Buy.com wants to make sure its services and products end up being the lowest prices in everyone's search. To deliver on its promises, Buy.com uses software to monitor price changes for products on competing sites. When these price changes occur, the software then recommends price adjustments to Buy.com. The process is automated, but the decision to change prices is made by a manager, usually once a day rather than moment to moment. Buy.com relies on this strategy in highly competitive online categories such as computer software. The software makes recommendations throughout the day, and decisions are made the next morning. Prices tend to fall more often than they go up.

DINING WITH DYNAMIC PRICING

Flexible, or dynamic, pricing in the restaurant industry involves changing menu prices by hour or time of day to attract diners in nonpeak hours, such as afternoons between 2 P.M. and 6 P.M. or late evenings. Restaurants may use discounts, such as 15 to 30 percent off the total check, to build traffic during off-hours. Typically the restaurants use a "dining aggregator," a site that collects and coordinates information about all restaurants in an area that want to offer dynamic pricing. For example, www.DinnerBroker.com, a novel dynamic-pricing website, represents 700 restaurants in 40 major metropolitan areas that use off-peak discount programs to gain incremental business and new customers. DinnerBroker.com has an easy-to-use graphic matrix that allows users to see on one page all participating restaurants and the discounts they offer. The site also enables customers to make online reservations and offers access to prime-time tables. To participate in these services, DinnerBroker.com requires restaurants to pay a subscription of $49 a month and $1 for every off-hour reservation booked and fulfilled by the service.

Another discount diner aggregator, iDine Rewards Network of Miami, recently reported a 45 percent increase in dining sales, to $82 million, generated through its consumer rewards program. Its website, www.idine.com, promotes discounts that run as high as 20 percent for particular times of day at thousands of participating restaurants.

Sources: Michael Bazeley, "eBay has Strong Earnings in Quarter," *Knight Ridder Tribune Business News,* October 21, 2004, p. 1; Georgia Perakis, "Third Informs Revenue Management and Pricing Conference," *Journal of Revenue and Pricing Management,* January 2004, p. 388; Vaidyanathan Jayaraman and Tim Baker, "The Internet as an Enabler for Dynamic Pricing of Goods," *IEEE Transactions on Engineering Management,* November 2003, p. 470; Alan J. Liddle, "Using Web for Discounting Clicks with Digital Diners," *Nation's Restaurant News,* May 19, 2003, p. 172; Christopher T. Heun, "Dynamic Pricing Boosts Bottom Line," *Informationweek,* October 29, 2001; Michael Vizard, "With So Very Few Internet Players, Is Dynamic Pricing Good for Our Economy?" *InfoWorld,* March 26, 2001; Michael Vizard, Ed Scannel, and Dan Neel, "Suppliers Toy with Dynamic Pricing," *InfoWorld,* May 14, 2001.

world. Pricing in Europe provides one of the most compelling examples of the pricing challenges that marketers face internationally.

Historically, Europe was considered to be a loosely aligned group of more than 12 separate countries, and a services marketer could have as many different pricing approaches as it had countries in which it offered the services. Although pricing was complex to administer, the marketer had full flexibility in pricing and could seek the profit-maximizing price in each country. Prices across countries tended to vary widely, both in services and in products: "In most markets, [there are] still enormous price differentials between countries. For identical consumer products, prices show typical deviations ranging between 30 and 150 percent—for example 115 percent for chocolate, 65 percent for tomato ketchup, and up to 155 percent for beer in Europe."[21] The European Community created a single internal market, holding the potential to simplify marketing in the area but also creating grave concerns about pricing. The largest concern is that marketers will be required to offer all services at a single European price—the lowest price offered in any European country—which could dramatically reduce revenues and profits.

PRICING STRATEGIES THAT LINK TO THE FOUR VALUE DEFINITIONS

In this section we describe the approaches to services pricing that are particularly suited to each of the four value definitions. Exhibit 17.2 presents research approaches to setting prices.

Pricing Strategies When the Customer Means "Value Is Low Price"

When monetary price is the most important determinant of value to a customer, the company focuses mainly on price. This focus does not mean that the quality level and intrinsic attributes are always irrelevant, just that monetary price dominates in importance. To establish a service price in this definition of value, the marketer must understand to what extent customers know the objective prices of services in this category, how they interpret various prices, and how much is too much of a perceived sacrifice. These factors are best understood when the service provider also knows the relative dollar size of the purchase, the frequency of past price changes, and the range of acceptable prices for the service. Some of the specific pricing approaches appropriate when customers define value as low price include discounting, odd pricing, synchro-pricing, and penetration pricing (Figure 17.3).

FIGURE 17.3
Pricing Strategies When the Customer Defines Value as Low Price

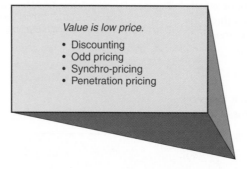

Value is low price.

- Discounting
- Odd pricing
- Synchro-pricing
- Penetration pricing

As described in this chapter, pricing a service in line with what customers perceive it is worth is often difficult. Two approaches that have gained favor in recent years are modular service pricing and service tiering.

MODULAR SERVICE PRICING

One of the reasons that pricing of services is more difficult than pricing of goods is that service units are more variable and difficult to identify than units of goods. Units of goods—automobiles, jeans, gallons of milk, and microwaves—are easy to define. Units of service are more difficult in part because they are sold by a variety of units. Information services, for example, are sold by the minute, the web page, the file (as in buying online music), or the search (as in finding and purchasing magazine articles). The services of your doctor are sold by the length and type of the visit, the test performed, the shot given, and the X-rays taken. Cable television is sold by the month (basic fees, premium charges for HBO and Showtime), by the type of equipment leased (digital video recorders or DVRs, remote controls, digital cable boxes), and by the unit (pay-per-view movies). One approach to dealing with the complexity of pricing services is to develop modular service bundles.

Modular service pricing involves first identifying the basic and value-added services of a provider as components or building blocks for pricing. To create modules, the company first defines the full range of services both that could meet customer needs and for which customers will pay. In the airlines, for example, the base price is set for a seat, but customers will also pay for excess baggage, special ticketing, class of seats, animals, alcoholic beverages, and food (Delta now offers meals on flights at different prices). Customers of rental car companies pay by the day but also buy additional services such as liability insurance, collision insurance, drop-off services, and refueling services.

To create modular pricing, firms need

1. A viable price for each different service

2. The ability to combine prices and services using easy rules

3. Minimum overlap among the service elements so that customers do not pay twice or more for the same service

Graphically, good modular pricing looks like the left side of the accompanying figure, which approximates the pricing for Time Warner's cable services. Each component has a price that is in line with customers' perceptions of the worth of that service, and the components can be selected individually by customers or combined in bundles. The right side of the figure shows poor building blocks for modular pricing—the components are in different units that are hard to combine and there appears to be overlap among them (for example, the annual subscription and the monthly fee seem to be covering the same service, and three months of HBO and the monthly charge for three premium stations also overlap). With good modular pricing such as Time Warner's, the customers can mix or match the services and get exactly what they desire.

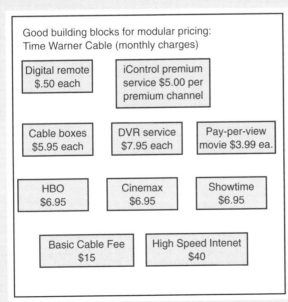

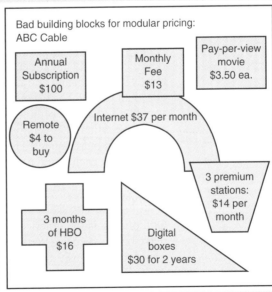

SERVICE TIERING

Sometimes even good modular pricing can become too complex, and simpler ways to present the company's prices are needed. Service tiering, usually called versioning when applied to the pricing of goods, involves creating a set of prices that corresponds to the price points and value bundles of different customer segments. For example, Time Warner Cable offers service tiers that correspond to service components that are typically desired together. Notice that when customers buy the bundles, they receive discounts from what the services would cost individually.

1. **Standard Package @ $20 per month:** Includes basic cable, one cable box, and digital remote

2. **Program Tier Package @ $30 per month:** Includes all services in Standard Package plus choice of two premium channels (HBO, Showtime, Cinemax)

3. **Premium Package @ $50 per month:** Includes all services in Program Tier Package plus a Digital Video Recorder and iControl Premium Service on two premium channels (iControl is video-on-demand service that offers all the shows on a premium channel at any time the customer wants to watch them)

4. **Premium Combo Package @ $85 per month:** Includes all services in Program Tier Package plus one additional premium channel with iControl Premium Service plus high-speed Internet.

In general, service tiers allow customers to quickly and simply match their desires and the price they are willing to pay with an offering from the company. The customer perceives a benefit in choosing one of the tiers because each tier provides a discount over individual services. The company enjoys a benefit because customers typically buy more services when they are sold in tiers than when they are offered individually. The customer can also easily add components—for example, additional cable boxes and remotes—to the packages, which then provides additional profit to the firm.

Modular pricing and service tiering allow the company to maximize sales from all parts of a service that the customer desires without having to create unique service bundles for each different customer.

Sources: R. Docters, M. Reopel, J. Sun, and S. Tanny, "Capturing the Unique Value of Services: Why Pricing of Services is Different," *The Journal of Business Strategy* 25, no. 2 (2004), pp. 23–28; Time Warner Cable price list, Durham, North Carolina 27706, 2005.

Discounting

Service providers offer discounts or price cuts to communicate to price-sensitive buyers that they are receiving value. Colleges are now providing many forms of discounting to attract students. Lehigh University allows top students to get a fifth year of undergraduate or graduate education free, and also offers scholarships based on criteria other than financial need. The business school also cut tuition 22 percent for its master's program and allows graduates to take two-thirds off the regular tuition price.[22] Discount pricing has become a creative art at other educational institutions. The University of Rochester offered a $5,000 grant to all New York State residents enrolling as freshmen. Miami University (in Ohio) now lists only one tuition for *all* students (both in-state and out-of-state). The university offers a discount to in-state students. The end result is that each group of students pays the same as before, but the perception is that in-state students get a discount.

Odd Pricing

Odd pricing is the practice of pricing services just below the exact dollar amount to · make buyers perceive that they are getting a lower price. Dry cleaners charge $2.98 for a shirt rather than $3.00, health clubs have dues priced at $33.90 per month rather than

$34, and haircuts are $9.50 rather than $10.00. Odd prices suggest discounting and bargains and are appealing to customers for whom value means low price.

Synchro-Pricing

Synchro-pricing is the use of price to manage demand for a service by capitalizing on customer sensitivity to prices. Certain services, such as tax preparation, passenger transportation, long-distance telephone, hotels, and theaters, have demand that fluctuates over time as well as constrained supply at peak times. For companies in these and other industries, setting a price that provides a profit over time can be difficult. Pricing can, however, play a role in smoothing demand and synchronizing demand and supply. Time, place, quantity, and incentive differentials have all been used effectively by service firms, as discussed in Chapter 15.

Place differentials are used for services in which customers have a sensitivity to location. The front row at concerts, the 50-yard line in football, center court in tennis or basketball, ocean-side rooms in resort hotels—all these represent place differentials that are meaningful to customers and that therefore command higher prices.

Time differentials involve price variations that depend on when the service is consumed. Telephone service after 11 P.M., hospital rooms on weekends, airline tickets that include a Saturday night stay, and health spas in the off-season are time differentials that reflect slow periods of service. By offering lower prices for underused time periods, a service company can smooth demand and also gain incremental revenue.

Quantity differentials are usually price decreases given for volume purchasing. This pricing structure allows a service company to predict future demand for its services. Customers who buy a booklet of coupons for a tanning salon or facial, a quantity of tokens for public bridges, or packages of advertising spots on radio or television are all responding to price incentives achieved by committing to future services. Corporate discounts for airlines, hotels, and rental cars exemplify quantity discounts in the business context; by offering lower prices, the service provider locks in future business.

Differentials as incentives are lower prices for new or existing clients in the hope of encouraging them to be regular users or more frequent users. Some professionals—lawyers, dentists, electrologists, and even some physicians—offer free consultations at the front end, usually to overcome fear and uncertainty about high service prices. Other companies stimulate use by offering regular customers discounts or premiums during slow periods. Sports teams are now using differential prices as incentives to attract customers who would otherwise not be able to afford the high cost of attending sports events. For example, in 2004 the average price of an NBA ticket was $44.68, an NHL ticket was $44.22, and an NFL ticket was $52.95. The Phoenix Suns, in claiming that "You should have pricing for every pocketbook," revamped its ticket pricing by raising premium seats by 26 percent, decreasing arena seats by 31 percent, and adding 500 $10 tickets. The net result was a 6 percent increase in the average ticket price (paid for by the premium seat holders), but more attendance at the games because more fans in different segments could afford the seats.[23]

Penetration Pricing

Penetration pricing is a strategy in which new services are introduced at low prices to stimulate trial and widespread use. The strategy is appropriate when (1) sales volume of the service is very sensitive to price, even in the early stages of introduction; (2) it is possible to achieve economies in unit costs by operating at large volumes; (3) a service faces threats of strong potential competition very soon after introduction; and (4) there is no class of buyers willing to pay a higher price to obtain the service.[24] Penetration

FIGURE 17.4
Pricing Strategies When the Customer Defines Value as Everything Wanted in a Service

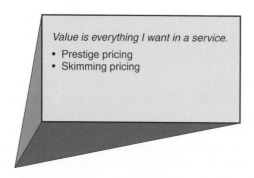

Value is everything I want in a service.
- Prestige pricing
- Skimming pricing

pricing can lead to problems when companies then select a "regular" increased price. Care must be taken not to penetrate with so low a price that customers feel the regular price is outside the range of acceptable prices.

Pricing Strategies When the Customer Means "Value Is Everything I Want in a Service"

When the customer is concerned principally with the "get" components of a service, monetary price is not of primary concern. The more desirable intrinsic attributes a given service possesses, the more highly valued the service is likely to be and the higher the price the marketer can set. Figure 17.4 shows appropriate pricing strategies.

Prestige Pricing

Prestige pricing is a special form of demand-based pricing by service marketers who offer high-quality or status services. For certain services—restaurants, health clubs, airlines, and hotels—a higher price is charged for the luxury end of the business. Some customers of service companies who use this approach may actually value the high price because it represents prestige or a quality image. Others prefer purchasing at the high end because they are given preference in seating or accommodations and are entitled to other special benefits. In prestige pricing, demand may actually increase as price increases because the costlier service has more value in reflecting quality or prestige.

Skimming Pricing

Skimming, a strategy in which new services are introduced at high prices with large promotional expenditures, is an effective approach when services are major improvements over past services. In this situation customers are more concerned about obtaining the service than about the cost of the service, allowing service providers to skim the customers most willing to pay the highest prices.

Pricing Strategies When the Customer Means "Value Is the Quality I Get for the Price I Pay"

Some customers primarily consider both quality and monetary price. The task of the marketer is to understand what *quality* means to the customer (or segments of customers) and then to match quality level with price level. Specific strategies are shown in Figure 17.5.

Value Pricing

The widely used term *value pricing* has come to mean "giving more for less." In current usage it involves assembling a bundle of services that are desirable to a wide group

FIGURE 17.5
**Pricing Strategies
When the Customer
Defines Value as
Quality for the Price
Paid**

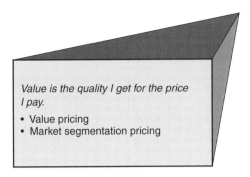

Value is the quality I get for the price
I pay.
- Value pricing
- Market segmentation pricing

of customers and then pricing them lower than they would cost alone. Taco Bell pioneered value pricing with a $0.59 Value Menu. After sales at the chain rose 50 percent in two years to $2.4 billion, McDonald's and Burger King adopted the value pricing practice. The menu at Taco Bell has since been reconfigured to emphasize plain tacos and burritos (which are easier and faster for the chain to make) for less than a dollar. Southwest Airlines also offers value pricing in its airline service: a low cost for a bundle of desirable service attributes such as frequent departures, friendly and funny employees, and on-time arrival. The airline offers consistently low fares with bare-bones service.

Market Segmentation Pricing

Market segmentation pricing, a service marketer charges different prices to groups of customers for what are perceived to be different quality levels of service, even though there may not be corresponding differences in the costs of providing the service to each of these groups. This form of pricing is based on the premise that segments show different price elasticities of demand and desire different quality levels.

Services marketers often price by *client category,* based on the recognition that some groups find it difficult to pay a recommended price. Health clubs located in college communities will typically offer student memberships, recognizing that this segment of customers has limited ability to pay full price. In addition to the lower price, student memberships may also carry with them reduced hours of use, particularly in peak times. The same line of reasoning leads to memberships for "seniors," who are less able to pay full price but are willing to patronize the clubs during daytime hours when most full-price members are working.

Companies also use market segmentation by *service version,* recognizing that not all segments want the basic level of service at the lowest price. When they can identify a bundle of attributes that are desirable enough for another segment of customers, they can charge a higher price for that bundle. Companies can configure service bundles that reflect price and service points appealing to different groups in the market. Hotels, for example, offer standard rooms at a basic rate but then combine amenities and tangibles related to the room to attract customers willing to pay more for the concierge level, jacuzzis, additional beds, and sitting areas.

Pricing Strategies When the Customer Means "Value Is All That I Get for All That I Give"

Some customers define value as including not just the benefits they receive but also the time, money, and effort they put into a service. Figure 17.6 illustrates the pricing strategies described in this definition of value.

FIGURE 17.6
Pricing Strategies When the Customer Defines Value as All That Is Received for All That Is Given

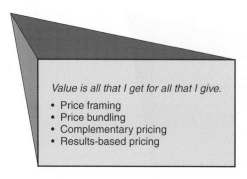

Value is all that I get for all that I give.
- Price framing
- Price bundling
- Complementary pricing
- Results-based pricing

Price Framing

Because many customers do not possess accurate reference prices for services, services marketers are more likely than product marketers to organize price information for customers so they know how to view it. Customers naturally look for price anchors as well as familiar services against which to judge focal services. If they accept the anchors, they view the price and service package favorably. Gerald Smith, a professor at Boston College, provided an enlightening example of the way price framing could have improved sales of the 1994 Olympic TripleCast, minute-by-minute coverage of different Olympic arenas that was a well-documented failure because customers were not willing to pay the price of $130. He suggested that if CBS had segmented the market, isolated meaningful packages of sports, and framed them in a way that was familiar to customers, the service might have been successful. He proposed a boxing package for $24.95, a skating package for $24.95, and equestrian and wrestling packages for $19.95. In each case the service could be framed in an appropriate price context. For example, boxing at $24.95 is priced somewhere between attending a boxing match and watching it on pay-per-view. Boxing aficionados would recognize that the price for the full package of matches was a value.[25]

Price Bundling

Some services are consumed more effectively in conjunction with other services; other services accompany the products they support (such as extended service warranties, training, and expedited delivery). When customers find value in a package of services that are interrelated, price bundling is an appropriate strategy. Bundling, which means pricing and selling services as a group rather than individually, has benefits to both customers and service companies. Customers find that bundling simplifies their purchase and payment, and companies find that the approach stimulates demand for the firm's service line, thereby achieving cost economies for the operations as a whole while increasing net contributions.[26] Bundling also allows the customer to pay less than when purchasing each of the services individually, which contributes to perceptions of value.

The effectiveness of price bundling depends on how well the service firm understands the bundles of value that customers or segments perceive, and on the complementarity of demand for these services. Effectiveness also depends on the right choice of services from the firm's point of view. Because the firm's objective is to increase overall sales, the services selected for bundling should be those with a relatively small sales volume without the bundling to minimize revenue loss from discounting a service that already has a high sales volume.

Approaches to bundling include mixed bundling, mixed-leader bundling, and mixed-joint bundling.[27] In *mixed bundling,* the customer can purchase the services individually or as a package, but a price incentive is offered for purchasing the package. As an example, a health club customer may be able to contract for aerobics classes at $10 per month, weight machines at $15, and pool privileges at $15—or the group of three services for $27 (a price incentive of $13 per month).[28] In *mixed-leader bundling,* the price of one service is discounted if the first service is purchased at full price. For example, if cable TV customers buy one premium channel at full price, they can acquire a second premium channel at a reduced monthly rate. The objective is to reduce the price of the higher-volume service to generate an increase in its volume that "pulls" an increase in demand for a lower-volume but higher-contribution margin service. In *mixed-joint bundling,* a single price is formed for the combined set of services to increase demand for both services by packaging them together.

Complementary Pricing

Services that are highly interrelated can be leveraged by using complementary pricing. This pricing includes three related strategies—captive pricing, two-part pricing, and loss leadership.[29] In *captive pricing* the firm offers a base service or product and then provides the supplies or peripheral services needed to continue using the service. In this situation the company could off-load some part of the price for the basic service to the peripherals. For example, cable services often drop the price for installation to a very low level, then compensate by charging enough for the peripheral services to make up for the loss in revenue. With service firms, this strategy is often called *two-part pricing* because the service price is broken into a fixed fee plus variable usage fees (also found in telephone services, health clubs, and commercial services such as rentals). *Loss leadership* is the term typically used in retail stores when providers place a familiar service on special largely to draw the customer to the store and then reveal other levels of service available at higher prices.

Results-Based Pricing

In service industries in which outcome is very important but uncertainty is high, the most relevant aspect of value is the *result* of the service. In personal injury lawsuits, for example, clients value the settlement they receive at the conclusion of the service. From tax accountants, clients value cost savings. From trade schools, students most value getting a job upon graduation. From Hollywood stars, production companies value high grosses. In these and other situations, an appropriate value-based pricing strategy is to price on the basis of results or outcome of the service.

The most commonly known form of results-based pricing is a practice called *contingency pricing* used by lawyers. Contingency pricing is the major way that personal injury and certain consumer cases are billed; it accounts for 12 percent of commercial law billings.[30] In this approach, lawyers do not receive fees or payment until the case is settled, when they are paid a percentage of the money that the client receives. Therefore, only an outcome in the client's favor is compensated. From the client's point of view, the pricing makes sense in part because most clients in these cases are unfamiliar with and possibly intimidated by law firms. Their biggest fears are high fees for a case that may take years to settle. By using contingency pricing, clients are ensured that they pay no fees until they receive a settlement.

In these and other instances of contingency pricing, the economic value of the service is hard to determine before the service, and providers develop a price that allows them to share the risks and rewards of delivering value to the buyer. Partial contingency pricing, now being used in commercial law cases, is a version in which the client pays a lower fee than usual but offers a bonus if the settlement exceeds a certain level.

Bickel and Brewer, a commercial law firm, agreed to cap fees for legal work at $800,000 but to split with its client, Prentiss Properties, any judgment over $10 million. When the federal judge awarded Prentiss $100 million in settlement, the law firm walked away with $45 million more in payment for taking the risk.[31]

Sealed Bid Contingency Pricing Companies wishing to gain the most value from their services purchases are increasingly turning to a form of results-based pricing that involves sealed bids guaranteeing results. Consider the challenge of a school district with energy bills (including heating oil, gas, and electricity) so high that money was diverted from its primary mission of educating students. In its most recent year, costs for energy were $775,000, and the proposed budget for the coming year was $810,000. The school board wanted a long-term solution to the problem, desiring to expend less of their budget on energy and more on direct education expenses. The EMS Company, an engineering firm providing services to control and reduce energy use in large buildings, was one of three companies submitting bids to the school district. EMS proposed a computer-controlled system that monitored energy use and operated on/off valves for all energy-using systems. The proposal specified a five-year contract with a fixed price of $254,500 per year, with the additional guarantee that the school district would save at least that amount of money each year or EMS would refund the difference. Included in the proposal was a plan to take into account energy prices, hours the buildings were in use, and degree days so as to provide a basis of calculating the actual savings occurring. After five years the school district would own the system with the option of purchasing a management operating service for an annual fee of $50,000.[32]

Although two other firms submitted lower multiyear bids of $190,000 and $215,000 annually, neither bid provided any guarantee for energy savings. The school board was intrigued by the EMS approach, because at worst the cost of the service was zero. EMS was awarded the bid. During the first year, actual calculated savings exceeded $300,000. A cost-plus bid by EMS would have been priced at $130,000 per year. The use of contingency pricing by EMS removed the risk from the school board's decision and added profits at EMS.[33]

Money-Back Guarantees Vocational colleges offer one major promise: to get students jobs upon graduation. So many schools commit to this promise—often blatantly in television advertising—that prospective students have come to distrust all promises from these colleges. To give substance to its promise, Brown-MacKenzie College, a for-profit vocational college, offered a tuition-back guarantee to any graduate who, after due effort, failed to obtain a suitable position within 90 days of program completion. Although other educational institutions cannot do this, largely because the results desired do not often arrive within a 90-day period, other results-based plans are taking shape. A future-income-dependent payment plan has been considered by many schools. Under such a plan, a student would receive a full scholarship and, after graduation, pay a fixed percentage of salary for a set period—for example, 5 percent of salary for 20 years. Under this plan, the more "value added" by education and the more money-oriented the student, the more the student and the institution would benefit financially.[34]

Commission Many services providers—including real estate agents and advertising agencies—earn their fees through commissions based on a percentage of the selling price. In these and other industries, commission is paid by the supplier rather than the buyer. Advertising agencies are paid 15 percent commission by the print and broadcast media (newspaper, radio, TV, magazines) for the amount of advertising that they place

FIGURE 17.7
Summary of Service Pricing Strategies for Four Customer Definitions of Value

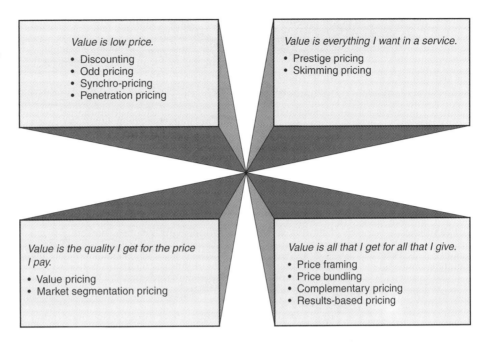

Value is low price.
- Discounting
- Odd pricing
- Synchro-pricing
- Penetration pricing

Value is everything I want in a service.
- Prestige pricing
- Skimming pricing

Value is the quality I get for the price I pay.
- Value pricing
- Market segmentation pricing

Value is all that I get for all that I give.
- Price framing
- Price bundling
- Complementary pricing
- Results-based pricing

with the media, but agencies are not paid by their clients. Real estate agents are paid 6 percent of the selling price of a house.

The commission approach to services pricing is compelling in that agents are compensated most when they find the highest rates and fares. It would seem that agents have an underlying motivation to avoid the lowest fares and rates for their clients.

Summary

This chapter began with three key differences between customer evaluation of pricing for services and goods: (1) customers often have inaccurate or limited reference prices for services, (2) price is a key signal to quality in services, and (3) monetary price is not the only relevant price to service customers. These three differences can have profound impact on the strategies that companies use to set and administer prices for services. The chapter next discussed common pricing structures, including (1) cost-based, (2) competition-based, and (3) demand-based pricing. Central to the discussion were the specific challenges in each of these structures and the services pricing techniques that have emerged in practice.

Finally, the chapter defined customer perceptions of value and suggested appropriate pricing strategies that match each customer definition. Figure 17.7 summarizes these definitions and strategies. The four value definitions include (1) value is low price, (2) value is whatever I want in a product or service, (3) value is the quality I get for the price I pay, and (4) value is all that I get for all that I give.

Discussion Questions

1. Which approach to pricing (cost-based, competition-based, or demand-based) is the most fair to customers? Why?
2. Is it possible to use all three approaches simultaneously when pricing services? If you answer yes, describe a service that is priced this way.

3. For what consumer services do you have reference prices? What makes these services different from others for which you lack reference prices?

4. Name three services you purchase in which price is a signal to quality. Do you believe that there are true differences across services that are priced high and those that are priced low? Why or why not?

5. Describe the nonmonetary costs involved in the following services: getting an automobile loan, belonging to a health club, having allergies diagnosed and treated, attending an executive education class, and getting braces.

6. Consider the specific pricing strategies for each of the four customer value definitions. Which of these strategies could be adapted and used with another value definition?

Exercises

1. List five services for which you have no reference price. Now put yourself in the role of the service providers for two of those services and develop pricing strategies. Be sure to include in your description which of the value definitions you believe customers will possess and what types of strategies would be appropriate given those definitions.

2. In the next week, find three price lists for services (such as from a restaurant, dry cleaner, or hairstylist). Identify the pricing base and the strategy used in each of them. How effective is each?

3. Consider that you are the owner of a new private college and can prepare a value/price package that is appealing to students. Describe your approach. How does it differ from existing offerings?

4. Go to the priceline.com Internet site and become familiar with the way it works.

Notes

1. Peter Lewis, "Pay to Play," *Fortune*, January 7, 2002, pp. 115–17.
2. Robert Barba, "Apple's Online Music Store Sells 150 Millionth Song," *Knight Ridder Tribune Business News,* October 15, 2004, p. 1.
3. Fred Goodman, "Will Fans Pay for Music Online?" *Rolling Stone*, January 31, 2002, pp. 17–18.
4. "MusicRebellion.com Inc.: Dynamic Pricing for Music Starts with 10-Cent Tunes," *The Wall Street Journal* (Eastern edition), January 9, 2004, p. 1.
5. K. Monroe, "The Pricing of Services," *Handbook of Services Marketing,* ed. C. A. Congram and M. L. Friedman (New York: AMACOM, 1989), pp. 20–31.
6. Ibid.
7. "Pet Depressed? Call Us," *Newsweek,* May 22, 1989, p. 60.
8. "Rent a Star for the Holidays," *People,* December 15, 2003.
9. M. A. Ernst, "Price Visibility and Its Implications for Financial Services," presentation at the Effective Pricing Strategies for Service Providers Conference, Institute for International Research, Boston, October 1994.
10. M. Chase, "Whose Time Is Worth More: Yours or the Doctor's," *The Wall Street Journal,* October 24, 1994, p. B1.
11. Monroe, "The Pricing of Services."
12. V. A. Zeithaml, "The Acquisition, Meaning, and Use of Price Information by Consumers of Professional Services," in *Marketing Theory: Philosophy of Science Perspectives,* ed. R. Bush and S. Hunt (Chicago: American Marketing Association, 1982), pp. 237–41.

13. C. H. Lovelock, "Understanding Costs and Developing Pricing Strategies," *Services Marketing* (New York: Prentice Hall, 1991), pp. 236–46.
14. A. Stevens, "Firms Try More Lucrative Ways of Charging for Legal Services," *The Wall Street Journal,* November 25, 1994, pp. B1ff.
15. K. H. Bacon, "Banks' Services Grow Costlier for Consumers," *The Wall Street Journal,* November 18, 1993, p. B1.
16. Ibid.
17. J. L. Fix, "Consumers Are Snarling over Charges," *USA Today,* August 2, 1994, pp. B1–B2.
18. C. L. Grossman, "The Driving Forces behind Rental Car Costs," *USA Today,* October 25, 1994, p. 50.
19. V. A. Zeithaml, "Consumer Perceptions of Price, Quality, and Value: A Means-End Model and Synthesis of Evidence," *Journal of Marketing* 52 (July 1988), pp. 2–22.
20. All comments from these four sections are based on those from Zeithaml, "Consumer Perceptions," pp. 13–14.
21. H. Simon, "If the Price Isn't Right," *World Link,* September–October 1994.
22. "Colleges Get Creative in Price-Cutting," *St. Petersburg Times,* December 27, 1994, pp. B1, B6.
23. G. Boeck, "Teams Woo Fans with Cheaper Seats," *USA Today,* August 31, 2004.
24. Monroe, "The Pricing of Services."
25. G. E. Smith, "Framing and Customers' Perceptions of Price and Value in Service-Oriented Businesses," presentation at the Effective Pricing Strategies for Service Providers Conference, Institute for International Research, Boston, October 1994.
26. Monroe, "The Pricing of Services."
27. Ibid.
28. J. P. Guiltinan, "The Price Bundling of Services: A Normative Framework," *Journal of Marketing* 51 (April 1987): 74–85.
29. G. J. Tellis, "Beyond the Many Faces of Price: An Integration of Pricing Strategies," *Journal of Marketing* 50 (October 1986): 146–60.
30. A. Stevens, "Clients Second-Guess Legal Fees," *The Wall Street Journal,* January 6, 1995, pp. B1, B6.
31. Example adapted from P. J. LaPlaca, "Pricing That Is Contingent on Value Delivered," given at the First Annual Pricing Conference, The Pricing Institute, New York, December 3, 4, 1987, and described in Monroe, "The Pricing of Services," p. 23.
32. Ibid.
33. Ibid.
34. K. Fox, *Service Marketing Newsletter* (Chicago: American Marketing Association, 1984), pp. 1–2.

SERVICE AND THE BOTTOM LINE

Chapter 18: The Financial and Economic Impact of Service

In this final section of the text, we discuss one of the most important questions about service that managers have been debating over the past 25 years: Is excellent service profitable to an organization? We pull together research and company experience, virtually all of it from the past decade, to answer this question. We present our own model of how the relationship works and show you alternative models that have been used in companies such as Sears. Our model shows how service quality has offensive effects (gaining new customers) and defensive effects (retaining customers).

We also discuss several important performance models in this chapter. Return on service quality (ROSQ) is a modeling approach that allows a company to gauge the return on investments in different service activities. Customer equity is an extension of the ROSQ approach that compares investments in service with expenditures on other marketing activities. The balanced performance scorecard is an approach that includes multiple company factors including financial, customer, operational, and innovative measures. The balanced performance scorecard allows a company to measure performance from the customer's perspective (Chapter 10), from the employee's perspective (Chapter 12), and from an innovation and new service perspective (Chapter 9). Thus, in Chapter 18 we synthesize the measurement issues that underlie the provision of service and offer a way for companies to demonstrate that service is accountable financially. We also present an approach called strategic performance mapping that helps companies integrate all elements of their balanced scorecards. These models help companies understand more accurately their benefits from investments in service excellence.

18

The Financial and Economic Impact of Service

This chapter's objectives are to

1. Examine the direct effects of service on profits.

2. Consider the effect of service on getting new customers.

3. Evaluate the role of service in keeping customers.

4. Discuss what is known about the key service drivers of overall service quality, customer retention, and profitability.

5. Discuss the balanced performance scorecard that allows for strategic focus on measurements other than financials.

6. Describe the role of strategy maps in implementing the balanced performance scorecard.

"What return can I expect on service quality improvements?"

—A typical CEO

All authors of this text work with companies to improve their service quality and better meet their customers' expectations. The two most frequent questions asked by executives of these companies are

"How do I know that service quality improvements will be a good investment?"
"Where in the company do I invest money to achieve the highest return?"

For example, a restaurant chain, after conducting consumer research, found that service quality perceptions averaged 85 percent across the chain. The specific items receiving the lowest scores on the survey were appearance of the restaurant's exterior (70 percent), wait time for service (78 percent), and limited menu (76 percent). The company's CEO wanted to know, first of all, whether making improvements in overall service quality or to any of the specific areas would result in revenues that exceeded their costs. Moreover, he wanted guidance as to which of the service aspects to tackle. He could determine how much each of the initiatives would cost to change, but that was as far as his financial estimates would take him. Clearly, the restaurant's exterior was most in need of change because it was rated lowest; but would it not also be by far the most expensive to change? What could he expect in return for improvements in each service area? Would adjustments in the other two factors be better investments? Which of the three service initiatives would generate noticeable improvements to raise the overall customer perceptions of the restaurant?

Ten years ago, these questions had to be answered on the basis of executive intuition. Today, fortunately, more analytical and rigorous approaches exist to help managers make these decisions about service quality investments. The best known and most widely respected approach is called return on service quality (ROSQ) and was developed by Roland Rust, Anthony Zahorik, and Tim Keiningham, a team of researchers and consultants.[1] The ROSQ approach is based on the following assumptions:

1. Quality is an investment.

2. Quality efforts must be financially accountable.

3. It is possible to spend too much on quality.

4. Not all quality expenditures are equally valid.

Their approach looks at investments in services as a chain of effects of the following form:

1. A service improvement effort will produce an increased level of customer satisfaction at the process or attribute level. For example, expending money to refurbish the exterior of the restaurants will likely increase customers' satisfaction level from the current low rating of 70 percent.

2. Increased customer satisfaction at the process or attribute level will lead to increased overall customer satisfaction. If satisfaction with the restaurant's exterior goes from 70 to 80 percent, overall service quality ratings may increase from 85 to 90 percent. (Both these percentage changes could be accurately measured the next time surveys are conducted and could even be projected in advance using the ROSQ model.)

3. Higher overall service quality or customer satisfaction will lead to increased behavioral intentions, such as greater repurchase intention and intention to increase usage. Customers who have not yet eaten at the restaurant will be drawn to do so, and many who currently eat there once a month will consider increasing their patronage.

4. Increased behavioral intentions will lead to behavioral impact, including repurchase or customer retention, positive word of mouth, and increased usage. Intentions about patronizing the restaurant will become reality, resulting in higher revenues and more positive word-of-mouth communications.

5. Behavioral effects will then lead to improved profitability and other financial outcomes. Higher revenues will lead to higher profits for the restaurant, assuming that the original investment in refurbishing the exterior is covered.

The ROSQ methodology can help distinguish among all the company strategies, processes, approaches, and tactics that can be altered. The ROSQ approach is informative because it can be applied in companies to direct their individual strategies. Software has been developed to accompany the approach, and consulting firms work with companies to apply it. No longer do firms like the restaurant discussed here have to depend on intuition alone to guide them in their service quality investments.

In the current era of accountability and streamlining, virtually all companies hunger for evidence and tools to ascertain and monitor the payoff and payback of new investments in service. Many managers still see service and service quality as costs rather than as contributors to profits, partly because of the difficulty involved in tracing the link between service and financial returns. Determining the financial impact of service parallels the age-old search for the connection between advertising and sales. Service quality's results—like advertising's results—are cumulative, and therefore, evidence of the link may not come immediately or even quickly after investments. And, like advertising, service quality is one of many variables—among them pricing, advertising, efficiency, and image—that simultaneously influence profits. Furthermore, spending on service per se does not guarantee results because strategy and execution must both also be considered.

In recent years, however, researchers and company executives have sought to understand the relationship between service and profits and have found strong evidence to support the relationship. For example, a recent study examined the comparative benefits of revenue expansion and cost reduction on return on quality. The research addressed a common strategic dilemma faced by executives: whether to reduce costs through the use of quality programs such as Six Sigma that focus on efficiencies and cost cutting, or to build revenues through improvements to customer service, customer satisfaction, and customer retention.[2] Using managers' reports as well as secondary data on firm profitability and stock returns, the study investigated whether the highest return on quality was generated from cost cutting, revenue expansion, or a combination of the two approaches. The results suggest that firms that adopt primarily a revenue expansion emphasis perform better and have higher return on quality than firms that emphasize either cost reduction or both revenue expansion and cost reduction together.[3]

Executives are also realizing that the link between service and profits is neither straightforward nor simple. Service quality affects many economic factors in a company, some of them leading to profits through variables not traditionally in the domain of marketing. For example, the traditional total quality management approach expresses the financial impact of service quality in lowered costs or increased productivity. These relationships involve operational issues that concern marketing only in the sense that marketing research is used to identify service improvements that customers notice and value.

More recently, other types of evidence have become available on which to examine the relationship between service and profitability. The overall goal of this chapter is to synthesize that recent evidence and to identify relationships between service and profits. This chapter is divided into six sections, paralleling the chapter's objectives. In each

FIGURE 18.1
The Direct Relationship between Service and Profits

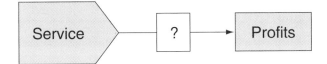

section we assess the evidence and identify what is currently known about the topics. The chapter is organized using a conceptual framework linking all the variables in the topics.

SERVICE AND PROFITABILITY: THE DIRECT RELATIONSHIP

Figure 18.1 shows the underlying question at the heart of this chapter. Managers were first interested in this question in the 1980s when service quality emerged as a pivotal competitive strategy. The executives of leading service companies such as Federal Express and Disney were willing to trust their intuitive sense that better service would lead to improved financial success. Without formal documentation of the financial payoff, they committed resources to improving service and were richly rewarded for their leaps of faith. In the 1990s, the strategy of using service for competitive advantage and profits was embraced by forward-thinking manufacturing and information technology companies such as General Electric and IBM. However, executives in other companies withheld judgment about investing in service, waiting for solid evidence of its financial soundness.

Because tools such as return on quality analysis did not exist at the time, individual firms turned for insight to a group of early 1990s studies that explored total quality management (TQM) effects across a broad sample of manufacturing and service firms. The news was not encouraging. McKinsey and Company found that nearly two-thirds of quality programs examined had either stalled or fallen short of delivering real improvements.[4] In two other studies, A. T. Kearney found that 80 percent of British firms reported no significant impact as a result of TQM, and Arthur D. Little claimed that almost two-thirds of 500 U.S. companies saw "zero competitive gain" from TQM.[5]

Partially in response to early versions of these studies, the U.S. General Accounting Office (GAO) sought grounds for belief in the financial impact of quality in companies that had been finalists or winners of the Malcolm Baldrige National Quality Award. The GAO found that these elite quality firms had benefited in terms of market share, sales per employee, return on sales, and return on assets. Based on responses from 22 companies who won or were finalists in 1988 and 1989, the GAO found that 34 of 40 financial variables showed positive performance improvements while only 6 measurements were negative or neutral.[6]

In later years, evidence from more rigorous research showed the positive impact of service. One study showed the favorable financial impact of complaint recovery systems.[7] Another found a significant and positive relationship between patient satisfaction and hospital profitability. In this study, specific dimensions of hospital service quality, such as billing and discharge processes, explained 17 to 27 percent of hospital earnings, net revenues, and return on assets.[8] Extending the definition of financial performance to include stock returns, another study found a significant positive link between changes in customer quality perceptions and stock return while holding constant the effects of advertising expenditures and return on investment.[9]

Exhibit 18.1 **THE EMPLOYEE–CUSTOMER–PROFIT CHAIN AT SEARS**

One way to view the relationship between service and profit has been developed by a group of Harvard professors and is called the "service-profit chain." The professors who created it argue many of the same points made in this chapter—that the longer customers stay with companies, the lower the costs to serve them, the higher the volume of purchases they make, the higher the price premium they tolerate, and the greater the positive word-of-mouth communication they engage in. The professors have provided evidence from in-depth studies in multiple companies such as Sears, Intuit, and Taco Bell to document these relationships. We take one of these companies, Sears, and illustrate the approach used both to examine the relationships among employees, customers, and profits as well as to improve the overall financial performance of the organization using these relationships.

The year 1992 was the worst in the history of Sears, with a net loss of $3.9 billion on sales of $52.3 billion. Between 1993 and 1998, however, Sears transformed itself into a company built around its customers. Using an ongoing process of data collection and analysis, the company created a set of total performance indicator (TPI) measures that show how well it is doing with customers, employees, and investors. Because of the extensive analysis the company undertook, it understood the influence of each of these measures on the others and ran the business on the basis of the indicators.

Early on, Sears recognized that everyone—managers and employees—must feel a sense of ownership in the program. After extensive work in teams, managers were aligned because they created the model around which the system was built—called the 3 Cs and 3 Ps. The 3 Cs were known as the three "compellings": make Sears into a "compelling place to work, shop, and invest." The 3 Ps were the company's three shared values—"passion for the customer, our people add value, and performance leadership."

As the accompanying figure shows, sets of specific objectives and measures captured the 3 Cs so that the company could be managed according to them. These objectives include many of the priorities we discuss in this chapter, including customer loyalty and excellent service. Believing that these objectives could be obtained only if employees were committed and involved, parallel goals and measures were established for that group of internal customers. Sears management spent a great deal of time and effort in communication and education to store-level personnel about their value and the worth of the customer. In 1998, the company declared the model successful:

> We use the TPI at every level of the company, in every store and facility; and nearly every manager has some portion of his or her compensation at risk on the basis of nonfinancial measures . . . . [I]n the course of the last 12 months, employee satisfaction on the Sears TPI has risen

Exhibit 18.1 shows how some of these relationships have been examined at Sears in the context of the "employee–customer–profit chain" that has been discussed earlier in this textbook. Although some companies continued to approach the relationship at a broad level, others began to focus more specifically on particular elements of the relationship. For example, executives and researchers soon recognized that service quality played a different role in getting new customers than it did in retaining existing customers.

OFFENSIVE MARKETING EFFECTS OF SERVICE: ATTRACTING MORE AND BETTER CUSTOMERS

Service quality can help companies attract more and better customers to the business through *offensive marketing*.[10] Offensive effects (shown in Figure 18.2) involve market share, reputation, and price premiums. When service is good, a company gains a positive reputation and through that reputation a higher market share and the ability to charge more than its competitors for services. These benefits were documented in a multiyear, multicompany study called PIMS (profit impact of marketing strategy). The PIMS research shows that companies offering superior service achieve higher-than-normal market share growth and that service quality influences profits through increased market share and premium prices as well as lowered costs and less rework.[11] The study found that businesses rated in the top fifth of competitors on relative service quality average an 8 percent price premium over their competitors.[12]

To document the impact of service on market share, a group of researchers described their version of the path between quality and market share, claiming that satisfied customers spread positive word of mouth, which leads to the attraction of new customers and then to higher market share. They claim that advertising service excellence without sufficient quality to back up the communications will not increase market share. Further, they confirm that there are time lags in market share effects, making the relationship between quality and market share difficult to discern in the short term.[13]

DEFENSIVE MARKETING EFFECTS OF SERVICE: CUSTOMER RETENTION

When it comes to keeping the customers a firm already has—an approach called *defensive marketing*[14]—researchers and consulting firms have in the last 15 years documented and quantified the financial impact of existing customers. In Chapter 7 we explained that

FIGURE 18.2
Offensive Marketing Effects of Service on Profits

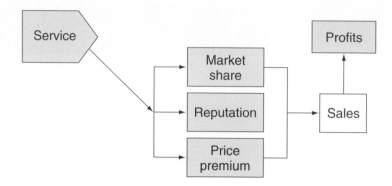

customer defection, or "customer churn," is widespread in service businesses. Customer defection is costly to companies because new customers must replace lost customers, and replacement comes at a high cost. Getting new customers is expensive; it involves advertising, promotion, and sales costs as well as start-up operating expenses. New customers are often unprofitable for a period of time after acquisition. In the insurance industry, for example, the insurer does not typically recover selling costs until the third or fourth year of the relationship. Capturing customers from other companies is also an expensive proposition: A greater degree of service improvement is necessary to make a customer switch from a competitor than to retain a current customer. Selling costs for existing customers are much lower (on average 20 percent lower) than selling to new ones.[15]

In general, the longer a customer remains with the company, the more profitable the relationship is for the organization:

> Served correctly, customers generate increasingly more profits each year they stay with a company. Across a wide range of businesses, the pattern is the same: the longer a company keeps a customer, the more money it stands to make.[16]

The money a company makes from retention comes from four sources (shown in Figure 18.3): costs, volume of purchases, price premium, and word-of-mouth communication. This section provides research evidence for many of the sources.

Lower Costs

Attracting a new customer is five times as costly as retaining an existing one. Consultants who have focused on these relationships assert that customer defections have a stronger effect on a company's profits than market share, scale, unit costs, and many other factors usually associated with competitive advantage.[17] They also claim that, depending on the industry, companies can increase profits from 25 to 85 percent by retaining just 5 percent more of their customers. The General Accounting Office study of semifinalists in the Malcolm Baldrige competition (described earlier in this chapter) found that quality reduced costs: Order processing time decreased on average by 12 percent per year, errors and defects fell by 10 percent per year, and cost of quality declined by 9 percent per year.

Consider the following facts about the role of service quality in lowering costs:

- "Our highest quality day was our lowest cost of operations day" (Fred Smith, Federal Express).

- "Our costs of not doing things right the first time were from 25 to 30 percent of our revenue" (David F. Colicchio, regional quality manager, Hewlett-Packard Company).[18]

FIGURE 18.3
Defensive Marketing Effects of Service on Profits

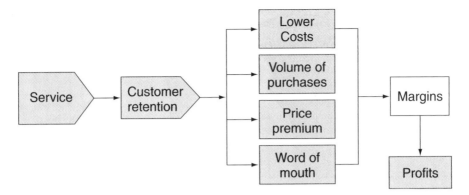

- Profit on services purchased by a 10-year customer is on average three times greater than for a 5-year customer.[19]
- Bain and Company, a consulting organization specializing in retention research, estimates that in the life insurance business, a 5 percent annual increase in customer retention lowers a company's costs per policy by 18 percent.

Volume of Purchases

Customers who are satisfied with a company's services are likely to increase the amount of money they spend with that company or the types of services offered. A customer satisfied with a broker's services, for example, will likely invest more money when it becomes available. Similarly, a customer satisfied with a bank's checking services is likely to open a savings account with the same bank and to use the bank's loan services as well.

Price Premium

Evidence suggests that a customer who notices and values the services provided by a company will pay a price premium for those services. Graniterock, a winner of the Baldrige Award, has been able to command prices up to 30 percent higher than competitors for its rock (a product that many would claim is a commodity!) because it offers off-hour delivery and 24-hour self-service. In fact, most of the service quality leaders in industry command higher prices than their competitors: Federal Express collects more for overnight delivery than the U.S. Postal Service, Hertz rental cars cost more than Avis cars, and staying at the Ritz-Carlton is a more expensive undertaking than staying at the Hyatt.

Word-of-Mouth Communication

In Chapter 3 of this text, we described the valuable role of word-of-mouth communications in purchasing service. Because word-of-mouth communication is considered more credible than other sources of information, the best type of promotion for a service may well come from other customers who advocate the services provided by the company. Word-of-mouth communication brings new customers to the firm, and the financial value of this form of advocacy can be calibrated by the company in terms of the promotional costs it saves as well as the streams of revenues from new customers.

Many questions remain about defensive marketing, among them the ones shown in Exhibit 18.2. Although research has come a long way in the last decade, researchers

Managers of service firms are only beginning to understand the topics discussed in this chapter. For each of the sections on the service quality/profitability relationship in this chapter, Exhibit 18.3 lists an inventory of questions that managers and researchers most want to know. To give you an idea of the specific questions that managers are asking, we elaborate here on the topic of defensive marketing.

1. *What is a loyal customer?* Customer loyalty can be viewed as the way customers feel or as the way they act. A simple definition is possible with some products and services: Customers are loyal as long as they continue to use a good or service. For washing machines or long-distance telephone service, customers are deemed loyal if they continue to use the machine or telephone service. Defining customer loyalty for other products and services is more problematic. What is the definition of loyalty to a restaurant: always eat there, eat there more times than at other restaurants, or eat there at least once during a given period? These questions highlight the growing popularity of the concept of "share of wallet" that company managers are very interested in. "Share of wallet" means what percentage of the spending in a particular service category is made on a given service provider. The other way to define loyalty is in terms of the customer's sense of belonging or commitment to the product. Some companies have been noted for their "apostles," customers who care so much about the company that they stay in contact to provide suggestions for improvement and constantly preach to others the benefits of the company. Is this the best way to define loyalty?

2. *What is the role of service in defensive marketing?* Quality products at appropriate prices are important elements in the retention equation, but both these marketing variables can be imitated. Service plays a critical role—if not the critical role—in retaining customers. Providing consistently good service is not as easy to duplicate and therefore is likely to be the cementing force in customer relationships. Exactly how important is service in defensive marketing? How does service compare in effectiveness to other retention strategies such as price? To date no studies have incorporated all or most factors to examine their relative importance in keeping customers. Many companies actually have survey data that could answer this question but either have not analyzed the data for this purpose or have not reported their findings.

3. *What levels of service provision are needed to retain customers?* How much spending on service quality is enough to retain customers? Initial investigations into this question have been argued but have not been con-

and companies must continue working on these questions for a more complete understanding of the impact of service on defensive marketing.

CUSTOMER PERCEPTIONS OF SERVICE AND PURCHASE INTENTIONS

In Chapter 5 we highlighted the links among customer satisfaction, service quality, and increased purchases. Here we provide more research and empirical evidence supporting these relationships. For example, researchers at Xerox offered a compelling insight about the relationship between satisfaction and purchase intentions during the company's early years of customer satisfaction research. Initially, the company focused on satisfied customers, which they identified as those checking either a "4" or a "5" on a five-point satisfaction scale. Careful analysis of the data showed that customers giving Xerox 5s were six times more likely to indicate that they would repurchase Xerox equipment than those giving 4s. This relationship encouraged the company to focus on increasing the 5s rather than the 4s and 5s because of the strong sales and profitability implications.[20] Figure 18.4 shows this relationship.

firmed. One consultant, for example, proposed that when satisfaction rose above a certain threshold, repurchase loyalty would climb rapidly. When satisfaction fell below a different threshold, customer loyalty would decline equally rapidly. Between these thresholds, he believed that loyalty was relatively flat. The material discussed in Chapter 4 of this text offered a different prediction. The zone of tolerance in that chapter captured the range within which a company is meeting expectations. This framework suggests that firms operating within the zone of tolerance should continue to improve service, even to the point of reaching the desired service level. This hypothesis implies an upward-sloping (rather than flat) relationship with the zone of tolerance.

4. *What aspects of service are most important for customer retention?* The only studies that have examined specific aspects of service and their impact on customer retention have been early studies looking at customer complaint management. A decade ago such a study was appropriate because service was often equated with customer service, the after-sale function that dealt with dissatisfied customers. But today, most companies realize that service is multifaceted and want to identify the specific aspects of service provision that will lead to keeping customers.

5. *How can defection-prone customers be identified?* Companies find it difficult to create and execute strategies responsive enough to detect customer defections. Systems must be developed to isolate potential defecting customers, evaluate them, and retain them if it is in the best interest of the company. One author and consultant advises that companies focus on three groups of customers who may be candidates for defection: (a) customers who close their accounts and shift business to a competitor, (b) customers who shift some of their business to another firm, and (c) customers who actually buy more but whose purchases represent a smaller share of their total expenditures. The first of these groups is easiest to identify, and the third group is the most difficult. Among the other customers who would be vulnerable are any customer with a negative service experience, new customers, and customers of companies in very competitive markets. Developing early warning systems of such customers is a pivotal requirement for companies.

Source: Reprinted with permission from V. A. Zeithaml, "Service Quality, Profitability and the Economic Worth of Customers," *Journal of the Academy of Marketing Science,* January 2000, © 2000 by the Academy of Marketing Science.

Evidence also shows that customer satisfaction and service quality perceptions affect consumer intentions to behave in other positive ways—praising the firm, preferring the company over others, increasing volume of purchases, or agreeably paying a price premium. Most of the early evidence looked only at overall benefits in terms of purchase intention rather than examining specific types of behavioral intentions. One study, for example, found a significant association between overall patient satisfaction and intent to choose a hospital again.[21] Another, using information from a Swedish customer satisfaction barometer, found that stated repurchase intention is strongly related to stated satisfaction across virtually all product categories.[22]

More recently, studies have found relationships between service quality and more specific behavioral intentions. One study involving university students found strong links between service quality and other behavioral intentions of strategic importance to a university, including behavior such as saying positive things about the school, planning to contribute money to the class pledge on graduation, and planning to recommend the school to employers as a place from which to recruit.[23] Another comprehensive study examined a battery comprised of 13 specific behavioral intentions likely to result from perceived service quality. The overall measure was significantly correlated with customer perceptions of service quality.[24]

FIGURE 18.4
The Effects of Service

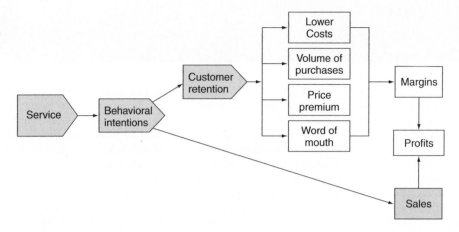

Individual companies have also monitored the impact of service quality on selected behavioral intentions. Toyota found that intent to repurchase a Toyota automobile increased from a base of 37 to 45 percent with a positive sales experience, from 37 to 79 percent with a positive service experience, and from 37 to 91 percent with both positive sales and service experiences.[25] A similar study quantitatively assessed the relationship between level of service quality and willingness to purchase at AT&T. Of AT&T's customers who rated the company's overall quality as excellent, more than 90 percent expressed willingness to purchase from AT&T again. For customers rating the service as good, fair, or poor, the percentages decreased to 60, 17, and 0 percent, respectively. According to these data, willingness to repurchase increased at a steeper rate (by 43 percent) as the service quality rating improved from fair to good than when it went from poor to fair (17 percent) or from good to excellent (30 percent).[26]

Exhibit 18.3 shows a list of the questions that businesses still need to know more about on this topic and the others in this chapter.

THE KEY DRIVERS OF SERVICE QUALITY, CUSTOMER RETENTION, AND PROFITS

Understanding the relationship between overall service quality and profitability is important, but it is perhaps more useful to managers to identify specific drivers of service quality that most relate to profitability (shown in Figure 18.5). Doing so will help firms understand what aspects of service quality to change to influence the relationship, and therefore where to invest resources.

Most evidence for this issue has come from examining the aspects of service (such as empathy, responsiveness, and tangibles) on overall service quality, customer satisfaction, and purchase intentions rather than on financial outcomes such as retention or profitability. As you have discovered in this text, service is multifaceted, consisting of a wide variety of customer-perceived dimensions including reliability, responsiveness, and empathy and resulting from innumerable company strategies such as technology and process improvement. In research exploring the relative importance of service dimensions on overall service quality or customer satisfaction, the bulk of the support confirms that reliability is most critical; but other research has demonstrated the importance of customization and other factors. Because the dimensions and attributes are

Exhibit 18.3 **SERVICE QUALITY AND THE ECONOMIC WORTH OF CUSTOMERS: BUSINESSES STILL NEED TO KNOW MORE**

Topic	Key Research Questions
Service quality and profitability: the direct relationship	1. What methodologies need to be developed to allow companies to capture the effect of service quality on profit? 2. What measures are necessary to examine the relationship in a consistent, valid, and reliable manner? 3. Does the relationship between service quality and profitability vary by industry, country, category of business (e.g., in services companies versus goods companies, in industrial versus packaged goods companies), or other variables? 4. What are the moderating factors of the relationship between service quality and profitability? 5. What is the optimal spending level on service in order to affect profitability?
Offensive effects of service quality	1. What is the optimal amount of spending on service quality to obtain offensive effects on reputation? 2. To obtain offensive effect, are expenditures on advertising or service quality itself more effective? 3. In what ways can companies signal high service quality to customers to obtain offensive effects?
Defensive effects of service quality	1. What is a loyal customer? 2. What is the role of service in defensive marketing? 3. How does service compare in effectiveness to other retention strategies such as price? 4. What levels of service provision are needed to retain customers? 5. How can the effects of word-of-mouth communication from retained customers be quantified? 6. What aspects of service are most important for customer retention? 7. How can defection-prone customers be identified?
Perceptions of service quality, behavioral intentions, and profits	1. What is the relationship between customer purchase intentions and initial purchase behavior in services? 2. What is the relationship between behavioral intentions and repurchase in services? 3. Does the degree of association between service quality and behavior change at different quality levels?
Identifying the key drivers of service quality, customer retention, and profits	1. What service encounters are most responsible for perceptions of service quality? 2. What are the key drivers in each service encounter? 3. Where should investments be made to affect service quality, purchase, retention, and profits? 4. Are key drivers of service quality the same as key drivers of behavioral intentions, customer retention, and profits?

delivered in many cases with totally different internal strategies, resources must be allocated where they are most needed, and study in this topic could provide direction.

Some companies and researchers have viewed the effect of specific service encounters on overall service quality or customer satisfaction and the effect of specific behaviors within service encounters. As we discussed more fully in Chapters 5 and 8,

FIGURE 18.5
The Key Drivers of Service Quality, Customer Retention, and Profits

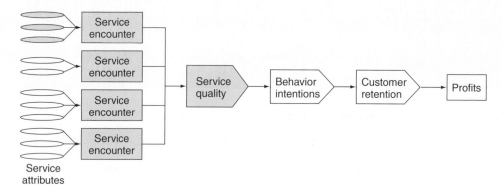

Service attributes

Marriott Hotels conducted extensive customer research to determine what service elements contribute most to customer loyalty. They found that four of the top five factors came into play in the first 10 minutes of the guest's stay—those that involved the early encounters of arriving, checking in, and entering the hotel rooms. Other companies have found that mistakes or problems that occur in early service encounters are particularly critical, because a failure at early points results in greater risk for dissatisfaction in each ensuing encounter. Both AT&T and IBM found that the sales encounter was the most critical of all, in large part because salespeople establish expectations for the remaining service encounters.

Another way of looking at the problem, based largely in the operations and management literature, involves investigating the effect of service programs and managerial approaches within an organization on financial measures such as profitability. A new customer-focused approach to metrics is described in the Strategy Insight. For example, one study estimated the effect of continuous improvement programs on profits in 280 automotive suppliers and found a 17 percent increase in profits over a two- to three-year period.[27] Another revealed that delegated teams were particularly effective at improving people and that statistical process control was most effective in improving processes in TQM programs.[28]

COMPANY PERFORMANCE MEASUREMENT: THE BALANCED PERFORMANCE SCORECARD

Traditionally, organizations have measured their performance almost completely on the basis of financial indicators such as profit, sales, and return on investment. This short-term approach leads companies to emphasize financials to the exclusion of other performance indicators. Today's corporate strategists recognize the limitations of evaluating corporate performance on financials alone, contending that these income-based financial figures measure yesterday's decisions rather than indicate future performance. This recognition came when many companies' strong financial records deteriorated because of unnoticed declines in operational processes, quality, or customer satisfaction.[27] In the words of one observer of corporate strategy:

> Financial measures emphasize profitability of inert assets over any other mission of the company. They do not recognize the emerging leverage of the soft stuff—skilled people and employment of information—as the new keys to high performance and near-perfect customer satisfaction . . . . If the only mission a measurement system conveys is financial discipline, an organization is directionless.[30]

Although the marketing concept has articulated a customer-centered viewpoint since the 1960s, marketing theory and practice have become incrementally customer-centered over the last 40 years. For example, marketing has only recently decreased its emphasis on short-term transactions and increased its focus on long-term customer relationships. Much of this refocus stems from the changing nature of the world's leading economies, which have undergone a century-long shift from the goods sector to the service sector.

Because service often tends to be more relationship based, this structural shift in the economy has resulted in more attention to relationships and therefore more attention to customers. This customer-centered viewpoint is starting to be reflected in the concepts and metrics that drive marketing management, including such metrics as customer value and voice of the customer. For example, the concept of brand equity, a fundamentally product-centered concept, is now being challenged by the customer-centered concept of *customer equity*.

> *Customer equity* is the total of the discounted lifetime values summed over all the firm's customers.

In other words, customer equity is obtained by summing up the customer lifetime values of the firm's customers. In fast-moving and dynamic industries that involve customer relationships, products come and go but customers remain. Customers and customer equity may be more central to many firms than brands and brand equity, although current management practices and metrics do not yet fully reflect this shift. The shift from product-centered thinking to customer-centered thinking implies the need for an accompanying shift from product-based metrics to customer-based metrics.

USING CUSTOMER EQUITY IN A STRATEGIC FRAMEWORK

Consider the issues facing a typical marketing manager or marketing-oriented CEO: How do I manage my brand? How will my customers react to changes in service and service quality? Should I raise price? What is the best way to enhance the relationships with my current customers? Where should I focus my efforts? Determining customer lifetime value, or customer equity, is the first step, but the more important step is to evaluate and test ideas and strategies using lifetime value as the measuring stick. At a very basic level, strategies for building customer relationships can affect five basic factors: retention rate, referrals, increased sales, reduced direct costs, and reduced marketing costs.

Rust, Zeithaml and Lemon have developed an approach based on customer equity that can help business executives answer their questions. The model that represents this approach is shown in the accompanying figure. In this context, customer equity is a new approach to marketing and corporate strategy that finally puts the customer—and, more importantly, strategies that grow the value of the customer—at the heart of the organization. The researchers identify the drivers of customer equity—value equity, brand equity, and relationship equity—and explain how these drivers work, independently and together, to grow customer equity. Service strategies are prominent in both value equity and relationship equity. Within each of these drivers are specific, incisive actions ("levers") that the firm can take to enhance the firm's overall customer equity.

continued

The Customer Equity Model

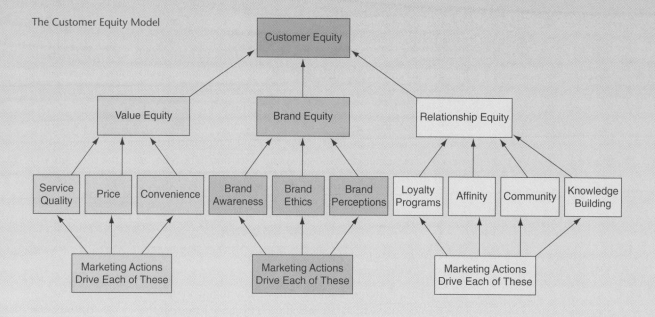

WHY IS CUSTOMER EQUITY IMPORTANT?

For most firms, customer equity—the total of the discounted lifetime values of all the firm's customers—is certain to be the most important determinant of the long-term value of the firm. Although customer equity will not be responsible for the entire value of the firm (consider, for example, physical assets, intellectual property, research and development competencies, etc.), the firm's current customers provide the most reliable source of future revenues and profits—and provide a focal point for marketing strategy.

Although it may seem obvious that customer equity is key to long-term success, understanding how to grow and manage customer equity is much more complex. Growing customer equity is of utmost importance, and doing it well can lead to significant competitive advantage.

CALCULATING RETURN ON MARKETING USING CUSTOMER EQUITY

At the beginning of this chapter, we told you about an approach called return on quality that was developed to help companies understand where they could get the biggest impact from quality investments. A more general form of that approach is called return on marketing, which enables companies to look at all competing marketing strategy options and trade them off on the basis of projected financial return. This approach allows companies to not just examine the impact of service on financial return but also compare the impact of service with the impact of branding, price changes, and all other marketing strategies. Using the customer equity model, firms can analyze the drivers that have the greatest impact, compare the drivers' performance with that of competitors' drivers, and project return on investment from improvements in the drivers. The framework enables what-if evaluation of marketing return on investment, which can include such criteria as return on quality, return on advertising, return on loyalty programs, and even return on corporate citizenship, given a particular shift in customer perceptions. This approach enables firms to focus marketing efforts on strategic initiatives that generate the greatest return.

Sources: R. T. Rust, K. N. Lemon, and V. A. Zeithaml, "Return on Marketing: Using Customer Equity to Focus Marketing Strategy," *Journal of Marketing* 68, no. 1 (January 2004), pp. 109; R. Rust, V. Zeithaml and K. Lemon, *Driving Customer Equity* (New York: The Free Press, 2000).

For this reason, companies began to recognize that *balanced performance scorecards*—strategic measurement systems that captured other areas of performance—were needed. The developers of balanced performance scorecards defined them as follows:

> . . . a set of measures that gives top managers a fast but comprehensive view of the business . . . . [that] complements the financial measures with operational measures of customer satisfaction, internal processes, and the organization's innovation and improvement activities—operational measures that are the drivers of future financial performance.[31]

Having a firm handle on what had been viewed as "soft" measures became the way to help organizations identify customer problems, improve processes, and achieve company objectives.

Balanced performance scorecards have become extremely popular. One recent report indicates that 70 percent of the *Fortune* 1,000 companies have or are experimenting with balanced performance scorecards and more than one-half of the largest companies worldwide use them. Another study by the Institute of Management Accountants showed that 64 percent of U.S. companies anticipate using a new performance measurement system. Furthermore, according to a report called "Measures That Matter" from Ernst and Young's Center for Business Innovation, investors give nonfinancial measures an average of one-third the weight when making a decision to buy or sell any given stock,[32] strongly demonstrating to companies that investors recognize the value of the new forms of measurement.

As shown in Figure 18.6, the balanced performance scorecard captures three perspectives in addition to the financial perspective: customer, operational, and learning. The balanced scorecard brings together, in a single management report, many of the previously separated elements of a company's competitive agenda and forces senior managers to consider all the important measures together. The scorecard has been facilitated by recent developments in enterprise-wide software (discussed in the Technology Spotlight) that allow companies to create, automate, and integrate measurements from all parts of the company.

Methods for measuring financial performance are the most developed and established in corporations, having been created more than 400 years ago. In contrast, efforts to measure market share, quality, innovation, human resources, and customer satisfaction have only recently been created. Companies can improve their performance by developing this discipline in their measurement of all four categories.

Technology Spotlight
Automating the Balanced Scorecard

A study of the usage of balanced scorecards by North American organizations, sponsored by six organizations that are involved in their preparation and use (AICPA, CAM-I, CMA Canada, IQPC, Targus Corporation, and Hyperion Solutions), examined the factors that make the use of scorecards successful. One of the most important factors was software automation of the scorecards, and the study found that 70 percent of organizations who use balanced scorecards currently use some form of off-the-shelf or in-house software. The use of software allows companies to collect and report information quickly and continuously, removing the time-consuming task of updating data and freeing employees and management to focus on the strategic aspects of the scorecard.

Thirty-six percent of organizations that use software, and virtually all that have been using scorecards for more than five years, use Microsoft Excel spreadsheets, largely because they are easy to use, widely available, inexpensive, and flexible. Spreadsheets are flexible because a template can be created into which multiple parts of the organization can enter their data. Organizations also tend to add, eliminate, or change measures, and spreadsheets offer the flexibility of adapting. However, users have found that spreadsheets make benchmarking scorecards across performance units difficult because departments can interpret measures differently and can engage in gamesmanship. Spreadsheets are also difficult to maintain because the data are not collected electronically and must be updated by area.

The second most popular software is Hyperion's Performance Scorecard, one of the off-the-shelf packages that has been developed by software companies. Hyperion Solutions reports that 88 of the Fortune 100 companies, 66 of the Nikkei top 100, 53 of the Financial Times Europe Top 100, 10 of the top 10 banks and 5 of the top 5 industrial equipment companies use the company's Balanced Performance Scorecard software. These packages have the following advantages over spreadsheet software: better data security, a more focused tool, and more consistent information across the firm. These off-the-shelf programs can extract data from multiple transactional systems and integrate it into one version of the company's financial and operational performance. Therefore, all managers have the same facts and metrics, giving them a common understanding of the factors affecting overall performance.

Organizations use five different ways to communicate scorecard results: paper, e-mail, the Web, LANs, and WANs. The method used by a company tends to be related to organizational size and the use of software. The smallest organizations (fewer than 100 employees) typically use paper-based reporting. Medium-sized companies use e-mail and the Web to report the results of spreadsheet software, and companies that use the Web are the most likely to report success. The largest organizations use technologically sophisticated techniques like the Web and LANs, which are easy to use in combination with off-the-shelf software.

Changes to Financial Measurement

One way that service leaders are changing financial measurement is to calibrate the defensive effect of retaining and losing customers. The monetary value of retaining customers can be projected through the use of average revenues over the lifetimes of customers. The number of customer defections can then be translated into lost revenue to the firm and become a critical company performance standard:

> Ultimately, defections should be a key performance measure for senior management and a fundamental component of incentive systems. Managers should know the company's defection rate, what happens to profits when the rate moves up or down and why defections occur.[33]

Companies can also measure actual increases or decreases in revenue from retention or defection of customers by capturing the value of a loyal customer, including expected cash flows over a customer's lifetime or lifetime customer value (as described in Chapter 7). Other possible financial measures (as shown in Figure 18.6) include the value of price premiums, volume increases, customer referrals, and cross sales.

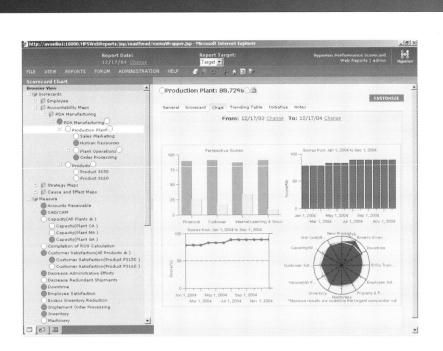

The survey showed that the most important feature related to success in using software for balanced scorecards is the ability to provide Web-based reporting. This feature was followed by the ability to drill down to root data, the ability to customize reports, and the ability to link scorecards and roll them up. The system also needs to be able to access data from multiple legacy systems and other data sources and must be flexible enough to easily accommodate future changes to the scorecarding system.

Sources: R. Lawson, W. Stratton, and T. Hatch, "Automating the Balanced Scorecard," *CMA Management* 77, no. 9 (2004), pp. 39–44; www.Hyperion.com.

Customer Perceptual Measures

Customer perceptual measures are leading indicators of financial performance. As we discussed in this chapter, customers who are not happy with the company will defect and will tell others about their dissatisfaction. As we also discussed, perceptual measures reflect customer beliefs and feelings about the company and its products and services and can predict how the customer will behave in the future. Overall forms of the measurements we discussed in Chapters 5 and 6 (shown in the customer perspective box of Figure 18.6) are measures that can be included in this category. Among the measures that are valuable to track are overall service perceptions and expectations, customer satisfaction, perceptual measures of value, and behavioral intention measures such as loyalty and intent to switch. A company that notices a decline in these numbers should be concerned that the decline will translate into lost dollars for the company.

Operational Measures

Operational measures involve the translation of customer perceptual measures into the standards or actions that must be set internally to meet customers' expectations.

FIGURE 18.6   **Sample Measurements for the Balanced Scorecard**

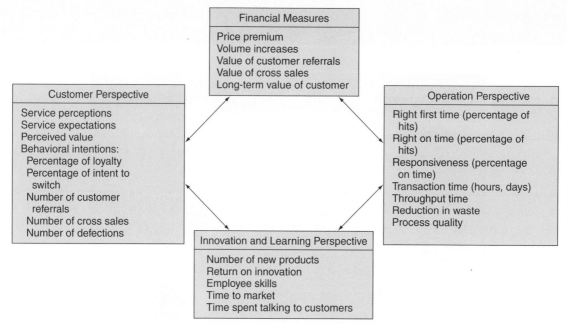

Although virtually all companies count or calculate operational measures in some form, the balanced scorecard requires that these measures stem from the business processes that have the greatest effect on customer satisfaction. In other words, these measures are not independent of customer perceptual measures but instead are intricately linked with them. In Chapter 10 we called these customer-linked operational measures *customer-defined standards*—operational standards determined through customer expectations and calibrated the way the customer views and expresses them.

Innovation and Learning

The final area of measurement involves a company's ability to innovate, improve, and learn—by launching new products, creating more value for customers, and improving operating efficiencies. This measurement area is most difficult to capture quantitatively but can be accomplished using performance-to-goal percentages. For example, a company can set a goal of launching 10 new products a year, then measure what percentage of that goal it achieves in a year. If four new products are launched, its percentage for the year is 40 percent, which can then be compared with subsequent years.

The Global Feature shows that implementation of the balanced performance scorecard can vary by culture.

The Balanced Scorecard in Practice

The balanced scorecard has been implemented not only in corporations but also in government and nonprofit organizations as well. In 2001 the University of Virginia Library (UVL), a system of 11 different libraries with holdings of four million volumes, became the first library in North America to begin using a balanced scorecard to improve its performance.[34]

As China continues to develop into a world economic power, its organizations are recognizing the value of strategic management concepts to help them formulate and execute effective and competitive strategies. Chinese organizations are now joining the organizations in the world that have adopted the balanced performance scorecard.

Companies in China face many of the same external and internal challenges as Western companies face, including rapidly changing business conditions, increasing competition, and increasing customer expectations. However, many Chinese organizations are unfamiliar with the building blocks needed for strategy development—such as analysis of the business life cycle, SWOT (strengths, weaknesses, opportunities, and threats) analysis, and development of value propositions for target markets. Chinese companies had been successful largely based on entrepreneurship, intuition, or prior market dominance, approaches that have been unsuccessful as competition has intensified.

Consultants and companies that have implemented balanced scorecards in China recognize special challenges:

1. Goal-setting processes are not flexible enough to allow companies to adapt quickly, largely because companies lack the ability to track, analyze, and change goals.
2. Measurement data is either not readily available or is scattered across the organization, with no single system for recording or displaying the information. Enterprise software systems usually have data in the financial and operational areas but lack data in the customer and learning/growth perspectives.
3. Performance appraisal systems in China are particularly susceptible to the problems created by organizational silos, and managers are compensated based on functional performance.
4. Companies are less likely to have information technology systems to record data for employee evaluations. Therefore, human resource professionals or managers must manually calculate performance scores and bonuses.

Irv Beiman and Yong-Ling Sun of e-Gate Consulting Shanghai, consultants who have applied the balanced performance scorecard to workplaces in China, identify six critical success factors in implementing the scorecard methodology in workplaces: (1) committing and involving top management; (2) overcoming implementation hurdles; (3) overcoming functional silos; (4) establishing linkages to competency development and variable pay; (5) developing infrastructure to communicate the strategy, track performance, and make adjustments based on results; and (6) elevating human resources to the status of a strategic partner to line management. All these criteria are important for a firm in any country to have a successful balanced scorecard, but the challenges in China are harder to overcome, particularly in the area of human resources.

One of the biggest human resource issues is the way that executives, directors, and managers are paid. Variable pay, which creates incentives to aim for common goals, is infrequently used, and compensation is almost always based on individual departments' sales and revenue goals. For example, Chinese sales personnel are almost always paid exclusively for sales volume or revenue. Because of the way they are paid, they do not cooperate with other departments, which results in conflict and tension, particularly with production departments. Consider the experience of a private entrepreneurial company in China. Each

continued

department in the firm had developed its own way of approaching work, without coordinating with other departments. Compensation was based on each department's performance rather than common performance. When faced with increasing pressure from international competition in their domestic markets, the firm recognized that it needed to revise its strategy and focus on external customer needs. The company adopted the balanced scorecard methodology and initially found that managers constantly complained about employees in other departments, placing the blame on them. After implementation of the scorecard, managers began working more cooperatively with each other by sharing objectives across departments, improving cross-functional business processes, and fostering teamwork. Measurable improvements in company performance resulted.

Another human resource issue involves performance appraisal, performance management, and job descriptions, which do not always exist in Chinese firms. When they do exist, they are created in each individual department, meaning that each department knows only a piece of the work done by the organization. As a result, training across departments is not connected with a focus on the customer or the firm's overall strategy. In situations in which the balanced performance scorecard approach has been used effectively, the human resource function assumes the responsibility for job descriptions, performance appraisals, variable compensation, and other policies that support strategy execution.

Sources: I. Beiman and Y. L. Sun, **"Using the Balanced Scorecard for Strategy Execution in China,"** *China Staff* 9, no. 8 (2003), pp. 10–14; I. Beiman and Y. Sun, *"Implementing a Balanced Scorecard in China: Steps for Success,"* China Staff 9, no. 9 (2003), pp. 11–15. Used with permission.

Lynda White, associate director of management information services at UVL, says that the scorecard is currently used as a management tool to assess the health of the organization, to indicate areas in which it is doing well and other areas that need attention, and to assemble information in a meaningful way. The organization began development of the scorecard by prioritizing the many numbers in the statistics and data that it had collected over the years.

The library's scorecard uses four categories of measures: the user perspective, the internal processes perspective, the financial perspective, and the learning and growth perspective. Each of the four perspectives has four to six measures that tell the organization how well the library is doing in each area. The first two categories, focusing on users and internal processes, were easy for the library to understand and measure. The metrics for user perspective helped the library improve customer service, as White describes:

> We measure how well we do in customer service, what faculty and students think of services and collections, what students think of user instruction, how much special collections is used, how much patrons use new books and electronic resources, how quickly we turn around requests (for searches, recalls, library electronic ordering [LEO] document delivery, interlibrary loan, scanning for e-reserves, new books), how fast and accurately we re-shelve, Web-site usability, renovation of public-service areas, increasing access to digital materials. And of course, measuring the unit cost of various services affects them as taxpayers or donors. It addresses whether we are using their money wisely and efficiently.[35]

According to Jim Self, director of management information services at the library, the other two categories were more difficult. Because UVL, like most libraries, is non-profit, the financial perspective was the most challenging. In determining what to measure, the scorecard gave the library an opportunity to look at the financial aspects of its operation that had not been emphasized before, such as processing costs incurred in cataloging and acquisitions and transaction costs in reference, circulation, and inter-library loan.

The organization realized the value of the scorecard when it compared its actual performance to its assumed performance. It found out, for example, that turn-around times for ordering books requested by users were much slower than its promises. It had been promising users that it could get new books for them in one week, but it found that only 17 percent of new books it ordered on request were ready in seven days. Through this comparison and others, the balanced scorecard helped the library look at its priorities, goals, and vision statements, align them with each other, and simplify its priority list. The library's special website (www.lib.virginia.edu/bsc) describes the history, measures, and implementation of the scorecard.

Strategy Maps to Enhance Balanced Scorecards

The strategy map is a concept that was recently developed to help companies deploy the balanced scorecard more effectively. A strategy map provides a single-page visual representation of a firm's strategy (see Figure 18.7) that links the four perspectives of the balanced scorecard and thereby shows the cause-and-effect relationships among them.[36] Instead of merely showing the four clusters of metrics as separate categories linked by arrows, as shown in Figure 18.7, the strategy map shows how the typical 20 to 30 measures in a balanced scorecard are integrated in the creation of a single unified strategy and clearly demonstrates which variables lead, lag, and feed back into other variables. The map also identifies the capabilities of the organization's intangible assets—human capital, information capital, and organization capital—that are required for superior performance.

The essence of the map is that financial outcomes are possible only if targeted customers are satisfied, a complicated process achieved with a set of interrelated capabilities. The mapping process forces managers to identify cause and effect and to clarify the logic of how the company will create value and for whom.[37] As part of the process, companies must identify the customer value proposition and then describe how it will generate sales and loyalty from targeted customers. The company then must link the critical internal processes that are most important to deliver the value proposition. Mapping helps identify any of the four categories in which management has not thought through metrics and strategies. Strategies are typically executed through a structure of strategic themes developed during the mapping.

Effective Nonfinancial Performance Measurements

According to field research conducted in 60 companies and survey responses from 297 senior executives, many companies do not identify and act on the correct nonfinancial measures.[38] One example involves a bank that surveyed satisfaction only from customers who physically entered the branches, a policy that caused some branch managers to offer free food and drinks in order to increase their scores. According to the authors of the study, companies make four major mistakes:

1. *Not linking measures to strategy*. Companies can easily identify hundreds of nonfinancial measures to track, but they also need to use analysis that identifies the

FIGURE 18.7   **A Strategy Map Helps Companies Align Strategy with Performance**

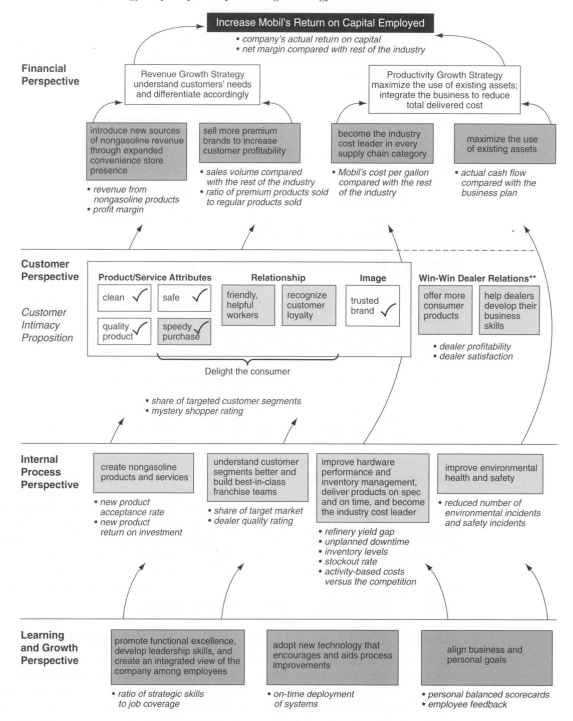

FIGURE 18.8
The Measures That Matter Most:
A causal model for a fast-food company shows the critical drivers of performance and the concepts that lead to shareholder value.

Source: Christopher D. Ittner and David F. Larcker, "Coming Up Short on Nonfinancial Performance Measurement," *Harvard Business Review,* November 2003, pp. 88–95.

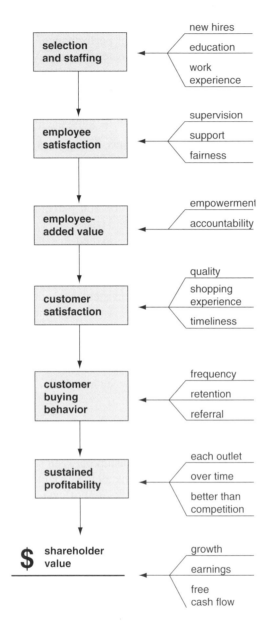

most important drivers of their strategy. Successful organizations use value driver maps, tools that lay out the cause-and-effect relationships between drivers and strategic success. Figure 18.8 shows the causal model developed by a successful fast-food chain to understand the key drivers of shareholder value. The factors on the right were identified as most important in leading to the concepts on the left, and the sequence of concepts from top to bottom show the relationships among company strategies (such as selection and staffing) and intermediate results (such as employee and customer satisfaction) that result in financial results (such as sustained profitability and shareholder value). The study found that fewer than 30 percent of the firms surveyed used this causal modeling approach.

2. *Not validating the links.* Only 21 percent of companies in the study verify that the nonfinancial measures lead to financial performance. Instead, many firms decide what they are going to measure in each category and never link the categories. Many managers believed that the relationships were self-evident instead of conducting analysis to validate the linkages. This chapter's Strategy Insight shows one way that companies can create this type of linkage. In general, it is critical that companies pull together all their data and examine the relationships among the categories.

3. *Not setting the right performance targets.* Companies sometimes aim too high in setting improvement targets. Targeting 100 percent customer satisfaction might seem to be a desirable goal, but many companies expend far too many resources to gain too little improvement in satisfaction. The study's authors found that a telecommunications company aiming for 100 percent customer satisfaction was wasting resources because customers who were 100 percent satisfied spent no more money than those who were 80 percent satisfied.[39]

4. *Measuring incorrectly.* Companies need to use metrics with statistical validity and reliability. Organizations cannot measure complex phenomenon with one or two simple measures, nor can they use inconsistent methodologies to measure the same concept, such as customer satisfaction. Another problem that companies may encounter is trying to use quantitative metrics to capture qualitative results for important factors such as leadership and innovation.

Creating a balanced scorecard in and of itself does not improve performance. Companies will not reap the benefits of techniques such as the balanced scorecard unless they address these four issues.

Summary

This chapter is divided into six sections, five of which assess the evidence and identify what is currently known about the relationship between service and profitability. The chapter used a conceptual framework to link all the variables in these topics: (1) the direct relationship between service and profits; (2) offensive effects of service quality; (3) defensive effects of service quality; (4) the relationship between service quality and purchase intentions; (5) key drivers of service quality, customer retention, and profits. Considerable progress has been made in the last 10 years in the investigation of service quality, profitability, and the economic worth of customers, but managers are still lacking many of the answers that would help them make informed decisions about service quality investments. The chapter concluded with a discussion of the balanced performance scorecard approach to measuring corporate performance, which offers a strategic approach for measuring all aspects of a company's performance.

Discussion Questions

1. Why has it been difficult for executives to understand the relationship between service improvements and profitability in their companies?
2. What is the ROSQ model, and what is its significance to corporate America?
3. To this day, many companies believe that service is a cost rather than a revenue producer. Why might they hold this view? How would you argue the opposite view?
4. What is the difference between offensive and defensive marketing? How does service affect each of these?

5. What are the main sources of profit in defensive marketing?

6. What are the main sources of profit in offensive marketing?

7. How will the balanced performance scorecard help us understand and document the information presented in this chapter? Which of the five sections that discuss different aspects of the relationship between service quality and profits can it illuminate?

Exercises

1. On the Internet, use a search engine to locate three companies that make balanced scorecard software. What are the software companies' current offerings? How can the software firms help individual companies understand the concepts and relationships discussed in this chapter? Which of the three companies would you select based on the information you locate?

2. Interview a local firm and see what it knows about its key drivers of financial performance. What are the key service drivers of the firm? Does the company know whether these service drivers relate to profit?

3. Select a service industry (such as fast food) or a company (such as McDonald's) that you are familiar with, either as a customer or employee, and create a balanced scorecard. Describe the operational, customer, financial, and learning measures that could be used to capture performance.

Notes

1. R. T. Rust, A. J. Zahorik, and T. L. Keiningham, *Return on Quality* (Chicago: Probus, 1994).

2. R. T. Rust, C. Moorman, and P. R. Dickson, "Getting Return on Quality: Revenue Expansion, Cost Reduction, or Both?" *Journal of Marketing* 66, (October 2002), pp. 7–24.

3. Ibid.

4. J. Matthews and P. Katel, "The Cost of Quality: Faced with Hard Times, Business Sours on Total Quality Management," *Newsweek,* September 7, 1992, pp. 48–49.

5. "The Cracks in Quality," *The Economist* 18 (April 1992), pp. 67–68.

6. *Management Practice, U.S. Companies Improve Performance through Quality Efforts,* Report No. GAO/NSIAD-91-190 (Washington, DC: U.S. General Accounting Office, 1992).

7. R. Rust, B. Subramanian, and M. Wells, "Making Complaints a Management Tool," *Marketing Management* 3 (1993), pp. 40–45.

8. E. Nelson, R. T. Rust, A. Zahorik, R. L. Rose, P. Batalden, and B. Siemanski, "Do Patient Perceptions of Quality Relate to Hospital Financial Performance?" *Journal of Healthcare Marketing,* December 1992, pp. 1–13.

9. D. A. Aaker and R. Jacobson, "The Financial Information Content of Perceived Quality," *Journal of Marketing* 58 (May 1994), pp. 191–201.

10. C. Fornell and B. Wernerfelt, "Defensive Marketing Strategy by Customer Complaint Management: A Theoretical Analysis," *Journal of Marketing Research* 24 (November 1987), pp. 337–46; see also C. Fornell and B. Wernerfelt, "A Model for Customer Complaint Management," *Marketing Science* 7 (Summer 1988), pp. 271–86.

11. B. Gale, "Monitoring Customer Satisfaction and Market-Perceived Quality," *American Marketing Association Worth Repeating Series,* no. 922CS01 (Chicago: American Marketing Association, 1992).

12. Ibid.

13. R. E. Kordupleski, R. T. Rust, and A. J. Zahorik, "Why Improving Quality Doesn't Improve Quality (or Whatever Happened to Marketing?)," *California Management Review* 35 (1993), pp. 82–95.

14. Fornell and Wernerfelt, "Defensive Marketing Strategy by Customer Complaint Management," also Fornell and Wernerfelt, "A Model for Customer Complaint Management."

15. T. J. Peters, *Thriving on Chaos* (New York: Alfred A. Knopf, 1988).

16. F. Reichheld and E. Sasser, "Zero Defections: Quality Comes to Services," *Harvard Business Review,* September–October 1990, p. 106.

17. Ibid., p. 105.

18. D. F. Colicchio, regional quality manager, Hewlett-Packard Company, personal communication.

19. S. Rose, "The Coming Revolution in Credit Cards," *Journal of Retail Banking,* Summer 1990, pp. 17–19.

20. J. L. Heskett, W. E. Sasser, Jr. and L. A. Schlesinger, *The Service Profit Chain* (New York: The Free Press, 1997).

21. A. Woodside, L. Frey, and R. Daly, "Linking Service Quality, Customer Satisfaction and Behavioral Intentions," *Journal of Health Care Marketing* 9 (December 1989), pp. 5–17.

22. E. W. Anderson and M. Sullivan, "The Antecedents and Consequences of Customer Satisfaction for Firms," *Marketing Science* 12 (Spring 1992), pp. 125–43.

23. W. Boulding, R. Staelin, A. Kalra, and V. A. Zeithaml, "Conceptualizing and Testing a Dynamic Process Model of Service Quality," report no. 92-121, Marketing Science Institute, 1992.

24. V. A. Zeithaml, L. L. Berry, and A. Parasuraman, "The Behavioral Consequences of Service Quality," *Journal of Marketing* 60 (April 1996), pp. 31–46.

25. J. P. McLaughlin, "Ensuring Customer Satisfaction Is a Strategic Issue, Not Just an Operational One," presentation at the AIC Customer Satisfaction Measurement Conference, Chicago, December 6–7, 1993.

26. Gale, "Monitoring Customer Satisfaction."

27. C. Fitzerald and T. Erdmann, *Actionline,* American Automotive Industry Action Group, October 1992.

28. R. Mann and D. Kehoe, "An Evaluation of the Effects of Quality Improvement Activities on Business Performance," *International Journal of Quality and Reliability Management* 11, (1994), pp. 29–45.

29. R. S. Kaplan and D. P. Norton, "The Balanced Scorecard—Measures That Drive Performance," *Harvard Business Review,* January–February 1992, pp. 71–79.

30. Kaplan and Norton, "The Balanced Scorecard."

31. S. Silk, "Automating the Balance Scorecard," *Management Accounting,* May 1998, pp. 38–42.

32. D. A. Light, "Performance Measurement: Investors' Balance Scorecards," *Harvard Business Review,* November–December 1998, pp. 17–20.

33. Reichheld and Sasser, "Zero Defections," p. 111.

34. A. Willis, "Using the Balanced Scorecard at the University of Virginia Library: An Interview with Jim Self and Lynda White," *Library Administration and Management* 18, (2004), pp. 64–67.

35. Ibid., p. 66.

36. R. Kaplan and D. Norton, "Plotting Success with 'Strategy Maps,'" *Optimize,* 2004, pp. 61–65.

37. R. S. Kaplan and D. P. Norton, "How Strategy Maps Frame an Organization's Objectives," *Financial Executive* 20, (2004), pp. 40–45.

38. The material in this section comes from C. D. Ittner and D. F. Larcker, "Coming Up Short on Nonfinancial Performance Measurement," *Harvard Business Review,* November 2003, pp. 88–95.

39. Ibid., page 92.

EASYCAR.COM

> At easyCar we aim to offer you outstanding value for money. To us value for money means a reliable service at a low price. We achieve this by simplifying the product we offer, and passing on the benefits to you in the form of lower prices.[1]

This quotation was the stated mission of car rental company easyCar.com. EasyCar was a member of the easyGroup family of companies founded by the flamboyant Greek entrepreneur Stelios Haji-Ioannou, who was known to most people simply as Stelios. Stelios founded low-cost air carrier easyJet.com in 1995 after convincing his father, a Greek shipping billionaire, to loan him the £5 million (Note: In January 2003, £1 = €1.52 = U.S.$1.61) needed to start the business.[2] EasyJet was one of the early low-cost, no-frills air carriers in the European market. It was built on a foundation of simple point-to-point flights booked over the Internet and of the aggressive use of yield management policies to maximize the revenues it derived from its assets. The company proved highly successful, and as a result, Stelios had expanded this business model to industries with characteristics similar to the airline industry. EasyCar, founded in 2000 on a £10 million investment on the part of Stelios, was one of these efforts.

EasyCar's approach, built on the easyJet model, was quite different than the approaches used by the traditional rental car companies. EasyCar rented only a single vehicle type at each location it operated, whereas most of its competitors rented a wide variety of vehicle types. EasyCar did not work with agents—more than 95 percent of its bookings were made through the company's website, with the remainder of bookings being made directly through the company's phone reservation system (at a cost to the customer of €0.95 per minute for the call). Most rental car companies worked with a variety of intermediaries, and their own websites accounted for less than 10 percent of their total booking.[3] And like easyJet, easyCar managed prices in an attempt to have its fleet rented out 100 percent of the time and to generate the maximum revenue from its rentals. EasyCar's information system constantly evaluated projected demand and expected utilization at each site, and the system adjusted price accordingly. Because of its aggressive pricing, easyCar was able to achieve a fleet utilization rate in excess of 90 percent[4]—much higher than other major rental car companies. Industry leader Avis Europe, for example, had a fleet utilization rate of 68 percent.[5]

EasyCar had broken even in the fiscal year ending September 2002[6] on revenues of £27 million.[7] These revenues represented a significant improvement over 2001, when

By John J. Lawrence (University of Idaho) and Luis Solis (Instituto de Empresa).

easyCar had lost £7.5 million on revenues of £18.5 million.[8] Although pleased that the company had broken even in only its third year in operation, Stelios in January 2003 had set aggressive financial goals for easyCar for the next two years. Plans called for a quadrupling of revenues in the next two years in preparation for a planned initial public offering in the second half of 2004. EasyCar's goal was to reach £100 million in revenue and £10 million in profit for the year 2004. Stelios felt that the £100 million revenue goal and £10 million profit goal were necessary to obtain the desired return from an IPO. He thought that with this level of performance, the company might be worth about £250 million.[9] In order to achieve these financial goals, the company was pushing to open an average of two new sites a week through 2003 and 2004 to reach a total of 180 sites by the end of 2004.[10]

THE RENTAL CAR INDUSTRY IN WESTERN EUROPE

The Western European rental car industry consisted of many different national markets that were only semi-integrated. Although many companies competed within this European rental car industry, a handful of companies held dominant positions, either across a number of national markets or within one or a few national markets. Industry experts saw the sector as ripe for consolidation.[11] Several international companies—notably Avis, Europcar, and Hertz—had strong positions across most major European markets. Within most countries, there was also a primarily national or regional company that had a strong position in its home market and perhaps moderate market share in neighboring markets. Sixt was the market leader in Germany, for example, whereas Atesa (in partnership with National) was the market leader in Spain. Generally these major players accounted for more than half the market. In Germany, for example, Sixt, Europcar, Avis, and Hertz had a combined 60 percent of the €2.5 billion German rental car market.[12] In Spain, the top five firms accounted for 60 percent of the €920 million Spanish rental car market. These top firms targeted both business and vacation travelers and offered a wide range of vehicles for rent. Exhibit 1 provides basic information on these market-leading companies.

In addition to these major companies in each market, many smaller rental companies were operating in each market. Germany, for example, had more than 700 smaller companies,[13] whereas Spain had more than 1,600 smaller companies. Many of these smaller companies operated at only one or a few locations and were particularly prevalent in tourist locations. A number of brokers, such as Holiday Autos, also operated in the sector. Brokerage companies did not own their own fleet of cars but managed the excess inventory of other companies and matched customers with rental companies that had excess fleet capacity.

Overall, the rental car market was composed of two broad segments: a business segment and a tourist/leisure segment. Depending on the market, the leisure segment represented somewhere between 45 percent and 65 percent of the overall market, and a large part of this segment was very price conscious. The business segment made up the remaining 35 percent to 55 percent of the market. It was less price sensitive than the tourist segment and more concerned about service quality, convenience, and flexibility.

THE GROWTH OF EASYCAR

EasyCar opened its first location in London on 20 April 2000 under the name easyRentacar. In the same week, easyCar opened locations in Glasgow and Barcelona. All three locations were popular easyJet destinations. Vehicles initially could be rented

EXHIBIT 1   Information on easyCar's Major European Competitors

	easyCar	Avis Europe	Europcar	Hertz	Sixt
Number of Rental Outlets	46	3,100	2,650	7,000	1,250
2002 Fleet Size	7,000	120,000	220,000	700,000	46,700
Number of Countries	5	107	118	150	50
Largest Market	U.K.	France	France	U.S.	Germany
Who Owns Company	EasyGroup/ Stelios Haji-Ioannou	D'Ieteren (Belgium) is majority shareholder	Volkswagen AG	Ford Motor Company	Publicly Traded
European Revenues	€41 million	€1.25 billion	€1.12 billion	€910 million	€600 million
Company Website	www.easycar. com	www.avis-europe.com	www.europ car.com	www.hertz. com	ag.sixt.com

Source: Information in this table came from each company's website and online annual reports. European revenues are for vehicle rental in Europe and are based on market share estimates for 2001 from Avis Europe's website.

for as low as €15/day plus a one-time car preparation fee of €8. Each of these locations had a fleet consisting entirely of Mercedes A-class vehicles. It was the only vehicle that easyCar rented at the time.

EasyCar had signed a deal with Mercedes, amid much fanfare, at the Geneva Motor Show earlier in the year to purchase a total of 5,000 A-class vehicles. The vehicles, which came with guaranteed buy-back terms, cost easyCar's parent company a little over £6 million.[14] Many observers in the car rental industry were surprised by the choice because they were expecting easyCar to rely on less expensive models.[15] In describing the acquisition of the 5,000 Mercedes vehicles, Stelios had said:

> The choice of Mercedes reflects the easyGroup brand. EasyRentacar will use brand new Mercedes cars in the same way that easyJet uses brand new Boeing aircraft. We do not compromise on the hardware, we just use innovation to substantially reduce costs. The car hire industry is where the airline industry was five years ago, a cartel feeding off the corporate client. EasyRentacar will provide a choice for consumers who pay out of their own pockets and who will not be ripped off for traveling mid-week.[16]

EasyCar quickly expanded to other locations, focusing first on those locations that were popular with easyJet customers, including Amsterdam, Geneva, Nice, and Malagra. By July of 2001, a little over a year after its initial launch, easyCar had fleets of Mercedes A-class vehicles in 14 locations in the United Kingdom, Spain, France, and the Netherlands. At this point, easyCar secured £27 million from a consortium of Bank of Scotland Corporate Banking and NBGI Private Equity to further expand its operations. The package consisted of a combination of equity and loan stock.

Although easyCar added a few sites in the second half of 2001 and early 2002, volatile demand in the wake of the September 11 attacks forced easyCar to roll out new rental locations somewhat slower than originally expected.[17] Growth accelerated, however, in the spring of 2002. Between May 2002 and January 2003, easyCar opened 30 new locations, to go from 18 sites to a total of 48 sites. This acceleration in growth also coincided with a change in easyCar's policy regarding the makeup of its fleet. By May of 2002, easyCar's fleet consisted of 6,000 Mercedes A-class vehicles across 18 sites. Beginning in May, however, easyCar began to stock its fleet with other types of vehicles. It still maintained its policy of offering only a single vehicle at each location, but now the vehicle the customer received depended on the location. The first new vehicle that easyCar introduced was the Vauxhall Corsa. According to Stelios,

> Vauxhall Corsas cost easyCar £2 a day less than Mercedes A-Class so we can pass this saving on to customers. Customers themselves will decide if they want to pay a premium for a Mercedes. EasyGroup companies benefit from economies of scale where relevant but we also want to create contestable markets among our suppliers so that we can keep the cost to our customers as low as possible.[18]

By January 2003, easyCar was also using Ford Focuses (four locations), Renault Clios (three locations), Toyota Yarises (three locations), and Mercedes Smart cars (two locations) in addition to the Vauxhall Corsas (seven locations) and the Mercedes A-Class vehicles (28 locations). Plans called for a further expansion of the fleet from the 7,000 vehicles that easyCar had in January to 24,000 vehicles across 180 rental sites by the end of 2004.[19]

In addition to making vehicles available at more locations, easyCar had also changed its policies for 2003 to allow rentals for as little as one hour and with as little as one hour's notice of rental. By making this change, Stelios felt that easyCar could be a serious competitor to local taxis, buses, trains, and even car ownership. EasyCar expected that if it made car rental simple enough and cheap enough, some people living in traffic-congested European cities who only use their car occasionally would give up the costs and hassles of car ownership and simply hire an easyCar when they needed a vehicle. Tapping into this broader transportation market would help the company reach its ambitious future sales goals.

FACILITIES

EasyCar had facilities in a total of 17 cities in five European countries, as shown in Exhibit 2. It located its facilities primarily near bus and train stations in the major European cities, seeking out sites that offered lower lease costs. It generally avoided prime airport locations, because the cost for space at, or in some cases near, airports was significantly higher than most other locations. When easyCar did locate near an airport, it generally chose sites off the airport in order to reduce the cost of the lease. Airport locations also tended to require longer hours to satisfy customers arriving on late flights or departing on very early flights. EasyCar kept its airport locations open 24 hours a day, whereas its other locations were generally open only from 7:00 A.M. to 11:00 P.M.

The physical facilities at all locations were kept to a minimum. In many locations, easyCar leased space in an existing parking garage. Employees worked out of a small, self-contained cubicle within the garage. The cubicle, depending on the location, might be no more than 15 m² and included little more than a small counter and a couple of computers at which staff processed customers as they came to pick up or return their vehicles. EasyCar also leased a number of spaces within the garage for its fleet of cars. However, because easyCar's vehicles were rented 90 percent of the time, the number of spaces required for at an average site, which had a fleet of about 150 cars, was only 15 to 20 spaces.[20] To speed up the opening of new sites, easyCar had equipped a number of vans with all the needed computer and telephone equipment to run a site.[21] From an operational perspective, the company could open a new location by simply leasing 20 or so spaces in a parking garage, hiring a small staff, driving a van to the location, and adding the location to the company's website. Depending on the fleet size at a location, easyCar typically had only one or two people at a time working at a site.

EXHIBIT 2 **EasyCar Locations in January 2003**

Country	City	Number	Number Near an Airport
France	Nice	1	1
France	Paris	8	0
Netherlands	Amsterdam	3	1
Spain	Barcelona	2	0
Spain	Madrid	2	0
Spain	Majorca	1	1
Spain	Malagra	1	1
Switzerland	Geneva	1	1
United Kingdom	Birmingham	2	0
United Kingdom	Bromley	1	0
United Kingdom	Croydon	1	1
United Kingdom	Glasgow	2	1
United Kingdom	Kingston-Upon-Thames	1	0
United Kingdom	Liverpool	2	1
United Kingdom	London	15	0
United Kingdom	Manchester	2	1
United Kingdom	Waterford	1	0
Total	5 Countries, 17 Cities	46	9

Source: easyCar.com website, January 2003.

VEHICLE PICKUP AND RETURN PROCESSES

Customers arrived at a site to pick up a vehicle within a prearranged one-hour time period. Each customer selected this time slot when he or she booked the vehicle. EasyCar adjusted the first day's rental price based on the pickup time. Customers who picked their cars up earlier in the day or at popular times were charged more than were customers picking up their cars later in the day or at less busy times. Customers were required to bring a printed copy of their contract along with the credit card they used to make the booking and identification. Given the low staffing levels, customers occasionally had to wait 30 minutes or more to be processed and receive their vehicles, particularly at peak times of the day. Processing a customer began with the employee accessing the customer's contract online. If the customer was new to easyCar or to the site, the basic policies and possible additional charges were briefly explained. The employee then made copies of the customer's identification and credit card and took a digital photo of the customer. The customer was charged an €80 refundable deposit, signed the contract, and was on his or her way.

All vehicles were rented with more or less empty fuel tanks; the exact level was dependent on how much gasoline was left in the vehicle when the previous renter returned it. Customers were provided with a small map of the immediate area around the rental site that showed the location and hours of nearby gas stations. Customers could return vehicles with any amount of gas in them as long as the low fuel indicator light in the vehicle was not on. Customers who returned vehicles with the low fuel indicator light on were charged a fueling fee of €16.

Customers were also expected to return the vehicle within a prearranged one-hour time period, which they also selected at the time of booking. Although customers did not have to worry about refueling the car before returning it, they were expected to thoroughly clean the car. This clean car policy had been implemented in May 2002 as a way to further reduce the price that customers could pay for their vehicles. Prior to this change, all customers paid a fixed preparation fee of €11 each time they rented a vehicle (up from the €8 preparation fee when the company started operations in 2000). The new policy reduced this up-front preparation fee to €4 but required customers to either return the vehicle clean or pay an additional cleaning fee of €16. In order to avoid any misunderstanding about what it meant by a clean car, easyCar provided customers with an explicit description of what constituted a clean car, both for the interior and the exterior of the car. It had to be apparent that the exterior of the car had been washed prior to returning the vehicle. The nearby gas stations map that customers were provided when they picked up their cars also showed nearby car washes where they could clean the car before returning it. Although easyCar had received some bad press in relation to the policy,[22] 85 percent of customers returned their vehicles clean as a result of the policy.

When a customer returned a vehicle, an easyCar employee would check to make sure that the vehicle was clean and undamaged and that the low fuel indicator light was not on. The employee would also check the kilometers driven. The customer would then be notified of any additional charges. These charges would be subtracted from the €80 deposit and the difference refunded to the customer's credit card (or, if additional charges exceeded the €80 deposit, the customer's credit card would be charged the difference).

PRICING

EasyCar clearly differentiated itself from its competitors with its low price. In addition, pricing also played a key role in easyCar's efforts to achieve high utilization of its fleet of cars. EasyCar advertised prices as low as €5/day plus a per rental preparation fee of €4. Prices, however, varied by the location and dates of the rental, by when the booking was made, and by what time the car was to be picked up and returned. EasyCar's systems constantly evaluated projected demand and expected utilization at each site and adjusted price accordingly. Achieving the €5/day rate usually required customers to book well in advance, and these rates were typically available only on weekdays. Weekend rates, when booked well in advance, typically started a few euros higher than the weekday rates. As a given rental date approached, however, the price typically went up significantly as easyCar approached 100 percent fleet utilization for that day. Rates could literally triple overnight if there was sufficient booking activity. Generally, however, easyCar's price was less than half that of its major competitors. EasyCar, unlike most other rental car companies, required customers to pay in full at the time of booking, and once a booking was made, the payment was nonrefundable.

EasyCar's base price covered only the core rental of the vehicle—the total price customers paid was in many cases much higher and depended on how the customer reserved, paid for, used, and returned the vehicle. EasyCar's price was based on customers booking through the company's website and paying for their rental with their easyMoney credit card. EasyMoney was the easyGroup's credit and financial services company. Customers who chose to book through the company's phone reservation system were charged an additional €0.95 per minute for the call, and those who used other credit cards were charged €5 extra. All vehicles had to be paid for by a credit or debit card—cash was not accepted. The base rental price allowed customers to drive vehicles 100 kilometers per day; additional kilometers were charged at a rate of €0.12 per km. In addition, customers were expected to return their cars clean and on time. Customers who returned cars that did not meet easyCar's standards for clean were charged a €16 cleaning fee. Those who returned their cars late were immediately charged €120 and subsequently charged an additional €120 for each subsequent 24-hour period in which the car was not returned. EasyCar explained the high late fee as representing the cost that they would likely incur in providing another vehicle to the next customer. Customers wishing to make any changes to their bookings were also charged a change fee of €16. Changes could be made either before the rental started or during the rental period but were limited to changing the dates, times, and location of the rental and were subject to the prices and vehicle availability at the time the change was being made. If the change resulted in an overall lower price for the rental, however, no refund was provided for the difference.

Beginning in 2003, all customers were also required to purchase loss/damage insurance for an additional charge of €4 per day that eliminated the customer's liability for loss or damage to the vehicle (excluding damage to the tires or windshield of the vehicle). Through 2002, customers were able to choose whether to purchase additional insurance from easyCar to eliminate any financial liability in the event that the rental vehicle was damaged. The cost of this insurance had been €6 per day, and approximately 60 percent of easyCar's customers purchased this optional insurance. Those not purchasing this insurance had either assumed the liability for the first €800 in damages personally or had their own insurance through some other means (e.g., some credit card companies provide this insurance to their cardholders at no additional charge for short-term rentals paid for with the credit card).

EasyCar's website attempted to make all these additional charges clear to customers at the time of their booking. EasyCar had received a fair amount of bad press when it first opened for business after many renters complained about having to pay undisclosed charges when they returned their cars.[23] In response, easyCar had revamped its website in an effort to make these charges more transparent to customers and to explain the logic behind many of these charges.

PROMOTION

EasyCar's promotional efforts had through 2002 focused primarily on posters and press advertising. Posters were particularly prevalent in metro systems and bus and train stations in cities in which easyCar had operations. All this advertising focused on easyCar's low price. According to founder Stelios:

> You will never see an advert for an easy company offering an experience—it's about price. If you create expectations you can't live up to then you will ultimately suffer as a result.[24]

In 2002, easyCar spent £1.43 million on such advertising.[25]

EasyCar also promoted itself by displaying its name, phone number, and website address prominently on the doors and rear window of its entire fleet of vehicles and took advantage of free publicity when the opportunity presented itself. An example of seeking out such publicity occurred when Hertz complained that easyCar's comparative advertising campaign in the Netherlands that featured the line "The best reason to use easyCar.com can be found at hertz.nl" violated Dutch law that required comparative advertising to be exact, not general. In response, Stelios and a group of easyCar employees, dressed in orange boiler suits and with a fleet of easyCar vehicles, protested outside the Hertz Amsterdam office with signs asking "What is Hertz frightened of?"[26]

In an effort to help reach its goal of quadrupling sales in the next two years, easyCar had recently hired Jennifer Mowat for the new position of commercial director, which would take over responsibility for easyCar's European marketing. Ms. Mowat had previously been eBay's UK country manager and had recently completed an MBA in Switzerland. Previously, Stelios and easyCar's managing director, Andrew Fitzmaurice, had handled the marketing function themselves.[27] As part of this stepped-up marketing effort, easyCar also planned to double its advertising budget for 2003, to £3 million, and to begin to advertise on television. The television advertising campaign was to feature easyCar's founder, Stelios.[28]

LEGAL CHALLENGES

EasyCar faced several challenges to its approaches. The most significant challenge dealt with a November 2002 ruling made by the Office of Fair Trading (OFT) that easyCar had to grant customers seven days from the time they made a booking to cancel their booking and receive a full refund. The OFT was a UK governmental agency that was responsible for protecting UK consumers from unfair and/or anticompetitive business practices. The ruling against easyCar was based on The 2000 Consumer Protection Distance Selling Regulations. These regulations stipulated that companies that sell at a distance (e.g., by Internet or phone) must provide customers with a seven-day cooling-off period during which time customers can cancel their contracts with the company and receive a full refund. The law exempted accommodation, transportation, catering, and leisure service companies from this requirement. The OFT's ruling concluded that easyCar did not qualify as a transportation service company because the consumers had to drive themselves, and as such, they were not receiving a transport service, just a car.[29]

EasyCar had appealed the OFT's decision to the UK High Court on the grounds that it was indeed a transportation service company and was entitled to an exemption from this requirement. EasyCar was hopeful that it would eventually win this legal challenge. EasyCar had argued that this ruling would destroy the company's book-early–pay-less philosophy and could lead to a tripling of prices.[30] Chairman Stelios was quoted as saying:

> It is very serious. My fear is that as soon as we put in the seven-day cooling off periods our utilization rate will fall from 90% to 65%. That's the difference between a profitable company and an unprofitable one.[31]

EasyCar was also concerned that prolonged legal action on this point could interfere with its plans for a 2004 IPO.

OFT, for its part, had also applied to the UK High Court for an injunction to make the company comply with the ruling. Other rental car companies were generally unconcerned about the ruling, because few offered big discounts for early bookings or nonrefundable bookings.[32]

EasyCar's new policy of posting the pictures of customers whose cars were 15 days or more overdue was also drawing legal criticism. EasyCar had recently received public warnings from lawyers that this new policy might violate data protection, libel, privacy, confidentiality, and human rights laws.[33] Of particular concern to some lawyers was the possibility that easyCar might post the wrong person's picture, given the large number of customers the company dealt with.[34] Such a mistake could open the company to costly libel suits. The policy of posting the pictures of overdue customers on the easyCar website, initiated in November of 2002, was designed to reduce the losses associated with customers renting a vehicle and never returning it. The costs were significant, according to Stelios:

> These cars are expensive, £15,000 each, and we have 6000 of them. At any given time we are looking for as many as several tens which are overdue. If we don't get one back, it's a write-off. We are writing off an entire car, and it's uninsurable.[35]

Stelios was also convinced of the legality of the new policy. In a letter to the editor of the *Financial Times* in which he responded to the legal concerns raised in the press, Stelios said:

> From a legal perspective, we have been entirely factual and objective and are merely reporting the details of the overdue car and the person who collected it. In addition, our policy is made very clear in our terms and conditions and the photo is taken both overtly and with the consent of the customer . . . I estimate the total cost of overdue cars to be 5% of total easyCar costs, or 50p on every car rental day for all customers. In 2004, when I intend to float easyCar, this cost will amount to £5 million unless we can reduce our quantity of overdue cars.[36]

In the past, easyCar had simply provided pictures to police when a rental car was 15 days or more overdue. The company hoped that posting the picture would both discourage drivers from not returning vehicles and shame those drivers who currently had overdue cars into returning them. In fact, the first person whose photo was posted on the easyCar website did indeed return his car two days later. The vehicle was 29 days late.[37]

THE FUTURE

At the end of 2002, Stelios had stepped down as the CEO of easyJet so that he could devote more of his time to the other easyGroup companies, including easyCar. He had three priorities for the new year. One was to turn around the money-losing easyInternetCafe business, which Stelios had described as "the worst mistake of my career."[38] The 22-store chain had lost £80 million in the last two years. A second priority was to oversee the planned launch of another new easyGroup business, easyCinema, in the spring of 2003. And the third was to oversee the rapid expansion of the easyCar chain so that it would be ready for an initial public offering in the second half of 2004.

NOTES

1. EasyCar.com website.
2. "The big picture—an interview with Stelios," *The Sunday Herald* (UK), 16 March 2003.
3. "Click to fly" *The Economist,* 13 May 2004.
4. E. Simpkins, "Stelios isn't taking it easy," *The Sunday Telegraph* (UK), 15 December 2002.
5. Avis Europe plc 2002 annual report, p. 10. Accessed online at http://ir.avis-europe.com/avis/reports on 16 August, 2004.
6. Simpkins, "Stelios isn't taking it easy."
7. "Marketing: Former eBay UK chief lands top easyCar position," *Financial Times Information Limited,* 9 January 2003.

8. T. Burt, "EasyCar agrees deal with Vauxhall," *Financial Times*, 30 April 2002, p. 24.

9. N. Hodgson, "Stelios plans easycar float," *Liverpool Echo*, 24 September 2002.

10. Simpkins, "Stelios isn't taking it easy."

11. "Marketing Week: Don't write off the car rental industry," *Financial Times Information Limited,* 26 September 2002.

12. "EasyCar set to shake up German car rental market," *European Intelligence Wire,* 22 February 2002.

13. Ibid.

14. N. Hodgson, "Stelios plans easycar float."

15. A. Felsted, "EasyCar courts Clio for rental fleet," *Financial Times*, 11 February 2002, p. 26.

16. EasyCar.com website news release, 1 March 2000.

17. T. Burt, "EasyCar agrees deal with Vauxhall."

18. EasyCar.com website news release, 2 May 2002.

19. "Marketing Week: EasyCar appoints head of European marketing," *Financial Times Information Limited,* 9 January 2003.

20 Simpkins, "Stelios isn't taking it easy."

21. Ibid.

22. J. Hyde, "Travel View: Clearing up on the extras," *The Observer* (UK), 7 July 2002.

23. J. Stanton, "The empire that's easy money," *Edinburgh Evening News*, 26 November 2002.

24. "The big picture—an interview with Stelios," *The Sunday Herald.*

25. "EasyCar appoints head of European marketing," *Financial Times Information Limited.*

26. EasyCar.com website news release, 22 April 2002.

27. "EasyCar appoints head of European marketing," *Financial Times Information Limited.*

28. "Campaigning: EasyGroup appoints Publicis for easyCar TV advertising brief," *Financial Times Information Limited*, 31 January 2003.

29. J. Macintosh, "EasyCar sues OFT amid threat to planned flotation," *Financial Times,* 22 November 2002, p. 4.

30. "EasyCar appoints head of European marketing," *Financial Times Information Limited.*

31. Mackintosh, "EasyCar sues OFT amid threat to planned flotation."

32. Ibid.

33. B. Sherwood, B. & A. Wendlandt, "EasyCar may be in difficulty over naming ploy," *Financial Times*, 14 November 2002, p. 2.

34. Ibid.

35. "e-business: Internet fraudsters fail to steal Potter movie's magic and other news," *Financial Times Information Limited,* 19 November 2002.

36. S. Haji-Ioannou, "Letters to the Editor: Costly effect of late car return," *Financial Times,* 16 November 2002, p. 10.

37. M. Hookham, "How Stelios nets return of his cars," *Daily Post* (Liverpool, UK), 14 November 2002.

38. S. Bentley, "The worst mistake of my career, by Stelios," *Financial Times*, 24 December 2002.

Case

2

PEOPLE, SERVICE, AND PROFIT AT JYSKE BANK

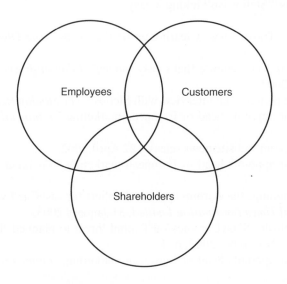

The Jyske Bank Group is managed and operated as a business. At the same time, we attach great importance to treating our three groups of stakeholders—shareholders, customers and employees—with equal respect. This is illustrated by three equally big overlapping circles which must remain in perfect balance. If the balance shifts in favor of one or two of the groups, this will be to the long-term detriment of all the groups.

—Jyske Bank Management Philosophy

This case was prepared under the auspices of the Scandinavian International Management Institute. It was written by Roger Hallowell. It is intended to be used as a basis for class discussion rather than to illustrate either effective or ineffective handling of an administrative situation.
© 2003 SIMI, Scandinavian International Management Institute.

EXHIBIT 1
Danish Banks
Shareholders' Equity
at January 1, 2002

Bank		Shareholders' Equity
1.	DDB	57.091
2.*	Jyske Bank	6.174
3.	Sydbank	3.435
4.	Nykredit Bank	2.708
5.	Spar Nord	1.692
6.	Arbejdernes Landsbank	1.518
7.	Amtssparekassen Fyn	994
8.	Amargerbanken	956
9.	Sparbank Vest	841
10.	Sparekassen, Kornjylland	816
11.	Ringkøbing Landbobank	794
12.	Alm. Brand Bank	749
13.	Forstædernes Bank	706
14.	Loskilde Bank	698
15.	Lån & Spar Bank	589
16.	Nørresundby Bank	583
17.	Sparekassen Sjælland	582
18.	Sparekassen Lolland	559
19.	Nordvestbank	545

*Note: Nordea is not shown as it was a Swedish bank with operations in Denmark, having acquired Unibank.
Source: Jyske Bank.

In 2003, Jyske Bank Group's primary operations consisted of Jyske Bank, which was the third largest bank in Denmark after Den Danske Bank and Nordea's Danish operations (see **Exhibit 1**). Jyske Bank was created in 1967 through the merger of four Danish banks having their operations in Jutland, Jyske being Danish for "Jutlandish." Jutland was the large portion of Denmark attached to the European mainland to the north of Germany. Until the late 1990s, Jyske Bank was characterized as a typical Danish bank: prudent, conservative, well-managed, generally unremarkable, and largely undifferentiated.

Beginning in the mid-1990s, Jyske Bank embarked on a change process that led to its no longer being characterized as either unremarkable or undifferentiated. By 2003 its unique "flavor" of service made it a leader in customer satisfaction among Danish banks (see **Exhibit 2**). At the heart of these changes was the bank's determination to be, in the words of one executive, "the most customer-oriented bank in Denmark." The bank achieved its goal by focusing on what it called *Jyske Forskelle*, or Jyske Differences.

DENMARK

At the onset of the twenty-first century Denmark had a population of approximately five million. A member of the European Union retaining its own currency (the Danish Kronor, DKK[1]), Denmark was the southernmost of the Scandinavian countries. Denmark had been a wealthy country for hundreds of years. This was originally due to its strategic location in the Baltic Sea (see **Exhibit 3**) enabling it to extract tolls from merchants who were forced to sail within cannon range of its shores. More recently, much of Denmark's wealth came from high-value-added goods such as agricultural products, pharmaceuticals, machinery, instruments, and medical equipment, in addition to a highly-developed service sector including shipping.

[1]Euro bought approximately DKK 7.4 and U.S. $1 bought approximately DKK 6.3 as of June 10, 2003.

EXHIBIT 2 **Danish Banks' Quality of Service Metrics**

		Part I: Analysis of Bank Image					
	Total Image	Willingness to Take Risk	Management	They Are a Strategic Coach for Me	Service and Customer Treatment	Expert in Advice and Competence	Chose This Bank If We Want to Change Banks
Jyske Bank	1	1	1	1	1	1	1
Sydbank	2	2	3	2	2	2	2
Spar Nord Bank	3	4	4	3	3	5	5
Midtbank/ Handeslbank	4	6	7	4	6	4	7
Amagerbanken	5	3	5	6	4	8	6
Amtssparekassen Fyn	6	5	6	5	5	7	8
Nordea	7	7	8	8	7	6	3
Danske Bank	8	8	2	7	8	3	4
BG Bank	9	9	9	9	9	9	9

Source: survey of 1,750 small companies conducted by the Danish newspaper *Erhvervs Bladet*, 22 March 2002, p. 2.

Part II: (A) Consumer Satisfaction Survey; Very Satisfied

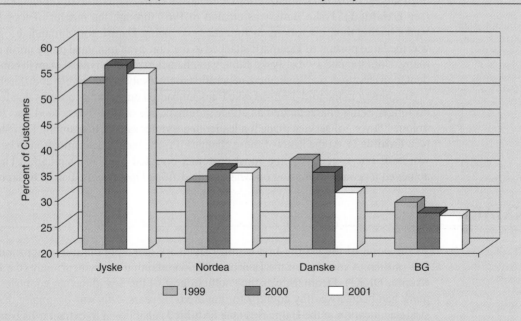

continued

Part II: (B) Consumer Satisfaction Survey; Satisfied and Very Satisfied

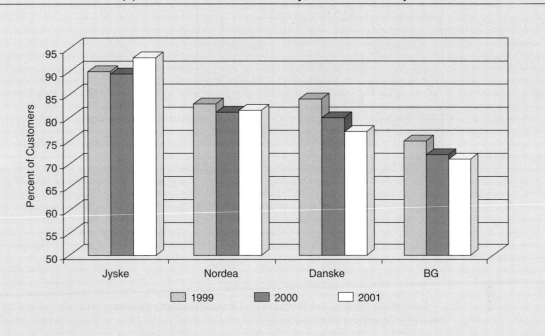

Part II: (C) Consumer Satisfaction Survey; Dissatisfied and Very Dissatisfied

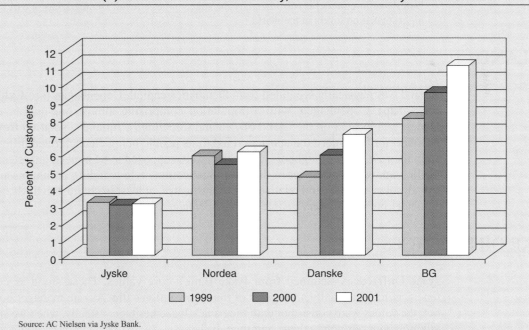

Source: AC Nielsen via Jyske Bank.

EXHIBIT 3
Denmark

Source: CIA World Factbook

Following the Second World War, Denmark adopted a social welfare system its government described as follows:

> The basic principle of the Danish welfare system, often referred to as the Scandinavian welfare model, is that all citizens have equal rights to social security. Within the Danish welfare system, a number of services are available to citizens, free of charge. . . . The Danish welfare model is subsidized by the state, and as a result Denmark has one of the highest taxation levels in the world.[2]

JUTLAND

Jutland was physically separated from Denmark's capital, Copenhagen (see **Exhibit 3** for a map). Copenhagen, with a population comprising almost one-quarter of all Danes, was located on the island of Zealand (*Sjaelland*). Jutland's isolation from the capital prior to modern transportation led to its people being characterized differently from their Zealander neighbors: Jutlanders were supposed to be honest, unpretentious, egalitarian, open and direct in their communication style (candid), commonsensical, frugal, sober-minded, and relatively unsophisticated, at least in contrast to those, as one Jutlander put it, "slippery people from Copenhagen."

JYSKE DIFFERENCES

Jyske Differences stemmed from Jyske Bank's core values. These stood as central tenets, guiding virtually all aspects of the organization's life. As one manager pointed out, the values were consistent with the bank's Jyske heritage: "Really, when we started talking about our core values, and their Jyskeness, we just became overt about values we had long held." Jyske Bank's core values, published for employees, customers, and

[2]See www.denmark.dk

shareholders, were that the bank should (1) have common sense; (2) be open and honest; (3) be different and unpretentious; (4) have genuine interest and equal respect for people; and (5) be efficient and persevering. See **Exhibit 4** for a more detailed description.

The core values led management to reevaluate how the bank did business with its customers. Managers determined that if the bank were to be true to its values, it would have to deliver service differently from both how it had in the past, and how other banks delivered service. Jyske Differences were thus operationalized as specific practices that distinguished Jyske Bank.

Competitive Positioning

Managers looked to Jyske values and differences for the bank's competitive positioning. This process was aided by a Dutch consultant, whose market research indicated that Jyske bank's core target market of Danish families and small-to-medium sized Danish companies (earnings were 40% commercial, 60% retail) generally liked the idea of a bank that was Jyske. Additional research suggested that what managers described as the "hard factors" of price, product, and location had become *sine qua non* in the eyes of customers. In contrast, "soft factors" relating to an individual customer's relationship with her service providers served as the basis for differentiation, specifically, "being nice," "making time for the customer," and "caring about the customer and his family."

Managers felt that the "genuine interest" component of the bank's values dictated a shift from traditional product focused selling to a customer-solution approach. They characterized the new approach by contrasting the statement, "Let me tell you about our demand-deposit account," with the question, "What do you need?"

Although the bank's core financial products remained essentially similar to those of other Danish banks,[3] the way they were delivered changed. This required significant changes in the branches, both tangible and intangible, and how they were supported. Tools were developed to support solution-based service delivery. For example, new IT systems helped employees take customers through processes to determine their needs and find appropriate solutions. In one, the customer and her banker filled out an on-line investor profile to determine what style of investment products were most appropriate for her based on risk aversion, time frame, and return goals, among other factors. A manager commented that, "The tools themselves aren't proprietary. We've seen other financial services with similar programs—it's how our people use them that makes the difference." Another stated, "Our tools are designed either to enhance our ability to deliver solutions, or to reduce administrative tasks and increase the amount of time our people can spend with customers—delivering solutions."

Finally, being overtly Jyske meant that the bank would no longer be a good place for any customer meeting its demographic criteria for two reasons. First, delivering this type of service was expensive. As a result, the bank charged a slight premium, and targeted only those customers who were less likely to represent a credit risk. Second, the bank would have a personality. According to one manager, "The danger in having a personality is, someone, inevitably, won't like you." Senior management considered this the price of being candid, and welcomed the effect it had on some customers. For

[3]Typical core financial products included house, car, and personal loans as well as cash management and investment services for individuals, as well as loans, cash management, and investment services for small-to-medium sized companies. Jyske Bank did not offer credit cards.

EXHIBIT 4   Jyske Bank's Core Values

Common Sense

>>With both feet placed firmly on the ground, we think before we act<<

That means that we:

- consider common sense our best guide
- apply common sense when solving problems and meeting daily challenges
- allow common sense to override awkward customs and routines
- take action whenever we encounter examples of bureaucratic procedures
- observe existing rules and regulations
- accept that control measures are necessary to a certain degree
- generate satisfactory short- and long-term financial results by pursuing sound business practices
- apply common sense whenever we incur group expenses

Open and Honest

>>*We are open and honest in both word and action*<<

That means that we:

- keep each other up-to-date on relevant matters, and do not misuse information obtained in the course of our work
- restrict the degree of openness only by business considerations or by consideration for other stakeholders
- respect agreements entered into and do not betray the Bank's confidence
- strive towards making important decisions concerning individual employees on the basis of a constructive dialogue
- communicate openly about the mistakes we make and the problems we encounter
- accept that mistakes are made, that they are corrected, and that focus is then on learning from the process
- listen openly to new ideas and constructive criticism

Different and Unpretentious

>>*We think and act differently and are generally unpretentious*<<

That means that we:

- encourage creativity and initiative by being untraditional
- are full of initiative, and are committed and proactive
- encourage relaxed and straightforward communication—both internally and externally

Genuine Interest and Equal Respect

>>*We demonstrate insight and respect for other people*<<

That means that we:

- recognize that no two people are alike
- seek lasting relations with shareholders, customers, and employees
- offer qualified advice matching the financial needs and requirements of each customer
- have job security based on mutual obligations and that we pay attention to individual and personal needs
- allow the highest possible degree of personal influence on assignments, working hours, and place of work

EXHIBIT 4   **Jyske Bank's Core Values—continued**

Efficient and Persevering

>>*We work consistently and with determination to reach our goals*<<

That means that we:

- use JB 2005 (the bank's core values) as a guide in our daily work
- are not blown off course because of external circumstances—but take a bearing and plot a new course when this is deemed appropriate
- adopt an organization which promotes efficiency
- consider security important to efficiency
- are convinced that efficiency increases with the level of personal responsibility
- allow employees to assume personal responsibility for day-to-day decisions—even when the basis for decision making may not be 100% perfect
- acquire the level of skills required through personal and professional development
- act on the basis of competence rather than organizational charge
- support our decisions by well-founded arguments

example, Jyske Bank's cash/debit card had a picture of a black grouse on it, black grouses being found in Jutland's rural countryside. When a few customers complained that the bird didn't seem very business-like, or wasn't hip (one was "embarrassed to pull it out at the disco") managers were happy to invite them to open accounts at competitor institutions. A manager noted:

> Actually, if no one reacts to our materials, they're not strong enough. Some people should dislike us. After all, we're only about 6% of the market. I don't want everyone to like us—we're not for everyone and don't want to be.

Tangible Differences

Account Teams

Delivering on the banks competitive positioning required a number of tangible changes in its service delivery system. These began with assigning each customer a branch employee to serve as primary point of contact. Over time, managers discovered that this created problems, because customers often arrived at a branch when their service provider was busy with other customers or otherwise unavailable. Nevertheless, managers were committed to providing individualized service. According to one, "How can we be honest in saying we care about customers as individuals if we don't get to know them as individuals? And without knowing them, we can't identify and solve their problems." The solution was found in account teams: each customer was assigned to a small team of branch bankers. These employees worked together to know and serve their customers, sitting in close physical proximity within the branch.

Branch Design

Jyske Bank planned to spend approximately DKK 750 million to physically redesign its branches (most of this had been spent by 2003). Danish observers described the new branches as looking "like an advertising agency" or "a smart hotel." These effects were accomplished through the use of modern, up-scale materials such as light wood, warm colors, and original art. Branch redesign also included changes in the way customers interacted with their bankers, made possible by architectural and design changes. For example, customers waiting for their banker could help themselves to fresh coffee in a small part of the branch resembling a café. A customer commented on the café, "It means more than you initially think—it makes you feel welcome, it says they're really interested in me." Fruit juice was available for children, who could amuse themselves with toys in the play center. Bankers' desks were now round tables, signifying equality. A team of three or four bankers sat at a single large round table, with customers making themselves comfortable between the bankers' work stations. Customers could see bankers' computer screens, reinforcing openness. Customers' ability to view the screens also facilitated the use of IT programs designed to structure interactions between account team members and customers. As equals, bankers and customers sat in the same type of chairs, and bankers no longer sat on a raised dais, the origins of which went back to feudal times when the heads of certain people were supposed to be higher than those of others. If a conversation required more discretion, specially designed meeting rooms giving the feeling of "home" were available. **Exhibit 5** contains pictures of a remodeled branch.

Details

Jyskeness was infused into the bank wherever possible, a formal policy requiring Jyske differences to be considered in all product and IT development. No detail was too small: for example, although employees' business cards had their pictures on them, as one manager put it, "They were bad pictures, really gray. They weren't warm—the people in them looked stiff and uncaring." To make them more Jyske, the bank hired a professional photographer who worked with each employee to "get the genuine interest in that employee's eye to come to life." Each picture was then tinted slightly yellow to make it resemble "an old family photo."

EXHIBIT 5
Pictures of a
Remodeled Branch

Source: Jyske Bank

(A)

EXHIBIT 5   **Pictures of a Remodeled Branch—continued**

(B)

(C)

(D)

Intangible Differences

Delivering the bank's new competitive positioning also required numerous intangible changes and other changes not immediately visible to the customer. Managers stated that the most important of these involved training and empowering those employees closest to the customer to serve the customer.

Training

Before a branch was remodeled, all staff took part in special training sessions. These included teambuilding and customer service, drawing on best practices from the "traditional" retail sector.

Empowering the Branches

Jyske Bank leadership examined its organizational structure, asking, "Where is value created?" and "Where should decisions be made in order to create the most value?" The answer to both questions was "in the branches."

Previously, almost all lending decisions of any consequence required approval at the branch, regional, and headquarters levels. Specifically, a customer would approach an employee for a loan. The request would be communicated to the branch manager. The branch manager would then make out the formal application, which if the loan was for more than DKK 3 million, was sent to a regional office with the branch manager's comments. The regional office would then comment on the application, and if the loan were for more than DKK 15 million, send it to headquarters for approval, where additional comments were added to the application. Loans of more than DKK 30 million also required approval from the head of credit for the bank as a whole. In examining this process, managers discovered that most of the debate and communication were among individuals in the middle, rather than between the employee closest to the customer (who presumably had the most information about the customer) and the ultimate decision maker.

After reviewing the situation, the bank's leadership stated, "If we are to be true to our value of using common sense, we shouldn't need so many people, and so many layers, reviewing loans." First, the process was changed so that the employee receiving the request for the loan completed the formal application. This empowered that employee by giving him ownership of the loan, which he was trained in how to handle. He was also put in charge of pricing the loan, as long as his suggested pricing was within a set range of where the final approval authority felt it should be. Most loans received final approval from the branch manager, who was either selected in part based on her credit skills or given additional training in credit. A few loans required approval at the regional level because of their size. In these instances, the employee completing the application sent it directly to the regional head of credit. 98% of loans were handled at the branch or regional levels, where loans of up to DKK 90 million were approved. The credit department at headquarters was disbanded, leaving only the bank's head of credit who reviewed loans of more than DKK 90 million. This additional review was retained for loans of this size because exposure to the customer would be so great that default could significantly affect the bank's capital.

The changes implemented were originally designed to affect internal processes. However, they also improved customers' experiences. For example, managers believed that because the employee in direct contact with the customer made the application, the quality of information in applications increased; as a result, more borrowers worthy of credit received it, and the quality of loans in the bank's portfolio improved. In addition, the time to reach a decision for the largest loans declined from a maximum of three weeks to ten days. Smaller loans able to be approved within the branch could be made almost instantly. Finally, customers' expectations regarding price and terms were more often included in the application. This helped the approving authority to see whether the loan, in a form acceptable to the bank, was likely to be accepted by the customer, saving time and effort when customers' expectations were inconsistent with the bank's requirements.

The streamlined approval process did not pose a credit risk, according to managers, because of the combination of: (1) improved branch credit skills, (2) lack of incentive to make poor loans (branch managers had no incentives immediately related to loan volume or quality), and (3) a robust internal auditing function that monitored credit quality.

At the same time that the credit process was redesigned, the bank consolidated from five regions to three, and increased spans of control so that between 35 and 45 branches reported to each business unit director, who had a staff of marketing, credit, human resources, and control professionals at the regional level (many of whom had previously been at headquarters).

A senior manager commented on the roles of headquarters, the regions, and the branches:

> Headquarters is where we transform our values and strategy into products, processes, and information technology. The three regions are where we make sure that what comes from headquarters is translated for the local marketplace, and where we ensure that Jyske Differences are being acted upon—that customers experience them. The 119 branches are where we serve customers and thus where value is really created. 20% of what we do is development at headquarters, and 80% is implementation in the field, supported by the regions. Given the small size of our branches we need the regional level to ensure that implementation is done right.

Empowerment throughout the Bank

Empowerment was not limited to the branches. Throughout the bank, employees were encouraged to make decisions of all sorts if they felt comfortable doing so. In general, employees were encouraged to ask themselves, "Does it make sense to ask for help or permission? Is there a business reason for asking? Is this something you've never done before? Is this a 'big' decision (big being relative)? Is it debatable, or is it a new principle?" In general, employees were told, "When in doubt, ask. However, if there is no doubt, go ahead." Managers were expected to set an example.

Examples of this policy in action included working hours and vacation time. One employee noted, "If your job makes it possible, you set your hours, you just have to agree with your colleagues, you don't need approval from your boss. You do the same with holidays." A manager noted, "The union[4] at headquarters didn't have a problem with this, but the union in Copenhagen worried that employees might misuse the flexibility."

Another example involved the amount employees were able to spend on meals and entertainment while traveling or entertaining customers. Previously, there had been a set amount, DKK 125, and bills consistently came to DKK 125. Consistent with its value of common sense, the bank changed the policy to be (paraphrased) "Spend what you need to spend." This resulted in what an executive stated was a "substantial decline in travel and entertainment expenses." When asked, "How do you get a system like this to work?" he replied:

> First, you tell people what's expected.
>
> Second, you check on their behavior. If they are buying expensive wine, you ask, "Why?" You explain what makes sense, and why. You do it in a way that tells them you honestly want to help them improve.
>
> Third, if there are continued problems, this person may not be right for the bank.

---

[4]As was typical in Scandinavia, most employees and managers were members of a union.

The real challenge is when we hire someone from another bank. We expect them to be up to speed quickly because of their background, but they aren't used to making these kinds of decisions—they have to be taught how.

Management Style

A senior manager commented:

You can train and educate all day long, but unless your managers and employees are committed to Jyske Differences, they just won't happen. Getting them committed required a great deal of my effort.

When we started this process there were times when it was hard—really hard. The branch managers didn't think strategically—they sat in their offices and focused on their day-to-day work. I wanted the branch manager to get up on a hill and look around, to get a bigger picture. To get them to change I asked them questions: What's the market? Where—and who—are your competitors? What are your strengths and weaknesses, how do they tie to Jyske Differences? Now, contrast what you need with what you have. Are the teams in your branch living up to the demands? What do you need to do to ensure that that they will? There will be resistance; understand where it is coming from. One way to deal with it is to make agreements with individuals on how they will develop new skills. If there is a complete mismatch you may need new team members, but for the most part, you can coach your people through this kind of change—you can lead them.

According to another executive:

The branch managers have to be able to motivate employees to work a little harder, and differently. The most successful give their employees a lot of latitude for decision making. They do a lot of training, 80% of which is on the job. When it isn't, it's mostly role playing. There aren't any high-powered incentives to offer, but there are really good tools coming out of IT. It's more *how the branch managers do it* than *what they do*. They constantly link the tools, training, and behaviors to our Jyske values. They get their employees to share the values and act on them.

A third noted:

When I have a difficult situation I look for what I call a "culture carrier." I try to put that person into the middle of it, because they live our values. What I usually see is that the other employees who are on the fence about the values start to come over—they see the example and they like what they see. This leaves the few people who really don't want to be Jyske on the outside, and they tend not to last long. Most people are willing to change, but they've got to be supported in the process.

Human Resources

Legal aspects of human resources, record keeping, and training were centralized at headquarters. In contrast, advice on how to deal with human issues was provided by human resource professionals located in the field (at the regional level). They delivered this advice to general managers in the field such as branch managers. The branches had to pay for this service, and they could choose to either buy the service or do without if they preferred.

Selection   An executive discussed employee selection at the bank:

It's very important. For most of the jobs, we're not only looking for banking skills, we're looking for social abilities—service mindedness and compatibility with our Jyske values: openness, genuine interest in other people. You can smell it when you speak with someone. We don't have a systematic approach to this, although when we're hiring someone from another bank we ask why they want to work for us and listen for answers consistent with Jyske values. We can train most banking skills, but we can't train these attitudes. Maybe our biggest challenge is hiring people with them, and getting a few of our established employees to adopt them.

Some departments of the bank asked potential hires to write about themselves. A manager noted, "We're looking to see whether they're engaged in what they do, or if they're promoting themselves."

Training   A manager in human resources commented:

> We have told every employee that his or her development is his or her responsibility. We believe development is incredibly important. While my peers at other Danish banks are cutting staff and saving every way possible, our goal is to get employees and managers to invest in more development. But it's up to the individual to decide what to invest in. We're outsourcing a lot of development activities, but we keep anything related to Jyske values in house.

Incentives   Managers pointed out that the bank had few monetary incentives. The few in place consisted of three types, stock, one-time payments, and annual raises.

> Stock incentives: if the bank's annual performance was above the average of the top ten Danish banks', a stock option grant valued at DKK 8.000 was made available to all employees and managers. In addition, any employee could use up to DKK 13.200 to buy company stock annually at a 20% discount. If the bank's annual performance was among the top three Danish banks', the discount rose to 40%.

> One-time payments: for truly exceptional work, employees could be awarded one-time payments. Fewer than 1% of individuals at the bank received this type of payment.

> Raise incentives: employees and managers received annual salary increases based on their manager's evaluation of their work. The highest raise practicably possible was 10%, although an employee or manager in the top 15% of performers (the highest level) typically received a raise of approximately 7%. Salary raises were eventually limited as total salary had to remain within the bands established for a particular position. Once an increase was granted it became a permanent part of the employee's salary.

Commitment   An employee commented on what it was like to work for Jyske Bank: "I'm not restricted. I don't have to leave my head at home—I can take it with me to work and I'm supposed to." Another commented:

> You're treated as a human being here. At other banks you have to be really careful what you say. Here, you can be open and honest—I can approach anyone—even the CEO.

> Jyske Bank is a way of life. You come in at 8:00 and you leave when you collect your pension. I pay a premium for this, I could earn more at another bank, but it's worth it for me. At some banks, bankers have prostituted themselves for higher pay, stuffing products down the throats of customers those customers may not need. We don't.

Anders Dam, Jyske Bank's CEO, stated:

> If you can create an environment in which people aren't talking about money, but where they gain value in their relationships with their colleagues and their customers, where the bank will take care of those who work hard even if they get sick, then people will be committed to the bank.

Metrics and Financial Results

Bank managers frequently referred to the importance of measuring performance, in both quantitative and qualitative ways, and at a variety of locations in the bank. Traditional financial measures were considered important, but not all-important. In addition to traditional measures, Jyske Bank implemented an information technology system to measure account profitability on a risk-adjusted basis (risk adjusted return on capital, or RAROC). This had been a considerable effort and was just coming on-line in 2003.

Customer and employee measures were also considered important. Managers reported that employee satisfaction was higher at Jyske Bank than at any of its major competitors based on data collected by independent third parties. Several sources of data indicated that Jyske Bank customer satisfaction was also the highest among the bank's major competitors (see **Exhibit 2**). Customer satisfaction could be tracked to the regional level. Plans were in place to be able to measure and report it at the branch, and eventually the individual customer, levels.

Financial and selected operating results are presented in **Exhibit 6.** Jyske Bank took a conservative approach to earnings, writing off its entire investment in remodeling branches, building a new headquarters, and new information technology systems in the years in which spending occurred. This amounted to DKK 302 million in 2002, DKK 253 million in 2001, DKK 194 million in 2000, and DKK 212 million in 1999. Results for 2002 also reflected an extraordinary tax payment of DKK 222 million, which was described as "a potential liability in light of discussions with the Danish tax authorities."[5]

Jyske Bank's statement of core values and principles included the following:

> . . . the aim is for Jyske Bank every year to be one of the top performing Danish banks
> . . . Jyske Bank is thus an excellent choice for shareholders who want to make a long-term investment and who do not attach great importance to decisions which generate only short-term price increases.

Communication

Management believed that most employees liked working for the bank and appreciated Jyske Differences as they affected their jobs. Sustaining Jyske Differences required the bank to remain independent, not an easy task in the Scandinavian banking market, which had consolidated considerably during the 1990s and early 21st century. Executives believed that they had taken the right steps to remain independent by investing in employees, systems, and infrastructure that would enable the bank to deliver superior value to its targeted customers, and thus achieve superior financial returns. This economic model was built on the bank's value chain (see **Exhibit 7**).

Delivering that value required considerable change. One manager stated a point that several alluded to:

> If you want employees to behave differently, you have to be sure they know what that means—how they should behave going forward, and why they should change. We can't ask people to change without communicating this kind of information to them—it's not fair.

Bank leadership believed that communication should be, in the words of an executive, "a car wash, not a waterfall—communication must come from all directions at once, not just cascade down from above." In that spirit, in 1997 communication

---

[5]According to an executive, "If we are right [and we eventually reverse the charge] we have an upside. If we are wrong it won't impact future results. All in all the tax issue is not related to the 2002 result and it would be more correct to judge the result before tax."

EXHIBIT 6   Jyske Bank Group Financial and Selected Operating Results

Five-Year Summary of Financial Results					
Summary of Profit and Loss Account (DKKm)	**2002**	**2001**	**2000**	**1999**	**1998**
Net interest income	2,826	2,623	2,350	2,078	2,133
Dividend on capital holdings	64	98	69	52	34
Net fee and commission income	758	668	759	646	594
Net interest and fee income	**3,648**	3,389	3,178	2,776	2,761
Revaluations	386	129	379	631	−361
Other ordinary income	203	213	162	175	219
Operating expenses and depreciation	2,598	2,443	2,142	2,014	1,764
Losses and provisions for bad debts	408	286	318	248	197
Revaluation of capital interests	−148	−112	−4	−44	52
Profit/loss on ordinary activities before tax	1,083	890	1,255	1,276	710
Tax	572	267	172	379	199
Profit/loss for the year	**511**	623	1,083	897	511
Summary of Balance Sheet (DKKm)	**2002**	**2001**	**2000**	**1999**	**1998**
Advances	95,302	82,537	75,362	49,790	39,762
Deposits	58,963	54,393	52,267	49,813	43,816
Issued bonds	43,362	36,964	26,902	192	623
Total assets	153,169	133,156	127,359	92,557	76,938
Shareholders' funds	6,658	6,174	5,887	5,391	5,108
Supplementary capital	2,000	2,663	2,110	1,395	434
Key Figures	**2002**	**2001**	**2000**	**1999**	**1998**
Per Jyske Bank share					
Core earnings	23.17	25.39	22.07	14.68	19.89
Profit/loss on ordinary activities before tax	29.32	24.11	31.86	29.58	15.77
Net profit/loss for the year	13.84	16.77	27.51	20.83	11.22
Dividend	0.00	0.00	0.00	3.20	2.80
Price at year-end	192	177	161	149	123
Book value	178	170	157	131	114
Price/book value	1.08	1.04	1.03	1.14	1.08
Price/earnings	13.8	10.5	5.9	7.2	10.9
The Jyske Bank Group					
Solvency ratio	11.3	11.4	11.0	10.5	10.4
Core capital ratio	8.2	7.9	8.0	8.2	9.5
Income on every krone of expenditure	1.36	1.33	1.51	1.56	1.36
Total provisions as % of total loans	1.8	1.9	2.0	2.7	3.0
Losses and provisions for the year as % of total loans	0.4	0.3	0.4	0.4	0.4

Source: Jyske Bank

continued

EXHIBIT 6 Jyske Bank Group Financial and Selected Operating Results—continued

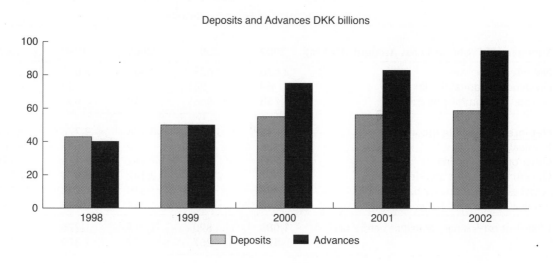

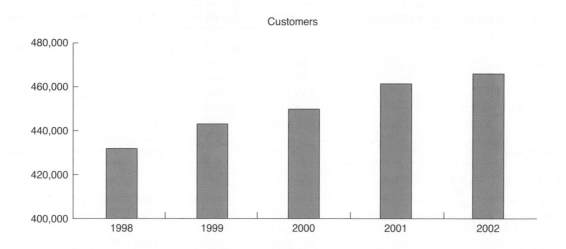

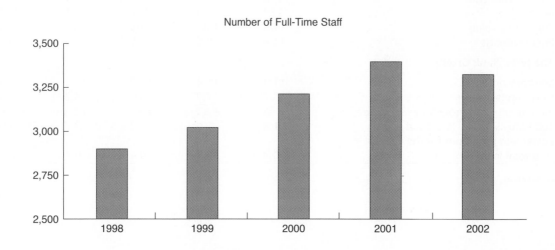

EXHIBIT 7
The Jyske Bank
Value Chain

Source: Jyske Bank's adaptation
of Heskett, Sasser, and
Schlesinger's Service Profit
Chain, see Heskett et al., 1997.

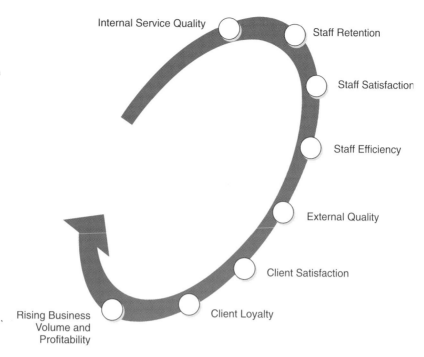

Internal Service Quality

Staff Retention

Staff Satisfaction

Staff Efficiency

External Quality

Client Satisfaction

Client Loyalty

Rising Business
Volume and
Profitability

reinforced Jyske values and differences when the bank produced a video tape on Jyske Differences made available to all employees. This was designed to look like a television talk show. The host was a prominent Danish television personality and the guests were Anders Dam and Danish experts on business. Each was interviewed and they discussed what Jyske Differences were, how they were being implemented, and what they meant to employees and customers, supported by video clips of employees and customers in the branches.

Communication efforts continued in 1999, executives planning a surprise for the bank's strategic meeting, to which all employees were invited every third year.

The Battle at Vejle   The 1999 strategic meeting took place in Vejle, the closest city to the bank's headquarters with an auditorium large enough for the 82% of the bank's 3107 employees who chose to attend. The meeting opened with a panel of senior executives, some of whom were from Jyske Bank, and others who were strangers. A grim-faced Anders Dam got up, and introduced one of the strangers as "the CEO of a large, very large, Swedish bank." Dam then continued, explaining that the Swedish bank had offered to buy Jyske Bank for almost twice its current stock market valuation, a premium of 2.3 times what other Danish banks had recently been acquired for. A fax was to be sent to the Copenhagen stock exchange, suspending trading in Jyske Bank shares immediately after the meeting. As he spoke, a sense of foreboding rose in the audience.

Non-Scandinavians should note that despite the currently cozy relationship between Swedes and Danes, they fought against one another for many centuries, Southern Sweden once having been a Danish possession.

The CEO of the Swedish bank took the podium and announced (in Swedish, which is very difficult for most Danes to understand) that his Danish was very poor, so that he would "speak Scandinavian, very slowly," after which he continued to deliver his address in Swedish.

He stated, among other things, that "You—Jyske Bank, you are good, very good. But are you good enough? For tomorrow? For the future? For a world without boarders across the continent?" After his speech Anders Dam took the podium again and asked for an "immediate and honest response" from the employees. Over the course of several questions and responses it became clear that although the takeover was friendly, the integration would be anything but. In the words of the Swedish CEO, "A merger has certain administrative advantages, which will require an adjustment in staffing." Eventually, a manager got up and said, "Do something for the environment. Put the Swedes on the ferry and send them back!" His suggestion received wild applause.

After a pause, Anders Dam returned to the podium and, now smiling, explained that it had all been a joke, which he called "Jyske Fun." He added that he was "proud, proud as a peacock of your reaction to the joke," being delighted that the vast majority of the audience flatly rejected the idea of being acquired. One questioner put it bluntly, stating that (paraphrased) "Jyske Bank couldn't live Jyske Differences, couldn't do the things for employees and customers they had been working so hard on, if it were to be acquired." Dam finished his speech by pointing out that if Jyske Bank were to remain independent in the increasingly-competitive environment Danish banks now faced, everyone would have to contribute.

Part of that contribution was an effort to diversify the bank's type of shareholders and increase their number in order to ensure that they shared its long-term perspective on financial performance. Employees encouraged customers to consider purchasing Jyske Bank Group shares. Between the "Battle at Vejle" and 2003, the number of shareholders increased from 150.000 to more than 210.000.

Managers and employees agreed that the message of the "Battle at Vejle" was heard throughout the organization and that Jyske Fun was a good idea. Subsequent examples of it included the only national advertising campaign the bank had engaged in during the past decade, which was effectively a dog beauty contest with entry requiring a visit to a local branch. When asked why advertising was so limited, an executive replied:

> Two reasons. First, we rely on word of mouth, so we don't need to advertise that much—our advertising cost as a percentage of revenue is half what banks of similar size spend. Second, we have to be absolutely sure we can consistently deliver Jyske Differences before we advertise them.

Later in 1999, communication efforts continued when managers created a video tape illustrating Jyske Differences in an unusual way. The tape introduces Max Performa, an ex-KGB agent hired by a mysterious and beautiful senior manager of a competitor bank. Performa is assigned to find out if Jyske Differences are actually being delivered at Jyske Bank's branches. He checks off each Jyske Difference as he experiences it, pretending to be a Jutlandish farmer wanting a loan (speaking Danish with a thick Russian accent). In the course of applying for the loan he discovers that Jyske Differences are being delivered, among them that the employee opening his account has the authority necessary to meet his needs (*common sense*), that the bank will go to great lengths to show *genuine interest* in him (he and the branch manager drink an entire bottle of vodka one afternoon), and that Jyske Bank *is different* and isn't for everyone: when he complains about the black grouse on his debit card he is politely told he might be happier banking with a competitor. At the end of the tape the viewer learns that the mysterious senior manager who hired Performa actually works for Jyske Bank.

Executives believed that they needed to constantly reinforce the message that remaining independent required every employee to work a little harder, and to behave in a manner consistent with Jyske Differences. To deliver that constant reinforcement, they printed the bank's values and Jyske Differences in materials that managers were asked to discuss with their employees. On one occasion, branch employees were asked to come in on a Saturday, without pay, to discuss the values and differences and their implications for day to-day behavior. 80% chose to come in.

In 2002, communication efforts included the bank's strategic employee meeting, called "Return to Vejle." The meeting, complete with live, high-energy music (a locally popular drum duo) and entertainment, celebrated the bank's accomplishments and served as a reminder of what still needed to be done.

Finally, in 2002 the bank introduced what it called a "tool box" for communicating value chain information to and from the branches. The tool box enabled each branch to select elements on the bank's value chain (see **Exhibit 7**) and measure the branch's performance against goals related to that element. The tool box delivered regularly updated information including guides such as green or red lights describing the branch's performance on the selected value chain elements. An executive described the tool box as "a way to operationalize the value chain so that everyone in the organization understands how they need to behave on a day-to-day basis in order to optimize it."

CONCLUSION

The bank's leadership believed that Jyske values and differences, and the bank's value chain, provided ways to achieve the balance they wanted among their three stakeholders: employees, customers, and shareholders. Several leaders commented that with the large capital investments behind them as of 2003, net income would increase considerably in the coming years, assuming the recession of 2001 and 2002 was over. Shareholders had received a 17.8% annual return on their investment for the ten years prior to year-end 2002. Anders Dam's 2002–2003 goal for shareholders was to increase the bank's stock multiple approximately 40% to the level of Danske Bank's, the largest and most richly-priced bank in Denmark. This was achieved in July 2003.[6] While the bank's leadership was pleased with the bank's success, they were more interested in determining how the bank would remain in a position of leadership while still keeping the interests of its key stakeholders in balance.

QUESTIONS TO THE JYSKE BANK CASE

1. As of the mid 1990s, what was Jyske Bank's competitive positioning, that is, what did it do for customers relative to its competitors?

2. As of 2003, what was Jyske Bank's competitive positioning?

3. What did Jyske Bank change to enable it to deliver its new competitive positioning?

4. How did Jyske Bank implement those changes?

[6]Managers attributed the increase in the bank's stock price multiple to recognition among stock analysts that investments in Jyske Differences made in the previous five years and expensed immediately were bearing fruit.

Case 3

GIORDANO

We are committed to provide our customers with value-for-money merchandise, professional customer service, and a comfortable shopping experience at convenient locations.

Giordano's Corporate Mission

Giordano is a retailer of casual clothes in East Asia, South-East Asia, and the Middle East. In 1999, it operated outlets in China, Dubai, Hong Kong, Macao, Philippines, Saudi Arabia, Singapore, South Korea, and Taiwan. Giordano's sales grew from HK$712 million in 1989 to HK$3,092 million in 1999 (see Exhibit 1). This case study describes the success factors that allowed Giordano to grow rapidly in some Asian countries. It looks at three imminent issues that Giordano faced in maintaining its success in existing markets and in its plan to enter new markets in Asia and beyond. The first concerns Giordano's positioning. In what ways, if at all, should Giordano change its current positioning? The second concerns the critical factors that have contributed to Giordano's success. Would these factors remain critical over the coming years? Finally, as Giordano seeks to enter new markets, the third issue, whether its competitive strengths can be transferred to other markets, needs to be examined.

This case was prepared by Jochen Wirtz as the basis for class discussion rather than to illustrate effective or ineffective handling of an administrative situation. Jochen Wirtz is Associate Professor of Marketing with the NUS Business School, Faculty of Business Administration, National University of Singapore, 17 Law Link, Singapore 117591, Tel: +65-8743656, Fax: +65-7795941, E-mail: fbawirtz@nus.edu.sg. Http://www.nus.edu.sg. Not to be reproduced or used without written permission.

The author acknowledges the generous support in terms of time, information, and feedback on earlier drafts of this case provided by Charles Fung, Chief Operating Officer and Executive Director of Giordano (Southeast Asia), and by Jill Klein, Associate Professor at INSEAD. Furthermore, the author gratefully acknowledges the input by Ang Swee Hoon, who co-authored earlier versions of this case published in the Asian Case Research Journal (2000), Volume 4, Issue 2, pp. 145–67, and in *Principles of Marketing: An Asian Casebook* (2000), Ang et al., Prentice Hall, pp. 80–87. Finally, the author also thanks Jerome S. W. Kho and Jaisey L. Y. Yip for their excellent research assistance in gathering much of the data and assisting with the write-up.

The exchange rates at the time the case was written (February 2001) were US$1 = HK$7.80 and S$1 = HK$4.49.

EXHIBIT 1 Financial Highlights (in Millions of HK$)

(Consolidated)	2000*	1999	1998	1997	1996	1995	1994
Turnover	1,661.4	3,092.2	2,609.2	3,014.4	3,522.0	3,482.0	2,863.7
Turnover increase (percentage)	16.2%	18.5%	(13.4%)	(14.4%)	1.2%	21.6%	22.7%
Profit after tax and minority interests	173.3	360.0	76.1	68.0	261.2	250.2	195.3
Profit after tax and minority interests increase (percentage)	31.1%	375.0%	11.9%	(74.0%)	4.4%	28.1%	41.9%
Shareholders' fund	NA	1,250.8	1,111.1	1,068.9	1,138.3	911.7	544.5
Working capital	701.1	762.3	700.6	654.2	670.3	496.0	362.0
Total debt to equity ratio	NA	0.5	0.3	0.3	0.4	0.7	0.9
Bank borrowings to equity ratio	NA	0	0	0	0	0	0.1
Inventory turnover on sales (days)	28	28	44	48	58	55	53
Return on total assets (percentage)	NA	18.8%	5.3%	4.8%	16.5%	16.4%	18.8%
Return on average equity (percentage)	NA	30.5%	7.0%	6.2%	25.5%	34.4%	39.1%
Return on sales	NA	11.6	2.9	2.3	7.4	7.2	6.8
Earning per share (cents)	24.5	51.3	10.8	9.6	36.9	38.8	30.9
Cash dividend per share (cents)	8.5	34.5	4.5	5.0	16.0	13.5	11.0

Note: "NA" indicates data were not available at time of print; *2000 figures are for the first six months of Giordano's 2000 financial year, ended 30 June 2000. Percentages for 2000 were calculated over the figures for same period in the previous year.(Consolidated)

COMPANY BACKGROUND

Giordano was founded by Jimmy Lai in 1980. To give his venture a more sophisticated image, Lai picked an Italian name for his retail chain. In 1981, Giordano started in Hong Kong selling casual clothes manufactured predominantly for the United States market by a Hong Kong–based manufacturer, the Comitex Group. Initially, it focused on wholesale trade of high-margin merchandise under the Giordano brand in Hong Kong. In 1983, it scaled back on its wholesale operation and started to set up its own retail shops in Hong Kong. It also began to expand its market by distributing Giordano merchandise in Taiwan through a joint venture. In 1985, it opened its first retail outlet in Singapore.

However, in 1987, sales were low and the business became unprofitable. Lai realized that the pricy retail chain concept was unprofitable. Under a new management team, Giordano changed its strategy. Until 1987, it sold exclusively men's casual apparel. When it realized that an increasing number of women customers were attracted to its stores, Giordano changed its positioning and started selling unisex casual apparel. It repositioned itself as a retailer of discounted casual unisex apparel with the goal of maximizing unit sales instead of margins, and sold value-for-money merchandise. Its shift in strategy was successful. Its sales almost quadrupled, from HK$712 million in 1989 to HK$3,092 million in 1999 (see Exhibit 1). A typical Giordano store is shown in Exhibit 2.

EXHIBIT 2
Typical Giordano Storefront

Source: Courtesy of Giordano.

MANAGEMENT VALUES AND STYLE

Being Entrepreneurial and Accepting Mistakes as Learning Opportunities

The willingness to try new ways of doing things and learning from past errors was an integral part of Lai's management philosophy. The occasional failure represented a current limitation and indirectly pointed management to the right decision in the future. To demonstrate his commitment to this philosophy, Lai took the lead by being a role model for his employees " . . . Like in a meeting, I say, look, I have made this mistake. I'm sorry for that. I hope everybody learns from this. If I can make mistakes, who the hell do you think you are that you can't make mistakes?" He also believed strongly in empowerment—if everyone is allowed to contribute and participate, mistakes can be minimized.

Treating Employees as an Asset

Besides the willingness to accept employees' mistakes, another factor that contributed to the success of Giordano was that it had a dedicated, trained, ever-smiling sales force. It considered front-line workers to be its customer service heroes. Charles Fung, Giordano's Chief Operations Officer and Executive Director (South-East Asia), said, "Even the most sophisticated training program won't guarantee the best customer service. People are the key. They make exceptional service possible. Training is merely a skeleton of a customer service program. It's the people who deliver that give it form and meaning."

Giordano had stringent selection procedures to make sure that only those candidates who matched the profile of what it looked for in its employees were selected. Selection continued into its training workshops. Fung called the workshops "attitude training." The service orientation and character of a new employee were tested in these workshops. These situations, he added, were an appropriate screening tool for "weeding out those made of grit and mettle."

Giordano's philosophy of quality service could be observed in its overseas outlets as well. Its Singapore operations, for example, achieved ISO9002 certification. Its obsession with providing excellent customer service was best described by Fung. "The only way to keep abreast with stiff competition in the retail market is to know the customers' needs and serve them well. Customers pay our paychecks; they are our bosses . . . Giordano considers service to be a very important element [in trying to draw customers] . . . service is in the blood of every member of our staff."

According to Fung, everyone who joined Giordano, even office employees, worked in a store for at least one week as part of his or her training. "They must understand and appreciate every detail of the operations. How can they offer proper customer assistance—internal and external—if they don't know what goes on in operations?"

In Singapore, for instance, Giordano invested heavily in training its employees. In 1998, it spent 3.9 percent of its overall payroll on training, with each employee receiving an average of 224 hours of training per year. It had a training room complete with one-way mirrors, video cameras, and other electronic paraphernalia. A training consultant and seven full-time trainers conducted training sessions for every new sales staff member, and existing staff were required to take refresher courses. Its commitment to training and developing its staff was recognized when it was awarded the People Developer Award in 1998.

However, providing training programs was not as important as ensuring the transfer of learning from the workshops and seminars to the store. As Fung explained, "Training is important. Every organization is providing its employees training. However, what is more important is the transfer of learning to the store. When there is a transfer of learning, each dollar invested in training yields a high return. We try to encourage this [transfer of learning] by cultivating a culture and by providing positive reinforcement, rewarding those who practice what they learned."

For Giordano, investment in service meant investment in people. It paid high wages to attract and keep its staff. Giordano offered what Fung claimed was "one of the most attractive packages in an industry where employee turnover is high. We generally pay more than what the market pays." With higher wages, there was a lower staff turnover rate. The higher wages and Giordano's emphasis on training resulted in a corps of eager-to-please sales force.

Managing its vital human resources (HR) became a challenge to Giordano when it decided to expand into global markets. To replicate its high service—quality positioning, Giordano needed to consider the HR issues involved in setting up retail outlets on unfamiliar ground. For example, the recruitment, selection, and training of local employees could require modifications to its formula for success in its current markets owing to differences in the culture, education, and technology of the new countries. Labor regulations could also affect HR policies such as compensation and providing welfare. Finally, expatriate policies for staff seconded to help run Giordano outside their home country and management practices needed to be considered.

Focusing Giordano's Organizational Structure on Simplicity and Speed

Giordano maintained a flat organizational structure. Fung believed that "this gives us the intensity to react to market changes on a day-to-day basis." It followed a relaxed management style, where management worked closely with line staff. There were no separate offices for higher and top management; rather their desks were located next to their staff's, separated only by shoulder-high panels. This closeness allowed easy communication, efficient project management, and speedy decision-making, which are all critical ingredients to success amidst fast-changing consumer tastes and fashion trends. Speed allowed Giordano to keep its product development cycle short. Similar demands in quickness were also expected of its suppliers.

KEY COMPETITIVE STRENGTHS

Giordano's home base, Hong Kong, was flooded with retailers, both big and small. To beat the dog-eat-dog competition prevalent in Asia, especially Hong Kong, Lai felt that Giordano must have a distinctive competitive advantage. Although many retail outlets in Hong Kong competed almost exclusively on price, Lai felt differently about Giordano. Noting successful Western retailers, Lai astutely observed that there were other key factors for success. He started to benchmark Giordano against best practice organizations in four key areas: (1) computerization (from The Limited), (2) a tightly controlled menu (from McDonald's), (3) frugality (from Wal-Mart), and (4) value pricing (from Marks & Spencer) (Ang 1996).

The emphasis on service and the value-for-money concept had proven to be successful. Lai was convinced that the product was only half of what Giordano sells. Service was the other half, and Lai believed that service was the best way to make customers return to Giordano again and again. Lai said, "We are not just a shirt retailer, we are not just an apparel retailer. We are also a service retailer because we sell feeling. Let's make the guy feel good about coming into here [our stores]"(Ang 1996).

Service

Giordano's commitment to excellent service was reflected in the list of service-related awards it had received. It was ranked number one by the *Far Eastern Economic Review,* for being innovative in responding to customers' needs, for three consecutive years— 1994, 1995, and 1996. And when it came to winning service awards, Giordano's name kept cropping up. In Singapore, it won numerous service awards over the years. It was given the Excellent Service Award for three consecutive years: 1996, 1997, and 1998. It also received three tourism awards: "Store of the Year" in 1991, "Retailer of the Month" in 1993, and "Best Shopping Experience—Retailer Outlet" in 1996. These were just some of the awards won by Giordano (see Exhibit 3).

How did Giordano achieve such recognition for its commitment to customer service? It began with the Customer Service Campaign in 1989. In that campaign, yellow badges bearing the words "Giordano Means Service" were worn by every Giordano employee. This philosophy had three tenets: We welcome unlimited try-ons; we exchange—no questions asked; and we serve with a smile. The yellow badges reminded employees that they were there to deliver excellent customer service.

Since its inception, several creative, customer-focused campaigns and promotions had been launched to extend its service orientation. For instance, in Singapore, Giordano asked its customers what they thought would be the fairest price to charge for a pair of jeans and charged each customer the price that they were willing to pay. This one-month campaign was immensely successful, with some 3,000 pairs of jeans sold every day during the promotion. In another service-related campaign, customers were given a free T-shirt for criticizing Giordano's service. Over 10,000 T-shirts were given

EXHIBIT 3   Recent Giordano Company Awards

Award	Awarding Organization	Category	Year(s)
Excellent Service Award*	Singapore Prodtivity and Standards Board	—	1996, 1997, 1998
American Service Excellence Award	American Express	Fashion/Apparel	1995
ISO9002**	SISIR	—	1994
People Developer Award	Singapore Productivity and Standards Board	—	1998
Ear Award	Radio Corporation of Singapore	Listeners' Choice (English Commercial)	1996
Ear Award	Radio Corporation of Singapore	Creative Merits (English Jingles)	1996
1999 HKRMA Customer Service Award	Hong Kong Retail Management Association	—	1999
The Fourth Hong Kong Awards for Services	Hong Kong Trade Development Council	Export Marketing & Customer Service	2000

Note: Awards given to the Giordano Originals Singapore.
*ISO9002 refers to the guidelines from the Geneva-based International Organization for Standardization for companies that produce and install products.
**To be nominated for the Excellent Service Award, a company must have had, among other things, significant training and other programs that ensured quality service. These include systems for recognizing employees and for customer feedback.

away. Far from only being another brand-building campaign, Giordano responded seriously to the feedback collected. For example, the Giordano logo was removed from
some of its merchandise, as some customers liked the quality but not the "value-for-
money" image of the Giordano brand.

Against advice that it would be abused, Lai also introduced a no-questions-asked
and no-time-limit exchange policy, which made it one of the few retailers in Asia outside Japan with such a generous exchange policy. Giordano claimed that returns were
less then 0.1 percent of sales.

To ensure that every store and individual employee provided excellent customer service, performance evaluations were conducted frequently at the store level, as well as
for individual employees. The service standard of each store was evaluated twice every
month, while individual employees were evaluated once every two months. Internal
competitions were designed to motivate employees and store teams to do their best in
serving customers. Every month, Giordano awarded the "Service Star" to individual
employees, based on nominations provided by shoppers. In addition, every Giordano
store was evaluated every month by mystery shoppers. Based on the combined results
of these evaluations, the "Best Service Shop" award was given to the top store.

Value for Money

Lai explained the rationale for Giordano's "value for money" policy: Consumers are
learning a lot better about what value is. Out of ignorance, people chose the brand. But
the label does not matter, so the business has become value driven, because when people recognize value, that is the only game in town. So we always ask ourselves how can
we sell it cheaper, make it more convenient for the consumer to buy, and deliver faster
today than yesterday. That is all value, because convenience is value for the consumer.
Time is value for the customer.

Giordano was able to consistently sell value-for-money merchandise through careful selection of suppliers, strict cost control, and resisting the temptation to increase retail prices unnecessarily. For instance, to provide greater shopping convenience to
customers, Giordano in Singapore located its operations in densely populated housing
estates in addition to its outlets in the traditional downtown retail areas.

Inventory Control

In markets with expensive retail space, retailers would try to maximize every square
foot of the store for sales opportunities. Giordano was no different. Its strategy involved not having a back storeroom in each store. Instead, a central distribution center
replaced the function of a back storeroom. With information technology, Giordano was
able to skillfully manage its inventory and forecast demand. When an item was sold,
the barcode information, identifying size, color, style, and price, was recorded by the
point-of-sale cash register and transmitted to the company's main computer. At the end
of each day, the information was compiled at the store level and sent to the sales department and the distribution center. The compiled sales information became the
store's order for the following day. Orders were filled during the night and were ready
for delivery by early morning, ensuring that before a Giordano store opened for business, new inventory was already on the shelves.

Another advantage of its IT system was that information was disseminated to production facilities in real time. Such information allowed customers' purchase patterns
to be understood, and this provided valuable input to its manufacturing operations, resulting in fewer problems and costs related to slow-moving inventory. "If there is a

slow-selling item, we will decide immediately how to sell it as quickly as possible. When the sales of an item hit a minimum momentum, we pull it out, instead of thinking of how to revitalize its [slow-selling] sales." Giordano stores were therefore well stocked with fast-moving items, and customers were happy as they were seldom out of stock of anything.

The use of technology also afforded more efficient inventory holding. Giordano's inventory turnover on sales was reduced from 58 days in 1996 to 28 days in 1999, allowing it to thrive on lower gross margins. Savings were passed to customers, thus reinforcing its value-for-money philosophy. All in all, despite the lower margins, Giordano was still able to post healthy profits. Such efficiency became a crucial factor when periodic price wars were encountered. Giordano was able to carve out ever-greater slices of the market, because it was easy money competing against companies that were used to relying on high gross margins to make up for slow inventory turnover.

Besides the use of IT and real-time information generated from the information system, Giordano's successful inventory control was achieved through close integration of the purchasing and selling functions. As Fung elaborated, "There are two very common scenarios that many retailers encounter: slow-selling items stuck in the warehouse and fast-selling popular items that are out of stock. Giordano tries to minimize the probability of the occurrence of these two scenarios, which requires close integration between the purchasing and selling departments."

But more than technology and inventory control, Giordano had another competitive edge over its competitors. As Fung explained, "In the 1980s and early 1990s, when few retailers would use IT to manage their inventory, the use of IT gave Giordano a leading edge. However, today, when many retailers are using such technology, it is no longer our real distinctive competitive strength. In a time when there is information overload, it is the organizational culture in Giordano to intelligently use the information that sets us apart from the rest." And this was further explained by Lai: "None of this is novel. Marks & Spencer in Britain, The Gap and Wal-Mart in America, and Seven-Eleven in Japan have used similar systems for years. Nowadays, information flows so fast that anybody can acquire or imitate ideas. What matters is how well the ideas are executed." Indeed, with rapid development in Internet and intranet technologies, packaged solutions (e.g., MS Office, point of sale [POS] and enterprise resource planning [ERP] software), and supporting telecommunications services (e.g., broadband Internet access), acquiring integrated IT and logistics technology has become easier and more cost-effective than ever before. Hence, a competitive advantage based on technology and its implementation is likely to become smaller and more difficult to maintain in the medium- to long-term future.

Product Positioning

When a business becomes successful, there would always be a temptation to expand into more products and services to meet customer needs. However, Giordano recognized the importance of limiting its expansion and focusing on one specific area. Fung said, "Focus makes the business more manageable: positioning in the market, keeping the store simple, better inventory management. And we can get the best out of limited resources." Simplicity and focus were reflected in the way Giordano merchandised its goods. "You'll see no more than 100 items in a Giordano store. We have 17 core items; other retailers have 200 to 300 items. Merchandising a wide range of products causes retailers to take a longer time to react to market changes."

Giordano's willingness to experiment with new ideas and its perseverance despite past failures could also be seen in its introduction of new product lines. Its venture into mid-priced women's fashion, Giordano Ladies', clearly illustrated this. With its line of smart blouses, dress pants, and short skirts, the company was hoping to attract young, stylish women and benefit from the fatter profit margins enjoyed in more upscale niches of women's clothing—about 50 to 60 percent compared with 40 percent for casual wear. Giordano, however, wandered into a market crowded with seasoned players. While there were no complaints about the look or quality of the line, it had to compete with more than a dozen established brands already on the racks, including Theme and Esprit. It also failed initially to differentiate its new clothing line from its mainstream product line, and even tried to sell both through the same outlets. Nevertheless, it persisted in its efforts and Giordano Ladies' made a successful comeback. In 1999, it took advantage of the financial troubles facing rivals such as Theme, as well as the post–Asian currency crisis boom in many parts of Asia, to aggressively relaunch its Giordano Ladies' line, which met with great success. As of June 30, 2000, the reinforced Giordano Ladies' focused on a select segment, with 14 stores worldwide offering personalized service (e.g., staff are trained to memorize names of regular customers and recall past purchases). It also had plans to expand its five more Giordano Ladies' outlets in Hong Kong, Taiwan, and the Middle East.

Giordano recently began to reposition its brand by emphasizing sensible but more stylish clothes and broadening its appeal by overhauling the stores and apparel. For instance, a large portion of its capital expenditure (totaling HK$56.9 million in the first six months of year 2000) went to renovating of its stores to enhance shop ambience. This indicated its intention to reinforce its image and to position it in line with its globalization strategy and changing consumer needs. A typical store layout is shown in Exhibits 4 and 5. Giordano's relatively mid-priced positioning worked well—inexpensive, yet contemporary looking outfits appealed to Asia's frugal customers, especially during the Asian economic crisis. However, over time, this positioning became inconsistent with the brand image that Giordano tried hard to build over the years. Says one of Giordano's top executives, "The feeling went from 'this is nice and good value' to 'this is cheap.' When you try to live off selling 100-Hong Kong-dollar shirts, it catches up with you."(*AsiaWeek,* 15 October 1999)

EXHIBIT 4
A Typical Store Layout

Source: Courtesy of Giordano.

EXHIBIT 5
A Typical Store Layout

Source: Courtesy of Giordano.

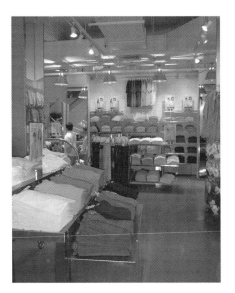

Nevertheless, while it gradually remarketed its core brand as a trendier label, Giordano continued to cater to the needs of customers who favored its value-for-money positioning. In 1999 it launched a new product line, Bluestar Exchange, to cater to the needs of its budget-conscious customers, after successful prototyping in Hong Kong and Taiwan. The good market responses to this new line, which targeted mainly families (similar to Gap's Blue Navy), triggered plans to expand from the 14 Bluestar stores in Hong Kong and 3 in Taiwan, to 20 in Hong Kong, 15 in Taiwan, 2 in Singapore, and up to 100 in mainland China (including franchised stores).

Aggressive Advertising and Promotion

Fung said, "Giordano spends a large proportion of its turnover on advertising and promotions. No retailer of our size spends as much as us." For the past five years, Giordano in Singapore had been spending about S$1.5 million to S$2 million annually on its advertising and promotional activities. It won the Top Advertiser Award from 1991 to 1994 (see Exhibit 3). Up to June 30, 2000, total advertising and promotional expenditure for the group amounted to HK$41.5 million, or 3 percent of the group's retail turnover. In addition to its big budget, Giordano's advertising and promotional campaigns were creative and appealing. One such campaign was the "Round the Clock Madness Shopping" with the Singapore radio station FM93.3 on 1 May 1994. Different clothing items were discounted from 10 to 60 percent at various times beginning at midnight. For example, jeans were offered at a 20 percent discount from 12 A.M. to 1 A.M., whereas polo shirts and T-shirts were given a 30 percent discount from 1 A.M. to 2 A.M. and then shorts at a 40 percent discount from 2 A.M. to 3 A.M. To keep listeners awake and excited, the product categories that were on sale at each time slot were released only at the specified hour, so that nobody knew the next items that would be on this special sale. Listeners to the radio station were cajoled into coming to Giordano stores throughout the night (Ang 1996). In 1996, Giordano won the Singapore Ear Award. Its English radio commercial was voted by listeners to be one of the best, with the most creative English jingle.

Another success was its "Simply Khakis" promotion, launched in April 1999, which emphasized basic, street-culture style that "mixed and matched" and thus fitted all occasions. In Singapore, within days of its launch, the new line sold out and had to be relaunched two weeks later. By October 1999, over a million pairs of khaki trousers and shorts had been sold. This success could be attributed partly to its clearly defined communications objectives. As Garrett Bennett, Giordano's Executive Director in charge of merchandising and operations, said, "We want to be the key provider of the basics: khakis, jeans, and the white shirt." Elsewhere in the region, sales were booming for Giordano, despite only moderate recovery experienced in the retail industry. Its strength in executing innovative and effective promotional strategies helped the retailer to reduce the impact of the Asian crisis on its sales and take advantage of the slight recovery seen in early 1999. Aggressive advertising and promotions also played a significant role in the successful remarketing of its core brand and relaunch or introduction of sister brands, Giordano Ladies', Giordano Junior, and Bluestar Exchange.

THE ASIAN APPAREL RETAIL INDUSTRY

Hit severely by the Asian crisis from 1997 to 1999, the Asian retail industry went through dramatic restructuring and consolidation. Many retailers reduced the number of shops in their chains, or closed down completely. Almost everyone in the industry implemented cost-cutting measures while at the same time cajoling reluctant customers with promotional strategies. Yet, there was a silver lining, as the more competitive firms were able to take advantage of lower rentals and the departure of weaker companies. Some firms, including Giordano, worked toward strengthening their positioning and brand image to compete better in the long run. Some retailers also explored opportunities, or accelerated their presence in markets that were less affected by the Asian crisis—mostly in markets outside Asia.

During the crisis and for the immediate future until a full recovery set in, industry analysts predicted that opportunities would continue to be driven by value. Thus, Giordano's value proposition appeared appropriate during these times. It was not surprising, then, that in spite of its problems, Giordano was ranked the 14th most competitive company overall in Asia by a regional business magazine (*Asia Inc.,* 6 June 1997). It even won a place on *Forbes Global*'s 1999 list of the World's 300 Best Small Companies, indicative of world-class performance, together with eight other Hong Kong companies. Giordano's performance was accredited to its management's swift cost-control strategies in the areas of rents, outsourcing, inventory control, cash management, and overseas travel. The economic downturn had indeed revealed the management's flexibility and responsiveness in making decisive moves.

The retailing environment was becoming more dynamic, a change that was perhaps led by growing sophistication of tastes and rapid advancements in the media, communications, and logistics environment. Giordano's response to these trends would be the key to its ability to compete in the future, especially as these trends seem to "commoditize" its current competitive edge in IT, stock control, and logistics.

GIORDANO'S COMPETITION

Until recently, Giordano's main competitors for low-priced apparel were Hang Ten, Bossini, and Baleno. However, its shift in positioning, and the squeeze of the retailing sector caused by the crisis, pushed formerly more upmarket firms such as Esprit and Theme to compete for Giordano's value-for-money segment. Exhibit 6 provides a list of their websites for more information regarding their product lines and operations.

EXHIBIT 6
Websites of Giordano
and Its Closest
Competitors

Firm	Website Address
Baleno	www.baleno.com.hk
Esprit	www.esprit-intl.com
The Gap	www.gap.com
Giordano	www.giordano.com.hk
Hang Ten	www.hangten.com
Theme	www.theme.com.hk

EXHIBIT 7
Competitive
Positioning

Firms	Positioning	Target Market
Giordano and The Gap	Value for money Mid-priced but trendy fashion	Unisex casual wear for all ages (under different brands)
Hang Ten	Value for money Sporty lifestyle	Casual wear and sports wear, teens and young adults
Bossini	Low price (comparable to Giordano)	Unisex apparel, both young and old (above 30s)
Baleno	Value for money Trendy, young age casual wear	Unisex appeal, young adults
Esprit	More upmarket than Giordano Stylish, trendy	Ladies' casual, but also other specialized lines for children
Theme	Upmarket, stylish	Ladies' smart fashion, ladies' business wear

EXHIBIT 8   Competitive Financial Data for 1999: Giordano, Esprit, The Gap, Theme and Bossini (Amounts Expressed in Millions of HK$)

	Giordano	Esprit	The Gap	Theme	Bossini
Turnover	3,092	5,994	90,756	319	1,109
Profit after tax and minority interests	360	430	8,791	(218)	18
Working capital	762	478	3,470	(243.0)	182
Return on total assets (percentage)	18.8%	NA	24.6%	NA	NA
Return on average equity (percentage)	30.5%	33.1%	59.2%	NA	6.5%
Return on sales (percentage)	11.6%	7.2%	9.7%	(68.3%)	1.6%
Price/sales ratio	2.07	1.33	1.97	.82	0.23
Sales growth	18.5%	17.8%	28.5%	(69.8%)	(22.4%)
No. of employees	6,237	4,471	NA	NA	869
Sales per employee	495,779	1,340,599	NA	NA	1,276,254

Note: Esprit reports its earnings in Euro and The Gap in US$. All reported figures have been converted into HK$ at the following exchange rate (as of Feb. 2001): US$1 = Euro$1.09 = HK$7.8. Sources: *Annual Report 1999,* Giordano International; *Financial Highlights 1999,* Esprit International; *Annual Report 1999.* The Gap Financial Report 1999, Bossini International Holdings Limited.

Exhibit 7 shows the relative positioning of Giordano and its competitors: The Gap, Bossini, Hang Ten, Baleno, Esprit, and Theme. Financial data for Giordano, Esprit, and The Gap are shown in Exhibit 8. The geographical areas these firms operate in are shown in Exhibit 9.

EXHIBIT 9 **Geographical Presence of Giordano and Current Competitors**

Country	Giordano	Hang Ten	Bossini	Baleno	Esprit	Theme
Asia						
HK/Macao	X	X	X	X	X	X
Singapore	X	X	X	—	X	X
South Korea	X	X	—	—	X	X
Taiwan	X	X	X	X	X	X
China	X	X	X	X	X	X
Malaysia	X	X	—	—	X	X
Indonesia	X	X	—	—	X	X
Philippines	X	X	—	—	X	X
Thailand	X	X	—	—	X	X
World						
US and Canada	—	X	X	—	X	X
Europe	—	X	X	—	X	X
Japan	X	X	—	—	X	X
Australia	X	X	—	—	X	X
Total	**750**	**NA**	**173**	**125**	**8,470**	**200**

Note: Data are as of February 2001; X indicates presence in the country/region; — indicates no presence; NA indicates data not available at time of print.

United States–based Hang Ten and Italy-based Bossini were generally positioned as low-price retailers offering reasonable quality and service. The clothes emphasized versatility and simplicity. But while Hang Ten and Baleno were more popular among teenagers and young adults, Bossini had a more general appeal. Their distribution strategies were somewhat similar, but they focused on different markets. For instance, according to Fung, while Hang Ten was only strong in Taiwan, Baleno was increasingly strong in China and Taiwan. On the other hand, Bossini was very strong in Hong Kong and relatively strong in Singapore but had little presence in Taiwan and China.

Esprit is an international fashion lifestyle brand, engaged principally in the image and product design, sourcing, manufacturing, and retail and wholesale distribution of a wide range of women's, men's, and children's apparel, footwear, accessories, and other products under the Esprit brand name. The Esprit name was promoted as a "lifestyle" image, and products were strategically positioned as good quality and value for money—a position that Giordano was occupying. As of 1999, Esprit had a distribution network of over 8,000 stores and outlets in 40 countries in Europe, Asia, Canada, and Australia. The main markets were in Europe, which accounted for approximately 65 percent of sales; and in Asia, which accounted for approximately 34 percent of 2000 sales. The Esprit brand products were principally sold via directly managed retail outlets, by wholesale customers (Including department stores, specialty stores, and franchisees), and by licensees for products manufactured under license, principally through the licensees' own distribution networks.

Theme International Holdings Limited was founded in Hong Kong in 1986 by Chairman and Chief Executive Officer Kenneth Lai. He identified a niche in the local market for high-quality, fashionable ladies' business wear, although it subsequently expanded into casual wear. The Theme label and chain were in direct competition with Giordano Ladies'. From the first store in 1986 to a chain comprising over 200 outlets in Hong Kong, China, Korea, Macao, Taiwan, Singapore, Malaysia, Indonesia, the Philippines, Japan, Thailand, Canada, and Holland, the phenomenal growth of Theme was built on a vertically integrated corporate structure and advanced management system. However, its ambitious expansion proved to be costly in view of the crisis, with interest soaring on high levels of debt. In 1999, the company announced a HK$106.1 million net loss for the six months up to 30 September 1998, and it closed 23 retail outlets in Hong Kong, which traded under its subsidiary The Clothing Shop. Theme International had since been acquired by High Fashion International, a Hong Kong–based fashion retailer specializing in upmarket, trendy apparel.

In general, although these firms had slightly different positioning strategies and targeted dissimilar but overlapping segments, they all competed in a number of similar areas. For example, all firms heavily emphasized advertising and sales promotion—selling fashionable clothes at attractive prices. Almost all stores were also located primarily in good ground-floor areas, drawing high-volume traffic and facilitating shopping, browsing, and impulse buying. However, Giordano clearly distinguished itself from its competitors with its high-quality service and cost leadership that together provided great customer value that none of its competitors had been able to match.

In a study by *Interbrand* on top Asian marquees, Giordano was Asia's highest-ranking general apparel retailer. It was ranked number 20. The clothing names next in line were Australia's Quicksilver at number 45 and Country Road at number 47. However, Giordano as a world label was still far off. As a spokesman on consumer insights for advertising agency McCann-Erickson said, "It is a good brand, but not a great one. Compared to other international brands, it doesn't shape opinion."

A threat from US–based The Gap was also looming. Giordano was aware that the American retailer was invading Asia. The Gap was already in Japan. After 2005, when garment quotas are likely to be abolished, imports into the region should become more cost-effective. Hence, Giordano had to examine whether its intention to shift toward a higher position from its current value-for-money position was viable.

GIORDANO'S GROWTH STRATEGY

As early as the 1980s, Giordano realized that it was difficult to achieve substantial growth and economies of scale if it operated only in Hong Kong. The key was in regional expansion. By 1999, Giordano had opened 740 stores in 23 markets, out of which Giordano directly managed 317 stores (see Exhibit 10). Until 2000, four markets dominated its retail and distribution operations—Hong Kong, Taiwan, China, and Singapore (see Exhibit 11). By 2000, Giordano had 895 Giordano stores in 25 markets.

Giordano cast its sights on markets beyond Asia, driven partially by its desire for growth and partially to reduce its dependence on Asia in the wake of the 1998 economic meltdown. In Giordano's first full year of operation in Australia, sales turnover reached HK$29 million (US$3.72 million) in December 2000. The number of retail outlets increased from 4 in 1999 to 14 in 2000. With the opening up of its first retail outlet in Sydney in September 2000, Giordano outlets could now be found in both Melbourne and Sydney. As part of Giordano's globalization process, it planned to open up its first shops in Germany and Japan during the first half of 2001. Currently, Giordano planned to focus its globalization efforts on new markets like Germany, Japan, Australia, Indonesia, and Kuwait.

When the crisis made Giordano rethink its regional strategy, it was still determined to enter and further penetrate new Asian markets. This determination led to the suc-

EXHIBIT 10 Operational Highlights for Retail and Distribution Division (Figures as at Year-End Unless Specified)

	1999	1998	1997	1996	1995	1994	1993
Number of retail outlets							
• Directly managed by the Group	317	308	324	294	280	283	257
• Franchised	423	370	316	221	171	77	481
Total number of retail outlets	740	678	640	515	451	360	738
Retail floor area directly managed by the Group (sq. ft.)	301,100	358,500	313,800	295,500	286,200	282,700	209,500
Sales per square foot (HK$)	8,400	6,800	8,000	9,900	10,500	10,600	12,600
Number of employees	6,237	6,319	8,175	10,004	10,348	6,863	2,330
Comparable store sales Increase/(decrease) (percentage)	21%	(13)%	(11)%	(6)%	8%	(9)%	15%
Number of sales associates	2,026	1,681	1,929	1,958	2,069	1,928	1,502

EXHIBIT 11 Regional Highlights

	Taiwan 1999	Hong Kong 1999	China 1999	Singapore 1999	Malaysia 1999
Net sales (HK$ millions)	953.1	681.7	543.7	349.2	66.6
Sales per sq. ft. (HK$)	6,000	9,400	22,500	13,800	3,600
Comparable store sales increase (percentage)*	31%	8%	4%	48%	69%
Retail floor area (sq. ft.)	165,700	100,000	24,700	24,400	20,400
Number of sales associates	827	441	350	228	115
Number of outlets					
• Directly managed	178	61	10	27	23
• Franchised	0	0	243	0	11

*Note: Figures as compared to previous financial year.

cessful expansion of Giordano in Mainland China, which saw the retail outlets grow from 253 stores in 1999 to 357 stores in 2000. Due to the expanded retail network in Mainland China and improvements made to the product line, sales turnover increased by 30.9 percent to HK$712 million (US$91.3 million) in 2000. Faced with the imminent accession of Mainland China to the World Trade Organization, Giordano's management foresees both challenges and opportunities ahead. In Indonesia, Giordano opened up 7 more stores in 2000, bringing the total number of retail stores to 10. These stores covered areas in Jakarta, Surabaya, and Bali. However, with the political and social instability in Indonesia, coupled with the downward pressure on the Rupiah, Giordano was cautiously optimistic about further expansion and planned to proceed with caution. In Malaysia, Giordano planned to refurnish its Malaysian outlets and intensify its local promotional campaigns to consolidate its leadership position in the Malaysia market.

Giordano's success in these markets would depend on its understanding of them, and consumer tastes and preferences for fabrics, colors, and advertising. In the past,

Giordano relied on a consistent strategy across different countries, and elements of this successful strategy included its positioning and service strategies, information systems and logistics, and human resource policies. However, tactical implementation (e.g., promotional campaigns) was left mostly to local managers in their respective countries. A country's performance (e.g., sales, contribution, service levels, and customer feedback) was monitored by regional headquarters (e.g., Singapore for South-East Asia) and the head office in Hong Kong. Weekly performance reports were made accessible to all managers. In recent years, it appeared that as the organization expanded beyond Asia, different strategies had to be developed for different regions or countries.

THE FUTURE

Giordano was confronted with some important issues as it prepared itself for the new millennium. Although it had been extremely successful, as its revenue, profits, and the many awards that it received clearly show, the question was how it could maintain this success in the new millennium. First, how, if at all, should Giordano reposition itself against its competitors in its existing and new markets? Would it be necessary to follow different positioning strategies for different markets (e.g., Hong Kong versus South-East Asia)?

The second issue was the sustainability of Giordano's key success factors. It clearly understood its core competencies and the pillars of its success, but it had to carefully explore how they were likely to develop over the coming years. Which of its competitive advantages would be sustainable and which ones were likely to be eroded?

A third issue was Giordano's growth strategy in Asia as well as across continents. Would Giordano's competitive strengths be transferable to other markets? Would strategic adaptations to IT strategy and marketing mix be required, or would tactical moves suffice?

STUDY QUESTIONS

1. Describe and evaluate Giordano's product, business, and corporate strategies.

2. Describe and evaluate Giordano's current positioning strategy. Should Giordano reposition itself against its competitors in its current and new markets, and should it have different positioning strategies for different geographic markets?

3. What are Giordano's key success factors (KSF) and sources of competitive advantage? Are its competitive advantages sustainable, and how would they develop in the future?

4. Could Giordano transfer its key success factors to new markets as it expanded both in Asia and the other parts of the world?

5. How do you think Giordano had/would have to adapt its marketing and operations strategies and tactics when entering and penetrating your country?

6. What general lessons can be learned from Giordano for other major clothing retailers in your country?

REFERENCES

"Aiming High: Asia's 50 Most Competitive Companies," *Asia Inc.,* 6 June 1997, pp. 34–7.

Ang, Swee Hoon (1996), "Giordano Holdings Limited," *Cases in Marketing Management and Strategy: An Asian–Pacific Perspective.* Quelch, John A., Leong, Siew Meng, Ang, Swee Hoon, and Tan, Chin Tiong (eds.): Prentice Hall, pp. 182–190.

"An All-New Dress for Success," *AsiaWeek,* 15 Oct. 1999, volume 25, no. 41.

"And the Winning Store Is, Again . . ." *The Straits Times* (Singapore), 2 Dec 1995.

"Asia: Giordano Plans Expansion," *Sing Tao Daily,* 29 June 1999.

"Asian IPO Focus: Analysts See Little to Like in HK's Veeko," *Dow Jones International News,* 12 April 1999.

Austria, Cecille (1994), "The Bottom Line," *World Executive's Digest,* 19 Dec, pp. 17–20.

"Casual-Wear Chain Prospers on Cost-Cutting Regime," *South China Morning Post,* 15 Oct 1999.

"China: HK Companies Commended by *Forbes* for Best Practices," *China Business Information Network,* 12 Nov 1999.

Clifford, Mark (1993), "Extra Large," *Far Eastern Economic Review,* 2 Dec 1993, pp. 72–76.

"Company Looks Outside Asia," *Dow Jones International News,* 12 Aug 1998.

"Creditors Push Struggling Theme Fashion Outlet into Liquidation," *South China Morning Post,* 11 March 1999.

Esprit International, *Financial Highlights 1999.*

"Fashion Free-Fall," *The Asian Wall Street Journal,* 9 Nov 1998.

"Giordano 12-Month Target Price Raised to 16.00 HKD," *AFX (AP),* 16 May 2000.

"Giordano's After-Tax Earnings Soared in First Half," *The Asian Wall Street Journal,* 27 July 1999.

"Giordano Comes Out of the Cold," *Business Week,* 31 May 1999.

"Giordano Details $700 Million Expansion," *South China Morning Post,* 4 Dec 1999.

"Giordano Dreams Up Sale for Insomniacs," *Business Times (Singapore),* 6 May 1994.

"Giordano Expects to Set Up Ops in Europe October," *AFX (AP),* 19 June 2000.

Giordano Holdings Limited, *Annual Report 1993.*

Giordano Holdings Limited, *Annual Report 1997.*

Giordano International Limited, *Announcement of Results,* 31 Dec 2000.

Giordano International Limited, *Annual Report 1998.*

Giordano International Limited, *Annual Report 1999.*

Giordano International Limited, *Interim Results 2000.*

"Giordano Intl 1998 Net Profit," *AFX (AP),* 25 March 1999 (from Dow Jones Interactive).

"Giordano Out of the Running to Buy Theme: High Fashion International Emerges as Favorite in Race for Control," *South China Morning Post,* 25 Nov 1999.

"Giordano Predicts Further Growth as Net Profit Reaches $46.3 Million," *Asian Wall Street Journal,* 3 March 2000.

"Giordano Scores with Smart Moves," *The Straits Times (Singapore),* 11 Sept 1993.

"Giordano Seeks to Acquire Chain Stores in Australia," *AFX (AP),* 8 February 2000.

"Giordano Spreads Its Wings," *The Straits Times (Singapore),* 13 March 1994.

"Good Service Has Brought Giordano Soaring Sales," *Business Times (Singapore),* 6 Aug 1993.

"High-End Training to Get More Funding," *The Straits Times,* 1 Oct 1998.

"HK Bossini International Fiscal Year Net Profit HK$17.6 Million vs. HK$45.5 Million Loss," *Dow Jones Business News,* 16 July 1999.

"HK Giordano Gets Green Light to Reopen in Shanghai," *Dow Jones International News,* 9 June 1999.

"Hong Kong: High Fashion to Take Over Theme," *Sing Tao Daily,* 26 Nov 1999.

"Hong Kong Retailer Raced to New Markets, Spurring Everbright Loan," *The Asian Wall Street Journal,* 7 April 1998.

"Hubris Catches Up to Theme," *The Globe and Mail,* 7 April 1998.

"In HK: Retail Shares Win Praise Amid Companies' Losses," *The Asian Wall Street Journal,* 25 June 1999.

"Interview," by Frances Huang, *AFX (AP),* 16 Sept. 1998 (from Dow Jones Interactive).

Mills, D. Quinn, and Richard C. Wei (1993), "Giordano Holdings Ltd.," *Harvard Business School,* N9-495-002.

"Old Loss Masks Giordano Growth," *South China Morning Post,* 5 March 1999.

"Service Means Training," *The Straits Times,* 7 Oct 1998.

"Simple Winning Formula," *Business Times,* 6 Aug 1993.

The Gap, *Annual Report 1999.*

"The Outlook for Asian Retailing," *Discount Merchandiser,* May 1999.

"Theme International Unit to Close 23 Stores," *The Asian Wall Street Journal,* 4 Aug 1998.

"US News Brief: Benetton Group," *The Wall Street Journal Europe,* 17 Dec 1998.

"What Is the People Developer," *The Straits Times,* 30 Sept 1998.

Case 4

THE QUALITY IMPROVEMENT CUSTOMERS DIDN'T WANT

Jack Zadow, the consultant, was persuasive. Wrapping up the hour-long presentation, he still seemed as energized as he had in the first five minutes. "Your biggest competitor, HealthCare One, has already begun using a computerized reception system in 14 of its 22 facilities," he said, pointing to the overhead projection illuminating the darkened conference room. The image was a regional map with red stars on every Health-Care One facility and yellow circles around the ones using the new system. "When their members come in the door, they go right to a computer and slide their identification card through. Then the computer leads them through a set of questions about their current medical condition, the reason for the visit, and so on. Everything is done electronically: The computer pulls the member's record, processes the new information, and then routes the member to the appropriate staff person for consultation."

He slipped the next image over the map. It showed Quality Care's own facilities in dull brown. "HealthCare One will have all its facilities up and running on the new system by June. The number two player, MediCenters, is planning to install a similar system by January 1997. I think you should consider it seriously—it's really the wave of the future."

The last overhead. A model of a "new and improved" Quality Care reception area. No more crowded waiting room. Patients talking with nurses in the privacy of small, partitioned cubicles. Other patients checking in, paying bills, even having their blood pressure taken at attractive computer stations.

"I think this one speaks for itself." Jack let the image sink in for a moment. "But I'll comment anyway. With this system, you take a giant step forward in the quality of your service. Your staff will be able to devote more energy to making sure that each patient receives prompt, unhurried, personal attention." He switched off the projector and stepped back to flip on the lights.

Blinking, Allan Moulter accepted the report summary Jack handed him. He had been the CEO at Quality Care for nine years—how many meetings did that mean he had attended? He looked at Pat Penstone, the company's CIO. She seemed enraptured. He rubbed his forehead. "Thanks, that was informative," he said. "You've given us a good overview of an intriguing trend in service delivery in the industry—at a regional level and at a national level. But can you tell us a little more about the specifics of installing a system like that? How is HealthCare One handling the transition? How has it measured the improvements in service quality? How much has the company invested in training? Computer consultants? Troubleshooters? HealthCare One is a staff-model HMO like us, so I know we can look at them for comparison, but I have to say that I'm a little concerned. You seem to be telling us that our image as a quality health care provider will suffer if we don't make this move, but we're talking about an important change in a lot of daily routines. We have just under 3,000 employees and 200,000 members. Think of the procedural changes. The timing changes. And with more automation, wouldn't we want to think about cutting the administrative staff by what, by two at each facility? Four? Six?"

"You could cut several positions from each location," Jack said. "But HealthCare One isn't cutting staff—this is strictly a quality improvement, and it's paying for itself in increased customer retention over the long term. What's more, the transition isn't difficult. In the pilot location, they're already testing the next generation of the system: artificial intelligence diagnostic programs. They're incorporating scales and the blood pressure machines you saw in the last overhead. That saves a step or two for the nurse practitioner, so it simplifies service operations. They're also going to upgrade so that the computer will be able to produce records that can be standardized for insurance companies. Within a few months, the nurses and physicians will be experimenting with a prototype for their own notes on patients, which will streamline follow-up care as well."

"If they're not cutting staff, and they're investing in new generations of the system, where's the real advantage? There is a cost-control element to consider as well, isn't there?" Allan looked around the room, then back at Jack. "The system itself is a big investment—it would run the company more than $350,000 when you include development, installation, training, consulting, and so forth. What's more, the network would have to operate across all of our locations. And if we wanted to do it right, we would probably tackle a whole host of ancillary projects at the same time, things like rethinking the design of our reception areas and our workstations.

"I'm not sure it's worth it. Our customer retention rates are good. They've been steady for the past two years. And our customers are satisfied with the service—on a scale of one to five, 86 percent of our customers are either a four—that's satisfied—or a five—that's completely satisfied. We survey them constantly.

"Frankly, I'm not convinced that investing in a new system will improve the quality of our care. As I said, you're talking about a major shift in how our people get their work done—all the way up the line. That's disruptive. Would the gains be worth it?"

"Ultimately," Jack said patiently, "if your staff is less stressed and your care is more personalized, your quality improves. And—this is almost more important, although it's going to sound strange—the *image* of your quality also improves. Remember, the top two HMOs in this region are installing this system. Quality Care is the number three player—you can't afford to look as though you're behind the times."

Pat could not contain herself.

"I'd hate to see the industry moving toward this technology while we sit on our hands doing nothing," she said, straight to Allan. "I mean, okay, it's just the reception function, but what if a patient assumes that because we're not high tech with our sign-in procedures, we're also not up to speed on our medical procedures? The reception area, taken alone, isn't a big deal. But as a part of our whole offering, it's critical. It's the first thing our customers see. It tells them what we are and how we work."

She nodded at Jack and continued. "Not to mention that we'll have to install a system like this at some point anyway, as soon as the government or the insurance companies decide that it's the way to go. Once a method is standardized, we don't want to be playing catch-up."

"Right. Well." Allan looked at his watch, an impassive expression on his face. "I can see this warrants some further discussion, but we'll have to leave it for the time being." He stood up, ending the meeting. "Jack, thanks," he said again. "We'll go over the reports and I'll see you later this week."

Back in his office, Allan swallowed two aspirins with the one gulp of coffee he had left in his mug. Then he reached for the box of crackers he kept in his top drawer. He knew he should get some lunch, but he wanted to think about this issue some more without distraction. The afternoon was booked solid; then he wanted to catch at least part of his son's ice hockey game at 5:30, and he had to be back in town to participate in a panel discussion on health care for the elderly at 8:00. Munching, he thought about Quality Care's position in the market and the kinds of things that had made the company successful to date.

Quality Care had never been the region's largest or most profitable HMO. But it was doing well. This past year, its total revenues were $450 million, with profits of $8.1 million after expenses. And it did have a good track record when it came to customer retention. Businesses kept the contract because their employees were satisfied with Quality Care, and Allan liked to think that he had played an important role in creating that loyalty.

Allan had begun his career with a large manufacturer of electronics equipment, where talking with customers had been his passion. He had brought that passion to Quality Care. During his tenure, the HMO had instituted regular customer satisfaction surveys. Patients were asked how they felt about the service they received: Were they waiting too long to see a doctor? Were they satisfied with the location and upkeep of the facilities? Did they want more information on health clubs or wellness programs? One survey had revealed the need for increased communication with pregnant members. Now expectant mothers received regular newsletters geared to provide timely advice and support during their pregnancies. The company had also provided a dedicated toll-free number so that pregnant customers would have easy access to advice and information. Allan was proud of the program.

And the surveys weren't the only way the company solicited information from its customers. Each facility also had a "feedback box" in the waiting area—paper and pens were provided, and patients were encouraged to offer anonymous comments on any aspect of their experience with the company. In addition, Quality Care frequently and systematically surveyed other constituents: its corporate members, affiliated hospitals and health clubs, even its own employees.

His peers often complained about how hard it was to increase customer satisfaction these days. Allan knew why it was so hard—keeping all the constituents happy was an insane balancing act. Still, Allan figured it was the open communication and the feedback that kept the company effective and competitive.

That's why he was more than a little concerned about Jack's presentation. Quality Care's own marketing staff hadn't turned up any dissatisfaction with the current reception procedures. And yet Allan was drawn to the possibilities presented by the new system. He picked up his phone and punched in Ginger Rooney's extension. Ginger was the vice president of marketing for Quality Care. She was part of the team that was scoping out locations for expansion and possible new alliances. She had flown in from Pittsburgh that morning—too late to attend Jack's presentation.

"Do you have a minute right now to hear about that meeting?" Allan asked. She was in his office moments later, folder in hand.

"Cracker?" he offered, holding out the box. She declined. He took another one and plunged into the topic.

"I'm not entirely convinced we need this system," Allan said. "But I'll tell you, I was playing devil's advocate in there, and I was having a hard time. I don't want us to fall behind the curve."

"We're ahead of the curve, if anything," said Ginger, holding a familiar survey report out for his inspection. "Why you and Pat are so gung ho about this computerized reception area, I'll never know. If you'll remember, we were approached by a sales rep from the Technomedic Software Company 18 months ago. We looked into a similar system then and dismissed the idea. We took the concept to our members in a special survey and they said they'd hate it."

"But then why would HealthCare One go forward with it? They're the one to beat. I know they must have done their homework on this—maybe better than we did. Don't take this the wrong way, but they've got a more sophisticated organization. I'm sure they've weighed the risks against the benefits. Our study might have been inaccurate. Is it possible that the results are out of date already?"

Ginger didn't take offense. "I doubt it," she said mildly. "Think about why the customers said they wouldn't like it. Human contact versus machine. Health care is a personal field—one-on-one attention is what makes a satisfied customer. They just didn't like the idea of a computer, at least for this part of their interaction with the HMO. They come into one of our facilities for some health-related exam. Often it's just routine, but sometimes they're a little nervous and they appreciate all the human contact they can get. It's reassuring. The idea of having the first 'person' they meet when they come in the door turn out to be a machine was quite disconcerting to many of the people we surveyed. Especially the seniors." She fell silent, but spoke again as she saw Allan framing a response. "We spent a lot of time and money on that special study—why are you so willing to disregard it?"

"Look at ATMs," Allan said. "Older people got used to them."

"I'm not sure that's true. And even so, does that mean that we'll try to encourage all our members to use the computer but that we'll need human receptionists anyway for older members? Isn't that making the operation more complicated, not less? That doesn't sound like cost savings or quality improvement to me."

"We've invested a good deal in Zadow's research as well," Allan said. "HealthCare One hasn't reduced staff, but we could. And what happens when all the other organizations have signed on and the government or the insurance companies start requiring standardized reports? Pat brought that up in the meeting. It's a valid concern."

"There's more than one way to create a standard report." Ginger began to look frustrated. "I'll bet half the time, the patients enter information incorrectly anyway. Someone would have to double-check the files on a daily basis."

She returned to his earlier point. "If HealthCare One hasn't cut staff, how can you be sure that we would be able to? And keep in mind whom we should really be talking about—the customers. Their perception is what's important. Remember, our *employees* were the only ones who really liked the idea. The administrative staff thought that a computerized reception area would make their jobs easier. And the nurse practitioners have so many routine procedures to do that they're just racing patients by on a conveyor belt. They thought the system would give them time for the human touch."

"Now you sound like you're arguing for the system, Ginger. You can't disregard employee input. Our employee turnover rate is average for this industry, but it has increased over the last two years. That's a reason to reconsider the system in light of Jack's report," Allan said. "It's important to keep our employees happy—we want to keep good people. In fact, as I recall, it took a lot of tap dancing to explain to them why we weren't proceeding with the computer system last time."

"But the point still remains that the members didn't like the idea," Ginger said. "They thought that it was just another sign of big corporate America depersonalizing something that in this case happens to be one of the most personal services there is. You mentioned us retaining our 'leading edge' image. But a computer sends an impersonal image as well. I just don't think that a computer at the front desk will make or break us. You know that my department's reports consistently show favorable customer satisfaction results. They already think we're doing a good job by them. If I can be blunt, I think that you've been romanced by a consultant's very savvy presentation. And I think that we've spent so much money on the consultant that you feel we wouldn't get our money's worth if we didn't follow his recommendations. I seem to be the only one thinking about what's right for the company."

"Ginger, what happens in a year or so when everyone but us has this system installed?" Allan threw up his hands. "Don't you find it strange that we're trying to choose between installing a system that we think might enhance our quality as a provider and not installing a system because we want to please our members?"

Ginger spotted Pat in line at the cafeteria on the first floor of the building that housed Quality Care's administrative offices. She caught up with her just as Pat was paying for lunch. "Not to ruin your digestion, but I have a problem I'd like to talk about with you for a few minutes. Do you mind?"

"Not at all," Pat smiled. Ginger knew the smile was strained. The two had just never really gotten along. For people whose departments were usually in agreement about new initiatives and plans for the company, Pat and Ginger had often found themselves holding opposing views, or at least misunderstanding each other's motives.

"I'll get right to the point, and I won't take much of your time. I know that you support the idea of a computerized reception area, but I'd like to know more about why. You know that the customers are not in favor of it."

"No, I don't really know that." Pat looked uncomfortable for a moment and then seemed to gain resolve. "I may as well say this. I know that Allan has a personal interest in how the company communicates with customers, but I have some serious doubts about the way all of those customer satisfaction surveys are carried out. You don't personally oversee the surveys, do you? That's Mike Farrow's bailiwick, isn't it?"

"Yes, it is," Ginger said. "But we use the same sorts of surveys as most companies do. Frankly, I do agree with you about some of that. I don't put much stake in some of the information we get from the complaint boxes, for example. Those comments reflect the views of only one person. 'Change the night you're open late from Monday to Thursday.' 'Change the color scheme in the examining rooms.' Those comments aren't significant. But we asked a significant number of our members straight out, in a special study, how they would feel about a computerized system. They said they wouldn't like it."

"I just don't have a sense that any of that information is to be trusted. People need to be told what they want—and people will recognize quality care when they see it. That's why I think we need this system."

"I'm thinking about the bottom line," Ginger said. She wished she had waited until later in the afternoon to approach Pat. In fact, she wished she had written her a memo and sent it over by e-mail. "Why go through all the trauma if we already know how the customers will receive the change?"

Pat hadn't yet touched her lunch. She picked up a packet of salad dressing and pulled it open. "You say you're thinking of the bottom line, but which one?" she asked. "Today's or tomorrow's?"

Case 5

CUSTOM RESEARCH INC. (A)

INTRODUCTION

Custom Research Inc. (CRI) had just passed its 16th birthday, but without much to celebrate. Profitability as a percentage of sales had been declining for several years and revenue growth had been flat recently. CRI partners Jeff Pope and Judy Corson had reached a turning point. They had just completed an extensive financial analysis and found that a large majority of their clients were clients who only did a few projects a year and while profitable, the small client project revenue did not add up to a big part of their total company revenue. They had started the company with, and continued to espouse, a "take all comers" philosophy as to prospective clients. "We've been operating under the presumption that there's no such thing as a 'bad' client. They all pay our bills," said Jeff Pope, "but we are now beginning to question this assumption." Should they stop working with these smaller clients? What would happen if they did? Could the company survive if they did not?

Furthermore, there were serious questions as to CRI's organizational structure. For example, staff members responsible for selling projects were also responsible for implementing project design, interviewing, and analysis. Did this structure make sense moving into the future? These were just a few of the questions senior staff were raising during a series of off-site meetings with Sam Marcus, currently Managing Partner—Brecker & Merryman, Inc., a New York management consulting firm.

BACKGROUND

Judith Corson, fresh from completing a liberal arts degree at the University of Minnesota in 1964, decided she didn't want to be a "nurse or a teacher like everyone else." Through her sorority network, she was contacted by Norma Friedrichs, the manager of project administration in commercial research at The Pillsbury Company. Corson was promptly hired as one of three project directors in charge of project implementation of marketing research for Pillsbury.

Pillsbury, unlike a number of its competitors at this time, had a comprehensive internal research department. Marketing research analysts would request a study and Pillsbury's own internal research department would then implement the entire process from designing the methodology to composing the questionnaire to hiring interviewing services to tabulating results. Most other consumer products companies only had a group of in-house marketing research analysts who would contract their studies out to an independent research firm.

Corson led Pillsbury's new-product marketing research implementation effort on and off for a period of 10 years (she had a stint in marketing research at Scott Paper in Philadelphia from 1967 to 1969 before returning to Pillsbury). In the late 1960s, Pillsbury established a central telephone interviewing capability in-house. Soon it became obvious that the peaks and valleys in Pillsbury's marketing research work volume made it impossible to staff this telephone facility. Operating as a stand-alone profit center funded by charging its time to various departments that needed its services, the marketing research department's problem of having a "single client" made it difficult to generate enough studies for the telephone center staff and therefore difficult to retain personnel.

In 1968, two marketing research analysts left Pillsbury to work for Johnson Wax. Without any internal marketing research department to turn to at their new firm, the analysts called Judy Corson to ask if she could continue to do studies for them. Her boss, Dudley Ruch, gave her permission to do so (and to seek other outside clients). Judy's outside research client business was soon profitable (enjoying 15 to 20 percent profit margins while the company as a whole averaged approximately 4 to 5 percent). This outside research group was able to supplement funding for developing new commercial research techniques.

After a few years, it became necessary to structure the outside research group's relationship to the company in a more formal way. Management demanded that the outside research group become a separate free-standing business—in essence, a line organization, paying corporate taxes to the firm. Seeing this as unfair (marketing research did their own accounting, HR, etc.), Corson became increasingly frustrated with the status of her department. "We were paying corporate taxes, but we weren't getting any services in return!"

Furthermore, industry diversification was giving rise to a number of potential conflicts of interest that prevented Corson from accepting more outside business from other consumer research companies. For example, after Pillsbury bought Burger King, Corson was forced to turn down lucrative marketing research work from McDonald's. This prevented her from growing the outside research business as quickly as she wished.

In January 1974, when Dudley Ruch left Pillsbury to work for Quaker Oats and Corson had no one to report to, she decided it was finally time for a change. She approached Norma Friedrichs, her original boss, to ask her if she would like to go into business together. At that time, Norma was responsible for project implementation of all Pillsbury marketing research. They, in turn, asked Jeff Pope, a Pillsbury product manager who, prior to joining Pillsbury, had also done marketing research for an independent research company and KPMG, to join the team. Custom Research Inc. was founded in August 1974.

Immediately upon beginning the firm, the trio hired a lawyer to implement a buy-sell agreement which proved to be a wise first step—two years later, Norma Friedrichs left the company and Judy Corson and Jeff Pope exercised the agreement, buying out Friedrichs and becoming 50/50 partners in CRI.

THE INDUSTRY

While the marketing research industry began as an in-house function of the larger consumer goods companies, CRI's experience was typical of the trend in the late 1960s and 1970s as companies began to contract with independent research firms. During this period, the industry was very fragmented, with a multitude of small, one- or two-person firms and a few well-established larger organizations.

In the recent decade, however, the trend was toward consolidation, with a few larger firms at the top able to complete all aspects of the research process from data collection to analysis and literally thousands of very small firms competing for data collection and tabulation business only. Furthermore, in a 1987 study of Council of American Survey Research Organizations (CASRO) member firms, a large majority expected custom research spending to grow slowly or remain the same over the next few years. (See Exhibit 1 for industry breakdown.)

THE MARKETING RESEARCH STUDY

A marketing research study typically includes the following steps:

1. *Study design:* Establishes client's research and information needs, determines the limitations of available research tools and methods, and draws up plans for implementing the study. Includes development of detailed client questionnaire.

2. *Proposal:* Explains study design to client, offers cost and timing estimate within 10 percent of final cost to client.

3. *Data collection:* Uses questionnaire to gather data necessary to determine what information a client needs to know about a new product idea, a price increase, or other types of information. Typically done by outside interviewing services, either over the phone or in person (for example, at shopping malls). Other data collection methods include mail.

4. *Tabulation:* Results from data collection stage are tabulated according to variables laid out during study design stage.

5. *Analysis:* Study results are analyzed for their relevance to client—should client develop the new product? Why or why not? What are the real implications of the study results?

At its inception, CRI did almost exclusively data collection and tabulation. The process went as follows: first, a research analyst from a client firm would request a

EXHIBIT 1
Council of American Survey Research Organizations—Quarterly Bookings Report—Firms May 26, 1987

Size of Firm	(N)	1Q87	% Change	% Change vs. Year Ago
		115,139	*+2*	*—*
10mm and over	16	119,436	+6	+4
4mm to 10mm	21	33,892	+6	−4
		11,524	*−13*	*−1*
2mm to 4mm	16	10,955	−17	−6
		2,897	*−5*	*−22*
1mm to 2mm	9	2,697	−10	−28
		2,445	*−19*	*−32*
Under 1mm	14	3,035	—	−15
		165,897	*+1*	*−2* ·
TOTAL	76	170,015	+4	—

| *Italics* | — Represent analysis adjusted for outliers.

Comparison of Two- or Three- Year Outlook on Primary Research Spending

Percentage that said custom research spending by their organization in the next two or three years would:

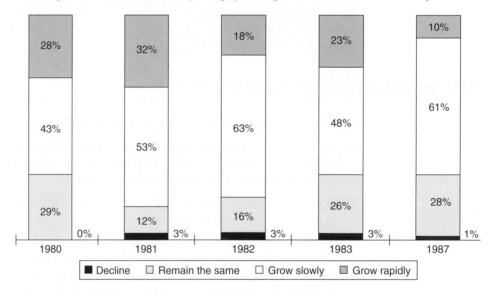

study to test a new product idea with a certain number of consumers (e.g., the design stage was already completed by the client). CRI would receive the request and would, according to the size and scope of the study, develop a proposal with a cost and timing estimate for data collection and tabulation. At the beginning, clients would typically do the first step—study design—and the last step—analysis of the results—themselves. Later, in the early 1980s, as their client companies began to downsize, CRI began to perform the design and analysis functions as well. (See Exhibit 2 for a typical study request, results, and analysis.)

EXHIBIT 2

Mr. Joe Leim
Great Foods Company
2 White Pine Road
Jonesville, WV

Dear Joe:

Well, it's time for another wave of Pancake Mix Price Increase Awareness Study. This is the *second* of four waves. The following is our understanding of the study specifications for this study. Also included are the associated study costs and timing. Joe, please note that the costs did go up for this wave (and for each subsequent wave).

Background and Study Purpose

Due to current low supplies of the ingredients for pancake mix worldwide, the wheat futures market is extraordinarily volatile. The purpose of this study is to help you understand consumer awareness of pancake mix pricing increases and how these increases affect consumers' usage habits. You will conduct a series of four telephone surveys at six-week intervals. This study is the first of the four waves.

Specifications

Methodology

Telephone study conducted on weeknights, and weekends, using standard random digit dialing sampling procedures.

Locations

National (total U.S., excluding Alaska and Hawaii)

Quota

150 Head of Household (female/male if no female) who have bought any type of pancake mix in the past three months for use in their homes.

Each wave will consist of 150 interviews for a total of 600 interviews after completing all four waves.

Sample

RDD sample will be provided by SSI.

Incidence

When the study was costed, incidence was estimated at 70 percent. However, during the Wave 1 study, incidence was falling out at 60 percent.

Questionnaire and Interview Length

Interview length is estimated at six minutes.

Coding

There is one open-end question.

Data Tables

We will provide data tables and a top line report upon completion of the study.

continued

EXHIBIT 2 *(continued)*

Schedule and Budget

Schedule

We are operating under this timetable for Wave 2:

Sample at CRI	February 6
Final q'aire approved	n/a (same as Wave 1)
Data collection start	February 9
Data collection finish	February 16
Data tables and top line report to you	February 23

Budget

Joe, due to the lower than estimated incidence, the cost of each additional wave has increased from our earlier estimate. If the incidence should go up, we will adjust the costs accordingly. But, as of now, our projected costs for this wave of research (and each additional wave) will be within 10 percent of the following:

Data collection start	$6,400
Sample	$300
Data processing	$700
Total	*$7,400*

Did I get everything, Joe? If not, please let me know and I'll make the necessary modifications.

Best regards,

Norma Brennan
Sr. Research Associate

continued

EXHIBIT 2 *(continued)*

Pancake Price Increase Awareness Study—Wave 2

Introduction (Base = All)

Good (morning/afternoon/evening). I'm (NAME) calling long distance from Custom Research Inc.

Today I'm collecting information for a marketing study about products used in the home.

(Are you/may I please speak with) the female head of the household (/lady of the house)?

IF THERE IS NO FEMALE HEAD OF HOUSEHOLD ASK:

(Are you/may I please speak with) the male head of the household (/man of the house)?

Q1. Gender (Base = All)

RECORD GENDER.
　　　'Female'/
　　　'Male'

Q2. Pancake Mix Bought Past Three Months (Base = All)

In the past three months, has pancake mix of any type been bought for use in your home?
　　　'Yes'/
　　　'No'

> REFER TO Q2. IF "NO," DISCONTINUE.
> ALL OTHER CONTINUE WITH Q3.

Q3. Usual Brand—Household Usage (Base = All)

In the past three months, what *one* brand of pancake mix was used most of the time in your home?

IF TWO OR MORE BRANDS: Was one of these brands used more often than the other(s), or were they both (all) used about equally?

IF TWO EQUALLY, ENTER BOTH.　　　IF THREE+, RECORD "NO USUAL."

RECORD ON BRAND LIST.

continued

EXHIBIT 2 *(continued)*

Q4. Next Brand—Household Usage (Base = All)

Thinking of the next time you buy pancake mix, as best as you can say, what *one* brand are you most likely to buy the next time you buy pancake mix?

IF RESPONDENT SAYS: "I buy what's on Sale/Coupon," RECORD "(50) Whatever on Sale/Coupon."

TWO OR MORE BRANDS: Would you be more likely to buy one of these brands than the other(s), or would you buy both (all) equally?

IF TWO EQUALLY, ENTER BOTH.   IF THREE+, RECORD "NO USUAL."

RECORD ON BRAND LIST.

Q5. How Often Will You Buy Pancake Mix (Base = All)

In the next three months, are you likely to buy pancake mix more often, about as often, or less often than you have in the past three months?

> "More often"/
> "About as often"/
> "Less often"/
> "NK/Ref" /

Q6. How Much Will Buy Pancake Mix (Base = All)

Now thinking of the next time you buy pancake mix, are you likely to buy more, about the same number of, or fewer boxes of pancake mix than the number you usually buy?

> "More"/
> "About the same number"/
> "Fewer"/
> "NK/Ref"/

Q7. What Size Will Buy (Base = All)

The next time you buy pancake mix, are you likely to buy a larger size, the same size, or a smaller size of pancake mix than the size you usually buy?

> "Larger"/
> "Same size"/
> "Smaller"/
> "NK/Ref"/

continued

EXHIBIT 2 *(continued)*

Q8. Price of Pancake Mix Last Bought (Base = All)

Now thinking about the last time you bought pancake mix, was the price of the pancake mix higher than, about the same, or lower than the previous time you had bought the same brand and type of pancake mix?

> "Higher"/
> "About the same price"/
> "Lower"/
> "NK/Ref"/

Q9. Price of Pancake Mix Increasing (Base = All)

Some people we've talked with recently mentioned hearing about an increase in the price of pancake mix. Have you seen or heard anything recently about pancake mix prices increasing, or not?

> "Yes"/
> "No"/

REFER TO Q9.   IF "YES," CONTINUE WITH Q10.   IF "NO," SKIP TO DEMOS.

Q10 Cause of Increase in Pancake Mix Prices (Base = All)

What do you think is causing the increase in pancake mix prices?
   PROBE AND CLARIFY FULLY.

DEMOGRAPHICS (Demos)   (Base = All)

My last few questions are for demographic purposes only.

Number in Household (Base = All)

In total, how many people live in your household, including children and yourself?

DO NOT READ LIST.

> Resp sp "One"/
> "Two"/
> "Three"/
> "Four"/
> "Five"/
> "Six"/
> "Seven or more"/
> "Refuse"/

continued

EXHIBIT 2 *(continued)*

Household Income (Base = 18+ Years Old)

Is the total yearly household income over or under $50,000?

UNDER: Is it over or under $25,000?

OVER: Is it over or under $70,000?

> "Under $25,000"/
> "$25,000–$49,999"/
> "$50,000–$69,999"/
> "$70,000 and over"/
> "Refuse"/

Education (Base = All)

What was the last grade of school that you, yourself, completed?

IF NECESSARY, READ LIST.

> "Grade School or Less"/
> "Some High School"/
> "High School Graduate"/
> "Some College"/
> "College Graduate"/
> "Post Graduate"/
> "Refuse (DO NOT READ)"/

Those are all of the questions I have for you today. Thank you for participating in this study. We value your opinion.

continued

EXHIBIT 2 *(continued)*

Pancake Mix Price Increase Awareness: Waves 1 & 2
Market Research Department Report

Research Purpose: To track: (1) consumer awareness of pricing changes in the pancake mix category, (2) consumer perceptions for the reasons for the price increase, and (3) expected claimed habit changes due to pancake mix pricing volatility.

Success Criteria/Expected Results: Will be used with other data to aid brand management in decisions about product, promotion, pricing, and public relations responses to the pricing increases.

Initiated By: Brand management.

Locations of Data Collection: Continental United States.

Market Research Contact: Joe L.

Background: The wheat futures market is extraordinarily volatile with the spring futures increasing by over 50 percent, the second highest level ever. Unlike the most recent 1996 run-up, which was weather-related, this market is being driven by fundamental supply and demand issues as worldwide stocks of higher quality wheat are at critically low levels and estimates for this year's crop are 10 percent lower than last year. We expect continued volatility over the next three months. In an effort to understand consumer awareness of pancake mix pricing increase and how the price increase affects consumers' usage habits, we will conduct a series of four telephone surveys at six-week intervals.

Method/Test Description: Interviews were conducted via telephone. In order to track awareness of the price increases, perceptions of the causes and changes in claimed/expected behaviors over time, four waves of this study will be conducted at six-week intervals. A total of 600 heads of households (150/wave for four waves) who have bought any type of pancake mix in the past three months for use in their home will be interviewed.

Key Dates: Wave 1 fieldwork—2/9/98 through 2/16/98. Wave 2 fieldwork—3/30/98 through 4/6/98.

continued

EXHIBIT 2 *(concluded)*

Market Research Department Report
Summary
Pancake Mix Increase Awareness: Waves 1 & 2

Research Purpose: To track: (1) consumer awareness of pricing changes in the pancake mix category, (2) consumer perceptions for the reasons for the price increase, and (3) expected claimed habit changes due to pancake mix pricing volatility.

The request states that the results will be used: with other data to aid brand management in decisions about product, promotion, pricing, and public relations responses to the pricing increases.

Respondents are: Heads of Household, age 18+.

Key data for Waves 1 & 2 are shown below.

	Heads of Household Who Purchased Pancake Mix in Past Three Months	
	Wave 1 2/98	Wave 2 4/98
Base = Total Interviews	150	152
	%	%
Predicts change in habits (undup.)	**30**	**24**
Amount planned to buy in next three months		
More often	4	5
About as often	77	85
Less often	18	11
Number of packages plans to buy next time		
More	4	3
About the same number	87	87
Fewer	8	9
Size of packages plans to buy next time		
Larger size	8	9
Same size	88	89
Smaller size	3	1
Noticed pancake mix price increase (aided)	**66**	**56**
Price compared to last bought pancake mix		
Compared to previous time		
Higher	41	43
About the same price	39	37
Lower	6	9
Reasons for price increase		
(Base = Noticed price increase)	(99)	(85)
Freeze/Frost/Bad weather	25	29
Manufacturer greed/Taking advantage of customer	10	11
Brand usage		
Most often past three months brand	42	43
Next brand will purchase	39	39

Market Research Department Report

ORGANIZATIONAL STRUCTURE

Once the proposal was accepted by a client, the CRI project manager would deploy staff to implement the study. Project managers were organized by industry into two main divisions. The first division included Business to Business (companies that sold products to other companies; i.e., auto parts suppliers, corporate service firms, etc.) and Medical (pharmaceutical, hospital supplies, etc.). This division accounted for only 25 percent of CRI's total revenues. Clients such as Johnson & Johnson were among CRI's first clients in the medical marketing research business.

The second division, representing the other 75 percent of CRI's business, was Consumer Research. Clients included Quaker Oats, Land O'Lakes, and Johnson Wax. A third division, Corporate Services, provided support services to the research function, such as data tabulation, copying, shipping, etc.

CRI's project managers also served as salespeople—the company had not established an independent sales department. One reason for this structure was the nature of the business. As Judy Corson explained, "At CRI, salespeople must first be researchers—you must understand the methodology and the technology or you will not be taken seriously by the client. It normally takes five years to learn the business and there is no substitute for actually doing the studies."

EXPANDING BUSINESS, DECLINING PROFITS

From 1974 to 1990, CRI's customer base expanded steadily. With a number of large corporate clients, CRI had developed a reputation as one of the premier market research firms in the United States. However, during these years, a somewhat disturbing trend had developed. The results of an extensive profitability analysis completed in 1990 showed that while new bookings, closed sales, and overall operating profit were all on the rise, the crucial measure of profit as a percentage of sales was slowly declining. (See Exhibit 3 for analysis.)

From its formation, CRI had used a detailed activity-based costing system to assign costs to each marketing research study or project. Each employee or associate recorded time spent on each job using one of more than 30 different charge rates depending on the work done. Time spent on selling projects was charged first to a "zero" account and charged back later to jobs accepted. Using this system, CRI had a record of profitability for each research study or project.

EXHIBIT 3
Fiscal 1990 Review—
Custom Research
Inc.—Confidential
(Company Total—
Fiscal 1990 Review[a])

	Actual	Plan	$ Difference	% Difference
Bookings[b]	$10,899.3M	$11,547.0M	$ −647.7M	−6%
Closings[b]	10,297.0M	10,792.0M	−495.9M	−5%
Gross margins	1,677.6M	1,871.5M	−193.9M	−10%
General and administrative	729.8M	708.2M	−21.6M	−3%
Operating profit	$947.8M	$1,163.3M	$ −215.5M	−19%
	9%	11%		−2%

continued

[a]All data and numbers in Exhibit 3 are disguised.

[b]"Bookings" refers to work under contract which in turn becomes work in progress. "Closings" is the revenue figure recorded once all costs are allocated. Typically, closings lag bookings by 5 to 10 percent as this small percentage of booked business closes in the following fiscal year.

EXHIBIT 3
(continued)

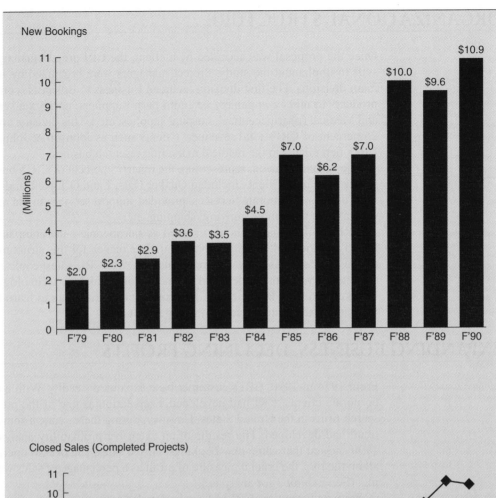

New Bookings

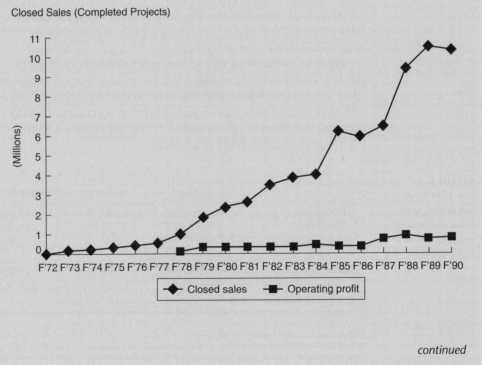

Closed Sales (Completed Projects)

continued

EXHIBIT 3
(continued)

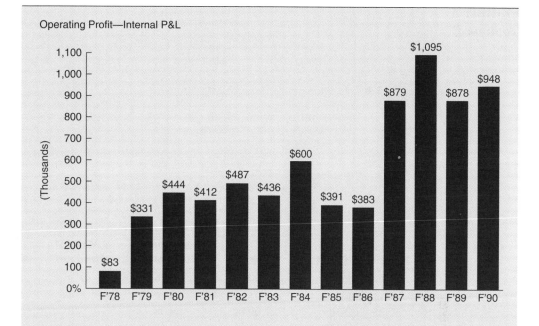

Operating Profit—Internal P&L

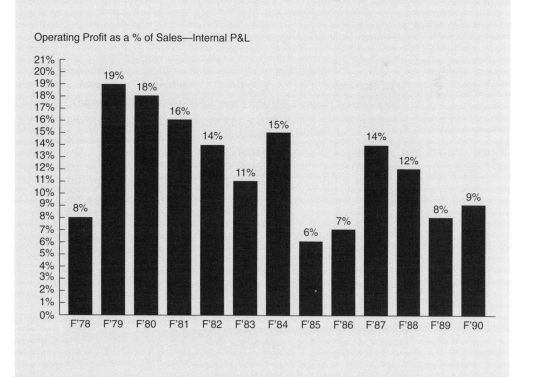

Operating Profit as a % of Sales—Internal P&L

continued

EXHIBIT 3
(continued)

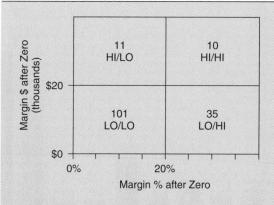

Number of Clients		$ Volume	$ Margin[a] after Zero	$ Margin[a] after Zero	% of Total CRI Margin
10	HI-HI	$3,001K	$744K	25%	44%
11	HI-LO	2,919K	411K	14	25
35	LO-HI	1,094K	310K	28	18
101	LO-LO	3,283K	213K	6	13
157	Total	$10,297K	$1,678K	16%	100%

[a]"$ margin after zero" refers to the profit margin after all direct project costs (salaries, data collection and tabulation, copying, shipping, etc.), as well as sales costs (e.g., all costs involved in selling the project) have been deducted. "Margin" refers to profit margin before sales costs have been deducted.

I.D. Number	$ Volume	% Margin	% Margin[a] after Zero	$ Margin[a] after Zero
F-90 Closed Projects—HI/HI (over $20K/under 20% Margin)				
30	$989,387	28%	26%	253,184
29	505,426	29	26	129,440
39	410,098	24	21	86,244
15	184,700	35	30	54,560
44	266,650	23	20	54,343
45	231,300	21	20	45,450
31	156,000	27	25	39,718
12	99,815	34	30	30,234
7	81,102	36	36	29,294
18	76,600	33	29	22,000
Total 10	$3,001,077			$744,466

continued

EXHIBIT 3
(continued)

I.D. Number	$ Volume	% Margin	% Margin after Zero	$ Margin after Zero
F-90 Closed Projects—HI/LO (over $20K/over 20% Margin)				
46	$460,311	26%	19%	$88,518
60	206,125	19	16	49,531
61	281,962	22	16	45,255
54	252,269	22	18	44,904
71	276,608	15	12	32,640
78	293,600	10	10	28,685
73	232,300	20	12	26,877
68	189,358	23	14	26,529
79	258,535	22	9	24,406
76	223,681	13	10	22,592
67	144,500	15	15	21,155
Total 11	$2,919,249			$411,090
F-90 Closed Projects—LO/HI (under $20K/over 20% Margin)				
13	$61,250	32%	30%	$18,449
2	32,500	57	54	17,596
8	51,940	36	34	17,576
28	65,980	31	26	17,221
27	57,300	32	27	15,282
4	39,500	46	38	15,121
23	52,200	28	28	14,376
36	62,835	26	23	14,320
19	48,521	31	28	13,785
43	56,700	22	20	11,555
17	38,150	32	29	11,144
16	36,985	32	29	10,837
41	48,151	22	21	10,054
9	30,750	35	32	9,963
24	34,900	41	27	9,580
14	31,730	35	30	9,532
34	38,000	29	23	8,900
32	35,236	25	25	8,675
42	38,660	24	21	8,022
40	37,300	24	21	7,844
20	26,922	31	28	7,552
10	23,000	34	32	7,349
22	21,300	32	28	5,924
6	15,985	38	36	5,820
26	20,300	27	27	5,475
35	21,350	26	23	4,893
3	10,600	50	46	4,862
1	4,700	100	100	4,677
25	16,500	27	27	4,455
37	16,055	38	22	3,550
11	9,250	33	31	2,831
5	3,400	43	37	1,264
21	3,650	28	28	1,018
33	1,389	100	24	332
38	800	26	21	172
Total 35	$1,093,788			$310,003

continued

EXHIBIT 3
(continued)

I.D. Number	$ Volume	% Margin	% Margin after Zero	$ Margin after Zero
F-90 Closed Projects—LO/LO (under $20K/under 20% Margin)				
72	$153,650	16%	12%	$18,438
66	113,780	19	15	17,067
83	186,680	17	9	16,801
59	102,501	21	16	16,400
84	203,320	14	7	14,232
47	57,900	24	19	11,001
55	59,789	22	18	10,762
82	115,925	16	9	10,433
64	57,165	24	15	8,575
49	42,100	24	19	7,999
70	62,800	22	12	7,536
63	45,850	24	16	7,336
80	74,547	11	9	6,709
58	40,650	21	16	6,504
52	35,600	23	18	6,408
56	36,660	28	17	6,232
87	110,885	7	5	5,544
69	38,494	16	14	5,389
57	31,284	23	17	5,318
53	29,000	26	18	5,220
65	29,300	20	15	4,395
75	27,500	22	11	3,025
50	15,600	27	19	2,964
62	18,000	20	16	2,880
92	91,900	12	3	2,757
81	30,600	21	9	2,754
85	36,500	13	7	2,555
96	47,250	10	5	2,363
134	38,600	30	6	2,316
123	45,000	20	5	2,250
77	19,100	22	10	1,910
48	9,685	29	19	1,840
157	31,950	6	5	1,598
125	30,150	17	5	1,508
91	36,675	17	4	1,467
155	35,800	16	4	1,432
120	22,994	26	6	1,380
74	12,350	15	11	1,359
51	7,600	26	17	1,292
94	125,055	3	1	1,251
115	23,775	22	5	1,189
114	23,500	18	5	1,175
86	18,510	15	6	1,111
128	20,700	15	5	1,035
89	18,500	17	5	925
88	16,030	5	5	802
150	15,895	5	5	795
98	15,650	20	5	783
93	36,300	3	2	726
129	11,900	25	6	714
130	35,475	5	2	710

continued

EXHIBIT 3
(continued)

I.D. Number	$ Volume	% Margin	% Margin after Zero	$ Margin after Zero
F-90 Closed Projects—LO/LO (under $20K/under 20% Margin)				
95	11,500	9	6	690
141	8,900	15	7	623
127	11,100	11	5	555
153	10,990	12	5	550
90	6,100	16	9	549
144	9,100	33	6	546
142	10,400	21	5	520
119	6,750	56	7	473
131	8,350	17	5	418
156	6,100	32	6	366
160	12,100	9	3	363
97	11,739	6	3	352
100	8,700	9	4	348
136	6,900	34	5	345
148	6,300	12	5	315
132	7,800	12	4	312
113	14,922	6	2	298
122	5,500	51	5	275
121	4,800	60	5	240
106	5,000	31	4	200
126	3,900	28	4	156
118	3,100	22	5	155
110	3,800	25	3	114
117	1,778	40	6	107
149	2,080	38	5	104
158	2,500	26	4	100
101	2,000	43	4	80
151	1,700	28	4	68
152	1,225	44	5	61
104	1,200	18	5	60
116	1,200	58	5	60
112	1,000	12	5	50
109	500	31	5	25
140	210	76	5	11
135	13,000	5	0	0
124	1,200	−1	−6	−72
139	7,800	4	−1	−78
111	2,000	−4	−9	−180
108	3,100	−4	−10	−310
147	3,900	−27	−32	−1,248
133	10,900	−5	−13	−1,417
159	9,800	−17	−19	−1,862
143	28,000	0	−7	−1,960
103	19,981	−3	−10	−1,998
138	12,100	−17	−22	−2,662
154	68,470	−2	−5	−3,424
102	43,180	−4	−9	−3,886
107	113,600	−1	−4	−4,544
99	54,450	−11	−12	−6,534
105	145,800	−5	−9	−13,122
Total 101	$3,282,949			$213,353

As Executive Vice President Diane Kokal explained, profit as a percentage of sales was the main way that CRI measured its success:

> Working for a client that doesn't actually clear a profit is no fun. Obviously what you want is the highest possible profit margin, particularly in our business where the game is definitely not market share. The research business is a very fragmented one so market share is not such a meaningful measure. We knew we had to grow consistently but we also knew we must grow more profitably.

Jeff Pope further organized these data into a quadrant analysis that provided even more insight into the problem. Two-thirds of all clients were in the "Low/Low" quadrant, meaning that they contributed less than $20,000 in margin contribution and less than a 20 percent profit margin (as a percentage of sales). Thus, these were either small clients or small projects or both.

DIRECTION

The Steering Committee, made up of the two partners and the two executive vice presidents—Diane Kokal and Jan Elsesser—decided it was time to hire an outsider to facilitate the process of establishing the right direction for the future. They hired Sam Marcus, formerly of the Delta Group in New York, and the four members of the Steering Committee went off-site over a year for a series of one-day strategy meetings.

Questions were many. If a large percentage of clients contributed little or nothing to overall profit, should CRI neglect them? What would be the repercussions of such a strategy? What if the remaining clients experienced an economic downturn and cut back on their research budgets? Could CRI grow under this strategy? Jeff Pope thought CRI could focus on and grow the business of the larger, more profitable clients.

What choices must be made if the Steering Committee were to terminate relations with some predetermined group of their existing clients? What criteria should they use to decide whom to keep and whom to drop? Should they in fact maintain all profitable clients and drop all unprofitable clients? Perhaps the choice was not that simple.

Furthermore, how exactly would they explain all this to their clients? Was it their responsibility to refer those smaller clients to someone else for service? What else did the Steering Committee need to address before making this very important decision about the company's future?

And finally, what about CRI's organizational structure? While it seemed to make sense that "doers" were also sellers, the research function was quite different, and in some respects, required very different skills, than did the sales function. Furthermore, while the project managers were out selling projects, they were unable to implement others and while directing research, they were unable to sell. This seemed rather inefficient. However, everyone agreed that it was crucial that CRI's salespeople all understand (and have experience in implementing) research projects.

General Electric Medical Systems— Establishing an Ongoing Dialogue with Customers

GE Medical Systems (GEMS), a $4 billion division of General Electric Company (GE), is at the forefront of GE's transition from a manufacturing company to a services company. This case study examines how GEMS has used its customer education services to establish an ongoing dialogue with customers that has resulted in dramatic improvements in customer satisfaction and has contributed to market gains. GEMS took its "number-one *dissatisfier*," applications training, and turned it into its "number-one *satisfier*." GEMS is incorporating customer feedback and other information gained during the delivery of customer education services to fuel marketing programs that better address customer needs. A culture of innovation and a commitment to serving the customer has enabled the GEMS customer education organization to cross internal boundaries to work with the GEMS sales organization, services delivery, services marketing, and even NBC, to develop new, creative marketing and customer training programs.

INTRODUCTION

The medical systems market, especially in the United States, has been characterized by slow growth and intense competition. To get ahead, market participants need to develop deeper customer relationships that engender loyalty. Through the creative use of technology, GEMS has dramatically increased the number of times it "touches" each of its customers with virtually no increase in costs. The company has invested in new product and service offerings development, despite the industry downturn, to position itself for growth. In fact, GEMS innovations such as comprehensive multivendor services solutions, sophisticated software applications, and customer satellite TV training are fueling a rejuvenation of the market. The company's strong 1996 operating results will provide the momentum needed to support continued growth.

This case study describes a number of original programs implemented by the GE Medical Systems' customer training organization. The customer satellite training network, in particular, is highlighted. All of the programs described in this Best Practice Case Study have something in common: They provide a means for GE to communicate with its customer base and use the knowledge it gains to improve its relationship with customers. The ensuing dialogue builds a foundation for trust and loyalty—an undeniable competitive advantage.

CASE BACKGROUND

GE Medical Systems designs, manufactures, sells, and services a wide range of diagnostic medical imaging systems, radiation therapy systems, and diagnostic information management systems. Products include magnetic resonance (MR) and computed tomography (CT) scanners, positron emission tomography (PET), X-ray, nuclear imaging, ultrasound, and other diagnostic imaging equipment. Global revenue in 1996 was approximately $4 billion. About half of GE Medical Systems global revenue is derived from services.

Services revenue is growing faster than total revenue. Total revenue growth in the last few years has been modest due to weakening of the U.S. and European markets. Market growth in the United States has slowed because of economic pressures impacting the health care industry and relative maturity and saturation of the market. Consequently, the company has placed a greater emphasis on growing its non-U.S. business. In 1996, slightly more than half of total revenue came from nondomestic markets, including Europe and Asia/Pacific. Furthermore, the company has implemented initiatives to rejuvenate its growth. The 1995 annual report states: " . . . three-quarters of 1996's orders and sales will be generated from offerings introduced in just the past two years." In addition to new medical products, GE has introduced a number of major new service initiatives, setting the company apart as a leader: multivendor diagnostic imaging services and biomedical services. The company also continues to innovate within its existing service product lines.

Medical Systems: A Software- and Services-Driven Business

Historically, the medical equipment industry has not been considered a computer or software business. Today, however, medical systems are driven by CPUs and software. Similar to the mainstream computer industry, the medical equipment hardware technology is fast becoming a commodity. It is the software and services that will differentiate the players. Consequently, vendors of diagnostic imaging systems are learning how to develop and deploy sophisticated applications. These applications are often networked with the main hospital information systems, allowing access to centralized databases and digitized medical records.

The Medical Systems Customer

GEMS' customers range from doctors' offices and clinics to large multihospital systems. Some major trends impacting these customers have had a double effect on GEMS, resulting in a slowdown in its revenue growth while also creating some new and exciting opportunities:

- There is an enormous amount of pressure to reduce health care costs. Health care institutions are looking for ways to increase efficiency, but at a lower cost. Return on capital investments is of great concern. Assets need to be productive from day one. Many customers are putting off purchases of new equipment to eke out another year or two of use from existing assets.

- More health care is being provided beyond the walls of the hospital. This is creating a need for networks to link satellite clinics, doctors' offices, HMOs, etc.

- Hospitals and other major health care institutions are consolidating at a breakneck pace to eliminate redundant costs and take advantage of economies of scale. Consequently the number of potential customers is shrinking.

- Larger, more powerful health care institutions are looking for strategic suppliers.

Medical Equipment Services: At a Turning Point

As the medical equipment systems market shifts from a hardware-driven business to a software- and services-driven business, the strategic importance of services is intensifying.

- Until 1996, growth in the medical systems equipment market had been flat to negative. The market is essentially a replacement market for hardware with growth coming primarily from software upgrades and services.

- Customers are increasingly looking for one-stop shopping in the form of multivendor services.

- Customer–vendor interactions are evolving from a series of transactions to long-term relationships. Outsourcing relationships are becoming more commonplace.

- Traditional maintenance services are expanding to include more value-added enhancement services, such as asset management and equipment utilization management.

- There is a burgeoning need for software and network support as the software and networking content of the equipment expands. Systems are becoming significantly more sophisticated.

- Health care institutions are implementing comprehensive computerized medical records, including diagnostic imaging. Integration of the medical imaging equipment with centralized databases is increasingly demanded.

- In an environment that prizes system uptime and reduced costs, remote system diagnostics and repair are becoming essential.

- With intense margin pressure on the hardware, medical products companies can no longer afford to include services with the equipment purchase. Services are transitioning from "free" to "fee."

GEMS TRAINING IN PARTNERSHIP (TIP™)

GEMS recognized early on that a well-trained customer is a happy customer. Furthermore, there is an inverse relationship between the amount of training customers receive and the cost to support them (Exhibit 1). For example, statistical analysis led GEMS management to conclude that 10 percent of service calls resulted from operator error. Improved training would eliminate those service calls. With multiyear, fixed rate contracts, any reduction in the number and costs of service calls goes straight to the bottom line.

GEMS customers have some unique training needs that directly impact their satisfaction with GE equipment and, ultimately, their tendency to repeat purchase. GE faces many challenges in its quest to train its customers:

- The buyers and users (technologists and doctors) of medical diagnostic equipment are relatively computer illiterate. GEMS is incorporating computer hardware and software technology in its products at a rapid pace. One of the more recently developed GEMS educational programs is designed to teach elementary computer skills, such as how to use a mouse.

- Computer users of office productivity software can usually get away with learning just enough about their software to "get the job done." Medical users, on the other hand, can continuously improve patient care, job satisfaction, and productivity if they take the time and have the opportunity to learn new applications and system features.

- GEMS business is global. The skill level of users varies greatly from country to country. This makes staffing and managing the resources of a global customer training organization very complex.

In 1990, Jack Albertson, Applications Program Manager, was hired by GEMS to develop a new, formal customer education program to address the changing needs of the customer base. He began this task by surveying GEMS customers to determine their wants and needs and current impressions of GE Medical Systems' customer education services. The surveys uncovered a number of problems:

EXHIBIT 1
Well-Trained Customers Can Be Supported At Lower Costs

Source: ITSMA, 1997.

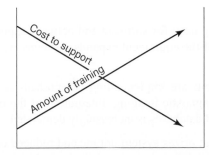

One Benefit of High-Performance Customers

- Customers did not perceive that the training they received was sufficient. They wanted more training to increase their comfort levels with using the new, sophisticated equipment and applications.

- Education and training services were one of the top dissatisfiers with GEMS.

- Customers wanted more contact with GEMS to learn about new products, upgrades, and applications.

- Despite the desire for more training, many customers lacked a commitment to education, making it difficult to free up equipment and staff for training sessions. Customer education budgets were insufficient to cover the costs of training.

At the time, training was being provided almost exclusively at the customers' sites. Training, included in the purchase price of the medical systems, was delivered in a one-week, intensive dose with little or no follow-up. GE could not afford to include additional on-site training with the equipment purchase. Furthermore, staff resources to provide the on-site training were limited. GE needed to find a way to reach its customers more economically, without the requirement of dramatically increasing staffing levels. Thus, the GE Training in Partnership (TiP™) program was born.

The TiP™ program is more than training classes and multimedia materials. The company takes a very broad view of customer education. Its education services incorporate help desk services and user documentation, which together with training classes, seminars, and multimedia materials influence the customers' ultimate success in using GEMS products (Exhibits 2 and 3). GE's philosophy is to extend classroom learning into the job—to provide support before, during, and after the traditional on-site training. GEMS provides educational support throughout the life cycle of the product. The ultimate goal is to provide "just-in-time" training—training at the precise moment it is needed.

For instance, user documentation, formerly written exclusively by the engineers, is now much more "user friendly." User manuals are now written in both computer-based tutorial and quick reference formats by application specialists who have an extensive background in training customers on system operations and applications. The new documentation essentially integrates all knowledge of the global TiP™ applications team. In addition, the user documentation can be integrated into product training and continuing education, as well as used by the applications support specialists staffing the

EXHIBIT 2
GEMS' Broad View of Customer Education

Source: ITSMA, 1997.

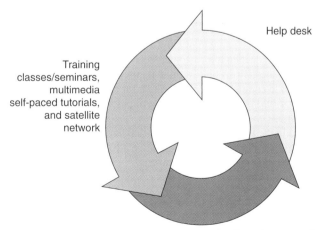

Help desk

Training classes/seminars, multimedia self-paced tutorials, and satellite network

User documentation

EXHIBIT 3
GEMS' TiP™
Customer Education
Product Offerings

Source: GEMS, 1997.

- On-site training: Product-specific, competency-based training for complete system and clinical applications.
- Education center classroom training: Hands-on and didactic training in modality-specific theory and product use.
- Computer tutorials: Individual, self-paced product training through interactive computer-based tutorials on product consoles.
- Videotapes: Product-specific videotapes.
- Online services: Nonemergency phone assistance for questions regarding system operation.
- Telephone conference training: Customized telephone training to fit specific customer training needs.
- Local and national seminars: Guest presenters and GE experts provide current information on clinical procedures and software updates.
- Consultant services: Customized applications training services to assist in departmental analysis and productivity.
- User documentation: Manuals provide applications training, reference materials, and "quick look-up" sections.
- TV satellite training: Interactive training broadcasts ranging from general to advance topics transmitted directly to health care facility. Broadcasts can be custom tailored for large multihospital systems customers.

customer support lines. User documentation in the form of TiP™ Applications Operator Information becomes the foundation, or core, for all other TiP™ customer education products.

Moreover, GE recognizes that its education programs are crucial for developing a closer relationship with the customer. GE uses its education services to identify ways to add value to the customer–vendor relationship and seed future business. As a result, GEMS customer education programs are a strong contributor to customer satisfaction.

HIGH-PERFORMANCE CUSTOMERS

Organizations that treat their customers as only end-user consumers of their services will lose the service game to organizations that involve their customers in a variety of other roles that deepen the customer–service provider relationship. . . . Although it is obvious that these firms highly value their customers as consumers, they have gone beyond that to create other opportunities for collaboration and partnership. . . . Managers would benefit from thinking of customers as possible "partial employees" of the firm or as "co-producers" of services . . . the payoff then comes from having the best customers in the business. We propose that having the most competent customer base can be a source of sustainable competitive advantage just like having the most skilled employee base. (Schneider and Bowen, *Winning the Service Game,* Harvard Business School Press, 1995)

High-performance customers are customers that have the ability and motivation to actively contribute to their relationships with their vendors. High-performance customers are not just satisfied; they are committed and loyal. GEMS' customer education programs aim to create high-performance customers.

CUSTOMERS AS "COPRODUCERS"

GEMS has certain expectations of its customers as contributors to the service process and as owners and users of GE medical systems. As such, customers act as "coproducers" of the services they receive. GE provides the enabling knowledge and resources to ensure their success. Even the name of GE's customer education organization denotes this philosophy: "TiP™: Training in Partnership." For example, prior to delivery, TiP™ on-site education customers are responsible for readying the installation site. GE provides information, checklists, manuals, and guidance. Furthermore, the GEMS Customer Education Center classes use the "train the trainer" format. GE trains the "master trainer" from the customer site. The master trainer is then responsible for training the remainder of the staff. This results in transferring a good deal of the training responsibility to the customer.

After the initial equipment installation and training, GE expects customers to continue training to further their skills and maximize their use of the sophisticated equipment. This training is not mandatory; however, GE has provided the necessary motivation (through improved job performance and continuing education accreditation by professional associations) and convenience, to keep its customers in the training loop.

GE even encourages its customers to take an active role in the marketing of its TiP-TV™ satellite customer education network. At each customer site, a coordinator is assigned to take on the marketing role. The coordinator is responsible for posting announcements and scheduling training sessions.

GEMS conducts an ongoing appraisal of its customers' performance through its TiP™ OnLine phone support. Questions and problems are logged and categorized in a comprehensive database that is used to remedy problems and provide input to TiP™ curriculum development. GEMS takes corrective action when performance problems are unearthed through a variety of programs, some of which are described in this case study. Left untouched, low-performing customers become frustrated and dissatisfied. Customers that are "touched" become advocates.

TIP™ ORGANIZATION

The GEMS customer education organization, TiP™, is structured as a cost center. Its mission is to cost-effectively create educational opportunities to improve customers' growth and productivity. A primary goal of customer education is customer satisfaction. The key measurements of success are customer satisfaction survey results and the number of times the customer is "touched" by GE.

The TiP™ organization itself is part of the GEMS services organization, reporting directly to the Vice President of Service (Exhibit 4). At this time, the TiP™ program is developing two types of products: training products that come as entitlements with the purchase of hardware and software; and training products that are fee for service.

Exhibit 5 summarizes the vision and mission statements for GEMS and its primary service organizations.

ENTREPRENEURIAL SPIRIT AND INTERNAL PARTNERING

GE's top corporate management aims to create "a new kind of company—one that has, and uses, all the strengths of a big company while moving with the speed, hunger and

EXHIBIT 4   **GEMS Service Organization Chart**

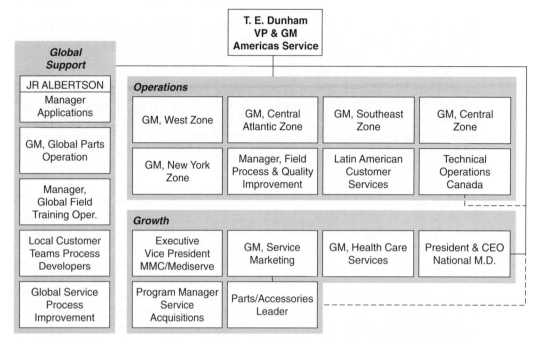

Source: GEMS, 1997.

EXHIBIT 5
Vision and Mission Statements for GEMS Total Business and GEMS Services

Source: GEMS, 1997.

GEMS Vision: To grow as the global leader in quality, productivity, information, and technology solutions to the health care industry, providing superior customer and patient satisfaction delivered by energized employees who meet commitments.

GEMS Services Mission Statement: To be the recognized global leader in the health care equipment services industry, achieving sustained profitable growth by maximizing customer satisfaction and providing the highest quality and value-added services for the customer.

GEMS Services Marketing Mission Statement: Lead the development and implementation of customer-focused integrated marketing strategies and offerings that sustain profitable growth and position GEMS as the recognized leader in the health care equipment service industry.

GEMS TiP™ Vision: To be the worldwide leader in marketing applications education products that support the delivery of quality health care/imaging solutions for productivity and growth of GEMS and our customers.

GEMS TiP™ Mission Statement: To develop and market global, quality, state-of-the-art education products for GEMS and our customers:

- that promote solutions for productivity and growth;
- which improve health care delivery;
- in a cost effective manner.

urgency of a small company" (1995 Annual Report). The result is an entrepreneurial environment that is conducive to risk taking. Thomas Dunham, the Vice President and General Manager of GEMS Service, allows his managers to operate with a great deal of autonomy. If someone has a good idea, GEMS finds a way to make it happen. Seed money is available pending approval of a review board. GE funds new programs that will do one or more of the following:

- Provide profitable growth.

- Improve productivity/reduce costs.

- Increase customer satisfaction.

- Drive quality.

Within these guidelines, GEMS has introduced a number of new services and marketing programs. What sets these programs apart from the ordinary is the fruitful collaboration of multiple GEMS organizations and other organizations within the GE family of businesses. The goals of increased customer satisfaction, revenue growth, and improved productivity appear to supersede individual departments' objectives.

ITSMA has identified the partnerships between marketing, sales, customer education services delivery, and ultimately the customer as best practices contributing to extraordinary results. GEMS has cost-effectively increased the number of times it "touches" its customers, improved customer satisfaction, and increased revenue growth and market share. The information obtained during customer interactions easily crosses organizational boundaries. The ensuing dialogue builds a foundation for trust and loyalty—an undeniable competitive advantage.

TiP-TV™: UTILIZING TECHNOLOGY TO COST-EFFECTIVELY INCREASE CUSTOMER "TOUCHES"

Prior to 1992, GEMS had already used its internal TV network acumen (GE is the parent company of NBC) to produce and transmit training programs for GE-employed field engineers. This system had an abundance of excess capacity. An incremental $4 million investment, on top of a $25 million lease investment for a new GEMS education center, launched TiP-TV™. Fourteen pilot programs were produced, and the program was tested at hospitals already equipped for satellite transmission. The pilot program was an overwhelming success (Exhibit 6). GEMS had uncovered a customer need and a way to fulfill it. TiP-TV™ was introduced for general availability in 1993. After the first six months, GE had signed up six paying customers. It now has nearly 1,700 (Exhibit 7).

What Is TiP-TV™?

TiP-TV™ is a paid hospital subscription satellite training network. It offers live, interactive training programs on both GEMS-specific equipment and applications, and more general health care and management topics. Courses range from basic to advanced. TiP-TV™ is sold on a flat rate, annual basis for a specified number of live

EXHIBIT 6
TiP-TV™ Facts and Figures

Source: GEMS, 1997.

Number of TV shows aired	125 annually
Number of subscribers	1,635
Subscribers with multiyear educational service commitments	95%
Renewal rate	90%
Viewers claiming continuing education credits	83%

EXHIBIT 7
TiP-TV™ Subscriber Growth

Source: GEMS, 1997.

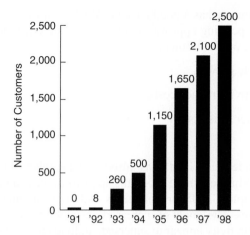

program broadcasts. Discounts are offered for multiyear subscriptions. Alternatively, TiP-TV™ can be purchased through a GEMS services contract with programming specific to the equipment type on the contract. Approximately 80 percent of subscribers purchase TiP-TV™ through their service contracts.

TiP-TV™ is accredited by all of the major professional organizations for continuing education credits. GEMS provides its subscribers with all of the required paperwork and submits the paperwork to the appropriate organizations.

Fees range from $3,000 for a one-year subscription including 10 customer-selected broadcasts to $22,800 for a five-year, 30 program per year package.

TiP-TV™ Growth and Expansion Plans

There are approximately 5,700 American Hospital Association (AHA) short-term hospitals in the United States. GE has sold its medical systems to 3,700, or nearly two-thirds, of these hospitals. Just under half (1,700) of GE's medical systems customer base subscribes to TiP-TV™. In other words, GE has a 50 percent penetration of its original target market. In 1997, GE expects to have 2,100 subscribers.

TiP-TV™ currently generates approximately $4 million in revenue. In comparison, TiP-TV™ on-site training sold after the initial equipment installation generates $700,000. (The bulk of the on-site equipment installation, or turnover, training performed by GEMS is included with the equipment purchase and is not contained in the customer education revenue numbers.) Although the revenue numbers for TiP-TV™ seem small in relation to GEMS' overall revenue, TiP-TV™, in a few short years, now accounts for just over 80 percent of GEMS' total customer education revenue (Exhibit 8).

While there is clearly more room for growth for TiP-TV™ within the GEMS installed base, GEMS managers are in the beginning stages of broadening TiP-TV™'s scope and target market. Future revenue growth will come from two sources:

• Signing up additional—especially global—hospital subscribers.

• Selling TiP-TV™ network access to other content providers that want to address the same health care audience in the network.

GEMS has already forged an agreement with several health care companies that have produced original programs to be aired on the TiP-TV™ network. In many cases,

EXHIBIT 8
1996 TiP-TV™
Revenue Sources

Source: GEMS, 1997.

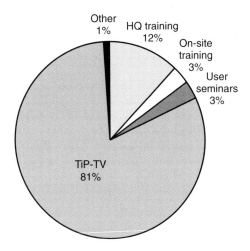

the programs will be offered to subscribing hospitals free of charge. GEMS will charge the health care companies a fee to use its TiP-TV™ network access. The intent is to address more needs within the hospital beyond radiology, and at the same time defray TiP-TV™ radiology programming production costs.

TiP-TV™ Customer Benefits

TiP-TV™ is designed to be a customer-driven service product. GEMS customers regularly contribute to program production in partnership with GE. Through TiP-TV™, GEMS is able to demonstrate a total commitment to customer support through the entire product life cycle. The specific benefits to customers include these:

- Cost-effective training: The average hospital has 14 diagnostic imaging technologists. The average cost of sending one of these technologists to a GEMS training class program at the GEMS Education Center is $1,900. A more economical solution is on-site training, which costs, on average, $1,100 per day. On-site trainers will train up to four technologists for this price. The primary drawback is that the hospital's equipment must be taken out of production to be used for training. An average subscription to TiP-TV™ is $3,000 per year. For this price, all 14 technologists can receive the benefits of training either live or through videotaped programs.

- Point of need training: GE encourages TiP-TV™ subscribers to videotape the initial, interactive program broadcasts. Subscribers can build their own library of programs to be used when needed, such as for new hires and refresher courses.

- CEU credits (continuing education units): Coincident with the full-scale launch of TiP-TV™, the ARRT (American Registry of Radiologic Technologists) passed a mandatory requirement for continuing education credits. In addition, the Society of Nuclear Medicine and the Society of Diagnostic Medical Sonographers also require continuing education. TiP-TV™ is approved by all of the major professional organizations and state licensing bodies for continuing education credits.

- Improved quality of patient care through more knowledgeable technologists and fewer retakes.

EXHIBIT 9
An Actual Letter
from the Field

Source: GEMS, 1997.

February 3, 1997

Dear Jack,

I am the service manager covering Tennessee. Not too long ago I was visiting with Sherry Brown,* Radiology Manager for one of my major medical center customers. During our visit, Sherry brought up the subject of TiP-TV™. At the time, the medical center did not have a TiP-TV™ subscription. Sherry told me she was prompted to ask me about TiP-TV™ after interviewing a person for a technologist position in the radiology department. She said the person being interviewed asked if the medical center had TiP-TV™. The interviewee also stated she ultimately wanted to work at a place which offered continuing education opportunities, specifically TiP-TV™!

Sherry immediately realized the value of TiP-TV™ not only as continuing education for her staff but also as a "recruiting" tool. Well, not too long after our conversation, I had customized a nice TiP-TV™ subscription for Sherry. They are now on-line and I have received VERY positive feedback from Sherry on the broadcasts which have been viewed so far!

From a service manager's perspective, TiP-TV™ rates right up there with InSite™ when it comes to demonstrating value to our customers! Keep up the good work!

Ron

*fictional name

- Higher hospital employee satisfaction—with TiP-TV™, hospitals are more willing to invest in continuing education (Exhibit 9).

Sales and Marketing for TiP-TV™

GEMS services are sold either by the product salesforce or the dedicated service salesforce. Telesales are also involved. The dedicated service salesforce, which reports to the service delivery organization, sells most of the subscriptions. TiP-TV™ was built into a service contract offering package for GEMS equipment service customers. The majority (80 percent) of subscribers purchase TiP-TV™ in conjunction with their equipment service contracts. The other 20 percent of subscribers purchase TiP-TV™ services a la carte.

TiP™ coordinates its marketing efforts with those of GEMS' Services Marketing Department. The marketing strategy is based on leveraging multiple channels to accelerate market penetration. Typical marketing communications and promotional activities include

- Trade journal ads.
- Trade show exhibits.
- Videos.
- Course catalogs.
- Customer testimonials.

- Descriptive brochures.

- Direct mail.

- Customer tours of the GEMS education center.

- Internet/intranet.

A Marketing Strategy to Move from Free to Fee

GE has historically provided "free" application training. GEMS is challenged to shift to a direct fee-for-service model in its education offerings. Diagnostic medical systems are large, complex, and expensive. It is not possible for technologists to use the equipment without thorough training. Consequently customers believe that the training should be "free." At the same time, the customer wants to start running patients through its new $1.5 million systems as soon as possible to start generating revenue. Customers are not willing to invest time, money, and resources into training.

ITSMA has often noted that when a company moves its services from "free" to "fee," it is often the salespeople, not the customer, who are most resistant to the change. GEMS recognized that it needed to convince the sales representatives of the benefits of TiP-TV™ to their customers. The marketing strategy included providing sales representatives with a laptop software program that does a cost–benefit analysis for TiP-TV™. The program demonstrates how the customer will save money because of reduced pilot error and image retakes, better equipment utilization, and improved diagnostic quality.

TiP-TV™ Competition

Competition for TiP-TV™ comes from two sources:

- Television networks, such as HSTN Network/Wescott Communications, Lambert (now defunct), Voluntary Hospitals of America (VHA): In comparison to these competitors, GEMS TiP-TV™ has a larger subscriber base and provides a greater breadth of coverage and, GE believes, better quality programming.

- Imaging and medical systems companies, such as Philips, Picker, Siemens, and Toshiba: These companies are not currently offering customer satellite training. Therefore, the competition is in the form of traditional on-site training classes and seminars.

No other medical systems company has a customer satellite TV training program. Even four years after the launch of TiP-TV™, no other manufacturers have entered the market. Consequently, TiP-TV™ continues to be a key differentiator for GEMS in a market where much of the core technology has reached competitive parity.

Results

The initial goals of the TiP-TV™ program were to

- Increase the number of times GEMS "touches" the customer.

- Increase customer satisfaction and loyalty.

- Improve the skill level of the customer.

In light of the large up-front capital investment, TiP-TV™ was not expected to be profitable. It was expected to be virtually self-funding by reallocating the TiP™

applications organization's resources. At this time, TiP-TV™ breaks even. The program has the potential to turn profitable in 1997 or 1998.

GEMS has achieved its initial goals for TiP-TV™. The number of times GEMS "touches" the customer has increased dramatically since the inception of the program. There are three ways that TiP-TV™ has positively impacted GE's contact with customers. TiP-TV™ has increased the number of

- Times one customer site can be touched.

- People per customer site "touched."

- Sites that can be touched with a single effort.

Four years ago the average number of customer training "touches" per customer was nine days per year. Today, GEMS estimates the average number of "touches" per year to be 21 days.

Customer training satisfaction, the primary measurement, is at an all-time high. GEMS surveys its customer base on a regular basis. Applications education was the number one dissatisfier five years ago. Today, applications education is the number one *satisfier.* Over half of the customers surveyed rate education a "five" on a one-to-five scale (Exhibit 10).

The increases in customer satisfaction and times customers are "touched" are even more impressive when one considers that the costs of serving the customers have remained virtually flat. By substituting technology for on-site visits, GEMS has succeeded in solidifying its customer relationships without incremental cost (Exhibit 11).

A secondary benefit of TiP-TV™ is slowing the erosion of service-contract average sale price (ASP) in a very competitive market. Furthermore, better-trained, high-performance customers are less likely to commit pilot error and need support center assistance.

Through a combination of excellent product support and new product technology, GEMS has succeeded in gaining market share. Every avenue to sustain or grow market share is significant in a low growth market. In the last few years, GEMS estimates that it has gained approximately four to five points of market share in the United States.

TiP-TV™ is not the only best practice program coming from GEMS' customer education organization. There are other TiP™ programs that demonstrate how partner-

EXHIBIT 10
GEMS' Customer
Satisfaction Survey
Results

Source: GEMS, 1997.

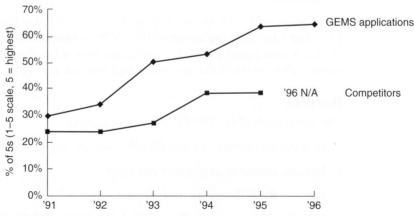

♦ Application training is now one of GEMS' top customer satisfiers.
■ GEMS is widening its competitive advantage.

EXHIBIT 11
Technology-Based Training (TBT) Plays a Key Role in TiP™ Educational Offerings

Source: GEMS, 1997.

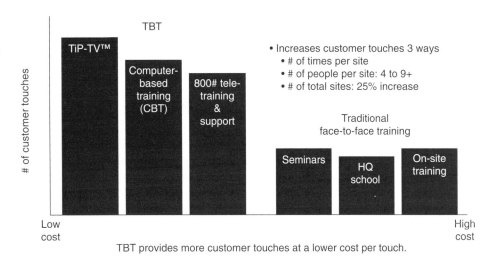

ships between multiple functional departments to create learning relationships with customers can lead to superior business performance and customer satisfaction.

TWO TELEPHONE HELP LINES, ONE SUPPORT CENTER

GEMS' OnLine Center houses two distinct customer support answer lines:

- OnLine Center Engineers.

- TiP™ Applications OnLine.

The OnLine Center Engineers telephone support organization is staffed with 180 engineers who are prepared to resolve any *emergency* repair or equipment maintenance issues. They use the specialized, proprietary technology called InSite™ to perform remote maintenance on customer imaging systems. GEMS remote diagnostic system, InSite™, is a cornerstone in GEMS' maintenance services strategy. InSite™ technology also plays a major role in training customers, as will be discussed in the paragraphs that follow.

The GEMS customer education organization runs a toll-free help line called TiP™ Applications OnLine. This is a *nonemergency* information source. Applications support specialists are available to answer questions regarding the everyday operation of the equipment, as well as the support services available from GEMS. TiP™ Applications OnLine functions as the centerpiece of GEMS' TiP™ educational programs. Its applications experts have the primary responsibility for building and maintaining the dialogue with customers. The information collected by the Applications OnLine staff is collected and analyzed, forming the basis of the ongoing *learning* relationships that help GEMS customize its marketing and educational services.

Although the OnLine Center Engineers and TiP™ Applications OnLine support lines perform two very different functions and report to two distinct organizations, they are colocated at a centralized support center. In fact, TiP™ Applications OnLine services support specialists sit in the same work areas with OnLine Center Engineers. Consequently, they work together to solve applications and repair problems in a way that is transparent to the customer. For example, a customer called the OnLine Center Engineers with what appeared to be a malfunction of the equipment; the images did not look right. GE avoided a time-consuming and costly troubleshooting process due to the close working relationship with the applications specialists. The Applications OnLine specialist viewed the images and advised the customer that the patient was positioned in the machine backward for the particular application!

CUSTOMER EDUCATION AND INSITE™: TELETRAINING

GEMS has developed a remote customer training program, TiP™ Telephone Conference Training. The TiP™ training team uses the GEMS InSite™ technology as the foundation of these cost-effective training sessions. With the remote diagnosis tools, the GE trainers can dial directly into some customers' equipment consoles to demonstrate the use of product features and capabilities. Teletraining is offered to customers free of charge. It is a cost-effective way to spend concentrated time with customers, responding to their individual training needs. GE conducts approximately 2,200 to 2,500 training teleconferences each year. Still, the full potential of this training modality has yet to be tapped. There is a great opportunity to use this powerful teaching tool globally.

The applications support specialists that staff the TiP™ Applications OnLine help desk identify training deficiencies in the installed customer base. They track the questions they receive and suggest TiP™ programs the customers may take advantage of for further training. GE uses the information it receives from the service relationship to deliver customized training to correct knowledge or usage problems. GE is identifying and satisfying a customer need that the customer may not even be aware of. This is yet another way for GE to "touch" the customer, gain intelligence, and ensure satisfaction with GE products and services.

"TRY IT, YOU'LL LIKE IT" PROGRAM

People do not often think of education and training services as a channel of distribution. Nevertheless, some at GE have realized that education services provide an ideal access point to the equipment installed base. By modifying an existing program and taking advantage of already developed technology, GE has created a very successful sales and marketing "try it, you'll like it" program called Flex-Trial.

One of the TiP™ educational offerings, described above, is teletraining—a formal training session conducted by telephone. GEMS uses the InSite™ technology to communicate interactively with the equipment at the customer's site, making this a very effective medium. The teletraining program has recently been expanded to support the Flex-Trial program.

GEMS has developed approximately 20 different software applications that are "add-ons" to the basic applications that come with its equipment. The economics of the direct GEMS salesforce do not allow them sufficient time for selling the new software. Consequently, GEMS has established a telemarketing team to aid in the sale of its more advanced applications software. Telemarketing representatives identify appropriate customers that are interested in learning more about the new applications software programs. They are sent a copy of the software that is good for 60 days after installation. Once the software is installed, a 1.5 hour "TiP™ Teledemo" is scheduled with the prospect to introduce the features of the software. After the telephone conference training session, the telemarketing team follows up with the customer to get feedback, and hopefully, close the sale.

The Flex-Trial program has been operational for approximately eight months. By all accounts it has been very successful. In addition to selling the software applications, GEMS has increased the number of customer "touches." In the process, GE has gleaned some very important feedback from the customers about its products and services, and any other issues important to the customers. Customer satisfaction improves as customers have more opportunity to learn about the capabilities of their GE equipment.

The Flex-Trial program is a wonderful example of a partnership between marketing, sales, and a services delivery organization. The program itself is structured as a marketing/sales program. The customer education organization receives no revenue for its services, but does get some help from marketing to offset costs. Beyond the cost recovery, GEMS customer education believes that the value of the information it obtains from the additional customer interactions and the impact on customer satisfaction are well worth its time and resources.

THE TiP™ GUARANTEE

TiP™ offers its on-site applications training customers an unconditional, easy to understand, and easy to invoke training services guarantee:

> Should you feel that any fully participating attendees in a guaranteed TiP™ on-site training program are not competent in performing at least 95% of the tasks required for the basic operation of the system, we'll return for up to two days to revisit the areas in which they need additional work. There will be no charge, provided you notify us of deficiencies within two months of course completion.

Despite the unpredictability inherent in providing services, GEMS has chosen to guarantee its customer education services. No other medical imaging vendor has an explicit customer education guarantee. The message conveyed is that GEMS has confidence in its ability to deliver customer satisfaction. The guarantee supports the notion of a committed partnership between GEMS and the costumer.

Approximately 5 percent of GEMS on-site training customers invoke the TiP™ training guarantee. In many of these cases, GEMS can use its carefully documented training logs to trace the nonperformance issues back to failure of the customer's technologists to "fully participate" in training. Still, GEMS honors these guarantees as part of its mission to maximize customer satisfaction.

To reduce the number of times customers invoke the training guarantee without justification, GEMS is challenged to better set customers' expectations. There are a number of avenues to influence customer expectations that span marketing, sales, and services delivery. TiP™ collateral and trainers carefully describe the need for full participation. Working closely with the GEMS sales organization, TiP™ aims to educate its customers about the importance of training and the need for "full participation." However, initiatives for getting the salesforce to focus on this issue have been only partially effective to date.

Case 7

STARBUCKS: DELIVERING CUSTOMER SERVICE

In mid-2002, Christine Day, Starbucks' senior vice president of administration in North America, sat in the seventh-floor conference room of Starbucks' Seattle headquarters and reached for her second cup of *toffee nut latte*. The handcrafted beverage—a buttery, toffee-nut flavored espresso concoction topped with whipped cream and toffee sprinkles—had become a regular afternoon indulgence for Day ever since its introduction earlier that year.

As she waited for her colleagues to join her, Day reflected on the company's recent performance. While other retailers were still reeling from the post-9/11 recession, Starbucks was enjoying its 11th consecutive year of 5% or higher comparable store sales growth, prompting its founder and chairman, Howard Schultz, to declare: "I think we've demonstrated that we are close to a recession-proof product."[1]

Day, however, was not feeling nearly as sanguine, in part because Starbucks' most recent market research had revealed some unexpected findings. "We've always taken great pride in our retail service," said Day, "but according to the data, we're not always meeting our customers' expectations in the area of customer satisfaction."

As a result of these concerns, Day and her associates had come up with a plan to invest an additional $40 million annually in the company's 4,500 stores, which would allow each store to add the equivalent of 20 hours of labor a week. "The idea is to improve speed-of-service and thereby increase customer satisfaction," said Day.

In two days, Day was due to make a final recommendation to both Schultz and Orin Smith, Starbucks' CEO, about whether the company should move forward with the plan. "The investment is the EPS [earnings per share] equivalent of almost seven cents a share," said Day. In preparation for her meeting with Schultz and Smith, Day had asked one of her associates to help her think through the implications of the plan. Day

[1] Jake Batsell, "A Grande Decade for Starbucks," *The Seattle Times,* June 26, 2002.

noted, "The real question is, do we believe what our customers are telling us about what constitutes 'excellent' customer service? And if we deliver it, what will the impact be on our sales and profitability?"

COMPANY BACKGROUND

The story of how Howard Schultz managed to transform a commodity into an upscale cultural phenomenon has become the stuff of legends. In 1971, three coffee fanatics—Gerald Baldwin, Gordon Bowker and Ziev Siegl—opened a small coffee shop in Seattle's Pike Place Market. The shop specialized in selling whole arabica beans to a niche market of coffee purists.

In 1982 Schultz joined the Starbucks marketing team; shortly thereafter, he traveled to Italy where he became fascinated with Milan's coffee culture, in particular, the role the neighborhood espresso bars played in Italians' everyday social lives. Upon his return, the inspired Schultz convinced the company to set up an espresso bar in the corner of its only downtown Seattle shop. As Schultz explained, the bar became the prototype for his long-term vision:

> The idea was to create a chain of coffeehouses that would become America's "third place."
> At the time, most Americans had two places in their lives—home and work. But I believed
> that people needed another place, a place where they could go to relax and enjoy others, or
> just be by themselves. I envisioned a place that would be separate from home or work, a
> place that would mean different things to different people.

A few years later, Schultz got his chance when Starbucks' founders agreed to sell him the company. As soon as Schultz took over, he immediately began opening new stores. The stores sold whole beans and premium-priced coffee beverages by the cup and catered primarily to affluent, well-educated, white-collar patrons (skewed female) between the ages of 25 and 44. By 1992, the company had 140 such stores in the Northwest and Chicago and was successfully competing against other small-scale coffee chains such as Gloria Jean's Coffee Bean and Barnie's Coffee & Tea.

That same year, Schultz decided to take the company public. As he recalled, many Wall Street types were dubious about the idea: "They'd say, 'You mean, you're going to sell coffee for a dollar in a paper cup, with Italian names that no one in America can say? At a time in America when no one's drinking coffee? And I can get coffee at the local coffee shop or doughnut shop for 50 cents? Are you kidding me?'"[2]

Ignoring the skeptics Schultz forged ahead with the public offering, raising $25 million in the process. The proceeds allowed Starbucks to open more stores across the nation.

By mid-2002, Schultz had unequivocally established Starbucks as the dominant specialty-coffee brand in North America. Sales had climbed at a compound annual growth rate (CAGR) of 40% since the company had gone public, and net earnings had risen at a CAGR of 50%. The company was now serving 20 million unique customers in well over 5,000 stores around the globe and was opening on average three new stores a day. (See **Exhibits 1–3** for company financials and store growth over time.)

What made Starbucks' success even more impressive was that the company had spent almost nothing on advertising to achieve it. North American marketing primarily consisted of point-of-sale materials and local-store marketing and was far less than the industry average. (Most fast-food chains had marketing budgets in the 3%–6% range.)

---

[2]Batsell.

EXHIBIT 1   **Starbucks' Financials, FY1998 to FY2002 ($ in millions)**

	FY1998	**FY1999**	**FY2000**	**FY2001**	**FY2002**
Revenue					
Co-Owned North American	1,076.8	1,375.0	1,734.9	2,086.4	2,583.8
Co-Owned Int'l (UK, Thailand, Australia)	25.8	48.4	88.7	143.2	209.1
Total Company-Operated Retail	1,102.6	1,423.4	1,823.6	2,229.6	2,792.9
Specialty Operations	206.1	263.4	354.0	419.4	496.0
Net Revenues	1,308.7	1,686.8	2,177.6	2,649.0	3,288.9
Cost of Goods Sold	578.5	747.6	961.9	1,112.8	1,350.0
Gross Profit	730.2	939.2	1,215.7	1,536.2	1,938.9
Joint-Venture Income[a]	1.0	3.2	20.3	28.6	35.8
Expenses:					
Store Operating Expense	418.5	543.6	704.9	875.5	1,121.1
Other Operating Expense	44.5	54.6	78.4	93.3	127.2
Depreciation & Amortization Expense	72.5	97.8	130.2	163.5	205.6
General & Admin Expense	77.6	89.7	110.2	151.4	202.1
Operating Expenses	613.1	785.7	1,023.8	1,283.7	1,656.0
Operating Profit	109.2	156.7	212.3	281.1	310.0
Net Income	68.4	101.7	94.5	181.2	215.1
% Change in Monthly Comparable Store Sales[b]					
North America	5%	6%	9%	5%	7%
Consolidated	5%	6%	9%	5%	6%

Source: Adapted from company reports and Lehman Brothers, November 5, 2002.
[a]Includes income from various joint ventures, including Starbucks' partnership with the Pepsi-Cola Company to develop and distribute Frappuccino and with Dreyer's Grand Ice Cream to develop and distribute premium ice creams.
[b]Includes only company-operated stores open 13 months or longer.

EXHIBIT 2   **Starbucks' Store Growth**

	FY1998	**FY1999**	**FY2000**	**FY2001**	**FY2002**
Total North America	1,755	2,217	2,976	3,780	4,574
Company-Operated	1,622	2,038	2,446	2,971	3,496
Licensed Stores[a]	133	179	530	809	1,078
Total International	131	281	525	929	1,312
Company-Operated	66	97	173	295	384
Licensed Stores	65	184	352	634	928
Total Stores	1,886	2,498	3,501	4,709	5,886

Source: Company reports.
[a]Includes kiosks located in grocery stores, bookstores, hotels, airports, and so on.

EXHIBIT 3   **Additional Data, North American Company-Operated Stores (FY2002)**

	Average
Average hourly rate with shift supervisors and hourly partners	$ 9.00
Total labor hours per week, average store	360
Average weekly store volume	$15,400
Average ticket	$3.85
Average daily customer count per store	570

Source: Company reports.

For his part, Schultz remained as chairman and chief global strategist in control of the company, handing over day-to-day operations in 2002 to CEO Orin Smith, a Harvard MBA (1967) who had joined the company in 1990.

THE STARBUCKS VALUE PROPOSITION

Starbucks' brand strategy was best captured by its "live coffee" mantra, a phrase that reflected the importance the company attached to keeping the national coffee culture alive. From a retail perspective, this meant creating an "experience" around the consumption of coffee, an experience that people could weave into the fabric of their everyday lives.

There were three components to this experiential branding strategy. The first component was the coffee itself. Starbucks prided itself on offering what it believed to be the highest-quality coffee in the world, sourced from the Africa, Central and South America, and Asia-Pacific regions. To enforce its exacting coffee standards, Starbucks controlled as much of the supply chain as possible—it worked directly with growers in various countries of origin to purchase green coffee beans, it oversaw the custom-roasting process for the company's various blends and single-origin coffees, and it controlled distribution to retail stores around the world.

The second brand component was service, or what the company sometimes referred to as "customer intimacy." "Our goal is to create an uplifting experience every time you walk through our door," explained Jim Alling, Starbucks senior vice president of North American retail. "Our most loyal customers visit us as often as 18 times a month, so it could be something as simple as recognizing you and knowing your drink or customizing your drink just the way you like it."

The third brand component was atmosphere. "People come for the coffee," explained Day, "but the ambience is what makes them want to stay." For that reason, most Starbucks had seating areas to encourage lounging and layouts that were designed to provide an upscale yet inviting environment for those who wanted to linger. "What we have built has universal appeal," remarked Schultz. "It's based on the human spirit, it's based on a sense of community, the need for people to come together."[3]

Channels of Distribution

Almost all of Starbucks' locations in North America were company-operated stores located in high-traffic, high-visibility settings such as retail centers, office buildings, and university campuses.[4] In addition to selling whole-bean coffees, these stores sold rich-brewed coffees, Italian-style espresso drinks, cold-blended beverages, and premium teas. Product mixes tended to vary depending on a store's size and location, but most stores offered a variety of pastries, sodas, and juices, along with coffee-related accessories and equipment, music CDs, games, and seasonal novelty items. (About 500 stores even carried a selection of sandwiches and salads.)

Beverages accounted for the largest percentage of sales in these stores (77%); this represented a change from 10 years earlier, when about half of store revenues had come from sales of whole-bean coffees (See **Exhibit 4** for retail sales mix by product type; see **Exhibit 5** for a typical menu board and price list).

[3]Batsell.

[4]Starbucks had recently begun experimenting with drive-throughs. Less than 10% of its stores had drive-throughs, but in these stores, the drive-throughs accounted for 50% of all business.

EXHIBIT 4
Product Mix, North
American Company-
Operated Stores
(FY2002)

	Percent of Sales
Retail Product Mix	
Coffee Beverages	77%
Food Items	13%
Whole-Bean Coffees	6%
Equipment & Accessories	4%

Source: Company reports.

Starbucks also sold coffee products through non-company-operated retail channels; these so-called "Specialty Operations" accounted for 15% of net revenues. About 27% of these revenues came from North American food-service accounts, that is, sales of whole-bean and ground coffees to hotels, airlines, restaurants, and the like. Another 18% came from domestic retail store licenses that, in North America, were only granted when there was no other way to achieve access to desirable retail space (e.g., in airports).

The remaining 55% of specialty revenues came from a variety of sources, including international licensed stores, grocery stores and warehouse clubs (Kraft Foods handled marketing and distribution for Starbucks in this channel), and online and mail-order sales. Starbucks also had a joint venture with Pepsi-Cola to distribute bottled Frappuccino beverages in North America, as well as a partnership with Dreyer's Grand Ice Cream to develop and distribute a line of premium ice creams.

Day explained the company s broad distribution strategy:

> Our philosophy is pretty straightforward—we want to reach customers where they work, travel, shop, and dine. In order to do this, we sometimes have to establish relationships with third parties that share our values and commitment to quality. This is a particularly effective way to reach newcomers with our brand. It s a lot less intimidating to buy Starbucks at a grocery store than it is to walk into one of our coffeehouses for the first time. In fact, about 40% of our new coffeehouse customers have already tried the Starbucks brand before they walk through our doors. Even something like ice cream has become an important trial vehicle for us.

Starbucks Partners

All Starbucks employees were called "partners." The company employed 60,000 partners worldwide, about 50,000 in North America. Most were hourly-wage employees (called *baristas*) who worked in Starbucks retail stores. Alling remarked, "From day one, Howard has made clear his belief that partner satisfaction leads to customer satisfaction. This belief is part of Howard's DNA, and because it's been pounded into each and every one of us, it's become part of our DNA too."

The company had a generous policy of giving health insurance and stock options to even the most entry-level partners, most of whom were between the ages of 17 and 23. Partly as a result of this, Starbucks' partner satisfaction rate consistently hovered in the 80% to 90% range, well above the industry norm,[5] and the company had recently been ranked 47th in the *Fortune* magazine list of best places to work, quite an accomplishment for a company with so many hourly-wage workers.

---

[5]Industrywide, employee satisfaction rates tended to be in the 50% to 60% range. Source: Starbucks, 2000.

EXHIBIT 5 Typical Menu Board and Price List for North American Company-Owned Store

Espresso Traditions	Tall	Grande	Venti
Classic Favorites			
Toffee Nut Latte	2.95	3.50	3.80
Vanilla Latte	2.85	3.40	3.70
Caffe Latte	2.55	3.10	3.40
Cappuccino	2.55	3.10	3.40
Caramel Macchiato	2.80	3.40	3.65
White Chocolate Mocha	3.20	3.75	4.00
Caffe Mocha	2.75	3.30	3.55
Caffe Americano	1.75	2.05	2.40

Espresso	Solo		Doppio
Espresso	1.45		1.75

Extras		
Additional Espresso Shot		.55
Add flavored syrup		.30
Organic milk & soy available upon request		

Frappuccino Ice Blended Beverages	Tall	Grande	Venti
Coffee	2.65	3.15	3.65
Mocha	2.90	3.40	3.90
Caramel Frappuccino	3.15	3.65	4.15
Mocha Coconut (limited offering)	3.15	3.65	4.15

Créme Frappuccino Ice Blended Créme	Tall	Grande	Venti
Toffee Nut Créme	3.15	3.65	4.15
Vanilla Créme	2.65	3.15	3.65
Coconut Créme	3.15	3.65	4.15

Tazo Tea Frappuccino Ice Blended Teas	Tall	Grande	Venti
Tazo Citrus	2.90	3.40	3.90
Tazoberry	2.90	3.40	3.90
Tazo Chai Créme	3.15	3.65	4.15

Brewed Coffee	Tall	Grande	Venti
Coffee of the Day	1.40	1.60	1.70
Decaf of the Day	1.40	1.60	1.70

Cold Beverages	Tall	Grande	Venti
Iced Caffe Latte	2.55	3.10	3.50
Iced Caramel Macchiato	2.80	3.40	3.80
Iced Caffe Americano	1.75	2.05	3.40

Coffee Alternatives	Tall	Grande	Venti
Toffee Nut Créme	2.45	2.70	2.95
Vanilla Créme	2.20	2.45	2.70
Caramel Apple Cider	2.45	2.70	2.95
Hot Chocolate	2.20	2.45	2.70
Tazo Hot Tea	1.15	1.65	1.65
Tazo Chai	2.70	3.10	3.35

Whole Beans: Bold Our most intriguing and exotic coffees	½ lb	1 lb
Gold Coast Blend	5.70	10.95
French Roast	5.20	9.95
Sumatra	5.30	10.15
Decaf Sumatra	5.60	10.65
Ethiopia Sidame	5.20	9.95
Arabian Mocha Sanani	8.30	15.95
Kenya	5.30	10.15
Italian Roast	5.20	9.95
Sulawesi	6.10	11.65

Whole Beans: Smooth Richer, more flavorful coffees	½ lb	1 lb
Espresso Roast	5.20	9.95
Decaf Espresso Roast	5.60	10.65
Yukon Blend	5.20	9.95
Café Verona	5.20	9.95
Guatemala Antigua	5.30	10.15
Arabian Mocha Java	6.30	11.95
Decaf Mocha Java/SWP	6.50	12.45

Whole Beans: Mild The perfect introduction to Starbucks coffees	½ lb	1 lb
Breakfast Blend	5.20	9.95
Lightnote Blend	5.20	9.95
Decaf Lightnote Blend	5.60	10.65
Colombia Narino	5.50	10.45
House Blend	5.20	9.95
Decaf House Blend	5.60	10.65
Fair Trade Coffee	5.95	11.45

In addition, Starbucks had one of the lowest employee turnover rates in the industry—just 70%, compared with fast-food industry averages as high as 300%. The rate was even lower for managers, and as Alling noted, the company was always looking for ways to bring turnover down further: "Whenever we have a problem store, we almost always find either an inexperienced store manager or inexperienced baristas. Manager stability is key—it not only decreases partner turnover, but it also enables the store to do a much better job of recognizing regular customers and providing personalized service. So our goal is to make the position a lifetime job."

To this end, the company encouraged promotion from within its own ranks. About 70% of the company's store managers were ex-baristas, and about 60% of its district managers were ex-store managers. In fact, upon being hired, all senior executives had to train and succeed as baristas before being allowed to assume their positions in corporate headquarters.

DELIVERING ON SERVICE

When a partner was hired to work in one of Starbucks' North American retail stores, he or she had to undergo two types of training. The first type focused on "hard skills" such as learning how to use the cash register and learning how to mix drinks. Most Starbucks beverages were handcrafted, and to ensure product quality, there was a pre-specified process associated with each drink. Making an espresso beverage, for example, required seven specific steps.

The other type of training focused on "soft skills." Alling explained:

> In our training manual, we explicitly teach partners to connect with customers—to enthusiastically welcome them to the store, to establish eye contact, to smile, and to try to remember their names and orders if they're regulars. We also encourage partners to create conversations with customers using questions that require more than a yes or no answer. So for example, "I noticed you were looking at the menu board—what types of beverages do you typically enjoy?" is a good question for a partner to ask.

Starbucks "Just Say Yes" policy empowered partners to provide the best service possible, even if it required going beyond company rules. "This means that if a customer spills a drink and asks for a refill, we'll give it to him," said Day. "Or if a customer doesn't have cash and wants to pay with a check (which we aren't supposed to accept), then we'll give her a sample drink for free. The last thing we want to do is win the argument and lose the customer."

Most barista turnover occurred within the first 90 days of employment; if a barista lasted beyond that, there was a high probability that he or she would stay for three years or more. "Our training ends up being a self-selection process," Alling said. Indeed, the ability to balance hard and soft skills required a particular type of person, and Alling believed the challenges had only grown over time:

> Back in the days when we sold mostly beans, every customer who walked in the door was a coffee connoisseur, and it was easy for baristas to engage in chitchat while ringing up a bag. Those days are long gone. Today, almost every customer orders a handcrafted beverage. If the line is stretching out the door and everyone's clamoring for their coffee fix, it's not that easy to strike up a conversation with a customer.

The complexity of the barista's job had also increased over time; making a *venti tazoberry and crème,* for instance, required 10 different steps. "It used to be that a barista could make every variation of drink we offered in half a day," Day observed.

"Nowadays, given our product proliferation, it would take 16 days of eight-hour shifts. There are literally hundreds of combinations of drinks in our portfolio."

This job complexity was compounded by the fact that almost half of Starbucks' customers customized their drinks. According to Day, this created a tension between product quality and customer focus for Starbucks:

> On the one hand, we train baristas to make beverages to our preestablished quality standards—this means enforcing a consistent process that baristas can master. On the other hand, if a customer comes in and wants it their way—extra vanilla, for instance—what should we do? Our heaviest users are always the most demanding. Of course, every time we customize, we slow down the service for everyone else. We also put a lot of strain on our baristas, who are already dealing with an extraordinary number of sophisticated drinks.

One obvious solution to the problem was to hire more baristas to share the workload; however, the company had been extremely reluctant to do this in recent years, particularly given the economic downturn. Labor was already the company's largest expense item in North America (see **Exhibit 3**), and Starbucks stores tended to be located in urban areas with high wage rates. Instead, the company had focused on increasing barista efficiency by removing all non-value-added tasks, simplifying the beverage production process, and tinkering with the facility design to eliminate bottlenecks.

In addition, the company had recently begun installing automated espresso machines in its North American cafés. The *verismo* machines, which decreased the number of steps required to make an espresso beverage, reduced waste, improved consistency, and had generated an overwhelmingly positive customer and barista response.

Measuring Service Performance

Starbucks tracked service performance using a variety of metrics, including monthly status reports and self-reported checklists. The company's most prominent measurement tool was a mystery shopper program called the "Customer Snapshot." Under this program, every store was visited by an anonymous mystery shopper three times a quarter. Upon completing the visit, the shopper would rate the store on four "Basic Service" criteria:

- **Service**—Did the register partner verbally greet the customer? Did the barista and register partner make eye contact with the customer? Say thank you?

- **Cleanliness**—Was the store clean? The counters? The tables? The restrooms?

- **Product quality**—Was the order filled accurately? Was the temperature of the drink within range? Was the beverage properly presented?

- **Speed of service**—How long did the customer have to wait? The company's goal was to serve a customer within three minutes, from back-of-the-line to drink-in-hand. This benchmark was based on market research which indicated that the three-minute standard was a key component in how current Starbucks customers defined "excellent service."

In addition to Basic Service, stores were also rated on "Legendary Service," which was defined as "behavior that created a memorable experience for a customer, that inspired a customer to return often and tell a friend." Legendary Service scores were based on secret shopper observations of service attributes such as partners initiating conversations with customers, partners recognizing customers by name or drink order, and partners being responsive to service problems.

During 2002, the company's Customer Snapshot scores had increased across all stores (see **Exhibit 6**), leading Day to comment, "The Snapshot is not a perfect measurement tool, but we believe it does a good job of measuring trends over the course of a quarter. In order for a store to do well on the Snapshot, it needs to have sustainable processes in place that create a well-established pattern of doing things right so that it gets 'caught' doing things right."

COMPETITION

In the United States, Starbucks competed against a variety of small-scale specialty coffee chains, most of which were regionally concentrated. Each tried to differentiate itself from Starbucks in a different way. For example, Minneapolis-based Caribou Coffee, which operated more than 200 stores in nine states, differentiated itself on store environment. Rather than offer an upscale, pseudo-European atmosphere, its strategy was to simulate the look and feel of an Alaskan lodge, with knotty-pine cabinetry, fireplaces, and soft seating. Another example was California-based Peet's Coffee & Tea, which operated about 70 stores in five states. More than 60% of Peet's revenues came from the sale of whole beans. Peet's strategy was to build a super-premium brand by offering the freshest coffee on the market. One of the ways it delivered on this promise was by "roasting to order," that is, by hand roasting small batches of coffee at its California plant and making sure that all of its coffee shipped within 24 hours of roasting.

Starbucks also competed against thousands of independent specialty coffee shops. Some of these independent coffee shops offered a wide range of food and beverages, including beer, wine, and liquor; others offered satellite televisions or Internet-connected computers. Still others differentiated themselves by delivering highly personalized service to an eclectic clientele.

Finally, Starbucks competed against donut and bagel chains such as Dunkin Donuts, which operated over 3,700 stores in 38 states. Dunkin Donuts attributed half of its sales to coffee and in recent years had begun offering flavored coffee and noncoffee alternatives, such as Dunkaccino (a coffee and chocolate combination available with various toppings) and Vanilla Chai (a combination of tea, vanilla, honey, and spices).

CAFFEINATING THE WORLD

The company's overall objective was to establish Starbucks as the "most recognized and respected brand in the world."[6] This ambitious goal required an aggressive growth strategy, and in 2002, the two biggest drivers of company growth were retail expansion and product innovation.

Retail Expansion

Starbucks already owned close to one-third of America's coffee bars, more than its next five biggest competitors combined. (By comparison, the U.S.'s second-largest player, Diedrich Coffee, operated fewer than 400 stores.) However, the company had plans to open 525 company-operated and 225 licensed North American stores in 2003, and Schultz believed that there was no reason North America could not eventually expand to at least 10,000 stores. As he put it, "These are still the early days of the company's growth."[7]

---

[6]Starbucks 2002 Annual Report.
[7]Dina ElBoghdady, "Pouring It On: The Starbucks Strategy? Locations, Locations, Locations," *The Washington Post,* August 25, 2002.

EXHIBIT 6   **Customer Snapshot Scores (North American stores)**

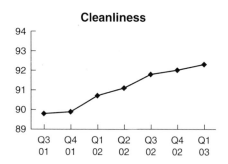

GEMS applications

Competitors

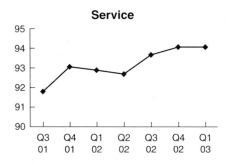

Service

Cleanliness

Product Quality

Average Wait Time
(in minutes.seconds)

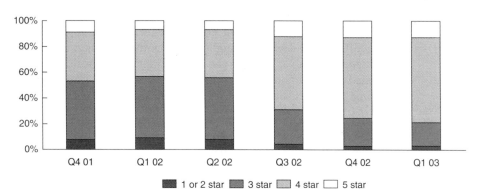

Legendary Service Scores

■ 1 or 2 star   ■ 3 star   □ 4 star   □ 5 star

Source: Company information.

EXHIBIT 7   **Total U.S. Retail Coffee Market (includes both in-home and out-of-home consumption)**

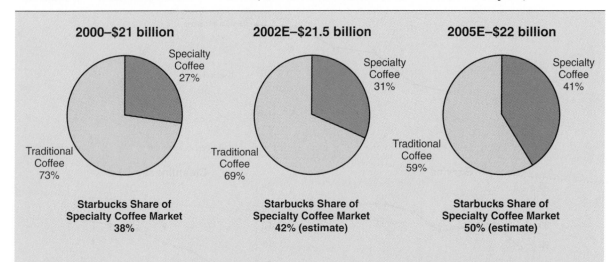

Other estimates[a] for the U.S. retail coffee market in 2002:

- In the home, specialty coffee[b] was estimated to be a $3.2 billion business, of which Starbucks was estimated to have a 4% share.

- In the food service channel, specialty coffee was estimated to be a $5 billion business, of which Starbucks was estimated to have a 5% share.

- In grocery stores, Starbucks was estimated to have a 7.3% share in the ground-coffee category and a 21.7% share in the whole-beans category.

- It was estimated that over the next several years, the overall retail market would grow less than 1% per annum, but growth in the specialty-coffee category would be strong, with compound annual growth rate (CAGR) of 9% to 10%.

- Starbucks' U.S. business was projected to grow at a CAGR of approximately 20% top-line revenue growth.

Source: Adapted from company reports and Lehman Brothers, November 5, 2002.
[a]The value of the retail coffee market was difficult to estimate given the highly fragmented and loosely monitored nature of the market (i.e., specialty coffeehouses, restaurants, delis, kiosks, street carts, grocery and convenience stores, vending machines, etc.).
[b]Specialty coffee includes espresso, cappuccino, latte, café mocha, iced/ice-blended coffee, gourmet coffee (premium whole bean or ground), and blended coffee.

The company's optimistic growth plans were based on a number of considerations:

- First, coffee consumption was on the rise in the United States, following years of decline. More than 109 million people (about half of the U.S. population) now drank coffee every day, and an additional 52 million drank it on occasion. The market's biggest growth appeared to be among drinkers of specialty coffee,[8] and it was estimated that about one-third of all U.S. coffee consumption took place outside of the home, in places such as offices, restaurants, and coffee shops. (See **Exhibit 7.**)

- Second, there were still eight states in the United States without a single company-operated Starbucks; in fact, the company was only in 150 of the roughly 300 metropolitan statistical areas in the nation.

[8]National Coffee Association.

- Third, the company believed it was far from reaching saturation levels in many existing markets. In the Southeast, for example, there was only one store for every 110,000 people (compared with one store for every 20,000 people in the Pacific Northwest). More generally, only seven states had more than 100 Starbucks locations.

Starbucks strategy for expanding its retail business was to open stores in new markets while geographically clustering stores in existing markets. Although the latter often resulted in significant cannibalization, the company believed that this was more than offset by the total incremental sales associated with the increased store concentration. As Schultz readily conceded, "We self-cannibalize at least a third of our stores every day."[9]

When it came to selecting new retail sites, the company considered a number of criteria, including the extent to which the demographics of the area matched the profile of the typical Starbucks drinker, the level of coffee consumption in the area, the nature and intensity of competition in the local market, and the availability of attractive real estate. Once a decision was made to move forward with a site, the company was capable of designing, permitting, constructing, and opening a new store within 16 weeks. A new store typically averaged about $610,000 in sales during its first year; same-store sales (comps) were strongest in the first three years and then continued to comp positively, consistent with the company average.

Starbucks' international expansion plans were equally ambitious. Starbucks already operated over 300 company-owned stores in the United Kingdom, Australia, and Thailand, in addition to about 900 licensed stores in various countries in Asia, Europe, the Middle East, Africa, and Latin America. (Its largest international market was Japan, with close to 400 stores.) The company's goal was to ultimately have 15,000 international stores.

Product Innovation

The second big driver of company growth was product innovation. Internally, this was considered one of the most significant factors in comparable store sales growth, particularly since Starbucks' prices had remained relatively stable in recent years. New products were launched on a regular basis; for example, Starbucks introduced at least one new hot beverage every holiday season.

The new product development process generally operated on a 12- to 18-month cycle, during which the internal research and development (R&D) team tinkered with product formulations, ran focus groups, and conducted in-store experiments and market tests. Aside from consumer acceptance, whether a product made it to market depended on a number of factors, including the extent to which the drink fit into the "ergonomic flow" of operations and the speed with which the beverage could be handcrafted. Most importantly, the success of a new beverage depended on partner acceptance. "We've learned that no matter how great a drink it is, if our partners aren't excited about it, it won't sell," said Alling.

In recent years, the company's most successful innovation had been the 1995 introduction of a coffee and non-coffee-based line of Frappuccino beverages, which had driven same-store sales primarily by boosting traffic during nonpeak hours. The bottled version of the beverage (distributed by PepsiCo) had become a $400 million[10]

[9]ElBoghdady.
[10]Refers to sales at retail. Actual revenue contribution was much lower due to the joint-venture structure.

franchise; it had managed to capture 90% of the ready-to-drink coffee category, in large part due to its appeal to non-coffee-drinking 20-somethings.

Service Innovation

In terms of nonproduct innovation, Starbucks' stored-value card (SVC) had been launched in November 2001. This prepaid, swipeable smart card—which Schultz referred to as "the most significant product introduction since Frappuccino"[11]—could be used to pay for transactions in any company-operated store in North America. Early indications of the SVC's appeal were very positive: After less than one year on the market, about 6 million cards had been issued, and initial activations and reloads had already reached $160 million in sales. In surveys, the company had learned that cardholders tended to visit Starbucks twice as often as cash customers and tended to experience reduced transaction times.

Day remarked, "We've found that a lot of the cards are being given away as gifts, and many of those gift recipients are being introduced to our brand for the first time. Not to mention the fact that the cards allow us to collect all kinds of customer-transaction data, data that we haven't even begun to do anything with yet."

The company's latest service innovation was its T-Mobile HotSpot wireless Internet service, which it planned to introduce in August 2002. The service would offer high-speed access to the Internet in 2,000 Starbucks stores in the United States and Europe, starting at $49.99 a month.

STARBUCKS' MARKET RESEARCH: TROUBLE BREWING?

Interestingly, although Starbucks was considered one of the world's most effective marketing organizations, it lacked a strategic marketing group. In fact, the company had no chief marketing officer, and its marketing department functioned as three separate groups—a market research group that gathered and analyzed market data requested by the various business units, a category group that developed new products and managed the menu and margins, and a marketing group that developed the quarterly promotional plans.

This organizational structure forced all of Starbucks' senior executives to assume marketing-related responsibilities. As Day pointed out, "Marketing is everywhere at Starbucks—it just doesn't necessarily show up in a line item called 'marketing.' Everyone has to get involved in a collaborative marketing effort." However, the organizational structure also meant that market- and customer-related trends could sometimes be overlooked. "We tend to be great at measuring things, at collecting market data," Day noted, "but we are not very disciplined when it comes to using this data to drive decision making." She continued:

> This is exactly what started to happen a few years ago. We had evidence coming in from market research that contradicted some of the fundamental assumptions we had about our brand and our customers. The problem was that this evidence was all over the place—no one was really looking at the "big picture." As a result, it took awhile before we started to take notice.

Starbucks' Brand Meaning

Once the team did take notice, it discovered several things. First, despite Starbucks' overwhelming presence and convenience, there was very little image or product dif-

---

[11]Stanley Holmes, "Starbucks' Card Smarts," *Business Week,* March 18, 2002.

ferentiation between Starbucks and the smaller coffee chains (other than Starbucks' ubiquity) in the minds of specialty coffeehouse customers. There *was* significant differentiation, however, between Starbucks and the independent specialty coffeehouses (see **Table A** below).

More generally, the market research team discovered that Starbucks' brand image had some rough edges. The number of respondents who strongly agreed with the statement "Starbucks cares primarily about making money" was up from 53% in 2000 to 61% in 2001, while the number of respondents who strongly agreed with the statement "Starbucks cares primarily about building more stores" was up from 48% to 55%. Day noted, "It's become apparent that we need to ask ourselves, 'Are we focusing on the right things? Are we clearly communicating our value and values to our customers, instead of just our growth plans?'" (see **Table B** below).

The Changing Customer

The market research team also discovered that Starbucks' customer base was evolving. Starbucks' newer customers tended to be younger, less well-educated, and in a lower income bracket than Starbucks' more established customers. In addition, they visited the stores less frequently and had very different perceptions of the Starbucks brand compared to more established customers (see **Exhibit 8**).

Furthermore, the team learned that Starbucks' historical customer profile—the affluent, well-educated, white-collar female between the ages of 24 and 44—had expanded. For example, about half of the stores in southern California had large numbers

TABLE A
Qualitative Brand Meaning: Independents vs. Starbucks

Independents:
- Social and inclusive
- Diverse and intellectual
- Artsy and funky
- Liberal and free-spirited
- Lingering encouraged
- Particularly appealing to younger coffeehouse customers
- Somewhat intimidating to older, more mainstream coffeehouse customers

Starbucks:
- Everywhere—the trend
- Good coffee on the run
- Place to meet and move on
- Convenience oriented; on the way to work
- Accessible and consistent

Source: Starbucks, based on qualitative interviews with specialty-coffeehouse customers.

TABLE B
The Top Five Attributes Consumers Associate with the Starbucks Brand

- Known for specialty/gourmet coffee (54% strongly agree)
- Widely available (43% strongly agree)
- Corporate (42% strongly agree)
- Trendy (41% strongly agree)
- Always feel welcome at Starbucks (39% strongly agree)

Source: Starbucks, based on 2002 survey.

EXHIBIT 8 **Starbucks' Customer Retention Information**

% of Starbucks customers who first started visiting Starbucks . . .

In the past year	27%
1–2 years ago	20%
2–5 years ago	30%
5 or more years ago	23%

Source: Starbucks, 2002. Based on a sample of Starbucks' 2002 customer base.

	New Customers (first visited in past year)	Established Customers (first visited 5+ years ago)
Percent female	45%	49%
Average Age	36	40
Percent with College Degree +	37%	63%
Average income	$65,000	$81,000
Average # cups of coffee/week (includes at home and away from home)	15	19
Attitudes toward Starbucks:		
High-quality brand	34%	51%
Brand I trust	30%	50%
For someone like me	15%	40%
Worth paying more for	8%	32%
Known for specialty coffee	44%	60%
Known as the coffee expert	31%	45%
Best-tasting coffee	20%	31%
Highest-quality coffee	26%	41%
Overall opinion of Starbucks	**25%**	**44%**

Source: Starbucks, 2002. "Attitudes toward Starbucks" measured according to the percent of customers who agreed with the above statements.

of Hispanic customers. In Florida, the company had stores that catered primarily to Cuban-Americans.

Customer Behavior

With respect to customer behavior, the market research team discovered that, regardless of the market—urban versus rural, new versus established—customers tended to use the stores the same way. The team also learned that, although the company's most frequent customers averaged 18 visits a month, the typical customer visited just five times a month (see **Figure A** on next page).

Measuring and Driving Customer Satisfaction

Finally, the team discovered that, despite its high Customer Snapshot scores, Starbucks was not meeting expectations in terms of customer satisfaction. The satisfaction scores were considered critical because the team also had evidence of a direct link between satisfaction level and customer loyalty (see **Exhibit 9** for customer satisfaction data).

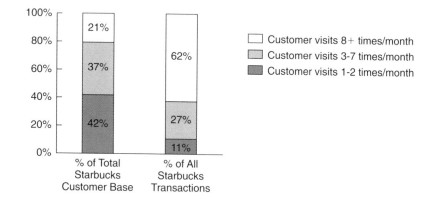

FIGURE A
Customer Visit Frequency

Source: Starbucks, 2002.

- Customer visits 8+ times/month
- Customer visits 3-7 times/month
- Customer visits 1-2 times/month

EXHIBIT 9   **Starbucks' Customer Behavior, by Satisfaction Level**

	Unsatisfied Customer	Satisfied Customer	Highly Satisfied Customer
Number of Starbucks Visits/Month	3.9	4.3	7.2
Average Ticket Size/Visit	$3.88	$4.06	$4.42
Average Customer Life (Years)	1.1	4.4	8.3

Source: Self-reported customer activity from Starbucks survey, 2002.

While customer satisfaction was driven by a number of different factors (see **Exhibit 10**), Day believed that the customer satisfaction gap could primarily be attributed to a *service gap* between Starbucks scores on key attributes and customer expectations. When Starbucks had polled its customers to determine what it could do to make them feel more like valued customers, "improvements to service"—in particular, speed-of-service—had been mentioned most frequently (see **Exhibit 11** for more information).

REDISCOVERING THE STARBUCKS CUSTOMER

Responding to the market research findings posed a difficult management challenge. The most controversial proposal was the one on the table before Day—it involved relaxing the labor-hour controls in the stores to add an additional 20 hours of labor, per week, per store, at a cost of an extra $40 million per year. Not surprisingly, the plan was being met with significant internal resistance. "Our CFO is understandably concerned about the potential impact on our bottom line," said Day. "Each $6 million in profit contribution translates into a penny a share. But my argument is that if we move away from seeing labor as an expense to seeing it as a customer-oriented investment, we'll see a positive return." She continued:

> We need to bring service time down to the three-minute level in all of our stores, regardless of the time of day. If we do this, we'll not only increase customer satisfaction and build stronger long-term relationships with our customers, we'll also improve our customer throughput. The goal is to move each store closer to the $20,000 level in terms of weekly sales, and I think that this plan will help us get there.

EXHIBIT 10 **Importance Rankings of Key Attributes in Creating Customer Satisfaction**

To be read: *83% of Starbucks' customers rate a clean store as being highly important (90+ on a 100-point scale) in creating customer satisfaction.*

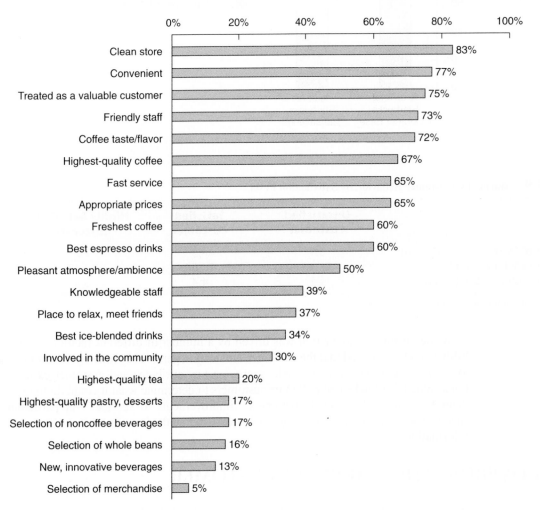

Attribute	Percentage
Clean store	83%
Convenient	77%
Treated as a valuable customer	75%
Friendly staff	73%
Coffee taste/flavor	72%
Highest-quality coffee	67%
Fast service	65%
Appropriate prices	65%
Freshest coffee	60%
Best espresso drinks	60%
Pleasant atmosphere/ambience	50%
Knowledgeable staff	39%
Place to relax, meet friends	37%
Best ice-blended drinks	34%
Involved in the community	30%
Highest-quality tea	20%
Highest-quality pastry, desserts	17%
Selection of noncoffee beverages	17%
Selection of whole beans	16%
New, innovative beverages	13%
Selection of merchandise	5%

Source: Self-reported customer activity from Starbucks survey, 2002.

In two days, Day was scheduled to make a final recommendation to Howard Schultz and Orin Smith about whether the company should roll out the $40 million plan in October 2002. In preparation for this meeting, Day had asked Alling to help her think through the implications of the plan one final time. She mused:

> We've been operating with the assumption that we do customer service well. But the reality is, we've started to lose sight of the consumer. It's amazing that this could happen to a company like us—after all, we've become one of the most prominent consumer brands in the world. For all of our focus on building the brand and introducing new products, we've simply stopped talking about the customer. We've lost the connection between satisfying our customers and growing the business.

EXHIBIT 11   **Factors Driving "Valued Customer" Perceptions**

How could Starbucks make you feel more like a valued customer?	% Responses
Improvements to Service (total)	**34%**
Friendlier, more attentive staff	19%
Faster, more efficient service	10%
Personal treatment (remember my name, remember my order)	4%
More knowledgeable staff	4%
Better service	2%
Offer Better Prices/Incentive Programs (total)	**31%**
Free cup after x number of visits	19%
Reduce prices	11%
Offer promotions, specials	3%
Other (total)	**21%**
Better quality/Variety of products	9%
Improve atmosphere	8%
Community outreach/Charity	2%
More stores/More convenient locations	2%
Don't Know/Already Satisfied	**28%**

Source: Starbucks, 2002. Based on a survey of Starbucks' 2002 customer base, including highly satisfied, satisfied, and unsatisfied customers.

Alling's response was simple: "We know that both Howard and Orin are totally committed to satisfying our retail customers. Our challenge is to tie customer satisfaction to the bottom line. What evidence do we have?"

Case 8

SHOULDICE HOSPITAL LIMITED (ABRIDGED)

Two shadowy figures, enrobed and in slippers, walked slowly down the semi-darkened hall of the Shouldice Hospital. They didn't notice Alan O'Dell, the hospital's managing director, and his guest. Once they were out of earshot, O'Dell remarked good naturedly, "By the way they act, you'd think our patients own this place. And while they're here, in way they do." Following a visit to the five operating rooms, O'Dell and his visitor once again encountered the same pair of patients still engrossed in discussing their hernia operations, which had been performed the previous morning.

HISTORY

An attractive brochure that was recently printed, although neither dated nor distributed to prospective patients, described Dr. Earle Shouldice, the founder of the hospital:

> Dr Shouldice's interest in early ambulation stemmed, in part, from an operation he performed in 1932 to remove the appendix from a seven-year-old girl and the girl's subsequent refusal to stay quietly in bed. In spite of her activity, no harm was done, and the experience recalled to the doctor the postoperative actions of animals upon which he had performed surgery. They had all moved about freely with no ill effects.

By 1940, Shouldice had given extensive thought to several factors that contributed to early ambulation following surgery. Among them were the use of a local anesthetic, the nature of the surgical procedure itself, the design of a facility to encourage move-

Professor James Heskett prepared the original version of this case, "Shouldice Hospital Limited," HBS No. 683-068. This version was prepared jointly by Professor James Heskett and Roger Hallowell (MBA 1989, DBA 1997). HBS cases are developed solely as the basis for class discussion. Cases are not intended to serve as endorsements, sources of primary data, or illustrations of effective or ineffective management.

ment without unnecessarily causing discomfort and the postoperative regimen. With these things in mind, he began to develop a surgical technique for repairing hernias[1] that was superior to others; word of his early success generated demand.

Dr. Shouldice's medical license permitted him to operate anywhere, even on a kitchen table. However, as more and more patients requested operations, Dr. Shouldice created new facilities by buying a rambling 130-acre estate with a 17,000-square foot main house in the Toronto suburb of Thornhill. After some years of planning, a large wing was added to provide a total capacity of 89 beds,

Dr. Shouldice died in 1965. At that time, Shouldice Hospital Limited was formed to operate both the hospital and clinical facilities under the surgical direction of Dr. Nicholas Obney. In 1999, Dr. Casim Degani, an internationally-recognized authority, became surgeon-in-chief. By 2004, 7,600 operations were performed per year.

THE SHOULDICE METHOD

Only external (vs. internal) abdominal hernias were repaired at Shouldice Hospital. Thus most first-time repairs, "primaries," were straightforward operations requiring about 45 minutes. The remaining procedures involved patients suffering recurrences of hernias previously repaired elsewhere.[2] Many of the recurrences and very difficult hernia repairs required 90 minutes or more.

In the Shouldice method, the muscles of the abdominal wall were arranged in three distinct layers, and the opening was repaired—each layer in turn—by overlapping its margins as the edges of a coat might be overlapped when buttoned. The end result reinforced the muscular wall of the abdomen with six rows of sutures (stitches) under the skin cover, which was then closed with clamps that were later removed. (Other methods might not separate muscle layers, often involved fewer rows of sutures, and sometimes involved the insertion of screens or meshes under the skin.)

A typical first-time repair could be completed with the use of preoperative sedation (sleeping pill) and analgesic (pain killer) plus a local anesthetic, an injection of Novocain in the region of the incision. This allowed immediate post-operative patient ambulation and facilitated rapid recovery.

THE PATIENTS' EXPERIENCE

Most potential Shouldice patients learned about the hospital from previous Shouldice patients. Although thousands of doctors had referred patients, doctors were less likely to recommend Shouldice because of the generally regarded simplicity of the surgery, often considered a "bread and butter" operation. Typically, many patients had their

[1]Most hernias, known as external abdominal hernias, are protrusions of some part of the abdominal contents through a hole or slit in the muscular layers of the abdominal wall which is supposed to contain them. Well over 90% of these hernias occur in the groin area. Of these, by far the most common are inguinal hernias, many of which are caused by a slight weakness in the muscle layers brought about by the passage of the testicles in male babies through the groin area shortly before birth. Aging also contributes to the development of inguinal hernias. Because of the cause of the affliction, 85% of all hernias occur in males.
[2]Based on tracking of patients over more than 30 years, the gross recurrence rate for all operations performed at Shouldice was 0.8%. Recurrence rates reported in the literature for these types of hernia varied greatly. However, one text stated, "In the United States the gross rate of recurrence for groin hernias approaches 10%."

problem diagnosed by a personal physician and then contacted Shouldice directly. Many more made this diagnosis themselves.

The process experienced by Shouldice patients depended on whether or not they lived close enough to the hospital to visit the facility to obtain a diagnosis. Approximately 10% of Shouldice patients came from outside the province of Ontario, most of these from the United States. Another 60% of patients lived beyond the Toronto area. These out-of-town patients often were diagnosed by mail using the Medical Information Questionnaire shown in **Exhibit 1.** Based on information in the questionnaire, a Shouldice surgeon would determine the type of hernia the respondent had and whether there were signs that some risk might be associated with surgery (for example, an overweight or heart condition, or a patient who had suffered a heart attack or a stroke in the past six months to a year, or whether a general or local anesthetic was required). At this point, a patient was given a operating date and sent a brochure describing the hospital and the Shouldice method. If necessary, a sheet outlining a weight-loss program prior to surgery was also sent. A small proportion was refused treatment, either because they were overweight, represented an undue medical risk, or because it was determined that they did not have a hernia.

EXHIBIT 1 Medical Information Questionnaire

FAMILY NAME (Last Name)	FIRST NAME	MIDDLE NAME

STREET & NUMBER (or Rural Route or P.O. Box)	Town/City	Province/State

County	Township	Zip or Postal Code	Birthdate: Month Day Year

Telephone Home .... Work .... If none, give neighbour's number	Married or Single	Religion

NEXT OF KIN: Name	Address	Telephone #

SHOULDICE HOSPITAL

7750 Bayview Avenue
Box 370, Thornhill, Ontario L3T 4A3 Canada
Phone (418) 889-1125

(Thornhill - One Mile North Metro Toronto)

MEDICAL

INFORMATION

INSURANCE INFORMATION: Please give name of Insurance Company and Numbers.	Date form completed

HOSPITAL INSURANCE: (Please bring hospital certificates) O.H.I.P. BLUE CROSS Number _____ Number _____	OTHER HOSPITAL INSURANCE Company Name _____ Policy Number _____
SURGICAL INSURANCE: (Please bring insurance certificates) O.H.I.P. BLUE SHIELD Number _____ Number _____	OTHER SURGICAL INSURANCE Company Name _____ Policy Number _____

WORKMEN'S COMPENSATION BOARD Claim No.	Approved Yes No	Social Insurance (Security) Number

Occupation Name of Business	Are you the owner? If Retired – Former Occupation Yes No

How did you hear about Shouldice Hospital? If referred by a doctor, give name & address)

Are you a former patient of Shouldice Hospital? Yes No	Do you smoke? Yes No
Have you ever written to Shouldice Hospital in the past? Yes No	

What is your preferred admission date? (Please give as much advance notice as possible)
No admissions Friday, Saturday or Sunday.

Patients who live at a distance often prefer their examination, admission and operation to be arranged all on a single visit – to save making two lengthy journeys. The whole purpose of this questionnarie is to make such arrangements possible, although, of course, it cannot replace the examination in any way. Its completion and return will not put you under any obligation.

Please be sure to fill in both sides.

FOR OFFICE USE ONLY

Date Received	Type of Hernia	Weight Loss lbs.

Consent to Operate ☐ Heart Report ☐	Special Instructions	Approved

Referring Doctor Notified	Operation Date

This information will be treated as confidential.

(continued on next page)

EXHIBIT 1 Medical Information Questionnaire—continued

THIS CHART IS FOR EXPLANATION ONLY

Ordinary hernias are mostly either
at the navel ("belly-button") - or just above it ►

or down in the groin area on either side ►

An "inclsional hernia" is one that bulges through
the scar of any other surgical operation that has
failed to hold - wherever it may be.

Right Groin *Left Groin*

THIS IS <u>YOUR</u> CHART – PLEASE MARK IT!

(MARK THE POSITION OF EACH HERNIA
YOU WANT REPAIRED WITH AN "X")

Right Groin *Left Groin*

APPROXIMATE SIZE . . .
Walnut (or less)
Hen's Egg or Lemon
Grapefruit (or more)

ESSENTIAL EXTRA INFORMATION
Use only the sections that apply to your hernias and put a √ in each
box that seems appropriate.

NAVEL AREA (AND JUST ABOVE NAVEL) ONLY   Yes   No
Is this navel (bellybutton) hernia your FIRST one?   ☐   ☐

If it's NOT your first, how many repair attempts so far? ☐

GROIN HERNIAS ONLY   RIGHT GROIN   LEFT GROIN
                                          Yes   No   Yes   No
Is this your FIRST GROIN HERNIA ON THIS SIDE? ☐   ☐   ☐   ☐

How many hernia operations in this groin already? Right ☐   Left ☐
DATE OF LAST OPERATION   [   ]

INCISIONAL HERNIAS ONLY (the ones bulging through previous operation scars)
Was the original operation for your Appendix? ☐ . or Gallbladder? ☐ .
or Stomach? ☐ . or Prostate? ☐ . or Hysterectomy? ☐ . or Other? . . . .
. . . .
How many attempts to repair the hernia have been made so far? ☐

PLEASE BE ACCURATE: Misleading figures, when checked on a
admission day, could mean postponement of your operation till your weight
is suitable.

HEIGHT . . . . ft . . . . ins.   WEIGHT . . . . lbs. Nude   Recent gain? . . . . lbs.
                                    or just pyjamas   Recent loss? . . . . lbs.

Waist (muscles relaxed) . . . . ins.   Chest (not expanded) . . . . ins.

GENERAL HEALTH

Age . . . . years   Is your health now GOOD ☐ . FAIR ☐ . or POOR ☐

Please mention briefly any severe past illness — such as a
"heart attack" or a "stroke", for example, from which you
have now recovered (and its approximate date) . . . .
. . . .

We need to know about other present conditions, even though your admission is
NOT likely to be refused because of them.

Please tick   √ any condition   Name of any prescribed
for which you are having regular   pills, tablets or capsules you
treatment: take regularly: –

Blood Pressure   ☐

Excess body fluids   ☐

Chest pain ("angina")   ☐

Irregular Heartbeat   ☐

Diabetes   ☐

Asthma & Bronchitis   ☐

Ulcers   ☐

Anticoagulants   ☐
(to delay blood-clotting
or to "thin the blood")

Other . . . .

Did you remember to MARK AN "X" on your body chart to show us where
each of your hernias is located?

Arriving at the clinic between 1:00 P.M. and 3:00 P.M. the day before the operation, a patient joined other patients in the waiting room. He or she was soon examined in one of six examination rooms staffed by surgeons who had completed their operating schedules for the day. This examination required no more than 20 minutes, unless the patient needed reassurance. (Patients typically exhibited a moderate level of anxiety until their operation was completed.) At this point it occasionally was discovered that a patient had not corrected his or her weight problem; others might be found not to have a hernia at all. In either case, the patient was sent home.

After checking administrative details, about an hour after arriving at the hospital, a patient was directed to the room number shown on his or her wrist band. Throughout the process, patients were asked to keep their luggage (usually light) with them.

All patient rooms at the hospital were semiprivate, containing two beds. Patients with similar jobs, backgrounds, or interests were assigned to the same room to the extent possible. Upon reaching their rooms, patients busied themselves unpacking, getting acquainted with roommates, shaving themselves in the area of the operation, and changing into pajamas.

At 4:30 P.M., a nurse's orientation provided the group of incoming patients with information about what to expect, including the need for exercise after the operation and the daily routine. According to Alan O'Dell, "Half are so nervous they don't remember much." Dinner was then served, followed by further recreation and tea and cookies at 9:00 P.M. Nurses emphasized the importance of attendance at that time because it provided an opportunity for preoperative patients to talk with those whose operations had been completed earlier that same day.

Patients to be operated on early were awakened at 5:30 A.M. to be given preop sedation. An attempt was made to schedule operations for roommates at approximately the same time. Patients were taken to the preoperating room where the circulating nurse administered Demerol, an analgesic, 45 minutes before surgery. A few minutes prior to the first operation at 7:30 A.M., the surgeon assigned to each patient administered Novocain, a local anesthetic, in the operating room. This was in contrast to the typical hospital procedure in which patients were sedated in their rooms prior to being taken to the operating rooms.

Upon the completion of their operation, during which a few patients were "chatty" and fully aware of what was going on, patients were invited to get off the operating table and walk to the post-operating room with the help of their surgeons. According to the director of nursing:

> Ninety-nine percent accept the surgeon's invitation. While we use wheelchairs to return them to their rooms, the walk from the operating table is for psychological as well as physiological [blood pressure, respiratory] reasons. Patients prove to themselves that they can do it, and they start their all-important exercise immediately.

Throughout the day after their operation, patients were encouraged to exercise by nurses and housekeepers alike. By 9:00 P.M. on the day of their operations, all patients were ready and able to walk down to the dining room for tea and cookies, even if it meant climbing stairs, to help indoctrinate the new "class" admitted that day. On the fourth morning, patients were ready for discharge.

During their stay, patients were encouraged to take advantage of the opportunity to explore the premises and make new friends. Some members of the staff felt that the patients and their attitudes were the most important element of the Shouldice program. According to Dr. Byrnes Shouldice, son of the founder, a surgeon on the staff, and a 50% owner of the hospital:

> Patients sometimes ask to stay an extra day. Why? Well, think about it. They are basically well to begin with. But they arrive with a problem and a certain amount of nervousness, tension, and anxiety about their surgery. Their first morning here they're operated on and experience a sense of relief from something that's been bothering them for a long time. They are immediately able to get around, and they've got a three-day holiday ahead of them with a perfectly good reason to be away from work with no sense of guilt. They share experiences with other patients, make friends easily, and have the run of the hospital. In summer, the most common after-effect from the surgery is sunburn.

THE NURSES' EXPERIENCE

34 full-time-equivalent nurses staffed Shouldice each 24 hour period. However, during non-operating hours, only six full-time-equivalent nurses were on the premises at any given time. While the Canadian acute-care hospital average ratio of nurses to patients was 1:4, at Shouldice the ratio was 1:15. Shouldice nurses spent an unusually large proportion of their time in counseling activities. As one supervisor commented, "We don't use bedpans." According to a manager, "Shouldice has a waiting list of

Nurses wanting to be hired, while other hospitals in Toronto are short-staffed and perpetually recruiting."

THE DOCTORS' EXPERIENCE

The hospital employed 10 full-time surgeons and 8 part-time assistant surgeons. Two anesthetists were also on site. The anesthetists floated among cases except when general anesthesia was in use. Each operating team required a surgeon, an assistant surgeon, a scrub nurse, and a circulating nurse. The operating load varied from 30 to 36 operations per day. As a result, each surgeon typically performed three or four operations each day.

A typical surgeon's day started with a *scrubbing* shortly before the first scheduled operation at 7:30 A.M. If the first operation was routine, it usually was completed by 8:15 A.M. At its conclusion, the surgical team helped the patient walk from the room and summoned the next patient. After scrubbing, the surgeon could be ready to operate again at 8:30 A.M. Surgeons were advised to take a coffee break after their second or third operation. Even so, a surgeon could complete three routine operations and a fourth involving a recurrence and still be finished in time for a 12:30 P.M. lunch in the staff dining room.

Upon finishing lunch, surgeons not scheduled to operate in the afternoon examined incoming patients. A surgeon's day ended by 4:00 P.M. In addition, a surgeon could expect to be on call one weekday night in ten and one weekend in ten. Alan O'Dell commented that the position appealed to doctors who "want to watch their children grow up. A doctor on call is rarely called to the hospital and has regular hours." According to Dr. Obney:

> When I interview prospective surgeons, I look for experience and a good education. I try to gain some insight into their domestic situation and personal interests and habits. I also try to find out why a surgeon wants to switch positions. And I try to determine if he's willing to perform the repair exactly as he's told. This is no place for prima donnas.

Dr. Shouldice added:

> Traditionally a hernia is often the first operation that a junior resident in surgery performs. Hernia repair is regarded as a relatively simple operation compared to other major operations. This is quite wrong, as is borne out by the resulting high recurrence rate. It is a tricky anatomical area and occasionally very complicated, especially to the novice or those doing very few hernia repairs each year. But at Shouldice Hospital a surgeon learns the Shouldice technique over a period of several months. He learns when he can go fast and when he must go slow. He develops a pace and a touch. If he encounters something unusual, he is encouraged to consult immediately with other surgeons. We teach each other and try to encourage a group effort. And he learns not to take risks to achieve absolute perfection. Excellence is the enemy of good.

Chief Surgeon Degani assigned surgeons to an operating room on a daily basis by noon of the preceding day. This allowed surgeons to examine the specific patients that they were to operate on. Surgeons and assistants were rotated every few days. Cases were assigned to give doctors a non-routine operation (often involving a recurrence) several times a week. More complex procedures were assigned to more senior and experienced members of the staff. Dr Obney commented:

> If something goes wrong, we want to make sure that we have an experienced surgeon in charge. Experience is most important. The typical general surgeon may perform 25 to 50 hernia operations per year. Ours perform 750 or more.

The 10 full-time surgeons were paid a straight salary, typically $144,000.[3] In addition, bonuses to doctors were distributed monthly. These depended on profit, individual productivity, and performance. The total bonus pool paid to the surgeons in a recent year was approximately $400,000. Total surgeon compensation (including benefits) was approximately 15% more than the average income for a surgeon in Ontario.

Training in the Shouldice technique was important because the procedure could not be varied. It was accomplished through direct supervision by one or more of the senior surgeons. The rotation of teams and frequent consultations allowed for an ongoing opportunity to appraise performance and take corrective action. Where possible, former Shouldice patients suffering recurrences were assigned to the doctor who performed the first operation "to allow the doctor to learn from his mistake." Dr. Obney commented on being a Shouldice surgeon:

> A doctor must decide after several years whether he wants to do this for the rest of his life because, just as in other specialties—for example, radiology—he loses touch with other medical disciplines. If he stays for five years, he doesn't leave. Even among younger doctors, few elect to leave.

THE FACILITY

The Shouldice Hospital contained two facilities in one building—the hospital and the clinic. On its first level, the hospital contained the kitchen and dining rooms. The second level contained a large, open lounge area, the admissions offices, patient rooms, and a spacious glass-covered Florida room. The third level had additional patient rooms and recreational areas. Patients could be seen visiting in each others' rooms, walking up and down hallways, lounging in the sunroom, and making use of light recreational facilities ranging from a pool table to an exercycle. Alan O'Dell pointed out some of the features of the hospital:

> The rooms contain no telephone or television sets. If a patient needs to make a call or wants to watch television, he or she has to take a walk. The steps are designed specially with a small rise to allow patients recently operated on to negotiate the stairs without undue discomfort. Every square foot of the hospital is carpeted to reduce the hospital feeling and the possibility of a fall. Carpeting also gives the place a smell other than that of disinfectant.
>
> This facility was designed by an architect with input from Dr. Byrnes Shouldice and Mrs. W. H. Urquhart (the daughter of the founder). The facility was discussed for years and many changes in the plans were made before the first concrete was poured. A number of unique policies were also instituted. For example, parents accompanying children here for an operation stay free. You may wonder why we can do it, but we learned that we save more in nursing costs than we spend for the parent's room and board.

Patients and staff were served food prepared in the same kitchen, and staff members picked up food from a cafeteria line placed in the very center of the kitchen. This provided an opportunity for everyone to chat with the kitchen staff several times a day, and the hospital staff to eat together. According to O'Dell, "We use all fresh ingredients and prepare the food from scratch in the kitchen."

The director of housekeeping pointed out:

---

[3]All monetary references in the case are to Canadian dollars. $1 US equaled $1.33 Canadian on February 23, 2004.

I have only three on my housekeeping staff for the entire facility. One of the reasons for so few housekeepers is that we don't need to change linens during a patient's four-day stay. Also, the medical staff doesn't want the patients in bed all day. They want the nurses to encourage the patients to be up socializing, comparing notes [for confidence], encouraging each other, and walking around, getting exercise. Of course, we're in the rooms straightening up throughout the day. This gives the housekeepers a chance to josh with the patients and to encourage them to exercise.

The clinic housed five operating rooms, a laboratory, and the patient-recovery room. In total, the estimated cost to furnish an operating room was $30,000. This was considerably less than for other hospitals requiring a bank of equipment with which to administer anesthetics for each room. At Shouldice, two mobile units were used by the anesthetists when needed. In addition, the complex had one "crash cart" per floor for use if a patient should suffer a heart attack or stroke.

ADMINISTRATION

Alan O'Dell described his job:

We try to meet people's needs and make this as good a place to work as possible. There is a strong concern for employees here. Nobody is fired. [This was later reinforced by Dr. Shouldice, who described a situation involving two employees who confessed to theft in the hospital. They agreed to seek psychiatric help and were allowed to remain on the job.] As a result, turnover is low.

Our administrative and support staff are non-union, but we try to maintain a pay scale higher than the union scale for comparable jobs in the area. We have a profit-sharing plan that is separate from the doctors.' Last year the administrative and support staff divided up $60,000.

If work needs to be done, people pitch in to help each other. A unique aspect of our administration is that I insist that each secretary is trained to do another's work and in an emergency is able to switch to another function immediately. We don't have an organization chart. A chart tends to make people think they're boxed in jobs.[4] I try to stay one night a week, having dinner and listening to the patients, to find out how things are really going around here.

Operating Costs

The 2004 budgets for the hospital and clinic were close to $8.5 million,[5] and $3.5 million, respectively.[6]

THE MARKET

Hernia operations were among the most common performed on males. In 2000 an estimated 1,000,000 such operations were performed in the United States alone. According to Dr. Shouldice:

When our backlog of scheduled operations gets too large, we wonder how many people decide instead to have their local doctor perform the operation. Every time we've expanded

---

[4]The chart in **Exhibit 2** was prepared by the casewriter, based on conversations with hospital personnel.
[5]This figure included a provincially mandated return on investment.
[6]The latter figure included the bonus pool for doctors.

EXHIBIT 2 Organization Chart

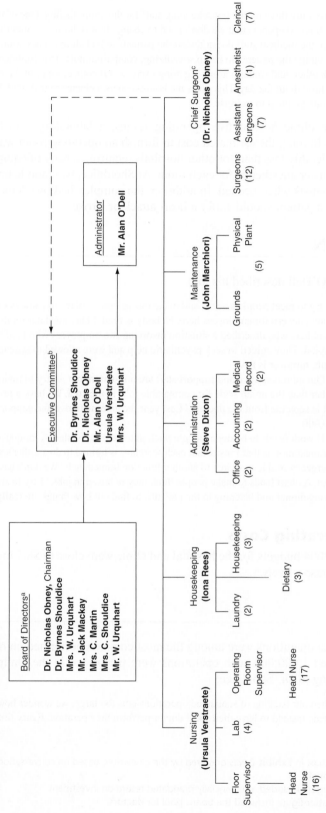

Board of Directors[a]

Dr. Nicholas Obney, Chairman
Dr. Byrnes Shouldice
Mrs. W. Urquhart
Mr. Jack Mackay
Mrs. C. Martin
Mrs. C. Shouldice
Mr. W. Urquhart

Executive Committee[b]

Dr. Byrnes Shouldice
Dr. Nicholas Obney
Mr. Alan O'Dell
Ursula Verstraete
Mrs. W. Urquhart

Administrator
Mr. Alan O'Dell

Nursing
(Ursula Verstraete)

Floor Supervisor — Head Nurse (16)

Lab (4)

Operating Room Supervisor — Head Nurse (17)

Housekeeping
(Iona Rees)

Laundry (2)

Housekeeping (3)

Dietary (3)

Administration
(Steve Dixon)

Office (2)

Accounting (2)

Medical Record (2)

Maintenance
(John Marchiori)

Grounds

Physical Plant (5)

Chief Surgeon[c]
(Dr. Nicholas Obney)

Surgeons (12)

Assistant Surgeons (7)

Anesthetist (1)

Clerical (7)

[a]Meets three times a year or as needed.
[b]Meet as needed (usually twice a month).
[c]Informally reports to Executive Committee.

our capacity, the backlog has declined briefly, only to climb once again. Right now, at 2,400, it is larger than it has ever been and is growing by 100 every six months.

The hospital relied entirely on word-of-mouth advertising, the importance of which was suggested by the results of a poll carried out by students of DePaul University as part of a project (**Exhibit 3** shows a portion of these results). Although little systematic data about patients had been collected, Alan O'Dell remarked that "if we had to rely on wealthy patients only, our practice would be much smaller."

Patients were attracted to the hospital, in part, by its reasonable rates. Charges for a typical operation were four days of hospital stay at $320 per day, and a $650 surgical fee for a primary inguinal (the most common hernia). An additional fee of $300

EXHIBIT 3   **Shouldice Hospital Annual Patient Reunion Data**

Direction: For each question, please place a check mark as it applies to you.

1. Sex   Male _41_ 95.34%   Female _2_ 4.65%

2. Age   20 or less ___   21-40 _4_ 9.30%   41-60 _17_ 39.54%   61 or more _22_ 51.16%

3. Nationality
   Directions: Please place a check mark in nation you represent and please write in your province, state or country where it applies.
   Canada _38_ Province 88.37%   America _5_ State 11.63%   Europe ___ Country ___   Other ___ ___

4. Education level
   Elementary _5_ 11.63%   High School _18_ 41.86%   College _13_ 30.23%   Graduate work _7_ 16.28%

5. Occupation ___

6. Have you been overnight in a hospital other than Shouldice before your operation?   Yes _31_   No _12_

7. What brought Shouldice Hospital to your attention?
   Friend _23_ 53.49%   Doctor _9_ 20.93%   Relative _7_ 16.28%   Article ___   Other _4_ 9.30% (Please explain)

8. Did you have a single _25_ 58.14% or double _18_ 41.86% hernia operation?

9. Is this your first Annual Reunion? Yes _20_ 46.51%   No _23_ 53.49% (2-5 reunions -11 47.83%, 6-10 reunions - 5 21.73%, 11-20 reunions - 4 17.39%, 21-36 reunions - 3 13.05%)
   If no, how many reunions have you attended? ___

10. Do you feel that Shouldice Hospital cared for you as a person?
    Most definitely _37_ 86.05%   Definitely _6_ 13.95%   Very little ___   Not at all ___

EXHIBIT 3 Shouldice Hospital Annual Patient Reunion Data—continued

11. What impressed you the most about your stay at Shouldice? Please check one answer for each of the following.

A. Fees charged for operation and hospital stay
Very Important _10_   Important _3_   Somewhat Important _6_   Not Important _24_

B. Operation Procedure
Very Important _33_   Important _9_   Somewhat Important _1_   Not Important ___
_76.74%_   _20.93%_   _2.33%_

C. Physician's Care
Very Important _31_   Important _12_   Somewhat Important _−_   Not Important _−_
_72.10%_   _27.90%_

D. Nursing Care
Very Important _28_   Important _14_   Somewhat Important _1_   Not Important ___
_65.12%_   _32.56%_   _2.33%_

E. Food Service
Very Important _23_   Important _11_   Somewhat Important _7_   Not Important _2_
_53.48%_   _25.59%_   _16.28%_   _4.65%_

F. Shortness of Hospital Stay
Very Important _17_   Important _15_   Somewhat Important _8_   Not Important _3_
_39.53%_   _34.88%_   _18.60%_   _6.98%_

G. Exercise; Recreational Activities
Very Important _17_   Important _14_   Somewhat Important _12_   Not Important _−_
_39.53%_   _32.56%_   _27.91%_

H. Friendships with Patients
Very Important _25_   Important _10_   Somewhat Important _5_   Not Important _3_
_58.15%_   _23.25%_   _11.63%_   _6.98%_

I. "Shouldice Hospital hardly seemed like a hospital at all."
Very Important _25_   Important _13_   Somewhat Important _5_   Not Important ___
_58.14%_   _30.23%_   _11.63%_

12. In a few words, give the MAIN REASON why you returned for this annual reunion.

was assessed if general anesthesia was required (in about 20% of cases). These charges compared to an average charge of $5,240 for operations performed elsewhere.

Round-trip fares for travel to Toronto from various major cities on the North American continent ranged from roughly $200 to $600.

The hospital also provided annual checkups to alumni, free of charge. Many occurred at the time of the patient reunion. The most recent reunion, featuring dinner and a floor show, was held at a first-class hotel in downtown Toronto and was attended by 1,000 former patients, many from outside Canada.

PROBLEMS AND PLANS

When asked about major questions confronting the management of the hospital, Dr. Shouldice cited a desire to seek ways of increasing the hospital's capacity while at the same time maintaining control over the quality of service delivered, the future role of government in the operations of the hospital, and the use of the Shouldice name by potential competitors. As Dr Shouldice put it:

> I'm a doctor first and an entrepreneur second. For example, we could refuse permission to other doctors who want to visit the hospital. They may copy our technique and misapply it or misinform their patients about the use of it. This results in failure, and we are concerned that the technique will be blamed. But we're doctors, and it is our obligation to help other surgeons learn. On the other hand, it's quite clear that others are trying to emulate us. Look at this ad. [The advertisement is shown in **Exhibit 4.**]
>
> This makes me believe that we should add to our capacity, either here or elsewhere. Here, we could go to Saturday operations and increase our capacity by 20%. Throughout the year, no operations are scheduled for Saturdays or Sundays, although patients whose operations are scheduled late in the week remain in the hospital over the weekend. Or, with an

EXHIBIT 4
Advertisement by a Shouldice Competitor

investment of perhaps $4 million in new space, we could expand our number of beds by 50%, and schedule the operating rooms more heavily.

On the other hand, given government regulation, do we want to invest more in Toronto? Or should we establish another hospital with similar design, perhaps in the United States? There is also the possibility that we could diversify into other specialties offering similar opportunities such as eye surgery, varicose veins, or diagnostic services (e.g. colonoscopies).

For now, we're also beginning the process of grooming someone to succeed Dr. Degani when he retires. He's in his early 60s, but at some point we'll have to address this issue. And for good reason, he's resisted changing certain successful procedures that I think we could improve on. We had quite a time changing the schedule for the administration of Demerol to patients to increase their comfort level during the operation. Dr Degani has opposed a Saturday operating program on the premise that he won't be here and won't be able to maintain proper control.

Alan O'Dell added his own concerns:

How should we be marketing our services? Right now, we don't advertise directly to patients. We're even afraid to send out this new brochure we've put together, unless a potential patient specifically requests it, for fear it will generate too much demand. Our records show that just under 1% of our patients are medical doctors, a significantly high percentage. How should we capitalize on that? I'm also concerned about this talk of Saturday operations. We are already getting good utilization of this facility. And if we expand further, it will be very difficult to maintain the same kind of working relationships and attitudes. Already there are rumors floating around among the staff about it. And the staff is not pleased.

The matter of Saturday operations had been a topic of conversation among the doctors as well. Four of the older doctors were opposed to it. While most of the younger doctors were indifferent or supportive, at least two who had been at the hospital for some time were particularly concerned about the possibility that the issue would drive a wedge between the two groups. As one put it, "I'd hate to see the practice split over the issue."

INDEX